Exploring Mass Communication

Connecting with the World of Media

Vincent F. Filak

University of Wisconsin-Oshkosh

FOR INFORMATION:

2455 Teller Road
Thousand Oaks, California 91320
E-mail: order@sagepub.com

1 Oliver's Yard
55 City Road
London, EC1Y 1SP
United Kingdom

Unit No. 323-333, Third Floor, F-Block
International Trade Tower
Nehru Place, New Delhi – 110 019
India

18 Cross Street #10-10/11/12
China Square Central
Singapore 048423

Printed in the United States of America

Library of Congress Cataloging-in-Publication Data

ISBN 978-1-5443-8563-1

Acquisitions Editor: Charles Lee

Content Development Editor: Megan OHeffernan

Production Editor: Aparajita Srivastava

Copy Editor: Jim Kelly

Typesetter: Diachritech

Cover Designer: Scott Van Atta

Marketing Manager: Victoria Velasquez

This book is printed on acid-free paper.

23 24 25 26 27 10 9 8 7 6 5 4 3 2 1

Exploring Mass Communication

To my mom, Lynn, my dad, Frank, and my wife, Amy.

I would never get anywhere in life without your love and support.

Thank you for everything.

And for Zoe.

I love everything you are and the amazing young woman you have become.

You truly represent the best of everything for your mom and me.

BRIEF CONTENTS

DETAILED CONTENTS

PART III DIGITAL MEDIA

PART V RULES AND VALUES

PREFACE

Exploring Mass Communication was written for *you* as a student and user of media in all its many forms. As you are fully aware, the media world today is rapidly changing, and there are many new opportunities to express yourself, through both traditional and cutting-edge platforms. You are bombarded with messages every day, from your social media feeds to email, blog postings, push alerts, and breaking news. This makes it even more important for you to become an active and savvy consumer and creator of media. Knowing the history of mass communication and how it has changed over the centuries is key to understanding the challenges and opportunities that it offers today. While the platforms may be changing, the content—what creators are trying to say—continues to raise social, ethical, and legal issues that students need to know. *Exploring Mass Communication* is designed to give you the knowledge and tools you'll need to survive and flourish in this ever changing environment.

While your instructors are looking for a book that will meet their course goals—to cover a list of topics that are important for you to understand and to help you to master them—I have written this book specifically to reach students with content that is relevant, useful, and interesting, to help you see why it should matter to you. Whenever possible, I have tried to highlight fresh and interesting trends—including focusing on student-created materials—while at the same time ensuring that the key topics and achievements of past innovators are not slighted. The goal is to make this history come alive for you.

MY APPROACH

This book covers the key aspects of mass communication in a way that provides you with both a historical backdrop and a current examination of the field. In doing so, it gives you the background you need to take a long view of the field as well as a set of personal touchstones that connect the content to your daily lives.

Rather than take an encyclopedic approach to the field, which might overwhelm you with facts and details that you "need to learn," I have focused on a specific element of mass communication in each chapter, using an approach that is rooted in three key concepts:

- Simplify
- Clarify
- Apply

Here is how each of those elements works within a chapter and throughout the book.

Simplify

By their very nature, introductory texts can't provide a comprehensive guide to every topic in a particular field. Your instructor will probably have their own particular areas of professional interest, and they may focus on those areas when they teach this course. Rather than emphasize my own background and interests, I have tried to give you a broad overview of the field to hopefully inspire you to do more deep investigating as you focus on specific areas to pursue in your college career.

I have chosen to take an approach that values simplifying concepts, paring down overly broad historical discussions, and streamlining content to make it easier for you to handle. This is not about "dumbing down" material, nor is it an attempt to gloss over important topics. It *is* about helping introductory students better see the forest for the trees, rather than feeling like they are forced to know every plant they encounter along the way.

Clarify

When it comes to education, knowing is one thing, and understanding is another. Textbooks can often leave students feeling tied to memorizing names and dates instead of seeing the importance of those people and events. In each chapter, I don't just give you things that you should "know for a test" but also help you clearly see why you should care about the information—and how it applies to your own life. Each concept is clearly paired with a specific answer to the basic question "Why does this matter to me?"

Apply

People tend to retain and value information when they can see its practical value. I have leveraged this concept in the approach I have taken in this text. Each chapter provides you with discussion and writing prompts that require you to directly apply what you have experienced. You can see the impact of each subject on how you live every day.

In addition, I have tied the theoretical to the practical in meaningful ways, helping you take what you learn here and apply it to real-life situations. Media literacy—the ability to interpret information in real time as it is presented to you—is one of the most important skills you can learn in college. My goal is to give you the enhanced tools to be successful media consumer or creators—no matter what career you ultimately pursue.

ORGANIZATION

Each chapter begins with a series of questions that are intended to "prime the pump" before you dive into a topic. These questions ask you to draw on your own experience and knowledge before you are exposed to the historical and practical ideas that will be explored in the chapter as a whole.

A series of learning objectives follows, with the idea that each objective will be fully explored in a particular section of the chapter. Each one of these matches up directly with one of the main topic headings in the chapter, so you can see how each section fits with what I thought was helpful and important on the topic. I hope this will also make it easier to study for tests and to ultimately succeed in class.

Each chapter provides a brief bit of history on its topic, touching on specific items that set a solid foundation for learning. Then, the chapter moves into the "how" and "why" issues of the topic, exploring not just what happened but how it occurred over the years and why you should care about it as a reader. Within each chapter, I provide a robust view of the topic that goes beyond the traditional mainstream history, tapping into a diverse stream of often overlooked groups and individuals.

Each chapter concludes with a brief overview of key points, providing a list of "need-to-know" terms, as well as a few more questions for discussion. You may be surprised at how your approach to these final questions is similar to or different from those you answered at the beginning of the chapter.

KEY CHAPTER FEATURES

Keeping with the "right tool for the job" approach, the features in this book are used as needed. Let's take a quick look at what features you will see in most of the chapters.

Key Names: Understanding history and the people who forged it matters a great deal, but some books tend to get lost in so many names and dates that students tend to get overwhelmed. To make this a bit easier, most chapters have a breakout feature that showcases a few people who have done important things in the field. Some names might be familiar, while others might be new to you. In the spirit of the "exploring" nature of the text, the goal was to find both the big names you need to know and some valuable figures who never quite got their due. As we have become more conscious of the need to critically examine history for those people and events that were "left out" through a traditional focus on "big names" and "key events," it is ever more important to acknowledge everyone who has contributed to our collective achievements.

A Deeper Look: Introductory texts need to cover a lot of material quickly, but some topics would be better served by some additional attention. In cases in which some depth and context matter a great deal, this feature gives you deeper content. You may be fine with the basic coverage in the main part of the text, but if you want or need to know more, that's where this element enters the mix.

Media Literacy Moment: In today's media world, it's not so much about what people know, but what they understand. In the predigital world, memorizing tons of names, dates, and places was the only way to really hold onto information. Today, a quick search on a phone provides the basic information that you need to know. However, *why* those names, dates, and places matters requires some additional thinking. Furthermore, it's crucial to understand the ways in which people use media, the ways in which some folks in the media use people, and how we can make sense of the seemingly endless amount of media generated on a 24/7 basis. The goal of this feature is to make you a savvier media consumer and feel more self-assured in your interactions with it.

Job Availability: Speaking of "why," many students want to know why they need to take a class in mass media basics. At the point they take a class like this one, they don't always know what they want to do or what careers are available to them. They also know that they have anxious parents back home who are asking, "You dropped your (fill in the name of a slam-dunk job field) major? What are you going to do now? Can you get a job in that?" Each practical chapter comes with a list of potential jobs in the field, as well as some things a person in that job would likely do as part of their daily work life. Students interested in pursuing a media career might not find the perfect gig here, but at least they'll have an answer to the question "Can you get a job in that?"

DIGITAL RESOURCES

This text includes an array of teaching materials designed to save instructors time and to help them keep students engaged. To learn more, visit sagepub.com or contact your SAGE representative at sagepub.com/findmyrep.

ACKNOWLEDGMENTS

Even though my name is on the cover, this book is far from being mine alone. Without the help, kindness, tough love, human decency, and occasional kick in the rear from a lot of people, this book would never have gotten done.

I always tell anyone who listens that I learn far more from other people than they learn from me, and this book is a testament to that fact. I am grateful for all my students here at UW Oshkosh, who keep me up to date on what media they're using, why they're using it, and why it matters to them. Getting to teach these students has been one of the luckiest breaks in my life.

The editorial team at SAGE has gone far beyond the call of duty on this one, particularly my editor, Richard Carlin. Also, Lily Norton, Charles Lee, and Jennifer Jovin-Bernstein did important work in putting this package together for a variety of platforms, based on feedback from a disparate group of reviewers. It takes a special kind of person to put up with me and my writing process, and these folks managed to do just that. Also, shout-outs to Jim Kelly for some truly great copy-editing saves, Megan O'Heffernan for getting this thing to the finish line in decent shape, and Naomi Kornhauser for making the book visually appealing. Last, but certainly not least, I am eternally grateful to Staci Wittek and the sales crew at SAGE for getting the word out on this book.

SAGE would like to thank the following instructors for their invaluable feedback during the development of this book:

Adam Rugg, Fairfield University
Amber Chiang, California State University, Bakersfield
Amy Rawson, Century College
Andrea Clark Mason, Arapahoe Community College
Anthony G. Aggimenti, Mercy College
Arpan Yagnik, Penn State University
Barbara J. Irwin, Canisius College
Brand Rawlins, Arkansas State University
Chandra Massner, University of Pikeville
Christina DeWalt, Florida Atlantic University
Colin Agur, University of Minnesota
Dale Zacher, St. Cloud University
Darina Sarelska, University of Tennesee
Donald Diefenbach, Weber State University
Dorrian Baber, Valdosta State University
Douglas Ferguson, College of Charleston
Douglas Ferguson, University of Oklahoma
Edward T. Arke, Messiah University
Frances Gateward, California State University, Northridge
Geoff Carr, North Idaho College
Greg Barnes, Broward College
Hojin Song, California State University, Monterey Bay
Jack Breslin, Iona College
Jason Piscia, University of Illinois, Springfield
Jenny L. Hanson, Augsburg University
John Chapin, Penn State University
John Williams, Northeast Lakeview College
Jon Arakaki, Portland Community College

Jordan Stalker, Fort Hays State University
Judith G. Curtis, University of North Carolina, Pembroke
Karyn Beyer, City College of San Francisco
Katherine Lehman, Albright College
Kevin E. Curry, Linfield University
Kristen Chamberlain, Augsburg University
Kurt Odenwald, Wentworth Institute of Technology
Laura K. Davis, Harrisburg Area Community College
Marti Maguire, William Peace University
Martin D. Sommerness, Northern Arizona University
Matthew Donahue, Bowling Green State University
Maxwell Foxman, University of Oregon
Melanie Wilderman, University of Oklahoma
Mike Van Esler, University of Wisconsin Oshkosh
Nancy DiTunnariello, St. John's University
Nancy Stillwell, Madison College
Nathan Rodriguez, University of North Carolina, Asheville
Nathan Rodriguez, Weber State University
Rebecca Lind, University of Illinois at Chicago
Robert Herklotz, Kingsborough Community College
Ryan Eanes, Klein College of Media and Communication, Temple University
Samuel Ebersole, Colorado State University, Pueblo
Sharaf Rehman, University of Minnesota
Sharaf Rehman, University of Texas, Rio Grande Valley
Sonali Kudva, University of Tampa
Stephen Swanson, McLennan Community College
Suzanne Martens, Muskegon Community College
Taciane Batista, Sacred Heart University
Timothy Molina, Northwest Vista College
Timothy Posada, Saddleback College
Valerie Kretz, St. Norbert College
Wendy Maxian, Xavier University

ABOUT THE AUTHOR

Vincent F. Filak, Ph.D., is an award-winning teacher and scholar who serves as a professor of journalism at the University of Wisconsin Oshkosh, where he primarily teaches courses on media writing and reporting. Prior to his arrival at UWO, he served on the faculty at Ball State University and also taught courses at the University of Missouri and the University of Wisconsin–Madison. He also previously worked for the *Wisconsin State Journal* and the *Columbia Missourian* newspapers.

The Associated Collegiate Press honored him as part of the organization's inaugural class of Pioneer Award Winners in 2022. The Scholastic Journalism Division of the Association for Education in Journalism and Mass Communication presented him with the Educator of the Year award in 2021, a year after he was honored by the National Society of Leadership and Success with an Excellence in Teaching award. In 2019, he received the Friend of KEMPA award for his work with high school journalism students through the Kettle Moraine Press Association. In addition, he has received awards from the College Media Association (CMA) and the National Scholastic Press Association for his work as a college media adviser and a mentor to high school journalists.

As a scholar, Filak has received thirteen top conference paper awards, including those from the Association for Education in Journalism and Mass Communication, the Broadcast Education Association, and the International Public Relations Society of America. He has published more than thirty scholarly, peer-reviewed articles in top-tier journals, including *Journalism and Mass Communication Quarterly, Journalism and Mass Communication Educator*, the *Newspaper Research Journal*, the *Atlantic Journal of Communication, Journalism: Theory, Practice and Criticism*, the *Howard Journal of Communication, Educational Psychology*, and the *British Journal of Social Psychology*. He is also the winner of CMA's Nordin Research Award, which goes to the best research paper completed on a topic pertaining to media advisers within a given year.

He has published several textbooks in the field of journalism, including *Dynamics of Media Writing* (SAGE), *Dynamics of News Reporting and Writing* (SAGE), *Dynamics of Media Editing* (SAGE), *Convergent Journalism* (Focal), and *The Journalist's Handbook to Online Editing* (with Kenneth Rosenauer; Pearson). He also blogs about media-related topics at DynamicsOfWriting.com.

He lives outside Auroraville, Wisconsin, with his wife, Amy, and their daughter, Zoe.

Zoom became an almost essential platform for communication during the COVID-19 pandemic, with everything from education and business to public relations and news reports relying on it to connect with others while in isolation.

Alistair Berg/DigitalVision/Getty images

MEDIA BASICS: MODELS AND THEORIES

INTRODUCTION

1. *How well do you feel you communicate with others through a platform like Zoom? Does it improve your interaction with others or limit you in certain ways?*
2. *As you see when someone on Zoom turns off their camera or uses a different name, certain forms of communication allow you more or less anonymity. What do you see as the benefits and drawbacks associated with anonymity in communication efforts?*
3. *How much do you rely on mass media platforms like this one to connect with people in your life?*

Media platforms like Zoom play a vital role in our lives, as they inform, entertain, and connect us in ways that continue to grow and expand, thanks to innovation and technology. This chapter will explore how communication has evolved from early oral traditions to digital media platforms. It will also outline basic communication models, explaining how they work and which ones work best in different situations. In addition, it will examine media theories that can help us understand the ways in which media affect our lives.

LEARNING OBJECTIVES

After completing this chapter, you should be able to:

1. Describe the concept of media and the ways in which it developed over time.
2. Illustrate the basic communication models and analyze the models' key components.
3. Assess the role of each media theory in understanding mass media.
4. Understand the value of media in terms of employment opportunities.

WHAT IS MEDIA?

LEARNING OBJECTIVES

LO 1: Describe the concept of media and the ways in which it developed over time.

The definition of **media** can be tricky to understand because the word itself covers several basic concepts. The term "media" can include:

- The *content* we receive through various devices, like a class meeting on Zoom or an episode of *The Bachelor* we stream.
- The *platform* on which the material is delivered, such as a printed newspaper or a vinyl album that rotates on a record player.
- The *information* we receive, whether we read it on a smartphone, hear it on a podcast, or see it in a thirty-second video.
- Some combination of content, platform, and information.

Regardless of how you want to think about media, at the core of this concept is an inherent desire to communicate with other people. Throughout the remainder of this chapter, as well as the rest of this book, we will look at two fundamental questions to help better explain the presence, relevance, and usefulness of media itself:

1. What do we do with media and what does media do to us?
2. What value does media have for us as a society and as individuals?

The Evolution of Storytelling

Before we can begin to understand today's media world, it's worth taking a look back at how communication evolved from the simple sounds humans relied on hundreds of thousands of years ago to the complex digital media transmissions we use today. Although communication and media have changed radically over the millennia, at the heart of it all is our basic need to tell people who matter to us something we want them to know.

Oral communication goes back to the days of cavemen, telling stories around the fire.

iStockPhoto.com/estt

In short, it's all about storytelling.

Long before there was mass media, human beings had a strong desire to communicate with one another. The forms of communication they used are thought to have developed in three stages (see Table 1.1).

TABLE 1.1 ■ Three Forms of Communication

Oral Communication	Visual Communication	Written Communication
Originated between 500,000 and 200,000 BC	Originated between 60,000 and 40,000 BC	Originated around 4000 BC
• Began with humans mimicking sounds they heard in nature • Grew to the development of languages	• Individuals drew images that represented important objects in their environments • Used to permanently retain information for future generations	• Humans used marks and images to record information • Began with reeds pressed into clay tablets before evolving to include materials like papyrus and parchment marked with ink quills and paint brushes

In the earliest days of communication, writers and artists often produced only a single piece that could be shared among audience members in a limited geographic area. It required a great deal of effort and time to make copies of these original items. What helped communication and media grow was the arrival of technology that allowed messages to be copied more easily and spread across larger geographic areas.

Early written communication, like this cuneiform tablet, took a great deal of time to create and could not be widely distributed.

iStockPhoto.com/swisshippo

A Leap into Mass Communication

The arrival of **mass communication**, a technique of disseminating information from one source to many receivers, applied technology to communication, allowing content to reach a much wider audience. **Oral**, **written**, and **visual communication** remained the core ways in which stories passed from sender to receiver, but new technologies made it easier for more people to receive this content more quickly than ever before (see Table 1.2).

For much of the twentieth century, mass media was defined as consisting of primarily print (books, magazines, newspapers), recorded (records, movies), and broadcast (radio, television) media. The **platform**—or the *way* the media was shared—was foremost, with the content or information that was being shared molded to fit each format. This would all change with the introduction of a revolutionary new technology: the World Wide Web.

In the early 1990s, the internet emerged as a viable way of communicating, and media outlets saw the benefit of having a presence on the World Wide Web. This new information platform had mass media outlets looking for ways to reach more people with improved content in ways they hadn't initially thought of before. What emerged from these efforts to improve storytelling and take advantage of different storytelling tools was a concept called convergence (see Figure 1.1).

Convergence saw print, broadcast, and online resources coming together as collective entities instead of separate media outlets. News broadcasters relied on print reporters to provide them tips on key stories, while broadcast journalists provided video clips for web distribution. Online

The printing press, invented by Johannes Gutenberg, signalled the beginning of the mass communication era.

http://istockphoto.com/dja65

TABLE 1.2 ■ Mass Communication's New Technologies

Printing Press	Telegraph	Phonograph	Radio	Television
• Invented in 1450 by Johannes Gutenberg • Allowed the mass production of printed material, instead of relying on hand-copying content • Improved access for all people to printed material and helped boost mass literacy	• Invented in 1836 by David Alter and popularized by Samuel Morse in 1837 • Allowed messages to be sent through physical communication lines across great distances • Improved the speed at which information was shared	• Invented in 1877 by Thomas Edison and improved upon by Alexander Graham Bell in the 1880s • Allowed the recording of words and music for sharing and preservation • Improved access to music and speech, similar to how the printing press helped share text	• Invented and patented in 1896 by Guglielmo Marconi • Allowed the transmission of messages across great distances without the use of wires • Improved opportunities to share content with a wider audience across a greater physical distance	• An all-electric version was invented in 1927 by Philo Farnsworth • Allowed sound and pictures to be transmitted across the airwaves • Improved on the radio model by adding visuals

FIGURE 1.1 ■ Traditional Versus Converging Media

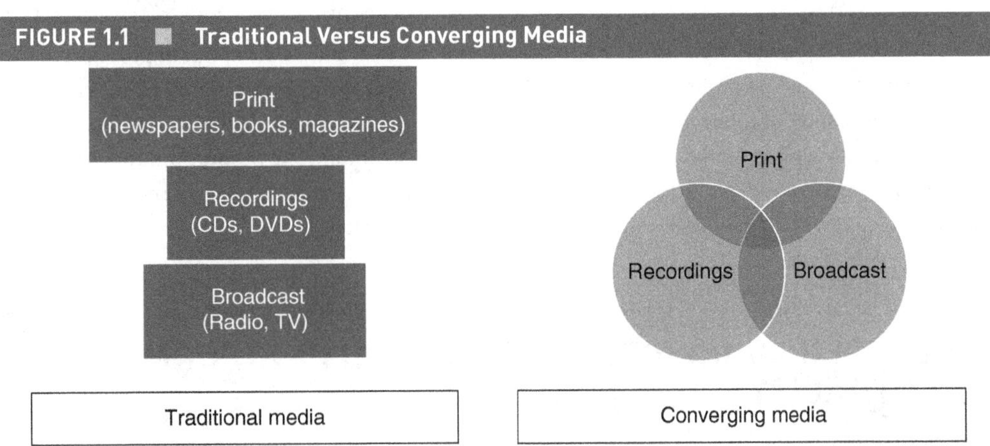

outlets posted print stories before they hit the press, giving newspaper reporters the opportunity to "scoop" the competition.

Critics of convergence have noted that the continued concentration of ownership prevents a wide array of voices from being heard, homogenizes content for the sake of profit, and has led to the dumbing down of information. Those who favor this approach note that giving owners the ability to operate multiple types of media allows them to provide more content across more platforms in shorter times and with better audience satisfaction.

The Digital Media Age

As the internet grew in terms of available content and ease of use, people began to see huge benefits to working with information that wasn't anchored to one place, one device, or one point in time. The ability to access the web through wireless internet, the growth of mobile devices that relied on apps to provide content to users, and the explosion of options to both send and receive content worked together to create the **digital media** era.

When media was still viewed as being defined by its physical format—such as newspapers or movies—users had to consider three key elements when consuming it:

1. Geography: The location of the market a media outlet served, such as the circulation area of a newspaper or the reach of a radio station's signal.
2. Time: The period when content was available, such as the hour a television program would air or the week when a movie would be available in a theater.
3. Scarcity: The limitation of available media, such as the number of copies of a book the library keeps or the number of copies of a magazine available at a bookstore.

These elements placed limitations on access for users, thus forcing them to make decisions regarding where they physically could go to get information, what information was available to them, and how long they could access that information before it was gone. When digital media arrived, it eliminated those concerns and limitations, as media practitioners applied technology and provided content in a way that allowed more people to access a greater volume of material.

Today's digital media realm provides content creators and users the ability to share information with anyone and everyone. It allows people to send and receive information that can be used, modified, and reshared across multiple platforms for the benefit of its audience members. The content is transferred electronically, and it can be easily replicated without a loss of quality. It can also be reconstructed, repurposed, and shared with a whole new audience for a purpose entirely different from that of its original creator.

As digital media continued to gain prominence, most traditional media organizations looked for ways to take advantage of it. Newspapers invested more in a digital-first mentality, posting breaking news content online prior to its running in the next day's print edition. Broadcast journalists relied on social media to provide live video of unfolding stories and to alert viewers about important stories. Book publishers sought ways to make their volumes more accessible on e-readers and other digital devices. Television and movie producers shifted away from traditional distribution approaches and standard episodic-delivery models. This opened the door for improved innovation and enhanced content-consumption opportunities as media users embraced **platform neutrality**: the concept of placing more value on the content than the device on which it is delivered.

A DEEPER LOOK: DIGITAL MEDIA AND PLATFORM NEUTRALITY

Digital media relies on several important tenets of traditional mass media, such as expanding the reach of the content, serving the needs of an audience, and providing content more quickly than was previously possible. However, the key distinction between traditional mass media and digital media is in the concept of platform neutrality.

Platform neutrality helps us focus on the primacy of information, meaning that the content we consume is more important than the way we consume it. For most of the twentieth century, information was conveyed through physical objects. If you found a funny cartoon in your local newspaper and wanted to share it with a friend, you'd have to physically cut it out and send it through the mail. If you wanted to send it to multiple people, you needed to photocopy it and then mail the copies out. When digital media emerged, computers made it easier to store, share, and replicate content without having to rely on tangible products. Now, with the click of a mouse or a touch on your screen, you could copy the information, save it to your device, and ship it off to hundreds or thousands of people in an instant.

The shift to digital media made platform distinctions and barriers less important and thus changed people's thinking to focus more on content than on devices. We now saw the benefit of the information itself and sought media outlets and distributors who could best meet our needs with regard to when and how we wanted this information. This not only gave rise to more media organizations and platforms that vied for our attention, but it also pushed traditional mass media practitioners to take advantage of digital options.

In a digital realm, the audience is free to consume content how, when, and where they want. For example, in the pre-internet world, a film was shown to a large audience at specific show times during a limited theater run, or an episode of a TV show was presented on a certain day or at a certain time. You had to physically travel to the theater or sit by your TV set at the specific time to watch. Today, we binge-watch shows through streaming services, record our favorite shows to a cloud-based DVR, and download episodes of long-canceled programs from Amazon or iTunes. Even more, we watch these shows and films on TVs, computers, tablets, and mobile devices in almost every public or private place imaginable. We can pause, save, rewatch, and stash content however we choose. The ability to platform-hop and time-shift has made content king in a way that wasn't possible for prior generations.

HOW DO WE USE MEDIA TO INTERACT?

LEARNING OBJECTIVES

LO 2: Illustrate the basic communication models and analyze the models' key components.

Thousands of times each day, we communicate using a wide variety of means without even thinking about it. A quick "snap" to a friend could help set up a study meeting or simply brighten their mood with a laugh. A discussion with your family at the dinner table could help them learn all about your day. A quick handwave could tell another driver who just arrived at a four-way intersection that you want them to go first.

These interactions contain several key components researchers have identified in most basic communication. Let's take a look at those components and several basic communication models to see how they explain what we do instinctively every day.

Communication Components

Defining the basic components of communication is one of the more difficult aspects of understanding these media models. Communication is something you have done for your entire life without giving much thought to it, so trying to explain it might seem awkward. It's like describing how to tie your shoes to a little kid: you've done it so often, it's essentially muscle memory. When you have to explain how to hold the laces at the beginning or how tight to pull the bow, it can feel strange.

To help explain how communication works, several theorists developed models to describe this process. Table 1.3 outlines the basic process through which a message is sent to a receiver.

All media models retain some form of these basic elements, even though the more complex models rely on different approaches and alternative terms to explain how the communication occurs.

Linear Model of Communication

Initial models of communication sought to explain how information started at Point A and reached Point B. As the shortest distance between two points is a straight line, scholars sought to explain communication using a **linear model**.

In the late 1940s, Claude Shannon and Warren Weaver developed the initial linear model of communication based on a mathematical approach to understanding how radio and television waves travelled most efficiently.[1] These researchers stated that a message starts with a **source**, travels along a **medium** of some form, and then reaches a **receiver** at the other end. This approach to communication is often referred to as a **transmission model**, because it described how a message is sent, or transmitted, from a source to a receiver.

TABLE 1.3 ■ Communication Models

Component	What It Is	Also Known As	Examples
Sender	The source of a message or its starting point	• Source • Communicator • Encoder • **Originator**	• A teacher delivering a lecture • A television station sending out a nightly news broadcast • A baby crying in its crib
Message	The information that is being communicated	• Content • Information • Transmission	• A story in a newspaper • A push alert on your phone • A statement a friend makes • A "thumbs up" gesture
Channel	The format that you use to send the message	• Media • Platform	• Smartphone • TV set • Newspaper
Receivers	The end point of a message	• Communicators • Decoders • **Recipients**	• A crowd at a rally • A waiter taking your order • A student in a class
Noise	Anything that interferes with the sender's message reaching the receiver		• Advertising meant to negate the sender's message • Other messages competing for the receiver's attention • Literal noise (such as a lawn mower drowning out speech)

The model eventually expanded to consider additional elements, such as the influence of outside interference, which is often referred to as **noise**. From a technological standpoint, noise included any elements that could block signals, such as a mountain range limiting access to radio signals.

In the 1960s, David Berlo's theories helped shift the linear approach to focus more on human orientation. His **Sender-Message-Channel-Receiver (SMCR) model**[2] considered various contributing factors in each stage of communication that would either enhance or diminish the likelihood of its success (see Figure 1.2).

FIGURE 1.2 ■ Sender-Message-Channel-Receiver Model of Communication

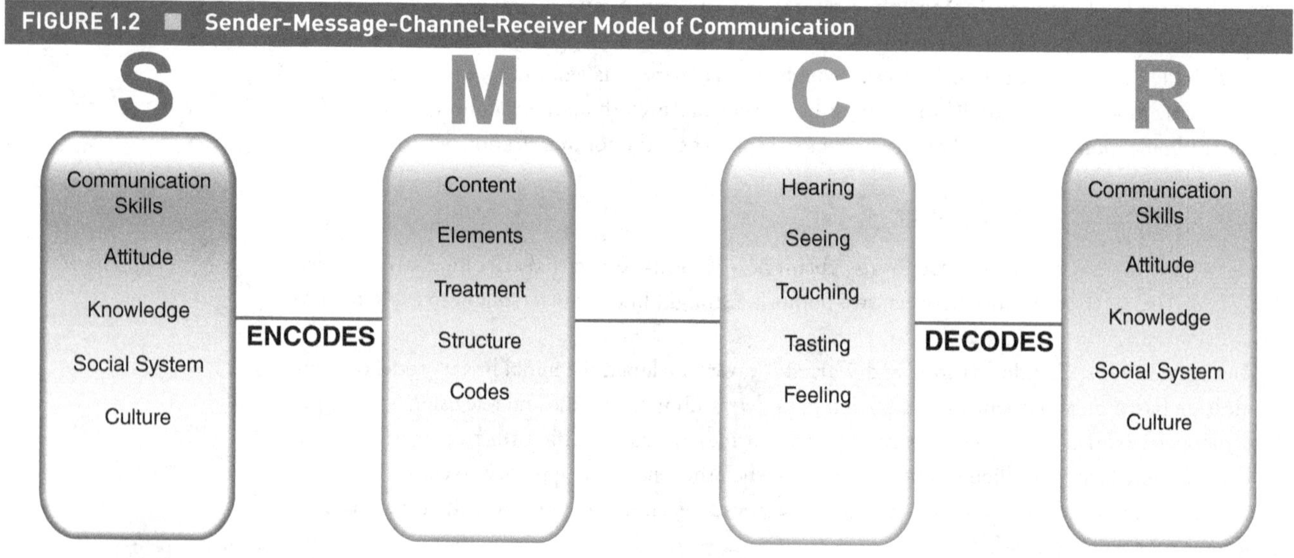

David Berlo's model of communication helps outline the ways in which information is shared between people. Although it is criticized for its simplicity, it was one of the first models to clearly capture the interpersonal communication process.

Here's how the model works:

- The sender begins the process with the intent of sharing a message. The sender's level of communication skill and attitude can enhance or limit potential success. In addition, the sender's knowledge of the topic, the message, and the receiver can play an important role in this communication process.
- The message is sent, having been encoded by the sender with elements that can improve or detract from its quality. The content itself plays a vital role in the message's success, but other elements, like nonverbal gestures and the tone of the speaker, matter as well. How the message is packaged and structured also matter as do coding elements, such as language usage.
- The message is sent through a channel, such as a magazine, a website, or a computer. The channel must be able to reach the person through one of the five senses humans rely on for sensory perception.
- The receiver gets the message and decodes it using their communication skills, attitudes, knowledge, social system, and culture. The more the sender and receiver share similar traits in these areas, the more likely the communication effort will be successful.

Berlo's critics noted that the simplicity of his approach fails to consider the way in which interpersonal communication actually functions. People rarely serve as only senders or receivers. In addition, the quality of the communication can wax and wane according to a variety of interactions that occur between sender and receiver, as well as additional outside forces. The linear model adequately represents the technical process Shannon and Weaver had described, but it clearly lacks the nuances experienced in human interactions.

Interactive Model of Communication

To deal with the shortcomings of the linear model, Wilbur Schramm and his research colleagues began to look at communication as a shared process between participants. Communication became less of a straight line from a single sender to a single receiver but rather a circular movement of shared engagement between participants. This **interactive model** also is known as the **Osgood-Schramm model** (see Figure 1.3):

FIGURE 1.3 ■ Osgood-Schramm Model of Communication

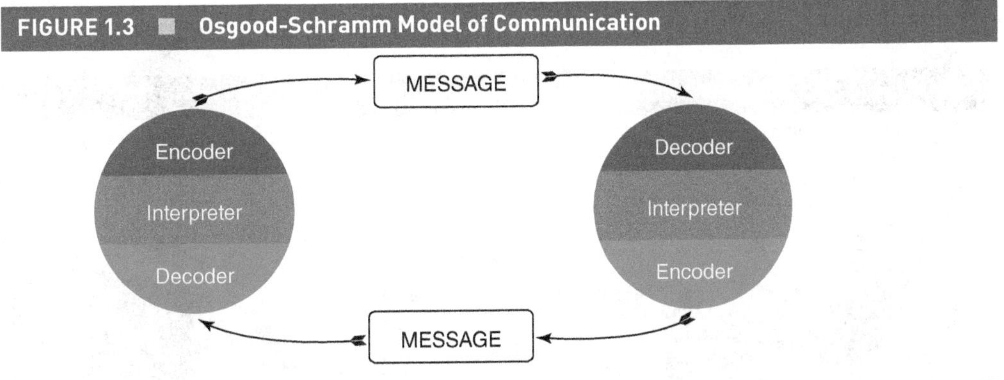

The Osgood-Schramm model of communication was one of the earliest attempts to explain how communication was more interactive and less unidirectional.

- Communication begins with a message the sender **encodes** with meaning and value, indicating a sense of purpose within the communication.[3]
- The sender than puts the message into some form that will be sent through a channel, with the intention of reaching the receiver.
- The receiver then takes the message and **decodes** it, attempting to understand the content of the message, as well as the source's meaning.

- As that occurs, the receiver becomes the sender of a secondary message, known as **feedback**, which will determine how successful the original sender has been.
- Between the sender and receiver, forces that are not tied directly to the message can increase or decrease the likelihood of the message's success.

If you think about your last interaction with a professor, you could see this model playing out something like this:

You: I'm confused about my midterm paper assignment. What am I supposed to do?
Professor: Well, you need to be able to discuss media communication theory by referring to the many different approaches that we've discussed in class.
You (Looking puzzled): I know that, but I'm not sure how to begin...
Professor: Do you mean you don't know how to describe these theories or don't know which theories to discuss?
You: I don't know which ones to discuss.
Professor: Well, choose one that you think is particularly important. You can briefly mention how it relates to the others at the end of your paper.
You: Thanks!

In this model, communication is a dynamic process that views individuals as simultaneously being senders and receivers. It also allows participants to succeed or fail based on misunderstandings or other problems occurring within the interaction. External "noise" issues, proposed in the earlier linear model, remain possible here, but this model also accounts for additional interpersonal and psychological factors, such as shared experiences, contextual clues, and emotional elements. Thus, what you might consider to be a simple request to your roommates to turn down the music could be construed as a passive-aggressive complaint about how they live their lives.

Transactional Model of Communication

The **transactional model** of communication presents the most dynamic approach to communication. Instead of either a linear or circular pattern of information sharing, this model looks at individuals as sharing space within a communication zone, allowing them to serve as both senders and receivers at various points and times within the process. The communication that results occurs as part of a cooperative action that leads to a mutually beneficial result (see Figure 1.4).[4]

FIGURE 1.4 ■ The Transactional Model of Communication

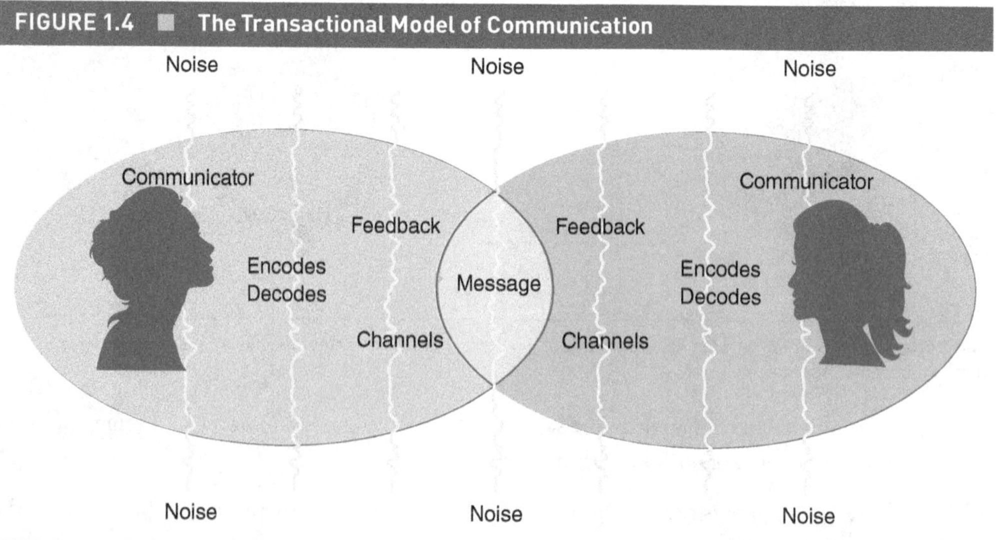

The transactional model incorporates more real-world elements, including individual experiences, the presence of noise, and the lack of "turn-taking" in communication.

Source: Guerrero and McEwan, *Interpersonal Encounters*, 1e, Sage Publishing, 2022.

As is the case with the interactive model, outside "noise" can limit the success of the communication, and the communication has an overall goal couched in purposeful contact between the individuals. However, unlike the interactive model, this approach acknowledges that the "turn-taking" associated with messages and feedback tends to oversimplify the communication process. In addition, this model requires individuals to have a shared understanding when they engage with each other. This could be as simple as both sharing a common language or as complex as a long-term relationship in which preexisting knowledge and understanding are essentially baked into every communication effort.

This best represents what many of us do every day, whether it's engaging in a group chat with friends or working together around a table on a group project. The shared space and understanding allows us to react to how others are presenting information as well as how they present themselves as communicators to the group. You might choose to speak a lot because others are silent, or you might become silent when it is clear you are annoying other people with your chatter. You might show deference to one member of the group who is older or smarter, or you might take over the conversation because you are the only person who knows what's going on. This model considers all these potential elements—and much more.

WHAT DOES MEDIA DO TO US?

LEARNING OBJECTIVES

LO 3: Assess the role of each media theory in understanding mass media.

Even as the media landscape continues to radically shift in this new digital world, the concept of how media affects us as individuals is crucial. Given how much media we consume, the wide array of choices available to us, and the potential outcomes that result from media consumption, we all need a working understanding of media theories. The reason theories matter is that they provide us with a set of shared expectations of what is likely to occur in a given situation, based on what researchers found has happened consistently in similar situations in the past. Table 1.4 outlines some of those theories, with basic explanations of how they are supposed to work. Let's dig into these ideas more deeply.

TABLE 1.4 ■ Media Theories

Theory	Basic Explanation	Example
Magic bullet/"hypodermic needle"	Media messages are simple and direct, penetrating the minds of consumers and creating specified actions.	You see an ad for Diet Coke and you go out and buy one.
Gatekeeping	Media messages pass through a series of decision points that determine if they get to the audience.	A newspaper editor decides there isn't enough room to run a story on a high school basketball game, so no one in the community knows who won.
Agenda setting	Media establishes the key topics in our day-to-day lives. However, it doesn't necessarily change our opinions about those events.	The media's coverage of the U.S. withdrawal from Afghanistan keeps that story on your mind, but it doesn't change whether you support or oppose the withdrawal.
Framing	Media practitioners place emphases on specific aspects of a topic, thus coloring the way in which consumers view it.	The construction of a new apartment complex is framed as "bad for the environment," focusing our attention on ecological issues.
Spiral of silence	The more a person's opinion is in the majority, the more likely that person is to speak out. The less a person's opinion is in the majority, the quieter they remain about the issue.	A group of your friends support Bill Smith for homecoming court. You don't like Bill, but you keep that to yourself.
Third-person effect	People drastically overestimate the influence messages have on other people while underestimating the impact the messages have on themselves.	Your roommate says the violent video games he plays online never bother him, but he worries about "all those weirdos I play against."

The Magic-Bullet Theory

One of the earliest media effects theories to gain traction was also one of the most frightening in terms of the potential damage media could do. The **magic-bullet theory**, which is often called the **hypodermic-needle model**, saw media messages as both direct and impactful. In this model, a message was essentially "injected" into the heads of the people who saw it, thus allowing it to penetrate their minds and create specified outcomes. Although he didn't use these terms specifically, researcher Harold Lasswell outlined this theory in his 1927 book *Propaganda Technique in the World War*, which essentially said that a propagandist could force people to bend to the will of the propagandist through proper media messaging.[5]

The idea that media owners could essentially shoot messages into audience members' minds and leave them helpless but to obey sounded terrifying at the time, even if it seems laughable today. In an attempt to poke holes in the theory, researcher Paul Lazarsfeld and his colleagues conducted research on the 1940 presidential election. The study, which looked at voting patterns and exposure to media messages created by Franklin D. Roosevelt's campaign, determined that the campaign didn't turn people into mindless zombies who did as they were told.[6] Instead, Lazarsfeld found that people can choose which messages affect them and which ones don't, thus starting a research path known as the **limited-effects model**. (All of the theories we will discuss in this chapter fall into this category.)

By the mid-1950s, the magic-bullet theory had fallen out of favor with researchers, who found that interpersonal relationships and social norms had much more influence over people than direct media messages. However, a few researchers continue to study the idea of a direct cause-and-effect connection between media use and personal actions.[7]

Gatekeeping

To understand what media can do to us, it is important to understand how information gets to us, which is explained by **gatekeeping**: how media professionals decide what content the public gets to see. Although many changes have occurred since the theory came into play more than seventy years ago, gatekeeping retains an important role in helping us understand information flow.

In 1950, David Manning White published a study that examined the ways in which editors and newsroom routines and processes influenced what people saw in their daily newspapers.[8] He followed the actions of a single editor, dubbed "Mr. Gates," who would make decisions about what made it into the publication. At the end of the week, only about 10 percent of the material Mr. Gates examined got published. The 90 percent that was rejected, White found, came as a result of the editor's own personal definition of what mattered and what didn't, as opposed to a clear set of rules and regulations within the newsroom. This study helped solidify the concept of gatekeeping, which explains the ways in which content makes it through a series of checkpoints before the public gets access to it through a media outlet.

The originator of gatekeeping theory was social psychologist Kurt Lewin, who developed it while studying the grocery-shopping habits of Midwestern housewives during World War II.[9] He noted that the women had a wide array of choices at the market, but only so many things would make it into their carts and thus become part of their families' meals. In studying this, Lewin found that individual choices made it possible for food to get into the cart or to be kept out.

Whether it was food in a grocery cart or copy across an editor's desk, this decision-making process made sense in a traditional media platform that had limited space or time, such as newspapers or radio broadcasts. Editors were under pressure to find ways to limit content, because not all of it could "fit in." In addition, the number of media outlets available to the public were limited, because even the largest cities had relatively fewer newspapers or radio stations compared with the sources we now have in the digital era.

The concept of gatekeeping can seem dated in a digital age, with the idea that only a few people can hold sway over whether information gets out to the public. However, scholars note that gatekeeping still exists, in large part due to the very technology that supposedly eliminates it. Information still begins at a source and ends up in the hands of the audience, even though the amount of content and the processes for moving it along have shifted. In White's day, the gatekeepers were humans; today, they are algorithms and selection tools.

In addition, when we consume and share media, we act as gatekeepers for our family, friends, and colleagues. A study published in 2021 showed that people who share content via social media platforms with people they know have essentially taken on the role of gatekeeper that once belonged only to editors like Mr. Gates.[10] Instead of relying on a newspaper editor to choose what we see or read, we now rely on what our friends post, retweet, or up-vote on a variety of platforms.

Agenda Setting

Agenda setting means that the media tends to focus on a small number of current events or issues, which thus become important to the public. Max McCombs and Donald Shaw began studying how the media can shape public attitudes through a series of studies in the late 1960s. Their work on the 1968 presidential election revealed a strong correlation between what the news media in Chapel Hill, North Carolina, heavily reported on and what residents of that area saw as important.[11] Although the media did not persuade people to think about the issues in a specific way, it did highlight and draw attention to those topics, thus leading the authors to note its agenda-setting function.

The concept of agenda-setting theory is based on one of McCombs's key influences, Bernard Cohen. Cohen famously noted that the media isn't successful about telling the people what to think, "but it is stunningly successful in telling its readers what to think about."[12] To that end, media outlets select areas they see as mattering a great deal and cover them vigorously. This puts the issues front and center for media consumers, who then decide for themselves how they feel about the topics.

For example, the 2020 presidential election tended to focus on the impact of the coronavirus pandemic and the way in which U.S. officials handled it.[13] While President Donald Trump touted his successes in fast-tracking a vaccine, challenger Joe Biden noted the slow response Trump's administration initially had to the outbreak. The degree to which voters reading about the topic agreed with either man varied, but the fact remains that COVID-19 stayed front and center in election discussions.

Framing

Similar to agenda-setting theory, the concept of framing suggests that media practitioners emphasize certain topics or ideas while ignoring others, thus eliciting specific responses from consumers. Erving Goffman discussed the concept of framing at length in his 1974 book *Frame Analysis*, in which he explained the way in which frames can exist for us and how they shape our understanding of what we see. For the sake of our discussion here, let's consider the ideas of physical frames and social frames.

A physical frame expands or limits our ability to physically observe something. For example, a peephole in a hotel door frames what we can see outside of our room, presenting an extremely restricted visual corridor. Conversely, a picture window in an oceanside home widens the field of vision and allows us to take in a wide array of elements outside of the house.

Physical frames can shift the way in which we consume content in the media and thus change how we think about what we have seen. For example, during the 2017 inauguration of President Donald Trump, the media and the White House argued vehemently about the size of the crowd and how it was photographed. Images taken from the back of the National Mall less than an hour before the ceremony showed large swaths of open space and few people milling around the area. Images taken from the same vantage point at approximately the same point in time during President Barack Obama's 2009 ceremony showed a mall flooded with people.[14] In the days that followed Trump's inauguration, the White House tried to "reframe" this by releasing photos of the event that were significantly cropped, making it seem like the crowd filled the whole frame and thus packed the Mall.[15]

Social framing relates to how people, organizations, and the media draw attention to certain events, focus on specific aspects of them, or portray them for the public at large. To do this, these individuals and groups apply social constructs to specific actions as a way of translating content for the audience. This translation relies on a number of things, including the experiences of the sender, the expectations of the receiver, and the goals associated with the communication.[16]

Several media organizations published side-by-side comparisons of the crowds at the first inauguration of President Barack Obama in 2009 versus the crowd at President Donald Trump's inauguration.

Reuters/Alamy Stock Photo

Let's look at a simple example that might help this make more sense. Your university wants to buy five houses near campus so it can knock them down and build a science center for its students. The people who own those houses have lived there for decades and do not want to move. When the school initially pitched this idea, the state's environmental protection agency stated that the proposed new science building would create high levels of ecological damage to the area, with a limited benefit. Finally, the city's historical society noted that three of the five homes feature a form of architecture that is rare and irreplaceable if lost.

The various organizations involved could frame the situation in different ways.

- The university could say that the new science building offers opportunity for growth and educational advancement.
- The homeowners could frame it as the big, bad university pushing around a few elderly people who can't fight back.
- The environmental agency could frame this as an issue of growth versus environment, arguing a need for balance.
- The historical society could frame it as an issue of progress destroying history.

The local media could pick up on any one of these themes or any one of a dozen others in its portrayal of this situation. In short, the message that the audience receives will be in some way influenced by the frame itself. Therefore, the framing of the issue will go a long way toward how people will come to support or reject this proposal.

If you stop and think about it, we see this almost everywhere in media coverage, particularly when it comes to political issues or topics of social conflict. Immigrants trying to escape war and poverty by coming to the United States can be framed as a "flood of illegal immigrants"[17] or as migrants who "bravely risk their lives and safety…sustained only by the hope that somehow they might find a better life."[18] Gun laws can be framed as an issue of constitutional freedoms or as an issue of public safety. Even how we see sporting events can come down to framing: Did your team have a miraculous comeback, or did the other team choke at end of the game? It depends on how you want to see it and how people in the media portray it. This is why framing can be a powerful tool in shaping public opinion and personal ideology.

Spiral of Silence

If you walked into a classroom and found four or five of your classmates loudly discussing support for a political candidate whom you despise, would you enter the discussion and voice your opinion? What if it was twenty people? The whole class? If you can understand the tension between your desire to speak and your fear of being in the minority opinion, you will start to understand how the **spiral of silence** works.

Elisabeth Noelle-Neumann discussed this concept in detail back in 1974 to explain when people decide to voice their opinion on important topics.[19] She believed that people generally fear social isolation, so they constantly try to remain aware of the majority's opinions. (Noelle-Neumann referred to this ability to feel the mood of the people around them as a "quasi-statistical sense" of public opinion.) The more people feel that their opinions on a given topic are in the majority, the more likely they are to speak out about it. Conversely, people who feel they are in the minority will resist the urge to express their opinions for fear of social rejection. This leads to fewer and fewer opinions' emerging, thus creating a spiral of silence toward one dominant view.

Media outlets play a crucial role in how people come to understand whether they are in the majority or minority on an issue. Polls can demonstrate that a topic is gaining ground as the dominant ideology. Stories about a topic can drive a point of view. Advertising that appears on billboards all over town or in social media feeds can reinforce the idea that everyone is talking about a certain topic in a certain way. This leads people who might normally express themselves to remain quiet.

Noelle-Neumann's theory has met with resistance over the years because researchers have had difficulty consistently replicating it. Even more, recent research has taken issue with how much influence the larger public has on people in this hypersegmented society. More often than not, other social groupings, such as close friends and family members, hold higher levels of sway over people than the general public.[20] Also, research into digital communication and social media has had a mixed bag of results, with some people feeling more empowered than in face-to-face communications, while others report a tendency toward self-censorship.[21] However, the premise behind the theory, that of individuals' willingly censoring themselves in the face of withering public support, remains a vital one to understand in this digital media age.

Third-Person Effect

People generally understand that messages spread through the media can create influence, shape opinions, and drive actions. They also tend to think that those effects happen only to other people, not them. This overestimation of the impact media has on "those people" while feeling like the media can't influence "me personally" is the core of what is called the **third-person effect**.

W. Phillips Davison coined this term in a 1983 research article that laid out the basic tenets of the theory.[22] He conducted four small experiments in which he analyzed the degree to which people felt that a message could influence them as opposed to the general public. His findings revealed that participants felt "others with 'more impressionable minds'...will be affected" rather than themselves. People who have studied this phenomenon have found that it applies in everything from social media use[23] to the viewing of direct-to-consumer advertising.[24]

A 2023 study revealed that heavy users of social media were not only likely to blame others for perpetuating fake news content but also more likely to overestimate their own abilities to separate fact from fiction on social media compared with people they saw as not being like them.[25] This supports findings in numerous other studies, including one by the Pew Research Center, which revealed that more than 80 percent of people felt confident in their ability to differentiate fake news from factual information. However, 64 percent of those surveyed stated that fake news causes "a great deal of confusion about basic facts of current issues and events."[26] In other words, the participants feel that they personally could figure out what is and isn't true, even as most of them thought the general public is confused by these fake stories.

The third-person effect has been used as a rationale for censoring even real information.[27] For example, researchers have found that people who report larger gaps between the level of impact messages have on themselves and others are more likely to support the censorship of television violence and pornography.[28] Their rationale is that it's clear that the general public (namely, you people out there who aren't me) will become violent porn addicts if "we" let them see this kind of material, and thus we have to put up some sort of barrier between it and them. It's basically for them own good.

Each of these theories falls into the category of what researchers call "effects theories," because they examine the effect that media use has on us. In Chapter 2, we will discuss a theory that looks at what we do with media itself and the ways in which all of these theories can help us be smarter and better media consumers.

MEDIA LITERACY MOMENT: PRACTICAL APPLICATIONS OF THEORETICAL CONCEPTS

Media theories can appear to have little personal relevance when you read about them in a book like this. The benefit of understanding media theories is that you can better appreciate how you and others can be influenced by the content you consume. In addition, you can apply these theories to the behaviors you see in society and analyze your own behavior as well.

For example, during the coronavirus pandemic, some areas of the United States implemented mandates that required people to wear masks in certain environments. Some people viewed this as a necessary first step toward preventing the spread of the virus, while others saw it as a pointless infringement on their personal freedom.

If you read the news stories or watch television reports on this topic, you can see how framing theory applies here. News outlets that presented the story in a "personal freedom" frame were more likely to feature individual citizens who resented the mandates, providing personal anecdotes about problems with the masks. News outlets that presented it with a "health care" frame were more likely to interview scientists and doctors to present data and research findings to support their position. Understanding these frames can help you understand how people will perceive the issue and which sources they gravitate toward in this debate.

The third-person effect can also be applied to our everyday media experiences. People in a city or town often protest when someone wants to open a business there that has negative social connotations to it, such as a marijuana dispensary or a strip club. News stories will often quote people who say things like, "We can't have this around our children" or "We don't know what kinds of people will come here to frequent this establishment." Nobody ever tells a reporter, "If they open this strip club so close to my house, I'm probably going to spend my entire paycheck one dollar at a time on a dancer named Delight," or "With such easy access to weed, I'm probably going to get stoned more often than I should." In other words, the protesters believe they will be fine but others will sustain significant damage.

These theories can help you understand media in a more meaningful fashion as you closely study what media outlets do when they disseminate content, as well as how and why people react to information in the way that they do.

THE NEXT STEP: Find a news article or news broadcast story on a topic that matters to you. Review the theories listed in this section and find one you think you can best use to analyze that story. Explain how the story fits within the parameters of that theory as well as how understanding this theory helped you better assess the material. Write a short essay that sums up your findings.

FROM MEDIA CONSUMER TO MEDIA CREATOR

LEARNING OBJECTIVES

LO 4: Understand the value of media in terms of employment opportunities.

The importance of understanding what we consume as media users and what it does to us matters a great deal in understanding the vital role this field plays in society. Understanding the history of communication, the theories that govern it, and the practical application of communication in the real world all have value and merit. However, real people create the content you consume every day in a wide array of jobs that might be of interest to you, so it is important to give you a look at that element of mass communication as well.

The media field is not only rich with employment opportunities for writers, editors, photographers, videographers, and digital producers, but it is continuing to widen in terms of the variety of jobs that require the skills media professionals garner in their education. Being able to understand both the long-view aspects of the field as well as the opportunity for hands-on employment could give you a leg up in this field, if you are interested.

Let's take a look at a couple ways in which you could shift from media consumer to a media creator:

Traditional Media Jobs

Media fields offer graduates a wide array of potential career options, with many areas in those fields showing expansive growth. News fields are showing declines in traditional positions, like newspapers and broadcast television, but digital jobs that rely on skills common in those fields are continuing to grow. Filmmaking, sound engineering, and other technical fields in media are showing significant growth, as are the fields of advertising, public relations, and technical writing.

These jobs offer people the opportunity to produce content for a wide array of audiences through the use of their writing, audio, video, and social media skills. Table 1.5 offers a handy overview of some of the most common positions open today. We will dig into each of these areas, as well as a number of specific jobs within each of them, in later chapters of the book.

TABLE 1.5 ■ Expected Growth in Media Jobs Over the Next Decade.

Field	Expected Growth/Decline by 2029
Advertising and marketing	+6 percent
Public relations	+7 percent
Broadcast news	−11 percent
Print news	−7 percent
Digital news	+3 percent
Film making	+10 percent
Videography	+18 percent
Radio and sound engineering	+9 percent
Technical writing	+7 percent
Book publishing	+2 percent

Source: Bureau of Labor Statistics.

Valuable Skills for Other Careers

Even if you don't plan to spend your life as a film producer, a news reporter, or an advertising executive, the media-related tools you can pick up during your time in school will make a huge difference in becoming a viable member of the workforce. The rise in digital media, coupled with the growth of digital natives who are consuming it, makes it crucial for employers to seek people who can understand how media works.

For example, social media growth within the United States continues to explode and diversify, with more than 246 million users taking part at some level in 2023. That number represents approximately three-fourths of the country's population and a 20-million-user increase since 2017.[29] To connect with these people, employers are consistently seeking applicants who can use social media to connect with potential audience members in an effective fashion. The ability to use these platforms, as well as video, audio, and photo tools for capturing and editing content, is at a premium across all industries.

Beyond technological acumen, employers are looking for people who can think critically and write well. According to the National Association of Colleges and Employers, 73 percent of hiring mangers want their employees to have strong writing skills. Experts note that the ability to write well demonstrates both effective communication abilities and clear-thinking skills. Other surveys of employers showed that critical thinking and problem solving were among other necessary skills for successful employees.[30] Education in this field can provide you with these attributes and make you a sought-after applicant in many fields.

CHAPTER REVIEW

LO1 **Describe the concept of media and the ways in which it developed over time.**

- Media encompasses the tools, platforms, and content we use to communicate thoughts, ideas, and information from one individual or group to another.
- Oral (spoken), visual (images), and written (text) communication evolved over a long period of time as the need developed for new media to communicate more efficiently.
- Mass communication began around 1450 with the development of the printing press and expanded with other technological advances that made it easier to copy and share media.
- Digital media relies on technological devices and methods to send and receive information that can be used, modified, and reshared across multiple platforms.
- Information primacy and platform neutrality helped give rise to the digital media era. The development and sharing of content took precedence over the physical platform that was used to deliver it.

LO2 **Illustrate the basic communication models and analyze the models' key components.**

- Most communication models contain a source, a message, a channel, and a receiver.
- The linear communication model describes how information moves from Point A (sender) to Point B (receiver). An example of this would be a radio signal being broadcast from a station to a radio receiver in someone's car.
- The interactive communication model focuses on how participants share roles as senders and receivers. This "turn-taking" approach includes the encoding of information by the sender and the decoding of information by the receiver. The receiver, in turn, provides feedback to the initial sender. An example of this would be a question-and-answer session between a professor and a student.
- The transactional model serves as a less structured approach to communicating in which individuals share space within a communication zone. This model allows the participants to act as both senders and receivers at various points in the process without fixed roles. An example of this would be a group chat on your phone with your friends.

LO3 **Assess the role of each media theory in understanding mass media.**

- The magic-bullet theory suggests that mass media messages are essentially "shot" into the minds of consumers, who then act on those messages. This theory has fallen out of favor as being too simplistic and easily disprovable.
- Gatekeeping examines the ways that media professionals determine what content reaches the public. Only about 10 percent of all potential content is published for public consumption. Each media's rationale for what should see the light of day helps explain how information moves within a media system.
- Agenda-setting theory proposes that the media isn't good at telling people *what* to think, but it can be valuable in telling what people should think *about*.
- Framing examines the way in which the media presents content for public discussion, placing emphasis on certain elements of a topic and deemphasizing others.

- The spiral-of-silence theory addresses why people choose to speak or not speak publicly about a specific topic. People who feel that their opinion is in the majority will speak out, while those in the minority will keep their thoughts to themselves.
- Third-person effect states that people drastically overestimate their own ability to resist the influence of mass communication messages compared with the general public.

LO4 Understand the value of media in terms of employment opportunities.

- Media can provide you with vast opportunities for employment, including radio, television, film, publishing, newspapers, magazines, and video games.
- Even people who lack an interest in media careers can benefit from improving their critical thinking and writing skills through the study of media.

KEY TERMS

Agenda setting
Decode
Digital media
Encode
Feedback
Framing
Gatekeeping
Hypodermic-needle model
Interactive model
Limited-effects model
Linear model
Magic-bullet theory
Mass communication
Media
Medium
Noise
Originator
Oral communication
Osgood-Schramm Model
Platform
Platform neutrality
Receiver
Recipient
Sender-Message-Channel-Receiver model
Spiral of silence
Source
Third-person effect
Transactional model
Transmission model
Visual communication
Written communication

DISCUSSION QUESTIONS

1. When you think of your media use, how much do you think of it in terms of the devices you use, and how much do you think of it as the content you consume? In other words, if you say, "I want to watch a TV show," do you think of it being related to the television or other screen on which it is showing, or do you think of it as the story you are viewing, regardless of where you're seeing it?

2. Given the many models outlined, do you think is important to understand how communication functions in order to be successful at it? Can people who don't understand the components of these models or the way in which information flows between senders and receivers effectively communicate?

3. Which of the communication theories outlined in the chapter do you think makes the most sense in relation to your own use of media? Which elements are most pertinent to you, and which do you think are either outdated or problematic?

4. How varied is your media diet, and what do you think it does to your point of view on important issues? Do you think an improved effort toward media literacy will benefit you in any meaningful way? Why or why not?

A group of people gather to watch a television program together.

MBI/Alamy Stock Photo

MEDIA AUDIENCES AND USES

INTRODUCTION

1. *What are some of the reasons you think people have for choosing to watch certain shows or movies? What benefits do you think they get from this kind of activity? What is the difference between watching as a group and watching on your own?*
2. *How often do you think about who creates the content you consume?*
3. *Are you ever worried about what effects the amount or type of media you consume is having on you? Why or why not?*

Consumers today take in exponentially more media content than those of previous generations. As a result, they need to better understand who is sending the content to them, what benefits they get from that content, and what concerns they should have about their media diets. This chapter will explain how to define a mass media audience, outlining the key factors that help place individuals into useful groupings. It will also explain what drives people to consume media, what benefits they get out of consuming it, and what drawbacks are associated with it. It will also introduce the idea of "demassification," the process through which media has become more individualized and how individuals can reach interested audiences without going through traditional media conglomerates. Finally, it will outline why understanding these basic media concepts can help you better navigate the media world around you.

LEARNING OBJECTIVES

After completing this chapter you should be able to:

1. Define a mass media audience using demographic, psychographic, and geographic information.
2. Describe the importance of media literacy.
3. Explain why people consume media content, including the specific needs it satisfies.
4. Assess the concerns people have about media consumption and its effects on users.
5. Explain the concept of "demassification" and how it relates to today's media world.

FROM AGE TO INTERESTS: A BRIEF LOOK AT HOW TO DEFINE AN AUDIENCE

LEARNING OBJECTIVES

LO 1: Define a mass media audience using demographic, psychographic, and geographic information.

As a culture and a species, we have an innate need to know what's going on around us and why it matters, although what we care about and why we care can vary greatly from person to person. When we seek information from traditional and digital content outlets that is relevant, useful, and interesting to us, we become part of a mass media **audience**.

For generations, the public relied on what was defined as traditional mass media: forms of communication like newspapers, radio, and television that provided the public with the same information in a prescribed way. However, as we will see throughout this text, the way in which we think about mass media has changed greatly over the past few decades, thanks to technological innovation and the massive increase in media outlets.

When we consider how best to reach audiences through any form of media, three key elements are crucial in helping media professionals understand and target an audience:

1. Demographics
2. Psychographics
3. Geographics

Let's take a deeper look at each of these items and why they matter.

Demographics

If you think about any survey you have filled out, it probably included questions about your age, your gender, your race, and your education. These are just a few of the facts contained in your **demographics**. Collectively, these data points allow researchers to categorize people based on information about their identity.

Demographics are relatively stable personal elements that allow researchers to create basic categories in hopes of forming smaller groups within a population. For example, children under the age of six are limited in their social experiences and basic knowledge, so a television show aimed at them will likely rely on simple themes that are easily resolved. Conversely, individuals over the age of forty have a wider array of personal and professional interactions, thus allowing a television producer to use more complex themes, plot twists, and layered narratives.

Color choices and word selection can be shaped by demographics as well. According to web design expert Jennifer Kyrnin, blue-collar workers prefer common color tones and direct language to create a sense of stability and familiarity. Highly educated people, however, find inspiration in rare color hues and complex verbiage that pique their interests and create excitement.[1] So, you would want to take a different overall approach to developing a website for a steelworkers' union than you would for one targeting postdoctoral physicists.

Overall, demographics provide a good way to make some rough judgments about your audience in a way that serves to eliminate the people you don't plan to reach. Think about it like an artist carving a statue from a block of marble: the initial chiseling effort doesn't do much to define what the statue will look like, but it does eliminate material that doesn't need to be there. With that in mind, if you want to get a more refined look at your audience, you need to dig more deeply into its interests and values.

Psychographics

If you look around your classroom, you will likely see why demographics can tell researchers only so much about a group of people. In the most basic sense, the room probably contains people of similar ages and levels of education. However, if your professor said, "You folks are all exactly the same," it would likely get a big laugh from you all. Your interests, cultures, and connections all vary widely. While demographics can be helpful in defining an audience, psychographics matter a lot more.

Psychographics are defined as those things that "focus on the interests, affinities, and emotions of a group of people—exactly the things marketers need to understand to best position their product."[2] These traits can shed light on people's "passion points" that help define their individual identities and differentiate them from other people in any particular setting. It's the reason you can't assume that people who live in Boston will all be Red Sox fans or that every person who lives in a rural town will love country music.

While demographics can tell you what surface-level connections people have to certain characteristics, psychographics will help you understand the degree to which something resonates with them. For example, if two people select "Catholic" as their religion of choice on a survey form, you can assume they both have some connection to that faith. However, psychographics will help you see the degree to which they identify with the faith. Person A might be an avid churchgoer, who never misses a Sunday mass, attends all holy days of obligation, and takes part in various outreach efforts. All of Person A's children are named after saints, and they have all taken part in the sacraments at the appointed times of life. On the other hand, Person B might attend church only on Easter and Christmas because their family members force them to go. Other than that, Person B has no interest in anything having to do with the church or its tenets.

While demographics tell us "what" someone is, psychographics can fill in the "how" and "why" elements that make it easier to reach that person. Although these are more difficult to gather and interpret, the rewards for doing so are much more valuable.

Geographics

Geographics refers to a group of individuals' physical location. Although the internet has freed us from the bonds of geographic isolation, where we live and work still influences our personal experiences. According to the U.S. Department of Transportation, approximately seventeen thousand car crashes occur on an average day,[3] a bit of information that might or might not interest you. However, when you are stuck in highway traffic, unable to move more than a few feet at a time for an hour, you are probably *really* curious about what happened on the road ahead and how long it's going to take for you to get out of there.

When something occurs in a geographic area that somehow relates to us, we find it much more interesting than things happening elsewhere. For example, if you hear about a man on the news who was using a ladder to break into homes and steal people's pets, you might have a vague interest. If that report mentions your current neighborhood or your hometown, your interest is immediately heightened. This is why placing a premium on understanding geography matters in assessing an audience.

MEDIA LITERACY

LEARNING OBJECTIVES

LO 2: Describe the importance of media literacy.

The amount and type of media we consume can have short- and long-term effects on our overall sense of being. How media consumption affects our overall health starts to make a lot more sense when we think about it like the food we eat or the air we breathe. For example, on a hot, humid day, you might grab a soda pop out of your refrigerator and start guzzling away. The expected effects are easy to spot: the cold liquid quenches your thirst and makes you feel less overheated. The unexpected outcomes could be varied and undetectable in the short term. Gulping down that can of soda tosses an additional 170 to 200 calories into your body, or somewhere close to one-tenth of your recommended caloric intake for the day. If you drink a six-pack or more per day, you're likely to pack on a few pounds (or more) over time.

The sugar and caffeine in the beverage add a jolt to your system, pepping you up in the short term until you crash out a bit later. The chemicals in the soda might eventually lead to negative circulatory and digestive problems when you hit your fifties, sixties, or seventies. Heavy sugar ingestion can lead to the development of type 2 diabetes. And that's just a short list of what might occur. The point is, if you know all of these potential risks and benefits as you make your choice about whether to drink that soda, you're going to make better overall choices.

Media literacy follows the same basic premise, with the goal of helping you ask important questions about the media you encounter and allowing you to make smart choices about what you consume. The Media Literacy Now project defines this term as the ability to decode messages within the media, determine how those messages can create personal influence, and then act based on those understandings. In addition, the group notes that media literacy allows the creation of thoughtful and conscientious media content.[4] When individuals can thrive as literate consumers of media, they feel empowered to make improved media selections, analyze questionable media messages, and engage in improved personal and societal behavior.

To better understand this topic, here are a series of issues related to media literacy:

1. Credibility
2. Bias
3. Fairness
4. Outcome
5. Critical thinking

Let's take a deeper look at each of these issues and how they affect your media literacy.

Issues of Credibility: Who Gets Our Trust?

In life, we tend to develop relationships based on trust from an early age. Depending upon our personal experiences in those situations, we determine whom we are willing to trust, how much we are willing to trust them, and what it will take to make or break those bonds of trust. Making those choices helps us define who and who does not have **credibility**. Credibility is the nature of being trustworthy, believable, and dependable. It reflects an honesty of character and reliability.

Think about the primary relationships you experienced as a child. It might be with a parent or a grandparent who showered you with affection or kept you from hurting yourself. That person's repeated "good acts" gave you confidence that future interactions with them would be being worthy of trust. For example, if your grandmother gave you a cookie, you would probably not question it and eat it. The idea is that the source is true and good, therefore, the cookie is probably tasty and safe.

However, if you had an older brother who constantly tricked you by making you smell his gym shoes or drink milk laced with hot sauce, you would probably not trust anything he gave you. Thus, if the cookie came from your brother, you would likely see those previous "bad acts" as pretty good reasons to reject the cookie. You expect that source to be untrustworthy and you know six seconds after you ate the cookie, he'd start laughing and say, "The *dog* just *sat* on that!"

From the 1960s into the 1980s, Walter Cronkite was a mainstay at the CBS News anchor desk and earned the title of "the most trusted man in America." A trusted source can be more important than the information itself when it comes to what some people believe.

MBI/Alamy Stock Photo/Getty Images

We apply similar concerns to choose people to trust in our daily media diet. Trust builds when someone achieves a consistent level of living up to the expectations of the audience. When Walter Cronkite anchored the CBS evening news, he was deemed "the most trusted man in America," because he provided content in a way that gave people a reason to believe him.[5] Today, Lester Holt, David Muir, Norah O'Donnell, and Anderson Cooper are frequently among the anchors cited as being the "most trusted" in the field.[6]

Other sources aren't so lucky, because they have committed acts that led media consumers to view them as untrustworthy. Jayson Blair was a young and promising reporter for the *New York Times* in the early 2000s, when he covered everything from the Washington, DC, sniper case to the return home of fallen soldiers. However, when it turned out he had fabricated much of his reporting, the *Times* fired him and published a 7,000-word correction and retraction of his work. In 2022, *USA Today* found that reporter Gabriela Miranda likely fabricated interviews and sources in multiple stories. The paper pulled twenty-three of Miranda's stories from its website after conducting an internal audit of her work, and Miranda resigned from her position at the paper.[7]

Today, you have more media sources vying for your trust and attention than ever before. Traditional outlets such as newspapers, magazines, and broadcast news stations provide you with opportunities to consume their content on **legacy platforms**, such as print publications and televisions. In addition, they offer opportunities for you to engage with them via social media platforms and hosted websites. If that's not enough, the individual broadcasters, writers, reporters, editors, and other staff members can provide you with chances to follow their individual thoughts through those same social media venues.

Those sources, however, are dwarfed by the swarm of nonaffiliated media outlets and single-source **citizen journalists** who provide you with content solely through digital media. A citizen journalist can be anyone who serves as a source of information through an internet connection and a digital media device. Those people can be the goofy uncles who forward conspiracy tweets about how the government is behind a Twinkie shortage or venerable professors and media experts who host respected podcasts. Perhaps the most important citizen journalists are individuals who use the media tools at their disposal to capture important events that are unfolding in front of them. In 2021, the Pulitzer Prize board presented teenager Darnella Frazier with a special citation for recording George Floyd's murder on her phone. While walking to a store, she saw Minneapolis police officer Derek Chauvin kneeling on Floyd's neck for about nine minutes while handcuffing him. The video captured Floyd pleading for his life, saying "I can't breathe," and it became a touchstone for subsequent protests against police brutality. The board noted that the video demonstrated "the crucial role of citizens in journalists' quest for truth and justice.[8]

George Floyd protests.

Robert K. Chin/Alamy Stock Photo

The traditional media outlets are often the subject of attacks by these outside sources, who sometimes raise reasonable questions about the fairness and equity of their coverage. Others use social media to demean any factual reporting they dislike or distrust as **fake news**.

A DEEPER LOOK: FAKE NEWS AND MEDIA TRUST

During his 2016 presidential campaign and subsequent time as president, Donald Trump derided the mainstream media as perpetually providing incorrect information to the American people. Trump popularized the term "fake news" in his speeches, news conferences, and social media posts, arguing that newspapers, television stations, and other venerable institutions were lying to audiences. Trump is not unique in his attacks on the media as being "fake news," as politicians throughout the legislative hierarchy and across party lines have openly argued that the media isn't being honest and accurate.

In the wake of this assault on the free press, researchers and media professionals wondered what kind of impact this was having on how citizens came to think of the media they consumed. What they found was that people often had varying definitions of what "the media" actually included, but overall, they didn't trust "the media" very much anymore. A 2018 *Columbia Journalism Review* study placed the media among the least trusted social institutions in the United States. Only Congress ranked lower, while the president, the Supreme Court, the military, and law enforcement all received higher ratings.

Media trust appeared to peak in the mid-1970s at just over 70 percent of people saying they believed what they read in newspapers and saw on broadcast news. After a slow and steady decline in trust over the next few decades, Gallup polls revealed that media trust hit rock bottom in 2016, with only 32 percent of respondents reporting faith in journalism.

So how can media professionals regain trust? Researchers at Louisiana State University found that these outlets can start by simply fighting back. Their field experiment revealed that the importance of fact-checking content and media transparency remain valuable in showing the public that it should trust journalism. The study also revealed that when journalists responded to accusations of bias from the public, people tended to trust the journalists more. In addition, media practitioners who used honesty, transparency, and clarity in their interactions with the public tended to fare much better than those who did not.

Issues of Bias: Does the Source Have an Agenda?

The goal of journalism is to remain objective in the reporting, editing, and publishing of content, regardless of the source or the platform. It's an admirable goal, but it's a lot like trying to catch sand in a sieve: It's almost impossible and, even if you succeed, you still won't be perfect.

Bias, a prejudice for or against a specific topic, individual, or concept, has a way of seeping into all sorts of media coverage in big and little ways. For example, a reporter might write, "Fortunately, firefighters were able to extinguish the blaze before it destroyed the house." Someone could easily argue that if this were truly a "fortunate" situation, the fire wouldn't have happened in the first place. Still, this kind of opinion inclusion isn't going to land a reporter in front of an ethics panel.

Other forms of bias are much more problematic. For example, Instagram influencer and celebrity Kendall Jenner endorsed the failed Fyre Festival via her Instagram account. Jenner intimated that she

Influencer and celebrity Kendall Jenner promoted the Fyre Festival event.

Kristin Callahan/ZUMA Press/Newscom

and other major celebrities would be there, and that her brother-in-law, musician Kanye West, would be performing as part of the festivities. Jenner failed to disclose to her followers that she was paid $275,000 to make that post and that she hadn't researched the festival before endorsing it.[9] The festival turned out to be a disaster that cost participants and investors more than $26 million, and Jenner paid $90,000 in 2020 to settle a lawsuit regarding her involvement with the event.

Controversies like these have underscored the need for basic rules to promote honest content. Sources in a story that promote the benefits of a project should disclose their attachment to that project. When a news organization investigates a topic, it should disclose if its parent company has any connections to that topic or the organizations associated with it. If they don't tell you about these potential **conflicts of interest**, there is a risk that you are being played when you consume the content. Who knows if a star athlete really enjoys drinking Gatorade or if a musician really loves playing a Gibson guitar? It could be they enjoy chugging milk and strumming a homemade six-string instead, but they were paid to endorse those brand-name products.

Being media literate is about looking for biases within the sources you use and the content they provide. Then, you can better assess the degree to which you should trust those sources, even if they aren't perfectly objective.

Issues of Fairness: Just Because We Can, Does It Mean We Should?

The Society of Professional Journalists' code of ethics states that media professionals should "show compassion for those who may be affected by news coverage."[10] The goal is to remind journalists that just because we can do something, it doesn't necessarily mean that we should do so. This goal has taken on new meaning in the age of digital content sharing and the lack of shared ethical standards.

For example, in 2006, a teenager named Nikki Catsouras slammed the black Porsche she was driving into a concrete toll booth while driving nearly one hundred miles per hour. The crash scene was so grisly, her parents weren't allowed to identify her body. However, photos of her bloody body, still wedged into the crumpled wreck, leaked to the internet. Although many legacy media outlets did not reproduce the images, many websites posted them for public consumption. As Nikki's family pleaded with outlets to take them down, the question became less what was legally right and more what was ethically responsible.[11] Similar concerns became the focal point of a 2022 court case involving the widow of basketball great Kobe Bryant. After Bryant died in a helicopter crash in 2020, first responders took unnecessary close-up photographs of his body and that of the Bryants' daughter, Gianna, and then shared the images with other people. Vanessa Bryant sued Los Angeles County as a result, with her lawyer arguing that these images could go viral at any point if one person decided to post them online. The jury sided with Vanessa Bryant and awarded her sixteen million dollars.[12]

The same responsibility that individuals have to consider the implications of their online behavior applies to media outlets. What lengths did a media organization go to in order to get content for a story? Does the outlet have a sense of public decency that matches your personal sense of right and wrong? How would you personally feel if this content were about someone you knew or loved? What standards does the outlet ascribe to in every part of its content gathering and dissemination process? These questions and others should play a large role in what you consider to be an acceptable media source and how much merit you ascribe to its content.

Issues of Outcome: What Happens as a Result of Media Use and Content?

Every generation thinks that the next generation is being corrupted by overindulgence in certain types of media. In the postwar era, parents thought comic books would make kids dumb. In the 1960s and 1970s, social critics feared that TV would lead to the widespread "dumbing down" of society. In the 1980s and 1990s, some felt that video games were going to be the downfall of children everywhere.

Today, portable digital media devices are ubiquitous, with every generation of people seemingly plugged into laptops, tablets, and phones on a twenty-four/seven basis (see Figure 2.1). The ability to remain connected to the world at large anywhere and at every time can lead to a variety of outcomes. Being aware of those outcomes is crucial to understanding media literacy.

FIGURE 2.1 ■ Growth in Media Use, 2008 to 2018

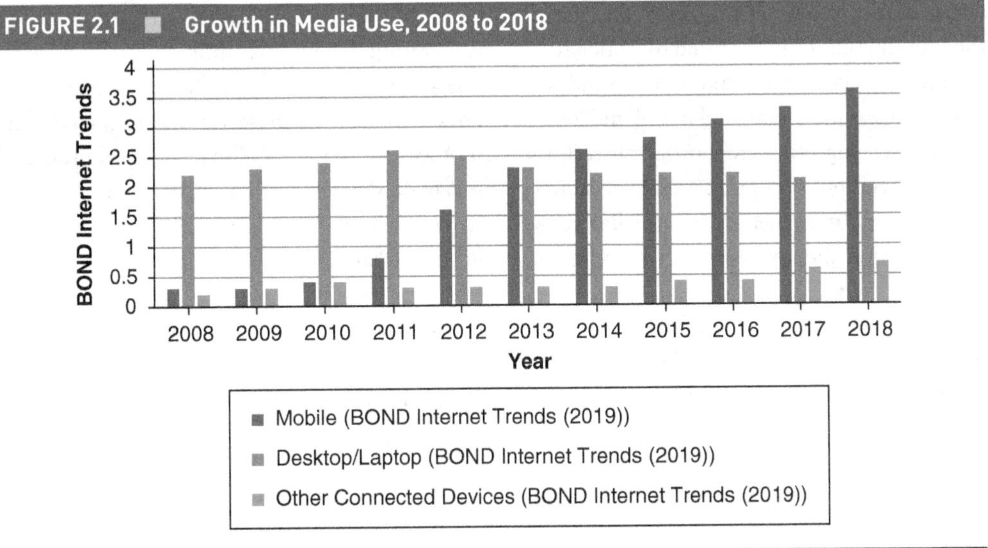

With increased media use, researchers are concerned about the impact the sheer volume of content is having on people.

Source: "Daily Hours Spent With Digital Media, United States, 2008 to 2018." Our World in Data, https://ourworldindata.org/search?q=daily+hours+spent+with+digital+media.

The Pew Research Center asked experts on digital life how technology affected their own lives. The experts noted that they were stunned at how long they were attached to computers and other digital devices during the day. In addition, individuals who were deprived of access to digital media for a protracted period of time noted a personal shift in terms of what they experienced in other parts of their daily lives. Some noted that they were less distracted and more able to focus. Others said they felt a level of withdrawal symptoms akin to being taken off an addictive substance, with one person noting, "I can't seem to get my brain to calm down and focus. It is all over the place."[13] Beyond the outcome associated with the technology itself, the content spread by this technology can make life psychologically problematic. Douglas Massey, a professor of sociology at Princeton University, told Pew researchers that information overload, hate mail, and personal attacks make it difficult for people to remain social and productive.[14]

Pew's 2022 look at teenagers and social media reflected similar concerns, with respondents saying they felt overwhelmed by the need to project only a positive version of themselves. In addition, teens reported high levels of interpersonal drama while interacting with their peers online.[15] Although the students reported making valuable connections to friends via social media, nearly half (46 percent) said they have experienced cyberbullying on these platforms.[16] Even more, instances of online harassment have led to severe negative outcomes for teens, including self-harm and even suicide.

Researchers have found social media to be psychologically harmful, even when people aren't being harassed. Social media users across multiple platforms reported that the more they used social media, the more socially isolated they felt. In other words, the more "social" they were online, the less connected to other people they actually felt. This can be a serious problem, as the researchers point out, because perceived social isolation is associated with substantial levels of morbidity and mortality.[17]

How much thought we put into the idea of consuming media and what it does to us is crucial for our ability to become media literate. As we will explain later in the chapter, media use doesn't have an immediate impact, but rather it leads to a gradual mental shift for consumers. The difference between direct and cumulative effects is the difference between downing a bottle of poison and eating fifty Twinkies a day for life: both will kill you, but the former is more immediate and obvious, so we perceive it as a risk and avoid it. The latter, however, still can do serious damage, even though we might not see it as problematic until it is too late.

Issues of Critical Thinking: How Much Do We Question Our Media Content?

One of the crucial elements of media literacy involves critical thinking. The Foundation for Critical Thinking defines **critical thinking** in a variety of ways, but the simplest of these calls it "the art of taking charge of your own mind."[18] The goal of critical thinking is to overcome the laziness of human thought and thus train the mind to work harder to avoid mistakes in how we think.

From an activity standpoint, the mind wants to be a cognitive miser. Just like it's so much easier to sleep in, eat junk food, and play games on our phones than it is to exercise, eat healthful foods, and read challenging literature, our minds seek the path of least resistance when taking in information. This creates problems in that we rely on stereotyping to make decisions, allow misinformation to pass unchallenged, and generally accept whatever we are given without thinking twice. In doing so, we fail to really think about what it is that we are consuming and what we are doing with that information once we get it.

Let's take a look at a real-life example of how this could play out. In February 2022, an email purported to be from Pollard Middle School stated that school would be canceled that day because of icy roads.[19] The cognitive miser within each of us would likely be willing to accept that information for a variety of reasons:

- It comes on a platform you're used to using (email).
- It appears to comes from a trustworthy source (the school).
- It supports an idea you like (no school).

Thus, you're likely to share that message through your various media platforms and start planning your day of binge-watching the latest Netflix series that all your friends have already gotten into. However, it's clear that very little critical thinking has occurred here.

Media literacy and critical thinking would have you digging deeper into this email and the information it provides to you. Some of this mental pushback could be relatively easy, such as carefully reading the email for nuance and tone. (One of the parents quickly noted that the email wasn't written in the same way as other emails from the school administration.) Additionally, you could look outside and see if the streets are really icy or if traffic is moving around on clear streets like any other day. However, true critical thought would involve a few bigger questions for you:

- What are other sources saying about this cancellation, particularly official sources like the school's website or social media accounts? (A subsequent email from the principal quickly debunked this "no school" claim.)
- How has the school historically treated weather situations like this, and does this fit with that pattern?
- As much as I want this to be true, how likely is it that we will no school, given what I know about other important factors, such as our school's "snow-day policy" and its use of digital technology for distance learning options instead of simply canceling school?

These are just a few of the critical thinking questions we would want to ask before deciding to quickly retweet the information and pass it along as fact. The Media Literacy Project emphasizes the importance of examining all possible issues in any news source and then reaching rational conclusions about what it is we expect to see happen as a result. The more often something is repeated, regardless of its truthfulness, the more likely it is people will start to believe it. That makes it important for us to understand what it is we are sharing, how we have examined it before we share it, and what we think will come out of it after we share it.

Building Critical Thinking Skills: The Three "A's"

Building critical thinking skills can seem to be a daunting task, but it becomes easier if you break down your analysis using three basic concepts called the three "A's": accuracy, association, and approach. You can apply each of these approaches to the content you receive to make sure that it passes muster.

Accuracy: Fact-checking the content you receive is probably the most important thing you can do prior to believing the information or forwarding it on to other people. You want to make sure the content itself has a clear and coherent set of facts that would allow you to rely upon them if you were to share this content with other people.

Here are some questions to help you assess the accuracy of the content:

- Is this the only source that is telling me this, or do other media reports support it?
- Does the information fit with other things I have learned about this topic over a long period of time?
- Does the piece cite primary sources, or is it relying on a few cherry-picked pieces?
- Is everything cleanly written, including grammar, spelling, and style?
- Is the material up to date, or is it too old to remain valid?

Association: Where the information comes from is often vital in determining how believable it is. Most people who put content out for public consumption have associations with groups or organizations that can create bias in their work. For example, if your mother works as a salesperson at a Toyota dealership, it's likely she thinks Toyotas are better than Hondas, Fords, and Chevys, because she's associated with the brand. Additionally, it likely follows that if you love your mother and you've heard her talking about how great Toyotas are, you'd be more inclined to think more highly of them than other brands.

Questions to ask about association:

- Does this author acknowledge a potential bias based on their association with the topic?
- Does the group the author is associated with benefit by convincing me the content is right?
- Are other nonaffiliated sources of information providing me with the same or different information?
- Am I giving this source too much credit because the material here supports the things I already believe or with which I am also associated?
- Is this information associated with a source that has proved credible in the past?

Approach: How someone communicates information to you can be almost as important as what it is they are trying to say. Quality media outlets rely on supportable, coherent information that will help you analyze the topic and come to your own logical conclusions. Weak media outlets will attempt to coerce you through less-than-scrupulous methods or apply propaganda techniques to cajole you into buying into what they're selling.

Questions regarding a source's approach include:

- Is this meant to be a fact-based piece, or is it based primarily on the author's opinions and assertions?
- Does the author rely on data and sourcing or on hyperbolic and exaggerated language to make key points?
- Is the content backed by information that can be proved true or false?
- Has the author engaged in labeling techniques, such as name-calling or glittering generalities meant to push me toward agreeing with them?
- Does the piece ignore or dodge relevant counterarguments instead of addressing and defeating them?

This process is meant as guide, more than a checklist, so keep that in mind as you assess the media you consume. An opinion piece can be perfectly valid, while one based on facts can lead you to erroneous conclusions. The point of media literacy is to help you make smarter choices through critical thinking. To help you improve in this area, we will be applying these methods of analysis throughout the text.

MEDIA LITERACY MOMENT: EXPLORING OUR BIASES

When you are media literate, you can understand the meaning behind the content you consume, evaluate the sources of the messages, determine the value of the messages, and react accordingly. Like most good habits, media literacy requires you to engage in certain activities repeatedly until they become second nature to you.

The benefit to strong media literacy is that you will become a critical thinker, a good communicator, and a quality producer of media content. People who lack media literacy often find themselves victims of scams, lies, and other fake-outs because they take what they have been given at face value and never look more deeply into it.

Here are four key biases that can affect your media literacy.

Anchoring bias	• The first piece of information people receive on a topic will "anchor" their judgment, regardless of that information's accuracy. • Additional arguments presented to people are judged in relationship to that initial piece of information, not on their own merits.
Confirmation bias	• People favor and recall information that supports their prior viewpoints, regardless of the validity of those viewpoints. • Regardless of the options available, people tend to select the ones that tell them what they want to hear.
Familiarity bias	• People prefer things they see most frequently, choosing the familiar item over the unfamiliar item. • The more often people receive specific information, regardless of the message's accuracy, the more likely they are to believe it.
Availability bias	• People place added importance on things they can most easily recall, regardless of their true relevance and value. • The more recently people received a message, the more concerned they are about its content, and they will likely act irrationally because of that information.

Most of these biases are intrinsic, meaning we cannot "cure" ourselves of them. However, knowing they exist makes us more able to push back against them when we get messages through the media. This is where the application of the three A's comes into play.

For example, a popular meme that floated around the internet pitched the incredible health value of pineapple juice. It noted:

> *Did you know that pineapple juice is 500% more effective at helping you to stop coughing than cough syrup is? Well, it's true, and it's all on account of the fact that fresh pineapples contain a substance known as Bromelain: a specific type of enzyme that has anti-inflammatory characteristics which can combat infections and eradicate bacteria.*

When we see a claim like this online, it's often the first time we are hearing about the topic, thus creating a potential anchoring bias. For people who dislike medicine or the corporations that market it, this could trigger a confirmation bias that there are better, natural cures than what "Big Pharma" sells us. The ease at which a meme like this can be shared can help it go viral quickly, which can give us a chance to see it frequently and subsequently trigger familiarity and availability biases.

To push back against those biases, let's go through each "A" to assess this piece of information.

Accuracy would have us look into other potential media sources that would support this information. A quick search of the internet shows multiple other media sources that directly contradict this statement and outline the research that supports the reasons why the original statement is false. Conversely, the original statement does not provide any reference to where this information originated or when it came about, thus violating two other tenets of accuracy.

Association requires us to examine how the source of this message is tied to the message itself. In this case, we don't have any sense of where the original information came from. We can't determine to what degree this source is credible in and of itself.

Approach has us determine how this message is presented. The message is meant to be fact based, but it lacks the supporting data one would expect for a medical claim of this type. The message also relies on hyperbole, such as the use of "500%" to draw readers in and engage them, even though this number's source is unclear. The author has engaged in a technique meant to provide readers with a baseless claim that is supported only through the author's repetition of phrases like "it's true" or "the fact that."

It will always take additional effort to critically examine the content of media messages and determine to what degree you should believe them. However, improved efforts to push back against biases and analyze this material before you believe it or share it can make a big difference in the quality of content we consume.

THE NEXT STEP: Select a media message that matters to you from a media source you frequently use. Go through the four forms of bias and analyze how each of these relates to the message and why you selected it. Then, go through the three A's and examine the message based on the questions listed under each A. How many of these did you answer with "I don't know" or something similar? How much do you think you know about the sources and messages you consume, based on the outcome of this examination? Compose an essay that outlines your findings and details your own sense of how media literate you feel.

WHY DO WE CONSUME MEDIA?

LEARNING OBJECTIVES

LO 3: Explain why people consume media content, including the specific needs it satisfies.

Most early research into mass communication tried to understand what media did to us. Did it push us to do or buy things we wouldn't normally do or buy? Did it have a direct effect with a singular message creating a singular action, like a hammer breaking through a pane of glass? Did it have a cumulative effect, like a lake eroding a shoreline?

A second form of media research emerged in the middle of the twentieth century, flipping the question and the approach of communication studies on its head: why do we consume media? This approach, often referred to as **uses and gratifications** research, saw the audience members as taking an active role in consuming media.

Uses and gratifications theory is one of the most significant innovations in the field of media scholarship because of its approach to how people and media content interact. Researchers found that people related to media the same way that they related to other things they needed. In short, just as a thirsty person knew enough to drink water without drowning, media consumers could find content that satisfied their needs without becoming zombies.

Studies in this area showed that media users made choices about what they read, saw, and heard with the goal finding content that met their needs.[20] When media users found content that satisfied those needs, they returned to that source when the need arose again. For example, let's say you found a person on TikTok who posted something that made you laugh. You would not only follow that person, but you would likely go back to that person's channel when you found yourself in need of a laugh.

This active-audience approach to understanding media use has become particularly important in the digital era, because the media people use most has a strong interactive component to it. Traditional media platforms, like television and radio, gave the audience few options, so people pretty much had to take what they got, much like when your dinner comes with a choice of green beans or Brussels sprouts for a side dish. Today's media is like a never-ending buffet of content, and it requires people to actively seek media on various social media platforms and internet sites. This means that understanding what the audience members want, how they make their choices, and why they continue to use certain media will matter a lot to anyone studying mass media.

Uses and gratifications researchers found several needs (or gratifications) that people satisfied (or tried to satisfy) through their media use. The terms have shifted over time, and the nomenclature has varied based on the researchers. Table 2.1 outlines a few reasons people tend to use media.

TABLE 2.1 ■ Needs Frequently Studied in Uses and Gratifications Research

Need	Explanation	Example
Surveillance	People feel a need to be aware of what is happening around them.	Checking a traffic app to see if any accidents have occurred that might make your daily commute longer.
Education	People have a need to become more informed on topics that matter to them.	Reading a blog post to learn how to keep your plants from dying.
Entertainment	People want to content to amuse them and make them feel good.	Watching a YouTube video of cats that can play the piano.
Social utility	People need to feel connected to other people in society.	Reading a "book of the month" to discuss it at an upcoming book club meeting.
Personal identity	People enjoy seeing content from people to whom they can relate.	Listening to a podcast from a fellow college student who talks about how bad the food is on campus.
Escape	People want to mentally free themselves from the problems they experience in their daily lives.	Playing a video game in which the main character flies through space and saves the universe.

Let's a deeper look at each of these needs.

Surveillance and Education

Surveillance is a term that describes people's need to be aware of their surroundings. While this need goes back to the days of cave dwellers, who needed to know when wild animals could cause danger or when rival groups might attack them, today, surveillance is less about base-level survival. Nonetheless, some concerns that mattered to early humans remain part of our surveillance interests. For example, we check the weather before we leave home to make sure what we're wearing will keep us comfortable.

Education takes the need for surveillance a step further, in that it attempts to deepen our understanding of a concept. People have an innate need to improve themselves both for their own edification as well as the needs of other people who matter to them. This could be anything from an infant's learning how to crawl to a physicist's journey in self-discovery that could improve all humankind. Education builds our knowledge of a subject. For example, you could visit YouTube to watch a video of how to fix a toilet after one of your roommates had a massive party and "somehow" the toilet got clogged. You could grab a tablet to read your textbook in advance of a quiz you have in a class later today.

Self-awareness is also a byproduct of education. Watching a television show could inspire you to try working out more often to shed unwanted pounds or get in shape to run a marathon. Listening to a meditation app could lead to a breakthrough in a problem that previously stumped you.

Entertainment

In 1961, Federal Communications Commission chairman Newton Minow spoke at a National Association of Broadcasters meeting and complained that television had become a "vast wasteland" of content that added little to the sum of human knowledge. Minow's speech did little to stop television from gaining a prominent place in the homes and lives of American citizens, primarily because people have an overwhelming desire for entertainment, events and performances that provide amusement and escape.

In some cases, media users are less interested in being entertained and more interested in avoiding boredom. Researchers have found that people will often consume media or interact with digital devices when they have nothing else to do. You might find yourself playing a simple puzzle game while waiting to get through the line at the grocery store. You might also find yourself texting friends or flipping through your Twitter feed while your professor is trying to explain something to the class.

Social Utility

Humans are social animals: we find value in connecting with other people in meaningful ways. Social utility relates to how we use media to stay connected with the people in our lives. This could be by seeing the movie or reading the book everyone is talking about, just so when someone asks us, "Have you read X yet?" we can say, "*Yes*! Can you believe the ending?" This kind of social need to connect with meaningful others is often thought of as a sense of belonging, with our goal of not losing the ability to connect.

In other cases, it might be that we actually want to be part of a group that is watching or reading something. This could be reading a book so we can discuss it at a monthly book club or going to a Sunday Night Football party to watch a game with people at an area bar. Whether we are physically present with people to share a moment or if we want just to talk about it with people later, the social needs connected to media consumption are valuable to us.

Personal Identity

For some media users, the connections can run more deeply between themselves and the content they consume than those they form with other people. Individuals who begin watching videos or listening to podcasts so they can gain knowledge or to pass the time can also make connections with the people showcased in the media itself. For example, a person with an interest in cooking on a limited budget could watch a series of videos on how to turn two cans of tuna, a few overripe tomatoes, and a box of pasta into a feast for her friends. After watching those videos, she also might buy the host's book, sign up for the host's newsletter, and even attend a local event the host is presenting. The connection between the individual and the material has now become more of a connection between the viewer and the host, based on the sense of a shared personal identity.

People can find themselves in parasocial relationships when they draw strong parallels between the lives of a novel's protagonist or a movie character with their own lives. For some people, this is simply finding comfort in seeing people who are like them living lives to which they aspire. Viewers can enjoy seeing themselves and their friends reflected in a show that presents four single women living their best lives as they take on the big city. These kinds of connections can become problematic for some media users who have difficulty separating fiction and reality. However, in most cases media use based on finding people of similar backgrounds, interests, or activities can give people that sense of socialization they used to only find in human-to-human contact.

Escape

Sometimes, life isn't all that great. School provides stress, with a huge pile of tests and homework. The boss is being a real pain at work, and no matter how much you work, you always seem to be broke. The person you really like in one of your classes isn't interested in talking to you, while all your friends seem to be enjoying perfect relationships. Things can seem downright miserable and depressing.

Media users often turn to various platforms to **escape** from the day-to-day misery of their lives. A video game offers the student who has failed four tests an opportunity to be successful in keeping aliens from colonizing what's left of Earth. A TV show featuring some loser who can't ever get a date can make a two-month dry spell on the dating market seem a lot better by comparison. That parking ticket you got last week? That's nothing compared with what happened to the people in the movie about street racers who got caught in an international plot to assassinate the president, and their only hope is to drive really, really fast.

Escape can be simply about getting away from the doldrums of life or the things that make your life feel lousy. It can also be about feeling better through downward social comparison, which allows you to look at other people and think, "Wow. My life isn't nearly as screwed up as theirs are." Some reality TV shows present characters who give viewers aspirations for themselves, but even more of them showcase human disasters who serve as cautionary tales, giving the audience a chance to feel superior.

IS MEDIA USE RISKY?

LEARNING OBJECTIVES

LO 4: Assess the concerns people have about media consumption and its effects on users.

As you can see, people use media for many reasons, and as you will see elsewhere in the book, media has specific effects on people over time. Here are some of the primary questions and concerns associated with media use and what researchers have found in studying these issues:

1. Will negative media imagery harm us?
2. Do we end up in our own media bubbles?
3. Is there such a thing as too much media?

Let's go through each of these questions and try to answer them.

Will Negative Media Imagery Harm Us?

One of the primary concerns about media use relates to what we see and how it affects us. As noted in Chapter 1, several studies have examined what media does to us in general. Some researchers, however, are more interested in the specific impact of content that exposes us to negative images and outcomes.

Scholars have long examined the relationship between viewing violent television actions and increased aggression among viewers, noting that individuals often mimic behavior that they observe.[21] In the early 1960s, psychologist Albert Bandura conducted a series of studies that assessed how children would react to violent behavior in different situations. His "Bobo doll" study had a group of students watch a video of a person acting violently toward a human-sized doll that looked like a clown. After watching the video, these children were placed in a room that had a similar doll as well as other toys. Bandura found that the kids who watched the violent video behaved much more aggressively toward the clown-doll compared with a control group that did not see the film.[22] A follow-up study revealed that when the violent film included someone rewarding the child for attacking the doll, the research participants subsequently acted more aggressively toward the doll themselves. Conversely, participants who saw a video in that the child attacking the doll was punished were less likely to hit the doll themselves.[23]

Media images can have a long-term effect on viewers. Research has indicated that watching violent or sexually explicit material not only inspires viewers to replicate the behavior, but it also desensitizes them to the content itself. In other words, it's not just a stimulus-response situation in which a person

Participants in Albert Bandura's media experiment who saw a video of a child acting violently toward a "Bobo doll" mimicked the actions of that child when placed in a room with a similar doll.

REUTERS/Alamy Stock Photo

sees one violent act, replicates it, and then returns to "normal." The additive nature of content can lower people's sense of concern when observing violence in real life; they may have fewer emotional reactions themselves when dealing with violence and act out violently, even when not directly primed to do so.[24]

A greater concern about media use emerged about thirty years ago when video games became not only more prevalent in daily life but also far more visually graphic. Cartoonish 1980s games like Dig Dug, in that you could use a bicycle pump to overinflate an enemy, were replaced with 1990s fighting games like Mortal Kombat, in that the player could tear the spinal column out of a foe as a "finishing move." Although studies varied in terms of the direct and indirect effects associated with playing these games, large-scale studies like the one conducted by psychologist Craig A. Anderson showed that playing violent video games is linked to aggressive behavior and thought processes and a lack of empathy for victims of violence.[25] A follow-up analysis that looked at specific elements, like racial or gender differences, supported these concerns.[26]

The question that remains for media consumers is where the line exists between occasionally playing a game of Pac-Man or glimpsing a swimsuit model in a catalog and becoming fully immersed in a world of violence and sexual degradation. It is clear that the more people use media that provides these, and other, negative images, the more problematic it is for users and the people with whom they associate. However, it remains unclear where a specific breaking point occurs or whether it varies based on individual factors that remain unknown.

Do We End Up in Our Own Media Bubbles?

The explosion of media channels at our disposal has allowed us to become much more finicky in our approach to the content we consume. Although this ability to pick and choose as we see fit has many benefits, it can limit our ability to understand large swaths of society that we aren't exposed to. This continual filtering of content can produce what researchers refer to as **media bubbles**, where we exist in an isolation chamber of information and fail to see beyond it.

Social media often takes the blame for breeding bubbles, but this concept of filtered digital content reaches back to the mid-1990s. Nicholas Negroponte, a pioneer in the field of computer-aided design, proposed the concept of a "Daily Me" in his 1995 book *Being Digital*.[27] Negroponte foresaw a future in which people would tell their computers the topics they wanted to read about, as well as subjects they

Mortal Kombat's Scorpion character executes a "fatality move," in which he tears his opponent in half. Researchers have found that playing violent games is linked to aggressive behavior and lack of empathy toward others.

Contraband Collection/Alamy Stock Photo

disliked. The computers would search the media world each day, collecting stories on each person's likes and avoiding those the person disliked. Then, the computer would print a personalized newspaper for each individual with nothing but the preferred information. This vision reflects the way in which algorithms push content into our social media feeds. It also illustrates how our media choices can eliminate things we either don't care about or actively dislike.

The problem associated with creating media bubbles, in which we each exist in our own little world, is that it makes it more difficult to reach a collective understanding about key events or topics. For example, a Pew Research Center report regarding the 2020 U.S. presidential election noted that about one-fifth of Democrats and Republicans were fully entrenched in political media bubbles. The survey data revealed that partisans in each party actively filtered out content that provided positive information about the other party or that reflected negatively upon their own party. In addition, they sought content only from outlets that like-minded political peers relied upon for information.[28]

Media practitioners note that this continued exclusion of information outside of our comfort zones will make us "victims to our own biases" and lead to the destruction of democracy.[29] At the very least, the lack of connective tissue between what we consume in a society can limit our ability to discuss important topics, settle crucial debates, and create shared values.

Is There Such a Thing as Too Much Media?

Aside from looking at concerns related to the use of specific platforms or viewing certain types of content, researchers often wonder if the omnipresence of media in our lives will have negative consequences.

One of their primary concerns is the degree to which people consume "too much" media. What accounts for too much media is up for debate, but several factors have contributed to increased use. The effect of that use has led to serious concerns regarding physical, mental, and emotional impacts.

According to a Pew study, the amount of time people in most age groups are engaging with social media platforms continues to grow each year.[30] Although the platforms may differ—with people over age fifty using Facebook, while those in the eighteen-to-twenty-four demographic are spending time on Snapchat—the overall findings suggest that media use continues to grow each year. Research conducted by eMarketer revealed that in 2019, the average U.S. consumer spent twelve hours and nine minutes per day online, up slightly from the year before, but by 2021, that number had reached thirteen hours and thirteen minutes and continued to hold steady through the first half of 2022.[31] If we were to assume that the average adult gets about seven hours of sleep per night,[32] this means that less than four hours of our days are spent without media. Put another way, we spend more than three times the amount of our waking hours engaging with media than we do without it.

Researchers have not found conclusive proof that social media use or the advent of the digital era has destroyed cognitive abilities or permanently crippled our attention spans. (Parents complaining about their kids' media use is nothing new. A previous generation of adults would tell children that watching too much TV would "rot your brain.") However, scholars have noted that the brain is malleable with regard to operating techniques and information intake.[33] This has led to concerns regarding how heavy media use, particularly the content consumed constantly through ubiquitous digital devices, will affect society. The overstimulation of our minds with the constant influx of content has led to concerns that our brains are becoming overloaded and overstressed.[34] For example, studies of human empathy indicate that although most people feel they have compassion and caring for others, heavy digital media use has actually led to a drop in concern for the problems of other people.[35]

Social media use has also been shown to overwhelm people, leading to feelings of despair and anxiety. A study of social media use in the workplace showed that individuals often have trouble finding ways to cope with mental overload and the invasion of work into their lives, and they experience anxiety related to uncertainty in their lives.[36] Research involving children produced similar results, with heavy digital media use being tied to anxiety and depression.[37]

This is not to say that media use itself is not beneficial, or that being on your phone will lead to some sort of irreversible degeneration of your ability to think clearly. Also, as we noted in our discussion of media violence, scholars have not established a clear bright line in which people who use exactly X hours and Y minutes of any media will sustain serious cognitive impairment. However, as with most habits, heavy use tends to inspire continued and expanded use over time. When we will max out on time spent with media or what its ultimate impact on our well-being will be is not known, but it is something that should concern all of us.

THE ERA OF "DEMASSIFICATION"

LEARNING OBJECTIVES

LO 5: Explain the concept of "demassification" and how it relates to today's media world.

Starting at the end of the twentieth century and continuing to this day, the mass media model has changed dramatically and irrevocably. The giants of media operation, like newspapers and network news outlets, found themselves struggling financially and unable to maintain a stronghold on information dissemination. Investments in traditional platforms and media products became unwise, as citizens suddenly seemed to become disinterested in what these venerable outlets were able to provide.

What we have experienced over the past twenty-five years or so can best be described as the era of **demassification**, a time in which a multitude of choices and options for media consumption have broken down content-based monopolies while at the same time mergers and financial maneuvers have created ownership monopolies. The ability of digital publishers to reach giant audiences without investing giant sums of money has allowed more people to enter the media space as content providers.

One way to think about this change is to consider the change that has occurred in family dining patterns. It used to be that "Mom" made a single meal that everyone ate at the same time, sitting around the dining room table. Today, families are less likely to gather at a single time to eat, and with a multitude of options for home delivery and online ordering, we all can eat whenever and wherever we want. In this way, people who enjoy salads get their salads, while other people can fill up on sweets and ice cream. The benefits are clear, but so are the drawbacks. For now, let's look at what constitutes this era of demassification and what it provides to us as content consumers.

One-to-Many Becomes Many-to-Many

The communication models we discussed in Chapter 1 outline a direct pathway from a sender to a receiver. This approach made sense in explaining the way in which humans interacted individually, such as in a conversation between a parent and a child or a letter written from one friend to another. As mass media became a prevalent form of communication, society saw a shift from a **one-to-one** to a **one-to-many model**. A newspaper could print thousands of copies that were disseminated from its printing plant to subscribers throughout a metropolitan area. A radio station broadcast news and music through its tower, its signal reaching anyone within range, providing information and entertainment to anyone with a receiver. Each form of mass media, from book publishers to television operations, could provide material to a wide group of the public.

In the one-to-many model, the entire audience received essentially the same content from a singular source. This model gave these sources importance because the audience members trusted that what they learned from the television anchors or the newspaper reporters was correct. In addition, the model provided significant power to the source, as advertisers, politicians, and celebrities understood how the media outlets could draw attention to positive or negative news. Thus, they often placed advertisements with those media, curried favor with their reporters, and sought to gain value through connections with these outlets. The one-to-many model stood for decades, for reasons we will discuss later in the chapter and later in the book.

However, as communication technology continued to develop and access to audiences no longer relied on monolithic sources of content, the model of communication shifted from a one-to-many to a **many-to-many model** (see Figure 2.2). Initial changes began with the growth of the cable television industry, when viewers received dozens of channels, thus breaking the oligopoly held by the three broadcast networks. The advent of the internet allowed readers to access publications online that were once available only to citizens in certain geographic areas. Social media allowed audience members to pick and choose among their interests in ways that had previously not existed.

Suddenly, the major media outlets that had once enjoyed an exalted status needed to fight harder to keep their audiences. Many of them have failed, as you can see from the losses in revenue among broadcast stations and the crumbling of the print industry. Consumers no longer said, "We will rely on

FIGURE 2.2 ■ From One-to-Many to Many-to-Many

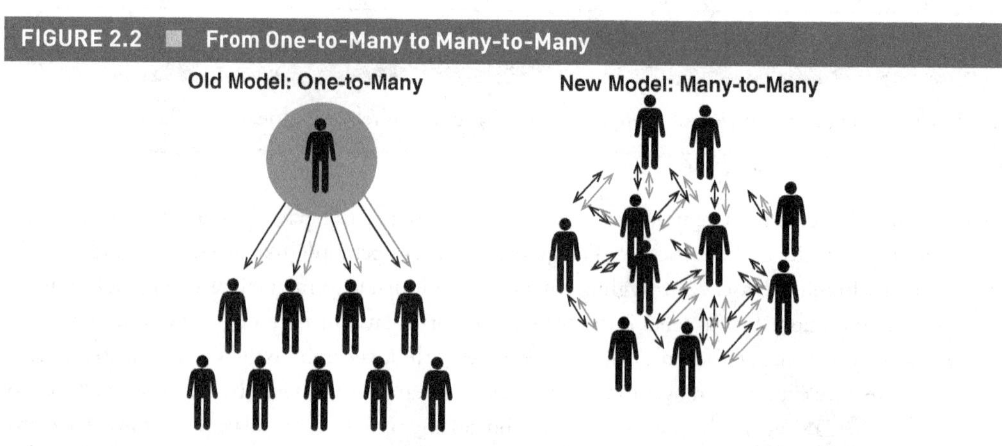

In traditional mass media, a singular source, like a newspaper or TV station, serves as the sender of content, with audience members serving as receivers. The many-to-many model enables multiple individuals and organizations to operate as senders and receivers of content.

you because we have always relied on you," but rather, "What have you done for us lately?" Sources that provided content the audience members valued retained their audiences, while those that failed to pass muster were cut loose.

Barriers to Media Entry Fall

One of the primary reasons a many-to-many model could succeed was because it took a lot less time and effort for people to become sources within the communication ecosystem. The easier and cheaper it became for people to participate in forms of mass communication, the more people took advantage of the opportunities that were once only afforded to a select few.

Prior to the full emergence of digital communication, reaching a mass audience was prohibitively expensive. Publishing a newspaper required obtaining a printing press, a staff to run it, workers to fill it with content, and a network of individuals to distribute it. To reach people through the airwaves was even more problematic because the costs were even higher than those associated with printing and the technology was much more complex. In addition, the Federal Communications Commission oversaw who had the right to broadcast, on which channels, and with what strength of signal. It became virtually impossible for anyone without significant financial backing to make inroads in these media spheres.

The internet offered a democratization of media because many of the costs of media creation or distribution were eliminated or significantly reduced. Smaller and cheaper devices came on the market, so anyone could print a flyer or record a song. Suddenly, anyone who had the ability to code a webpage and pay for internet access was able to take part in a global discussion.

As the digital age moved from the 1990s into the early 2000s, barriers continued to fall. Computer software eliminated the need for people to learn HTML or other coding languages to build websites. The WYSIWYG (what you see is what you get) movement did for web design and creation what Apple's graphic interfaces did for the personal computer. Furthermore, the costs of internet access began to fall. With lower costs associated with access, as well as cheaper web hosting, more people were willing to take chances to create content. Furthermore, those who sought to monetize their efforts were able to do so by selling advertising that not only reached specific people but did so at a much lower cost than that associated with legacy media.

For example, social media star Raye Boyce began with a Tumblr blog, where she and others exchanged hair and beauty tips. Her popularity encouraged her to expand to full video tutorials on YouTube when the video site was more of a hobby with limited financial opportunities. However, after establishing her own channel, ItsMyRayeRaye, she found a strong following that now exceeds 1.8 million subscribers. Her Instagram account also has approximately 1.6 million followers, and her estimated net worth has grown to more than one million dollars.[38]

Beauty influencer Raye Boyce.

Tasia Wells/Contributor/Getty Image

Beyond costs, the explosion of mobile technology opened even more doors for senders and receivers of content. Users found themselves able to consume content whenever and wherever they saw fit. Instead of having to buy a large desktop computer and a device to connect it to the web, consumers could access content on their phones or other portable digital devices. Thus, instead of making active choices to connect with content, by sitting down at a desk in a specific "computer room," people developed habits that allowed them to check in on websites via their phones when they were bored in class, stuck in a long line, or sitting at stoplights while driving.

Today, anyone with a thought in their head and a phone on which to type, film, or record can enter a global discussion without making a heavy financial investment. The degree to which this is a good or a bad thing will likely be the source of debate for generations to come. However, much like inexpensive newspapers brought information to the masses in the 1800s, these changes brought publishing opportunities to more financial classes of people.

Microtargeting

With lower costs to enter the market and improved ways to reach exponentially more readers and viewers, people with an interest in publishing online found themselves able to shift their focus away from a mass media model. Instead, they were able to engage in **microtargeting** efforts that provided interested individuals with a deep dive on narrow topics.

In the dominant days of mass media products, publishers had to be wary of maintaining too narrow of a focus in their work. If the topics being discussed in a newspaper or magazine failed to appeal to a wide audience, the publication wouldn't sell enough copies or draw enough advertising dollars to remain economically viable. Thus, newspapers that covered everything of interest in a geographic distribution area and general interest magazines, like *Time* and *Life*, attempted to be all things to all people.

The rise of the digital era gave almost anyone the chance to publish anything they wanted with lower costs and fewer risks. In addition, many groups, organizations, and individuals had felt ignored or marginalized by the mass media efforts of large metropolitan newspapers or broadly focused magazines. Now, they could provide content of interest on previously uncovered topics in a way that would reach fewer people but do so on a grander scale.

The concept of reaching an audience that had an interest in a topic with quality content written at their level remained constant from the approach that legacy media took. However, additional options helped make these microtargeted sites a success. For example, people who loved cooking could share thoughts, hints, tips, suggestions, and experiences every day, all day, on websites dedicated to food preparation. More focused information could be provided on even more specialized sites on specific types of cuisine, cooking for special events, or even discussions about cooking appliances and utensils. Advertisers could reach these special-interest groups more efficiently or engage them through chatrooms and contact forms on these sites.

The exponential growth of direct-contact apps also helped lower barriers that prevented senders and receivers from connecting. Rather than having to recall a website or bookmark a place on the web that we liked going, apps gave us the ability to simply click and go. Even more, the development of free apps for content consumption helped the social media revolution emerge on an extremely large scale. Aggregating platforms like Hootsuite or TweetDeck helped pull social media channels and interests into a single access point for consumers. These digital media operations helped give people a better opportunity to operate in a "pull" environment, in which they sought content, decided what mattered, and filtered out the rest.

CHAPTER REVIEW

LO 1 Define a mass media audience using demographic, psychographic, and geographic information.

- A mass media audience is a collection of individual information consumers who seek content that is relevant, useful, and interesting to them.
- Demographic information helps determine the composition of a mass media audience through measuring personal characteristics, such as age, gender, and level of education.
- Psychographic information helps determine the composition of a mass media audience by measuring individuals' interests, goals, and passions. While demographics measure the presence of a trait (religious preference), psychographics measure the degree of importance an individual places on that trait.
- Geographic information helps determine the composition of a mass media audience based on the physical location of the person or that person's connections to specific places.

LO 2 Describe the importance of media literacy.

- Media literacy is the ability to decode messages within the media, determine how those messages can create personal influence, and act based on those understandings.

- Gaining media literacy allows individuals to make improved media selections and examine media messages for their value and accuracy.
- Media literacy also allows individuals to act better as informed members of society.
- The application of the three "A's" (accuracy, association, and approach) can inspire critical thinking about the media you are consuming.

LO 3 Explain why people consume media content, including the specific needs it satisfies.

- People have psychological needs they can satisfy through the consumption of media content.
- Surveillance is the need people have to be aware of their surroundings and what is happening in them.
- Education is the need to gain knowledge about topics that have a societal or personal value.
- Entertainment is the need people have to enjoy performances or be amused by content they consume.
- Social utility is the need people have to find meaningful connections to others in their social groups.
- Personal identity is the need people have to find content that relates to who they are and what they value.
- Escape is the need to get away from things happening in everyday life.

LO 4 Assess the concerns people have about media consumption and its effects on users.

- Researchers have found that people who consume graphic content are likely to mimic what they see in a negative way.
- People who are repeatedly exposed to graphic content will become desensitized to it and show less empathy toward others.
- People often gravitate toward content that supports their way of thinking, creating their own "media bubbles." These bubbles limit encountering important information or alternative viewpoints that might provide a wider and more diverse view of a subject.
- People continue to increase their overall media consumption each year, which has some scholars worried that we are becoming more socially isolated from one another.

LO 5 Explain the concept of "demassification" and how it relates to today's media world.

- Demassification is the breakdown of media dominance from a few, large, traditional content providers and the emergence of a wide array of smaller, narrow media options.
- The ability for anyone to enter the media world as a source has given rise to more opportunities to create content and more options for the creation of specialized content.

KEY TERMS

Audience
Bias
Citizen journalist
Conflict of interest
Credibility
Critical thinking
Demassification
Demographics
Entertainment
Escape
Fake news
Geographics
Legacy platform
Many-to-many model
Media bubble
Media literacy
Microtargeting
One-to-many model
One-to-one model
Parasocial relationship
Personal identity
Psychographics
Self-awareness
Social utility
Surveillance
Uses and gratifications

DISCUSSION QUESTIONS

1. What are some of the key demographic, psychographic, and geographic elements you think influence your specific interests in what media content you consume?
2. How media literate do you feel you are, especially when compared with others around you, such as your peers and your family members?
3. Of the specific needs listed in the chapter that media use is known to satisfy (surveillance, education, personal identity, social utility, and escape), which one is most compelling to you when it comes to your consumption habits and why? Which is the least important to your media consumption and why?
4. Based on the research noted in the chapter, how concerned are you about the issues of media mimicry, media bubbles, and overuse of mass media?
5. What do you see as the benefits and drawbacks of demassification?

This is Shari Redstone, a person you likely have never seen, met, or even heard of. In spite of this, as the president of National Amusements, she has great influence over your media content, as she oversees a media conglomerate that holds majority ownership in CBS, Paramount, Viacom, Showtime, and hundreds of other media properties and subsidiaries.

Jared Siskin/Contributor/Getty Images

3 MEDIA SYSTEMS AND CORPORATE OWNERSHIP

INTRODUCTION

1. *How often do you think about who owns or controls the media content you consume on a daily basis?*
2. *What benefits and drawbacks do you think exist in owning a media outlet, like a newspaper, a television station, or a social media platform?*
3. *Do the media outlets available to you provide you with enough choices that you feel satisfied with what you consume, or do you feel that some things are missing?*

A line attributed to Doors vocalist Jim Morrison perfectly captures the importance of media ownership: "Whoever controls the media, controls the mind."[1] As we discussed in Chapter 1, when people receive a message repeatedly, they place significant value on it. A message can be presented from a variety of angles, each of which can shift the way in which readers and viewers perceive that message as well as the larger issue at hand.

Who decides which topics receive heavy coverage and which ones never see the light of day is an issue of media control, and that control is determined by media ownership. Whether it be a single individual in charge of a single publication or a multinational **conglomerate** with tentacles that reach across all forms of media, this ironic "Golden Rule" applies to content creation and distribution: "The person with the gold makes the rules."

This chapter will begin with an overview of the different types of media systems found around the world. It will then explore the history of media ownership in the United States, the rise of digital media as a disruptor, and the impacts of the overly consolidated media landscape in the country today.

LEARNING OBJECTIVES

After completing this chapter, you should be able to:

1. Compare and contrast the basic global media systems.
2. Identify the key phases in the history of U.S. media ownership and control.
3. Explain the impact of digital developments on the media landscape.
4. Understand the negative consequences of overly consolidated media ownership.

A BASIC OVERVIEW OF GLOBAL MEDIA SYSTEMS

LEARNING OBJECTIVES

LO 1: Compare and contrast the basic global media systems.

Who controls the media and to what ends are in large part based on how the government sees the role of media. In some countries, media outlets exist to support and enhance the ideas of the people in charge, while in other places, they provide a check on the power of the country's leaders. Scholars Fred Siebert, Theodore Peterson, and Wilbur Schramm examined the different media systems in place throughout the world and attempted to define and categorize them.[2] Not every country's approach to press freedom or information control fits neatly into a specific category. Here are the four systems that Siebert and his colleagues identified in their work:

Let's take a quick look at each of these briefly.

TABLE 3.1 ■ A Quick Look at the World's Four Basic Media Systems

Model	Features	Examples
Authoritarian	• Extremely limited or nonexistent freedom of expression • Strict control of content • Punishment for those who create content that questions or runs contrary to the government's interests	• North Korea • Iran • China
Libertarian	• Media is controlled by the people, not governmental interests • Content is free from censorship and governmental suppression • Supports the idea that everyone should be free to express themselves	• Finland • The Netherlands
Social-responsibility theory	• Private ownership groups control and operate media outlets • Journalists police themselves based on professional and ethical standards • Media outlets are free to serve the interests of their audiences	• England • United States • Japan
Soviet-communist	• Government owns and operates all media • Media outlets support the governmental ideology • Negative information about the government is suppressed	• The former Soviet Union

Authoritarian

In the **authoritarian system**, content is controlled by the elites and authorities for the supposed good of the society as a whole. As is the case with other aspects of authoritarian regimes, the ruling class believes it possesses superior knowledge to those in the lower classes and thus has both a duty and a right to impose its will upon those lesser individuals.

A North Korean television broadcast. North Korea's governmental control over its news media has placed it squarely in the authoritarian category of media systems.

JUNG YEON-JE/Contributor/Getty Images

In this system, media outlets are subject to strict oversight from the ruling class. Governmental censorship is common, and media outlets operate under constant threat of being shut down if they produce content that runs contrary to the wishes or ideologies of those in charge. The government justifies this level of control with the logic that information intended to question the country's leadership could create harm for the nation as a whole as well as individual citizens. Thus, the limitation of what people read, hear, and watch is a necessary and logical trade-off for the overall safety of the collective.[3]

Libertarian

The **libertarian system** runs counter to that of the authoritarian model, with the media resting in the hands of the public. In this model, media outlets not only have the freedom to produce content without governmental interference, but they have the right to examine, question, and even mock the ruling class.[4]

The rationale behind a libertarian system is that when people can produce content free of prior restraint from the government, the audience members can trust this content more completely. In an authoritarian model, if a website runs a story about how great a government program is, the readers will likely be suspicious of the program because they know the media must support it. However, in a libertarian system, that positive review of a governmental program carries more weight because the website is free to publish as it sees fit. Conversely, criticism of a governmental program is also allowed and likely to be believed. This model puts the responsibility of media content into the hands of the citizenry, not the leadership, but laws still exist to prevent abuses of the system. (We'll talk more about media law in Chapter 14.)

Social-Responsibility Theory

Social-responsibility theory seeks to balance the rights of a free press with the responsibilities to stakeholders within the social group. In this model, media outlets are free from government oversight and government ownership, but they do operate under a set of professional tenets that impose restrictions upon their behavior. In addition, the private controls of the media come from ownership groups and other stakeholders that can dictate an approach to content as they see fit, making this approach not as truly free as the libertarian model.[5]

For example, let's say a television station plans to run a story on how a local property manager is cheating people out of their security deposits. The journalists looking into that story must abide by their professional code of ethics while researching the story, interviewing sources, and creating their piece. Accuracy, truth, and fairness are crucial, so the journalists must diligently check their facts, attempt to interview sources on both sides of the issue, and present a story that goes only as far as the information they have can take them.

Under this model, even if that story were to meet those professional standards, the news director might think it's not good enough to run, or the owners of the station could kill it because the property managers buy a lot of advertising on the station.

Soviet-Communist

The **Soviet-communist system** is a nationalistic model in which the government owns and controls all media outlets for the purpose of enhancing and promoting the actions of the ruling class. While the authoritarian model allows private ownership that the government watches like a hawk, the Soviet approach simply avoids the need for censoring private owners by not allowing any to exist.

This approach relies on propaganda that highlights the benefits of the communist system, while it ignores or downplays any cultural, governmental, or social problems within the country. As such, citizens are unable to question or criticize the government through the media. Furthermore, the media does not provide a check on the actions of the government.

When Siebert and his colleagues developed their four models in 1956 and when they updated and refreshed them in 1984, the Soviet Union was a dominant player on the world stage. In addition, the media of the time existed in a predigital world. After the collapse of the Soviet Union in the early 1990s, the world no longer had a pure form of this model, with most dictatorial and nondemocratic regimes leaning more heavily toward the authoritarian model. The current model in Russia, the primary hub of the old Soviet Union, contains both state-run and privately owned media outlets today, although accusations of censorship and suppression linger to this day.

A BRIEF HISTORY OF MEDIA OWNERSHIP AND CONTROL

LEARNING OBJECTIVES

LO 2: Identify the key phases in the history of U.S. media ownership and control.

Even before they pushed for the creation of an independent nation, the founders of the United States understood the significant impact media could have on a society. Who could control what the people heard and read would make the difference in how citizens saw government and society. It is therefore no accident that the freedom of speech and of the press are among the dictates laid out in the First Amendment to the Constitution.

The idea of a free and unfettered media system isn't as simple and direct as it would seem in this country. In terms of media development in the United States, media ownership has gone through several key stages:

- Governmental control
- Independent ownership
- Corporate ownership
- Convergence and conglomerates
- Hedge fund ownership

Let's look at each of those in more depth.

Governmental Control

During the colonial days of the country, individuals had no rights to a free and independent press. The first attempt to create a newspaper died on the vine in 1690, when Benjamin Harris printed *Publick Occurrences in Boston*. The British governor declared that Harris had failed to secure a printing license from the government and forced him to shut the paper down.[6]

Laws pertaining to press ownership and governmental control were common throughout Europe during that time period, because governments understood the importance of limiting information. The more people could learn, the argument went, the less they would rely unquestioningly on their leaders' decisions. In America's colonial period, the ability to print and produce content without governmental approval and oversight created a clear and present threat to the rulers back in England.

Independent Ownership

Newspapers, leaflets, and other forms of press were vital in galvanizing support for the American Revolution as well as the establishment of the United States in the late 1700s. The founders understood this power and saw it as a vital right that should be in the hands of the citizenry. Thus, when they developed the Bill of Rights in 1789, the founders codified that right for the nation. This opened the floodgates for independent citizens to own and operate newspapers throughout the country.

Approximately two hundred newspapers were in operation as of 1800, with that number growing to three thousand by 1860. As the country continued to grow and transportation saw technological

Charles "Doc" Herrold became the first person to use the radio for regular entertainment broadcasts, beginning in 1912. He also taught students how to handle ship-to-shore broadcasting equipment, starting in 1909. Herrold's approach to radio communication typified the "one person, one operation" approach that preceded the corporate ownership model

Bettmann/Contributor/Getty Images

improvements, the number of papers and their cumulative circulation climbed exponentially.[7] The use of steam power to print newspapers and distribute them along the railways improved their speed and reach, while the government's decisions not to tax the press and to offer publishers favorable postal rates also gave them the ability to expand.[8]

Still, even well-known publishers like Horace Greeley and James Gordon Bennett tended to remain locked into specific geographic areas, because they owned and operated individual print shops. The impact of a publication tended to be based on the size of the city in which the newspaper operated as well as the overall appeal it had to its people. In other words, instead of gathering a bunch of outlets together, most owner-operators concentrated on maximizing the value of one high-level media property.

Independent ownership wasn't limited to the newspaper industry. As each form of media developed in this country, it was often inventors and innovators who made the first steps to own and operate single outlets. In the unregulated era before World War I, radio pioneers Lee de Forest and Charles "Doc" Herrold used their transmitters to provide entertainment programming to listeners in their geographic areas. De Forest and Herrold both returned to the air in the early 1920s, after the conclusion of the war and the end of the governmental ban of civilian transmissions. Thomas Edison had his hand in film production, with the production of individual kinetoscope machines that displayed "moving pictures," while the Lumière brothers in France developed and operated a movie company of their own. (We will take a deeper look at radio in Chapter 6 and at movies in Chapter 7.)

Corporate Ownership

The individual most responsible for the shift from the "one owner, one outlet" model to that of the media baron is William Randolph Hearst. The son of a millionaire, Hearst began his publishing career at the *San Francisco Examiner*, a paper his father had acquired in 1880. After improving the fortunes of the *Examiner*, he purchased the *New York Journal* in 1895 and began a circulation war with Joseph Pulitzer's *New York World*. Hearst continued his expansion over the next two decades, and by the mid-1920s, he had controlling interests in a variety of media outlets throughout the country. His nationwide chain of newspapers included operations in Boston, Chicago, Los Angeles, and Detroit, while he also invested heavily in magazines and book publishing. Hearst saw the opportunities for growth in newer media industries as well, buying radio station WINS in New York, a film company named Cosmopolitan Productions, and multiple syndication services that produced and shared illustrations and other media content.

Although Hearst's empire collapsed during the Great Depression, costing him control over his properties, the corporation that bears his name rebounded in the World War II era and remains a prominent media organization to this day. Hearst Communications currently has ownership stakes in newspapers, magazines, television operations, and internet companies, with an annual revenue upward of eleven billion dollars.[9]

In the 1920s, radio was also shifting away from the amateur movement and toward corporate ownership as well. In 1920, Westinghouse Electric & Manufacturing Company launched KDKA in Pittsburgh after finding success with its experimental radio operations. The company quickly added three additional stations—WJZ in Newark, New Jersey; KYW in Chicago; and WBZA in Boston—capitalizing on the interest listeners in Pennsylvania were showing and the company's success in selling radio receivers.

Westinghouse was also a part owner of the Radio Corporation of America (RCA), which launched the National Broadcasting Company in 1926. The twenty-four radio stations under the NBC flag represented the first network of its kind in the United States. Both Westinghouse and NBC, along with the Columbia Broadcasting System and the American Broadcasting Company, continued this pattern of corporate organization during the rise of television, each of which held significant positions in the world of broadcast TV. The corporate domination of television gave individual companies a stranglehold on what people saw at home, given the three major networks went unchallenged for more than thirty years.

In the realm of film, a few individual companies maintained a similar grip on the industry. In the 1930s and 1940s, five major organizations controlled ruled Hollywood with an iron fist, owning every aspect of the filmmaking and exhibiting process in a structure known as the studio system. MGM, Warner Brothers, Paramount, Fox, and RKO each owned production companies that signed actors, directors, and crew members to exclusive contracts, with the studios dictating who was allowed to work on which films. This was particularly difficult for actors because this system held them in service to a single studio that would determine what their images would be and how they would be portrayed publicly.[10]

Beyond the indentured servitude of the stars to these companies, the big five studios also maintained a strong grip on what people could see at the theaters. In owning not only the production but the dissemination and exhibition operations in the field, the studios were able to determine where and when their films would be shown. This total level of control was called vertical integration and served the studios well, while making life difficult on everyone else involved in the field. This system came to an end in 1948, when the courts ruled that the studios' efforts constituted a violation of the country's antitrust laws against monopolies.[11] The studios were forced to sell off their theatrical chains, and now individual theater owners could decide which movies to show.

Convergence and Conglomerates

In early 1970s, the Federal Communications Commission (FCC) became concerned that too many media outlets were owned by too few people. The commission worried that if one ownership group came to dominate a geographic area, it could eliminate competing outlets and silence other voices. In an attempt to prevent this kind of monopoly, the FCC initiated the cross-ownership rule in 1975, forbidding a newspaper from owning a television station in the same media market. Although a few media outlets that already owned both newspaper and TV outlets were allowed to continue operating them, and some media outlets were able to purchase stations in other markets, the rule provided a firewall that prevented print and broadcast consolidation within key markets.

As a journalist at the *Washington Post*, Ben Bagdikian had a key role in the Watergate reporting that led to the end of the Nixon presidency. In later life, he grew concerned at the ways in which media consolidation was harming citizens' access to a wide array of information.

San Francisco Chronicle/Hearst Newspapers via Getty Images/Contributor

When Congress passed the Telecommunications Act of 1996, it required the FCC to review all ownership regulations, including the cross-ownership rule. During its 2001 examination of this rule, the FCC struck down this rule, noting that it had become antiquated, given the rise of digital communication and the globalization of media. This was the first of several decisions the FCC made to relax ownership rules and allow increased media mergers. Researchers have noted that although the number of media outlets has significantly increased since 1975, the ownership of media outlets has become increasingly concentrated.[12]

These consolidation efforts created media conglomerates, because they had their tentacles in multiple areas of mass media. On the journalism side of media, these conglomerates put former competitors together into a single newsroom during the early 2000s, leading to the birth of the convergence movement in the early 2000s. Convergence occurs when media organizations from print, broadcast, and online operations work collectively to maximize a parent company's market share while improving information dissemination.[13] When organizations like the *Tampa Tribune*, WFLA-TV, and Tampa Bay Online first attempted to combine their operations in 2001, the internet was considered a tangential partner to the legacy media operations. As the importance of the internet grew over the next decade, and laws continued to allow larger and more integrated mergers, the focus on owning media enterprises across the digital spectrum became more enticing to investors.

On the entertainment side of media, media conglomerates were able to collect properties that had global distribution and networking opportunities, thus increasing access to previously untapped parts of the world. Much of the movie industry today focuses less on U.S. box office sales and more on how well a film will do on a global scale.

As cable giants like Viacom and entertainment titans like Fox were scooping up more and more properties, media critics began to worry about the overconsolidation of media into the hands of fewer and fewer owners. Long before the number of media conglomerates reached the single digits, a journalist and media critic named Ben Bagdikian was sounding the alarm bell on this issue.

A DEEPER LOOK: BEN BAGDIKIAN AND "THE MEDIA MONOPOLY"

In 1983, author Ben Bagdikian wrote a book titled *The Media Monopoly* in which he outlined his concerns about how fewer and fewer people were controlling many media outlets. His position was that the control these men and women had over what we read, saw, and heard was dangerous for democracy and independent thinking. Critics decried his work as alarmist, noting that while the number of people owning outlets seemed small, the public still had plenty of choices. At that time, approximately 50 corporate interests controlled the media in the United States, a number that continued to dwindle each time Bagdikian revised his book.

As of 2022, six corporate giants controlled upward of 90 percent of the U.S. media landscape: Comcast, Walt Disney, AT&T, National Amusements, Sony, and Fox.[14] Even more, these companies have stronger global ownership ties than they could when Bagdikian sounded the alarm on ownership consolidation, and they own media platforms that were not available back then, such as the internet and streaming services.

In his final version of the book, *The New Media Monopoly*, Bagdikian noted that this tiny cabal of media conglomerates wasn't the first oligopoly the United States had experienced. He also noted that many operations exist like this in finance, manufacturing, and other production sectors of the country. His concern, however, was that media was a completely different beast in terms of its impact on society. Put another way, he explained, "Media products are unique in one vital respect. They do not manufacture nuts and bolts: they manufacture a social and political world."[15]

A small handful of media conglomerates own and control the preponderance of the media we consume. Given the state of the financial markets and the appetite many media operations have for mergers and acquisitions, the top ownership outlets are always subject to change. That said, here is a brief look at some of the major organizations that dominated the top tier of media ownership in the early 2020s and some of the key media properties they own.

TABLE 3.2 ■ The Major Players

Conglomerate	Comcast	Disney	National Amusements	Sony	Fox
Key media properties	• Comcast Cable • Xfinity Internet • NBC Universal • Sky Group • DreamWorks	• ABC • ESPN • Pixar • Marvel • Lucasfilm	• CBS • Paramount Pictures • Simon & Schuster (publishing) • Viacom	• Columbia Pictures • Sony Music • Crunchyroll (streaming)	• Fox Sports • Fox News • Tubi (streaming) • TMZ

Hedge Fund Ownership

Media owners have become increasingly more concerned with the profitability of their outlets, as opposed to the ways in which these outlets serve consumers' political, sociological, and diversity needs. This is in large part because the owners of these outlets are becoming further and further removed from the media properties they own and the audiences the outlets serve.

The most recent and most concerning shift in media ownership has been the wide-scale purchasing of media outlets, particularly newspapers, through financial investment organizations that seek to maximize profit by any means necessary. These **hedge funds**, or private equity firms, are composed of individuals and corporations that pool their money to purchase various investments with the goal of earning significant returns in the shortest amount of time possible. Researchers have found that these kinds of funds own nearly half of all the daily newspapers in the United States, as of 2022. The most well-known and aggressive player in this area of the hedge fund market has been Alden Global Capital, which has invested in about two hundred newspapers.[16]

Protesters express their displeasure with Heath Freeman, the managing partner of Alden Global Capital, and his purchase of more than 260 daily newspapers since 2011. Journalists have decried the hedge fund's approach to slashing staff and liquidating "anything that wasn't nailed down."

AP Photo/Kassi Jackson

Since its first newspaper purchase in 2011, Alden's media acquisition strategy has demonstrated what stock market analysts call a **vulture capital strategy**: it found distressed or nearly bankrupt media outlets and purchased them at reduced prices. Then, rather than attempting to rebuild or rehabilitate each outlet, Alden picked through its bones for what little value remained before discarding the worthless carcass.[17] Or, as one writer put it, "The model is simple: gut the staff, sell the real estate, jack up subscriptions prices and wring out as much cash as possible."[18]

Although discussions of these kinds of purchases focus primarily on newspaper newsrooms, this shouldn't be seen as a minor concern for a dying aspect of journalism. Newspapers no longer exist in a silo, thanks to the convergence efforts of the early 2000s. Organizations that own newspapers also own television and radio stations as well as other media properties like magazines and websites. For example, when the hedge fund Chatham bought a controlling stake in American Media in 2016, it obtained not only several newspapers but also the tabloid the *National Enquirer* and several lifestyle and celebrity magazines.[19]

Corporations that find themselves ripe for hedge fund takeovers run the risk having to sever connections with less profitable media properties to remain viable. In the wake of Great Recession of 2008, for example, the Tribune Company separated its broadcast properties from the *Chicago Tribune* newspaper to make the company more attractive to investors. This approach made the *Tribune* a prime candidate for an Alden takeover in 2021. Shortly after the hedge fund acquired the newspaper, the newsroom staff was cut by 25 percent.

DIGITAL MEDIA DISRUPTORS

LEARNING OBJECTIVES

LO 3: Explain the impact of digital developments on the media landscape.

The business models that traditional media had built, including the rise of giant corporations, seemed destined to eternally rule the market. However, when the internet and other forms of digital media began to emerge, many of those traditional companies failed to see how these new media forces would transform their business models. The decline of print newspapers, glossy magazines, network television, terrestrial radio, and movie theater attendance didn't occur all at once or even through the rise of competing media conglomerates. Instead, the incremental development and application of digital technology reconstructed the media landscape piece by piece and an inch at a time.

Here are four key areas in which digital media slowly pecked away at the old guard and disrupted the traditional approach to content creations and distribution:

- The decline of newspapers
- Digital music mayhem
- Social sharing development
- Video goes viral

Let's look at each of those areas of change.

The Decline of Newspapers

The period between the 1940s and 1980s is often thought of as the golden age of newspapers. Profits were high, circulation figures were strong, and staffing was robust. Journalism was expensive, but it was worth it, and the owners could afford it. Papers were fat with advertising from local and national businesses that wanted to get their messages in front of people, enticing them to purchase goods and services. Classified advertising revenue poured into papers, as individuals within their circulation areas used these text-based ads to seek employment, rent apartments, purchase items from other individuals, and even find love. Newspaper owners could set the ad rates as they saw fit, because often they were the only print game in town. Broadcast ads were rare and far more expensive during the golden age of newspapers, so owning a newspaper was a license to print money. However, multiple forms of internet services started to cut away at various aspects of newspapers' dominance over advertising and content.

The first challenge to print publications came in the form of online information competitors. Traditional print media initially dismissed the internet as a digital playground for a few tech nerds, with *Newsweek* infamously printing an excoriating critique of digital communication under the headline "The Internet? Bah!"[20] However, the web presented potential journalists with opportunities traditional media had not. It was far cheaper to launch a website than to own a printing press, buy paper, hire press operators, and build a media property. Furthermore, individuals could make their content available to a wider array of people for free.

Arianna Huffington cofounded the Huffington Post in 2005 and spent eleven years creating a new way to develop and aggregate news content for her readers.

Pier Marco Tacca/Contributor/Getty Images

One of the first websites to garner significant public attention for its news coverage was the Drudge Report, a political and entertainment website started in 1997 by Matt Drudge. In 1998, he broke the news that President Bill Clinton had engaged in a romantic relationship with intern Monica Lewinsky. Furthermore, the site noted that *Newsweek* magazine had this information and was refusing to publish it.[21] Additional cracks in the traditional print media's hold on information developed around this time, as the web demonstrated the ability to cater to specific topics. Websites like the Huffington Post and Salon.com delivered political and social commentary, while sites like ESPN.com made it easier for people to get the sports content they wanted. Not only were these sites providing interesting content to targeted audiences, but they did it mostly for free.

While some sites were undercutting print publications' supremacy on the content end, others were taking away their advertising revenue. In 1996, Craig Newmark launched a website meant to take the classified advertising newspapers had always produced and make it more user friendly. Craigslist started with Newmark using an email system to alert people to social events in the San Francisco area, but it quickly became a website on which people posted job opportunities, items for sale, apartment rentals, and more, all for free. The company expanded rapidly beyond the San Francisco area and currently serves 570 cities in 70 countries. From 2000 to 2019, newspaper classified advertising revenue fell from $19.6 billion per year to $2.3 billion per year.[22] Experts in the field say today's classified advertising revenue rarely goes to newspapers; instead it goes to search ads and other targeted messaging online.[23]

As newspapers began to shrink their operations and lose market share, companies that traditionally placed advertising in their pages began looking elsewhere for opportunities. Newspaper publishers had always assumed that advertising came as a result of the quality of the product, but the truth was that advertisers were looking to "buy eyeballs." (We'll cover this concept in more depth in Chapter 13.) Therefore, as fewer people read newspapers, fewer advertisers placed ads in them. In 2005, advertising peaked at $49.4 billion per year, while as of 2021, that number had fallen to $7 billion. That number has been predicted to hit $4.9 billion by 2026, which would mark the first time in world history that a country's digital newspaper revenue surpassed its print newspaper revenue.[24]

Digital Music Mayhem

From 1974 to 1999, the music industry almost tripled its annual sales, with no end in sight.[25] The quality of musical sound had improved significantly, thanks to new digital production methods and the distribution of music on compact discs in the mid-1980s. By 1991, CDs had become the most popular music purchase on the market, having surpassed sales of both record albums and cassette tapes.[26] CDs were more resistant to damage than were vinyl records and cassettes and also were easier to use. Thanks to the individual digital files stored on the disc, users could quickly access their favorite songs, or shuffle the order of the entire album.

Those individual files would be the industry's undoing, when computer hackers began to find ways to separate the music (or audio files) from the medium (the physical CD) and share the content for free. In 1999, Shawn Fanning developed and launched Napster as a peer-to-peer file-sharing service for audiophiles. This allowed users to connect their music libraries to those of other people on Napster and download copies of songs they wanted.[27] In its first year, more than eighty million users logged on to Napster and other similar file-sharing sites, and sales of physical recordings dropped by nearly one-third in 2000 alone.[28]

Although the Recording Industry Association of America successfully sued Napster for copyright infringement and forced the site to cease operation by 2001, the digital music genie was out of the bottle, and users were not turning back. Stepping in to fill the void was Apple Computer and its visionary leader, Steve Jobs. In 2001, Jobs debuted the iPod, Apple's version of the portable MP3 player, that was pitched as being able "to hold a thousand songs in your pocket."[29] The device was more expensive than competing players and would at first connect only to Macintosh computers, leading to initially weak sales. However, what eventually drove this device to the top of the market, and also helped crush the CD market, was the debut of the iTunes Store in 2003. Apple collaborated with the owners of musical copyrights to create a legal marketplace for MP3s, giving music fans a way to buy songs they wanted in a format that fit their lives.

Apple founder Steve Jobs displays the first version of the iPod. Although industry insiders viewed the device as "just another MP3 player" at the time, the pairing of the device with a legal market for purchasing individual songs helped change the world of music.

REUTERS/Alamy Stock Photo

Although it only featured 200,000 tracks initially, the store sold more than 1 million copies of songs in its first week. The company continued its expansion offerings on iTunes and also made the software compatible for non-Apple devices. Although the recording industry reaped some benefits from this marketplace, it came at the expense of a sharp decline in traditional CD sales. In 2004, the first full year the iTunes store was operating, people bought more than 750 million CDs in the United States alone. In less than four years, that number had been cut in half, and by 2018, experts had declared CDs officially dead.[30] Figure 3.1 shows the change in music revenues from physical to digital sources over time.

The digitization of music also marked a financial turning point for terrestrial radio. While MP3 players operated as mobile jukeboxes that users could even plug into their car radios, streaming services like Pandora and Spotify allowed listeners to create playlists, find new artists, and curate their own radio stations. Experts noted in 2021 that audio consumption will continue to grow and expand but that most of that growth will come in the form of internet radio apps like iHeartRadio and digital streaming services. Most of this growth is expected to come at the expense of traditional AM/FM terrestrial radio, which will likely continue to see its share of the ad market and audience shrink.[31]

Social Sharing Development

Contrary to popular belief, Facebook was not a revolutionary concept whereby individuals socialized online. Prior to Mark Zuckerberg's launch of the social media site at Harvard in 2004, Friendster and MySpace had already found value in connecting people to one another based on friendships and shared interests.[32] While Facebook thrived and eventually overtook these and other social media platforms, it also created havoc for traditional media platforms.

FIGURE 3.1 ■ Changes in Music Revenue Sources since 1980

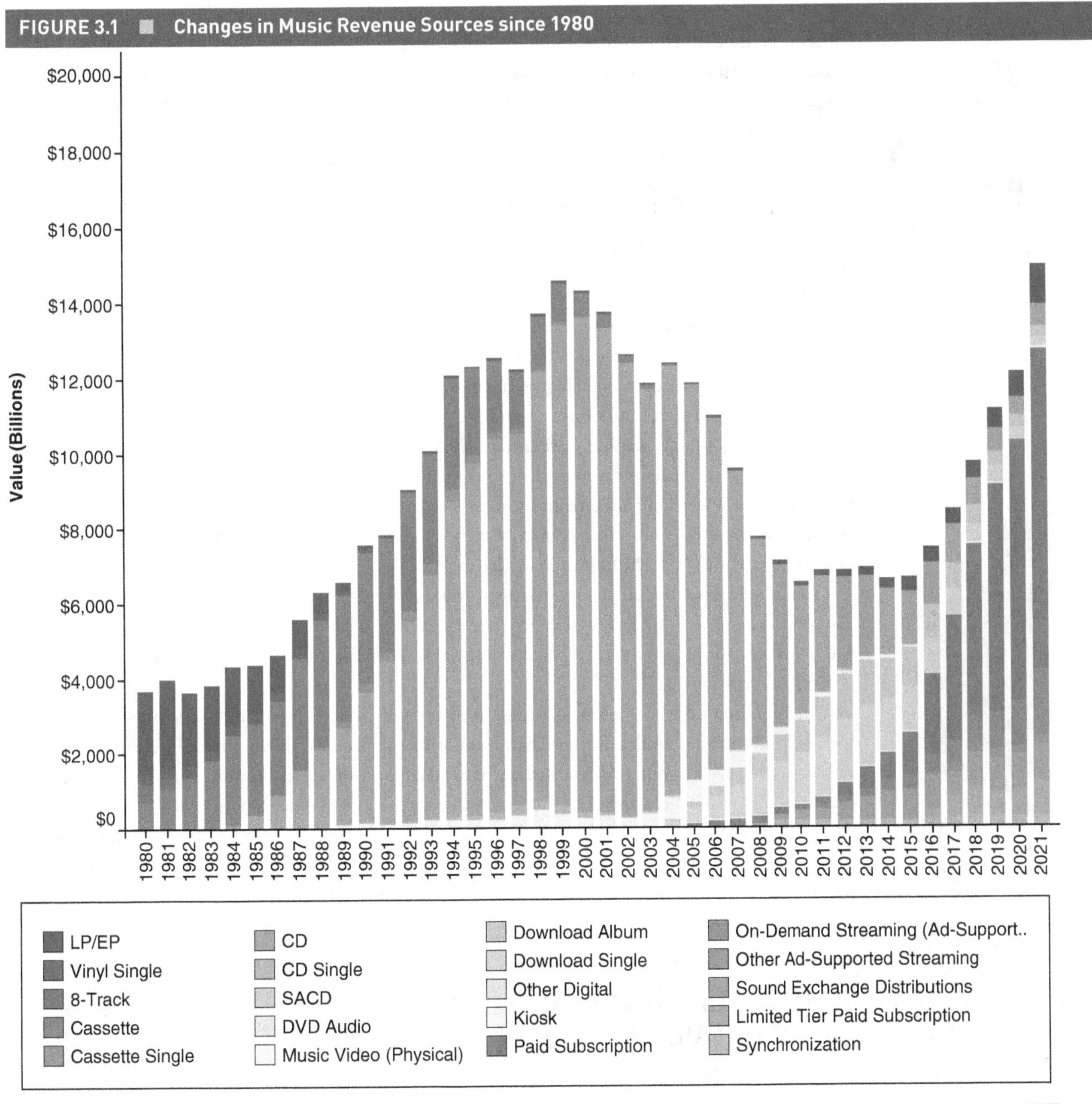

Music sales grew substantially from about 1980 into the start of the new millennium. Over the past twenty years, the music industry has seen a significant shift in how people purchase music, relying more now on digital downloads and subscriptions than on traditional physical purchases like vinyl records and CDs.

Based on data from https://www.riaa.com/u-s-sales-database/

With the decline of traditional media, advertisers were looking for ways to reach people with targeted messages for specific interests. While general-interest publications like newspapers and demographically focused television programs could deliver a large number of people, the specific data people shared on social media sites gave advertisers the ability to target the most interested potential consumers, making better use of the companies' advertising dollars. In addition, Facebook users were selecting content from old-media websites and sharing it on this new platform. Thus, an article from the *New York Times* might be shared hundreds of times on Facebook among various interested parties, but Facebook was collecting the traffic, the clicks, and the advertisers that would have previously gone into the paper.

Other social media platforms emerged during this time as well, including Twitter, Instagram, and Tumblr, each of which provided individuals with the ability to connect with similar individuals and share content through these sites. Each time another platform emerged, it meant more competition for revenue and thus less money for traditional platforms that were struggling to keep their audience share.

Video Goes Viral

As newspapers and the music corporations saw their grip on their industries weaken, television operations remained relatively stable. In 2005, people were spending more than 4.5 hours per day watching television, a number that had been part of an ever increasing trend.[33] That year, broadcast TV generated nearly $46 billion in advertising revenue. However, that same year, three PayPal workers started a side project that would shift video consumption forever: YouTube.

When Chad Hurley, Steve Chen, and Jawed Karim launched YouTube in 2005, they thought it could serve as a video online dating platform. While the dating portion didn't work, internet users enjoyed the idea of watching short, entertaining video clips, and the site took off.[34] In reflecting on YouTube's impact in the decade since its launch, YouTube executive Robert Kyncl noted in 2016 that online video consumption was not only growing at the rate of 50 percent per year, but it would overtake broadcast television as the primary source of entertainment by 2020.[35] A global study of video consumption in 2020 found that prediction to be relatively accurate, with online video hours per week overtaking broadcast for the first time in history.[36]

YouTube was not the only video-sharing service that began to erode the domination of traditional television. The rise of TikTok, which began in its current form in 2018, and other social sharing apps had people spending upward of 70 percent of their time on their mobile devices viewing social media or photo/video apps in 2021.[37]

The shift to online video forced entertainment professionals to rethink their approach to content and their advertising model. Rather than promoting movies and shows through television commercials, entertainment companies released trailers and clips online for consumption on these mobile sites. In addition, commercials had to be cut down to better deal with the impatient nature of online users who didn't want to wait through a thirty-second ad to see a fifteen-second video. Although television and movie revenues have remained relatively stable in nonpandemic years, the approach these industries have taken to keeping an interest in their programming continues to evolve.

MEDIA LITERACY MOMENT: THE AUDIENCE BECOMES THE PRODUCT

The earliest media outlets looked for ways to cater to the audience as customers. If enough readers didn't buy the newspapers or the magazines the publishers were printing, the publications would quickly cease to exist. Radio and television programmers also found that the audience-interest model served them well in deciding which programs to renew each season and which ones to cancel.

Once the concept of advertising entered the mix, media outlets found themselves serving two distinct masters: the people consuming the content and the organizations advertising in it. The symbiotic relationship among the three groups operated in dynamic tension, with the outlets needing to appeal to the audience without alienating the advertisers. Conversely, advertisers needed to promote their products adjacent to media content that appealed to the consumers. For example, if a newspaper published stories that cast a negative light on big gas-guzzling vehicles, the local truck dealership might decide not to advertise in it, even if a lot of people were interested in reading those stories. On the other hand, a newspaper that ran boring stories that offended no one might be a relatively safe place to advertise those trucks, but if nobody read the newspaper because it was boring, the ads didn't get the exposure they needed.

This kind of traditional balance of editorial concerns, advertising desires, and audience interests worked well for several decades until digital media changed the playing field.

Social media platforms like Facebook and Instagram offered free access to their sites and provided users with a seemingly endless string of benefits. People could share photos, connect with friends, and buy items from neighbors. Websites like Google made it easy to find anything online using a few key search terms, and they even provided free email and digital storage to boot.

This shift from the pay-to-play model and traditional advertising services came with unforeseen consequences. These digital companies were collecting the data people put forth as part of their interactions with the platforms and selling the information to advertisers and other corporate interests. One infamous example of this was the Cambridge Analytica scandal on Facebook, in which this British consulting company was gathering reams of information from Facebook users without their permission.[38] The Federal Trade Commission charged Facebook with violating users' privacy with deceptive settings that allowed this and other data collections to occur. In 2019, Facebook settled with the FTC for a record $5 billion and agreed to make changes to its approach to privacy.[39]

Not every effort to collect data or reach audience members is as egregious as this, but these digital platforms do have the ability to learn a great deal about us and target us with content and advertising to a frighteningly specific degree. A quick search for what movies are coming out this week can lead to targeted Instagram ads for discounted tickets at a local theater. A search through one website for a particular book can generate multiple ads for that book throughout a user's Facebook feed.

As much as we like to think that as users, these operations are beholden to us, the truth is that we aren't the ones paying the bills. Or, to quote a now famous line about social media: "If you are not paying for it, you're not the customer; you're the product being sold."[40]

THE NEXT STEP: Look through your social media feeds for advertising and suggested content. Do these suggestions reflect the kinds of things you normally buy, read, watch, or consume? Then, do several searches on your computer for a variety of things that you probably wouldn't look for on a daily basis. Maybe look up how much it costs to fly to a country you've never visited, or where you can purchase a pair of shoes you think are horribly ugly. Then, start looking through your social media feeds at the advertising and suggested content. Do these items or other similar ones start showing up? Have the items in your feeds changed? Write a short essay on your findings.

IMPACT OF OWNERSHIP CONSOLIDATION

LEARNING OBJECTIVES

LO 4: Understand the negative consequences of overly consolidated media ownership.

Media consolidation provides owners with increased profits and greater overall control of content. As we've noted, six major media organizations now control the preponderance of media in the United States, a fact often obscured by layers and layers of subsidiary ownership. The inherent value to them is clear, but the underlying problems associated with this concentrated ownership can lead to significant harm for readers, listeners, and viewers.

Here are a few significant impacts associated with this level of ownership consolidation:

- News deserts
- Job losses
- Loss of diversity
- False sense of choice

Let's examine each of these in more depth.

News Deserts

Scholars at the Hussman School of Journalism and Media at the University of North Carolina began an investigation in 2016 to assess how global media giants and hedge fund investors had forced the media outlets under their control to shrink. To maximize profitability, ownership groups pulled back on newspaper coverage and distribution outside of large metropolitan areas and eliminated unprofitable smaller publications within their holdings. Figure 3.2 shows news deserts in the United States.

FIGURE 3.2 ■ Do You Live in a News Desert?

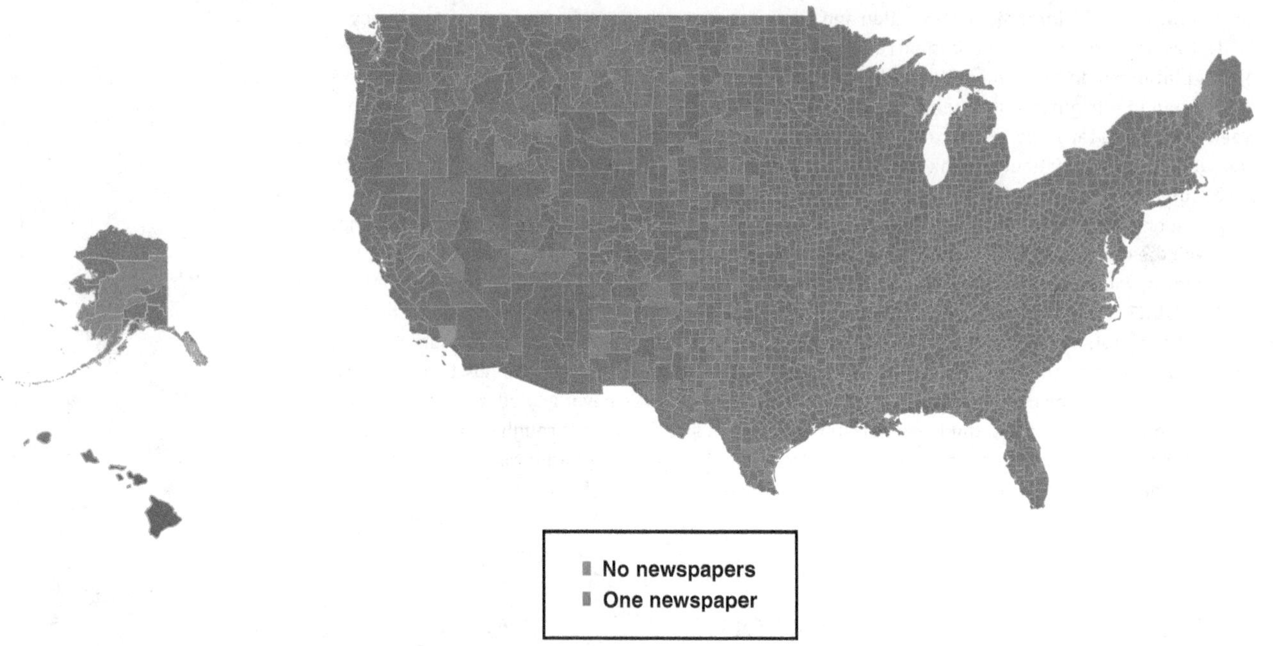

The consolidation of newspapers into corporate chains has left many areas of the United States with almost no local journalism. Researchers at the University of North Carolina found that 1,540 counties in the country have only one newspaper, which is usually a weekly publication. An additional 200 counties have no local newspaper.

Based on data from https://www.usnewsdeserts.com/#viz1626105082044

Although the broadcast industry saw continual profits as the newspaper industry continued to shrink, radio and television journalism saw a steady erosion of staff and coverage. The UNC researchers note that most daily newscasts don't present actual news, with about 90 percent of the content focused on soft features, crime, weather, and sports, primarily with a major metropolitan focus that gives outlying communities short shrift.[41] In addition, AM radio stations that once staffed news operations have moved toward syndicated talk radio programs or local commentators, because they are both more popular and less costly to produce than news gathering. These changes led to some communities' existing without viable, reliable media outlets, a phenomenon referred to as a **news desert**. The authors defined this term as an area of the country "with limited access to credible and comprehensive news and information that feeds democracy at the grassroots level."[42]

The UNC team found that more than two hundred counties in the United States have no newspaper at all, with about half of the remaining counties limited to one understaffed publication to serve the region. The authors also note that those publications that do remain do so as ghost newspapers, weakened versions of their former selves that do not adequately cover their communities.[43] TV stations also avoided community-level journalism, because it lacked broad appeal, instead venturing beyond the station's core coverage area only when large or odd events drew them to these smaller areas.

When people lack a reliable, quality source of information, they are at a distinct disadvantage in making intelligent decisions that can affect their lives. Citizens can learn a great deal about each major-party candidate running for president of the United States while simultaneously knowing almost nothing about the candidates for their town board, mayor, or municipal judge. In addition, local boards and committees that operate without concern that a local media outlet will provide critical coverage to engaged citizens can get away with almost anything.

Even more, when people don't know which outlet to trust, they can fall victim to any voice in the public sphere that speaks up. The concerns pertaining to the rise of fake news and other forms of misinformation stem from people's inability to discern fact from fiction. Stable, quality news outlets once provided people with a voice of reason and a source of verifiable facts, but as these outlets eroded or disappeared entirely, people lost their guiding force. As news deserts continue to emerge, more and more people will find themselves putting faith in unverified sources.

Job Losses

Research has shown that 2020 was the worst year for U.S. newsrooms, with more than 16,000 lost jobs occurring across print, broadcast, and online media operations. The researchers also noted that film production, television production, and advertising lost an additional 14,000 jobs in 2020, dealing another significant blow to the media industry.[44] Some of the blame for the layoffs rests on the impact the coronavirus pandemic had on the industry. Local businesses closed, costing news operations important advertising dollars, while social distancing inhibited television and film production and distribution. However, the shedding of jobs across the industry long predates the current situation and ties directly to the operational efforts of ownership.

The previous record for newsroom job cuts before 2020 was 14,265 jobs lost in 2008, with an additional 11,637 layoffs the following year. At no point between 2008 and 2022 did newsrooms have a net gain of jobs.

Media operations beyond the newsroom also saw losses in the pre-COVID era, as the economic impact of fewer production groups led to fewer opportunities for writers, camera operators, and other key personnel. The cycle of losses the music industry and the print news industry experienced in the decades prior had now struck the film industry. As far back as 2017, author Nick Bilton of *Vanity Fair* declared "Hollywood as we know it is already over."[45] In the era of individual or even smaller corporate ownership, these losses could be mitigated through a variety of methods that sought to preserve both the larger whole as well as the individual operations. However, conglomerates operate on both a larger scale and a shorter timetable, as failure to continually increase profitability is viewed as unacceptable. Therefore, losses in theater attendance, failure to reach news audiences, and the competition of streaming services led to significant cuts to projects and the people working on them.

Starting with Chapter 4, we will discuss potential job opportunities available to you in each media field we cover. Although the jobs provide a wide range of career options, the individual jobs available to you today are much fewer than they were prior to the age of media consolidation.

Loss of Diversity

The broad concept of diversity includes issues of race, gender, sexual orientation, religion, and political affiliation. The goal of a diverse society and the participation of individuals with a wide array of life experiences is to give each individual a more complete view of the world around them. For diversity to function, it requires individuals with differences to participate equitably within the culture to accurately reflect their positive and negative experiences.

The fewer participants exist within a system, the less likely diversity is to thrive and the narrower the view society will hold on to a vast array of topics. But research has shown that many media conglomerates often have the same people on their boards of directors, limiting diverse voices.[46] These entangling engagements make it even more difficult for outside individuals with distinctive viewpoints to influence what these organizations present to the public. With financial motives serving as the prime directive, conglomerates cater to what is most likely to appeal to the largest audience that will cost the least amount of money to create in hopes of maximizing profit. When this occurs, niche voices and diverse visions will fail to gain equal footing in the world of publication, television, film, and digital media.

False Sense of Choice

The ability to choose among seemingly endless media options can provide consumers with a sense of freedom and individuality, thus making them feel satisfied with the current media market. Cable and satellite dish television providers include hundreds of channels in even the lowest tiers of service, while streaming services include screen after screen of previously released films and original content for viewers. Satellite radio services serve up hundreds of channels of music, sports, talk, and weather, each of which serves a specific interest or focuses on a specific genre. The websites available to readers and viewers produce billions of stories, videos, podcasts, and images on hundreds of thousands of topics from the mainstream interests to the eccentric niches.

Although the choices themselves seem endless, individuals who fail to understand the true sources of those choices are operating under what psychologists call the **illusion of choice**. Illusion of choice gives people a false sense that they have more control over what they consume than they actually do. The goal of monopolistic conglomerates is to prevent people from challenging the ways in which they operate and the content they create through this illusion of overwhelming choice. Researchers note that this often harms the working and lower classes, as the choices individuals make all support and reinforce the values of the media owners.[47]

When a limited number of people or organizations control the media, the array of choices can seem excessive, but the true variety of content remains exceptionally limited, with some forms of content being completely eliminated. If none of those organizations deems it worthwhile to break from the standards that currently fund its global enterprise, no one will get to see content that challenges or runs counter to those standards.

CHAPTER REVIEW

LO1 Compare and contrast the basic global media systems.

- There are four models for global media systems.
- The authoritarian model places content control in the hands of the elites and authorities for the supposed good of the society as a whole. Media is censored, and critics of the controlling class are punished. The goal of the system is to promote the political, economic, and social status quo and retain a strong divide between the ruling class and the rest of the citizenry.
- The libertarian model places content control in the hands of the people, allowing a truly free press that exists without the threat of censorship or interference from the ruling class. The goal of this system is to provide everyone with the opportunity to express their opinions, thus allowing a well-rounded view of society as a whole and sponsoring a higher level of trust in the media.
- The social responsibility model balances the freedom of expression with the responsibilities of the media to key publics within the society. Media outlets in this structure do not fear government restriction, but they do operate under the control of private ownership groups that can determine what content is disseminated to the audience. In addition, the media practitioners abide by and respect a set of professional tenets that dictate how they act and what they will publish.
- The Soviet-communist model harkens to the days of the former Soviet Union, in which all media are owned and controlled by the state itself. The content produced reflects the propagandist nature of state media, as it highlights the benefits of the governmental system while ignoring negative aspects of life within the country. Citizens are not allowed to question or criticize the government through media.

LO2 Identify the key phases in the history of U.S. media ownership and control.

- During colonial times, the British government controlled the media through laws dictating who could own and operate a press. In addition, laws allowed governmental censorship of content that was deemed critical of the government or otherwise problematic to the ruling class.

- While developing its early ruling documents, the United States provided citizens with freedom of expression, in both speech and the press. As such, individuals with an interest in media ownership were able to purchase presses and create newspapers. During this time, individuals tended to own a single newspaper and seek to dominate a specific geographic location with it. A similar approach occurred during the advent of radio prior to World War I, as inventors took to the airwaves to connect with those in the area who owned and operated receivers.
- With the advent of the Federal Communications Commission, radio and television operations became part of larger corporate interests that owned chains of stations throughout the country. CBS, NBC, and ABC became dominant players, controlling the majority of broadcast operations in the United States from the 1940s through the 1980s. In a similar fashion, newspaper barons like William Randolph Hearst collected papers across the country under a single corporate entity. Other publishing giants would also develop newspaper chains that shared content throughout the organization.
- As U.S. laws regarding cross-ownership relaxed and digital media became more prominent, media investors began using convergence opportunities to merge newspaper, radio, television, and internet operations. This approach sought to maximize profitability of the media outlets while improving content distribution across multiple media platforms. As these media conglomerates continued to grow, ownership groups subsumed all forms of media under their control, including entertainment products and news operations.
- Investment groups saw distressed media properties, such as newspapers, as an opportunity for significant financial gain through cuts and consolidation. Hedge funds like Alden Global Capital have purchased hundreds of newspapers, only to sell off their real estate holdings and slash staff payroll, rather than rebuilding them. Other media outlets have suffered similar fates, as investors seek to maximize profits.

LO3 **Explain the impact of digital developments on the media landscape.**

- Advertising sites like Craigslist undercut newspapers by making classified advertising digital and free. In addition, independent websites like the Drudge Report and the Huffington Post showed people that interesting content could be obtained online for free. Traditional newspapers' loss of unilateral control of classified ads and content provision made them less interesting to audiences and thus less valuable to advertisers, who went elsewhere with their ads and dollars.
- Musical sharing services like Napster and the iTunes store forced the recording industry to grapple with the loss of traditional media purchases and reconceptualize how to make money from music. The addition of streaming services like Pandora and Spotify also unseated terrestrial radio as the dominant player in the music industry.
- Social media sites like Facebook and Twitter created places where people could share interesting information about themselves as well as content they found elsewhere. The information available to these platforms made it easy for advertisers to directly target users with individualized messages, thus making their ad buys more effective.
- Sites like YouTube and TikTok reshaped the way in which media consumers viewed video content, in terms of the devices they used and the types of material they watched. Traditional media platforms had to rethink their use of video clips, movie trailers, and even advertisements to meet the needs of the consumers who used these sites for entertainment and information.

LO4 **Understand the negative consequences of overly consolidated media ownership.**

- Parts of the country that do not have significant financial opportunities for media outlets have become news deserts. In these areas, citizens are without newspapers or other forms of traditional journalism that can keep them informed as to important events happening around them. Critics note that these deserts can lead to decreased knowledge among the citizenry and potential harms to the democratic process.

- Media consolidation for the purpose of profit can lead to significant cuts at media outlets across the spectrum of platforms. As salaries often account for a large portion of overall costs at media outlets, organizations seek to maximize the amount of content they can create while minimizing the number of people needed to do it. This leads to significant cuts in job opportunities, as noted throughout the chapter.
- Limitations to the number of people who get to own media often lead to a loss of diversity in an ownership group. Many of the individuals who serve at the highest levels of one media conglomerate hold similar positions at other conglomerates. In addition, the media ownership groups often form partnerships, thus further homogenizing the overall output from their properties. The lack of a broad swath of individual leaders that better represents the gender, racial, social, economic, and experiential makeup of society diminishes the opportunity for true diversity in these organizations.
- The limited number of media owners has led citizens to operate under an illusion of choice when it comes to their consumption habits. Despite a wider array of publications, channels, services, and media sites available to end users, the oligopoly that represents the ownership interests means that you get exactly what these few people want you to get, no more and no less. Failing to fully understand this can lead media consumers to allow the status quo to perpetuate without question.

KEY TERMS

Authoritarian system
Conglomerates
Convergence
Cross-ownership rule
Hedge funds
Illusion of choice
Libertarian system
News desert
Social-responsibility theory
Soviet-communist system
Studio system
Vertical integration
Vulture capital strategy

DISCUSSION QUESTIONS

1. Of the four media systems discussed in this chapter, which one do you think does the most good for a society? Which one do you like the least? Why?
2. What are the pros and cons of having more media in the hands of fewer people? Do you think the benefits outweigh the drawbacks? What do you think would be an appropriate number of media ownership groups and why?
3. How much has digital media changed the way in which you consume content, compared with what your parents or grandparents experienced? Have you lived through any major digital disruption that changed your media consumption habits? What was it like?
4. Of the four major negative consequences of media consolidation, which one concerns you the most for your own consumption habits? Which one concerns you the most regarding society as a whole?

The book *Maus*, a graphic novel that tells the story of the Holocaust during the Nazi regime in World War II, was banned from a Tennessee school district's curriculum in 2022.

MARO SIRANOSIAN/Contributor/Getty Image

BOOKS: THE ORIGINAL MASS MEDIUM

INTRODUCTION

1. *How do you react when you hear that a book has been banned? What thoughts or emotions does it evoke in you? Do you want to read the book even more, or do you want to avoid the book entirely?*
2. *Some books like* Maus *are meant to educate the reader or convey a message through language and visual imagery. What reasons do you have for reading books? Education? Escape? Amusement?*
3. *Do you think books still have a place in today's society, given the expansive use of shorter writing, digital platforms, and social media? Why or why not?*

In 2022, the McMinn County School Board voted unanimously to ban the graphic novel *Maus* from its eighth grade reading curriculum, citing inappropriate content for students of that age. The book tells the story of the Holocaust, using mice to represent Jewish people and cats as Nazis. Author Art Spiegelman wrote the novel to tell the story of his parents, who lived in Poland during World War II and survived internment in the Auschwitz death camp.[1] The book, which was first published in 1986, drew international acclaim and earned a Pulitzer Prize special citation in 1992, vaulting it to the top of multiple bestseller lists.

The concept of banning books can evoke imagery of Nazi rallies, in which government officials oversaw burning of texts deemed inappropriate for the public to read. Also, given that digital media gives more people access to texts of all kinds, it may seem impossible for any individual organization to prohibit certain people from reading specific books. However, in today's polarized political environment, experts note that the United States has seen a staggering rise in efforts to ban books from schools and libraries alike, with both sides of the divide trying to limit access to various texts.[2] The American Library Association Office for Intellectual Freedom noted in 2022 that requests for bans are up because some books challenge conventional thinking in certain regions of the country and make people uncomfortable.[3]

Books are often overlooked as a form of mass media, but they remain a crucial way in which people provide information, share culture, and create records for future generations. Even more, debates regarding what should or shouldn't be taught to each subsequent generation often place books and their authors in the crosshairs of society.

In this chapter, we will begin by examining the way in which society placed text-based communication at the core of its educational resources and historical records. We will then take a deeper look at the role of books regarding how they serve people's needs, both historically and today. We will also outline the ways in which books are developed and shared among people as part of the publishing process. Finally, we will look into the ways books have served as flash points for social movements throughout time and the ways in which people have sought to censor them for a variety of reasons.

LEARNING OBJECTIVES

After completing this chapter, you should be able to:

1. Identify the importance of key moments in the history of books and publishing.
2. Describe how books provide value to society.
3. Outline how books are developed, produced, and sold.
4. Understand the concept of censorship of books as well as the rationales used over time to justify it.

FROM STONE TABLETS TO DIGITAL TABLETS: A BRIEF HISTORY OF TEXT

LEARNING OBJECTIVES

LO 1: Identify the importance of key moments in the history of books and publishing.

We could spend hundreds of pages talking about the evolutionary and revolutionary steps that have influenced the written word and its development throughout history. Although we will touch on various elements of this story, the bigger issues we will tackle in this chapter are how societies used books to codify and advance their culture and history as well as how books helped shape societies through shared content that supported social norms, challenged societal convention, and enhanced collective knowledge.

Here are some key points in the development of books:

- Early writings
- Building a library, preserving knowledge
- Foundations of publication
- Pulp fiction and dime novels
- Paperback revolution
- Nonmainstream efforts
- Books on demand

Let's take a deeper look at these concepts.

Early Writings

As with most things humans invented, written text arose out of necessity. Scholars found that sometime in the middle of the fourth millennium BC, the people of Mesopotamia wanted to create a system that would help them keep track of resources, such as farming yields. Using what they had available to them, they relied on reeds from the Tigris and Euphrates rivers to create writing implements and used them to press iconic symbols into flat clay chunks that would retain the images. The wedge-shaped marks were the first known form of writing, dubbed **cuneiform** (from the Latin word *cuneus*, meaning

Egyptians relied on shapes and images to record important elements of their history. These hieroglyphics are an example of those detailed efforts.

DEA/S. VANNINI/Contributor/Getty Image

"wedge").[4] Writing formats continued to develop and adapt to the needs of the people, with everything from laws to literature being codified in this format throughout the region. The Mesopotamians wrote on stone as well, carving their language into rocks as a more permanent record.

The need to retain history and educate others about important aspects of one's culture emerged in other forms of written language moving forward from that point. Egyptians found other ways to use reeds in the creation of text, using them to create **papyrus**, an early form of paper. Upon scrolls of this fragile medium, scribes and artists shared religious rituals, denoted cultural expectations, and recorded historical achievements using **hieroglyphics**, an image-based form of language.

People saw the importance of cataloging the history of their societies, giving rise to improvements in language and preservation of texts. To overcome papyrus's frail nature, as well as the limited access to the reeds used to make it, humans found ways to craft other forms of this medium. As far back as AD 25, China developed a papermaking process to create a pulp-based, thin-stock paper on which officials would catalog information. In Europe, humans took to writing on dried animal skins, known as **parchment**, until papermaking technology reached that continent in the eleventh century. To help make content easier to consume and more widely accessible, humans developed a writing system that assigned sounds to letters, which could be combined to form words. In short, sometime around 1800 BC, the alphabet was created in what today is the Middle East, with the Greeks reshaping it into what scholars refer to as the first "true" alphabet by the eighth century BC.[5]

Building a Library, Preserving Knowledge

The word *library* has its roots in fourteenth-century Latin, coming from the word *librarium*, which translates roughly into "bookcase" or "chest for books." But the concept of a true library begins more than a millennium earlier in ancient Egypt.

In the third century BC, Alexander the Great was the king of Macedonia, known for his efforts in empire-building and military conquests. However, he also understood the power of knowledge to unify and advance society, which is why he hoped to develop the greatest repository of information ever known. He selected a site in the newly named city of Alexandria for the intellectual capital of the world and helped develop a library containing more than seven hundred thousand scrolls (approximately one hundred thousand modern printed books). Although the lighthouse installed at Alexandria receives accolades as one of the Seven Wonders of the World, the library was responsible for massive advances in humankind.[6]

Scientists, scribes, mathematicians, and other learned individuals throughout the world journeyed to the city for access to this repository of knowledge. The library served as an academy and a research center as well, where great minds like Euclid, Archimedes, Callimachus, and others established fields like geometry, physics, and library science. Many of their initial principles still provide the foundation of these fields to this day.

The scholars studied everything from poetry to medicine, and they saw the opportunity to work together to create a sense of organized, universal knowledge. Their mutual tolerance and respect for rational thought were furthered by this setting that prized reason and clarity above all else. The library's collection was seen as valuable content that future generations could rely upon to further their own efforts to educate and enhance society.

Although the library's prominence and holdings eroded near the turn of the century, it would endure until about AD 400, when it became a source of friction among various religious and governmental groups that viewed it as a threat to their power and standing. However, the library concept itself, in which the important works of a society are gathered in one place for the enjoyment and education of all, lives on throughout the world to this day.

Foundations of Publication

For generations, books were a true lifetime labor of love, with individuals copying texts by hand from trusted sources. These hand copies were then bound together to make books. This method was painstakingly difficult, was susceptible to the potential for variations among copies, and limited the number of volumes that could be produced in a certain amount of time.

The ability to create a consistent version of a book in a much easier and faster fashion didn't truly arrive until about 1450, when a goldsmith named Johannes Gutenberg developed the first viable printing press. Although woodblock printing dated back more than five hundred years, Gutenberg's innovation was to use a "press" to make an impression of an inked, metal block of type onto a blank piece of paper. He also pioneered the use of **movable type**, a process that advanced and improved publishing. Gutenberg cast multiple replicas of each of the letters of the alphabet by pouring heated lead into molds. The cast letters could be used to create a metal "plate" for printing each individual page of text. This made it easier to print hundreds of words that were composed of consistently sized letters, and it gave the printer the ability to reuse these letters as needed during the publication process. Gutenberg's invention allowed text to be transferred evenly and repeatedly onto paper, making the copies both consistent and legible.[7]

Although this approach to publishing launched the mass media industry, Gutenberg died penniless after he was sued over several bad business deals. That said, his press endured, inspiring other printing operations in France, Italy, and elsewhere.

Pulp Fiction and Dime Novels

As we have seen, once a new media format is cheap, and available to consumers in large quantities, it skyrockets in popularity. Books took off in this way in the 1860s with the rise of pulp fiction publications and dime store novels, both of which placed engaging content into the hands of people who weren't in the elite class.

In 1860, Beadle and Company began producing a series of paperback books that were cheap and short, known as **dime novels**. Their 10-cent price, which is equal to about $3.40 in today's economy, was significantly less than that of most other books of the day, which cost between $1 and $1.50, or roughly $33 to $50 today. The books ran about one hundred pages, and the series began by reprinting serialized copy from previous magazine publications, before eventually working with authors to tell original stories. The books followed the patterns of the **penny dreadfuls**, weekly texts published throughout the 1830s in England, telling wild tales focused on everything from pirates to mysteries.[8] Between 1860 and 1915, many other companies entered the field and collectively produced more than fifty thousand titles.[9]

Dime novels met their untimely end when magazine publication became easier and cheaper, allowing the content to reach more people, more cheaply, and through more venues than the dime novels could. Frank Munsey's magazine *Argosy*, launched in 1882 is often credited as the first **pulp fiction** publication, a no-frills magazine without illustrations or even a cover.[10] His publications covered similar topics as the dime novels: romance, adventure, and crime. Compared with the slick, colorful magazines and leather-bound, serious books of the time, these ragged and flimsy texts provided poorer people with greater access to reading opportunities.

Beadle's dime novels provided readers with fantastical stories about everything from pirates and explorers to gunslingers and frontier life.

Science History Images/Alamy Stock Photo

Paperback Revolution

Beginning with the invention of the printing press, publishing houses treated books as important tomes, sold to the literate upper class at prices that would be prohibitive for everyday citizens. These were hardcover texts that contained epic works of the historically valuable writers, such as William Shakespeare and Jane Austin. Dime novels, pulp fiction, and comic books made some inroads in the market, but most publishing houses saw these formats as being unworthy of their attention.

In 1939, Robert de Graff created Pocket Books, a publishing company that sold paperbacks that were of higher quality than the pulp novels from the turn of the century but much cheaper than the

Pocket Books told formulaic and often sexualized stories. Their low cost and easy access made them among the best-selling books in the paperback revolution.

Transcendental Graphics/Contributo/Getty Images

hardcovers of the day. The cost for each book was twenty-five cents, and the size of the book was standardized to fit in a person's pocket.[11] During World War II, other publishers followed de Graff's model, distributing thousands of free, pocket-sized texts to servicemen. The books fit into the pocket of the standard GI uniform and could be easily discarded or shared with others. De Graff built his empire with the idea of getting books out of bookstores and into dozens of other places people would visit, including grocery stores, drug stores, gas stations, and restaurants. To reach the mass market, he installed wire racks in many locations to showcase a variety of pocket-sized novels. The approach made books more of an impulse buy and appealed to a variety of reading tastes, from the classics to hard-boiled detective stories. Experts ascribed the success of these pocket-sized books to this down-market approach that provided fun, engaging stories for the masses.[12]

However, as other publishers jumped on the bandwagon, it put stress on the format's success. When de Graff started his Pocket Books experiment, he set the price at twenty-five cents because he felt that no one would miss a quarter, so that his product would not be a critical spending decision for consumers. However, with increased competition and low-cost products, these books had to sell exponentially more copies to break even than would the higher priced offerings of the bigger publishing houses. In the postwar era, the paperback publishers were selling tens of millions of units but were also seeing thousands of books shipped back each year, unsold. By the early 1960s, the era of pocket-sized books had ended, with the traditional publishers picking up the pieces of the market and incorporating them into their list of titles.

Nonmainstream Efforts

Despite an increased demand for books in the postwar era, a large amount of content didn't see the light of day. As discussed in Chapter 3, the massive presence of mainstream publishing companies and the consolidation of publishing houses made increased sales paramount, thus pushing authors to create material that had a wide appeal. In many cases, that wide appeal shut out voices of a diverse racial, social, and sexual nature.

In response, independent publishers created smaller niche publishing outlets that sought to showcase a greater array of work, especially that of engaging but unproven talents. For example, Haki R. Madhubuti founded the Third World Press Foundation in 1967 as a way to feature authors of color. An author and poet himself, Madhubuti wrote more than twenty books, while also mentoring some of the most important Black writers of the past fifty years. In the same vein, Jennifer Joseph also saw the importance of providing poets with a venue through which they could reach a wider audience. In 1984, she launched Manic D Press, which allowed everyone from poets to comic artists to produce content that discussed broader social and personal issues. Authors who published with Manic D have earned distinctions from multiple organizations for their efforts to produce quality LGBTQ+ content.

Books on Demand

As de Graff discovered, an important aspect of successful book sales is to make it as easy as possible to purchase the books. New technologies have allowed others to follow his lead in making books universally available to readers. In 1994, Jeff Bezos launched the first major online bookseller when he debuted Amazon.com. Like de Graff, Bezos saw the benefits of giving people wider access to reading material while also understanding the limitations of brick-and-mortar bookstores. His online library of titles could drastically exceed anything the major stores of the day could provide, and he could ship purchases directly to consumers wherever they lived or worked. Although critics questioned the

Haki R. Madhubuti's Third World Press Foundation gave authors of color one of their first venues to tell stories as they saw fit for readers with similar experiences.

Chicago Tribune/Contributor/Getty Images

viability of his approach, Bezos persisted, adding other forms of media to his online offerings. Bezos himself had warned early investors that there was a high probability the venture would fail.[13] However, today Amazon is the largest online retailer in the world, and Bezos is consistently listed among the five richest people on the planet.[14]

As digital media was becoming more prevalent and more portable, publishers looked for ways to transition traditional books onto new devices. In 1997, the E Ink Corporation developed the technology that allowed digital devices to operate without the need for a backlight.[15] This invention made the text on the screen read more like traditional print and significantly increased battery life for e-readers. This new "digital paper" saw limited success at first. However, when Amazon introduced the Kindle in 2007, the platform took off, due in large part to its ability to access Amazon's e-book library. Barnes & Noble followed in 2009 with the Nook, an e-reader with Wi-Fi and mobile cellular capabilities. Today, e-books account for about 20 percent of the sales and rental market, which comes out to about 191 million copies per year.[16] Researchers see the market for these digital products continuing to grow at about 6 percent annually between 2022 and 2025.[17]

These shifts in the publishing industry also helped provide authors with another way to reach an audience: self-publication. For example, Liberty University student Alexa Holsten self-published *Listening to the List* in 2019, which examined how people can improve their lives by examining their personal identities and relationships with others.[18] Although generations of authors have relied on **vanity presses**—which charged them to lightly edit, print, and to some extent advertise their books—the digital revolution made it much less financially risky to self-publish content. In 2010, Amanda Hocking began offering her young-adult, paranormal romance books as self-published e-books that could be read through digital devices. Her first collection of texts earned her $2 million in less than a year, making her the poster child for the self-publishing movement.[19] The "Kindle revolution" that followed provided authors with more freedom to determine the writing, editing, and approach to their work, while also allowing them to determine the most effective ways to market their efforts.[20]

TABLE 4.1 ■ A Few Key Names in Book Publishing

Johannes Gutenberg	Haki R. Madhubuti	Robert de Graff	Jennifer Joseph	Jeff Bezos
• A German inventor in the 1400s who revolutionized publishing through the development of a moveable-type printing press. • Introduced improvements to inks, typefaces, and molds for the press. • Began the print revolution and the ability to mass-produce media content.	• An African American author and poet who launched the Third World Press Foundation in 1967, which is the oldest independent Black-owned publishing house in the United States • Served as a mentor and publisher for world-renowned authors, poets, and editors, including Pulitzer Prize winner Gwendolyn Brooks. • Wrote and published twenty-eight books.	• Created the Pocket Books publishing empire in 1939, democratizing reading through cheap, small books. • Improved book marketing by placing books at a wide array of stores outside of traditional bookstores. • Saw reading as something all people should enjoy, not just the elite few, and published content that appealed to the masses.	• Founded Manic D Press in 1984 to provide an alternative press outlet for nonmainstream voices. • Books published at her press have earned multiple awards, including the Lambda Literary Award for Transgender Writing. • Remains an active writer and publisher in the alternative and independent press community.	• Founded Amazon in 1994 with the goal of creating an online bookstore that would give people greater access to more books than were available locally. • Expanded the services of his company to include music, movies, and millions of other products. • Purchased *The Washington Post* newspaper in 2013 and reshaped its approach to business through improved digital media and mobile content distribution.

ROLE OF BOOKS

LEARNING OBJECTIVES

LO 2: Describe how books provide value to society.

We've seen how innovations in printing and accessibility helped make printed materials a major means of distributing information and preserving knowledge. Over the centuries, books continued to evolve and improve in accessibility and format, including the advent of audiobooks and the development of e-readers that allow users to download a vast array of texts from all over the world in mere seconds. Even today, the concept of text-based content still retains specific important roles that are worth reviewing here, including the ability to:

- Record history
- Improve literacy and free thinking
- Expand education
- Provide entertainment and enjoyment

Record History

Humankind has long sought to preserve information about current events with the hope that future generations will benefit from that knowledge. Aside from using the material to educate others, humans have sought to track everything from mundane, small occurrences to once-in-a-generation events for their own edification as well as to pass along to others. Written records could be used to jog their memories and help them plan for the future. For example, from ancient times, shepherds kept track of how much wool their sheep yielded each year to be able to predict future production, enabling them to engage in trade and sales efforts more efficiently. Keeping track of upward or downward trends also would help them improve yields or limit losses through adjustments to their methods of animal care. When shepherds died, their knowledge could be passed down through written records to their heirs to continue the operation.

Major events—particularly historical "firsts"—often were preserved through written records. The first time a record is broken or a new technology is introduced tends to be more memorable than later occurrences. It's why schoolchildren know the name of Neil Armstrong, who was the first person to set foot on the moon, as opposed to that of Alan Bean, who was the fourth person to do it. It's why aspiring mountain climbers seek to summit Mount Everest, because it is the highest mountain above sea level, while few of them wax poetically about Cho Oyu, the sixth highest point on Earth. Firsts, lasts, and "onlys" serve as markers for societies to measure how far they have come or what they can accomplish. The term *record book* refers to the way in which we track these outcomes with the hopes of their lasting for generations and giving others something to which they can aspire. This can be on a global scale, as is the case with *Guinness World Records*, which covers a wide array of topics, or in a niche area like sports, television shows, theater, or video games. They provide a complete record so that we can understand larger patterns of events and then apply this knowledge to how we act in the future.

Improve Literacy and Free Thinking

Before books were easily accessible and inexpensive, only the upper classes and those privileged with the ability to read could access information. Many leaders took advantage of this situation, limiting publicly available information to what they wanted their subjects to know. Outside voices or contrary opinions were easily squashed, because those who spoke to the public in a way that displeased the rulers could be beaten, jailed, or killed. This shut off the source of the message and also sent a warning to the public. (As you will see later in the chapter, leaders who sought to maintain control in the face of improving literacy and a diversification of thought found other ways to do so: they banned or, in some cases, burned books.) Monarchs weren't the only ones who sought to limit literacy for their own gain. In the United States, plantation owners punished slaves who were caught reading, and several states passed laws that made it illegal to teach slaves how to read. The Alabama Slave Code of 1833 forbade any literacy instruction to any person of color, under penalty of a fine of up to five hundred dollars.[21]

As book publishing became freer from the strictures of government control, individuals could produce content that showcased a broader array of thought. Authors could provide readers with a view of life that was outside of their personal experience. For example, the novel *Uncle Tom's Cabin* by Harriet Beecher Stowe provided readers with an abolitionist's view of slavery through the characters' experiences. More than 160 years later, Ta-Nehisi Coates highlighted the struggles Black U.S. citizens continue to face in his book *Between the World and Me.*

Expand Education

Books are intended to make information available to people interested in a specific topic. Sharing information to improve knowledge goes beyond recording history or allowing individuals to think more freely. Books provide a written record of basic concepts and established methods of operation, saving individuals the time they would otherwise have to spend discovering this information on their own. Consider the way in which student media outlets produce informational guides for incoming freshmen and then distribute them on campus to help those new students learn about everything from residence hall life to which area restaurants offer the best student discounts. Written texts like these are more efficient in preserving and spreading information than other methods.

Researchers have found that individuals often gain knowledge differently, based on preferred learning styles. In the pre-text era, knowledge of how to properly grow crops or hunt animals for food was shared either in an oral format or through what is called a kinesthetic approach. In short, people were either told how to do something or they learned by doing it under the tutelage of experts who already possessed the skill. Books provided a key third way in which individuals could garner knowledge: self-education through reading.

While blog posts and YouTube videos have taken the place of many "self-help" or "how-to" texts, the use of books to improve oneself continues to thrive. For example, *Atomic Habits* by James Clear sold almost 1.3 million copies in 2022, placing it sixth on *Publishers Weekly*'s list of bestsellers that year. The book provides readers with ways to make small changes in their lives that can lead to better personal habits. The author notes that these changes can help with everything from stress reduction and personal achievement to weight loss and smoking cessation.[22]

Using visual and verbal tools that books provide allows individuals to learn at their own pace, reading as quickly or slowly as they like. In addition, they can work mentally through these processes before having to apply them to live situations. This gives individuals who learn best on their own the ability to gain and retain knowledge they can put into action. The visual/verbal approach also allows individuals to go back and reread a confusing passage or reexamine an image to improve understanding.

Without a written record, individuals would have to memorize a vast amount of material to be successful; books shift the educational burden from memorization to focusing on more specific aspects of tasks or activities. For example, an engineering text might contain specific measurements for certain materials at varied tensile strengths. Engineers could easily use this book as a reference guide to see if a certain material would be strong enough to accomplish a designated task, as opposed to either failing through trial and error or memorizing the strengths of all potential materials they might use in their work. Other fields, such as writing, rely on books for the spelling, definition, and style of certain terms, providing both definitive answers as well as a reassuring reference for the worker who is performing a task.

Finally, like other forms of mass media, books are more efficient in disseminating information than earlier formats. Oral tradition relied on single sources who shared content with multiple people at the same time, limiting its reach; books provide the opportunity both to reach more people and to time-shift the learning process for people who use books as sources of information.

The *Dog Man* series, by Dav Pilkey, frequently produces new stories that are among the most purchased books in the 2020s.

Patti McConville/Alamy Stock Photo

Provide Entertainment and Enjoyment

The ability to read has allowed people to entertain themselves with stories and tales for generations. Aside from the benefits reading can provide in terms of knowledge gain and social understanding, reading can help people escape from everyday life, laugh at the efforts of fictional characters, or try to figure out "whodunit" before the end of a mystery novel. Books can also allow readers to experience the lives of characters who are like themselves, in terms of social stratification, race, religion, sexual orientation, and more.

When it comes to what sells best, it turns out, children's books with humor and artistic engagement tend to draw the most eyeballs. For example, author and artist Dav Pilkey placed three books in the top twenty of *Publishers Weekly*'s list of bestsellers in 2021. *Mothering Heights* is part of his *Dog Man* series, which features a part-man, part-dog character who solves crimes, and it topped the charts with almost 1.3 million sales. *Cat Kid Comic Club* finished fifteenth on the list, with about half that many sales, and is a spinoff from the *Dog Man* books. Pilkey's final entry on the list is another from the *Dog Man* series, *Grime and Punishment*, which sold more than a half million copies and finished the year at number twenty.

Adults also entertain themselves by reading novels, with authors like John Grisham providing readers with legal thrillers and Kristin Hannah writing gripping historical fiction. As much as television shows and movies provide individuals with compelling storylines coupled with amazing visuals, books give individuals the ability to use their own imaginations to paint pictures in their minds without the translation of directors or actors.

THE PROCESS OF DEVELOPING, WRITING, PUBLISHING, AND SELLING BOOKS

LEARNING OBJECTIVES

LO 3: Outline how books are developed, produced, and sold.

If you have ever thought, "I would love to write a book someday," you're not alone. According to publishing data from the United Nations Educational, Scientific, and Cultural Organization, more than 2.2 million books are professionally published each year. ProQuest data reveal that, in the United States, more than 4 million books per year are self-published, meaning that the authors write, produce, publish, and distribute the books on their own. This level of growth has not led to a massive uptick in sales or book distribution, however; industry professionals note that, after a peak in 2007, book sales have remained flat or fallen each subsequent year.[23]

FIGURE 4.1 ■ The Book Publishing Process in Ten Easy Steps

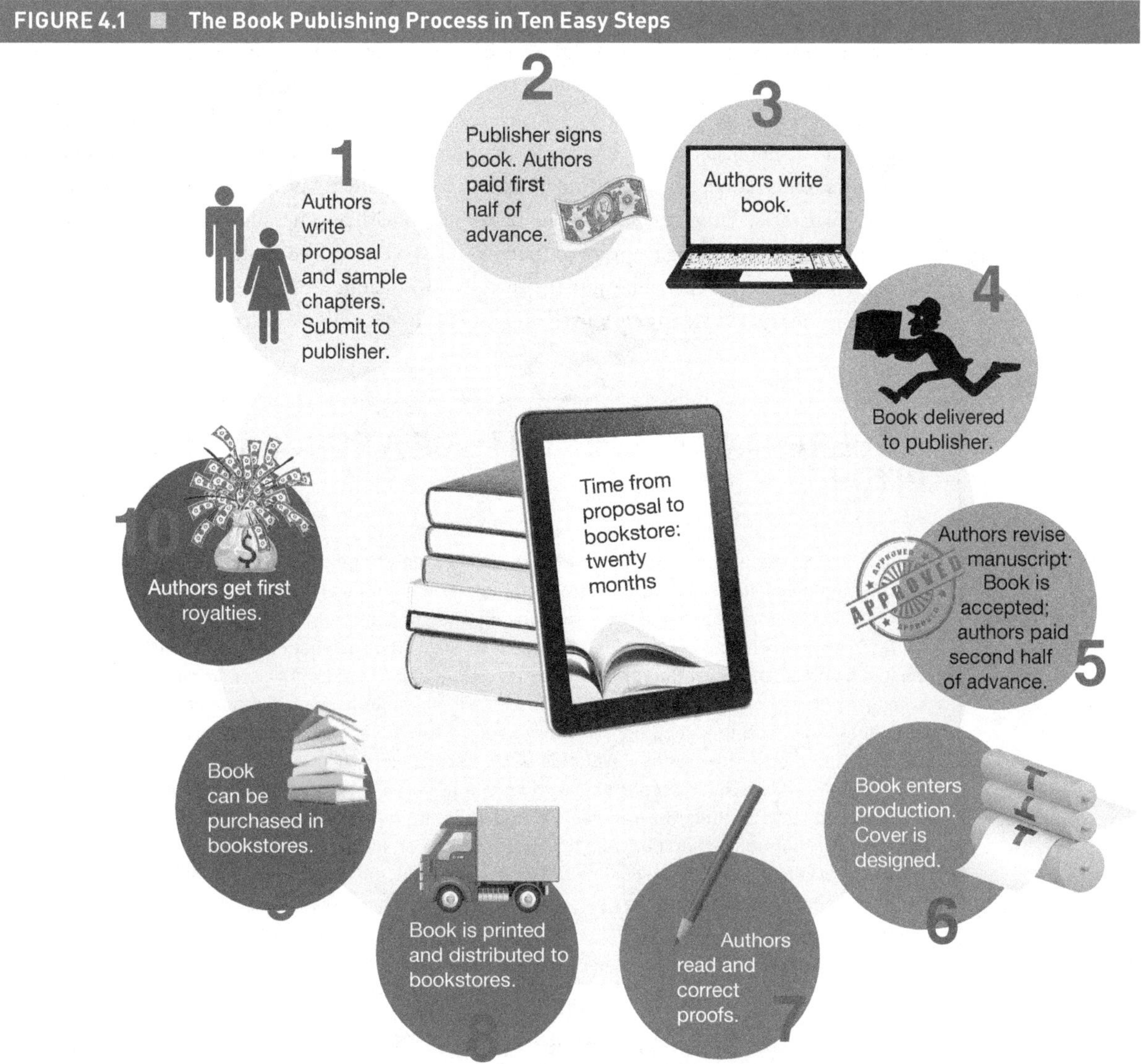

Several stages involving multiple types of editors and producers take place between the moment an author comes up with an idea for a book and the moment when an audience gets to enjoy it. Here are the most common steps a book sees on the way to publication.

Source: Hanson, Mass Communication 8e, Sage Publishing, 2019.

That said, authors show no sign of slowing down, and publishing houses are still reporting healthy profits as they take advantage of coronavirus-related boredom and a broader reliance on digital publishing to reach audience members instantly.[24] Let's look at some of the players in the publishing process:

- Authors
- Publishers
- Content and copy editors
- Booksellers

Authors

In most cases, the bookmaking process starts when an author identifies a topic, an idea, or a concept that could be addressed at length for the benefit of an audience of interested people. Authors then have the option of trying to get people excited about publishing the book before writing it, or writing out a first draft and then pitching it to those in the industry. Authors have to be willing and able to work with other people throughout the process, because a book is never completed in a single draft or by a single person. If the book is in draft form, publishers might want to send it out for review to get a sense of what potential readers would think about it. If the book is only a proposal, a publisher might require several chapters or some writing samples to demonstrate the author's skills and approach.

Authors must also be able to show that they can create a successful book. For example, author John Grisham has published more than three dozen books and has twenty-eight consecutive number one bestsellers to his name, demonstrating his ability to consistently produce publishable content that engages many readers. This means that when he comes up with another idea for a book, he will probably have an easier time getting it approved than would a recent college graduate who never wrote anything longer than a term paper. The author generally will include a timeline for the project, based on the publishing company's press cycle and the amount of time it will take to complete the work.

A DEEPER LOOK: ELEMENTS OF A SUCCESSFUL BOOK PITCH

Authors often create a **book pitch** or **proposal**, a document that allows potential publishers to analyze the likelihood of the text's success within the market. In this proposal, the author will identify a variety of key elements to make the book appealing to publishers.

An Overview: The author should have a fairly concrete idea of what the book will be before pitching it to a publisher. The author should be able to explain if the book is fiction or nonfiction, the size or length of the book, the core elements within the book, and the overall importance or value of the book itself. In short, this document should explain what the book is, what it hopes to accomplish, and why it matters. The proposal will also likely have to contain an outline of some kind that provides a skeleton for what the entire book will contain. In the case of nonfiction books, this could be a structured table of contents with additional details. In the case of fiction books, it could include several short summaries that explain the characters, plot, and other elements of the story.

The Market: According to book marketing research, the average book sells no more than five hundred copies. That number can seem small, but it gets even worse when you realize that this average is actually inflated thanks to blockbuster bestsellers like those by Stephen King or Margaret Atwood. If a publishing house is going to put up a good amount of time, effort, and energy to help an author publish a book, the people working there want to know that the book could sell.

Market research can include specific target audience demographic and psychographic information, which can assist the publisher in deciding if it can reach people in that group (see Chapter 2). The author can also explain what a particular genre or format is doing in terms of sales, growth, or interest. For example, if adult-themed graphic novels are among the most popular types of books sold through major outlets, an author proposing a new book in this format would want to showcase that for publishers. If young-adult, supernatural fiction books had shown exponential growth over the past five years, authors would likely have a good case that their proposed books in this genre would sell well.

Competition: In some areas of publishing, authors need to find a way to justify that their books are superior to others of a similar nature. In the case of romance novels, fans might read dozens of them each year from a variety of authors, so the sense of competition doesn't matter much. However, if a textbook author wants to enter a field where several dominant books already exist, that author needs to explain why this new text will supplant the ones professors are currently using. In cases like this, the author has to demonstrate how the book is "comfortably distinct," explaining that the book can serve the needs of people currently using the competitive texts, while providing specific benefits that they lack.

Credentials: A perfectly legitimate question most publishers will ask if you want to write a book for them is, "What makes you think you can do it?" Authors have to provide publishers with a sense that they have the background to produce quality content that will serve the audience well. In the case of books involving levels of expertise, authors should explain their background in the field as well as what makes them uniquely qualified to write on that topic. Grisham, for example, is known for legal thrillers such as *The Client, The Rainmaker*, and *The Pelican Brief*, and he has a law degree from the University of Mississippi and practiced law for about a decade before becoming a writer.[25]

Publishers

At the heart of the book creation system are publishers, companies that select books for creation and dissemination in various genres, geographic areas, and formats. Publishing houses employ a variety of people who take authors' ideas and shape them into material that has an appeal to a target audience. As you will see, numerous jobs exist in the publishing industry that go beyond what an author produces and what a bookstore sells.

At the start of the publishing process are acquisition editors, people who look for authors to create books that fit within the publisher's areas of interest. These editors work with the authors to create a book pitch, present it to an editorial review committee for consideration, and gather reviews from people willing to read the pitch. After this stage, the acquisition editors decide whether to present the author a contract to write the book, request additional work from the author for another set of reviews, or inform the author that the company is no longer interested in the project.

If an acquisition is successful, other members of the publishing team spring into action to help the author get the project under way. A project editor can work with the author to set deadlines for certain amounts of copy, determine how best to incorporate reviewers' ideas, and assist the author with the process of structuring the book. This editor often works with designers and art directors to find images to augment and improve the text, as well as to determine the layout of the book. A production team then comes into play, layering together all the work everyone has done into a finished product that can be disseminated in print or digital formats. Once the book is published, booksellers join the effort to make it successful.

FIGURE 4.2 ■ The Publishing Process

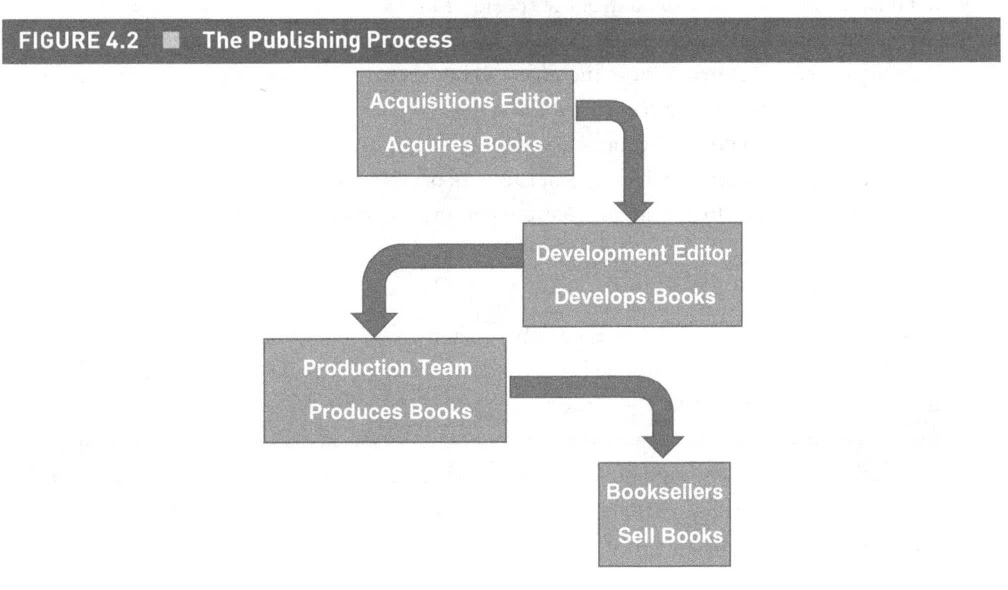

Content and Copy Editors

An author is responsible for whatever appears in any text that has their name on it, but much of the writing they do comes in the form of rewriting. This is where the role of the editor is vital in the completion of any project.

Editorial positions vary based on the specific needs of the author and the publisher in each project. A **content editor** (or **development editor**) might work with the author to flesh out characters, clarify plot points, or rework the conclusion of a book. A **copy editor** is attached to most projects, with the goal of fact-checking nonfiction, cleaning up grammatical errors, and standardizing style based on the approach the publisher deems appropriate. Editors serve as necessary team members who can provide a second set of eyes on the material in hopes of helping the writer's work shine.

Booksellers

Once a book is complete, or nearly so, the role of booksellers becomes crucial to the success or failure of the project. Publishers provide buyers at these media outlets with information, proof copies, and other elements associated with the project to entice them to purchase copies for broader distribution in their store or chain of stores, or on their website. The buyers then decide how many copies of a given title they will purchase for their bookselling organizations and how or where those copies will be sold. Each book has a specific price point at which it will be sold, or in some cases rented, through selling outlets. That price point is based on the format of the text, the competition within that niche, and the desirability of the book.

Sellers have the option of providing books to readers through various outlets, such as online giants like Amazon, where customers can shop without leaving their homes, as well as stores like Barnes & Noble, which remains the largest brick-and-mortar shop around. Textbooks can be rented through outlets like Chegg or through university-based bookstores, while libraries can also make available hardcover, paperback, and digital copies of new releases.

CENSORSHIP AND THE MOVEMENT TO BAN BOOKS

LEARNING OBJECTIVES

LO 4: Understand the concept of censorship of books as well as the rationales used over time to justify it.

Censorship is both a simple and a complex concept: if you can't see something, it won't have an effect on you. Thus, people who want to control the spread of knowledge or social norms of a society will attempt to censor things that operate outside of their sense of "decency" or "normalcy."

The ability to censor content prior to the advent of books was quite easy, as Socrates himself found out. Accused of corrupting the youth of society, Socrates was tried and convicted on these charges and forced to gulp down a fatal dose of hemlock as a penalty.[26] As it turned out, his students kept Socrates' teachings alive, and they survive to this day, but the work of every fatally censored source isn't as fortunate. Here is a look at efforts to prevent people from gaining access to books.

Early Censorship Efforts

The censorship of texts hearkens back to the rift between the Catholic Church and Protestant reformers in the mid-1500s. Pope Paul IV deemed authors like Martin Luther and John Calvin to be heretics and thus banned their writing.[27] By 1564, the church had crafted a list of books, noting that Catholics who owned them or were known to have read them were to be severely punished by their bishops. In addition, certain ancient books could not be read to children, lest they be corrupted by the content.[28]

Book banning and book destruction were often used to limit opinions that ran contrary to those of authoritarian figures. The first book believed to have been banned in what would become the United

States was *New English Canaan*, written by Thomas Morton in 1637. Morton came to Massachusetts in 1624 with a group of Puritans and quickly soured on the sect's strict values. He not only broke away to form his own colony, but he published this book as a sharp critique of Puritan life. The Puritans were aghast at Morton's writings and forbade anyone within the faith to read them.

In the United States, *Uncle Tom's Cabin* is cited by many historians as the first heavily banned book. The Confederate states believed that it promoted abolition and thus barred it, while other states in the Union prohibited its sale because it inflamed the passions associated with the slavery debate.[29] Other books in this era to be banned or censored included Mark Twain's *Adventures of Huckleberry Finn*, which drew immediate objections upon its publication for the use of "coarse language." Back in the 1880s, this complaint related to things like the use of the word *sweat* instead of *perspiration*, as opposed to its use of the N-word more than two hundred times.[30] Many argue that Twain used this offensive language as a parody of racist individuals, while others feel that there is never an excuse to use racially insensitive language.

Twentieth-Century Censorship

In 1933, members of the German Student Union burned more than twenty-five thousand books, stating that these texts were "anti-German" or reflected "extreme Jewish intellectualism." Authors whose works were incinerated included Albert Einstein, Helen Keller, and Ernest Hemmingway.[31] During the fires, Propaganda Minister Joseph Goebbels rallied the crowd with pro-Nazi ideology and promised that "we want to educate you." Interestingly, after the Germans were defeated in World War II, Allied forces confiscated all books that glorified Nazism or the military efforts that took place under Hitler's regime and destroyed them in May 1946. The textual purge encompassed millions of copies of more than thirty thousand titles.[32]

Nazi book burning.

Bettmann/Contributor/Getty Image

In the postwar United States, a significant debate over banned books occurred. The state of Georgia created a literature commission in 1953 that had the power to censor or remove books it believed violated the state's obscenity laws. Around that time, officials in Illinois demanded that more than four hundred titles be removed from the state's library system, citing obscenity and indecency within the texts. This wide-scale effort began after a girl from the town of Noble got a copy of *The Boy Came Back*, a novel by Charles Knickerbocker III that tells the story of an Army veteran who returns to his hometown after war and ends up beating his wife to death after she has several affairs with other men. The book came to the girl through the state library in 1953, and her mother was so displeased that she contacted the local sheriff.[33]

The American Library Association's website contains a running list of well-known books that were banned or censored in various schools, cities, and states. It also tracks **book challenges**, which are efforts to prevent a book from being used in school curricula or from being accessible within a school environment. Books like J. D. Salinger's *The Catcher in the Rye* received almost annual challenges throughout the country from 1975 through the end of the century for a wide array of reasons, including obscenity, sexuality, and being "centered around negative activity." A similar slew of challenges befell John Steinbeck's *Of Mice and Men*, which was challenged for the use of racist language and blasphemy.[34]

When the board of education of the Island Trees Union Free School District banned eleven books from the district's libraries, a group of students filed suit, claiming a violation of the First Amendment. The U.S. Supreme Court voted in 1982 in a narrowly structured five-to-four plurality that school boards could not remove books from school libraries based solely on their dislike of the material.[35] In that same year, the American Library Association began celebrating Banned Books Week, which encourages people to explore literature that is often banned and promotes the value of books that often stretch beyond the societal mainstream.[36]

Challenges and Bans Today

The concept of banning material from libraries or classrooms can seem almost quaint in the digital age, when pretty much anything that was ever written, photographed, or filmed can be at our fingertips in an instant. However, numerous groups across the United States are pushing school districts to limit student access to material they see as controversial more than at any time in the past few decades. In 2022, the Brooklyn Public Library pushed back against these bans, offering students across the country access to digital copies of books that were banned where they live.[37]

According to the American Library Association's most recent report, the country saw 330 book challenges at the start of the 2021–2022 school year, which represents a significant increase over

FIGURE 4.3 ■ Challenges by Reasons

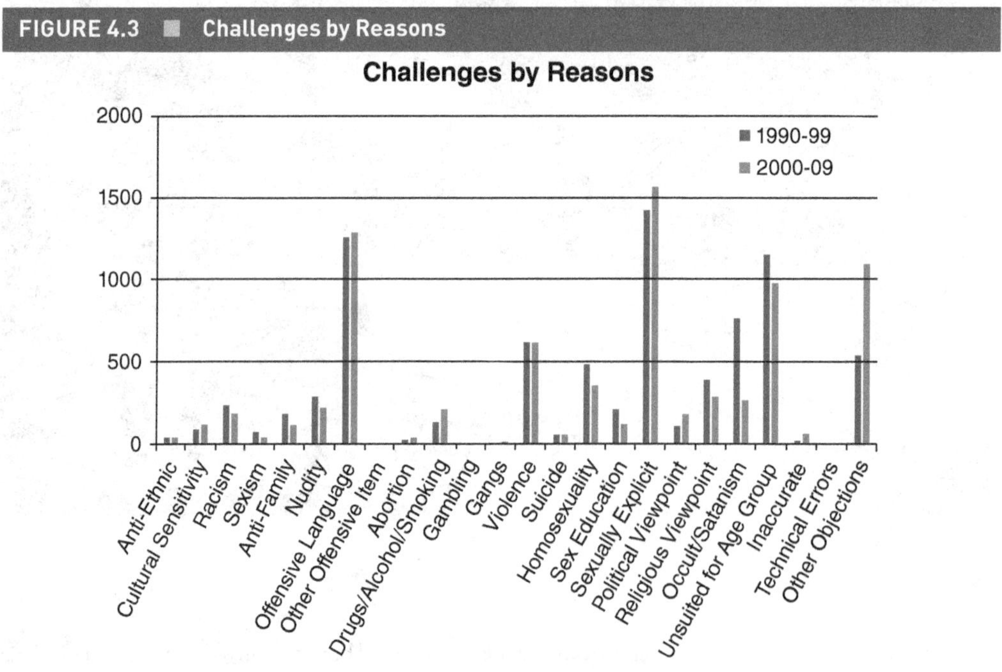

Based on data from https://www.ala.org/advocacy/bbooks/frequentlychallengedbooks/statistics/2000-09m and

previous years. As the year continued, parents' groups and activists have increased the pace at which they are challenging books for a wide array of familiar reasons, such as sexuality and profanity, as well as updated concerns, including racial disparities and political content.[38] Experts note that these numbers are likely underreported and fail to include efforts among educators to self-censor their reading lists and library offerings.

The state of Texas is among the most active in the movement to remove or restrict access to books in schools, according to organizations that track these challenges. According to a study by PEN America, the state banned 801 books in the 2021–2022 school year.[39] In November 2021, Texas governor Greg Abbott wrote to educational officials in the state, demanding that books containing "pornographic" content be removed from schools, although the letter did not specify what qualified as "pornographic." However, organizations like the Texas Association of School Boards, which was tasked by Abbott to lead this effort, stated publicly that it lacks the authority to take such actions.[40]

Banned Books Week takes place in September. Booksellers, teachers, and librarians around the country use the time to educate about the history of book banning and promote titles that have been challenged.

Patti McConville/Alamy Stock Photo

Why Are Some Books Frequently Banned?

What leads to a work's being labeled as a "controversial book" is often in the eye of the beholder. Most experts agree that social norms within a specific area, be it a school district or a state, provide citizens with a set of parameters that dictate what is acceptable for all people. Rightly or wrongly, when content attempts to stretch those norms or runs counter to them entirely, individuals and organizations seek to remove that content to prevent the status quo from being upended.

When it comes to banning or censoring books, several elements tend to trigger efforts to ban content with alarming frequency:

- Social or racial inequality
- Sex and violence
- LGBTQ+ characters

Social or Racial Inequality

Books are often censored or banned when they point out societal inequalities or attempt to showcase young people who do not "behave themselves." Salinger's protagonist in *The Catcher in the Rye*, Holden

Caulfield, is a young man who is dealing with the difficulties every adolescent faces while growing up. Rather than accepting that Caulfield's tumult was something normal for adolescents, censors have banned the book with complaints of its "vulgar language" and "promotion of sexual promiscuity."

Texts that propose bleak and dystopian futures also apparently get children too charged up for their own good. George Orwell's *1984* warns of a society in which totalitarian governmental officials engage in mass surveillance. Free will, open thought, and privacy are all prohibited in this world, which makes it a strange bit of irony that this book is frequently among the top ten most banned books in the United States. In 2014, the *Hunger Games* trilogy joined the list of the books most requested for banning, for many of the same reasons. Although people seeking to have the books banned cited "sexuality" among the reasons for their concerns, the majority of the complaints centered on the trilogy's emphasis on the social inequity between rich and poor, as well as the central theme of the book: a contest in which children kill one another for sport.

Books that point out racial inequalities within society often make the list of banned or challenged books.[41] An analysis by Diversity in YA (young adult literature) found that banned and challenged books tended to center on specific themes, with nearly one-fourth of the books challenged from 2010 to 2013 featuring nonwhite main characters and an additional quarter of the books including nonwhite secondary characters or non-Western settings.

Stamped: Racism, Antiracism, and You by Jason Reynolds and Ibram X. Kendi examines how racism was embedded in American society from its very beginnings and why it remains part of the country's fabric to this day. Critics who want the book banned note that it contains "selective storytelling incidents" and doesn't fully discuss racism against all people. Books like *The Hate U Give* by Angie Thomas and *All American Boys* by Jason Reynolds and Brendan Kiely have both been challenged under the premise that they promote antipolice messages.

Many of the challenges that come from the more liberal end of the political spectrum relate to social inequality as well, but often they relate to language. Books that use pejorative language or potential stereotyping related to race and sexual orientation end up on lists of challenged texts. Aside from *The Adventures of Huckleberry Finn*, Steinbeck's *Of Mice and Men* has met with opposition for its presentation of racial stereotypes and socioeconomic disparities.[42]

The Hate U Give by Angie Thomas, pictured, has been the target of frequent challenges and bans for promoting "antipolice" messages.

Paras Griffin/Stringer/Getty Images

Sex and Violence

In some cases, the issue is less about what children can or cannot handle and more of a societal sense of what should or should not be publicly available. Books that contain sexual or violent content are most likely to end up on lists of banned titles. While Salinger and James Joyce saw their books banned for being too sexually charged, Ernest Hemmingway had censors target his *A Farewell to Arms* for its realistic representation of the violence and bloodshed associated with World War I. More recently, Jay Asher's novel *13 Reasons Why* has been the target of banning efforts because of the main character's suicide, leaving behind the thirteen reasons why she ended her life.

In 2020, the book *The Absolutely True Diary of a Part-Time Indian* by Sherman Alexie made the top ten most challenged and most banned books for its use of sexual references and allegations of sexual misconduct by the author. *The Bluest Eye* by Toni Morrison was also banned and challenged for its presentation of sexually explicit material and its depictions of child abuse. Other texts banned or challenged for the presence of sexually explicit content include *The Handmaid's Tale* by Margaret Atwood and *This One Summer* by Mariko Tamaki and Jillian Tamaki.

LGBTQ+ Characters

The American Library Association keeps track of the most banned or challenged books each year through its Office for Intellectual Freedom. Most of the books targeted for removal in 2022 were cited as inappropriate because of the inclusion of LGBTQ+ content or characters who were not heterosexual or cisgender. Other complaints included the rejection of "traditional family structure," the inclusion of "political viewpoints," or the inclusion of ideas that don't reflect "the values of our community."[43] One such book was *George* by Alex Gino, a children's novel that follows a transgender fourth grader who struggles to understand her place in the world. (Gino changed the title to *Melissa* in 2022, to better identify with the gender identity the main character prefers for herself.)[44]

Another book facing bans based on the discussion of LGBTQ+ issues is George M. Johnson's *All Boys Aren't Blue*. The text contains a series of essays from the author, based on his life as a young, Black, noncisgender man living in New Jersey and Virginia. It discusses the difficulties he faced as a child, when he was attacked by bullies, as well as his breakthroughs in life as he became more confident in his true self.

MEDIA LITERACY MOMENT: LIMITATIONS LEAD TO LOST OPPORTUNITIES

The purpose of books and educators traditionally has been to broaden students' spectra of understanding by exposing them to a wide array of ideas. However, when these ideas clash with the experiences and values students grew up with, a state of discomfort and cognitive dissonance tends to emerge. Instead of considering the validity of those feelings, people often prefer to eliminate the source of the discomfort and cling to their previously held values.

At least 24 states are considering educational gag orders at the K–12 and college levels, making it more difficult to include issues of racism, sexism, and unpleasant elements of U.S. history in the classroom.[45] In addition, some states have passed laws that prohibit "ideological indoctrination" at public universities, with firings and budget cuts serving as penalties for violations.[46] As a result, a number of school districts and universities have taken proactive steps to remove any content that could run afoul of laws like these, further limiting viewpoints and potential learning opportunities.[47] Often these limits are couched in the language of protecting young people from mature content or avoiding confusion among people who aren't as "learned" as those people trying to ban the content.

If the goal of learning is to improve oneself, a larger amount and a wider array of information should give a person the best opportunity to do that. If becoming educated means thinking for oneself, information that runs counter to what "everybody else thinks" shouldn't be problematic, given that each person can choose to think or feel any way they see fit about anything they learn. The expansion of opportunities to read about things outside of an individual's comfort zone or own experience doesn't mean that person will adopt that way of thought or ideology. It isn't access to too much information that presents a problem; it's the exact opposite.

Think about it in another way: if you were given only peanut butter and jelly sandwiches to eat every day of your life, how would you know if you would like to choose something else to eat? Your parents might argue that you do have choices, in that you can pick any kind of jelly you want for your sandwich, or that they're just protecting you from foods that might upset your stomach. That said, if you didn't have the option to try a hamburger or a salad, you probably wouldn't know if you thought these items were better or worse than your sandwiches. If you didn't have a chance to try food from other cultures, you wouldn't know if you preferred certain flavors or spices not normally available in your area.

In the end, the goal of unfettered access to a variety of reading material is to show you a buffet of options and let you see which ones best help you understand the world in which you live.

THE NEXT STEP: Here is a list of books that have the distinction of being frequently challenged or banned for a variety of reasons. Examine the list and see if you have read any of them. If so, do an internet search for reasons the book has been banned and determine to what degree you agree or disagree with that rationale. If you have not, try to recall the last few books you have read and see if any of them have been the victim of an attempted challenge. If any of those books have been challenged or banned, decide if you believe the rationale for that effort was valid. (If you still are coming up empty, read one of the books on the list.) Write a short essay that outlines the topics covered in the book that created controversy and discusses the way you perceive the efforts to challenge or ban the book.

Uncle Tom's Cabin	*The Communist Manifesto*	*Mommy, Mama and Me*
Lolita	*Native Son*	*Black Like Me*
Go Ask Alice	*Go Tell It on the Mountain*	*The Catcher in the Rye*
The Bell Jar	*The Jungle*	*The Handmaid's Tale*
Fahrenheit 451	*Atlas Shrugged*	*The Crucible*
Night	*1984*	*I Know Why the Caged Bird Sings*
Brave New World	*Invisible Man*	*Incidents in the Life of a Slave Girl*
On the Road	*Feminine Mystique*	*Satanic Verses*
Things Fall Apart	*Crime and Punishment*	*Johnny Got His Gun*
Ball Four	*All Boys Aren't Blue*	*The Color Purple*
Monday's Not Coming	*Thirteen Reasons Why*	*The Hate U Give*
American Psycho	*George/Melissa*	*The Bluest Eye*
New Kid	*Maus*	
The *Fifty Shades* series	The *Hunger Games* series	

JOBS IN PUBLISHING

Now that you better understand books and the field of publishing, here's a handy overview of a few common positions in the field today.

Career Opportunity	Common Tasks
Acquisitions editor	• Locate authors with stories or ideas that could lead to successfully published texts • Assist writers in crafting texts to make them appealing to a target audience • Work with other departments in a publishing house to finalize the end product

Career Opportunity	Common Tasks
Developmental editor	● Assist the author in establishing a topic and approach for the book ● Work with the author in drafting and rewriting stages of the book ● Help create the structure of the text and develop an outline for how the book will proceed from chapter to chapter
Production editor	● Oversee the preparation of the text and its design and illustration ● Set deadlines for specific phases of the publishing process to ensure timely completion of the project ● Review final proof pages prior to publication to catch any last-minute errors or glitches
Sales representative	● Analyze the field a book will enter for potential competition or sales opportunities ● Pitch books to potential buyers, demonstrating the benefits of the text compared with alternatives
Art and design director	● Acquire or create images that supplement the author's text to enhance the book's appeal ● Design and develop page layouts and cover ideas to make the book readable and visually pleasing ● Select and apply design elements, such as fonts and color palettes, to improve the readability and tone of the book
Marketing and publicity	● Entice potential audiences to show interest in the book before and during its publication run ● Plan or attend events that provide an opportunity to personally connect with potential buyers ● Arrange marketing opportunities between interested parties and authors to promote their books

CHAPTER REVIEW

LO1 Identify the importance of key moments in the history of books and publishing.

- Writing began in Mesopotamia around 4000 BC with the use of reeds and clay tablets through cuneiform. This process allowed people to keep records of important things like livestock production and farming yields. The Egyptians improved upon this process between 3000 and 2000 BC using hieroglyphics and papyrus, making the content easier to transport and store.
- Around 300 BC, Alexander the Great developed the first library, in which scholars and experts gathered to share knowledge and develop society.
- Prior to AD 1450, much of the written word was transcribed by individuals who copied text from one bound volume to another. Johannes Gutenberg developed the first viable printing press around this time, making it faster and easier to create multiple copies of books.
- In the 1800s, the use of cheap materials and enticing storytelling brought books to the masses through the rise of pulp fiction and dime novels.
- In 1939, Robert de Graff developed a pocket-sized form of paperback that made it easier to carry and share novels of all genres. In addition, de Graff used a unique mass-marketing approach to make books more accessible, placing his novels in all sorts of stores instead of relying solely on book stores for sales.
- In 1994, Jeff Bezos launched Amazon.com, a service that allowed people to browse exponentially more titles online than any one brick-and-mortar store could provide. The company also shipped the books directly to people, making it fast and easy for them to

purchase and receive their items. Amazon was also important in the expansion of digital texts, known as e-books, through the development of its Kindle and the use of e-paper.

LO2 Describe how books provide value to society.

- Books allow people to record history, which helps them retain information beyond the life span of any one person's memory or any individual oral historian.
- Improved access to books led to increased literacy, giving people the ability to think for themselves and shape their own beliefs. Societies in which individuals had open access to material, as opposed to those in which authority figures suppressed content, enjoyed more varied and freer exchanges of ideas.
- Individual learning styles can benefit from the use of books as a part of education.
- Entertainment and enjoyment are often seen as benefits of novels and other published stories, because people can engage with stories that amuse, intrigue, or scare them.

LO3 Outline how books are developed, produced, and sold.

- An author comes up with an idea for a book and develops a framework for the material they want to produce and the stories they want to tell. They then create a book pitch or proposal for that book as part of soliciting a publishing partner.
- Publishers look for authors who have proposals that could lead to interesting books that would fill an underserved niche within a market. They also review proposals authors pitch to them to see if these ideas could lead to viable books. If both parties agree to work together, they develop a contract to outline the process by which the book will take shape.
- Content editors work with authors to craft books, solicit feedback from potential readers regarding drafts of books, and provide assistance in shaping books based on the needs of the readers. Copy editors review content for factual, grammatical, and style errors to improve the readability and consistency of the book.
- Booksellers work with the publishing company to purchase copies, find viable markets, and deliver the finished product to the consumers.

LO4 Understand the concept of censorship of books as well as the rationales used over time to justify it.

- Censorship is the effort to prevent individuals from consuming content that other people do not want them to see.
- Early efforts at censorship often involved religious or political groups' banning or burning books to prevent people from coming into contact with material that ran counter to established belief systems.
- More recent efforts to ban books relied on individuals associated with school systems, who sought to eliminate books they felt were too mature for students.
- The most frequent books people seek to ban are those with stories involving social inequality, race, sex, and violence, and those that include noncisgender characters

KEY TERMS

Book banning
Book challenge
Book pitch
Censorship
Content editor
Copy editor
Cuneiform
Development editor
Dime novels
Hieroglyphics
Movable type
Papyrus
Parchment
Penny dreadful
Proposal
Pulp fiction
Vanity press

DISCUSSION QUESTIONS

1. Have you ever thought about publishing a book? If so, what topics did you want to cover or what audiences did you want to reach? If not, what made you less interested in doing a larger writing project like this?
2. Of the key reasons books have value, which of the ones listed in the chapter do you feel is still most important to society? Which one do you feel matters least?
3. Are books still important to people in your generation, or are other forms of communication making them less and less valuable?
4. Given the reasons listed in the chapter for which people ban, censor, or challenge books, do you think any of those rationale have merit? If so, which ones and why?

Print newspapers roll off the press before they are physically distributed to readers.

iStock.com/industryview

5 PRINT JOURNALISM

Newspapers and Magazines

INTRODUCTION

1. *How important are newspapers in your daily life? Do you think they matter to people in your parents' generation? Your grandparents' generation?*
2. *When you think of a newspaper or a magazine, do you think more of the physical product or the information you receive from the reporters, editors, and photographers who work at the publication?*
3. *What future do you see for print publications over the next five or ten years?*

Print journalism encompasses the world of newspapers and magazines. The term refers both to the platform (the medium in which the information is presented) and the content (the information itself). In this chapter, we will be talking about both the content and the platform. In some cases, we will be discussing the products themselves: the tree pulp and ink or the glossy-format publications that land on doorsteps or in mailboxes. In other cases, we're going to be looking at the content: the print-style stories, photos, and graphics people consume, regardless of the platform upon which they are delivered. We will discuss not only the history of print journalism but also why it mattered to readers back then and should still matter to you today. We will explain how the various types of print journalism serve their readers in similar and different ways as well as how print can continue to thrive in the era of speedier competitors and declining readership.

LEARNING OBJECTIVES

After completing this chapter, you should be able to:

1. Outline key moments in the history of print journalism.
2. Understand how print journalism provides value to its readers.
3. Assess how newspapers and magazines can survive in the digital age.

A BRIEF HISTORY OF NEWS PUBLICATIONS

LEARNING OBJECTIVES

LO 1: Outline key moments in the history of print journalism.

Print journalism evolved over time, reaching its greatest success from the mid-nineteenth through the twentieth centuries. The history of how print journalism developed was influenced by changes in technology, education and literacy, and people's lives over a period of several centuries (see Table 5.1).

Early Efforts in Print

Newspapers were the first form of print journalism to arise, sometime in the mid-sixteenth to early seventeenth centuries. Determining when and where newspapers were first published depends on how you define what a newspaper is. Historians often point to ancient Rome, where governmental officials posted notices of importance around the city. Journalism researchers note that in 1566, handwritten information sheets in Venice, known as *avvisi* or gazettes, truly launched the idea of newspapers. The first regularly scheduled publication, *Relation aller Fürnemmen und gedenckwürdigen Historien* (*Account of All Distinguished and Commemorable Stories*), appeared in Germany in 1605. The first known English-language newspaper was a weekly newssheet called *Corante* that Nathaniel Butter published in London starting in 1620. The British government forbade the printing of news about

TABLE 5.1 ■ Overview of the History of Print Journalism

1550–1750	First print products appear, including early newspapers in Germany and England.
1750–1800	U.S. newspapers arise to challenge British authority and spread news about the early republic; pamphlets are printed to advance new ideas.
1800–1850	Rise of the penny press, inexpensive newspapers designed to appeal to a mass audience.
1827–1950	First Black-owned newspapers, advocating abolition; after the Civil War, papers like the *Chicago Defender* arise to express Black interests.
1900–1970	Rise of general and special-interest magazines and special-interest publications aimed at specific audiences.
1970 to today	Rise of newspaper and magazine chains, with a few large conglomerates owning most print outlets.
1990 to today	Revenues for print journalism decline as new digital producers arise in power and influence.

England, so Butter pulled information from several countries, including Italy, Germany, and France, to fill his paper.

Those early publications served specific audiences and did so with relatively narrow purposes. Only the very wealthy elite were literate, so newspapers reached only a tiny part of the overall population. In addition, the content often came from people or organizations promoting particular agendas, whether it was a governmental dictate or a publishing house seeking to promote specific information.

Colonial Times and Revolutionary Rhetoric

Before the United States became a country, a one-hit wonder of sorts got the ball rolling for colonial-era newspapers back in 1690: Benjamin Harris printed *Publick Occurrences*, which was suppressed after one issue. In this time period, publishers were required to be licensed by the British government, which oversaw the colonies, before they could print newspapers. That meant that the government maintained control over what was written, a key concern that the new country addressed upon its founding, with the inclusion of freedom of the press in the First Amendment to the Constitution.

During the colonial era, publishers used the written word and the printing press to distribute content of interest to citizens in hopes of shaping their opinions. The country's founders, such as Benjamin Franklin and Alexander Hamilton, had vested interests in the newspaper business, owning and operating presses and publications during the country's infancy. Franklin was connected to the *Pennsylvania Chronicle*, a paper often critical of English rule, which appeared around the time of the Revolutionary War.

Pamphleteers—people who published political arguments and distributed them to persuade others—were also key in stoking the fires of revolution. The most famous among these pamphlets was Thomas Paine's "Common Sense," printed in 1776, a persuasive argument in common language that helped galvanize support for U.S. independence.

Penny Press and Publication for the Masses

Newspapers massively expanded in the early 1800s, when publishers realized they had an untapped resource for both readership and news. With literacy becoming more common among all citizens, publisher Benjamin Day (see Table 5.2) bucked convention at the time by selling copies of his *New York Sun* for a penny apiece, as opposed to the six cents most papers charged. The goal of this penny press was to reach the mass market and make up for lost per-copy revenue with increased sales volume. With this approach, Day also shifted the tone of the editorial content, focusing on stories of crime and violence, as opposed to the political press aimed at the wealthy elites.

Other papers quickly followed Day's model after seeing what could be done with a true "mass medium" printed on the cheap. As competition raged in many larger media markets, publishers sought ways to speed up news gathering. Aside from the shift in sales, tone, and content, inventions and innovations related to pressing newspapers helped spur the mass media era into full speed. In 1814, the

TABLE 5.2 ■ A Few Key Names in Print Journalism

Benjamin Day	Henry Luce	John H. Sengstacke	Edythe Eyde	Gloria Steinem	John H. Johnson
• Founder of the *New York Sun*, the first "penny press" newspaper in the United States. • Shifted the focus of journalism toward sensationalism.	• Built a magazine empire, beginning with *Time* and *Life*. • Relied on vibrant photography to bring the world to people.	• Publisher and owner of the largest chain of U.S. Black press outlets. • Founded the National Negro Publishers Association. • Worked with President Franklin Roosevelt to gain press conference access for Black journalists.	• Created *Vice Versa*, the first lesbian publication in the United States. • Wrote for *The Ladder*, the first national lesbian magazine.	• Cofounded *Ms.* magazine in 1971. • Promoted women's participation in the popular press.	• Founded Johnson Publishing Company. • Developed *Ebony* (1945) and *Jet* (1951) magazines.

Times of London installed the first cylinder press, which drastically improved the speed of printing. The *Times* reported producing 1,100 sheets in an hour, or about four times what a traditional press could do.

Abolitionism, Civil Rights, and the Rise of the Black Press

The Black press began nearly two hundred years ago in New York when John Russwurm and Samuel Cornish started *Freedom's Journal* in 1827.[1] The publication lasted only two years, but it served as a template for subsequent papers of this kind. *Freedom's Journal* provided coverage of national and international topics germane to people of color at a time when New York had abolished slavery. Its editorials and current-events coverage sought to improve conditions for newly freed slaves and to address racist issues present in other media outlets of the day.[2]

In the lead-up to the Civil War, more than two dozen other Black-owned newspapers emerged in the United States, keeping Black citizens up to date on antislavery issues and efforts, as well as highlighting racist incidents that mainstream media outlets did not cover. Civil War–era publications often debated among themselves to what degree Black men should join in the fighting.[3] Frederick Douglass, an escaped slave who became one of the most influential Black abolitionists, founded the *North Star* in 1847, which served as a dominant force in the efforts of abolitionism.[4] In the postwar era, the Black press continued to provide information to freed slaves about their rights as well as informing citizens as to the illegal efforts of Jim Crow–style legislation.

At the turn of the twentieth century, the Black press continued to alert people of color to important social issues. The *Chicago Defender*, founded in 1905 by Robert Abbott, played a vital role in the movement of Black citizens from the South to northern cities that held promises of better financial and social opportunities for them.[5] The paper helped fuel the Great Migration with its posting of train schedules, job listings, and other relocation assistance.[6]

Publications such as the *Baltimore Afro-American* and the *Pittsburgh Courier* were part of a growing Black press in the 1940s and 1950s that drew attention to everything from racism in the military to the growing calls for civil rights. John H. Sengstacke, who oversaw multiple Black newspapers, including the legendary *Chicago Defender*, met with other publishers during this time period with the goal of finding "a common purpose for the benefit of Negro journalism." The organization came to be called the National Newspaper Publishers Association and remains an active organizing force within the Black newspaper community, with two hundred member publications. Student media outlets also contributed significantly to the Black press, as the Mississippi Freedom Schools project of 1964 gave students a powerful outlet to express themselves and share their experiences. Students at more than a dozen of these schools crafted their own newspapers, telling stories that went far beyond what white, mainstream media outlets told.[7]

Black-oriented magazines also emerged in postwar America to address issues of arts, sports, culture, and Black achievements. John H. Johnson launched *Ebony*, a publication tailored to middle-class African American readers, in 1945, making it the first magazine of its kind to be nationally circulated.[8] Johnson also created *Jet* magazine in 1951, covering news and society for more than six decades. Coupled with coverage of civil rights efforts were lifestyle tips and celebrity gossip. *Jet*'s popularity was so strong that it led to a saying among readers: "If it isn't in *Jet*, it didn't happen."[9]

John H. Johnson.

Bettmann/Contributor/Getty Images

Magazines Develop Broad Appeal and Niche Content

As photographic and printing technology advanced in the early twentieth century, magazines emerged as both a general-interest and niche-specific complement to newspapers. While newspapers kept people abreast of the day-to-day events occurring where they lived, magazines brought the world to their doorsteps with stunning photography and narrative writing.

In 1923, Henry Luce partnered with two Yale classmates to create *Time* magazine, the first weekly news magazine in the United States. The twenty-three-year-old entrepreneur saw the value of giving people quick bits of important information on a broad array of topics. He replicated this pattern of giving people what they needed to know through short bursts of information and high-quality visuals in other publications he either invented or reinvented, including *Fortune* (1929), *Life* (1936), and *Sports Illustrated* (1954).

In addition to **general-interest magazines** like *Time* and *Life* that flourished after World War II, publishers found opportunities to reach niche audiences with specialty content on a weekly or monthly basis. Most publications of this type fall into the category of **consumer magazines**, because they reach out to people who are interested in specific hobbies, cultures, or activities. Instead of being everything to everyone, they were able to specialize and find untapped markets.

A second form of niche press is that of **trade publications**, also known as business journalism, which provide relevant news to people who work in certain industries. Publications like *Advertising Age, Broadcasting & Cable*, and *Editor & Publisher* have value to people who work in specific areas of the mass media field. Legal practitioners (the *Law Society Gazette*), Dentists (*Dentistry* magazine), and even beauty salon workers (*Hairdressers Journal International*) rely on these targeted professional magazines to keep track of trends and innovations within an area.

Specialty Press: Journalism "by Us, for Us"

While general interest magazines and citywide daily publications serve mainstream interests, other publications cover issues for underrepresented segments of society. **Specialty publications** serve an important market that falls between the publications that cover the broadest interest of an area's citizenry and niche-specific topics of interest, such as hobbies and activities. In many cases, these outlets developed out of necessity, as publishers and writers recognized a market need. Thus, journalists with a deeper understanding of specific topics often struck out on their own to create a "by us, for us" form of media. As feminist pioneer Gloria Steinem said when asked why she helped launch *Ms.* magazine, "I realized as a journalist that there really was nothing for women to read that was controlled by women."[10]

Here are a few types of specialty press that found audiences outside of the media mainstream throughout U.S history.

Ethnic and Immigrant Press: The **ethnic press**, or immigrant press as it is sometimes known, served to connect people from "the old country" with fellow immigrants who had arrived in the United States. It also provided insight on numerous issues, including how to land a job, where to find a home, and how to adapt to their new surroundings.

In the 1800s, dozens of newspapers in multiple languages emerged with the goal of serving the new German, Irish, Polish, Italian, Czech, and Hungarian immigrants who began to enter the country in increasingly larger numbers. Researchers note that Germans alone were responsible for founding more than a thousand newspapers, helping connect each subsequent generation of their native kin that set down roots in the United States. Some archives of these early publications survive to this day and detail the anti-immigrant discrimination of the times, ranging from the Naturalization Act that required immigrants to learn English to the internment camps Japanese Americans were forced into during World War II.[11]

Today, the ethnic press remains vibrant and strong. A recent study of ethnic media use found that 29 million adults in the United States prefer this form of media to mainstream content. Although the languages and the issues may vary from group to group, the goal remains the same for each publication. As Yuru Chen, the editor in chief of the *World Journal* told the TV news program *Frontline* in the wake of this study, "The most important factor in developing any media is the same: How do you listen to the demands of your audience? Understanding how to serve the immigrant community is the best way for ethnic media to survive."[12]

Gay Press: Scholars have traced the roots of the **gay press** to Germany near the turn of the twentieth century, where *Der Eigene* (*The Exceptional*) was published beginning in 1896; it is believed to be the first "long-lasting gay journal."[13] Researchers note that the publication provided personal ads for gay men who wished to meet and also extensive coverage about the concerns facing gay men in society at that time. The first gay journal in the United States began in 1924, when Henry Gerber launched *Friendship and Freedom*. His efforts ended after two issues, when he was arrested on suspicion of running a "strange sex cult."

Lesbian journalism first began in North America when Edythe Eyde, working under the pseudonym Lisa Ben, created *Vice Versa* in 1947 with the promise of being "America's Gayest Magazine."[14] At the time, publishing content like this was dangerous, because both federal and state laws prohibited the promotion of gay and lesbian content. The publication, which lasted only nine issues, critiqued movies, novels, and other media that warned of the evils associated with same-sex relationships.

In 1953, Jim Kepner and W. Dorr Legg created the first issue of *ONE* magazine, a publication by and for members of the gay community. The magazine mirrored mainstream publications of the time, including feature articles, editorials, narrative pieces, and reviews.[15] *ONE* became vital in the cause of LGBTQ+ publications after it sued the U.S. Postal Service in 1954 for refusing to deliver the magazine and won a landmark Supreme Court case.[16]

LGBTQ+-based media flourished in post-1950s America, as it chronicled crucial moments in U.S. history that mainstream media outlets overlooked. The *Mattachine Midwest Newsletter* covered everything from social events and meetings to police raids of gay bars and legal issues pertaining to gay rights in the 1960s. In 1969, a police raid on a Greenwich Village gay bar, the Stonewall Inn, sparked a riot that served as a galvanizing force for members of the gay community. The *Advocate*, which began in 1967 and had published about two dozen issues by the time of the riot, chronicled the event in its September 1969 issue, which brought the incident into the national spotlight within the gay community.[17] In the book *Gay Press, Gay Power*, the authors argue that the *Advocate*, which remains the longest running LGBTQ+ publication in the United States, was "an important part of the growing gay media movement of the late 1960s and early 1970s."[18]

During the 1980s, LGBTQ+ media served as a vital resource for information during the AIDS epidemic. The *New York Native* published the first news report of any kind on the issue on May 18, 1981, beating the *New York Times* to the story by almost two months.[19] Playwright and author Larry Kramer's essay "1,112 and Counting" ran on the front page of the March 14, 1983, issue of the *New York Native*, loudly announcing that AIDS was an epidemic the world was ignoring at every level of political and social life.[20]

Although mainstream media outlets have given more attention to LGBTQ+ issues in the past two decades, advocates in the gay press continue to advance their own causes through a variety of print and digital media outlets. In assessing the current status of mainstream coverage, author Tracy Baim noted that mainstream media "are simply parachuting" into the community to cover a story, thus often painting an incomplete or inaccurate picture of LGBTQ+ issues.[21] Baim's statement could easily apply to most forms of specialty media, in that the people most involved in publishing this content are also deeply involved in the topics being covered. Freedom of the press makes it possible for individuals to express themselves in areas that often do not see coverage.

Perhaps one of the most interesting developments in print journalism involved people for whom freedom was not part of their lives: prisoners.

A DEEPER LOOK: PRISONERS LEARN A TRADE AND GET A VOICE

Near the turn of the twentieth century, criminal justice reformers floated the idea of allowing incarcerated men to produce newspapers for distribution within the prison walls. They noted that prisoners would eventually reenter the public world and should be informed about the important happenings of the day.[22] The *Summary*, a publication started at upstate New York's Elmira Reformatory in 1883, first tested this idea. However, the longest running of these publications originated in the Stillwater Prison in Minnesota: for almost 140 years, *The Prison Mirror* has walked the fine line between speaking truth to power and acquiescing to the concerns of prison officials.[23]

From 1904 to 1935, more than one hundred prisons and reformatory institutions launched their own newspapers, providing inmates with the opportunity to submit content, edit copy, draw images, and share ideas. The publications often included an array of sports, commentary, and national news. Others were published in magazine format and also included poetry and fiction that staff members and inmates contributed.

The use of newspapers within the prison walls had multiple purposes. For example, the *Candle*, a publication at the Waupun Prison in Wisconsin, was produced in 1934 as a part of its General Education Club's efforts to help prisoners improve themselves. The group saw the paper as a way for inmates to gain marketable skills, such as writing and editing, but also press operations. However, as it progressed, it became both a voice for inmates' concerns, addressing topics like the quality of the products offered in the prison canteen, and a way to keep prisoners' minds sharp. On the second page of every edition was the *Candle*'s mission statement: "to provide the prisoners with an outlet for their creative energies, to give them an opportunity to express their thoughts and attitudes, and to thus aid and encourage the mental and moral development of the individual and of the group as a whole."[24]

By the end of the 1950s, more than 250 prisons had inmate-staffed newspapers or magazines to call their own.[25] However, prison publications began to shrink in the 1960s and 1970s, because the public viewed them as a waste of tax dollars. Prisons underwent extensive privatization and financial reductions during the 1980s, thus laying waste to what was once a thriving area of publications. As of 2000, only a handful of publications written by prisoners and published within prison walls remained.[26]

Those that have survived, however, remain crucial to their audience and have reached far beyond the gates of the penitentiary. The *San Quentin News*, for example, has a readership of more than eleven thousand people and covers everything from criminal justice reform to transgender issues. Not only does the paper have a website that features its content, but it continues to engage in digital storytelling through podcasting and similar efforts.[27] The *Angolite* in Louisiana has also earned many awards over the past sixty years, including a George Polk Award in 1980 for outstanding journalism[28] and the Thurgood Marshall Journalism Award in 2007 for its coverage of capital punishment.[29]

The *San Quentin News* is a prison newspaper founded to give prisoners an opportunity to improve their writing talents as well as develop press operation and printing skills. Numerous penitentiaries have created "by us, for us" media outlets that cover inmates' lives.

AP Photo/Eric Risberg

The Growth of Chains and the Decline of Print

Newspaper **chains**—groups of newspapers that served different local markets—were a concept that publisher Frank Gannett made popular. Prior to Gannett, most publishers owned individual media outlets that serviced a specific geographic region, thus giving them a monopoly over a certain area's news coverage, but also a limited reach. Gannett realized that by owning more publications, he could expand his reach, share content among publications, and centralize his business operations in a way that would be more cost efficient. This created a chain of related papers across a broad area.

When Frank Gannett died in 1957, the media mogul had amassed a collection of twenty-two newspapers, along with television and radio stations in profitable markets. Shortly after his death, the Gannett corporation went on a buying spree, purchasing an average of one newspaper every three weeks by 1971. Gannett's chain approach served as a hint of what was to come in the postwar era of the United States, as other publishing groups and media moguls copied his model.

Entrepreneurs saw the success Gannett had achieved in developing chains of local publications and entered the market in the late 1980s and early 1990s, gobbling up small-town papers and midsized metros alike. By 1995, twenty chains controlled nearly 60 percent of the newspapers in the United States.[30] Approximately twenty-five years later, that number was reduced to just a few giant chains

USA Today began in 1982 with the goal of providing the country with a national newspaper. In its infancy, it relied on quick reads, informational graphics, and color images to draw readers into the previously dull black-and-white world of newspapers. The paper was immediately derided as "McNews" for being short on substance, but its approach of simplifying the news became an instant hit.

Paul Knivett/Alamy Stock Photo

thanks to mergers and takeovers. Gannett and GateHouse Media merged in 2019, resulting in a circulation nearly eight times larger than that of its closest competitor at the time.[31] McClatchy, a powerful chain for more than 150 years, declared bankruptcy in 2020 and was acquired by the hedge fund Chatham Asset Management, which already owned a large swath of newspapers throughout Canada. Alden MediaNews Group's acquisition of Tribune Media in 2021, along with its stake in Lee Enterprises and other media conglomerates, makes it a major player in this area as well.

Despite the growth of chains, newspapers and magazines have seen sharp declines in circulation over the past two decades. According to the Pew Research Center, U.S. newspaper circulation is at its lowest point since these statistics were first gathered in 1940.[32] The *New York Times* reported that one out of every five newspapers in the country has died off over the past fifteen years because of losses in advertising revenue and circulation.

ROLE OF NEWSPAPERS AND MAGAZINES

LEARNING OBJECTIVES

LO 2: Understand how print journalism provides value to its readers.

The purpose of news publications has varied greatly over the centuries. During colonial days, newspapers and pamphlets in the United States galvanized support for key aspects of the law and developments in the country. The goal was somewhere between persuasion and propaganda, depending on the methods the writers used to connect with their readers. Today, the concept of a **nonpartisan press**, neutral and based on the premise of fairness, is the goal of journalistic operations in this country. Although individual publications can vary widely in how they approach the goal of engaging their audience, a few underlying premises remain constant in print journalism. Table 5.3 lists the six bedrock goals of all news publications.

Let's take a deeper look at each of these concepts.

TABLE 5.3 ■ Six Goals of Print Publications

Goal	Example
1. Inform the public about important people, events, and outcomes that affect their lives	In early 2020, newspapers reported the dangers of the COVID-19 outbreak well before it reached the United States.
2. Advocate for societal change or against public actions that will affect citizens	In April 2020, the *Milwaukee Journal Sentinel* advocated that the in-person election set to take place at the height of the coronavirus epidemic should be postponed or conducted via mail-in ballots.
3. Investigate important stories that otherwise would remain out of the public eye	In 2021, a consortium of journalists reported on "Mississippi's Dangerous and Dysfunctional Penal System," revealing that prisons were drastically understaffed, making them unsafe for guards and prisoners alike.
4. Prevent corruption by shining a light on the bad actions of public figures	In 2017 and 2018, the *Carroll Times Herald* in Carroll, Iowa, ran a series of stories that shed light on a police officer who was having inappropriate relationships with teenage girls.
5. Entertain readers through engaging stories, photos, and graphics	In 2021, the *New Yorker* introduced a crossword puzzle into its weekly print publication, which had previously been available only on its website.
6. Provide a permanent, tangible record that serves as a first draft of history	When the 2016 Chicago Cubs won their first World Series since 1908, the *Chicago Tribune* celebrated the moment with a front-page treatment.

Inform

The First Amendment to the Constitution singles out freedom of the press as one of the key things vital to the survival of the country. Although many politicians owned or ran newspapers at that time, emphasizing the importance of this freedom wasn't simply an expression of self-serving, financial interest. The founders had a strong belief that an informed electorate was crucial to helping a democracy thrive. In other words, the country would run better and politicians would act more ethically if the people in that country knew what was going on around them.

Newspapers and magazines maintain that vital role today of informing the public about important topics. They seek facts, interview sources, and compose content with the purpose of helping readers understand what is happening that matters to them. National publications, such as *USA Today, Time* magazine, *Newsweek*, and the *New York Times*, cover political elections, global pandemics, and social concerns. Local publications, such as small-town weeklies, provide information on mayoral elections, school board actions, and area happenings that can affect the lives of people in a certain geographic region. Niche publications like *The Crisis, Out*, and *Christianity Today* connect people throughout the country (and the world) who share connective interests in race, sexual orientation, or religion.

For example, months before public officials found themselves grappling with the COVID-19 pandemic in early 2020, the *New York Times* and the *Washington Post* had extensively reported on the virus's rise in China and its spread to other countries. Early reports relied on scientists and health experts to explain the likely cause, frequent symptoms, and potential global spread of COVID-19.[33] By the time cases of COVID-19 were appearing in the United States, these newspapers had been writing about it for months.

Advocate

News publications have a purpose beyond conveying information to readers. In many cases, they also serve as a megaphone for issues that matter to the readers themselves. Columnists and editorial writers provide their audience with opinions that stimulate readers' interests in a topic, educate them about it, and then offer them ways to make their opinions known about it. This allows the audience to take part in civic, social, or moral actions based on this new information.

Additionally, newspapers often serve as the voice of the audience, speaking truth to power in the form of staff editorials. These editorials are based on the information gathered by reporters and the opinions of editorial board members who have a sense of what actions would best serve their readers. The editorial writers publish viewpoints and suggestions that explain how certain parts of the public should act or conduct themselves. For example, an editorial published in the *Milwaukee Journal Sentinel* in April 2020 argued that an in-person election set to take place at the height of the coronavirus epidemic should be postponed or conducted via mail-in ballots.[34] The election went on as planned, but the newspaper's editorial drew attention to the issue.

Publications have long served an advocacy role on a national scale, including suggesting the country take part in or avoid engaging in war. Local media outlets have engaged in similar efforts, arguing for the support of school referendum or putting their support behind local candidates for elected office.

Investigate

News reporters are inherently nosy, and the field of journalism allows them to satisfy their curiosity for the good of others. Journalists find important information and tell their readers about it. Writers and reporters often get "tips" from people they know or from citizens who know something that is going on that shouldn't be happening. They take these bits of information and dig into the topic, hoping to discover what is happening and who is involved. Through this investigative work, journalists can explain to their readers what is going on and why they should care.

Investigations can be of a watchdog nature, such as the work done by Bob Woodward and Carl Bernstein of the *Washington Post* that helped lead to the resignation of President Richard Nixon. In addition, they can be of a public-service nature, such as explaining how biases pertaining to gender and race need to be addressed.

They can focus on local issues, such as what an area school district is doing about low test scores or how it plans to meet the technological needs of its students during a budget crunch. In 2021, journalists from the Marshall Project, *Mississippi Today*, the Mississippi Center for Investigative Reporting, the *Jackson Clarion-Ledger*, and the *USA Today* network took home the distinguished Goldsmith Prize for their investigation of Mississippi's prison system. "Mississippi's Dangerous and Dysfunctional Penal System" revealed that prisons were drastically understaffed, making them unsafe for guards and prisoners alike. The story also revealed that the state still runs the country's only "debtor's prison," in which people are locked up for low-level crimes and forced to work off their court costs and fines.[35]

Student media outlets have also engaged in investigative journalism both on and off campus. In 2020, the *Red & Black* at the University of Georgia took a close look at the history of fraternities and sororities on campus and how systemic racism limited their ability to diversify their membership.[36] The *Daily Northwestern* at Northwestern University in Evanston, Illinois, dug into questions about water quality in one of the city's poorest districts. The investigation found that the Fifth District, composed primarily of poorer, Black citizens, received limited water testing over the years and was treated inequitably in other key ways as well.[37]

Prevent Corruption

The eighteenth-century British politician Edmund Burke is often credited for calling newspapers "the Fourth Estate," a term he used to demonstrate the way in which the press could provide a check against the three estates of Parliament, namely, the clergy, the nobility, and the commoners.[38] The term stuck, and today it represents the way in which an independent press serves a watchdog function in society, preventing the powerful from engaging in bad behavior.

For example, when burglars entered the Watergate complex in 1972 and attempted to bug the headquarters of the Democratic National Committee, early reports considered it to be nothing more than a minor case of dirty politics. However, when Woodward and Bernstein dug into the story, they found corruption and malfeasance that reached all the way into the Oval Office. By refusing to let the story die once the burglars had their day in court, the *Washington Post* duo showed the importance of keeping the public's eye on a story that wasn't as simple as some people might have thought.

The muckrakers of the Progressive Era took on powerful corporate interests around the turn of the twentieth century in publications like *McClure's Magazine, American Magazine*, and *Collier's Weekly*. Pioneering female journalist Ida Tarbell exposed the way in which Standard Oil used its power to monopolize the industry and crush potential competitors, leading the government to pass legislation to prevent further corporate abuse. Samuel Hopkins Adams wrote about the rampant fraud in the health arena, exposing fraudsters who peddled snake oil and other elixirs using grandiose and unsubstantiated claims. Upton Sinclair wrote *The Jungle*, which exposed the horrific condition of slaughterhouses and how workers in them were mistreated. These two efforts can be credited with the development of the Pure Food and Drug Act, whereby the quality and efficacy of the things we put in our bodies are monitored.

On a local level, the *Carroll Times Herald* in Carroll, Iowa, ran a series of stories in 2017 and 2018 that shed light on a police officer who was having inappropriate relationships with teenage girls. The paper revealed a pattern of bad behavior by Officer Jacob Smith that went back to a previous job he'd held in law enforcement. These articles led to Smith's resignation and demonstrated the importance of the press to hold public officials to account for their actions.[39]

Watchdogs like these in newspapers and magazines alert us to things we need to know so that corruption or other bad acts don't go unpunished.

Entertain

As much as newspapers and magazines work to create an informed citizenry, they also provide readers with the opportunity to relax and enjoy themselves. Serious publications offer leisure and lifestyle sections, where crossword puzzles and daily comic strips challenge the mind and tickle the funny bone. Tabloid publications, like the *National Enquirer*, use scandalous images and outrageous stories to ride the line between news-based content and partly truthful tales to help readers see how famous people are either living crazy lives or are "just like us." Some publications, like the *Weekly World News*, go a step further in publishing outrageous stories, running items like "Elvis Presley Found Alive" and "Bat Boy Found in West Virginia Cave."

The *Weekly World News* has blended satirical fiction and exaggerated facts to amuse and shock readers for more than forty years. The publication ceased its print edition in 2007, but lives on via the web.

Retro AdArchives/Alamy Stock Photo

Some media, like comic books and satirical publications, have the sole goal of entertaining readers through art, commentary, and fiction. For example, *The Onion*, which refers to itself as "America's Finest News Source," pokes fun at the news of the day through articles like "Biden Addresses Sexual Assault Allegations: 'My Advisors Told Me to Say They Aren't True,'" and "Zoom Crasher Becomes Too Engrossed in Sales Meeting to Scream Obscenities."

Provide Permanence

Print publications are the most likely to see the shortest shelf lives and are crafted on perishable materials. Weekly magazines get tossed once they are read. Newspapers are used to line birdcages, wrap glassware, and start campfires. Those that survive this secondary use will still grow brittle and yellow over time, crumbling or decomposing quickly in a variety of less-than-hospitable environments.

Thus, it seems oddly ironic that these forms of media actually serve as a way to preserve historic moments for future generations. Although people remember videos of Walter Cronkite announcing the death of President Kennedy or live footage of the terrorist attacks on September 11, 2001, very few people possess copies of those broadcasts. Internet sites offer the ability to share and copy material easily, causing certain elements online to go viral. However, in some cases, material can be easily altered or removed without maintaining a backup available. Newspapers and magazines, however, remain a prominent way in which people mark moments of significance, such as the election of Barack Obama as the first Black president of the United States. A digital bookmark or a file download has yet to replace the permanence associated with "dead-tree publications."

The word *new* is built into the word *newspaper*, which isn't an accident. The goal behind news publications is to alert citizens to important goings-on in areas that interest them, either geographically or topically. In doing so, they start the clock on what will become history for future generations. Declarations of war, approval of statehood, and deaths of iconic citizens arrive first on the front pages of newspapers and between the covers of magazines. As is often the case with first drafts of any form of writing, the information presented to the public in this format is sometimes incomplete and more than occasionally erroneous.

Weather: Chance of showers, 62/53 RACING ★ FINAL Wednesday, November 5, 2008

★★★★★ 32-PAGE ELECTION SPECIAL ★★★★★

DAILY NEWS

50¢ NYDailyNews.com

PRESIDENT OBAMA

Nation changes forever with historic victory

When Barack Obama became the first Black president of the United States, the *Daily News* celebrated the moment with a front-page treatment. Many citizens bought copies of the paper to preserve this historic moment.

New York Daily News/Contributor/Getty Images

MEDIA LITERACY MOMENT: THE LOSS OF LOCAL NEWS COVERAGE

When the Gannett corporation started the movement toward newspaper chains, consumers received a number of benefits, including access to information beyond their geographic locations and content from journalists who worked at other publications. Conversely, when a chain becomes too homogenized, it can lead to a lack of local content that is relevant to certain people, groups, or areas.

Look at the news section of any Gannett-owned newspaper and then compare it with the news section of any other Gannett paper, and you'll see significant overlap between them. Consider this list of the top news headlines from the Appleton (Wisconsin) *Post-Crescent*, which Gannett owns:

- Here's a running list of COVID-19 vaccination sites in Appleton, Fox Cities
- Why the county landfill is on track to expand, despite Little Chute residents' complaints
- Fans can vote now for photo to be displayed at Packers game
- History Channel's 'American Pickers' to film in Wisconsin in July
- Your home made simple
- Average COVID-19 cases declined over two weeks

Now compare this list with a list of the top headlines for the Oshkosh (Wisconsin) *Northwestern*, a paper also owned by Gannett, located thirty miles away:

- Here's a running list of COVID-19 vaccination sites in Appleton, Fox Cities
- Fans can vote now for photo to be displayed at Packers game
- History Channel's 'American Pickers' to film in Wisconsin in July
- Your home made simple
- Average COVID-19 cases declined over two weeks

How many of those stories focus on local content that differentiates the two cities, each of which has a different set of city administrators, law enforcement officials, industries, and educational facilities? How many of the stories are likely useful to their readers? How many of these stories perform the basic functions that papers are supposed to offer (inform, advocate, investigate, prevent corruption, entertain, provide permanence)?

Using your critical thinking skills and knowledge of the biases that can undercut media literacy, consider how this kind of approach to news could limit people's views on what matters most in their lives. Also consider how seeing this content repeated in different area papers could lead readers to place undue focus on certain events and ignore others.

THE NEXT STEP: Look at the newspaper (print or online edition) that covers your area and one that covers an area nearby to see what stories each one publishes in the news section for a week. Are these publications independently owned, or does the same chain operate them both?

How much overlap do you see between your paper and what the other paper prints? What elements of local news, like city government or area schools, get covered, and which ones don't? How well do these newspapers do in reflecting your interests and needs?

Similarities and Differences between Newspapers and Magazines

Journalists rely on several key interest elements to answer these questions and draw readers into their stories. These elements frequently appear in newspaper stories and magazine articles, and apply to all forms of media that attempt to engage and inform readers about ongoing events. Because this chapter is the first one of several to touch on news-based media, it makes sense to tackle this topic here, even though it applies to broadcast news, social media, public relations, and other areas of media.

A good way to remember these elements is with the mnemonic "FOCII," which is like the plural of "focus" but with two I's. If you can stay focused on the FOCII, you can see how best to attract readers.

Beyond those elements of interest, magazines and newspapers have a number of crucial things in common, while also using unique elements of their publication approach to serve their audiences in different ways. Table 5.5 lists a few ways traditional print magazines and newspapers are similar and yet different when it comes to serving their audiences.

TABLE 5.4 ■ Media FOCII

Interest Element	Explanation	Example
Fame	People, places, and things that are well known for good (or bad) reasons	• President Joe Biden • Serial killer Jeffrey Dahmer • Yankee Stadium • Mount Everest
Oddity	Strange things or novel and rare events, like the first, last, or only time something occurred	• A rat in New York City dragging a piece of pizza down some stairs • The smallest vertebrate on Earth (*Paedophryne amauensis*, a tiny frog) • The largest lottery jackpot ever won ($1.586 billion)
Conflict	When competing interests have mutually exclusive goals	• The Union and the Confederacy fighting in the Civil War • The New York Yankees playing the Atlanta Braves in the World Series • A city council reviewing an apartment building plan opposed by environmental activists
Immediacy	When news outlets provide timely information to the audience	• A newspaper putting out a special edition to announce the death of a president • A breaking news alert on a paper's website to alert viewers about an active shooter
Impact	The degree to which something affects the lives of the audience, which can be measured in terms of numbers (quantitative) or degree (qualitative)	• Two people from your school die in a car crash (qualitative) • Approximately four million people each year contract chicken pox (quantitative)

TABLE 5.5 ■ Similarities and Differences between Print Newspapers and Magazines

Topic	Similarities	Differences
Geographic reach	Both are limited to a geographic range, based on how far delivery services could ship them.	Newspapers publish on a daily basis, meaning a smaller circulation range of about the size of a city; magazines publish weekly or monthly and often use the U.S. Postal Service to extend their reach.
Informational focus	Both focus on content that they see as relevant and useful to a specific audience.	Although early "general interest" magazines covered a wide array of topics, most of these publications served topical niches based on special interests, like sports or food. Newspapers provide a wide array of content specified by the geographic zones in which they are based.

(Continued)

TABLE 5.5 ■ Similarities and Differences between Print Newspapers and Magazines (Continued)

Topic	Similarities	Differences
Material quality	Both rely on paper and ink printing to convey content.	Newspapers use cheaper rag-based or newsprint style paper; monthly magazines rely on glossy spreads with vibrant colors and images.
Writing approach	Both convey information in a clear, coherent fashion to their readers.	Newspapers rely heavily on an **inverted-pyramid** format, which places the most important information at the top of the story. The rest of the information is placed in the story in descending order of importance. They also use fewer words and a fact-based approach to content; magazines rely on narrative storytelling, with longer pieces and heavier reliance on description to tell their tales.

IS PRINT DEAD OR IS IT EVOLVING?

LEARNING OBJECTIVES

LO 3: Assess how newspapers and magazines can survive in the digital age.

This question of whether print can survive in the digital age has frequently been raised by publishers, media users, and pundits since the 1990s, when the World Wide Web entered the mainstream. As is the case with most technology, since that time, the costs associated with internet use have decreased, while computers and other digital devices have become faster and more ubiquitous. These advances in digital media allowed individuals with an interest in spreading messages, but who didn't own a printing press or a television transmitter, to engage audiences on a footing equal to that of traditional media barons.

Newspaper and magazine publishers were slow to react to the presence of the internet, often deriding it as inferior to print or inconsequential. This initial dismissal of the digital revolution proved costly, as entrepreneurs and nonmainstream voices took advantage of a fragmenting audience to chip away at the monoliths that published daily or monthly subscription products. According to researchers in the field, daily newspaper circulation fell from a high of sixty million printed copies in 1994 to thirty-five million print and digital readers in 2018.[40] However, in the wake of the COVID-19 outbreak, readership fell even more precipitously, with more than sixty local publications closing as a direct impact of the pandemic and revenue falling 42 percent compared with the same time a year earlier.[41] A California publisher who suspended his paper's fifty-year publishing run during the pandemic called the situation print's "death knell," while an industry analyst referred to it as "the 2009 recession on steroids."[42]

Those believing that print publications can adapt to the new digital world by taking a digital-first approach assert that online publication is similar to newspaper work, minus the paper and ink. Although the concept of sharing information through writing, photography, graphics, and design does translate well enough to make that case, the argument loses ground when publications cannot afford to hire and retain the people necessary to create content. Here are several key things that will likely determine if the print content of newspapers and magazines will not just live, but thrive, as it continues its long, slow movement into the digital realm.

Financial Support

For generations, the implied relationships among readers, publications, and advertisers went unchallenged. Publications produced content that readers bought as a matter of course. Businesses placed

FIGURE 5.1 ■ Newspaper Circulation since 1985

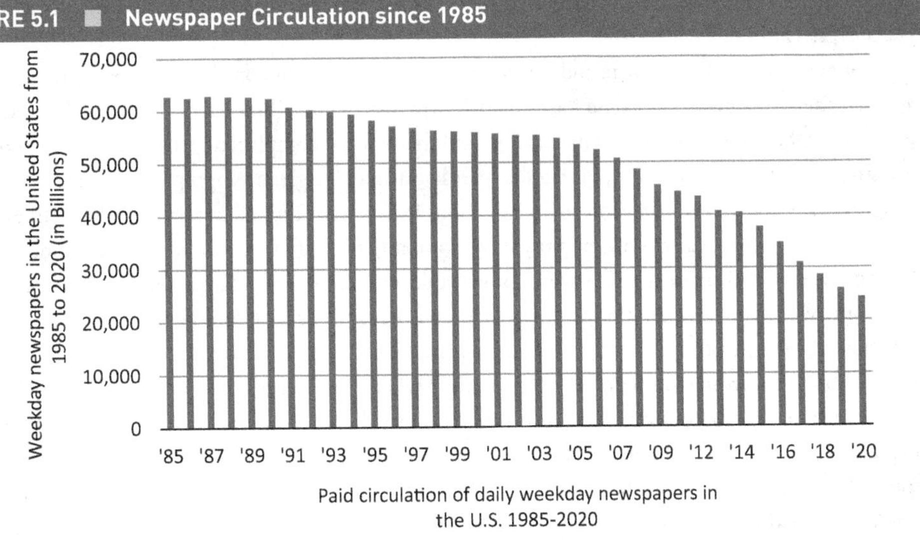

Over the past thirty-five years, U.S. newspapers have seen their print publications suffer massive losses in circulation. Daily print publications reach only a fraction of the media audience they once did.

Source: Based on data from https://www.statista.com/statistics/183422/paid-circulation-of-us-daily-newspapers-since-1975/

advertisements in these publications because that's where the eyeballs were, thus allowing these companies to reach potential purchasers. In most cases, these publications had a monopoly (or at least an oligopoly) in a given market, because it was cost-prohibitive to launch competitive products against an established brand.

Digital media challenged this financial model. Online information sources became a dime a dozen, while other services, like Craigslist, siphoned off lucrative revenue streams like classified advertising. Advertisers realized that not only was it cheaper to place ads in these digital publications, but the ads were also competitively successful. This led to a mass exodus of advertisers from print publications. From 2008 to 2018, magazine advertisers went from spending about twenty billion dollars a year on print ads to less than nine billion dollars.[43] Similarly, print revenue fell from about sixty-five billion dollars for newspapers in 2000 to less than nineteen billion dollars in 2016 and then eleven billion dollars by 2019.[44] Experts believe that by 2024, both newspapers and magazines will continue to see drastic losses, with their ad revenues being cut in half again.

Even when these traditional outlets shifted their publications to online platforms, they found that their advertising sales revenue was not enough to sustain the staff that print ads once supported. A 2013 examination of newspaper revenue in the United States found that newspapers lost sixteen dollars in print revenue for every dollar they gained in digital advertising dollars.[45] Although advertisers continue to invest in digital products more heavily, traditional news outlets no longer get the lion's share of the results. A 2019 Pew Research Center study revealed that Facebook and Google gobble up about half of the advertising dollars companies now spend, leaving news organizations fighting with all other online sites for their part of the remaining half.[46] Even math-averse journalists can see that the model can't hold.

In response to these financial losses, traditional print journalism has taken a variety of moves, from cutting staff to implementing paywalls, to try to increase revenue. News organizations have sought experts from financial fields as well as private investors to help find a way to monetize the news in a way that will sustain their publications. Until they can find a way to solve this puzzle, the future of newspapers and magazines, in any format, remains shaky.

Inherent Value to Readers

As we've outlined earlier in the chapter, certain things will draw an audience's attention: fame, oddity, conflict, immediacy, and impact. However, if more than one source is providing these items for the audience in a reasonably similar manner, it stands to reason that they will have to decide which one will get their attention.

For generations, newspapers and magazines had a stranglehold on that audience, providing coverage that met these needs, based on journalistic norms and values. This isn't to say they didn't do a good job or that the quality of these publications sank because of complacency. However, the competition for attention was relatively limited to a few media outlets in a given geographic area, all of which cost roughly the same amount of money. Think about it this way: the old media model was like deciding whether to buy a new car from Company A or Company B when features and costs are about the same. Your choices were limited and they were comparable, so it came down to personal preference or the flip of a coin. What the internet did was introduce a whole new car that could go a thousand times faster, fly above the roads, and cost almost nothing to buy. The question then became for the consumer, "Why would I buy a car from Company A or Company B when I can get this new and better thing for free?"

Traditional media outlets often provided value to the readers, but they didn't do a good job of explaining that value to them. Furthermore, when faced with competition from digital publications, journalists often ignored or belittled these start-up enterprises. In the meantime, these operations could run on almost no money and provide enough value to erode newspapers' and magazines' audiences. News outlets need to demonstrate why they are worth the price of a subscription or why their content is superior to that of the competition and do so in a clear and meaningful way. If newspapers and magazines can do this, they will be able to draw and retain readers and prevent cheaper or weaker competitors from eating away at their base of consumers.

Homogenization of Content

Much in the same way that newspapers have to demonstrate value, they have to demonstrate distinction. The continued concentration of media ownership, the heavy reliance on nonlocal coverage, and the lack of connection to local communities have led to the dilution of strong local journalism that readers will support.

The idea of putting out the same product repeatedly isn't new, and it isn't germane to newspaper or magazine business. When a style of music, be it rock, disco, or techno, becomes popular, artists and promoters rush to produce songs that fit that dynamic. When a movie or a television show becomes a hit, producers and executives green-light sequels and offshoots. (This is why we have something like ninety-two *Fast and Furious* movies and everything short of *CSI: Sioux Falls* on TV.) Newspaper chains rely on this principle: They find formulas that work in one realm and then transfer them to the next. This approach limits the cost of producing content and maximizes the use of successful content across multiple publications. However, in doing so, these corporations can limit the uniqueness that draws readers to certain papers and certain journalists.

For example, columnists Pete Hamill and Jimmy Breslin covered New York City in their own unique ways, drawing readers to the papers for which they wrote.[47] People would buy *Newsday* to find out what Breslin had to say or pick up the *New York Post* to get Hamill's take on what was going on in the city. (At one point, both men worked for the same paper, the New York *Daily News*, still competing for content and looking for scoops.) Today, columnists are mostly syndicated voices that address broader topics. Major stories are broken at one paper in the chain and then shared with others, often appearing on the front page of multiple papers under different headlines on the same day. Magazines rely heavily on formatted content, such as listicles, quizzes, and hot trends, replicating the successful approaches across various niches.

Meanwhile, independent digital outlets and independent bloggers write and report in ways that speak to different interests with different voices. Although successful models can be replicated, in the same way that stand-up comedians steal jokes from one another, these outlets put their own stamp on the content, making it unique for their readers. As people continue to crave distinctiveness, the degree to which newspapers and magazines can create content to fit these needs will determine how successful they will be in the next decade and beyond.

CAREERS IN PRINT JOURNALISM

Now that you better understand print journalism, here's a handy overview of a few common positions in the field of print journalism today.

Career Opportunity	Common Tasks
Reporter	• Find newsworthy events for the publication's audience. • Interview sources for facts and comments on topics of importance. • Write stories to engage readers, as you provide them with valuable information.
Copy editor	• Review stories reporters write for grammatical and style errors. • Fact-check copy to ensure its accuracy to avoid misinforming the readers. • Assess stories for balance and completeness prior to publication.
Section editor	• Assign stories to reporters and assist them in crafting their articles. • Work with other editors to determine the placement of stories and photos in the publication. • Manage a staff to ensure a consistent flow of content to the audience.
Photographer	• Capture newsworthy and visually engaging images for inclusion in the publication. • Select, tone, crop, and edit images to improve their aesthetic. • Work with other staff members to pair visuals with text-based stories.
Graphic designer	• Use illustration and photography software to build visual elements to improve storytelling. • Design newspaper pages, magazine spreads, and media webpages. • Select color palettes, font families, and design grids to create continuity within a publication.

CHAPTER REVIEW

LO 1 Outline key moments in the history of print journalism.

- In the 1500s and 1600s, print publications were usually created by people or organizations promoting a particular agenda, whether it was a government promoting a new law or a publishing house seeking to promote specific information.
- U.S. newspapers and pamphlets created in the 1700s and early 1800s were used to shape opinion, especially regarding English rule and politics in the post-Revolutionary society.
- The mid-1800s saw significant advances in print circulation and press technology. The advent of the penny press helped publishers reach an untapped market of common folks, while new technologies helped printers produce more papers, more cheaply, in less time.
- The rise of the Black press in the mid-1800s drew attention to the abolitionist movement and issues that were often ignored in mainstream media. During the twentieth century, it addressed everything from the movement of Blacks into northern states to the importance of the civil rights movement.
- In the mid-twentieth century, specialty media, such as the immigrant press, the gay press, and the prison press, provided an outlet for various groups to express their own experiences for others like them.
- By the latter half of the twentieth century, newspapers and magazines were primarily owned as parts of chains, allowing one owner to share resources among multiple outlets. Even as media conglomerates gained ownership, the standing of newspapers and magazines began to shrink as digital outlets arose that better served readers.

LO 2 Understand how print journalism provides value to its readers.

- Print journalists inform the public about important people, events, and outcomes that impact their lives.
- They advocate for societal change or against public actions that will help or harm citizens.
- They investigate important stories that otherwise would remain out of the public eye.
- Print journalists prevent corruption by shining a light on the negative actions of public figures.
- They entertain readers through engaging stories, photos, and graphics.
- They provide a permanent, tangible record that serves as a first draft of history.

LO 3 Assess how newspapers and magazines can survive in the digital age.

- Print journalism needs to build new sources of revenue. The digital age has created a significant loss of advertising revenue for traditional print products. For these publications to survive, they need to find ways to monetize their digital content and provide valuable advertising options across multiple platforms for their clients.
- Print journalism needs to demonstrate why its content is worth paying for. The advent of digital media has provided readers with more choices for information, on platforms that better fit their needs, and for little or no money. If newspapers and magazines are to survive, they must demonstrate why their work is superior to other forms of media and worth the cost of a subscription.
- Print journalism must find balance between giving readers things they are used to and accentuating the aspects of what makes each of their products unique.

KEY TERMS

Chain
Conflict
Consumer magazine
Cylinder press
Ethnic press
Fame
Gay press
General-interest magazines
Great Migration
Immediacy
Impact
Nonpartisan press
Oddity
Pamphleteer
Penny press
Specialty publication
Trade publications

DISCUSSION QUESTIONS

1. When you think of the media you consume, do you still consider it "reading a newspaper" when you consume it online instead of in print or "reading a magazine" if you access it through an app? Do you differentiate between the platform and the product or does it not matter to you, as long as the content is good?
2. Which of the six goals of print journalism is most important to you? Which one is least important? Why?
3. Of the five interest elements associated with newspaper and magazine coverage, which one is most appealing to you? Which one is least important? Why?
4. Where do you see newspapers and magazines being in 10 years? Do you think they will adapt to the digital environment and thrive or continue to sink under the financial weight of ink and paper? Or is there something in between those extremes that will be more likely to occur?

While you're driving in your car, listening to the radio, an announcer suddenly breaks in with a news report that there's a severe storm with tornado potential heading directly into your area.

iStockphoto.com/AHMET YARALI

RADIO AND OTHER AUDIO FORMATS

INTRODUCTION

1. *How often do you think of how important radio is in keeping you up to date wherever you go?*
2. *Are there types of content you prefer to consume by listening to them, as opposed to watching them? If so, what are they? If not, why do you think this is the case?*
3. *Where do you think radio broadcasting will be in the next few years? Is it going to fade away, shift to other forms of audio content dissemination, or develop new ways to satisfy its audience?*

The field of audio media has come a long way since the days of warbly recordings on metal cylinders and the use of crystals to capture sound from radio waves. The interwoven history of the recording and broadcasting industries has yielded a symbiotic relationship that has benefited the public in ways far beyond what inventors and scientists could have possibly imagined. Even more, as audio media has moved from physical recordings and broadcasted signals over the airwaves to the digital realm, the core essentials of broadcasting and recording continue to demonstrate the importance of audio as a form of mass media.

This chapter will explore the power of audio media as well as how it has benefited the public in mainstream and more specialized ways. In addition, we will discuss how the government grappled with regulating audio media, as it attempted to balance public needs and commercial interests. Finally, we will examine the role audio media has played in society and how it has continued to evolve with recent technological innovations.

LEARNING OBJECTIVES

After completing this chapter, you should be able to:

1. Identify the importance of key moments in the early history of audio-based media.
2. Describe how radio adapted to maintain its appeal during the rise of television.
3. Discuss the ways in which radio broadcasting has been regulated over time.
4. Articulate the societal value of radio as a mass medium.

A BRIEF HISTORY OF AUDIO MEDIA

LEARNING OBJECTIVES

LO 1: Identify the importance of key moments in the early history of audio-based media.)

Prior to the development of audio-based media, sound was an extremely limited form of communication. Oral storytelling tradition allowed stories to move from community to community, but the content could change in the retelling of stories. In addition, those stories moved slowly from group to group, according to the physical movement of the storytellers themselves. To make audio a truly viable mass media tool, inventors and innovators needed to find a way to capture the content verbatim for replay and then discover a way to transmit that content farther and faster than other forms of media.

Here are some key points in the history of audio-based media:

- Early recordings and broadcast discoveries
- The power of radio becomes clear
- The golden age of radio

- Diversity and expansion of programming
- Networks span the nation

Let's take a deeper look at these topics.

Early Recording and Broadcast Discoveries

The first attempts at recording sound came when Édouard-Léon Scott de Martinville developed his phonautograph machine in the 1850s, which captured audio vibrations by etching patterns onto a special medium. However, these recordings could not be played back. Thomas Edison's work in the late 1870s is often credited as the starting point of true audio-based media. In 1877, he developed a cylinder-based **phonograph machine** that could record and replay sounds, using a separate needle for each action. Edison and others continued to improve on his initial work through the early part of the twentieth century, experimenting with various recording media, recording approaches, and media size.

Thomas Edison's phonograph machine.

iStockPhoto.com/barbaraaaa

While some inventors were working on ways to capture sound, others were working on ways to broadcast it. The idea of sending audio content across large areas began in earnest when James Clerk Maxwell first proposed the theory of an electromagnetic field in 1864. The concept of using invisible waves to move sound from point to point set the stage for future inventors to build devices that could send communications through the air. Shortly after Heinrich Hertz established in 1866 that these waves did exist, other inventors were already looking for ways to use them for various communication efforts.

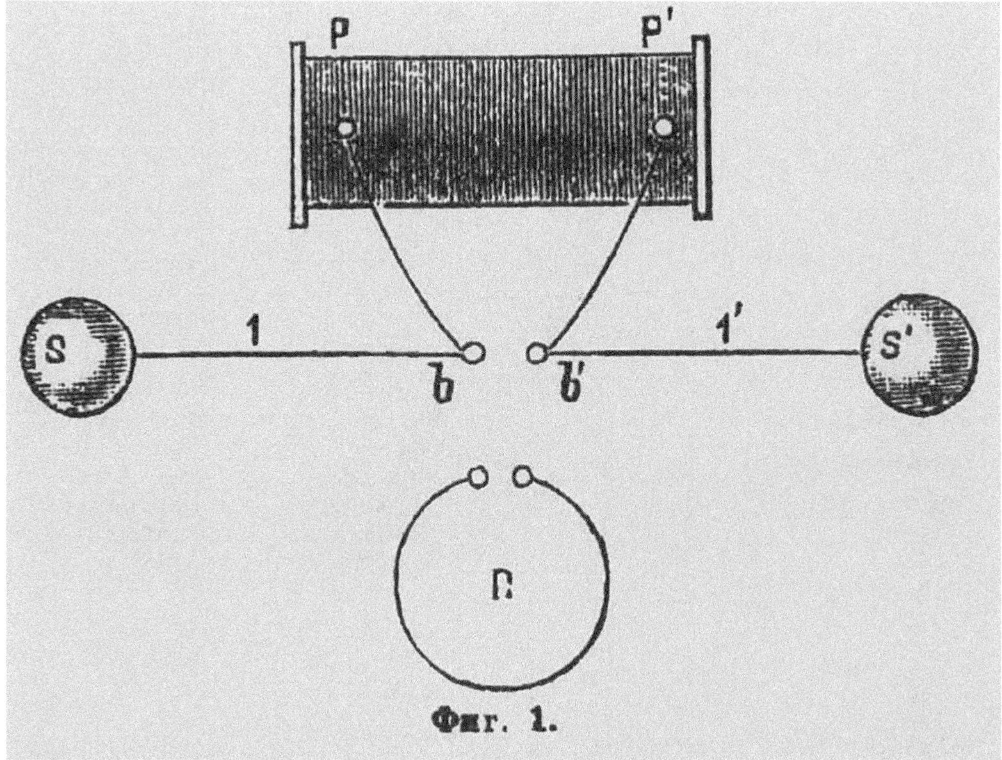

The existence of electromagnetic waves is proven.

Wikimedia Commons

TABLE 6.1 ■ Key Inventions and Discoveries in Audio Media

Item	Key Figure	What It Did	Why It Mattered
"A Dynamical Theory of the Electromagnetic Field"	James C. Maxwell	In 1864, Maxwell created equations that described the presence of an electromagnetic spectrum.	Maxwell's work is the foundation upon which all broadcasting rests. His efforts led to the discovery and use of radio waves and broadcast technology.
The phonograph	Thomas Edison	Edison's 1878 version of the phonograph allowed audio vibrations to be recorded onto cylindrical tubes.	The ability to capture and replay sound marked the start of audio recording. Edison's model was repeatedly improved upon, eventually giving us the vinyl records audiophiles still love.
The presence of electromagnetic waves is proved	Heinrich Hertz	In 1886, Hertz verified Maxwell's theories, establishing the concept of radio waves.	This added the practical component necessary to begin experimenting with over-the-air broadcasting using the radio spectrum, eventually creating the radio industry.
The Audion tube	Lee de Forest	This 1906 invention was the first practical audio amplifier, used widely in radio.	The Audion tube improved radio receivers by boosting the signal and improving the audio quality, making broadcasting much more practical.
Magnetic tape-based recording	Fritz Pfleumer	In 1928, Pfleumer developed a process of putting metal particles onto paper, which could be magnetized, leading to the development of tape-based recording.	Tape recording allowed users to record and rerecord their content on the same piece of tape without quality loss, and to edit that content.
The transistor radio	Texas Instruments	Introduced in 1954, the Regency TR-1 was the first mass-marketed version of the transistor radio.	The TR-1 was the first commercially viable radio that used on transistors instead of vacuum tubes. This revolution allowed radios to be much smaller, stronger, and portable.

The Power of Radio Becomes Clear

Although numerous scientists and inventors tinkered with the "**wireless telegraph**," Italian entrepreneur Guglielmo Marconi was the first to see its full commercial potential. In 1897, he formed his own firm to compete with the cable-based communication companies of the day. He saw the opportunity to reach

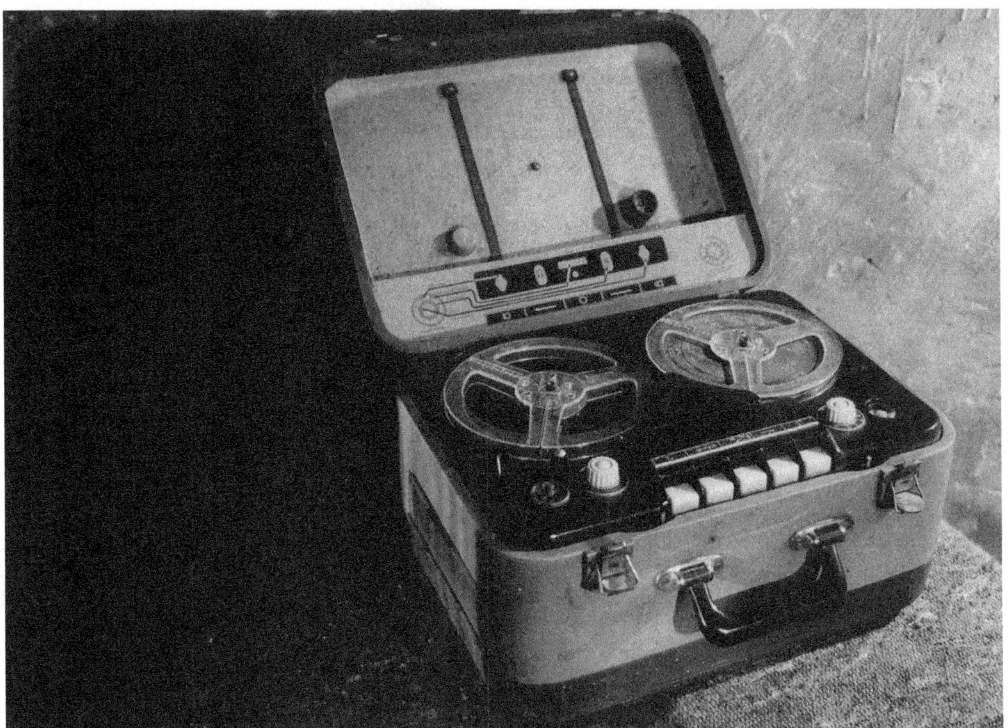

The invention of magnetic tape–based recording allowed users to record and edit content without a loss in sound quality.

iStockphoto.com/AndreasKermann

areas beyond where cabled communication could work, including the open sea. In December 1901, he sent a telegraphic message across the Atlantic Ocean, demonstrating the ability to move content wirelessly.

The early efforts of **broadcast radio**, also known as **terrestrial radio**, were limited in two key ways: first, the technology didn't allow people to send anything more than Morse code or other brief signals, and second, the receivers were relatively weak, so listeners had difficulty understanding whatever information they could get. In 1900, the first concern was addressed when a Brazilian priest named Roberto Landell de Moura first demonstrated that a voice could be transmitted wirelessly.

As with many of the innovations we'll discuss in this chapter, there are two conflicting stories of who was the first to solve the second issue, the problem of being able to amplify the signal so listeners could clearly hear the information that was broadcast. While many credit inventor Lee de Forest as the first to improve sound volume and quality through the invention of the **Audion** tube, engineer Reginald Fessenden claimed that he had beaten de Forest to the punch with the first broadcast of music and entertainment. Fessenden claimed in 1932 that ships at sea were able to pick up his 1906 radio broadcast, which included his playing "O Holy Night" on the violin and reading from the Bible.

A similar set of disputes arose in regard to the history of radio on college campuses, with multiple institutions staking claims as the first to avail themselves of this new medium. Beloit College lists the experiments of professor Charles Aaron Culver in 1907 as the first radio endeavors of this kind. St. Joseph's College in Philadelphia received the first experimental radio license for a college station back in 1912, even though it didn't construct a broadcast station for another decade. Union College in Schenectady, New York, claims on its website that its station, 2ADD, was the first in the nation to broadcast a show from a true station, back in 1920. Other institutions also claim to have been first, based on how they nuance the meaning of terms like *broadcast, radio, station*, and *operation*.[1]

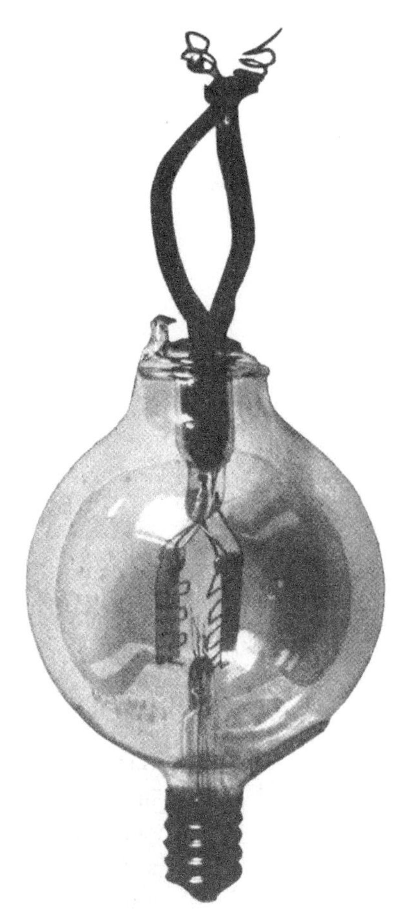

The Audion tube.

Wikimedia Commons

TABLE 6.2 ■ A Few Key Names in Radio

Guglielmo Marconi	David Sarnoff	Jack Gibson	Martha Jean Steinberg	Tara Ayres
• An inventor and engineer whose work on radio transmission and reception in the 1880s and 1890s earned him the title of "the inventor of radio." • Shared the Nobel Prize in 1909 for his work in developing wireless radio technology.	• Beginning in 1906, this pioneer in radio and television spent more than sixty years promoting the idea that these platforms are true "mass media." • Oversaw RCA and NBC for decades, through the golden ages of radio and television. • Known for "Sarnoff's law," which states that the value of a broadcast station is directly related to the number of people in its audience.	• Known as the father of Black-themed radio, because of his inclusive approach to Black music and issues in his broadcasts, starting with his first radio job in 1943. • A pioneering Black disc jockey who worked for multiple radio stations, including WERD, the first Black-owned station in the United States. • Fought against the appropriation of Black radio by opportunistic white stations, coining the phrase "Black from the ground up" to describe stations that were Black owned and operated.	• Nicknamed "The Queen," she began her forty-six-year career in radio in 1954 at WDIA in Memphis. • Co-owned WQBH in Detroit, where she broadcast gospel and talk programming. • Stayed on air for forty-eight straight hours during the 1967 Detroit riot, imploring listeners to stay inside.	• Spent thirty-five years in public radio, producing content that supported feminist and LGBTQ+ causes. • Helped pioneer one of the first recurring gay radio programs in the country, *Come Out Tonight*, which began in 1976 in Connecticut. • Ran *Her Turn* at WORT in Wisconsin, a program that began in 1978 and is one of the longest running radio programs dedicated to lesbian issues.

Regardless of which version of history you believe, it became clear that radio had potential as a broadcasting mass medium.

How Radio Works

Like all forms of mass communication, radio operates with a sender creating content that is sent through a channel to a receiver (see Chapter 1). From a technical standpoint, radio signals are limited in their reach by both the strength of the transmission and what is called **line of sight**, which means the signal can't bend around curves or climb over structures that impede the connection between sender and receiver. These limitations can be overcome in multiple ways, such as amplifying the power of the source and using several antennae to move the transmissions past obstacles. The process of how radio signals are effectively transmitted is shown in Figure 6.1.

FIGURE 6.1 ■ How Over-the-Air Broadcasting Works

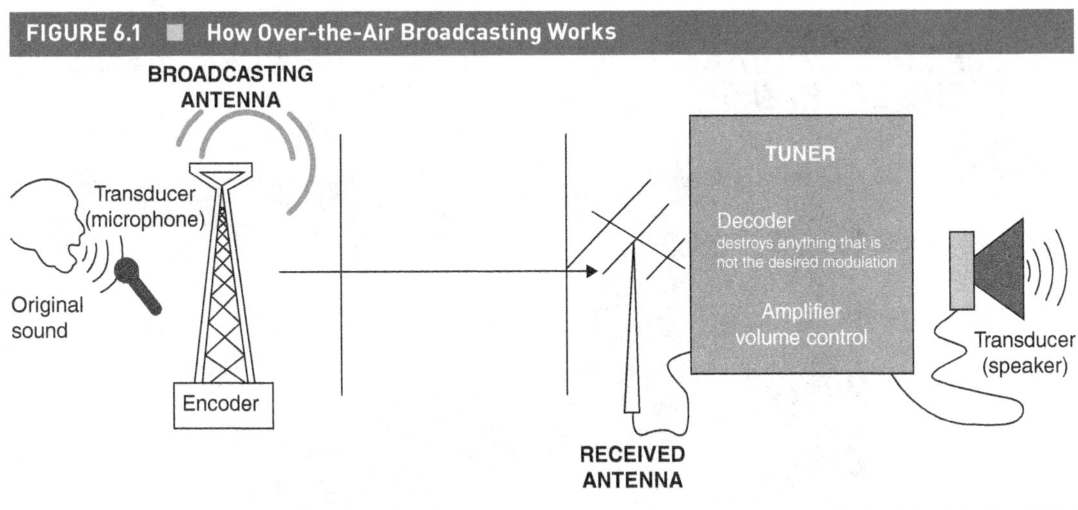

Here is a visual representation of how information moves from a broadcaster to an audience. (Table 6.3 provides additional detail.)

TABLE 6.3 ■ The Equipment Used in Over-the-Air Broadcasting

Item	What It Does
Microphone	Captures sound from a source and translates it into electrical energy
Transmitter	Combines the content from the microphone with radio signal for distribution over the air
Broadcasting antenna	Sends the signal to the public
Receiving antenna	Gathers the signals that broadcasters send out
Tuner	Selects the specific frequency of the broadcast waves the listener wants to hear
Decoder	Translates the radio waves back into sound for the listener
Amplifier	Allows the listener to increase the volume of the sound
Speaker	Presents the sound sent for the listener to enjoy

The Golden Age of Radio

During the 1920s, senders of content and sellers of radio receivers eagerly joined the race to gain market share in this new medium.[2] Radio stations became sources of entertainment, broadcasting shows and musical events, and also became prominent sources of information for the public. The ability to get free content after the initial investment in the receiver itself was appealing to citizens during the Great Depression. In addition, people did not need to be literate to understand the information or enjoy entertainment from the radio, making it more universal than newspapers or magazines.

Radio dominated the media landscape through the first half of the twentieth century, with many people and organizations taking advantage of the medium's capabilities. Politicians saw the benefit of bring a message directly to the people, something President Franklin D. Roosevelt did throughout the Great Depression with his fireside chats. Journalists saw it as a way to communicate information about the brewing conflict in Europe in the late 1930s and the United States' efforts during World War II. Radio programming brought people entertainment, such as variety shows, soap operas, and dramatic plays. According to the 1940 U.S. census, twenty-eight million households reported having a radio, a number that accounted for almost 83 percent of the population.[3]

MEDIA LITERACY MOMENT: *WAR OF THE WORLDS* AND THE SPREAD OF FALSE INFORMATION

Orson Welles rehearsing War of the Worlds.

Photo 12/Contributor/via Getty Images

Concepts like "fake news" and "deepfakes" have become part of our everyday experience today, as social media, biased websites, and internet trolls do their best to spread false information to achieve their goals. Orson Welles's 1938 *War of the Worlds* broadcast is often cited as "patient zero" for how false information was spread through mass media.[4]

Twenty-three-year-old Welles produced the *Mercury Theatre on the Air* for CBS, a series of programs that adapted literary classics for broadcast. In October 1938, for the Halloween broadcast, Welles chose the H. G. Wells classic *War of the Worlds*, which tells the story of aliens coming to Earth and colonizing the planet. Welles used standard radio techniques of the time, such as breaking into programs to report news bulletins, relying on "sources" who witnessed the alien attack, and natural sound that purported to be the aliens' spaceships, as if the invasion were a "real" event.[5] At the beginning of the show, Welles included a disclaimer explaining that this was a fictional reenactment, to appease the network's management. However, according to contemporary newspaper reports, people who tuned in late missed the disclaimer and thus thought they were listening to actual news. The following day, Welles held a news conference in an attempt to control the damage.[6]

For years, this event served as a reference point to showcase the power of radio at the time, with reports saying that almost twelve million people heard the broadcast and nearly one million thought it was real.[7] However, more recent examinations of the broadcast have called this conclusion into question. According to an investigation by *Slate* magazine in 2013, newspapers saw radio as a less worthy competitor for news and a financial drain on advertising revenue, and thus they sensationalized the story.[8] In other words, it could be a case of one good fake deserves another.

How do you think the radio station and the newspapers could have better handled the broadcast and its fallout? Do you think the radio broadcasters did enough to alert people as to the purpose of the piece they were performing? What kind of fact-checking could average listeners have done to determine the truth or falsity of *War of the Worlds*? How do the source of the original broadcast and the subsequent stories play a role in how this entire incident was presented to the public?

THE NEXT STEP: Take this concept a step further by finding the original broadcast. Based on what you heard, to what degree do you think people had a reasonable belief that this was an actual news event? What information was presented that could have clued in listeners that this was not real? Also, discuss if you think this broadcast led to an actual panic. If not, is it something worth learning about? Justify your position.

Diversity and Expansion of Programming: The Development of Black Radio

During the 1920s, radio programming was still in its infancy, but it was finding audiences across the racial spectrum. In 1929, Chicago's WSBC created *The All-Negro Hour*, which featured Black entertainers as well as music performed by Black artists. Jack L. Cooper served as the first Black radio announcer for this pioneering show.[9] Additional programs that catered to audiences interested in Black programming emerged over the next two decades, including the first all-Black radio soap opera, called *Here Comes Tomorrow*, which aired on WJJD in Chicago.

Radio personalities, often called **disc jockeys** or DJs, like Jack Gibson and Al Benson, became prominent figures in the Black community during the post–World War II era. Gibson, known as "Jack the Rapper," not only popularized Black-appeal radio, but he also hosted an annual Black radio convention that helped additional forms of Black music flourish. Benson's radio shows drew large audiences because he played the blues on the air before anyone else. His popularity with audiences and sponsors, first in radio and then on television, earned him the title of the "Godfather of Black Radio."[10]

The postwar era also saw the rise of radio stations that had completely shifted to Black-oriented content, such as R&B music and variety shows with all-Black casts. In 1948, stations like WDIA in Memphis and WLAC in Nashville moved to all-Black formats. In 1949, Atlanta's WERD became the nation's first Black-owned and programmed station when J. B. Blayton purchased the station.

Broadcaster Richard Durham used radio to demonstrate the importance of Black figures in American history with his *Destination Freedom* program.[11] Durham's scripted programming focused on influential individuals who were often lost to time, showcasing dignified scholars, political activists, and savvy business owners. The show told these stories using music, poetry, and narration, as Durham relied on strong research and a militant tone to establish the importance of these historical figures.

The presence of Black-oriented stations also provided women with opportunities that mainstream broadcasting did not. Black women broke down barriers in the 1950s on Black radio; they used their own ideas, names, and personalities to challenge stereotypes that women's roles should be limited to housekeeping or cooking.[12] Martha Jean "The Queen" Steinberg began her career at WDIA in 1954, where she was part of an all-Black staff at a white-owned radio station.[13] Her on-air work during the 1960s civil rights strife in Detroit provided a sense of connectivity for the Black community.

Martha Jean "The Queen" Steinberg

Nico Toutenhoofd/ZUMA Press/Newscom

Networks Span the Nation

Early radio technology—primarily the limits on how far a signal could reach—made it difficult for any one station to dominate the airwaves outside of a local geographic area. Even if a station were to receive an unfettered ability to increase its source power, the content could go only so far before it bounced off large buildings or was impeded by a set of mountains. One of the crucial ways in which radio companies overcame this problem was to create a **network**, a collection of stations that would share programming across portions of the country. Each station that was part of the greater whole was known as an **affiliate** station, which meant the owner would air the common content from the network but also provide local programming as well.

This system created benefits for everyone involved. Networks could increase their reach across the country while giving the public a common listening experience, wherever they lived. Popular programming now had a larger audience, which increased opportunities for advertising revenue for the network and its affiliates. Aside from a potential financial boost, affiliates got fresh, ready-made shows to fill the air and draw listeners to the station. In addition, these affiliates could weave local programming around the national content to increase audience interest in the homegrown material.

One of the first people who saw the potential for this kind of system was David Sarnoff, who was working for the Radio Corporation of America and saw radio as having mass media potential. When RCA purchased WEAF in New York, Sarnoff began building what would become a major radio empire: the National Broadcasting Company (NBC), establishing two networks, the Red and the Blue. Other early networks included NBC's main competitor, the Columbia Broadcasting System (CBS), founded in 1927 by William S. Paley, and the Mutual Broadcasting System (MBS), founded by a consortium of independent stations in 1934. In 1938, a Federal Communications Commission investigation revealed that NBC was a virtual monopoly, and the government forced NBC to sell its Blue network to Edward J. Noble, a candy baron, who renamed the company the American Broadcasting Companies (ABC). While NBC, CBS, and ABC all transitioned into television, MBS remained focused on radio until its sale to radio conglomerate Westwood One in 1985.

TELEVISION COMPETITION AND THE SHIFT TO THE NICHES

LEARNING OBJECTIVES

LO 2: Describe how radio adapted to maintain its appeal during the rise of television.

The popularity of radio began to wane in the 1950s, when television became a direct competitor that offered a distinct advantage: moving images. The visual medium took the place of radio in many homes, with radio shows moving over to the television side of broadcasting. Although these technological advancements did end what researchers call "the golden age of radio," radio retained its place as a valuable form of mass media.

Here are a few ways in which radio has evolved to keep it relevant to this day:

- Radio gains improved mobility
- AM and FM radio
- Going digital, filling niches

Let's take a look at how these innovations helped radio survive.

Radio Gains Improved Mobility

Although radios had become more portable since the days of de Forest and Marconi, they still operated on tube systems that tended to be bulky and could overheat. In 1948, U.S. scientists developed a solid-state signal amplifier that did the same job as tubes, but in a much smaller component and without creating heat issues. These **transistors** became the crucial element in Texas Instruments' quest to build a pocket-sized radio in 1954. More than one hundred thousand units were sold in the first year, inspiring the creation of smaller and more portable radio units. Audiences could now take music to the beach, listen to a ball game, and even listen to live events while attending them.

In the post–World War II era, teens with disposable incomes and a strong sense of self of often frequented malt shops or dance halls, where they could hear rock 'n' roll. When transistor radios allowed them to own radios of their own, they were able to hear this kind of music whenever and wherever they saw fit. Between the rise of Black radio stations and the influx of artists like Bill Haley and the Comets and Elvis Presley, teens flocked to transistor radios and helped boost the industry's growth, even as TV began to eat away at opportunities once reserved for radio.[14]

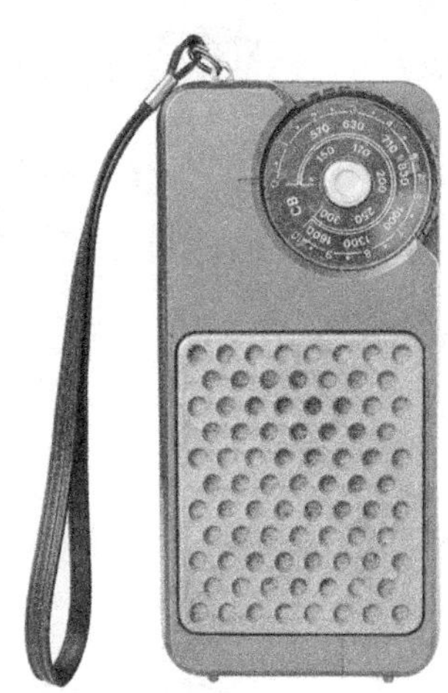

A transistor radio from the 1950s. These portable radios, coupled with the expanding musical genres that teens loved, made radio as popular as ever, even as televisions began to dominate the broadcast landscape.

iStockphoto.com/Ballun

AM and FM Radio

Originally, radio waves were limited to the so-called AM (**amplitude modulation**) range of frequencies. AM stations relied on variations in signal strength as part of the encoding process. As far back as the 1920s, the government recognized that the AM spectrum had only so many frequencies and was thus a limited public resource. Controlling who got the opportunity to broadcast and what they could produce was a large part of the Federal Radio Commission's (FRC) and Federal Communications Commission's (FCC) mandate, so most of what got broadcast fit within the mainstream interests.

A new innovation, FM (**frequency modulation**) radio, was introduced in the early 1940s. FM stations kept the signal the same, but altered the number of times a wave would move to send their content. Edwin Armstrong demonstrated a successful FM broadcast in 1936, and the FCC authorized the use of the FM band starting on January 1, 1941. The FM band provided an entirely untapped area for broadcasters seeking to enter the field of radio. Even more, the band provided improved sound quality, which appealed to stations that wanted to play music.

By the 1960s, the FCC had established the FM Non-Duplication Rule, which limited the amount of AM content that could be rebroadcast on FM stations. In addition, the rise of stereo-quality broadcast helped FM gain popularity among listeners. Another key factor in the rise of FM was its limited broadcasting range. When the FCC licensed an AM station, the commission had to limit other stations in much larger geographic areas to prevent overlapping between their signals. FM stations, which could broadcast over a significantly smaller area, could have multiple stations using the same frequency without interfering with one another.

Public broadcasters, who created programs outside of mainstream broadcasting interests, also benefited from the rise of FM, because the first twenty frequencies on the band had been dedicated for public broadcasting. This confluence of events expanded not only the amount of content available, thanks to the expansion of radio channels and limits on repetition, but also the variety of content, ranging from various musical tastes to public-interest talk shows.

You might think that AM is where you can hear talk radio, local sporting events, and music your grandparents like, while FM provides "morning zoo" DJs, music your parents like on "oldies" stations, and even stuff you might crank up while driving somewhere. However, the terms *AM* and *FM* have distinct technological elements embedded in them and provide different experiences in terms of quality.

The terms *AM* and *FM* relate to the way the radio signal is coded and mixed on a carrier wave. *AM* stands for "amplitude modulation" and works by altering the strength of the signal to encode the sound information as it is sent into the world. It uses less bandwidth than FM broadcasts and therefore provides less fidelity in the audio, which is why the AM format works best for sports events and talk shows, for which audio quality isn't as crucial for an individual's listening pleasure.

FIGURE 6.2 ■ How AM and FM Signals Differ

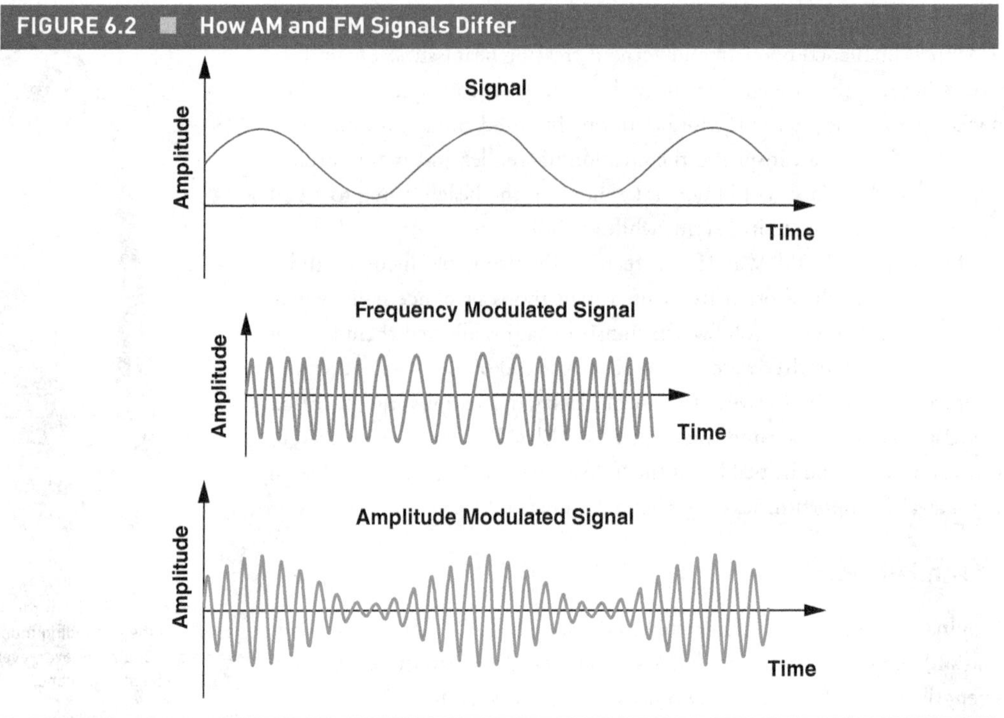

Both AM and FM radio signals carry content to an audience, but each does so in a specific way. AM signals alter the strength of the signal, thus using less bandwidth and having lower sound quality. FM signals alter the number of times the signal changes direction, thus taking up more bandwidth but limiting audio noise and enhancing sound quality.

FM stands for "frequency modulation" and works by keeping the strength of the signal constant, but manipulating the number of times the wave changes direction in a specific period of time. FM broadcasts require much more bandwidth than those on AM stations, but this approach provides two distinct advantages. First, the audio quality of the broadcast is much cleaner, making it a better fit for radio stations that rely heavily on music for their content. Second, FM radio has fewer problems related to changes in amplitude, such as audio noise.[15]

Going Digital, Filling Niches

Traditional AM and FM radio had technological limitations arising from the nature of the electromagnetic spectrum. Only a certain number of frequencies existed, channels operating on those frequencies had to be geographically limited to prevent overlapping among them, and distance from a source meant loss of signal quality. These concerns meant that only a few large, mainstream stations could operate in any given part of the country, pushing aside smaller, niche interests.

In the early 1990s, various pioneers began experimenting with the ability to broadcast content through digital platforms. As was the case with the start of terrestrial radio, several different people have claimed to pioneer internet radio. In 1993, Carl Malamud debuted *Internet Talk Radio*, a weekly program in which he interviewed computer experts for an online listening audiencc.[16] In 1994, WXYC in Chapel Hill, North Carolina, announced that it had begun simultaneously broadcasting its FM radio content online. In 1995, Scott Bourne launched NetRadio.com, stating that it was the first internet-only radio station.

Around this time, several corporate interests began lobbying Congress to open options for satellite radio broadcasting.[17] Although it took most of the 1990s to hash out the technological and regulatory specifics, satellite radio was launched in 2000 and quickly began to dominate the medium. Metrics indicate that SiriusXM, the primary source of satellite radio, had more than thirty-four million subscribers as of 2022.[18] Its roster of 150-plus channels includes decade-by-decade music offerings, talk radio of all kinds, traffic monitoring, religious programming, and more.

In addition to broadcast streaming services, technology aficionados began looking for ways to record and share digital audio content, much in the same way they previously had dubbed cassette tapes. What emerged was the podcast, a digital audio file that listeners can download to MP3 players and listen to at their leisure.[19] Former MTV personality Adam Curry helped develop the technology for this mass media in 2004, and since then, the popularity of the format has skyrocketed.

Research into podcasting revealed that more than 55 percent of the U.S. population has listened to at least one podcast, with half of those people stating that they listen to podcasts weekly.[20] As of 2022, approximately 384 million people around the world considered themselves podcast listeners, and they have plenty of options from which to choose. Data on podcasters reveal that there are more than 2.4 million podcasts, with more than 66 million episodes in total.[21] The most popular podcasts in the United States, according to Spotify's own data, include *The Joe Rogan Experience, Distractible, Pod Save America*, and *The Daily*. Joe Rogan's podcast alone draws an average of 11 million listeners per episode, making it the most popular Spotify podcast.[22]

Digital radio provided broadcasters with several distinct advantages over its terrestrial counterpart. The cost to begin an online station was a small fraction of what traditional AM or FM operations required. Digital radio did not use the electromagnetic spectrum for their broadcasts, and thus stations were not required to obtain FCC licenses. The digital realm was limitless in terms of space and opportunity, so broadcasters could choose specific niches of content to fill instead of trying to serve a mainstream audience.

A DEEPER LOOK: THE FUTURE OF TERRESTRIAL RADIO

When television debuted in the mid-twentieth century, it appeared to ring a death knell for radio as a viable form of mass communication. As noted earlier, radio evolved, pivoting toward other ways to serve the listening audience. However, recent statistics indicate that terrestrial radio could wither away, and that's not a good thing for any of us. A survey by Edison Research revealed that in 2008, 6 percent of people aged eighteen to thirty-four said that they had no terrestrial radio receivers in their homes. Ten years later, that number had grown to 50 percent, revealing that more and more people than ever before were looking elsewhere for their news and entertainment.[23]

One of the last true vestiges of security for terrestrial radio is even starting to dissolve: the automobile. The 2021 Infinite Dial study revealed that while audio use in cars has remained constant, digital platforms continue to weaken the grip terrestrial radio has on consumers. The data show that 75 percent of respondents reported listening to AM/FM radio while in the car in 2021, down from 81 percent the year before. The biggest gainer in this survey has been podcasting, which moved from 9 percent of respondents in 2008 to 41 percent in 2021.[24]

According to a 2019 report from Jacobs Media Strategies, this form of technological disruption has continued to push terrestrial radio further from the public consciousness.[25] Although radio and cars have gone together for many decades, it doesn't follow that terrestrial radio will continue to enjoy its place in our vehicles. Think about it this way: cigarette lighters and ashtrays used to be standard equipment in all vehicles. Now, they're still there in a way, but we call them power outlets and storage spaces.

So why does it matter if over-the-air radio disappears, as long as we can still hear the music we like, catch the big game when we want, and listen to our favorite talk radio celebrities?

For starters, the rules that govern terrestrial radio don't apply to the digital streaming services. The agreement struck between the government and broadcasters more than one hundred years ago dictates that radio operate in the public interest. The licensing process the FCC uses to determine which ownership groups get to use the radio spectrum to reach us helps keep stations operating with our best interests in mind. No such requirement exists online, so programmers can fill their stations with whatever gets the most listeners, to appease the most advertisers. It would be like hiring a company to run your school's nutrition program without requiring it to abide by any nutritional guidelines. If all the company cares about is selling stuff, it's goodbye broccoli, hello Reese's peanut butter cups!

In addition, the content we consume through digital platforms is rarely local, thus limiting our connections to other people in our geographic areas. Radio's geographic limitations created a drawback in one sense, in that the stations could broadcast only so far. However, in another sense, these limitations required the stations to focus more intensively on specific geographic areas for a good portion of their content. Channels like "I Love the '80s" or "All Baseball, All Day" can keep us entertained and engaged all day, but we'll never hear a breaking news story to let us know that the restaurant down the block just burned to the ground.

Local stations will get local information to us in a timely fashion to keep us connected with important community issues. It could be that a winter storm will require us to park on one side of the street tonight or that a maniacal killer is running through your neighborhood with an axe.

This loss of local content has already started, thanks to massive conglomerates' and hedge funds' swallowing up radio stations like they once did newspapers. In 2020, iHeartMedia, which owns more than 850 stations nationwide, announced that it would be making massive personnel cuts.[26] Estimates at the time noted that more than 1,200 on-air staff would be losing their jobs, as the company continued to rely more on national programming and artificial intelligence.[27] Cuts at the company continued through 2023, with losses in many metropolitan markets, including Chicago, Cleveland, and Dallas.[28] This makes it much less likely that a local DJ will get a news tip about a traffic jam or some breaking news about the city's mayor being arrested and break into the broadcast to tell you about it.

Finally, the ability to select personalized niche content can create a sense of isolation that terrestrial radio used to prevent. As noted earlier in the chapter, the use of network broadcasting gave people common media experiences, which helped bind them in cultural and social ways. Sociologist Robert Putnam explored this concept in his book *Bowling Alone*, in that he states that people benefit from social capital, the collective wisdom, information, action, and identities that emerge when people have shared experiences.[29] The more isolated people become from one another, the less likely they are to have a supportive and cohesive society. Rather than seeing a rich variety of content, we narrow our focus to a singular point that keeps us from broadening our horizons and connecting with a diverse group of individuals.

RULES AND REGULATIONS

LEARNING OBJECTIVES

LO 3: Discuss the ways in which radio broadcasting has been regulated over time.

Since the beginnings of the radio age, the federal government has sought to regulate the medium, balancing commercial considerations against the need to provide service to the people. The first federal regulations focused on safety for vessels operating at sea. In 1910, lawmakers passed the Wireless Ship Act, which required radio equipment and operators to be placed on certain ships that navigated the ocean waters. This law was meant to improve communication between ships at sea and the ports that served them. Two years later, radio played an instrumental part in one of the worst shipping disasters of all time. The use of Marconi's technology aboard the *Titanic* in 1912 is credited with saving hundreds of lives after the ship struck an iceberg. The telegraph operators on board were able to signal a nearby ship, the *Carpathia*, which was able to rescue many survivors. This tragedy underscored the importance of radio technology in saving lives.

As radio became more prominent as a mass medium, the question of regulation became important to resolve. Who had the right to broadcast? What could they or couldn't they broadcast? Where and when could broadcasting occur? These and other issues became important because the spectrum was a limited resource: only so many frequencies existed, so only so many stations could broadcast on those frequencies. With that in mind, the government set about building regulations that would both organize and refine broadcast radio.

Organization and Licensure

The effort to organize and apportion access to the airwaves began in earnest when the federal government passed the **Radio Act of 1912**. It mandated that anyone wishing to operate a radio broadcasting station had to obtain a license from the government. It also established a specific portion of the electromagnetic spectrum for emergency broadcasts and restricted amateur broadcasters' range of operation.

Table 6.4 outlines the various rules and regulations that were passed by the government as radio gained in popularity and use. Additional acts were passed to encourage more diversified content on radio. These included 1949's **Fairness Doctrine**, that demanded that the stations provide balanced and contrasting views on those issues, and 1967's **Public Broadcasting Act**, which created the Corporation for Public Broadcasting to create and distribute noncommercial content that was in the public interest.

TABLE 6.4 ■ Key Governmental Regulations

Date	Event	Outcome
1912	Radio Act of 1912	• Required broadcasters to be licensed by the government. • A distinct part of the spectrum was set aside for emergency services.
1927	Radio Act of 1927	• Created the Federal Radio Commission, which assigned radio stations specific frequencies, granted licenses to these stations, and established classes of stations, based on transmission power. • Provided the FRC with oversight powers. • Established that broadcasters who used this public resource had to do so with content "in the public interest."
1934	Communications Act	• Established the Federal Communications Commission (FCC) as an independent body to replace the FRC. • Empowered the FCC with the ability to oversee all telecommunications, including radio, television, and other broadcast forms that would emerge in the future, including those created by private companies.
1949	Fairness Doctrine	• Required provide a balanced perspective when discussing controversial issues of the day. • Attempted to address complaints that broadcasters were biased and presenting only one-sided stories. • Eliminated in 1987.
1967	Public Broadcasting Act	• Created the Corporation for Public Broadcasting, which had a mission of creating and disseminating noncommercial content that was in the public interest. • Provided a launch point for the Public Broadcasting Service (PBS) and National Public Radio (NPR).

THE ROLE OF RADIO IN SOCIETY

LEARNING OBJECTIVES

LO 4: Articulate the societal value of radio as a mass medium.

Although radio has evolved substantially over its history, it continues to have a vital place in society as it informs and entertains consumers.

Let's look at several things radio does that benefit society as a whole:

- Alert the public
- Bring events to people
- Create local connections

- Create cultural connections
- Galvanize social action

Here's a deeper look at each of these topics.

Alert the Public

Humans have always had a need to be aware of their surroundings, both to satisfy their innate curiosity and as a requirement for survival. Early tribes of humans often had to worry about invasions from rival clans or attacks from wild animals, so having individuals stand watch overnight allowed the tribes a sense of safety. If danger were to emerge, these sentries would alert the rest of the group. Although most of us today need not worry about hostile invasions or roving packs of wolves attacking us while we sleep, the desire to remain aware of crucial information can feel like a matter of life and death. The concept of "FOMO," or "fear of missing out," taps into that intrinsic need we have to be aware of our surroundings. When other people have information and we do not, we operate at a disadvantage.

For generations, broadcasters were the primary source of immediate information. "We interrupt this broadcast..." became the radio announcer's way of breaking into whatever normal content was on the air to alert the audience of something important. Special news briefs, breaking news coverage, and other similar alerts brought a sense of immediacy to the viewers and listeners regarding events that just couldn't wait to be reported until a regularly scheduled newscast.

Although social media, along with the ability to set up push notifications on key news apps, has taken over a great amount of the responsibility once purely within the domain of broadcasters, radio remains a vital part of people's lives. In rural parts of many sparsely populated states, radio remains the dominant way of reaching citizens.[30] From emergency alerts to local politics, the ability to remain aware of one's surroundings can be limited in many ways to the prominence of local radio offerings.

Bring Events to People

Broadcasting can bring the daily events directly to an audience anywhere those listeners can access the content. Whether it was a cluster of citizens crowding a radio to hear that World War II had ended or a group of people gathering around an iPhone to watch a video report from the George Floyd riots in Minnesota, the immediacy and vibrancy of broadcast can place people in the middle of that moment. These shared cultural moments create a sense of connectivity within society.

The power of broadcasting can shape how people remember history as well. For example, on October 3, 1951, Bobby Thomson of the New York Giants hit a home run off the Brooklyn Dodgers' Ralph Branca that was dubbed "the shot heard 'round the world." The cultural touchstone for generations to come was that of Giants announcer Russ Hodges screaming, "The Giants win the pennant! The Giants win the pennant!" Historians report that Hodges was one of about a dozen people broadcasting the game on that day, so most people didn't experience the moment through his euphoric announcement. However, because that is the most recognizable version of the audio from that day, it serves as the moment's historical marker.

Radio still can reach more people than any other form of traditional media, making it one of the key ways in which people can experience something from afar. Whether it's a sporting event, a political speech, or a news bulletin from the scene of a crime, radio can bring that event to people.

Create Local Connections

Broadcasters are part of people's lives within a community and throughout the world, thanks to the ability to connect to them through the power of audio and video. When local journalists cover events over time, they become more than conduits of information; they become friends and trusted partners for many viewers.

The ability to know what matters to the audience is crucial for all journalists, but in broadcasting, audience members often feel a strong relationship with on-air personalities that goes beyond merely a transactional one. The anchors arrive in people's homes every night and speak directly with them. The reporters who provide content move among an area's citizens and mingle with them as both interested investigators and champions of their causes. When people can put a face to a name and see a person working for them every day, it creates bonds of trust and a sense of friendship.

From a reporting point of view, broadcast journalists often operate as general-assignment reporters, which allows them to become familiar with the wants and needs of an audience. The technology that gave birth to broadcast news could send a signal only so far, thus limiting its reach beyond certain physical areas. When you combine this tradition of geographic beat coverage and the idea that reporters tended to cover everything, you can see how broadcasters became a one-stop shop for information in a given location. Reporters take this responsibility seriously when they seek information from sources in a given region and provide their viewers with valuable content based on what they have collected.

Create Cultural Connections

During the first half of the twentieth century, the airwaves were a place of endless possibilities for people interested in connecting with things beyond their small part of the world. Access to reading materials could be limited by what the local news stand stocked or what the library would permit on its shelves, but a radio tuner could give anyone a glimpse into whatever people were broadcasting.

Today, streaming and podcasting provide similar access for people who are seeking help from others who understand their cultural and personal experiences. LGBTQ+ groups have lauded podcasting as a medium that provides inclusive and diverse points of view in a safe environment for people within those communities. In particular, experts noted that podcasts in this area can shed light on a variety of issues pertaining to mental health, gender identity, and romantic relationship building.[31] Audio and video streaming services have provided additional access to programming that focuses on LGBTQ+ issues. Although media critics within these communities note that traditional streaming platforms are providing content that connects with their lives, the niche operations that specialize in LGBTQ+ programming have given audiences a wider array of options and forms of representation.[32] Stations like Pulse, GO! Live, and AOL LGBT Pride also provide niche-oriented music and shows aimed at the LGBTQ+ community.

Other marginalized communities have found similar opportunities in podcasting and streaming. With Black voices often underrepresented in traditional media outlets, a wide swath of the Black community has turned to podcasting and niche streaming channels as a way of getting messages out to a broader audience. Survey data show that nearly twelve million Black American adults listen to podcasts every month.[33] Of those listeners, 70 percent said that they find unique perspectives in podcasts from Black creators that are unavailable in other forms of media. Podcasts like Kitchen Table Talk examine issues of self-care for Black women, while those like For Colored Nerds dig into the geekier elements of pop culture within and outside the Black community. These kinds of podcasts provide listeners with access to "the conversations that Black people have when white people aren't in the room."[34]

Galvanize Social Action

The power of radio to entertain and inform was well established by the end of the 1950s, but its place in giving voice to the voiceless took on special meaning during the fight for equality. During the civil rights movement, some radio stations provided listeners with support as they mobilized against discrimination based on race, sexual orientation, and gender. In the early 1960s, DJs who represented underserved communities would use their programming to draw attention to the struggles of the people in need. Radio was far more accessible to people in these communities than television, which was expensive. Scholars also noted that it also was more potent than newspapers, because of the limited literacy in some communities.

Experts noted that Black radio improved the networking and mobilization efforts of protesters in the deep South. Some programs would feature and highlight the actions of civil rights leaders, while some DJs provided protesters with information about police and opposition forces during protests. For example, during the 1963 protests in Birmingham, Alabama, several Black DJs used coded language to move marchers around the city to help them avoid police roadblocks. One station went so far as to use a traffic helicopter to assist in this effort.[35]

In more recent times, podcasting has served as a way of shedding light on other forms of social injustice. In 2022, Adnan Syed was released from prison more than two decades after he was convicted of killing his ex-girlfriend. The case had been all but closed since early 2000s, but the podcast *Serial* and journalist Sarah Koenig dug into thousands of documents to reveal significant flaws with the judicial process.[36] (Syed's conviction was reinstated in early 2023, based on a procedural issue, and the case remains in flux as of this writing.[37] Regardless of the outcome, the influence of the podcast remains vital in this case.) In 2020, another true-crime podcast, *In the Dark*, helped free a Mississippi man wrongfully convicted of killing four people in a furniture store.[38] In these and other cases, the popularity of these podcast investigations drew enough attention to miscarriages of justice that authorities found themselves compelled to act.

A breakthrough occurred for gay rights in 1962, when a program featuring eight gay men discussing their lives aired on New York's WBAI. Earlier that year, the station aired a program titled *The Homosexual in America*, which featured heterosexual psychologists outlining the ways in which homosexuality was based on a series of mental defects. Gay activist Randy Wicker demanded equal time from the station to refute the allegations and explain the ways in which society had denied basic rights to people based on sexual orientation. The program, titled *Live and Let Live*, used a panel-discussion format for these gay men to share stories regarding police harassment and concerns with their social lives.[39]

By the 1970s, the expansion of programming related to LGBTQ+ issues had moved beyond single-episode installments and into recurring programs. WYBC on Yale University's campus, for example, aired *Come Out Tonight* every Sunday night, starting in 1976, while *Her Turn* debuted at Wisconsin's WORT in 1978 and provided listeners with expansive coverage of feminist and lesbian topics.[40] In 1980, Keith Brown launched *Gay Spirit Radio* on WWUH in Hartford, Connecticut, an LGBTQ+ community news and service program that remains active to this day.[41]

JOBS IN AUDIO MEDIA

Now that you better understand the various aspects of this field, here's a handy overview of a few common positions in audio media today.

Career Opportunity	Common Tasks
Program host/DJ	• Introduce songs, advertisements, and news segments as part of a broadcast show • Discuss topics of interest with a cohost or guest while inviting listeners to call in and express themselves
Producer	• Create content for news and entertainment shows • Coordinate with show hosts, interview subjects, and special guests to develop a special feature or show approach • Curate playlists for airing, based on the type of station you run and audience interests
Audio engineer	• Install and maintain equipment necessary to broadcast content • Upgrade and repair equipment for use in the studio or field
Record/music producer	• Organize the process of recording content for release, including choosing artists, booking studio time, and developing content • Work with audio equipment to fine-tune and edit content created within a studio
A & R director/manager	• Scout and book talent for recording labels, including singers, musicians, and composers • Serve as a liaison between musical talent and the organization for musical, promotional, and financial issues • Oversee the recording process, providing insight as to style, quality, and approach to the project

CHAPTER REVIEW

LO 1 Identify the importance of key moments in the early history of audio-based media.

- Édouard-Léon Scott de Martinville made the first known audio recording, but it wasn't until Thomas Edison's work in the late 1870s that both audio recording and playback were demonstrated.
- James Clerk Maxwell hypothesized the existence of an electromagnetic field in 1864, theorizing that content could be sent wirelessly on these electric waves. In 1866, Heinrich Hertz established that Maxwell was correct, marking the true beginning of over-the-air broadcasting opportunities.
- Italian entrepreneur Guglielmo Marconi's early work in point-to-point, over-the-air communication spurred on the radio industry.
- Inventors Lee de Forest and Reginald Fessenden began broadcasting audio content in 1906 and 1907, each claiming to be the first to do so. Both men made substantial technological innovations that improved broadcast quality and range.
- During the 1920s, radio sales boomed, as broadcasting helped bring information and entertainment to thousands of Americans. As the United States slogged through the Great Depression and World War II, the golden age of radio brought people great relief from the stresses of their daily lives.
- Black-oriented stations provided men and women of color with opportunities in the 1930s and 1940s that mainstream broadcasting did not. DJs like Jack Gibson and Al Benson became significant figures in the Black community, as they shared music and news with their communities.
- To expand the reach of large stations, companies like RCA developed networks of affiliates that would share common content. NBC, ABC, and CBS evolved in the 1930s and 1940s as radio stations and remain prominent players in broadcasting to this day.

LO 2 Describe how radio adapted to maintain its appeal during the rise of television.

- The invention of transistors made radios portable.
- The opening of the FM band allowed more stations to hit the airwaves, broadening the spectrum of content available to radio consumers and producing better sound quality than AM did, giving consumers a better listening experience.
- The emergence of digital radio continued to expand on the variety of content available to the listening public. The ability to produce radio-style shows without the daunting financial costs and legal concerns of traditional stations also helped turn radiophiles into broadcasters in their own right.

LO 3 Discuss the ways in which radio broadcasting has been regulated over time.

- The Radio Act of 1912 deemed the broadcasting spectrum to be a limited public resource. The federal government required people who wanted to broadcast to obtain a license to do so.
- The United States created the Federal Radio Commission (FRC) in 1927 to assign radio stations specific frequencies, grant licenses to these stations, and establish classes of stations, based on transmission power. It also established that licensees had to operate "in the public interest."
- The Communications Act of 1934 replaced the FRC with the Federal Communications Commission (FCC), an independent body that would oversee all telecommunications, including radio, television, and other forms of broadcasting.
- The Fairness Doctrine of 1949 demanded that broadcasters provide balance while discussing controversial issues of the day. It was eliminated in 1987.
- The Public Broadcasting Act of 1967 created the Corporation for Public Broadcasting, which had a mission of creating and disseminating noncommercial content that was in

the public interest. This act allowed the formation of the Public Broadcasting Service (PBS) and National Public Radio (NPR).

LO 4 Articulate the societal value of radio as a mass medium.

- *Alert the public:* Inform people immediately regarding items of public concern
- *Bring events to people:* Broadcast key events of the day to anyone who is listening anywhere the signal can reach.
- *Create local connections:* Provide people with a sense of community within a geographic area.
- *Galvanize social action:* Serve as a touchstone for people seeking the opportunity to share thoughts regarding social justice and inspire their actions

KEY TERMS

Affiliate
Amplitude modulation (AM)
Audion
Broadcast radio
Disc jockeys (DJs)
Fairness Doctrine
Frequency modulation (FM)
Line of sight
Network
Phonograph machine
Podcast
Public Broadcasting Act
Radio Act of 1912
Radio receiver
Terrestrial radio
Transistors
Wireless telegraphy

DISCUSSION QUESTIONS

1. To what degree do you think over-the-air broadcasting still has an impact on your daily life?
2. The federal government has repeatedly attempted to govern audio media, claiming that the electromagnetic spectrum upon which radio works is a scarce public resource. Given the shift toward digital media, which has no such limitations, do you think the government should continue to seek similar regulations regarding use and content? Why or why not?
3. What are the benefits and drawbacks you see in the network-affiliate model of broadcasting for the network, the affiliates, and the audience members?
4. Where do you see the future of terrestrial radio heading? What changes do you see coming and what things do you think will remain constant? Why?
5. Do you think the way you consume audio content is isolating you from the larger society in any of the ways outlined in the chapter? Do you think your approach to consumption is having a positive or negative impact on your sense of society as a whole? Why?

During the early days of the COVID-19 pandemic, many theaters closed down because of local restrictions or the inability to safely accommodate viewers. To keep the industry active, traditional movie studios relied on streaming services to present films to viewers who were stuck at home. This, coupled with the expansion of movies the streaming services themselves produced, changed the ways in which people got to experience movies, or which movies they were able to see.

Ted Hsu/Alamy Stock Photo

MOVIES

INTRODUCTION

1. *Is watching a movie in a full theater more or less fun for you than watching it alone at home? Why?*
2. *Given our ability to consume video content almost anywhere, at any time, and on any device, what do you think makes movies different from television shows in today's digital environment?*
3. *Do you think that traditional movie theaters still have a place in the media landscape? How do you think digital platforms and streaming services have changed the role of movies in society?*

Movies literally started with the goal of turning single images into moving ones, with no other sense of what such a process could provide. At the turn of the twentieth century, movies were a few seconds long, viewed by one person at a time, and simply demonstrated the ability of inventors to trick viewers into seeing something that wasn't there. At the turn of the twenty-first century, movies had become lengthy tales that millions of people flooded into theaters to experience as part of a shared social experience. In between these two milestones, an industry that entertained, informed, and connected us evolved in ways no one could have expected. Even now, as the movie industry grows outside of theaters and presents new opportunities to filmmakers and audiences alike, we can see how the basic principles of motion pictures remain part of our lives.

This chapter will examine the ways in the industry developed over the past 125 years and how it has benefited the public in that time. In addition, we will outline the ways in which movies get made and the methods by which some people have attempted to censor certain films. As they say in the business, let the show begin.

LEARNING OBJECTIVES

After completing this chapter, you should be able to:

1. Identify key moments in the history of movies.
2. Discuss the role of movies in society.
3. Understand the process through which movies get made today.
4. Explain the history of movie regulation.

A BRIEF HISTORY OF MOVIES

LEARNING OBJECTIVES

LO 1: Identify key moments in the history of movies.

The term *movie* comes from the shortened phrase "moving picture," the earliest way in which inventors described how they created action with images. The goal for these pioneers was to find a way to replicate motion from a series of still photographs.

As we have seen with so many other media forms, once the technology had been established, innovators took these early efforts and looked for practical applications for the invention. Over time, inventors found ways to improve upon the technology to enhance the applications of their work. Of all the forms of mass media we cover in this text, movies fit this pattern of cyclical improvements better than any of the others. Here are a few key moments that demonstrate that pattern of growth:

- Early inventions and the start of moving pictures
- Telling stories through edited film

- The introduction of sound and the talkies
- The move to color
- The VCR brings movies home
- Digital media and streaming

Let's look at each of these topics a bit more deeply.

Early Inventions and the Start of Moving Pictures

The multitalented inventor Thomas Edison served as a pioneer in movies. In 1888, Edison said, "I am experimenting upon an instrument which does for the eye what the phonograph does for the ear, which is the recording and reproduction of things in motion."[1] Four years later, he introduced the motion picture camera, known as the **kinetograph** and a viewer for his motion pictures called the **kinetoscope**.

Edison's inventions built on the work of Edward Muybridge, a photographer who discovered a way to take pictures in rapid succession. As part of a twenty-five thousand dollar challenge to prove if horses ever had all four hooves off the ground while in full gallop, Muybridge took individual images of a galloping horse and then rotated them quickly enough to simulate motion; in so doing, he proved that horses did manage to "fly" while racing along at top speed. Building on Muybridge's technique, Edison captured single images onto a strip of celluloid film at a consistent rate of speed. That strip could then be run through his playback device at the same speed, thus capturing movement. However, only one viewer at a time could view the moving images.

A series of kinetoscopes in a viewing parlor entertain patrons around 1895. The device was revolutionary but limited by its inability to allow more than one person view the film at a time.

Wikimedia Commons

Meanwhile, in 1895, two brothers from France, Auguste and Louis Lumière, publicly unveiled their **Cinématographe** machine, which projected the movie onto a screen so that an entire audience could see it at once. In addition, the Lumière brothers' invention combined the work of Edison's

Edison's coworker, William K. L. Dickson, captured this moment on film, known now as *Fred Ott's Sneeze*. Early movie technology significantly restricted the types of actions and the lengths of events that movies could capture. More than three hundred early films from Edison's company can be found here at the website of the Library of Congress: https://www.loc.gov/collections/edison-company-motion-pictures-and-sound-recordings/about-this-collection/.

Wikimedia Commons

machines into one box, functioning as a camera, a printer, and a projector.[2] Weighing in at about twelve pounds, compared with the thousand-pound monstrosity that Edison built, the device was much more portable and was much quieter and easier to use.[3]

Telling Stories through Edited Film

Early films showed viewers something they had never seen before: photographs in motion. The films often ran twenty or thirty seconds and featured a single action in a single shot. For example, the first copyrighted movie filmed on Edison's device lasted six seconds and recorded a man sneezing in front of the camera. However, what transformed the moving picture industry from a technological marvel into an entertainment industry was the introduction of storytelling techniques to film. French filmmaker Georges Méliès made several early narrative films beginning in the mid-1890s, culminating in his landmark *A Trip to the Moon* (1902). Edwin Porter's twelve-minute-long *The Great Train Robbery* (1903), built on inspiration from Méliès's work, incorporated multiple takes, camera movement, and continuously developing action, all of which advanced the medium significantly. The film was a huge success and is credited for making movies a form of valuable public entertainment.[4]

Movies from this point forward became longer and more complex, relying on scripted stories and complex editing processes. Film pioneers like director and actress Lois Weber experimented with techniques such as the **split screen** to show multiple characters performing different actions at the same time.[5] Director D. W. Griffith used techniques like **parallel construction**, which intercut scenes of two actions occurring at the same time to build drama and tell stories.[6] For example, a film

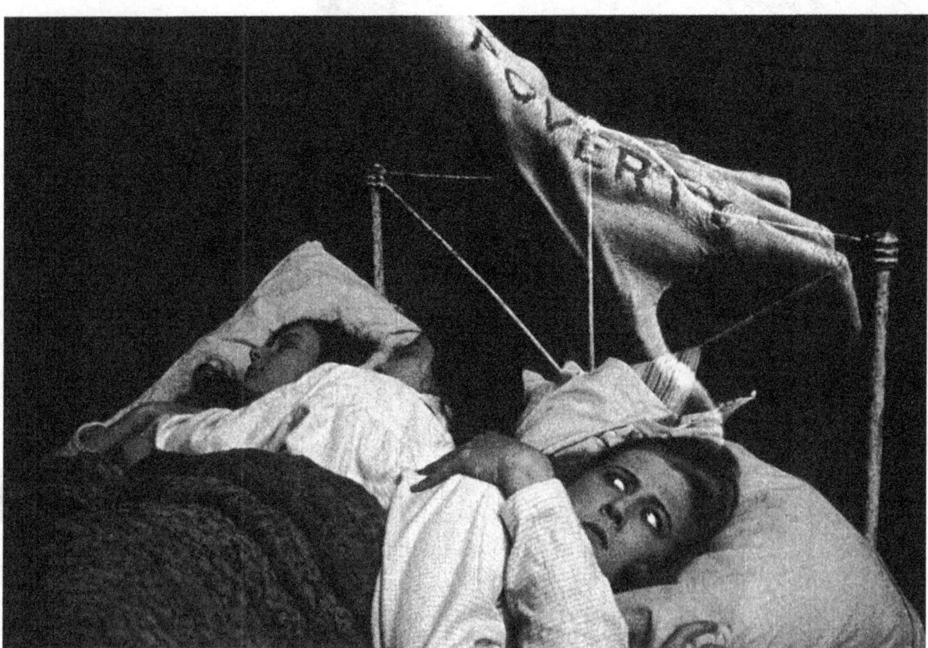

Lois Weber, known for films such as Suspense, The Blot and Hypocrites, used multiple editing techniques to tell stories in her films.

TCD/Prod.DB/Alamy Stock Photo

could show a cowboy racing on his horse to the rescue of a fair maiden who is tied to the railroad tracks in the path of an oncoming train. Each cut between the two actions would happen more quickly as the rider came closer and closer to saving the girl.

The Introduction of Sound and the Talkies

For more than thirty years, film and sound operated independently of each other. Storytelling relied heavily on the actors' exaggerated pantomiming and facial expressions, with brief written texts (called "title cards") inserted to augment the action. Sound could be provided separately in a theater by a pianist or an organist, who could play appropriate music to accompany a film.

In 1926, Warner Brothers Studio developed an approach that linked film's audio and visual elements electronically. Dubbed the **Vitaphone** system, the recordlike sound disk and the projected film acted in tandem to provide dialogue and music in perfect synchroneity. The system itself lasted only about five years, as Warner Brothers and other major studios moved to a sound-on-film system by 1931. That said, the ability to have sound and film working together was a major breakthrough in the movie industry. The first feature-length commercial film to have synchronized dialogue using this system was the 1927 hit *The Jazz Singer*, starring Al Jolson as a Jewish cantor's son who aspires to sing and dance for entertainment, despite his parents' objections.[7] Even though the Vitaphone system was short-lived, Jolson's declaration that "You ain't heard nothin' yet!" launched the era of **talkies**.[8]

Today, *The Jazz Singer* presents film historians with a dilemma. Although it served as a groundbreaking film, Jolson's character wears blackface as part of his act. This shameful reminder of racial insensitivity is just one of the ways in which technological triumphs of early film are associated with undignified reminders of the country's past.

TABLE 7.1 ■ A Few Key Names in Filmmaking

Oscar Micheaux	Alla Nazimova	Lois Weber	John Ford	John Waters
• Began making movies in 1919 and became the most successful African American filmmaker of the first half of the twentieth century. • Served as an author, a director, and a producer for more than forty-four films during his lifetime. • Produced movies that showcased the hardships Black people faced, including discrimination and exploitation.	• A Russian-born actress who began her career who starred in a series of successful films from 1918 to 1920. • Directed the 1923 film *Salome*, which critics credit as the first art film ever made in the United States. • Hailed as an LGBTQ+ icon who openly dated women and purposefully cast actors who were not cisgender or straight.	• Rose to prominence in the early twentieth century as an actress, a writer, a producer, and a director. • Achieved several firsts in film for an American woman, including directing a feature-length film and owning her own film studio. • Credited with writing, directing, or acting role in more than two hundred films.	• Deemed one of the greatest directors of all time, he worked in silents and talkies as well as working across a wide array of genres. • Earned a record four Best Director Academy Awards. • Developed and improved upon techniques like the wide shot and shooting in sequence to retain control over how the film would look.	• One of the earliest openly gay directors who met with both underground and mainstream success. • Known for surrealistic cult films that pushed the boundaries of social norms and acceptance beginning in the early 1970s. • Created films that were some of the first to have overtly LGBTQ+ characters in primary roles.

A DEEPER LOOK: HISTORICAL ACHIEVEMENTS MEET SHAMEFUL RACISM

Released in 1915, D. W. Griffith's best-known film is *The Birth of a Nation*, an expansive tale that was legendary for pioneering extensive new filmmaking techniques. From pan and zoom shots to close-ups and fade-outs, the film made camera movement and edits an essential part in storytelling.

For all of its technical achievements, the film drew rebukes from many sources, because it presents a pro-South narrative of the Civil War and Reconstruction. Played by white men in black-face, the African American characters are depicted as base-level animals, driven by stereotypical urges to violence, predatory sexual behavior, and drinking. The saviors of the white race are members of the Ku Klux Klan, who don their hoods and cloaks as they restore proper order to society.

Prior to its release, the NAACP called for the film to be censored, and the organization's members staged protests in multiple cities when it premiered. The film was banned in several cities, but some media outlets praised the movie, including the *Los Angeles Times*, which called it "the greatest picture ever made and the greatest drama ever filmed."[9] More than one hundred years later, the film remains the source of friction between those who marvel at the cinematographic revolution it introduced and others who remain appalled at the story's racist message.

Although famous for this dichotomy, *The Birth of a Nation* is not alone in its place among cinematic achievements that told stories laden with racism. As noted earlier, *The Jazz Singer* gained fame as the first feature-length "talkie." However, the main character dons blackface to help him build a career as a professional entertainer. Although the technological breakthrough was revolutionary at the time, the racism associated with the acceptance of minstrel actions and racial denigration are impossible to overlook.

Gone with the Wind is another classic film that has been reevaluated because of its racial content. At the time of its release in 1939, the movie was praised for bringing Margaret Mitchell's sprawling novel to the big screen. The movie broke every box-office record and established a new benchmark for Academy Award wins with eight competitive and two honorary Oscars. (Hattie McDaniel became the first African American to win an Academy Award for her portrayal of Mammy, even though as a Black woman, she was barred from the film's premiere in Atlanta and placed in segregated seating at the Oscar ceremony.)

Scholars have long grappled with how the technical achievements of these films have been celebrated, while their content goes uncriticized. University of Southern California film professor Todd Boyd notes that *Gone with the Wind*'s revisionist history swept the true horrors of slavery under the rug, while putting a softer focus on the southern "way of life" told from white people's perspective. In addition, its African American characters serve as stereotypical exemplars that remain relevant today.[10] Emory University film professor Nsenga Burton underscores how racist, on-screen depictions of Black people have led to long-term consequences for people of color in both cinema and society.[11] Students of these films must address both their technique and themes if they are to fully assess the impact these movies had.

The Move to Color

To make movies that felt truer to life, filmmakers knew they needed to present images that contained visual vibrancy. The addition of color to film would more intimately connect the actors on the screen to the viewers in the audience.

Early efforts near the turn of the twentieth century involved painstaking processes that were prohibitively expensive. In the early 1920s, the **Technicolor** process represented a breakthrough for color film. Early Technicolor was cumbersome and expensive to create, so it was used only sparingly. However, in the early 1930s, a three-color process was introduced that was cheaper and better than earlier efforts, with each color captured on a single roll of film. Anyone who ever owned an inkjet printer understands how three colors—cyan, magenta, and yellow—can be used to create a nearly infinite number of hues. This new technique produced more realistic color and could be shown in theaters on existing equipment.[12]

FIGURE 7.1 ■ Early Full-Color Creation in Film

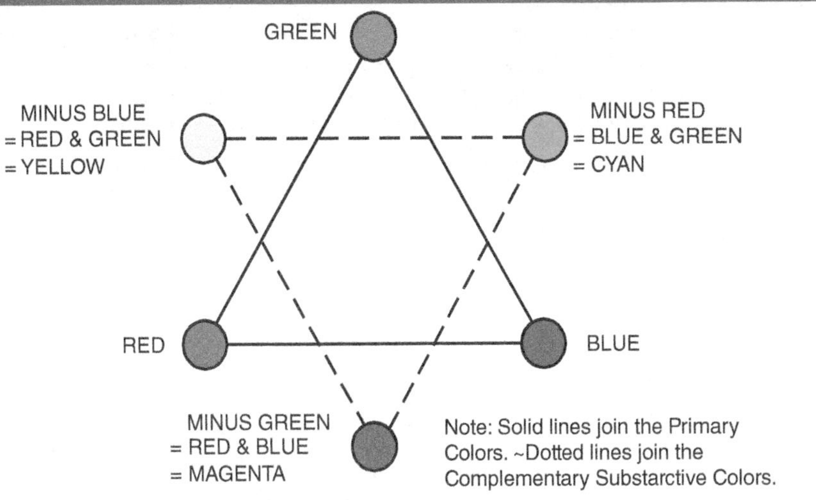

An illustration of the relation of the colors taken on the film reels to the colors used to print the final film stock for projection in theaters.

This three-layer process became the gold standard in the field until the 1950s, when Kodak and other film companies found cheaper and easier ways to create color on a single strip of film. However, the Technicolor approach remained prevalent in film until the mid-1970s.[13]

Fun Things We Tried at the Movies

Moviemakers were always looking for novel ways to draw audiences into the theater. In their attempts to make movies magical, a few ideas flourished, while others died quietly. Here are a few fun things the film industry experimented with over the years

3-D glasses, unlike other movie theater gimmicks, are still used in cinemas today, with a major resurgence in the 2000's.

Bettmann/Contributor/via Getty Images

Innovation	What It Did	How It Worked	What Happened to It
3D movies	Created the illusion of 3D images that leapt off the screen and into the audience.	Two images were created on film, one tinted red, one tinted blue. Viewers wore special glasses that created a 3D effect.	• *The Power of Love* (1922) was the first commercial 3D film, but its golden era was from about 1952 to 1956. • It remained relatively dormant until RealD Cinema emerged in about 2003. • 3D continues to be used in cinema and virtual reality technologies.
Scented movies	Used synchronized scent emission systems that would add smells into the theater to reflect the action on screen.	The aroma machine emitted different smells keyed to the action. For example, during a gun fight, it produced the smell of burnt gunpowder.	• AromaRama (1959) and Smell-O-Vision (1960) were two early attempts. However, the inability to clear the earlier scents from the room before new ones were released led to what one reviewer called "olfactory chaos." • Only a few other smell efforts have been attempted since, such as John Waters's use of scratch-and-sniff cards at screenings of his 1981 film *Polyester*.
Theater vibration	Mimicked on-screen movement (like volcanos or earthquakes) through various vibration techniques.	Theaters were equipped with either large sonic machines, akin to today's giant stereo subwoofers, or machines that shook the seats at various points in the film.	• The Percepto! device (1959) for the film *The Tingler* produced a vibration or an electric shock to the audience seats during particularly terrifying parts of the movie. • The Sensurround system (1974) in the film *Earthquake* created pulsing audio waves to simulate the feel of an earthquake. • Although these gimmicks were short-lived, the technology gave rise to the speaker systems used today, such as surround sound and 360-degree sound.

Scented movies posed challenges and did not last as a movie theater draw.

LMPC/Contributor/via Getty Images

The VCR Brings Movies Home

During the 1950s, as television was becoming a dominant platform, both films and TV programs were limited-run affairs. TV shows would air only once, at a given time on a specific network, never to be seen again (see Chapter 8). Movies had a limited run in theaters of a few days to a few weeks. Once that single engagement had ended, anyone who had missed the opportunity to see the movie was out of luck. Films were available only in movie houses, which meant that if people wanted to see the latest John Wayne western or James Dean drama, they had to go to the theater. All of this began to change when inventors found a way to make video recording devices more practical for home use.

The first true video cassette recorder, or VCR, boom began in the late 1970s, with the introduction of Panasonic's VHS and Sony's Betamax systems. The Betamax system used smaller tapes and delivered superior picture quality, but VHS won the day because of lower costs and the ability to record more content on a single tape. Its continually decreasing cost led to a boom of purchases of tapes and viewing equipment. In 1985, U.S. consumers bought approximately 11.5 million VCRs, more than a 50 percent increase over the previous year.[14]

At the time, movie executives railed against the new devices, filing copyright lawsuits and demanding high royalties from VCR manufacturers. At a 1982 congressional hearing, Motion Picture Association of America (MPAA) president Jack Valenti stated that the VCR was to the film industry what "the Boston Strangler is to the woman home alone."[15] Despite protests from the film industry, home video thrived, and eventually the industry saw profits by producing prerecorded versions of their movies.

Digital Media and Streaming

The VCR was just the first of many inventions that put the "home" in "home theater." The first viable challenger to tape-based supremacy was the "digital video/versatile disc" or DVD. This technology first hit stores in 1997 and was based on the same premise as the popular compact disc, or CD, which used a digital optical storage format.

DVDs had distinct advantages compared with VHS tapes. DVDs had higher quality picture and sound than tape did and weren't susceptible to wearing out the way a tape could. (On the other hand, a small nick on the disc could make it impossible to play any part of a movie, while VCR tapes could withstand a decent amount of abuse.) It was easier to quickly skip to a favorite scene. However, VCRs could record content, which DVDs initially could not do. The tapes allowed people to save a TV program and watch it later, or record the big game while they were doing something else. To address this shortcoming, the first DVD burners were commercially available by the early 2000s for people willing to spend four thousand dollars for the machine and about thirty-five dollars per disc, or about sixty-five hundred dollars in today's money.[16] As was the case with VCRs, as more people adopted them and the technology improved, DVD prices dropped significantly. By 2003, DVDs overtook VCR tapes as the preferred format for movie rentals,[17] and by 2006, major movie studios had stopped releasing films on VCR tapes.

The DVD market helped spawn two additional revolutions that would eventually lead to its own decline. The first was the movement to a completely digital model, making it possible to more easily keep and store content. The second was the streaming revolution that took advantage of the increased speed of and access to the internet to deliver on-demand content.

DVDs gave viewers more control over their content. However, you had to put them all somewhere; stacks of DVDs became an unwieldly part of a movie buff's entertainment collection, and discs often wound up in the wrong cases, making it a disorganized mess. The digital video recorder (DVR) captured the benefits of DVDs while eliminating their storage problems. The machine used a hard drive, akin to one a computer would contain, and stored the video content on the device itself. The first of these machines hit the market in 1999, when TiVo was introduced. These devices remain a crucial part of the at-home movie experience, even as the next revolution in the industry is taking place.

As videocassettes and then DVDs became popular, producers realized that most consumers wanted to watch each film only once, rather than owning their own personal copy. Rental chains like Blockbuster Video arose to service this market by allowing consumers to rent films for single viewing.

For a while, the chain dominated the market, but then two entrepreneurs realized that people didn't really want to leave their homes to get movies. They started Netflix in 1997 as a mail-order company. Customers could order DVDs of movies, which would be mailed to them with return envelopes so they could ship them back. Unlike traditional rental stores, people were guaranteed to get the movies they wanted, and they were able to keep it as long as they wanted. The approach became so popular that Netflix soon towered over physical retail rental giants like Blockbuster.

By 2006, more than 5 million people had accounts with Netflix, which was already planning for the future. In 2007, the company debuted its Watch Now service, which allowed users to stream content from the company on their computers. The idea of **streaming**, or using the internet to watch video content, appeared to have a limited market at the time. Computers were still mostly limited to hard-wired internet access, but as technology improved, the idea caught on. By the end of the year, Netflix had more than 7.5 million subscribers.[18]

As of 2022, Netflix dominates a congested streaming market with more than 213 million subscribers. Amazon's Prime Video service is next, with 175 million users, with services like Disney+, Hulu, and HBO Max each hosting more than 45 million subscribers per year. These services not only provide previously made content to consumers, but many make their own programming or contract for exclusive rights to show material. For example, Netflix's *Red Notice* and *Don't Look Up* dominated the streaming landscape in 2021, with more than 360 million hours of viewing time each. Apple TV+ also produced a number of original films, including *CODA*, which became the first movie distributed through a streaming service to win the Best Picture award at the Oscars. In all, it took home three Academy Awards in 2022: Best Picture, Best Supporting Actor, and Best Adapted Screenplay.[19]

THE ROLE OF MOVIES

LEARNING OBJECTIVES

LO 2: Discuss the role of movies in society.

Given the wide array of movie genres, films serve many different purposes. Here are just a few things movies do for people in society:

- Offer an escape
- Create inspiration
- Provide social commentary

Let's take a deeper look at each of those topics.

Offer an Escape

Movies offer the opportunity for people to forget their troubles for a short time, as they are transported from their daily lives to distant lands or connected with a group of new characters. This need for escape was never more prevalent than in the 1930s, when the United States fell into the depths of the Great Depression. Although millions of people suffered bankruptcies, job loss, and personal hardship, they found solace in the movies. Between sixty million and eighty million people in the United States attended a movie at least once a week throughout the 1930s, where they were treated to a newsreel, cartoon, a secondary feature, and a main attraction.[20] The films ranged from screwball comedies to gangster films, but each gave people something else to think about other than their own difficulties.[21]

Escapism was a recurrent theme in films in the following decades. During World War II, Hollywood churned out dozens of movies meant to distract people from stories of bloody battlefields overseas and rationed goods at home.[22] Bing Crosby and Bob Hope rolled out five of their seven *Road to...* musical comedies during this time period, providing a humorous lift to audiences. Crosby also starred in *Going My Way*, a sentimental film about a young priest coming to a new parish, which earned seven Academy Awards and the most money of any film in 1944.

Films in the 1970s also found ways to help people escape life filled with financial difficulties and social problems. In the wake of the Watergate scandal that led to the resignation of President Richard Nixon, the United States withdrew its troops from Vietnam, marking the first time the country had lost a military conflict. At home, inflation was making basic needs like food and gasoline expensive or unavailable. Science fiction films like George Lucas's *Star Wars* and Steven Spielberg's *Close Encounters of the Third Kind* gave people the opportunity to forget about those problems for a while.[23] In its original run, *Star Wars Episode IV: A New Hope* (1977) sold more than ninety-six million tickets and has since grossed more than $1.5 billion overall when adjusted for inflation.

In the wake of the September 11, 2001, terrorist attacks, movies like *Harry Potter and the Sorcerer's Stone* and *The Lord of the Rings* helped people find hope when all seemed lost. Today's blockbusters based on comic book characters have given people a sense of hope and an opportunity to take refuge in the exploits of heroes.[24] During the COVID-19 pandemic, only two films earned more than one hundred million dollars during their opening weekends: *Spider-Man: No Way Home* and *The Batman*. The most recent addition to the Caped Crusader anthology set the record for the best opening of 2022.[25]

Create Inspiration

People often relate to specific characters in films, which is why many movies showcase inspirational tales. These films inspire viewers that they can be successful and improve themselves as they break free from whatever is holding them back.

Directors like John Ford relied on all elements of film to compose stories that would enrapture audiences. His westerns, like *The Man Who Shot Liberty Valance* (1962), presented the societal clash between powerful lawless interests and the rights of individuals under the law. His adaptations of novels like *How Green Was My Valley* (1941) and *The Grapes of Wrath* (1940) told tales of perseverance in the face of grinding poverty and personal loss. In these adaptations, Ford often replaced the original stories' negative outcomes with more positive ones, to provide viewers with a sense of hope. Director Barry Levinson took a similar path in his version of *The Natural* (1984), which was based on Bernard Malamud's novel. In the book, the aging baseball superstar Roy Hobbs strikes out in his final at bat, costing his team a chance to go to the World Series and ending his career in disgrace. In Levinson's ending, Hobbs hits a home run that shatters the lights high atop the ballpark, raining down sparks upon him as he circles the bases while his team celebrates.

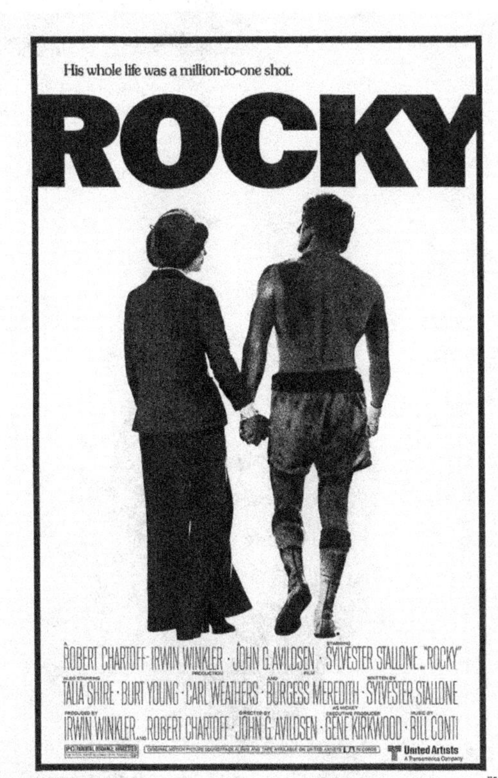

The original 1976 film *Rocky* was inspired by a true event, in which an underrated boxer named Chuck Wepner fought Muhammad Ali for the world championship.

BFA/Alamy Stock Photo

Sports films often tell stories of ordinary people doing extraordinary things. The 1976 Academy Award–winning film *Rocky* tells the story of a down-and-out boxer who is granted a once-in-a-lifetime chance to fight for the heavyweight championship. His quest isn't to win, as he explains to his girlfriend, but rather to survive all fifteen rounds facing a superior fighter. In the end, he completes his quest and finds the love of his life in the process. The story still resonates today through the *Creed* series, which had its latest installment in 2023 and follows the life of Adonis Creed, the son of Rocky's longtime opponent Apollo Creed.

Provide Social Commentary

Film producers have often presented controversial topics to their audiences to speak out against social ills. In 1923, film pioneer Dorothy Davenport coproduced the movie *Human Wreckage*, which told

The *Creed* saga picks up with Rocky training the son of his longtime opponent Apollo Creed, who ascends to the role of champion and faces his own challenges throughout the sequels. The third *Creed* film was released in 2023, starring and directed by Michael B. Jordan. Sports films often rely on underdog characters to provide inspiration to viewing audiences.

Kate Green / Stringer/via Getty Images

the story of how drug addiction can ruin the lives of drug users and the people around them. Davenport drew from her own experiences as the wife of actor and director Wallace Reid, who died that year addicted to morphine.[26] Over the next decade, Davenport covered a wide array of social issues, including prostitution and financial fraud.

The exploitation of underclass citizens was a common theme for directors wishing to dramatize people who had been marginalized because of their gender, race, or sexual orientation. For example, in some of her early films, Lois Weber touched on difficult topics such as abortion and birth control.[27] In another film, *Shoes* (1916), Weber examined the issue of money and power as it related to sexuality. The main character works in a shop but is so poor that she lacks the ability to replace her hole-filled, damaged shoes. She then makes the decision to sleep with a rich man who had been pursuing her for some time. Although we do not see what occurs between them, the next day, she is shown wearing new shoes.

Oscar Micheaux explored how Black citizens were treated in the United States more than fifty years after the Emancipation Proclamation. Micheaux wrote the novel *Homesteader* in 1917 and turned it into the first feature-length film created by an African American two years later. It tells the story of a lone Black settler who finds himself struggling to survive. At the same time as D. W. Griffith used stereotypes to denigrate people of color, Micheaux's films placed Black people in leading roles that showcased their intelligence and emotional strength. His work also called out the racism that was a constant burden to nonwhite citizens in their everyday lives.[28]

Oscar Micheaux.

Science History Images/Alamy Stock Photo

Director John Singleton also drew from his personal background to present his unique viewpoint. His debut film, 1991's *Boyz n the Hood*, presented a picture of urban youth, in which gangs were prevalent, violence was frequent, and people had limited ways of escaping their surroundings. His follow-up film, 1993's *Poetic Justice*, confronted issues of troubled relationships, drug addiction, and violence. Singleton noted that his desire to present Black culture in film came from a desire to humanize issues that were often ignored or stereotyped.[29] More recently, director Jordan Peele used his horror films, like *Get Out* (2017) and *Candyman* (2021), to reflect racial disparity and social injustice.

The degree to which films provide equal representation for all people is a large part of the social commentary element of filmmaking. In one case, it was a cartoonist who provided the motion picture industry with a key insight regarding limited opportunities for women in film and a "test" to prove that inequality exists in this regard.

MEDIA LITERACY MOMENT: THE BECHDEL TEST AND GENDER INEQUITY IN FILM

Alison Bechdel was not trying to start a sociological movement when she published a cartoon in 1985 that depicted two characters debating what movie they wanted to see.

However, her simple observation led to a phenomenon known as the **Bechdel test** (although she prefers the term *Bechdel-Wallace test*, as a nod to her friend Liz Wallace's role in the idea[30]) that scholars and media critics have used to evaluate sexism in films.

The test comes from one character's "rule" about what movies she is willing to see. It requires the following three things to be present in a movie:

1. The film must have two named female characters.
2. The women must talk to each other in the film.
3. The conversation must be about something other than a man.

Alison Bechdel. Scholars have used "the Bechdel test" to analyze the prevalence of sexism in individual movies.

WENN Rights Ltd/Alamy Stock Photo

Researchers have found that films that pass the test tend to receive lower budgets, even though they tend to do as well, or better, financially than films that don't pass it. Hollywood insiders have stated that the lower budgets and lesser support are because women will more willingly go to a "guys' movie" than men will go to a "women's movie." They also note that films with strong female characters tend not to "travel well" to international markets, despite financial data that refute that claim.[31]

An analysis of more than 9,300 movies produced since 1970 demonstrates that fewer than 57 percent of the films met all three criteria outlined in the test. In addition, approximately one-third of the movies met one or fewer criteria on the list.[32] (The character in Bechdel's cartoon notes that the last movie she was able to see was *Alien*, a film released six years before the cartoon was published.) A year-by-year analysis indicates that films are more frequently passing the test these days than in the past. From 1970 to 1974, fewer than one-fourth of the films studied satisfied all three requirements, while close to two-thirds of the films studied in 2021 passed the test. That said, this still means that more than one-third of the films people are seeing each year are unlikely to have two women in meaningful roles, having a meaningful conversation. It also doesn't account for the overall quality of those films or those roles, with horror films like *Night of the Living Dead* and the latest *Texas Chainsaw Massacre* making the cut. Critics also note that it doesn't account for breadth of representation of race, sexual orientation, or other elements associated with inclusion. However, this simple test has shined a light on a large, complex problem associated with what people see when they go to the movies.

THE NEXT STEP: Pick any of your favorite movies, or even just the most recent movie you watched, and apply the Bechdel test to it. Does it meet all three criteria? If it fails, which of the three requirements is lacking? If it passes, how significant do you think the characters and conversation involved are in regard to the overall premise of the film? Finally, in analyzing this movie, how well do you think it is doing in providing a broader sense of inclusion for those characters who help the film pass the test? Write a short essay on your findings.

HOW MOVIES ARE MADE

LEARNING OBJECTIVES

LO 3: Understand the process through which movies get made today.

The process of moviemaking involves more than what is going on in front of the camera. To be successful in creating any type of film, a filmmaker must use a great deal of planning, engage in smart choices during the filming process, and work diligently in composing the final product from the material available. Here are the four key stages of moviemaking:

- Planning and development
- Filming and production
- Editing and postproduction work
- Distribution

Let's look a bit deeper at what is involved in each stage.

Planning and Development

Like most forms of mass media, movies begin with storytelling. The first step in moviemaking involves deciding what story needs to be told and how best to tell it. This is the core of the development phase, in which the filmmaker conceptualizes the story, determines the length of the project, and organizes the approach they want to take to filming it. In addition, practical matters require consideration, such as how much money is available to make the film and where the film will be shot.

Scriptwriting and Storyboarding

- The basic story idea is developed first as an **elevator pitch** (a brief overview of the film's concept) to sell it to potential investors or producers.
- A fuller **treatment** is then written, including the title, the key characters, and a summary of the story.[33] It can include themes and tone, as well as sections of dialogue to further communicate the underlying premise of the film.
- **Storyboarding** shows how the filmmaker plans to set the scenes and portray the characters.[34] Storyboards use illustrations along with limited text to indicate the technical aspects of the image, such as how that portion of the film will be shot or specific camera movements.

Cast and Crew Selection

- Many of the higher level roles, such as director, producer, and cinematographer, are filled based on previous working relationships among like-minded professionals.
- Actors will often audition for their roles, although some major stars are actively pursued in order to give a film extra appeal.
- The other crew members either pitch their services or receive offers from the studios based on reputation.

Location Scouting

- **Location scouts** assess the viability of a potential filming site. They will review a list of specific shots crucial to the film, and the types of interior and exterior shots that are needed, along with other considerations. For example, a large valley in the country of Jordan has served as a popular film location when an open desert expanse is needed. The area featured prominently in *Dune* (2021) and *Star Wars: The Rise of Skywalker* (2019).
- Scouts often conduct **site survey** or **recce** (short for "reconnaissance"). If a scout finds a particularly promising site, other members of the crew will visit to see how well it meets their needs. If more than one location is under consideration, the crew will discuss each site's pros and cons with the scout to determine the best possible one.
- A location must not only fit the filmmaker's vision of what should be on screen, but it also must meet practical needs for power, lodging, and other basic human needs.

Budget and Financing

- The budget outlines the three stages of most movies' production:
  - Preproduction costs: covers the basics of scripting, storyboarding, location scouting, and talent rehearsals.
  - Production costs: covers location-related expenses, such as actor pay and equipment costs, basic human needs like food and lodging, and costumes and props.
  - Postproduction costs: covers all the editing costs associated with assembling the movie, as well as any music or effects required to bring the film to life.[35]
- Revenue and investment represent the other side of the financial coin in the budgeting process. Based on the overall costs associated with the film, how likely is it that it will break even or earn money? Investors want to know that the film can be made for the budgeted amount and that the revenue will provide them return on their investment. For example, 2021's *F9* worked with an estimated budget of $225 million. Although it was one of the most expensive films in the series, it also brought in more than $721 million in worldwide box-office receipts that year.[36] The next film in the franchise, 2023's *Fast X*, received a budget of more than $340 million.

Legal Concerns

- Due diligence is performed on all parts of the project as part of the preproduction process. This means that all potential legal issues are examined before filming begins, and a plan is made to address them.
- Contractual obligations must be finalized, ranging from making agreements with the film's actors to finalizing insurance policies to cover any unexpected events.
- Permission must be obtained to use the story and script. If an individual wrote the script specifically for this production, there are usually fewer issues as long as the story wasn't

plagiarized or taken from someone else without credit. If a prewritten script is selected for a film, the filmmaker needs to **option** it, which means securing the rights from its author. If all goes well, the film will be moved into production, and the film's production company and the writer will formalize a purchase agreement.

- Site permissions must be obtained. The studio must secure the location for the amount of time needed to shoot the film, work with legal authorities to determine how best to shoot the film within the parameters of local laws, and sign contracts that specify how much it will cost to shoot there.

Filming and Production

Once a film is approved to begin production, the shooting can begin. As much as this seems like the fun part of the process, experts say this can be an extremely stressful time for everyone involved.[37] With deadlines looming, actors and crew work against the clock to complete each shot as best they can, often dealing with unpredictable external forces, such as weather, or internal issues, like personality conflicts among the workers. Safety protocols need to be put into place in terms of stunts, props, and animals. Still, this is when the magic happens, so let's look at some of the aspects of filming a movie.

Principal Photography

Principal photography is when the visual and audio components of the movie are captured under the watchful eye of the writers, camera operators, and director. If the scene is captured to everyone's satisfaction, the production moves on to the next scene. If not, the scene will be reshot until either it is perfected or time runs out for that particular portion of filming.

- The main unit of the cast and crew works on the set each day to bring a director's vision to life.
- Actors often rehearse their lines and actions before a **take**, or a recording of their performance.
- Crew members practice the camera movements and placements, while also assessing the composition of each shot they plan to take.
- Experts on lighting, safety, and other production concerns weigh in on how best to complete the day's given tasks.
- Screenwriters may be asked to put together extra dialogue or rewrite a scene based on specific needs the director discovers during the filming process.
- The assistant directors keep track of what needs to be done in a given day and how much time each portion of filming can take. This job requires them to balance the art of the film with completing the work on time.

Secondary Filming

While the stars of the show film the main action of the movie, a **second unit** is taking care of other portions of the project.

- These crew members are responsible for filming sequences that don't involve the main talent of the film but are crucial in telling the story. These shots include any scenic filming, effects work, and stunts.
- While both the main and second unit collect additional footage to help tell the story, often called b-roll, the second unit is responsible for the majority of this work.
- Second-unit personnel face a specific challenge: to match the tone, feel, and movement of the main unit's vision, without seeing its footage. The second unit must ensure that the quality of the images, the continuity of the setting, and the choices of the main director are all reflected.[38]

Coverage and Sound

In filming a scene, *coverage* refers to how many different "takes" are created that can be used to construct the final sequence. To obtain proper coverage, a videographer needs to take enough footage of a variety of shots for every scene in the film.

Let's say you're watching a scene between Jill and Betty, who are talking over coffee. The scene starts with an establishing shot of both women, sitting at a table.

- As Jill begins talking, the screen now shows just her head and shoulders at first before cutting away to a shot of Betty for a reaction as Jill keeps talking.
- Upon returning to a shot of Jill, the screen now includes her entire body on the screen, allowing you to see her hand nervously stirring her coffee with a spoon.
- A quick cut back to Betty now focuses only on her eyes, staring down, presumably at the coffee cup.
- The next shot is focused on only on Jill's hand and the spoon in the coffee as she continues to speak.

This action takes place in one location and could all be covered by the initial shot without any of these other shots. However, using these additional shots can heighten the emotion of a scene or focus the audience's attention on specific aspects of it. Other ways to provide coverage is to shoot a scene from multiple perspectives, such as solely from Jill's or Betty's point of view. Directors often make decisions as to how shots play a role in the feel of a movie. Edgar Wright is known for his use of various editing techniques to shape a film. For example, in his 2021 film *Last Night in Soho*, he filmed a dance scene of more than a minute and a half in a single shot, with the camera circling the dancers as various actors move in and out of the shot. Conversely, in *Shaun of the Dead* (2004), Wright used one-second shots of a toilet, a toothbrush, a refrigerator, a utensil drawer, and a piece of jelly toast to show the main character's prework routine.

Sound is just as important to this kind of storytelling. A crew filming a movie about the Old West in the mid-1800s doesn't want to capture the sound of a massive airplane flying overhead, for obvious reasons. However, the sound of a train chugging down the tracks or sounding its horn might be just the right thing to add realism and feel to the production.

Other sounds can matter just as much. Returning to the previous scene, the sound of Jill's voice is obviously an important element of the storytelling process. However, other sounds, like the clinking of her spoon against the inside of her coffee cup, could add tension to the moment. The faster the clinks come, the more dramatic it could be, or the louder they become, the more concerned the audience might feel.

Editing and Postproduction Work

Once the film has wrapped up shooting, the filmmaker will begin the process of creating the final version of the film. Depending on how the principal photography panned out, this process can be relatively simple or extremely complex. Other factors also play a role in the completion of the film.[39] Let's dig into a couple of these key areas.

Editing

A common saying in the film community is that a film is made three times: once on paper, once while filming, and once in the editing.

- During the film edit, the filmmaker decides the order of the scenes, based both on the original outline in the script and any changes that occurred during the production process.
- The filmmaker also determines the overall length of the film as well as how it will start and end. This assembly process creates the primary skeletal structure of the entire film.

- The use of more shots that focus on details and create a quicker pace can create one type of atmosphere, while fewer shots that run longer can slow the progression of a movie or create a sense of stability within the film.

Special Effects

The special effects (sometimes "F/X") portion of postproduction helps flesh out the film through visuals and sounds created to improve the finished product.

- The level and importance of effects are determined largely by the movie's genre and the technological skill of the effects department. A love story involving two farmers, set in the early 1900s, will likely need significantly fewer special effects than an outer-space odyssey that includes alien invaders and laser battles.
- Computerization has made the effects process much better and less painstaking compared with earlier days, when filmmakers used plastic monsters and tiny model sets to create alien worlds.
- Stunts involving dangerous activities can be constructed in postproduction instead of filmed live. Additional elements can be added to the background, or certain elements can be removed.

One extreme example of this kind of digital alteration occurred in Zach Snyder's 2021 hit *Army of the Dead*. After filming had wrapped on principal photography, multiple underage girls charged actor Chris D'Elia with predatory sexual behavior. Rather than reshoot the whole film, Snyder had the effects team use digital editing techniques to remove D'Elia's character and replace it with one played by actor Tig Notaro. Although her character often is shown actively involved with the rest of the zombie-killing crew on screen, Notaro filmed most of her work alone against a plain backdrop.[40]

Actor Tig Notaro, third from left, was digitally inserted into multiple scenes of *Army of the Dead* after she replaced actor Chris D'Elia once principal photography had wrapped.

Moviestore Collection Ltd/Alamy Stock Photo

Music and Sound

A movie's auditory component includes everything people hear when they watch it. The primary sound element comes from the actors themselves through dialogue.

- Much of the dialogue is captured on the scene, although actors often have to **dub**, or rerecord, their lines in a studio environment, to make the words clearer to the audience.
- Actors might also be asked to rerecord lines to remove foul language or change the words in a line of dialogue.
- Narration, words spoken over the top of the film by an actor to provide context or information in a particular scene, may also be added.

Musical choices also play a crucial role in how a character is perceived.

- The entrance of Darth Vader in the *Star Wars* franchise is accompanied by John Williams's *Imperial March*, a foreboding and formal composition that elicits fear.
- Volker Bertelmann's score for *All Quiet on the Western Front* won him an Oscar in 2023. Bertelmann used a turn-of-the-century pump organ to create the "breathing" and "crackling" sound of "a war machine."[41]

Distribution

Once the film is ready for viewing, the filmmaker has to get it out to the public. This process, known as **distribution**, has evolved significantly over the past few years and entails more than just getting a film into a movie theater. Most studios and filmmakers contract with outside companies for their high-end films, putting the responsibility of marketing and distribution a film in the hands of professionals. Distributors will determine how many theaters should show the film, how long it should remain in theaters, and how much money to spend in hopes of generating buzz about the movie.[42]

In addition to this traditional path, distribution efforts can bypass the theater process entirely. Streaming services will often purchase the rights to show a movie early or exclusively, such as Netflix's distribution of 2022's *The Adam Project* and HBO Max's putting out *A Christmas Story Christmas*, the sequel to the 1983 classic holiday film, in 2022. During the COVID-19 pandemic, studios like Universal shifted their distribution strategies, releasing new films through streaming services at the same time as they released them in theaters.[43] Additional distribution efforts include where the movie will be available for viewing after the initial release, on what formats the final product will be available, and any ancillary product or rights opportunities.

VIEWER DISCRETION ADVISED: RATINGS AND SOCIAL ACCEPTABILITY

LEARNING OBJECTIVES

LO 4: Explain the history of movie regulation.

As discussed in Chapter 4, censorship often occurs when the ideas of media creators clash with the norms of society. In the case of film censorship, both governmental officials and industry officials struggled to balance commercial considerations with social acceptability. Let's take a look at how the regulation of film developed over time.

Early Censorship Efforts and the Production Code

Shortly after movies became available, some people started complaining about them. Between 1909 and 1922, religious groups across the country called for the censorship of "indecent" films. In an attempt to satisfy these individuals, the movie industry created several review boards, with the goal of policing itself to prevent outside interference and avoid federal censorship laws. In the early 1920s, the studios hired former postmaster general Will Hays to develop several different rules to enforce "decency" in films. However, he lacked the power to enforce these rules until the Great Depression hammered box-office receipts. Hays developed the Production (or Hays) Code, listing a series of things films should not include. The code forbade filmmakers from including in their movies sex, "perversion," profanity, "indecent" dancing, adultery, and more. In line with regulation and moral rectitude, the code also prohibited the display of brutal killings, illegal drug trafficking, and criminal actions that could be replicated.[44]

From 1930 to 1934, the enforcement of the Production Code was selective, at best, given that it had no bite when it came to penalizing violators. However, relentless pressure from all sides eventually forced the industry to make the regulation process mandatory.[45]

The code began to crumble in 1948, when a Supreme Court decision forced the end of the studio system (see Chapter 3), which gave theater owners more freedom to choose what films they wanted to screen. Four years later, in 1952, another Supreme Court case provided movies with the same free-speech protections afforded to other forms of media, further weakening the censors. In *Burstyn v. Wilson*, the court ruled that banning a film because of "sacrilegious" content violated the First Amendment.[46] This decision to give films the same rights as other media helped open the door to filmmakers who wanted to expose people to a wider variety of subjects.

Ratings Take Hold

When Jack Valenti became the president of the Motion Picture Association of America in 1966, he knew he had a problem. The Production Code was no longer enforceable, and yet the public was clamoring for someone to control the content coming out of Hollywood. Films had become more violent and sexually explicit during the late 1960s, and court decisions in the previous decade had all but stripped the industry of the ability to censor content.

Valenti's attempt to satisfy these critics remains in place today. Instead of censoring movies, he developed a rating system to inform the public about what was in them. A ratings board reviews films prior to their release and places each into a category. The original set of ratings contained four categories: general audience (G), mature audiences (M), restricted (R), and adults only (X). In 1970, the M rating became GP before flipping to PG (for "parental guidance") in 1972. In 1984, the industry introduced a midpoint between PG and R, creating the PG-13 rating. The last significant change of the ratings system occurred in 1990, when the X rating gave way to NC-17 (no one seventeen or younger admitted). This switch helped avoid confusion between mature content and the hardcore pornography industry that had adopted the XXX moniker as its own.

The MPAA further sought to assist parents in making decisions regarding a film's appropriateness by including information that accompanies a movie's promotional material, such as posters or newspaper advertisements, prominently highlighting the rating and providing language explaining its

FIGURE 7.2 ■ A Quick Breakdown of a Movie Rating

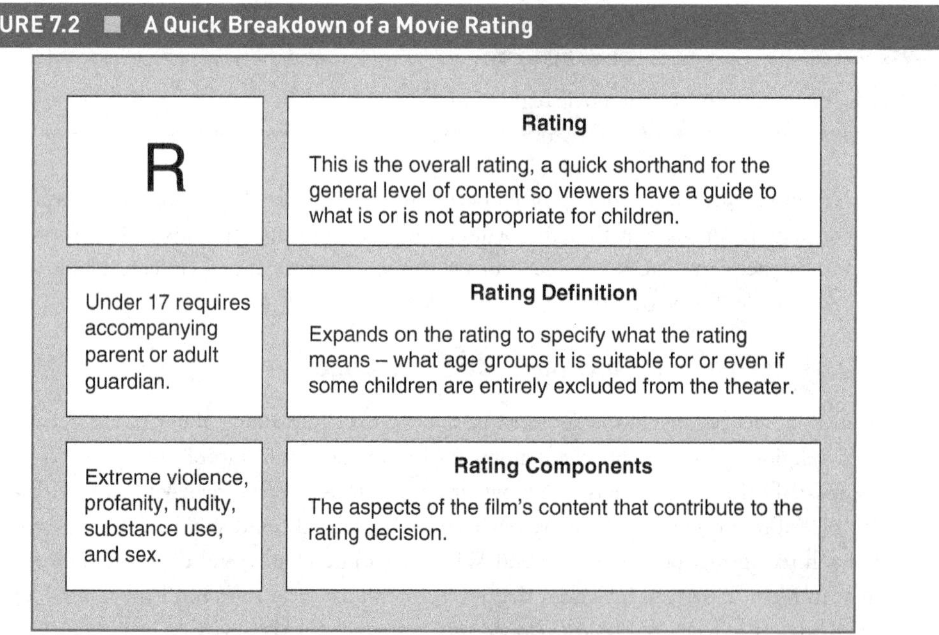

meaning. For example, a PG rating includes the statement "Parental Guidance Suggested. Some material may not be suitable for children." In addition, a box next to the rating contains specific information about what material might not be suitable for children, indicating whether the movie contains violence, disturbing images, sexual innuendo, coarse language, or anything else that led to that particular rating.

JOBS IN MOVIES AND FILM PRODUCTION

Now that you better understand the various aspects of this field, here's a handy overview of a few common positions in movies and film production today.

Career Opportunity	Common Tasks
Director	• Serves as head of the movie during its production • Instructs actors in their roles and performances • Works with cinematographers to compose and capture shots
Assistant director	• Creates and maintains schedules for filming operations for actors, cinematographers, and crew members • Manages equipment needed for daily shoots • Works with the director to oversee the smooth operation of filming activities
Production designer	• Develops the visual elements of the film, including scenes, costumes, and props • Assists in scouting locations for filming the movie • Coordinates with cinematographer on lighting and camera angles
Cinematographer	• Creates and chooses the visuals of the film, including lighting, color palettes, and camerawork • Composes shots and dictates movement to capture the action of the film • Oversees all aspects of the film's production, including preproduction, principal photography, and postproduction
Film editor	• Assembles multiple shots into coherent storytelling scenes of the film • Assists the director and cinematographer in production efforts
Screenwriter	• Composes dialogue for characters in the film • Collaborates with actors and directors to determine character development • Organizes and constructs plot development
Sound engineer	• Oversees the film's audio elements, including dialogue, special effects, and natural sound • Manages equipment on and off set • Mixes audio content from various sources to create a complete auditory experience for filmgoers

CHAPTER REVIEW

LO 1 Identify key moments in the history of movies.

- At the turn of the twentieth century, early inventions allowed people to view moving pictures individually. The films were single-shot actions, like two people kissing or one man sneezing.
- Starting in 1903 with Robert Porter's *The Great Train Robbery*, filmmakers began using multiple shots of film from multiple camera angles and assembled them together to tell a

story. These longer films were more involved and began what is considered the true start of filmmaking.

- In the early 1920s, inventors developed ways to add synchronized sound to silent films. The Vitaphone system became the first successful sound system, with 1927's *The Jazz Singer* being the first feature-length movie to include synchronized dialogue.
- The colorization processes used in early film involved dyes and stains being directly applied to small portions of film. By 1929, the Technicolor process had made it easier to produce vibrant and accurate color on film, marking the start of true color era.
- Movies had long been the realm of theaters, until the late 1970s with the advent of the videocassette recorder or VCR. The industry boomed into the mid-1980s, as people enjoyed taping shows and renting movies from local stores.
- The rise of digital media allowed the distribution of better quality copies of films that could be easily stored. It also spawned improvements, such as the digital video recorder and digital streaming services.

LO 2 **Discuss the role of movies in society.**

- Offer an escape: movies provide people an opportunity to enjoy something that takes them away from their troubles, even for just a short time.
- Create inspiration: movies present inspiring stories that provide people with a sense that they, too, can do more than they thought possible in life.
- Provide social commentary: movies shine a light on topics in society that might otherwise be ignored. Issues of discrimination on the basis of gender, race, and sexual orientation, and other forms of social injustice, can reach a larger audience when placed in the context of a film.

LO 3 **Understand the process through which movies get made today.**

- Planning and development: includes the creation of early drafts of a script, a budget, scouting potential locations for filming, and securing any legal permissions needed to film.
- Filming and production: the principal photography, conducted by the main unit, as well as the filming of stunts, b-roll, and scenic shots by the second unit is completed.
- Editing and postproduction work: the filmmaker assembles the shots captured during principal photography into a story, and special effects and other additional technical processes are finished.
- Distribution: the completed movie is distributed into theaters and onto streaming services, as well as promoted to its potential audience.

LO 4 **Explain the history of movie regulation.**

- Early censorship efforts began almost as soon as movies began to be made. Some cities and states enacted laws that allowed the banning or censoring of films.
- The Production Code, also known as the Hays Code, became a strictly enforced series of requirements on the film industry, starting in 1934. Movies made after this time could be censored, rewritten, and otherwise altered based on the demands of a board of censors.
- Two Supreme Court decisions, one in 1948 and one in 1952, removed the stranglehold the movie industry had on dictating content. Films were afforded the same free-speech protections as any other form of content, making censorship unconstitutional.
- To appease special-interest groups that sought to remove "indecent" content from movies, MPAA President Jack Valenti developed the ratings system for films in 1968, advising viewers of each film's content and its recommended viewing audience. It remains in place today.

KEY TERMS

Bechdel test
Cinématographe
Digital video recorder (DVR)
Distribution
Dub
DVD
Elevator pitch
Kinetograph
Kinetoscope
Location scout
Option
Parallel construction
Principal photography
Recce
Second unit
Site survey
Special effects
Split screen
Storyboarding
Streaming
Take
Talkies
Technicolor
Treatment
Video cassette recorder (VCR)
Vitaphone

DISCUSSION QUESTIONS

1. When it comes to regulating content or censoring films, do you think it should be the job of the film industry or the role of the government to make these kinds of decisions? Why?
2. Of all the roles available in filmmaking, which job would you most prefer to try in that industry? Which one is least appealing to you? Why?
3. How important is a film's rating to you in determining what to watch? Do you consider the rating as part of your selection process?
4. In examining the reasons listed in the chapter that explain why people watch movies, which one best matches with your reasons? Which one doesn't fit you at all? Why?

Streaming services like Netflix have given people access to complete seasons of their favorite television series, as well as new programming that is released only through those outlets. The ability to watch any television program, as often as we want and wherever we feel most comfortable, has changed the way in which we relate to our shows.

iStockphoto.com/Nicolas Maderna

8 TELEVISION

INTRODUCTION

1. *What types of television shows do you like to watch? What makes them worthy of your time?*
2. *Do you prefer to watch television on any particular device, or do you watch it on whatever screen is available when you feel like watching a show? Does the screen you choose to use affect your overall enjoyment of the programs?*
3. *How do you prefer to watch television shows: an episode at a time or full seasons at once? What makes you like your approach to consuming content in this way?*

Television combines features of many other forms of media. Like movies, it provides people with entertainment; like newspapers and magazines, it gives viewers important, newsworthy information; and like the internet and social media, it's got an immediacy to it, with content reaching audiences quickly. Many of the same issues that we discuss in terms of these other media will be relevant to our discussion of television and its impact.

What started as an experimental movement to add pictures to radio-style broadcasting has evolved into the constant companion and emotional weather vane for generations of people. The degree to which its constant presence in our lives is beneficial or detrimental varies based on who is examining the medium, what messages are the focal point of the study, and how much time study participants spend with the device.

This chapter will look into all of these issues, as well as to ways in which television has changed over time because of audience interests and technological breakthroughs.

LEARNING OBJECTIVES

1. Identify key moments in the history of television.
2. Understand the needs that television programming satisfies for its viewers.
3. Examine the importance of broadcast journalism.
4. Discuss the way in which technology has shifted television consumption habits.
5. Assess the criticisms levied against television programming over the years.

A BRIEF HISTORY OF TELEVISION

LEARNING OBJECTIVES

LO 1: Identify key moments in the history of television.)

Technology has long driven the ways in which broadcasting has served the public, as well as the range, reach, and clarity of the medium itself. The advancements, or in some cases limitations, involved with these technologies provided communicators with options and opportunities to try various things. Here are a few key advances in the field that brought us the television system we know today:

- Early mechanical efforts
- The beginning of over-the-air broadcasting
- The 1950s TV boom
- Satellite options emerge

- Cable becomes universally available
- Cord-cutting and internet TV develop

Let's take a look at how these delivery systems have evolved.

Early Mechanical Efforts

Even before radios emerged as a viable broadcast medium, inventors were looking for ways to transmit images from point A to point B. German engineer Paul Nipkow was an early pioneer who used mechanical devices and electric signals to convert images into electrical signals that could be sent over wire. However, this and many other mechanical approaches failed because of the limitations of early scanning equipment and the poor quality of the images they produced.

The Beginning of Over-the-Air Broadcasting

In 1927, Philo T. Farnsworth began developing a new all-electronic method of scanning images for broadcast with the creation of the **image dissector**. It allowed far better image quality through continually scanning of an image. Around the same time, Vladimir Zworykin pitched Farnsworth's concept to broadcasting pioneer David Sarnoff, who headed RCA. At the 1939 New York World's Fair, the public saw its first large-scale example of a televised broadcast, providing them a glimpse into the future.[1]

RCA launched the National Broadcasting Company (NBC) around that time and soon began selling television sets that could receive black and white images. Although slowed by the U.S. entry into World War II and patent suits over the new technology, RCA continued to play a large role in the television market.

Patrons at the 1939 World's Fair get a first glimpse at broadcast television. The opening ceremony was broadcast via NBC, as were other bits of content that drew the public to the RCA Pavilion.

Everett Collection Historical/Alamy Stock Photo

The 1950s TV Boom

Postwar America was characterized by the baby boom, as returning service members looked to set down roots and build lives for themselves. The growth of the American family and American prosperity was paralleled by the popularity of television. At the end of the war, in 1945, fewer than ten television stations existed, broadcasting to about seven thousand working sets. By 1950, five million sets were in American homes, with hundreds of stations operating associated with three major national networks: the Columbia Broadcasting System (CBS), the American Broadcasting Company (ABC), and NBC.

Programming reflected a wide array of interests. Many of the familiar radio programs, like *The Lone Ranger* and *Dragnet*, became part of the regular TV lineup in the 1950s. Shows specifically created for the new medium, like *I Love Lucy* and *The Honeymooners*, also delighted fans, who saw the physical aspects of comedy pairing wonderfully with amusing dialogue. Quiz shows became popular, as *I've Got a Secret* and *Beat the Clock* had fans cheering on favored champions. (That is, until the quiz show scandals of the late 1950s, when viewers discovered that shows like *Twenty-One* and *Dotto* had been rigged to favor certain players and eliminate others.)

High-quality programming graced the screen with shows like the *Kraft Television Theatre* and the *Philco Television Playhouse*, which delivered dramatic performances and musicals in primetime. Variety shows became popular, with Milton Berle, Jack Benny, and Ed Sullivan presenting a wide array of talented singers, dancers, and other performers. With three networks actively competing for the attention of a burgeoning audience, the 1950s were an exceptional time for television viewers.

Satellite Options Emerge

In 1962, AT&T paid NASA three million dollars to launch Telstar, a beach ball–sized object, into space to transmit signals across the entire world. While it worked for only about three hours a day, the concept of **satellite television** was born. Telstar allowed television broadcasts to reach overseas in a way that had not been previously possible. People throughout Europe tuned in on July 23, 1962, to see a live image of the Statue of Liberty, a few batters from a Cubs-Phillies game, an announcement from Walter Cronkite, and part of President John F. Kennedy's press conference.[2]

Although scientists and engineers from the United States, Canada, and the Soviet Union developed and tested various projects over the following decade, it wasn't until the mid-1970s that the satellite television industry demonstrated its potential. The system as we know it today, with subscribers owning or renting individual dishes for home use, got its start in 1979, when the Federal Communications Commission (FCC) allowed regular citizens to own a satellite dish without federal approval. The original dishes were large and expensive, ranging in diameter from ten to fifteen feet and costing anywhere from five thousand to thirty-five thousand dollars each. Coupled with weaker signals and lower quality than cable, satellite TV reached only a small slice of the TV-viewing audience through the 1980s.

As is the case with most technology, rapid improvements coupled with a sharp decrease in price made satellite TV a viable option for people to receive content. In the early 1990s, providers found a way to use medium-powered satellites to improve signal strength and thus decrease the sizes of the dishes. In 1991, four cable companies worked together to create PrimeStar, the first service to take advantage of this direct broadcast satellite approach. The service didn't last to the end of the decade, but it did serve as a precursor to DirecTV and Dish Network, which launched in 1994 and 1996, respectively. As of 2023, these two titans of satellite TV have nearly 21 million subscribers combined in the United States and are actively considering a merger.[3]

Cable Becomes Universally Available

In 1948, areas of Arkansas, Oregon, and Pennsylvania began installing cables that could run from a community antenna to homes that would otherwise be cut off from broadcast by mountains or distance. With this technology, known as **community antenna television** (CATV), cable companies could provide a broader array of programming unavailable to over-the-air television stations, creating an opportunity to distinguish themselves as unique content providers. This led to an expansion of cable operations in the 1950s and early 1960s, as more than 850,000 subscribers joined hundreds of providers.[4]

Out of fear that they would be overtaken by the competition, broadcast industry lobbyists convinced the FCC to restrict cable company's ability to provide certain services and programming for their viewers. While the government initially sided with the broadcasters, it eventually relaxed its restrictions in the mid-1970s. While earlier cable efforts were focused on providing local programming from distant stations, the 1970s saw the development of niche programming channels specifically for cable systems. Home Box Office (HBO) and Turner Broadcasting System (TBS) were early successful

TABLE 8.1 ■ A Few Key Names in Television

Vladimir Zworykin	Philo T. Farnsworth	Lucille Ball	Robert L. Johnson	Oprah Winfrey
• A Russian-American engineer who pioneered many of the early technologies that made television a practical form of mass media. • Beginning in 1930, he worked at David Sarnoff's RCA laboratories, where he developed first practical television camera tube.	• In 1927, this American inventor created the first practical completely electronic television system. • His work included the development of a fully functional video camera tube and a device that allowed images to be transmitted electronically.	• Known primarily as an actress, her efforts in multiple areas of the television business broke down many barriers for women. • Her decision to have *I Love Lucy* shot on film in front of a live audience helped create the first era of rerun and syndicated TV programming • In 1960, she took full control of Desilu Productions, making her the first woman to own a major TV studio.	• Saw the potential in niche marketing and cable TV when he launched Black Entertainment Television or BET in 1980. • Served as the head of BET when it became the first black-controlled company listed on the New York Stock Exchange in 1991. • Became the first African American billionaire in 2001.	• Oversaw *The Oprah Winfrey Show*, which revolutionized daytime talk shows and became TV's most popular nationally syndicated program from 1986 to 2011. • Serves as the chairwoman and CEO of Harpo Productions a multimedia operation that includes film, print, television, and radio divisions. • In 2003, she became the first female African American billionaire.

cable-only channels. Ted Turner, owner of TBS, launched another station pivotal to television and broadcast journalism in 1980: Cable News Network, or CNN.

The 1980s and 1990s saw exponential growth in terms of programming and access via cable. Congress continued its effort to deregulate the industry, which allowed additional players to get into the game. The number of channels grew from about 30 in 1980 to more than 170 in 1998, drawing more than sixty-five million subscribers before the turn of the millennium.[5]

Cord-Cutting and Internet TV Develop

In the earliest days of the internet, computers needed to hop on "the information superhighway," as it was called, through a telephone-based modem, leading to slow download speeds and limited applications for this platform. The cable industry was once again at the center of television innovation, although probably not in the way it had planned. The coaxial cables these companies used to pump television programs and movies into people's homes were equally adept at providing internet services that dwarfed the speeds telephone modems could provide. Suddenly, broadband internet gave quick access to online content, allowing people to upload and download audio and video content easily.

Consequently, users sought ways to bypass the bulky cable packages that usually charged high rates and were loaded with channels they infrequently watched. Much in the same way that the web allowed public relations practitioners and advertisers to bypass newspapers to get their message out to their audiences, streaming services and television networks saw the internet as an opportunity to bypass cable providers. In a twist of fate, high-speed internet accessed enabled people to "cut the cord" and unsubscribe from cable's television packages.

Improvements to mobile phones and the quality of the services they provided also helped democratize access to content. Websites like YouTube, which had provided video clips of all types to viewers, could now go mobile via apps. As the phone became the ubiquitous device to access the web for most Americans, other outlets began providing streaming video clips, breaking news, and other programming as it became available. High-speed mobile service allowed streaming content to be shown on handheld devices almost anywhere. Television had not only become liberated from the living room; it had been sent outside to play.

A number of key moments in television showcased its importance as a medium, created opportunities for social change, and made it part of everyday life for generations to come. Here are a few of those moments and why they mattered:

TABLE 8.2 ■ Several Important "Firsts" on Television

Year	Event	What Happened	Why It Mattered
1951	First scripted TV show shot on film in front of a live audience	*I Love Lucy* was filmed to capture the antics of stars Lucille Ball and Desi Arnaz.	• Film improved viewing quality. • Shows could be preserved for future reruns and syndication, a new concept at the time. • Early hits like *I Love Lucy* are still broadcast today thanks to this innovation.
1960	First televised presidential debate	Vice President Richard Nixon squared off against Senator John F. Kennedy on live TV, giving people their first opportunity to see the candidates speak to the nation.	• Set the stage for all future presidential elections. • Its impact was clear, based on data collected after the event: People who heard the debate on the radio generally thought that Nixon won, but those who watched it on TV believed that Kennedy won
1965–1974	First war coverage broadcast live	The Vietnam War was known as the "first TV war," in that all major networks were presenting daily coverage of battlefield actions for people back home to see.	• Previous war coverage was through print or radio, with heavy influence from the government. • When broadcasters presented the disturbing video from the war-torn country, American sentiment about the war became much more negative, leading to the eventual withdrawal of American troops.
1969	First Emmy nomination for an African American woman	*Julia*, which ran from 1968 to 1971, featured Diahann Carroll in the title role as a widowed mother and nurse.	• Carroll is viewed as a trailblazer in television, although some criticized the show for being not representative of Black America. • Other programs followed that demonstrated the interest in and viability of programming with women and strong Black actors in leading roles.
1972	First recurring gay character on a television show	*The Corner Bar*, a short-lived sitcom, included Peter Panama, an openly gay set designer, among its recurring cast members.	• Although Vincent Schiavelli's flamboyant portrayal of a gay man would be problematic today, no recurring character on a network show had previously been openly identified as being a member of the LGBTQ+ community. • In making his sexuality clear, the producers opened a door through which other shows would eventually follow.
1973	First "reality TV" show airs	*An American Family* provided viewers with a look at the Loud family of Santa Barbara, California, in a completely unscripted environment.	• The twelve-episode series was a forebear of what the late 1980s and early 1990s would bring with Fox's *Cops*, MTV's *The Real World*, CBS's *Survivor*, and other unscripted programming. • Reality TV's low production cost and high popularity have led to enormous profit margins for the networks.

Year	Event	What Happened	Why It Mattered
1995	First internet television show debuts	Bart Everson and Joe Nickell placed an episode titled "Global Village Idiots" of their Indiana-based public-access cable show, *Rox*, online in April.	● Predating YouTube by more than a decade, the episode sparked an interest in viewing programs via the web. ● Critics hailed their work as demonstrating the significant effect digital media could have on distributing video content.
1997	First use of content ratings on TV	Starting on January 1, television networks adopted a series of codes and labels for shows to indicate the acceptability of the programs for various age groups.	● As with the movie industry, television networks felt the pressure from groups that wanted to keep certain content away from children. ● The networks agreed to include ratings that would indicate both how age appropriate a show was as well as what potentially problematic content might be contained in a program.

THE MANY BENEFITS OF ENTERTAINMENT TELEVISION

LEARNING OBJECTIVES

LO 2: Understand the needs that television programming satisfies for its viewers.

Television programming aims to satisfy a wide range of its audience's cognitive and emotional needs. People turn to television for entertainment and information, but beyond those broad terms, several key things tend to drive our specific interests in what we view and when we view it. In addition, many of the key things that movies provide, like escape and inspiration, are also relevant here (see Chapter 7).

However, television also provides some specific benefits to viewers because of its constant presence in our lives. In looking simply at the scripted and unscripted, non-news programs available to people, here are a few key needs that people satisfy through watching TV:

- Mood management
- Social comparison
- Socialization and companionship

Let's take a deeper look at each one of these elements.

Mood Management

Television has the ability to present many options for people who are seeking to enhance or change how they are feeling, a concept known as **mood management**. A study in the *Journal of Consumer Research*, for example, revealed that people who repeatedly watched their favorite shows reported feeling more content with their lives and their emotional status.[6] Television gives us the ability to feel happier when we feel sad, to feel better about ourselves when we are experiencing lack of self-worth, and to have a good cry when our emotions feel bottled up inside.

Scholars Dolf Zillmann and Jennings Bryant researched this concept as part of their mood management theory, which states that people often select specific forms of entertainment to improve their overall emotional state of being.[7] Their earliest research demonstrated that people used exciting or relaxing television programs to overcome boredom or stress. Additional research showed that people might not even realize that they are actively seeking these mood shifts, but rather turn to pleasurable activities as opposed to remaining in a state of anxiety or discomfort. In short, people want to feel on an even keel when their emotions make them feel uncomfortable. Television programming has so many choices and is such an ever present force in our lives that we turn to certain familiar favorites to shift us away from emotional imbalance and back toward a state of pleasant normalcy.

Social Comparison

As the mid-1950s, research showed that people have a need to evaluate who they are and how they are doing in life. The primary way we do this is through **social comparison**, or comparing our own situations with those of others to see if we have nicer things, better friends, or more fulfilling lives. In this age of mediated content, people tend to focus less on their next-door neighbors and more on people they see on the screen. This kind of self-analysis can take the form of two very different forms of assessment: aspirational viewing and downward social comparison.

Aspirational viewing includes the many shows that focus on society's highest achievers. Shows like *Lifestyles of the Rich and Famous* and *Keeping up with the Kardashians* profile how these people live, providing a glimpse of material goods and social status that is far beyond the most viewers' reach. The audience gets a sense of what they could have or what would be nice to own if they were able to improve their lot in life. Other forms of aspirational viewing could include shows that accentuate intelligence, like quiz shows, or faith, like religious programming. In every case, the aspiration comes from the idea of wanting to measure up to the people on the screen.

Conversely, one of the strongest criticisms levied against reality television is that it is a voyeuristic opportunity for viewers to mock people to whom they feel superior. Whether they showcase a group of people who can't fix a car or a collection of meat-neck guys competing for the attention of one woman, shows like this allow people to engage in **downward social comparison**. This form of comparative analysis allows the viewer to take joy in the misfortunes of others, with the goal of bolstering the viewer's self-esteem. In short, you turn on the show because you feel that your life isn't going as well as you would like, but by the end of the program, you realize that at least you aren't as dumb, lazy, weird, or otherwise in as bad a situation as the people you just saw on TV.

Oprah Winfrey.

ZUMA Press, Inc./Alamy Stock Photo

Socialization and Companionship

Humans have an inherent need to connect with one another in meaningful ways. Television fulfills this need, either through gatherings where television watching is a part of the event, like Super Bowl or Oscar "watch parties," or through discussions of shared viewing experiences. In many cases, scholars have found that people will watch specific television programs because their friends or family members are watching them, with the goal of "having something to talk about" when they next meet.

People also seek companionship through watching programs. Daytime talk shows like *The Oprah Winfrey Show* gave people a sense of connection between the host and themselves, because Winfrey often shared personal details of her life with the audience. Her efforts to make viewers part of her life helped her build her brand through other endeavors, including cable networks and book clubs.

Individuals can also become heavily invested in fictional television characters and plots that have them seriously concerned for the outcomes of the shows. For example, in 2021, fans of the *Sex and the City* reboot, *And Just Like That*, were crushed when Carrie Bradshaw's long-time love interest, Mr. Big, died while riding his Peloton bike. The character had a series of heart ailments across both versions of the show, but killing him off just after the couple settled down appeared cruel to many viewers.[8] These kinds of relationships between viewers and programs can provide emotional bonds that are difficult for viewers to break, even as the actors move on to other projects.

THE ROLE OF BROADCAST JOURNALISM

LEARNING OBJECTIVES

LO 3: Examine the importance of broadcast journalism.

Broadcast journalists are expected to inform the citizenry of important happenings within their community and throughout the world. Each day, broadcasters offer multiple newscasts to cover everything from day-to-day governmental actions to chaotic events, such as crime, fire, and protests.

Broadcast journalism also has a wider role in providing content to the audiences it serves. Here are a few of the roles that broadcast journalism fulfills better than its print-based competitors:

- Alert the public
- Bring events to people
- Create local connections within a community
- Open the "window to the world" for people

Let's take a deeper look at each of these functions.

Alert the Public

As noted in Chapter 6, alerting the public to important information is a crucial aspect of broadcast journalism. Much of what was written in that part of the book applies here, including the innate desire to be aware of one's surroundings, the issue of "FOMO," and the ability for broadcasters to "interrupt this broadcast" with breaking news. That said, television broadcasters have the opportunity to more completely connect audience members with important, ongoing news items.

Television journalists remain vital in alerting the public to important local and national events. Television broadcasts provide up-to-the-minute coverage of major national elections as well as important local events, like nearby violent weather or emergency road closures.

For example, when a New York grand jury indicted former president Donald Trump on charges of fraud, connected with allegations that he paid an adult film star hush money, Trump was required to formally answer the charges in court. In April 2023, he traveled from his home in Florida to a New York courthouse, where he answered the charges, and television journalists documented each step of the journey as it happened. Although they were not allowed into the courtroom, they continued broadcasting by using the still images shot inside the building as well as those drawn by sketch artists to fill the space between Trump's arrival and departure, which they also covered. The broadcast stretched throughout the day, allowing anyone who turned on their TV to know not only what had happened, but what events were continuing to unfold.

MEDIA LITERACY MOMENT: THE ROPER QUESTION: EVALUATING INFORMATION

Starting back in 1959, the Roper Research Organization began assessing Americans' preferences when it came to media. The organization asked people to identify where they learned the most about what was happening in the world around them to see if radio, TV, newspapers, or magazines made the biggest impact. In addition, Roper asked people to consider a scenario in which they received conflicting reports from multiple media outlets on a topic of importance. If that happened, which one would they most likely believe? This eventually became known as the **Roper question** and served to create a kind of pecking order for the credibility of media outlets.

Television was rated as the most trusted source in that initial poll, with 51 percent of the respondents stating it was most trustworthy, even though it wasn't their primary source of information. By 1963, TV took over the top spot for information gathering and continued to dominate both that answer and the one related to trustworthiness for more than thirty years. The primary reason people gave for using and trusting TV news was simple: seeing is believing.

Today, people have trouble trusting not only television news but the media in general. As we noted earlier in the book, studies have shown the media's credibility to be at an all-time low, with many people saying they don't believe a lot of what media organizations present as fact.

Much of the reason for these issues comes down to the ability people now have to manipulate not just information but visuals as well. Propagandist programs that mimic the format of traditional news programs can shape the public's view on a wide array of issues. Experts in computer technology can create **deepfakes**, video and audio content that appears to be real but is created for the purpose of deceiving the public. In other words, simply seeing something these days doesn't necessarily mean you should believe it.

People who can manipulate you will likely take advantage of deepfakes if they lack a solid ethical code and they can benefit from this deception. A crucial way to prevent yourself from being faked out is to consider the source of the content, whether it is supported by information from outside sources, and your own level of media savvy. We will discuss ways to keep yourself rooted in facts and avoid fictions when we get to social media in Chapter 10.

THE NEXT STEP: Consider the sources of information you rely on in the media to inform you about important, fact-based issues. Which ones are primarily text-based media, like newspapers and Twitter posts, and which ones are more visually based, like television content, video clips, and Instagram posts? To what degree does the visual aspect play a role in what you tend to believe most? Does the source of the material give you the most confidence in it, or does "seeing is believing" matter more to you? Write a short essay on your experiences.

Bring Events to People

It can be one thing to read a newspaper reporter's interpretation of what happened at a baseball game, but it is another to see it unfold in front of you. Still images of a protest-turned-riot can bring slivers of the event to the readers, but a video report on the incident can put people in the middle of the chaos.

Broadcast journalism has the ability to bring the daily happenings of society directly to an audience anywhere those viewers can access the content. These shared cultural moments can create a sense of connection within a society. This occurs whether it is a cluster of citizens crowded around the window of a TV store to watch President John F. Kennedy's funeral in 1963 or a group of people gathering around an iPhone in 2022 to see the congressional hearings on the January 6 attack on the Capitol. The ability to connect people to events matters a great deal to those who can't experience these moments in person.

Broadcast news operations rely on video and audio to communicate effectively to their content to their audiences. While a print story can provide readers with a quotation from a source, broadcasters can use **sound bites** or **actualities**, which consist of video and audio clips from an interview with a person. Broadcast stories are written for the ear, meaning that they need to be constructed in a way that allows them to be easily heard. To do this well, and to vary their approach to the news, broadcast journalists use various story formats to tell their stories (see Table 8.3).

Create Local Connections within a Community

As noted in Chapter 6, broadcasters can become part of people's lives when they ply their trade on the airwaves. The anchors can become trusted sources of information, as viewers feel strongly connected to them over the years. Reporters who appear on air, broadcasting from the viewers' favorite grocery stores or city government buildings, can demonstrate a sense that they care about the same things the viewers do.

When local news operations conduct investigative reports or dig into malfeasance that viewers bring to their attention, viewers often feel that the journalists have their best interests in mind. The visuals of journalists confronting shady business owners or questioning ethically suspect politicians demonstrate the journalists' sense of responsibility to things that matter to the viewers. This kind of work further bonds the viewers and the reporters in a sense of shared values and community responsibility.

TABLE 8.3 ■ Forms of Broadcast Journalism Stories

Type of Story	Length and Elements	How It Works
Reader	• Ten to fifteen seconds • Anchor's voice only	The anchor of the newscast literally reads the story from start to finish, with no assistance from audio or video clips.
Voice-over (VO)	• Twenty-five to thirty-five seconds • Anchor's voice • Video	Video related to a story runs while an anchor reads the story over the top of the footage.
Voice-over/sound on tape (VO/SOT)	• Forty to fifty seconds • Anchor's voice • Video • Video and audio clip from an interview	As in the VO, the anchor's voice speaks over the top of video footage. Included in this format are a video and an audio clip taken from an interview with a source. This is often called a sound bite or an actuality.
Package	• Ninety seconds to two minutes • Reporter's voice • Video • Multiple video and audio clips from interviews	Completed in advance and placed into the newscast on the whole, this story is written and edited by a reporter, who includes their own voicing of a script, basic video to pair with the script, and several sound bites.

Open the "Window to the World" for People

In its golden days, television was called "the window to the world," referring to the way it could show people far away events and locations. Television could bring things happening in other cities, states, countries, and continents into the homes of people in ways that nothing could before. News programs and educational television offered insights into different cultures, events, and concepts beyond what viewers could experience firsthand.

Today, broadcast journalism continues to serve as a window to the world for people everywhere. According to the Nielsen ratings, in 2018, 29 million Americans watched the royal wedding of Prince Harry and Meghan Markle, with another 24 million watching in the United Kingdom.[9] Almost four decades earlier, 750 million people gathered around television sets throughout the world to see the prince's parents wed, when Prince Charles married Lady Diana Spencer in 1981.[10] In each case, television provided people a glimpse of something viewers never would have otherwise seen.

In terms of news, television shows people things beyond their own experiences. Journalists brought the Watts riots home to viewers in 1965 while also showing them daily battle footage from the Vietnam War throughout the latter part of the decade. In the 1990s, people gathered around television sets to find out if a jury would convict or acquit former football star O. J. Simpson of murdering his ex-wife and a friend. Even today, reporters and videographers risk life and limb to cover protests, like those sparked in the wake of the deaths of Eric Garner, George Floyd, and Amir Locke, to name a few.

Despite many journalists' efforts to provide fair, balanced, and accurate content to their audiences, the United States has seen a growing level of resentment toward them and their work. One of the more recent trends in calling the media's work into question is the phenomenon of "fake news," a term used to cast doubt onto content people dislike, regardless of its accuracy.

A DEEPER LOOK: BLAMING "THE MEDIA"

Although a broader array of media channels now exist, complaints against "the media" for coverage people find unfavorable these days are nothing new. At the turn of the century, investigative journalist Ida Tarbell wrote a series of articles about Standard Oil's monopolistic practices and the iron fist of its owner, John D. Rockefeller. President Theodore Roosevelt referred to Tarbell as a "muckraker," or a person who slung mud at a prominent figure. In the 1960s and 1970s, President Richard Nixon crafted an "enemies list" that included his political and media adversaries. In one famous moment, Daniel Schorr of CBS read a copy of the list live on air, stopping suddenly upon seeing his own name included as "a real media enemy."

Two crucial things are important to understand as they relate to journalistic coverage, particularly regarding broadcast news. First, there is no such thing as "the media" in the sense that critics use the term to attack reporting that they don't like. As *Washington Post* columnist Paul Farhi wrote, "Lumping these disparate entities under the same single bland label is like describing the denizens of the ocean as 'the fish.' It's true, but effectively meaningless."[11] Differences exist among media outlets, among shows on those outlets, and even among journalists on those shows.

Second, in attacking news journalists for unfavorable coverage, people in power are attempting to shift attention away from their shady actions. Disliking a story is not the same as its being wrong. In reviewing the stories Rockefeller, Roosevelt, Nixon, and others denounced, it is important to understand that history itself bore out the truth of those pieces. In Nixon's case, the stories he most directly assailed tied him to a "dirty tricks" campaign that led to his political downfall.

When considering the validity of a story, the source of that content matters significantly, so it is important to differentiate among the outlets, journalists, and platforms to better understand to what degree you should trust that source. At the very least, you should do your best to avoid labeling all forms of information as nothing more than "the media."

HOW TV HAS ADAPTED TO TECHNOLOGICAL ADVANCES

LEARNING OBJECTIVES

LO 4: Discuss the way in which technology has shifted television consumption habits.

Television originally gave people a sense of connectedness because of how the device itself functioned and how broadcasting worked. Early TVs were large pieces of furniture that sat in a single room of a home. Most homes had only one TV, which meant that family members would gather to view one show at a time. The programs ran only once at a specific time of the day and on a specific day of the week, which meant that if people wanted to see a show, they had to be in the room with the TV at that time. This was often called the **campfire TV model**, whereby people would gather around the TV whenever it was time to be entertained, much like campers would gather around a single campfire for warmth and camaraderie.

However, as is the case with most of the forms of mass media discussed in this book, technological advances altered this model significantly over the years, forcing broadcasters to adapt their approach to communicating with their audiences. From the rise of nonbroadcast options to the presence of multiple viewing devices in a single home, television has dealt with a wide array of challenges over the years. Here are a few things that have made waves in the industry over the years:

- Time-shifting
- Binge watching
- Subscription-based TV
- Niche content

Let's take a look at each of these issues in depth.

Time-Shifting

In the early days, television shows were performed and broadcast live, giving viewers one chance to see the content. The only true recordings or replays of the events took place when a live show was captured with a kinescope and then shipped to a market unable to view the live feed over the airwaves. Even in that situation, people had to be in front of the TV at a specific point in time if they wanted to watch *Bonanza* or *The Jackie Gleason Show*. If they weren't, they had to rely on other people to tell them what happened, as their one opportunity was gone.

When **video cassette recorders** (VCRs), which are discussed in depth in Chapter 7, became publicly available and reasonably affordable, people could not only rent movies and watch them at home but also record programs from their television sets and watch them whenever they liked. This was the first instance of **time-shifting**, or taking something presented at one point in time and consuming it at a different time.

Time-shifting gave people the ability to free themselves from the time demands television placed on them. It also allowed them to skip ahead past annoying commercials or rewind parts of a show they really liked. While the VCR was the first time-shifting device, it wasn't the last, as digital video recorders (DVRs) and on-demand programming became part of standard cable and satellite packages. These features gave people the ability to pick and choose when and how they watched shows. They could pause content for a quick bathroom break or stop watching altogether if they were tired and wanted to go to bed, all without missing any of the program they were watching.

Binge Watching

Television shows in the over-the-air broadcast era were doled out to viewers one at a time over an entire viewing season. This allowed people to develop specific viewing habits over time and become more involved in specific shows. The approach also allowed TV producers to build drama and excitement over the season, leaving viewers wanting more. The earliest instance of this was in the 1960s TV drama *The Fugitive*, which spent four seasons showing Dr. Richard Kimble running from authorities while trying to figure out who murdered his wife. As the show was poised to go off the air in 1967, the producers decided to finally let Kimble stop running and solved the mystery. Its two-part finale became the most watched show in TV history at that time and established a model for the cliffhanger approach to television.[12]

In this age of instant gratification and on-demand media, people have become increasingly impatient and tend to dislike being strung along for weeks or months, or even years. Services like Netflix began offering full seasons of popular shows that could be watched all at once. The instant availability of complete series gave rise to the concept of **binge watching**, in which people would watch multiple episodes or even a complete series all in one sitting.

Bridgerton, an original series aired on Netflix, offers viewers the opportunity to binge-watch the show, because all episodes of a single season are released at once.

LDNPix/Alamy Stock Photo

Binge watching in some form was always available to people, in that some cable channels would air marathons of old shows that allowed people to park in front of their TVs for hours on end. In addition, some shows were repackaged and released on VCR tapes or DVDs, so people could watch episode after episode at one time. The change came, however, when Netflix released the entire first season of *House of Cards* in February 2013. The story of political ambitions and ruthless betrayal in Washington, D.C., offered viewers both a compelling drama and the ability to watch an entire season of a first-run show in one sitting if they so desired. Additional series followed this model, including Netflix's *Bridgerton* and *Inventing Anna*, both of which were released in 2022.

This shift in approach made television producers reconsider how to package a show's episodes. In addition, this created a new model for scriptwriters, the people who are responsible for laying out storylines within an episode and writing dialogue for actors. Instead of taking a serialized approach, in which storylines develop and resolve in a single episode, conflicts can be stretched across as many episodes as the scriptwriter wants. The cliffhanger, once the staple of great dramas, became less important, as did the "previously on" approach to priming the audience's memory. One scriptwriter noted that building a bingeable series is like "breaking a 10-hour movie" into chunks.[13]

Subscription-Based TV

As was the case with radio, the portion of the electromagnetic spectrum upon which television signals were broadcast was limited. This meant that only so many broadcasters in a given area could provide content to viewers at home. Networks became the dominant players in the field, determining what people would see on the few available channels (see Chapter 6). Up until the 1980s, most televisions received three primary network feeds (ABC, CBS, NBC), a public television option (PBS), and maybe a few small, local channels operating on the lower-quality ultra-high-frequency (UHF) band.

Satellite and cable companies broke through these barriers that the networks had established, offering a wider variety of programming. The **subscription-based TV** model allowed people to receive content through cable outlets or via satellite dishes in their yards or on their roofs in exchange for a monthly fee. Over-the-air television was free, so these outlets knew they had to provide superior content and a lot more of it if they wanted people to spend money on their services.

The model also gave advertisers additional options for promoting their products. The additional channels increased competition and helped drive down pricing for ad placements. Advertisers could select specific channels and place more advertisements throughout the day for the same amount of money it would cost to place one ad on a traditional broadcast network during a single show.

Niche Content

One of the most popular forms of television in the 1950s golden age was the variety show, a form of television that had a little bit of everything in it to appeal to a wide array of interests. The idea was that if everyone in a house was watching one show on one TV, it made sense to give parents, grandparents, and even kids something to keep them entertained. These shows were popular not only with viewers but also with advertisers, because they could reach across wide swaths of demographic and psychographic interests with an ad on one program.

When families started owning multiple TV sets and subscription-based television began to take hold, the need to create one-size-fits-all television began to fade. With exponentially more channels available, programmers could provide **niche content** that appealed only to smaller groups of people. For example, in 1980, entrepreneur Robert L. Johnson started Black Entertainment Television, or BET, to provide programming intended to appeal to African Americans. Around that time, Entertainment and Sports Programming Network, or ESPN, also was added to people's cable and satellite packages, boasting that it would provide sports content 24/7, 365 days per year. Other networks, like CNN, promised nothing but news, while MTV offered 24 hours per day of music videos.

The proliferation of channel options and their niche-based content not only forced networks to rethink their programming, but it gave advertisers more options to target specific audiences that would be most interested in their content. The Columbia Record and Tape Club could pitch audiences a wide array of albums through ads on MTV, while *Sports Illustrated* could recruit magazine subscribers on ESPN. This targeted approach helped improve the effectiveness of the advertising and gave rise to programs that were successfully reaching larger, desirable niche audiences.

IS TELEVISION A "VAST WASTELAND"?

LEARNING OBJECTIVES

LO 5: Assess the criticisms levied against television programming over the years.

Adults of a certain generation will remember their parents admonishing them for watching too much TV, noting, "That stupid television will rot your brain." Interestingly enough, research has proven that watching too much television does, in fact, shrink the frontal cortex and entorhinal cortex of the brain.[14] It has also demonstrated that too much viewing can damage the quality of your remaining brain's health.[15] And that's not even accounting for the quality of the programming on the screen.

As noted in Chapter 2, critics like Newton Minow have referred to television's landscape as a "vast wasteland" of sex, violence, and stupidity. Even more disturbing, Minow made that statement back in 1961, long before we had shows about bickering housewives, people eating bugs, and contests to marry random strangers. When it comes to common complaints about television, here are some of the key things people see as problematic:

- Sex and violence
- Warped worldview
- Glorified consumerism
- Stereotypes and lack of diversity
- Unreal reality
- Blurred lines

Let's dig into each of these in more depth.

Sex and Violence

When the popular HBO series *Euphoria* aired its season 2 opener in 2022, fans flocked to watch at record rates. More than thirteen million people tuned in across the various HBO services to see a group of high school students deal with issues of sex, drugs, and personal trauma, more than double what the show averaged across all of its first-season episodes.[16] However, many critics complained that the raw presentation of nudity and violence can make the show hard to watch, even for people who consider themselves fans of the show.[17]

Complaints about television's portrayal of humanity's baser desires are nothing new. In 1956, singer Elvis Presley was threatened with banishment from popular variety shows hosted by Ed Sullivan and Steve Allen for his hip gyrations and supposedly obscene performances.[18] In 1961, the *Dick Van Dyke Show* was forced to portray the stars of the show, married couple Rob and Laura Petrie, sleeping in twin beds, separated by a nightstand, to prevent suggestions that they might have sex.

Subscription television programs, like HBO's Euphoria, are allowed to show more in the way of sex, drugs, and violence than over-the-air broadcast TV shows. Critics charge that the sheer volume of this type of content on the show makes the popular series hard to watch at times.

PictureLux/The Hollywood Archive/Alamy Stock Photo

In addition to sexual content, researchers have indicated that an average American will see more than two hundred thousand acts of violence on TV before they turn 18.[19] Research has shown negative effects related to early and heavy exposure to violent acts on television. One study showed that children who had early exposure to TV violence were more likely to become aggressive and violent adults.[20] Another revealed that kindergarten-age children who spent more time watching violent TV programs were more likely to have emotional problems and more difficulty with school work during their early grade school years.[21]

The studies are more mixed regarding sexual activity. Some studies showed that teens who watched more television that contained sexual content were more likely to begin sexual experimentation earlier in their lives than teens who did not watch those acts on TV.[22] However, other researchers have found that even with significant increases in sexual content in television programming, teens were actually waiting longer before having sex and relying on safer sex practices when they had sex. The data also revealed that teen pregnancy was at a historic low in the United States, even as TV was increasingly including sexually explicit content.[23]

Witnessing specific actions in the media does not directly inspire people to undertake actions they otherwise would not do (see Chapter 2). However, researchers have found that watching television can have a cumulative effect on people that can change the way they view the world around them.

Warped Worldview

Most of the theories we discussed at the beginning of the book apply broadly across multiple forms of mass media (see Chapter 1). However, one is geared directly for television, and it asks a question unlike any others: what is our reality?

Cultivation theory first emerged in the late 1960s when researcher George Gerbner began looking at what effect television had on heavy viewers. At that time, research had already shown that people who watched certain forms of TV were more likely to behave in certain ways or that actions shown on the screen led to replication in real life. (The Bandura experiment we discussed in Chapter 2 is an example of this.) Gerbner wanted to know whether television was essentially bathing people in an alternative reality so that they came to believe it to be true, even if their own lives did not reflect that reality.

Gerbner found distinct differences between the worldviews of light and heavy viewers of television. People who watched a great deal of television were more likely to think the world around them was more violent and dangerous than it actually was. In subsequent research, Gerbner and other scholars found that heavy viewers tended to believe most people in the world were just out for their own best interests, lacked empathy, and generally did not act in ways that would benefit society.[24] Other scholars applied this theory to issues of sexual behavior, representations of women, the behavior or LGBTQ+ people, and issues of race, all finding some level of negative distortions based on heavy viewing habits. These findings led to what scholars deemed a "**mean world syndrome**," in which heavy viewers saw a reality that was much worse than the one experience by lighter viewers.[25]

With the increased accessibility of television shows and video-based storytelling, through streaming services, on-demand programming, and smartphones, the ubiquity of programming is greater now than at any time in history. Researchers currently examining cultivation have accounted for this increased screen time. At the same time, screen time for young people has continued to increase over the years. As of 2009, researchers at the Kaiser Family Foundation noted that kids ages eight to eighteen watched approximately 4.5 hours of television per day.[26] Scholars in 2022 reported that teens in the United States saw their non-school-related screen time double during the COVID-19 pandemic.[27]

When experiencing the world primarily through the portal of television, people develop a sense of how things are based on what they see, and then they act accordingly. Thus, if a person thinks everyone else is out for themselves, they can view people who offer help suspiciously or mistrust what they learn from experts and politicians in other forms of media. It is worth examining to what degree you think your own world is shaped through the programs you see and to what degree you feel connected with the world at large based on these views.

Glorified Consumerism

Television and commercials have existed hand in hand since the first ad aired on TV in 1941, with products being either directly or indirectly connected to specific programs. Aside from direct sponsorship and the inclusion of ad breaks within programming, television shows have found a lot of value in product placement, in which certain brands and items are integrated into the shows themselves. (See Chapter 13 for a full discussion of these issues.) These connections have often raised criticism that TV's message is that happiness can truly be gained only through consuming material items. Researchers have found that television programs that showcase specific products, goods, and services can lead viewers to see these items as important in their own lives. A study that examined the effect of television programs on consumer desires showed that people who repeatedly see affluence on TV tend to see the goods and services the characters use as essential to living "a good life."[28]

As television evolved, its programming increasingly focused on characters who lived well beyond their means, without significant consequences. For example, the 1990s TV show *Friends* received significant criticism that the lifestyle of the cast members could not be replicated on the salaries their characters supposedly earned. No twenty-something just beginning a career could afford the lavish apartments and designer clothes these characters wore on the show.[29]

Scholars also found that much of the most popular television programming portrays wealth much more frequently than it truly exists in real life. In addition, research has demonstrated that viewers believe this level of affluence is both desirable and attainable in real life, even when it clearly is not. Frequent viewing of these kinds of programs has led to people aspiring to higher levels of wealth and holding much more materialistic values for their own lives.[30]

Stereotypes and Lack of Diversity

Casting directors, who are responsible for selecting actors for scripted series, have put significantly more emphasis on creating diversity on television shows of all genres. Despite these efforts, TV still faces charges that its programming fails to provide enough representation and inclusion in terms of race, ethnicity, and sexual orientation. ViacomCBS conducted a global poll and found that approximately 80 percent of the people surveyed thought more diversity needed to be included on television. In addition, more than half of those who participated in the survey felt that people "like them" were poorly represented because of lazy stereotypes or negative portrayals.[31]

For much of television history, critics found significant problems in how people of color and members of the LGBTQ+ community were portrayed. Some critics complained about a lack of diversified representation, meaning that shows often failed to have any characters who were not straight and white. Others noted that when diversity was addressed, it was as part of tangential and stereotyped roles. For example, gay characters portrayed in television shows were either demonstrated to be overly flamboyant oddities or presented in roles as the main character's "gay best friend."[32]

Recent data have shown that some television programming has made some significant moves to address this issue. A 2021 report from UCLA noted that while diversity has improved over the past decade in terms of acting, directing, and writing roles in television, certain groups, like Latinos, remain significantly underrepresented when compared with their overall percentages of the population.[33] Research by GLAAD in 2022 also found that LGBTQ+ representation has reached record numbers when it comes to television characters, but also noted that television still needed to widen its distinctive presentations of noncisgender characters and increase character diversity as well.[34]

Unreal Reality

For much of its existence, television relied on scripted programming, with actors performing roles to entertain their audiences. For example, audiences in the 1950s understood that actor George Reeves, TV's original Superman, was not "faster than a speeding bullet, more powerful than a locomotive, and able to leap tall buildings in a single bound." They understood that the bad guys the Lone Ranger shot didn't really die, and that Hugh Beaumont and Barbara Billingsley weren't really married and weren't raising a kid named Beaver Cleaver on *Leave It to Beaver*. The demarcation between fantasy and reality remained clearly in place.

In the early 1990s, however, those lines began to blur with the advent of **reality TV**. Although shows like *Cops*, which debuted in 1989, paired television with real-life situations, the idea of assembling a cast of real people to interact in a sort of social experiment came to life with MTV's *The Real World* starting in 1992. The producers had intended to make a traditional scripted teen-drama show, only to find that it was cost-prohibitive to hire actors and writers to bring their vision to life. Instead, they realized that hiring regular young people to live and interact with one another in a shared home could create a dramatic television experience. The show became a hit, making it the longest running series on MTV and spawning several spin-off shows.

Development executives, whose job it is to find and pitch potentially viable shows, suddenly recognized that reality TV was both popular and cheap to produce. From that point, the genre developed into numerous subgenres, such as reality relationship programs (*The Bachelor, The Bachelorette, Temptation Island*), talent competitions (*American Idol, Dancing with the Stars, Top Chef*), transformational shows (*The Biggest Loser, The Swan, Home Makeover, What Not to Wear*), and aspirational dramas (*Keeping up with the Kardashians*).[35] Reality programming dominated the TV landscape during the 2000s and is seeing renewed life in the streaming environment.[36]

Even as the first season of *The Real World* found a huge following, critics lambasted it as being fake or at least partially staged. Subsequent reality shows received similar criticisms, as scholars and media experts alike noted that this TV format promoted unrealistic beauty standards, irresponsible actions, and selfish behavior.[37] Researchers have found that viewing reality TV can lead to increased physical aggression, manipulative behavior, and bullying.[38]

Critics also have pointed out the negative effect these programs have on the participants. Even though these programs pitch themselves as being unscripted, contestants are given instructions as to how to perform or what actions will likely keep them on the show longer. In addition, participants have experienced severe negative impacts, including depression, anxiety, and suicidal thoughts, during and after working on the shows.[39]

Blurred Lines

As was the case with reality television, the lines between quality news content and other forms of entertainment became blurred over time. Starting with the talk shows of the 1950s and 1960s, nonjournalists became sources of information and ideology for television viewers. Talk shows like those hosted over the years by Dick Cavett made inroads by bringing people outside of the mainstream into the homes of Americans who otherwise might never have seen them. Even today, late-night talk shows like *Jimmy Kimmel Live!* and *The Late Show with Stephen Colbert* bring important public figures, celebrities, and even regular people into the public consciousness.

However, as formats evolved and tastes changed, the question of what was news and what wasn't became harder to define. Two key shifts in how information-based programming presented content blurred lines between fact and opinion for television viewers in ways that are potentially problematic: satirical news programs and the rise of pundits, who trade in opinion rather than facts.

Satirical News Programs

Comedian Jon Stewart was named the host of *The Daily Show* in 1999. Tapping deeply into the 2000 presidential election and the recount of votes in Florida, Stewart's "Indecision 2000" coverage helped establish the tone of the show, providing viewers with information while still mocking the system from which that information emerged. This form of **infotainment** bridged the gap for television viewers who would not otherwise engage with the events of the day.

Although Stewart went to great lengths to state that he was not a journalist, he became a trusted source of information for viewers who distrusted the traditional reporters and anchors on television. A Pew poll in 2007 had him tied with mainstream anchors Tom Brokaw, Dan Rather, Brian Williams, and Anderson Cooper as the most admired journalist in the United States.[40] A *Time* magazine poll two years later put him atop the list of America's most trusted newscasters.[41]

By the time Stewart called it quits in 2015, his approach to news-as-humor programming had given birth to multiple offshoots. HBO's *Last Week Tonight*, featuring John Oliver, usually recaps the week's

HBO's *Last Week Tonight* features comedian John Oliver using humor to tackle serious issues, like the dangerous world of coal mining and the seedy world of the payday loan industry.

Frederick M. Brown/Stringer

news before moving on to a main story that focuses on a single topic that transcends current events. In doing so, he was able to shift the focus of people's attention to everything from scandals in international soccer to the dark side of the coal mining industry.

Satirical newscasts have both proponents and detractors. Research conducted at the University of Pennsylvania and The Ohio State University demonstrated that people aged eighteen to thirty-four were more likely to engage with news when it was presented in a humorous fashion. In addition, these viewers were better able to recall facts about the material than were people who saw straightforward versions of the same stories.[42] Scholars also noted that a comedic approach to news helped provide a check on the news media itself, because it called for accountability among the public figures who often made news.[43]

However, other research demonstrated that humor undercut the accuracy of the messaging in some cases, leaving viewers confused about the veracity of the information they received. Research found that programs like *The Daily Show* increased viewers' knowledge of certain topics but also made them more cynical about those topics.[44] Satirical news programs also made viewers see traditional broadcast news programs as less credible and viewed them more negatively.[45]

The Rise of Pundits

Journalists have long relied on expert sources who were able to provide insight on complex issues for their viewers. Specialists were asked to explain complicated issues in a simple fashion, just as a professor would (or should) do with students in a classroom. When a terrorist organization became part of an international discussion, journalists would find people who studied that group and ask them to explain who was involved and what the terrorists wanted. When a plane crashed, journalists would seek aviation experts to tell the audience what happened in the crash and what, if anything, could be done to avoid it.

However, in many cases, journalists themselves step in and take the place of the experts, even if they don't know anything about the topic at hand. For example, when a breaking news event occurs, the network sends a correspondent to the scene and that reporter will give the anchor a live report on whatever is going on. The anchor and reporter then talk about "what we know at this point," much of it in the form of speculation.

In doing this, CNN, Fox News, MSNBC, and other cable news shows provide content that is rooted less in fact and more in opinion. In addition, these individuals are often less interested in informing the public than in promoting a point of view. Called **punditry**, this approach to news relies on hyperbolic language and heavy speculation.

In analyzing current punditry, the *Washington Post*'s Paul Farhi explained that these individuals "don't report the news as much as they talk and speculate endlessly about it." He found that CNN had approximately 100 pundits on its payroll, and it was likely that other networks cast in the same mold have a similar number in their ranks. In one eight-day span, he found that 602 pundits appeared across Fox News, CNN, and MSNBC, with 12 appearing on all three channels.[46]

This reliance on punditry raises major concerns because the general public often fails to differentiate between fact and opinion when it comes across on these networks. A 2018 Pew study[47] that asked U.S. adults to identify if a series of statements were fact or opinion revealed that only half of the participants successfully identified more than half of the factual statements; approximately one-third of the participants accurately identified all the opinion statements as such. Making things worse, political party identification shifted how people viewed facts and opinions, making errors in favor of statements that supported their worldview. Follow-up work in 2020 revealed that things weren't getting any better.[48]

In print publications, the news section is physically separated from the opinion section and the op-ed pages, where people can voice their thoughts on issues of the day. However, when a newsworthy event occurs and a reporter on the scene provides information, a quick switch to the pundit in the newsroom can leave viewers assuming that both are equally informed and neutral on the topic. Given the findings of the Pew study and the political leanings associated with specific cable television outlets, it is concerning that these channels continue to blur the lines between facts and opinions.

JOBS IN TELEVISION

Now that you better understand the various aspects of this field, here's a handy overview of a few common positions in television today.

Career Opportunity	Common Tasks
Casting director	• Read scripts to determine actors who might fit certain roles • Assist in the auditions and hiring of actors for shows • Work with directors and producers to build a cast for a show
Development executive	• Find ideas that have the potential to become good television programs • Work with screenwriters to improve scripts so they may be commissioned for production • Pitch projects to producers and directors based on their knowledge of the material
Screenwriter	• Create stories for television programs through the use of original ideas or by adapting existing content • Work with development executive to improve script and ready it for production • Rework aspects of scripts based on the needs of the director or the requirements of the production
Anchor	• Present information to the public that was gathered by reporters and videographers • Gather information for dissemination on newscasts • Serve as an unbiased and engaging source of information

Career Opportunity	Common Tasks
News director	● Plan the news broadcast in conjunction with other journalists at the television station ● Monitor stories for accuracy and clarity prior to their airing ● Abide by the rules of the FCC and other oversight agencies

CHAPTER REVIEW

LO1 Identify key moments in the history of television.

- Early television efforts helped establish the potential of transmitting images but ultimately proved to be impractical.
- Inventors like Vladimir Zworykin and Philo T. Farnsworth helped push television into the broadcast age, by developing electronic means of reproducing and transmitting moving images. At the 1939 World's Fair, early televisions demonstrated to people what would be in their own homes in a few short years.
- The big TV boom occurred in postwar America in the 1950s, as networks produced an array of content and TV sets became readily available. Over the next several decades, televisions would become ubiquitous in the lives of people around the world.
- Experiments in the early 1960s demonstrated that TV signals could use satellite technology to reach untapped markets and provide additional programming. Satellite TV systems posed the first of many challenges to the supremacy of the three primary broadcast networks.
- Cable television began as a way to reach homes blocked from direct signals because of geographical limitations. However, once Congress removed restrictions on who could receive cable TV, a proliferation of options emerged that gave people more channels and niche programming, ending the stranglehold broadcasters held on TV.
- As internet speeds increased and portable digital devices became prevalent, television shifted from a homebound appliance to a constant companion. Internet television and streaming services inspired viewers to move from subscribing to cable packages to take their programs on the go.

LO2 Understand the needs that television programming satisfies for its viewers.

- Mood management: people are able to watch programs that help them recalibrate their emotional state.
- Social comparison: people can either look up to or down on the characters in the shows they watch as a way of assessing their own status in society.
- Socialization and companionship: television provides viewers with something to talk about the next time they cross paths, encouraging socialization. People can also form basic relationships with their shows as they connect with their characters and storylines.

LO3 Examine the importance of broadcast journalism.

- Broadcast journalism can alert the public to newsworthy happenings in their areas or around the world, satisfying their need to be aware of their surroundings on a frequent basis.
- People often observe events through the media, such as assessing the damage a hurricane did several states away or seeing a baseball team win the World Series, allowing them to be present when actions occur that matter to them.
- Broadcasters often become a known entity within the community, because they present news on a daily basis and reach out to community members for information that will matter to viewers. These people create connections within the communities they serve.

- Television is often dubbed the "window to the world," because it gives people the opportunity to have experiences beyond their own lives. Watching royals wed or seeing how people in remote parts of the world live can expand the social experiences and knowledge base of viewers.

LO4 **Discuss the way in which technology has shifted television consumption habits.**

- Devices like the video cassette recorder and the digital video recorder have allowed users to determine when and how they watch programs, instead of having to show up at a time dictated by the broadcast networks.
- Streaming services have released full seasons of previously aired television shows as well as first-run content all at once, allowing viewers to binge-watch the material.
- Television once had three basic networks that all people received for free. Subscription-based television allowed the expansion of viewing options as well as the requirement that people pay for the privilege of watching certain content.
- Broad-based variety shows were once the staple of broadcast television, with the idea that everyone in the family would be watching one set at one time. With more television screens available to people on more devices than ever before, programmers took advantage of providing niche content to people, hoping to serve certain specific viewers' interests while also making it easier for advertiser to target these groups.

LO5 **Assess the criticisms levied against television programming over the years.**

- Television overemphasizes sexual and violent content. Researchers have shown heavy viewing of this material can have negative effects on the people who watch it.
- Television's reliance on social comparison can lead viewers to develop an overwhelming desire to buy a lot of things they don't actually need. Between the advertisements and the product placements, people are presented with a narrative that tells them the way to be happy is through consumerism.
- Television's presentation of stereotypical characters meant to represent marginalized groups can give viewers a warped view of these people. Both the quality and quantity of equitable representation across race, gender, class, sexual orientation, and other similar categories remain concerns for TV.
- Reality-based television programs raise the question of how "real" the people on the shows are. Reality TV often leads to negative consequences for both the viewers and participants alike.
- Lines between information and entertainment have been blurred over the years, with the advent of comedy-as-news shows and the rise of pundits on TV. People have had an exponentially difficult time discerning fact from opinion.

KEY TERMS

Actualities
Aspirational viewing
Binge watching
Campfire TV model
Community antenna television
Cultivation theory
Deepfake
Downward social comparison
Image dissector
Infotainment
Mean world syndrome
Mood management
Niche content
Punditry
Reality TV
Roper question
Satellite television
Social comparison
Sound bites
Subscription-based TV
Time-shifting

DISCUSSION QUESTIONS

1. Do you think that having more programming available through more channels than ever before makes for better or worse viewing experiences for you and the people you know? What are the benefits and drawbacks you see to this proliferation of options?
2. When you think of "watching television," how do you think this experience differs for you compared with your parents or your grandparents? Discuss everything including the devices you use, the channels you watch, and the motivations you have for viewing TV.
3. Has the blurring of lines between comedy and news or the use of pundits instead of straight news content made it better or worse for you as a news consumer? Why?
4. When you watch television content, which of the needs mentioned in the chapter are you most likely seeking to fulfill? How do your programming choices help you meet those needs?

Starting in 1993, America Online (AOL) sent computer disks through the mail that offered people fifteen free hours of internet time in the hope that they would subscribe to the company's monthly service. Subscribers would pay $9.95 per month for five hours online, with additional hours costing $2.95 each. In today's dollars and use rates, the average person would spend more than $1,200 per month for internet access.

R Kawka/Alamy Stock Photo

9 THE ALL-CONSUMING INTERNET

INTRODUCTION

1. *If America Online were being launched today, how would it market itself to its potential users?*
2. *If the internet ceased to exist, how much do you think this loss would affect your life and in what ways?*
3. *How much effort do you put into verifying the content that you see online before you believe the information or pass it on to other people?*

Few forms of media have developed as quickly or had as large an impact on society as has the internet. What started as a communications tool for military personnel in the 1960s has since become the way in which the majority of humankind stays connected, finds information, and communicates ideas. The internet today is as ubiquitous as electricity and as vital to communication as language itself. Even so, at its core, the internet is merely a tool, like every other form of media we have discussed to this point. Its inherent value resides in who controls the content that gets sent and the degree to which audience members receive benefit or harm from that content.

In this chapter, we will examine the rise of the internet, the functional benefits it provides its audience, and the specific impacts it has on society. In addition, we will examine the way in which this supposedly free and uncontrolled medium fell into the hands of a few monopolies. Finally, we will look into the negative consequences associated with providing anonymous individuals with unfettered access to other people's lives.

LEARNING OBJECTIVES

After completing this chapter, you should be able to:

1. Identify key moments in the history of the internet.
2. Understand specific ways the internet affects society.
3. Review the companies that have monopoly-like control over various aspects of the internet and the ways in which they have exercised that control.
4. Discuss the negative ramifications of online activities.

FROM MILITARY TOOL TO DAILY NECESSITY: A BRIEF HISTORY OF THE INTERNET

LEARNING OBJECTIVES

LO 1: Identify key moments in the history of the internet.

In the 1950s and 1960s, computers were large and exceptionally expensive. They usually could be used only by a single operator at a time, making them a precious and yet underused resource. To improve efficiency, researchers at various universities began looking for ways to allow multiple people to connect to a single computer, and then multiple computers, leading to the internet we know today.

Here are several key areas of internet development that took place over the past sixty years:

- The "intergalactic network," packet-switching theory, and ARPANET
- TCP/IP and the universal internet
- Welcome to the World Wide Web

- Interactivity and Web 2.0
- Wi-Fi and the untethering of devices

Let's dig into these topics a bit more deeply.

The "Intergalactic Network," Packet-Switching Theory, and ARPANET

Throughout the 1960s, researchers around the globe looked for ways in which they could make computer use more efficient, eventually developing a time-sharing system. **Time sharing** allows a mainframe computer to receive multiple users' commands from multiple input stations at the same time. It then processes the commands and responds to users in a prescribed order based on programming. This process is like having a Google document open with multiple users working on it at the same time.

The next step was to link all time-shared computers together. In 1962, J.C.R. Licklider began working on what he called the "intergalactic network" to solve this problem. He envisioned a system in which users would have immediate access to an interconnected series of machines around the world.[1] To make this work, Licklider and other researchers had to solve a couple of significant problems:

1. Computer networks were designed around a hierarchy (or structure) whereby the main computer is the "host" while others served as "guests" of that host. Think of this system like an octopus: there's the main body (the host) that deals with each tentacle (the guest) independent of each other tentacle. In this system, there's no ability for the tentacles to operate independently of the main body and communicate with one another.
2. Connections among computers were direct, meaning that only one guest could use a connection at a time to talk to the host computer. To make an interconnected set of computers, a system would need many connections at a time to accommodate different users.

A Rand Corporation researcher named Paul Baran provided the fix to both problems while working for the U.S. Air Force. The military relied on the telephone network to communicate and was worried that if a few specific hubs of the network were destroyed in an attack, the entire system could fail. Rather than creating a **decentralized network**, which breaks one central point into several smaller communication hubs, Baran discovered that the best way to keep a network functioning would be to create a **distributed network**, which allows each computer to talk to any computer along the network.[2] Also, Baran and his colleagues discovered that it would be quicker and simpler to break large pieces of

FIGURE 9.1 ■ Examples of Centralized, Decentralized, and Distributed Networks

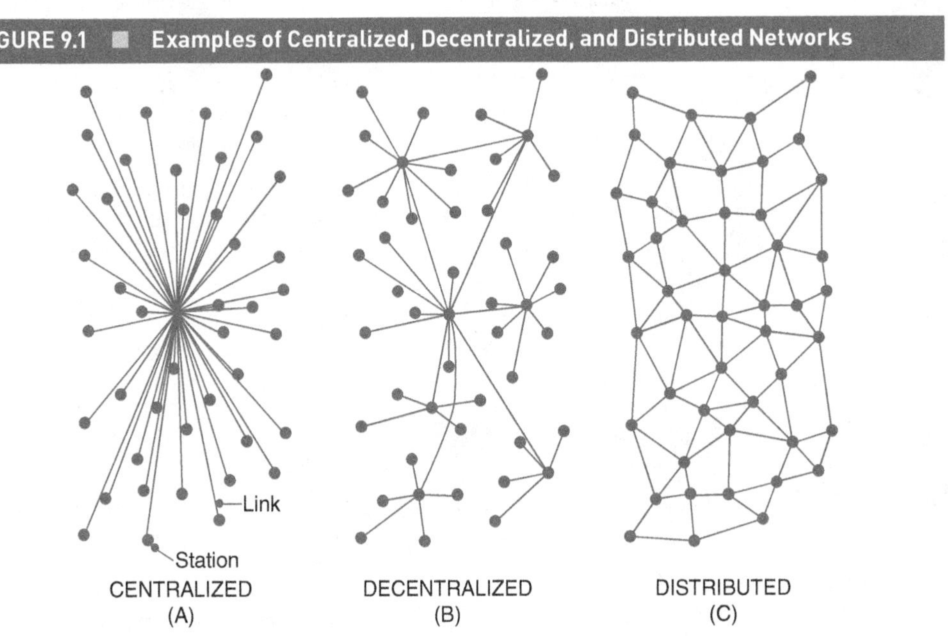

information into smaller chunks that could be sent individually to other machines along the network and reassembled later. This system came to be known as **packet switching**, and it revolutionized communication of all kinds.

Building on these discoveries, in 1966, researchers at the military's Advanced Research Projects Agency (ARPA) started building **ARPANET** (Advanced Research Projects Agency Network), a networking system built on packet switching that allowed individual computers to talk to one another. While the initial trial in October 1969 was not successful,[3] subsequent efforts succeeded, and soon permanent connections linked multiple universities in the western United States.

ARPANET was responsible for many "firsts" that remain valuable to computer users to this day. In 1971, the network was used to send the first email, and it also helped launch voice communication protocols and password encryption. ARPA's researchers built a structure and nomenclature for the

TABLE 9.1 ■ Key Moments in Internet Development

Date	What Happened	Why It Mattered
1962	Computer scientist J.C.R. Licklider proposes the development of a computer system in which all computers can connect to one another.	This shift in ideology proposed moving computers away from single main hubs with multiple input stations to a network of terminals that could talk to one another. This proposal is the foundation upon which the modern internet was built.
1964	Researcher Paul Baran presents a research paper that proposes a network in which content could be cut into small pieces and sent through the fastest routes available before being reassembled by the computer receiving it.	Baran's packet-switching model revolutionized digital content transmissions and is still in use today. In addition, his research explained the benefits of a distributed network, another crucial element in today's internet.
1969	The Advances Research Projects Agency launches ARPANET.	ARPANET became the first true internet system that connected computers across long distances. The researchers who developed this system also were responsible for many of the products and naming conventions we still use online today.
1983	The Department of Defense adopts TCP/IP as its official internet system.	To make all of the internets of the day talk to one another, they needed a common language. The transmission control protocol and internet protocol system became that language, something the Defense Department's adoption made official.
1989	Computer scientist Tim Berners-Lee invents the World Wide Web.	Berners-Lee's use of hypertext as well as the application of user-friendly browsers opened the world of the internet to regular people.
1996	America Online shifts its approach to buying internet access.	The primary internet provider of the day decided to charge a flat monthly fee for web surfing, replacing its pay-by-the-hour model. This made it cheaper for people to spend more time online, thus inspiring heavier use.
2004	Wi-Fi is approved for mobile phones.	The ability to make mobile phones essentially portable minicomputers is directly tied to the decision to give phones Wi-Fi access. Internet speeds and use on mobile devices dramatically increased because of this choice.

internet. Elizabeth "Jake" Feinler headed the team that created the naming functions of domains, including .com, .gov, and .edu.[4] By 1983, the service was divided between military and civilian use, leading to the first true use of the word "internet" to describe this digital networking system.[5] It was maintained until 1989, when it was shut down for good.

TCP/IP and the Universal Internet

The success of ARPANET led to the proliferation of other similar networking systems. This proliferation of networks gave more people greater access to computing power at a distance. However, as researchers tried to find ways to connect these disparate systems, they realized that these networks had no shared language or set of structure that allowed them to communicate.[6]

To address this problem, by 1978, the researchers had developed the transmission control protocol (TCP), which outlined the speed, structure, and format in which data would be sent and received between computers. In addition, the internet protocol (IP) outlined the system computers would use to represent themselves online and the ways in which computers could find one another. On January 1, 1983, the Department of Defense officially adopted this system, dubbed TCP/IP for short, for ARPANET and all its other networks. Other public and private networks joined this system over the subsequent decade, until it became the most common protocol among networks by the mid-1990s.[7]

Welcome to the World Wide Web

In 1989, British computer scientist Tim Berners-Lee proposed a way in which people without significant backgrounds in computer science could access and share data among themselves.[8] Through 1992, he developed and refined his hypertext system, which allowed files to be stored in one place but accessed through interactive links online. To improve access to these links, Berners-Lee constructed a web server, a digital repository where those files would be stored, and a web browser, a piece of software that would translate the computer code into easy-to-read pages of information. Together, these innovations became known as the World Wide Web, the familiar "www" prefix we encounter on webpages today.

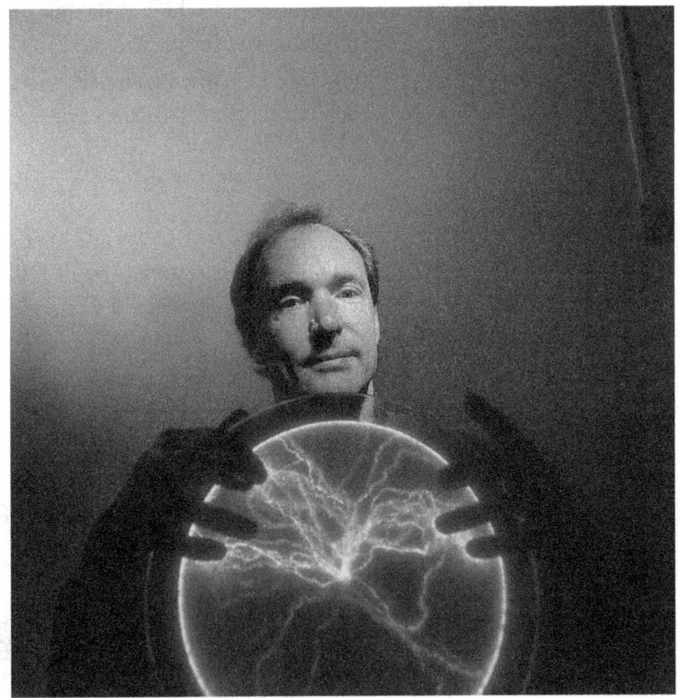

British computer scientist Tim Berners-Lee developed the three key innovations that became known as the World Wide Web.

Catrina Genovese/Contributor

Berners-Lee put the World Wide Web technology into the public domain in 1993 so that anyone could use it. This not only gave individuals and corporations the ability to use the web for their own interests, but it also led to a rapid expansion of the web's use around the world. By 1994, more than eleven million U.S. households had access to the web, joining millions more from around the world.

A small group of people initially created and published content on the web, with a larger group of people finding and consuming that content. This system, now known as Web 1.0, had very little interaction between creators and users, with many people treating the web like a collection of library books. Even early digital commerce was little more than pages of items for sale, with phone numbers or mailing addresses available for people to reach out and place orders.

Interactivity and Web 2.0

By the middle of the 1990s, the web began to shift from the model of "we write, you read" to one in which users were able to participate online more actively and interact more heavily with the content. This model of reading and writing online was dubbed Web 2.0 and remains the dominant paradigm for most internet users today.[9] This shift had several key elements that differentiated from the earlier days of the web.

For a start, more users were generating content for public consumption. In 1999, LiveJournal launched a platform that allowed users to write about any topic that interested them. The content presented newer material first, creating a web log of activity on the site. (This term would later be shortened to "blog," a concept we will discuss in more depth in Chapter 10.) In 2001, Larry Sanger and Jimmy Wales launched Wikipedia, the first open-source encyclopedia that allowed users from anywhere to contribute and edit content on a world of topics. Additionally, users were able to interact more with content other people had created. Individuals could comment on sites, discuss information they found with other users, and contact the site administrators and content creators. The internet was moving from a passive medium, like television, to an active one, in which participation was not just encouraged but necessary for proper use.

E-commerce became significantly easier around this time as well, with people being able to view and purchase items online. In 1995, electronic marketplaces like Amazon and eBay began making it easier for people to purchase products from the web. In 1997, online sales on sites like these were generating about $2.4 billion in revenue per year. As of 2022, global e-commerce sales hit $5.5 trillion and show no signs of slowing down.[10]

Perhaps the biggest change during this time was how people paid for online access. From 1993 through 1996, internet providers offered subscribers a set block of hours for a monthly fee, with each additional hour online costing an additional amount. This led people to carefully budget their online time; people would check their email, look for a recipe, read some chat room comments, or other similar activities and then disconnect. In October 1996, the largest internet provider at the time, America Online (AOL), shifted its model to a single monthly fee, allowing users to be online as much as they wanted. AOL's model has since become the standard operating practice for internet service providers.[11]

Wi-Fi and the Untethering of Devices

In the early, expansive days of the World Wide Web, people could go anywhere their minds could take them, but their computers had to stay tethered to power outlets and wired internet connections. "Hardwired" connections were slowly replaced as a new technology—the wireless internet, called Wi-Fi for short—was developed for home computers.[12] In 2004, the Wi-Fi trade body approved the use of the technology in mobile phones, starting the shift to more versatile portable devices.[13] The continual improvement of devices, and the increased number of Wi-Fi access points, led to Wi-Fi's exponential growth over the following decade. As of 2022, more than 4.95 billion people globally use the internet, with 5.31 billion using mobile phones to access it. These figures represent more than half of the 7.91 billion people who populate the Earth.[14] Experts note that these figures should climb to more than 6 billion over the next few years.

TABLE 9.2 ■ A Few Key Names in Internet History

J.C.R. Licklider	Elizabeth "Jake" Feinler	Tim Berners-Lee	Victor "Vic" Hayes	Elise Gerich
• Developed a way for computers to interact with each other. • Often called the "Johnny Appleseed of computing" for the ways his innovative thoughts planted the seeds that led to the internet age.	• Ran the group that was responsible for internet naming conventions, including the creation of the .gov, .edu, .org, and .com domains. • Created and edited the *ARPANET Resource Handbook*, the bible of documentation for the network service.	• Invented the World Wide Web, including the first web browser and web server. • Helped make the technology of the web public for all to use, helping the web expand exponentially.	• Established standards for wireless networking, earning him the nickname "the father of Wi-Fi." • His efforts to secure portions of the radio spectrum for wireless communication earned him multiple honors, including a place in the IT Hall of Fame.	• Assisted in the transition of the internet from a governmental service to commercial internet service providers. • Worked with commercial organizations to develop high-speed internet throughout the world.

ROLE OF THE INTERNET

LEARNING OBJECTIVES

LO 2: Understand specific ways the internet affects society.

The internet and the World Wide Web work in tandem but are distinct elements of the online experience. That said, in looking at the social ramifications of this platform, the terms can and will be used interchangeably.

When we discussed other forms of media in the book, we looked at specific uses people had and benefits they gained from each one. The internet is distinctively different from those media, because it can be used for all the reasons people use the other forms of media and meet even more needs than anything else. With that in mind, let's focus on specific things the internet does for us from a societal perspective in ways that go beyond what traditional media can provide:

- Broaden access to content
- Bypass censorship
- Provide voice to niche interests
- Archive information for future generations

Let's look at each one of those topics in depth.

Broaden Access to Content

As discussed in Chapters 5, 6, and 8, access to traditional media in the predigital era was limited significantly by geography. If you wanted to listen to a certain radio station or watch a certain TV station, you needed to be within the physical range of its broadcast waves. If you wanted to read a newspaper from a specific city or state, you needed to go to the area the newspaper served and buy it. At best, you could have the paper mailed to you, which got you Monday's news on Thursday. Researchers who wanted access to specific books or journal articles had to physically go to libraries where those books were kept or buy them from brick-and-mortar stores that had copies available for purchase.

The internet and the web brought content from the source to the individual as opposed to the individual needing to physically travel to the source. College libraries, for example, can provide information through Google Books, JSTOR, Academic Search Premier, and other digital collections. News content became available from across the country and around the world. In addition, content that was posted could be accessed at any point in time the user needed it, thus creating options for time-shifting information consumption. In other words, instead of being tethered to the TV to watch the 10 p.m. news at 10 p.m., users could catch video clips the next day or watch the entire program online a week later.

Bypass Censorship

People often think of censorship as being based on governmental or corporate interests' stamping out dissent in a direct fashion. However, a great deal of censorship comes from the uneven playing field on which most citizens operate in the media world. Individuals have a greater range of opportunity online, are given a broader array of options for publishing and easier access to platforms that reach greater numbers of people, and have the ability to sidestep interference from outside sources.

In some countries with government-controlled media, officials have attempted to limit all access to unapproved internet content. A 2022 study showed that China and North Korea were the heaviest censors of internet sites, with Iran, Belarus, Qatar, Syria, Thailand, and Turkmenistan among the next highest countries actively blocking access (see Figure 9.2).[15] While traditional media are much easier to seize and limit, citizens of some of these countries have found ways around the governmental online blockades to receive content from outside sources.[16] This helped break down the gatekeeping functions associated with traditional media in these realms.

FIGURE 9.2 ■ Countries with the Highest Levels of Governmental Internet Censorship

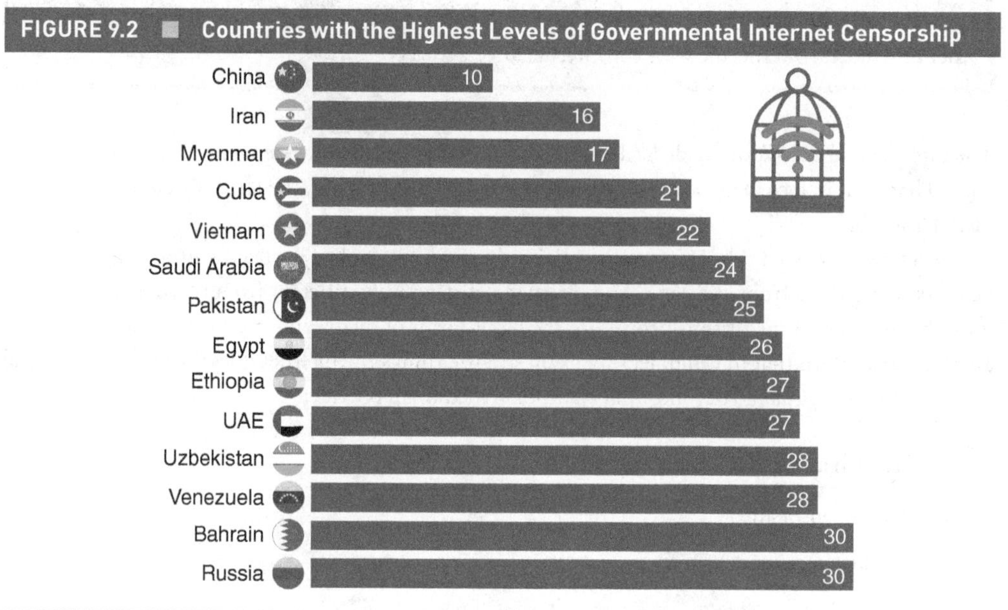

Adapted from Statista, https://www.statista.com/chart/3033/internet-freedom-index/

Even in parts of the world that operate under a free-press and free-speech system, traditional media often serves as a stumbling block of censorship for some individuals. As discussed in Chapter 1, traditional media outlets often served as gatekeepers for information. What they thought mattered got published or broadcast to a large swath of the public; what they didn't like never made it past the trashcan.

With traditional media, an individual seeking to get a message to a larger audience needs access to some high-priced equipment and in some cases governmental approval. To reach an audience through an online platform requires far less expensive equipment and far fewer experts in content dissemination. Through the creation of a website, participation in an internet chat room, the posting of a response to a news article, and a dozen other actions, individuals can bypass the limitations related to traditional media. Furthermore, as interest in a topic gains steam, online content providers can become vital sources of information to an interested and engaged public.

Provide Voice to Niche Interests

In 1995, technology futurist Nicholas Negroponte published the book *Being Digital*, in which he outlined a world in which computers provided a far more personalized experience for individual users. One of his predictions was that people would eventually receive individualized newspapers each day, based on what they told their computers they liked and didn't like. The computer would then seek information on each user's preapproved topics and print individualized newspapers each morning, a publication Negroponte dubbed "The Daily Me." Negroponte's understanding of how the internet could cater to niche interests was spot on. Not only has the internet created an opportunity for people to find content of a narrow interest, but it has provided people with the ability to publish content that might otherwise be ignored or overlooked by traditional media outlets.

When internet bulletin boards and chat rooms became available during the 1980s and 1990s, users often found connections to other people with similar interests. Many of the discussions in those digital meeting places mirrored the ones held by mainstream interests in larger society and included topics like politics, sports, the environment, entertainment, and so forth. However, some chat rooms provided a space in which underrepresented individuals could connect and discuss issues that mattered to them. For example, in 1987, Jean Marie Diaz created "the mother of lesbian lists" at Sappho.net, which provided a central hub for individuals interested in discussions on the topic. Chat rooms also provided a safe space for members of the LGBTQ+ community to discuss social concerns, ask personal questions, and connect with other community members in a way not possible elsewhere.[17]

Certain websites, like Quora, allow users to connect with individuals who have expertise in a topic to gain more information, and those like Goodreads provide topic-specific areas in which readers and authors can connect and discuss certain reading material.[18] Websites often establish chat forums and niche spaces for people interested in specific topics, thus helping them filter out irrelevant or distasteful posts.

Archive Information for Future Generations

Most traditional media contains information that is crucial to the ways in which we understand the societies that created it. Whether it was the clay tablets filled with cuneiform or the audio broadcast recordings of President Franklin Roosevelt's fireside chats, this material provides historians with insights as to what was happening in that part of the world at that time and what was valued. Even with significant preservation and discovery efforts, our views of past societies remain incomplete, because the information retained is a tiny fraction of the media that was created.

Digital librarian Brewster Kahle understood the importance of preserving as much of the web as was possible when he started the Internet Archive in 1996. Kahle hoped to collect websites and save them in their initial forms. The goal was to make sure the web could be accurately retained, much in the same way someone could save a book that was important, preserve a copy of a newspaper, or record an important event as it unfolded live on television. In 2001, Kahle opened the archives to the public through the Wayback Machine, which currently hosts more than 625 billion webpages. In addition, Kahle's team is working to digitize traditional forms of media; the archive now contains 38 million books, 14 million audio recordings, 7 million videos, and 4 million still images.[19]

The archiving of the web has become crucial because information that exists online can be a powerful tool in the search for truth. When the website Gawker closed down, the Freedom of the Press Foundation quickly archived its content to preserve stories that challenged powerful interests that had

President Harry Truman holds up a copy of the Chicago Daily Tribune, erroneously proclaiming that he lost the 1948 election. Copies of that paper still exist in private collections to this day.

Byron Rollins via AP Images

suddenly disappeared from the web.[20] When President Donald Trump claimed in 2018 that Google promoted former President Barack Obama's State of the Union address but refused to do so for his, news organizations used the Wayback Machine to quickly debunk the claim.[21]

Despite current efforts to retain online information, experts note that trying to preserve the internet in its entirety is like trying to catch water in a pasta strainer. Online content is both irrevocably permanent and fleetingly temporary, especially when compared with traditional media. For example, when the Chicago *Daily Tribune* incorrectly called the 1948 presidential election for New York governor Thomas Dewey, the error was preserved in black and white for all time. It was a mistake the paper could never live down. In today's media landscape, an error like that might be captured, screenshotted, and shared before the publication ever noticed it was online. It could be also turned into a series of memes, launch points for blog posts, and even a TikTok challenge. Conversely, if the content disappeared before someone noticed it, nobody might ever know it existed.

Archiving internet content can prevent the rewriting of history or the proliferation of falsehoods that exist simply because nobody has the original content to disprove them. What gets saved through archives like the Wayback Machine will provide future generations with the opportunity to see societal progression online.

MEDIA MONOPOLY 2.0

LEARNING OBJECTIVES

LO 3: Review the companies that have monopoly-like control over various aspects of the internet and the ways in which they have exercised that control.

In Chapter 3, we discussed Ben Bagdikian and his book *The Media Monopoly*, in which he made the case that a limited number of giant conglomerates controlled the majority of the world's media to the detriment of society. In his 2004 final edition of the book, Bagdikian saw the impact the internet could have on society through its explosive rate of spread throughout the culture. At the time, he was uncertain whether it would be a "liberator or Big Brother," to use his words, but he did note that its control or independence would prove vital to its value to society. Similar monopolies have since expanded to the online world. In 2020, a Democratic congressional staff report noted that four online giants wield monopoly-like power over specific areas of online engagement[22]:

- Apple
- Amazon
- Meta/Facebook
- Google

Let's look at what level of control each of these organizations has on our online experiences.

Apple

According to legend, the personal computer revolution started in Apple cofounder Steve Jobs's parents' garage in 1976 with the creation of the Apple I. In the following five decades, the company has waxed and waned in terms of relevance, market share, and innovation, as its leaders have sought to blend user-friendly experiences with quality products. In the late 1990s, the colorful iMac was both fun and practical, with internet connectivity integrated directly into the machine. The iBook provided users with the ability to connect wirelessly to the internet, a first in the field. However, it was the company's move to other digital devices that made Apple significantly profitable. The 2001 launch of the iPod and subsequent creation of the iTunes Store gave Apple a significant slice of the digital music market. The

FIGURE 9.3 ■ Internet Conglomerates That Dominated the Web over the Past Twenty-Five Years

INTERNET GIANTS THAT RULE THE WEB

The top 10 multi-platform online properties over time

RANK	1998	2003	2008	2013	2018	TODAY
1	AOL	YAHOO!	Google	YAHOO!	Google	Google
2	YAHOO!	AOL Time Warner	YAHOO!	Google	facebook	Microsoft
3	GeoCities	msn	Microsoft	Microsoft	Oath:	yahoo!
4	msn	EBAY	Aol.	facebook	Microsoft	facebook
5	Netscape	Google	FOX	Aol.	amazon	amazon
6	EXCITE	LYCOS	EBAY	amazon	COMCAST NBCUNIVERSAL	COMCAST NBCUNIVERSAL
7	LYCOS	amazon	ASK	GLAM MEDIA	CBS	Disney
8	Microsoft	ABOUT	amazon	WIKIMEDIA	Disney	cafe media
9	AMER. GREETINGS	EXCITE	GLAM MEDIA	CBS	Apple	VIACOMCBS
10	INFOSEEK	CNET	WIKIMEDIA	Turner	HEARST	Warner Media

Adapted from https://www.visualcapitalist.com/20-internet-giants-rule-web/

2007 creation of the iPhone, which essentially combined several successful products, pushed Apple's share value to an all-time high.[23] This trend continued over the next two decades, and as of 2022, Apple had a net worth of $2.45 trillion.[24]

Apple controls about 45 percent of the mobile phone market and 100 percent of the app market for their phones. This market share and exclusive marketplace has led to allegations that Apple operates as a monopoly, which was documented in a 2020 report by the U.S. House Judiciary Committee. The report noted that the company favored certain apps during searches, strong-armed app developers into disadvantageous financial agreements, and eliminated competitive forces in the market.[25] Several companies have filed lawsuits against Apple over the past few years, making similar claims.[26] App developers have stated they must pay up to a 30 percent commission to Apple to sell their products in the store. Furthermore, some have accused Apple of taking their ideas, creating similar apps, and promoting their copies at cheaper prices than the originals.[27] Despite rulings that Apple did not meet the textbook definition of a monopoly, courts and governmental bodies have expressed concern as to the impact Apple's level of control has on the overall digital marketplace.

Amazon

As discussed in Chapter 4, Amazon developed an online commerce model that changed how people purchase and read books. Jeff Bezos founded Amazon in 1994, and the company didn't record a profit for almost a decade, as it continued to invest in its e-commerce infrastructure and expand its product lineup.[28] Starting in 2011, the company began to increase its workforce exponentially, moving from thirty thousand full-time employees that year to more than one million a decade later.[29] It is currently a global e-commerce giant that has a hand in product sales, internet delivery, and streaming services. The company has a net worth of more than $1.2 trillion.[30]

According to market research, Amazon dominates nearly 50 percent of U.S. e-commerce sales, making it the go-to place for sellers of all kinds.[31] However, Amazon has been accused of harming independent sellers through a series of anticompetitive actions. One analysis showed that the search function on Amazon is biased toward products that benefit the company. In 60 percent of the cases, the top result went to a paid advertiser, and in the remaining 40 percent, the top search result went to Amazon-related products half of the time.[32]

The company also competes with independent sellers through its own private-label business. As of 2020, the company owned forty-five brands that produced more than 243,000 products.[33] Like Apple,

Amazon is accused of replicating successful products from third-party vendors and promoting their own versions. Despite statements from Amazon to the contrary, a series of leaked documents revealed that Amazon not only copied best-selling items but then leveraged its marketing efforts to promote and sell them ahead of the originals.[34] Sellers who find that Amazon is competing with them have said that they have no hope of surviving in the market.

Facebook/Meta

The story of Facebook is a well-known tale in which Harvard student Mark Zuckerberg and several friends developed a website in 2003 that let people connect with one another and share things about their lives. Well before people knew what social media was, Facebook had moved internet users and inspired a major social shift in how they lived their lives online. The site was initially limited to Harvard students before opening up in 2006 to anyone who was thirteen or older. Facebook, which also owns Instagram and WhatsApp, was valued at $538 billion in 2022, when it changed its corporate name to Meta.[35]

As of 2022, Facebook is the top social media platform, with more than 2.9 billion active users on the service each month. In other words, more than one-third of the Earth's population actively uses Facebook.[36] More than 30 percent of Americans reported getting their news directly from the site.[37] Thanks to its enormous market penetration, Facebook can shape what people see on a daily basis. In 2021, the Federal Trade Commission sued Facebook for illegally monopolizing the social media landscape through "an illegal buy-or-bury scheme."[38] The suit stated that the social media platform priced competitors out of the market, purchased potential threats to their dominance, and acted in other ways meant to prevent other social media developers to thrive. The goal was to keep Facebook as a singular dominant figure in this online realm.

Facebook can also shape what types of content people see most often because the platform's algorithm determines the types of content that get preferred treatment and which content is hidden from users. A 2021 *Wall Street Journal* series titled "The Facebook Files" revealed that angrier and more divisive content got significant boosts on the platform, thus creating the incentive for people seeking attention to create posts.[39] Despite the company's public statement that all content is treated equally, Facebook often failed to enforce rules against conservative and right-wing publishers for fear of user backlash.[40] Facebook's own researchers studied the impact the platform had on users, finding that one in eight people reported negative effects on their well-being. However, Facebook shut down its research arm shortly after those findings and did not disclose them.[41]

Facebook also has access to a significant amount of information about its users, creating concerns about what the company does with those data. In 2019, the Federal Trade Commission imposed a five billion dollar penalty on Facebook after determining that it illegally gave data company Cambridge Analytica access to personal information of more than thirty million people and then lied about the situation in public. The company paid an additional one hundred million dollars to settle charges from the Securities and Exchange Commission related to the scandal.[42] The SEC also began investigating complaints in 2021 from former employee Frances Haugen and several other whistleblowers, who provided documents showing that Facebook frequently put financial gains ahead of users' safety.[43]

Google

Stanford doctoral students Larry Page and Sergey Brin developed the idea for the Google search engine in 1996. Unlike other search engines of the day, they developed a better way to discover and rank webpages for users to quickly find the information that they needed. The pair incorporated Google in 1998 and continued to improve the search engine's performance. The company also added email services, an app store, and a news outlet over the next five years. The company went public in 2004 and is now valued at $1.6 trillion, which includes both its search-engine properties and branded smart devices like the Google Pixel mobile phone.[44] Its parent company, Alphabet, is among the top five information technology companies in the world.

In 2022, Google dominates the search-engine market, with estimates of market share ranging from 88 percent to nearly 93 percent of all searches. Experts note that Google's dominance comes from its heavy integration into platforms and apps, with Google making itself ever present and easy to use. As one writer put it, "Whenever users are searching, Google has never been far away."[45]

Google not only has a significant say over what people can find online, but also it is financially incentivized toward self-interest. Back in 2000, Google began offering advertising as part of its business model. Prior to that time, the founders had resisted this idea, instead stating that they preferred to give people the best options up front, without allowing people to buy their way to the front of the line. In 2004, cofounder Larry Page said that the goal of Google was to "get you out of Google and to the right place as fast as possible."[46] However, a recent examination of Google searches revealed that more than 40 percent of the first page of any search is dedicated to Google-related content, and nearly two-thirds of all Google searches ended without the user actually clicking on something Google didn't own.[47] Although other content was available to users beyond the first page, the majority of users do not go beyond the first page of results, with about 94 percent of the overall clicks going to the top results.[48]

In 2020, the Justice Department sued Google over what it saw as anticompetitive actions that made it "a monopoly gatekeeper for the internet."[49] This antitrust suit was one of several accusing Google of cutting deals with other companies and using its position of power to prevent any real challenges to its dominance. Ten state attorneys general sued the tech giant in 2020 for the way it overcharged for advertising and had colluded with Facebook to prevent competition for ads.[50] In 2021, thirty-six states and the District of Columbia filed suit against Google for monopolistic practices regarding the Android app store.[51] In each case, the suits note that Google has gone out of its way to make sure it remains the only game in town wherever it operates.

The control these organizations have on what people read, learn, buy, and find online has raised serious concern about the fairness of the internet playing field. However, a bigger concern could make this issue fairly minor: the current debate over **net neutrality** could determine who gets the best access to specific content and what it will cost to get into the fast lane. Net neutrality means that everyone who posts to the internet is treated equally; their data are moved at the same speed and are available to all users. Web providers could either favor or speed up some sites over others in exchange for higher fees or other incentives, which would discriminate against those who couldn't afford to pay for equal access.

A DEEPER LOOK: NET NEUTRALITY

When the original internet structures like ARPANET and NSFNET shut down and private enterprises stepped in to provide users with access, these companies sought to limit how the consumers would use their services. In the early 2000s, some service providers, like Comcast and AT&T, banned access to certain networks or treated specific online content less favorably than they did others.[52]

A 2003 journal article by Columbia law professor Tim Wu outlined the key arguments for and against these types of restrictions: people who wanted open access thought the internet should be an even playing field for all content, which would allow innovative growth, while people who opposed it thought open access would inhibit broadband internet expansion. In the paper, Wu coined the term "net neutrality," which meant that all content online should be treated the same by internet providers, regardless of its source or topic.[53]

In 2005, the Federal Communications Commission (FCC) developed a series of rules that prevented internet service providers from violating the premise of net neutrality, meaning that providers couldn't block legal content, slow down content from creators they didn't like, or prohibit users from attaching devices like Wi-Fi routers to their computer systems. In 2008, Comcast sued the FCC over these rules, and the courts decided the FCC didn't have the right to make or enforce them.

During the Obama era, the FCC reworked its approach to net neutrality regulations, arguing that the internet was as vital to the citizens as electricity and water and thus should be treated as such.[54] Businesses that provide these kinds of services are deemed **common carriers**, meaning that they receive specific legal benefits for their operations in exchange for equitable service to the public. In 2017, President Donald Trump's administration reversed the FCC's position on net neutrality, eliminating the common carrier designation for broadband internet providers and allowing them to control the speed of specific internet content. The FCC is looking to reverse its position once again, with FCC chair Jessica Rosenworcel saying in 2022 that she wanted to reinstitute the rules from the Obama presidency. Because the FCC's position is capable of changing at any moment based on who inhabits the White House, one FCC official noted in June 2022 that he would prefer that Congress take up this issue and codify it in law to prevent future flip-flops.[55]

THE DARK CORNERS AND NEGATIVE CONSEQUENCES OF THE INTERNET

LEARNING OBJECTIVES

LO 4: Discuss the negative ramifications of online activities.

The United States' founders made freedom of speech one of the key constitutional ideals because they believed it would promote a "marketplace of ideas." Ethicist John Stuart Mill believed that if people are all allowed to express themselves in an open and uncensored forum, the best ideas would prevail over bad ones. In other words, the more freedom we give people in an unfettered environment to test the value of their thoughts, the better the ideas that survive this process will be.[56] In the United States, significant court rulings have relied on this concept in striking down everything from the censorship of public speech to attempts to censor the internet. (We'll talk more about Mill in Chapter 15 and more about some of those legal cases in Chapter 14.)

From a pure concept standpoint, this approach makes sense, much in the same way that the most reliable cars will sell better than those that don't work. However, any human being who has spent more than five minutes online over the past twenty years can likely recall some terrible behavior that has gone unchecked and proliferated. From email scams to online harassment, the ability for everyone to do almost anything to anyone from the darkest corners of the internet has led to some negative consequences. (Although many of these behaviors thrive in the social media world, a topic we'll cover in Chapter 10, because most of them started long before social media became a thing, we'll cover them here.) Some particularly bad behavior includes:

- Cyberscamming and cybercrimes
- Hoaxes and frauds
- Harassment and cyberbullying

Let's look at each of these concepts individually.

Cyberscamming and Cybercrimes

Although crime has always been part of society, the computer has increased both the criminals' reach and the seriousness of their crimes. Data gathered through the Federal Trade Commission revealed that it had received more than 2.3 million reports of fraud through all forms of media in 2022, with more than half of those cases beginning with an online contact of some kind.[57] This came to a total loss of more than two billion dollars for people who were scammed digitally. The most frequent scams were **identity theft**, in which a criminal steals personally identifiable information about someone and uses it to commit financial fraud, and **imposter scams**, in which criminals trick people into sending them money through a variety of schemes.

One of oldest forms of cybercrime is **phishing**, an email-based attack in which a criminal sends a mass email to a potential target in hopes of gaining access to that person's personal or business data. A new twist, known as **spear phishing**, targets specific individuals in an organization and includes details to make them think the sender is someone they know. In some cases, people turn over information that gives the criminal access to the victims' computers or the company network, while in other cases, opening the mail installs viruses or other forms of destructive code that can cripple the organization's systems. Researchers found that in 2021, phishing of all forms was the second most expensive form of attack on businesses' data.[58]

Criminals can also **hack**, or gain illegal entry to, a system, through external attacks on a company's data system. Once they gain access, they can manipulate the network as they see fit, holding the company hostage for profit. This approach to cybercrime is called **ransomware** and occurs when hackers lock a company out of its own computer system until their financial demands are met. For example, in

2021, criminals engaged in a ransomware attack on the Colonial Pipeline, one of the most important oil distribution systems in the United States.[59] The hackers shut the pipeline down and demanded payment before they would return control to the company. Colonial Pipeline ended up paying the criminals nearly five million dollars to end the crisis.[60]

On a more individual level, some cybercriminals attack individuals for the purpose of public embarrassment or worse, an activity known as **doxing**. Doxing can include providing contact information, like phone numbers, email address, and physical addresses, of individuals for the purpose of inspiring others to harass these people. It can also include things like revenge porn, which is the release of personal private photographs or videos into the public realm, and document dumps that reveal internet activity. One of the most famous examples of this came in 2015, when hackers gained access to personally identifiable information of more than thirty-seven million users of Ashley Madison, a website developed as a place where people could cheat on their spouses.[61] The hackers released that information after the site refused to meet their demands, leading to a series of job resignations, divorces, and suicides.[62] Doxing is also done with the purpose of silencing commentary on political and social issues. For example, in 2022, students and faculty at multiple campuses, including Harvard University and Wellesley College, were doxxed after expressing their views about Palestine and Israel.[63]

Hoaxes and Frauds

People often lie to benefit themselves financially, make themselves feel more important than they really are, or just because they enjoy messing with others. Faked photos and fantastical tales have captured people's imagination and have fooled folks over the years. Today, the quality of these fakes has become significantly improved, thanks to enhanced digital technology. In addition, more and more outlandish true news stories have spread beyond their geographical homebase, making it much more difficult to determine which crazy things happened and which ones did not.

For example, an associate editor at *GQ* magazine started a Twitter account in 2013 that chronicled criminal activities in Florida that were beyond unbelievable. This created the "Florida man" phenomenon, in which internet users shared stories about men in Florida who had committed all sorts of strange acts. However, as the stories continued to spread, more than a few fake ones had entered the mix, making it difficult for users to know if stories like "Florida man charged with assault with a deadly weapon after throwing alligator through Wendy's drive-thru window" or "Florida man arrested for hanging from traffic lights, [pooping] on cars," are real. (In this case, one is and one isn't. Feel free to look them up.)

The ability for a story or an image to be constructed and fine-tuned to perfection can make it difficult for people to separate reality from fiction online. College students often have strong fraud detectors when it comes to online hoaxes, but even they have been victimized from time to time. For example, in 2020, students at various college campuses found themselves targeted by a fake-check program, which offered them advance payments on nonexistent jobs. After students deposited the checks and provided part of the money to a specific designee of the program, the banks determined that the checks were invalid, and the students were responsible for the cash loss.[64] The key to detecting scams like these often comes down to the ability to verify the source of the offers so you can figure out if it is a legitimate offer or a trick.

MEDIA LITERACY MOMENT: VERIFYING ONLINE INFORMATION

A common phrase heard in journalism circles is "If your mother says she loves you, go check it out." In other words, verifying information, regardless of how likely it is to be true or false, is at the heart of critical thinking and media literacy. Although lies and scams significantly predate the internet, digital media has made it much easier to create and spread extremely convincing content that has no basis in reality. Here are a few quick tips to help you better determine the accuracy of information you find online:

- **Examine the source:** Who tells you something is almost as important as what they tell you. As a child, you likely believed your parents more than your siblings or the kid across the street who said a UFO crash-landed in his backyard. Look for sources of information that are tied to respectable enterprises, which have a history of providing you with factually accurate information, and that provide you with source material you can investigate for yourself.
- **Click the links:** When online writers provide you with information, they will often link back to material that supports the statements they are making. The presence of those links can appear to provide support for the writers' assertions and make you feel more secure in what they are telling you. However, hyperlinks are only as good as the information they provide, so click the links and examine the source material. Does the linked content actually say what the writers say it does? Is it from an independent source, or is it a link to another piece on the same website? Always dig a little deeper into what people are telling you before you believe the story.
- **Check elsewhere:** If you see one story claiming that class is canceled today because your university has been overrun by zombies, the concept itself is weird enough for you to pay little attention to the story. However, if you saw a story stating that a massive sewer backup has forced your university to cancel classes today until the mess can be cleaned up, that might seem plausible. The best way to figure out if that source is accurate is to see if any other sources are reporting this information. Did the school newspaper run a short piece online about this? Have you received a push alert on the school's media app about a sewer issue? If one source is the only source for something, it doesn't always mean the information is wrong, but it's worth doing some verification.
- **Give the URLs a look:** Like other knockoff brands, people online who want to fool you will try to look like a more reputable product. Scammers and fraudsters will often grab a .co or .net domain that is similar to a well-known .com site. They will also tweak the name of the organization they are mimicking as part of the web address. For example, the *Washington Post*'s URL is www.washingtonpost.com, so a scammer might go with www.washington.post.com or www.washingtonpest.com. This is why it's important to verify the URL.

THE NEXT STEP: Find a story posted on a website with which you are unfamiliar but that covers a topic of interest to you. Work through the four steps listed here to determine how believable the information is. Does the site present information on its "About Us" page that you can verify? Can you find information about this site through an internet search? Does it rely on linked material to prove its points? Are those links taking you to outside support documents or just more of the writer's own musings? Does the information at the other end of the link match up with what the author says it does? Have other sources online covered the topic of this story, and do they parallel what this source is telling you? Are there any shenanigans going with the site's URL or the URLs of sources they link to? When you are done, write a short essay on your findings.

Harassment and Cyberbullying

Imagine for a moment walking up to your professor after class and saying, "You should not be allowed to reproduce, let alone teach,"[65] or "Your class is a serious health liability, meaning it makes me want to kill myself three times a week."[66] If you're like most students, the thought of that level of face-to-face hostility seems unfathomable. That said, people wrote both of these things about actual professors on the website Rate My Professor, which allows students to anonymously comment on faculty members.

The ability to act in the shadows with anonymity has emboldened a lot of people to act terribly toward one another without a thought as to the consequences of those actions. According to the Pew Research Center's 2021 assessment of online harassment, approximately four in ten Americans reported that they have been attacked online. This study looked into everything from offensive name-calling to physical threats. Approximately one-third of women younger than thirty-five said they have suffered sexual harassment online.[67]

A particularly dangerous form of harassment is **cyberbullying**, a persistent form of threats and intimidation sent through a variety of electronic communications that targets young adults. U.S. researchers have found that almost 60 percent of teenagers and another 14.5 percent of children between nine and twelve years of age reported being victims of cyberbullying of some kind.[68] Scholars found that teens and young adults who had experienced cyberbullying were twice as likely to have attempted suicide as those individuals who had not been victimized in this way.[69] Although school administrators and state governments continue to look for ways to eliminate these kinds of attacks, many admit that they are limited in what they can do and outmatched by students who have a better handle on the technology used to spread rumors and disparage classmates.

JOBS WORKING WITH ONLINE MEDIA

Now that you better understand the various aspects of this field, here's a handy overview of a few common positions for people who want to work in online-related areas of media today.

Career Opportunity	Common Tasks
Web designer	• Develop graphic and display elements for clients' websites • Create online content to inform and engage site visitors • Maintain user-facing elements to update the style and feel of the site, as well as keeping it user friendly
Web developer	• Design clients' websites to function effectively • Perform analyses to determine the efficiency of the site's "back end" systems • Learn and adopt new coding and development tools to improve overall user experience
Information technology specialist	• Design internal digital networks to serve clients' specific computer needs • Monitor networks for potential problems that would undermine peak efficiency • Install and update software as needed
Programmer	• Create software and applications that serve clients' needs • Facilitate communication between software and other parts of a computer network • Refresh products through updates and enhancements

CHAPTER REVIEW

LO 1 Identify key moments in the history of the internet.

- In 1962, researcher J.C.R. Licklider proposed a way of developing a series of interconnected computers he called the "intergalactic network," whereby all computers could speak to one another without needing to go through a central junction point.
- Starting in 1969, ARPANET connected researchers at universities throughout the country, providing them with interactive opportunities through the network.
- The creation of multiple independent networks made it difficult for computers to connect from one network to another. To fix this problem, technology experts worked on a universal language for online computers, eventually settling on the TCP/IP system.
- In the late 1980s and early 1990s, British computer scientist Tim Berners-Lee developed a form of hypertext that would allow people without significant computer knowledge to access information online. This served as the birth of the World Wide Web. In 1993, he made his technology open source, allowing others to adopt and improve upon the technology, sparking a rise in web use.

- In the mid-1990s, the web began shifting into a more interactive platform, allowing individuals to not only consume information they found online, but also to respond to it and create their own content. This marked the start of Web 2.0.
- The biggest leap in accelerating computer use occurred when people no longer had to be tethered to power outlets and modems to use the internet. In 1997, a committee of computer scientists released a set of standards they thought could make wireless connection to the internet workable.

LO 2 **Understand specific ways the internet affects society.**

- **Broaden access to content:** people are no longer tied to geographic limitations when it comes to which information they can access. Whether it is reading a newspaper published several states away or being able to view priceless works of art held in a museum halfway around the world, people can use the internet to go places without having to leave their homes.
- **Bypass censorship:** The internet has given people a broader array of options to publish content, easier ways to put their content into the public sphere, and the opportunity to reach larger audiences, making it more difficult for censors to stamp out dissention.
- **Provide voice to niche interests:** Individuals with interests that traditional mainstream media often ignored have the ability to create niche communities online and present content to others who have an interest in the topic.
- **Archive information for future generations:** With the internet serving as a primary form of communication, its cataloging and preservation can give future generations the opportunity to learn about the past. In addition, archiving of the web has become crucial because information that exists online can be a powerful tool in the search for truth.

LO 3 **Review the companies that have monopoly-like control over various aspects of the internet and the ways in which they have exercised that control.**

- **Apple:** The company controls about 45 percent of the mobile phone market. All app developers who wish to create content for those phones must go through its app store, paying a portion of their revenue to Apple. In addition, Apple often creates its own copies of successful apps, promoting their versions over those originally built by third-party developers.
- **Amazon:** The company controls approximately 50 percent of all e-commerce in the United States. Amazon has been accused of unfairly competing with its third-party sellers by manipulating which products get the most attention on its website. In addition, Amazon has been accused of making its own versions of popular products that other sellers have created and selling them for less than the originals.
- **Meta/Facebook:** Facebook serves approximately one-third of the Earth's population. The Federal Trade Commission sued Facebook for illegally monopolizing the social media landscape by buying potential competitors or using its size to crush new ones. Research into the company's business practices has revealed that the company knew that some of its actions could harm users but refused to change for fear of financial loss. In addition, the company was found to have illegally provided third-party companies with users' personal data without their permission.
- **Google:** The company controls between 88 percent and 93 percent of all online searches. Several government entities have sued the company for monopolistic practices, ranging from how it favors Google-related enterprises in its search algorithm to its unilateral control over the Android app market.

LO 4 **Discuss the negative ramifications of online activities.**

- **Cyberscamming and cybercrimes:** The Federal Trade Commission found that individuals and organizations lose as much as two billion dollars annually to cybercriminals. The most frequent scams were identity theft, in that a criminal steals personally identifiable information about someone and uses it to commit financial fraud, and imposter scams, in that criminals pretend to be someone they are not to obtain access to personal information.

- **Hoaxes and frauds:** Online content has allowed false stories and fraudulent content to develop and spread. The quality of computer-based fakes and the ease in which fraudsters can distribute this content makes it more difficult for people to determine what is and isn't true.
- **Harassment and cyberbullying:** Anonymous posting of hateful content has created an environment of fear for many online users. Approximately 440 percent of U.S. citizens have reported being harassed online, with that number rising to almost 60 percent of teens. Cyberbullying of preteen and teenage children has led to increases in depression and despondency. Teens who were harassed in this way reported that they were twice as likely to have attempted suicide as those who were not cyberbullied.

KEY TERMS

ARPANET
Browser
Common carriers
Cyberbullying
Decentralized network
Distributed network
Doxing
Hack
Hypertext
Identity theft
Imposter scams
Internet protocol
Net neutrality
Packet switching
Phishing
Ransomware
Server
Spear phishing
TCP/IP
Time sharing
Transmission control protocol
Web 2.0

DISCUSSION QUESTIONS

1. Internet operations began as a way to connect researchers and share knowledge. How far from that original mission do you think the internet has shifted? If you think it changed a lot, is that a good thing in your mind?
2. Of the societal contributions the internet has made, which one do you think has been the most important to you personally? To society as a whole?
3. How concerned are you about the ways in which four companies can control specific elements of internet access and operation? Have you personally encountered specific problems associated with how any of these four companies operate?
4. How much trust do you put in any piece of content you receive through online sources? To what degree do you check them for accuracy before believing them? How credible do you find the sources you use online as compared with more traditional media sources?
5. Of the three negative elements associated with the internet, which one is the most concerning to you? Why? Have you experienced any of these forms of negative treatment during your time online? If so, what were they and how did they affect you?

Participants at a Black Lives Matter protest display the hashtag that has rallied online attention to their cause. The use of social media has been instrumental in helping individuals with shared interests and ideologies connect with one another.

dpa picture alliance/Alamy Stock Photo

10 SOCIAL MEDIA

INTRODUCTION

1. *What makes social media more or less important to you than the other forms of media we have discussed in this textbook?*
2. *Which social media platform do you use most frequently, and what benefits do you get from using it?*
3. *How important are the people you follow on social media to what you do, think, or buy?*

LEARNING OBJECTIVES

After completing this chapter, you should be able to:

1. Identify key moments in the history of social media.
2. Discuss the elements that make social media distinctive from other forms of media.
3. Compare and contrast the various types of popular social media platforms.
4. Evaluate the role social media plays in the media ecosystem.
5. Assess the ways in which social media use meets people's needs.

FROM SIX DEGREES TO TIKTOK: A BRIEF HISTORY OF SOCIAL MEDIA

LEARNING OBJECTIVES

LO 1: Identify key moments in the history of social media.

At some level, all forms of media are **social media**, in that they require users to use a media outlet, consume content, and do something with the information they received. Technology experts have made two distinctions to separate this form of communication from its predecessors[1]:

1. Social media involves online communication, which ties the phenomenon directly to the internet era.
2. Social media offers opportunities for the creation of content by its users, thus making participants both senders and receivers in the model. This places social media's starting point squarely in the Web 2.0 era (see Chapter 9).

For the sake of our discussion, we're going to consider social media to operate under this set of parameters, with a few minor exceptions. Let's start looking at the history of social media by categorizing its development into a few basic eras:

- Social media's infancy
- The big players emerge
- Social goes mobile and visual

Let's take a look at each one of these individually.

Social Media's Infancy

As with most new phenomena, the trailblazers in social media often have been lost to history. Six Degrees is usually identified as the first social media outlet. Founded in 1996 by Andrew Weinreich,

Six Degrees took its name from the concept that any person can be linked to any other person through six social connections or fewer. Users were able to post information about themselves and connect with other users they knew. The site had many of the same features that more successful operations would have in the future, but it suffered from the fact that many potential users lacked internet access. YouthStream Media purchased the site in 1999 but shut it down for good in 2000.[2]

Many of the early social sites focused on teens and twenty-somethings who had both a high level of technological acumen and a strong interest in connecting with peers online. Friendster was launched in 2002 and boasted three million active users within the first few months of its existence. In 2003, Google offered to purchase the property for thirty million dollars, which founder Jonathan Abrams declined.[3] However, the company couldn't keep up with the heavy volume of site traffic and had difficulty fending off competing platforms, essentially closing up shop in most major markets by 2006.[4]

One of Friendster's competitors was MySpace, which followed a similar dramatic rise-and-fall saga. The platform was launched in 2003 and had more than five million registered users by the end of 2004. MySpace connected with young adults by offering them the ability to express themselves through creating their own pages. The site provided high customizability and integrated music options and made it easy for users to share content with others. In 2005, Rupert Murdoch's News Corp purchased the social media platform for $580 million. Despite growth over the next three years, the tension between the site's creative interests and its owner's financial considerations led to a lack of development and expansion to enable it to compete with other growing social media platforms.[5] In 2009, the company cut one-third of its workforce, and by 2011, what remained was sold to singer/actor Justin Timberlake and his partners for $35 million.[6] By then, the site was hemorrhaging users and had become a shell of its former self. It was sold once again in 2016 to Time, Inc., but never regained traction as a viable social media site.

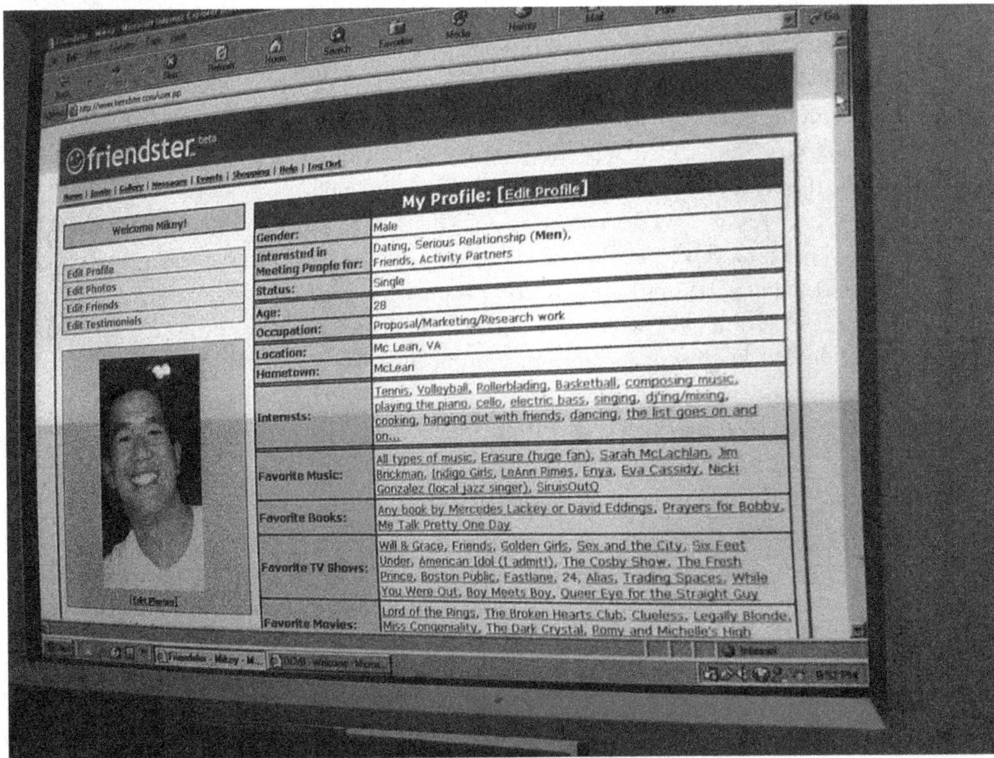

Social media sites like Friendster gave people the ability to find former classmates, family members, and other people with whom they wished to connect. Facebook eventually dominated this marketspace, relegating these other players to the ash heap of history.

The Washington Post/Contributor/via Getty Images

Not all social media launches during this time period targeted high school and college students who wanted to share music and funny photos. The concept of networking had long dominated the field of business, in which relationships were the coin of the realm. To move this form of corporate connectivity online, technology entrepreneur Adrian Scott started Ryze in 2001. Its purpose was to provide working professionals an online place to meet, share ideas, and find job opportunities.[7] The site claimed a membership of five hundred thousand people at its peak, with one thousand employer members, but it could never reach the popularity of other social media outlets Friendster and employment sites like LinkedIn.

A group of entrepreneurs who had previously found success with start-up ventures like PayPal launched LinkedIn in early 2003. The goal was to establish a professionals-only social media platform that allowed people to post résumés, organize events, and engage in career development.[8] In less than two years, the site claimed 1 million active members and continued to add features such as job postings, subscriptions, and recommended connections. When it went public in 2011, the site hosted more than 100 million individual users and 4.8 million paid corporate customers. At that point, LinkedIn was said to be adding members at a rate of one per second.[9] As of 2022, the site's annual revenue had reached slightly more than $8 billion, and it hosted 830 million members and 58 million registered corporate customers.[10]

The Big Players Emerge

With the exception of LinkedIn, most of the early social media efforts met a common fate: they were launched, got popular, grew too fast, hit some sort of organizational snag, and fell apart. The "information superhighway," as people back then called the online world, was littered with social media roadkill. However, in this second wave of Web 2.0 pioneers, several big players emerged that stood the test of time.

We discussed Facebook's development and almost monopolistic ownership of the social media realm in Chapter 9, so we won't repeat that here. Suffice it to say, Facebook's launch in 2004 and its subsequent growth have made it one of the most successful social media enterprises in the history of the platform and cofounder Mark Zuckerberg one of the most famous people on the planet. However, two other giants emerged during this time, each taking a specific angle on how people want to be connected and entertained.

YouTube was not the first video-sharing platform online, nor was it even supposed to be a video-sharing platform when its developers built it. The goal at the time was to make a dating site where people could view video clips of potential partners. While the dating part of the operation failed, people flocked to the site to see and upload video clips. The "aha" moment for cocreators Chad Hurley, Steve Chen, and Jawed Karim came after Janet Jackson's infamous "wardrobe malfunction" during the 2004 Super Bowl halftime show. The three men realized that there was no place online that had the clip available for viewing, thus inspiring the YouTube approach most users recognize today.

The site was launched in 2005 with a video titled "Me at the Zoo" showing YouTube cofounder Jawed Karim at the San Diego Zoo, commenting on the long trunks of the elephants; while hardly earth shattering, the video has earned its own Wikipedia page lauding its place in social media history.[11] YouTube has since expanded to include a wide array of short and long videos, with free and pay options for service. Google acquired the site in 2006, providing it both financial stability and additional development opportunities. Marketing agencies quickly saw the benefits of being attached to short videos, brokering deals to both post sponsored content and connect traditional video ads to popular clips. As of 2022, viewers watch nearly 5 billion videos every day, and three hundred hours of video are uploaded to the platform every minute.[12] Data analyses suggest that approximately 2.6 billion people use YouTube at least once a month,[13] making it the second most visited website in the world.

While YouTube went big, Twitter went small, as in 140 characters small. The platform started in 2006 as a **microblogging** service, allowing people to post short bursts of content as part of a stream of personal updates. Founder Jack Dorsey, a New York University college student, saw this platform as a way to communicate with a group of friends through a single text message. To inspire users, the initial prompt for the service told users to respond to the question, "What are you doing?" before changing it to "What's happening?"[14] Each posting was called a "tweet" in the spirit of the platform's name.

As the platform grew from a way to text a few friends into an expansive social media platform, the designers added features by the end of 2007 that drastically improved its usefulness and reach. For example, Twitter developed a system that allowed people to reshare things other people had sent them, a concept now known as a retweet. The developers also added the use of symbols to send direct messages to specific users (@) and to create an ongoing discussion through a shared term (#). These elements

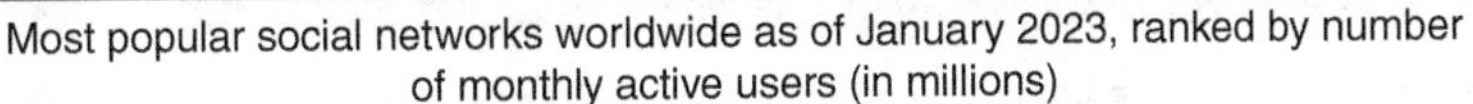

FIGURE 10.1 ■ Most Popular Social Media Platforms Worldwide as of 2023 Based on Number of Active Users (in Millions)

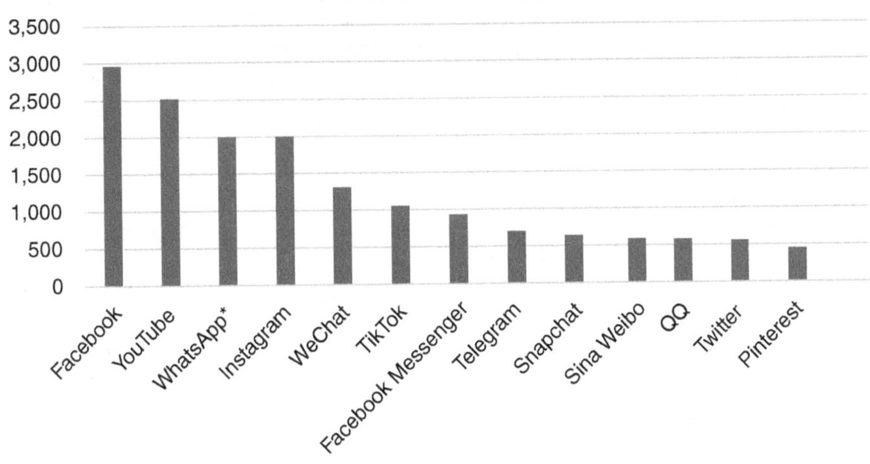

source: Based on data from Statista, https://www.statista.com/statistics/272014/global-social-networks-ranked-by-number-of-users/

became integral in several social and political movements, for which Twitter played a significant role in connecting like-minded individuals. The #MeToo hashtag was first used in 2006 but became a rallying call in 2017, when actor Alyssa Milano used it to raise awareness of sexual assault and harassment. The #BlackLivesMatter and #BLM hashtags became synonymous with the need to rectify racial inequality throughout all aspects of society. It first emerged in 2013 after seventeen-year-old Trayvon Martin's death and George Zimmerman's acquittal in the shooting and has been prominent in subsequent protests, including those related to the deaths of Michael Brown in 2014 and George Floyd in 2020.[15] Twitter's growth as a social media platform was due in large part to its simplicity and easy accessibility.

Twitter's initial 140-character limit was based on the amount of data that could be sent through a text message at the time, which allowed users to send and receive tweets wherever they went. However, developers soon augmented the platform with ways to add more content to users' messages. This included expanding the text limit to 280 characters in 2017, providing users with ways to include shortened links in tweets, and the addition of multimedia elements, including pictures and videos. Furthermore, Twitter opened up its service to third-party apps that could allow the management of multiple accounts and the categorizing of content into various streams.

Twitter went public in 2013 and immediately became worth twenty-four billion dollars, with more than 200 million people using the platform.[16] That number grew to more than 330 million in 2022, the same year entrepreneur Elon Musk purchased Twitter for forty-four billion dollars.[17] Musk's early days of ownership included laying off half of the staff, attempting to charge eight dollars for the "blue checkmark verification" element, and seeing more than 1.3 million users abandon the platform.[18] The future of the platform remains tenuous at best while many social media users shift to other traditional powers like Instagram and new upstarts like Mastodon.

Social Goes Mobile and Visual

YouTube and Twitter tapped into something that helped expand the reach of social media and make it a larger part of people's lives. YouTube demonstrated the importance of visual storytelling and the connections people made through sharing images and videos. Prior to YouTube, much of the content on social media sites lacked quality visual content. One of the crucial elements of Twitter's expansion was its ability to be accessed through mobile devices, making social media a consistent part of users' daily life. The users were no longer tethered to a computer to check in on their social media, so they could engage at a moment's notice through their phone.

TABLE 10.1 ■ Key Figures in Social Media History

Andrew Weinreich	Mark Zuckerberg	Ashley Weatherspoon	Whitney Wolfe Herd	Charli D'Amelio
• Founded Six Degrees, commonly deemed the first social media platform, in 1997. • Created the first patent in social media development for his system of constructing a social networking system. • Involved in seven technology startups, earning the moniker "serial entrepreneur."	• Cofounded Facebook, the most successful social media platform in the world, in 2004. • As Facebook's CEO, became the world's youngest self-made billionaire in 2007 at age twenty-three.	• A social media producer who runs Dear Young Queen, a site that encourages women to connect and share their experiences in life. • Is credited with the first social media post that launched the "Black Twitter" phenomenon in 2009.	• Cofounded Tinder, an online dating site, in 2012. • Founder and CEO of Bumble, an online dating social media app geared toward women, which began in 2014. • Became the world's youngest self-made female billionaire in 2021 at age thirty-one.	• A competitive dancer who started sharing social media posts in 2019, she became the first person to reach 50 million and then 100 million TikTok followers. • Dubbed "the reigning queen of TikTok," she has more followers on the platform than any other user as of 2022. • Earned $17.5 million in 2021, between her influencer efforts and other projects.

Pairing visual and mobile elements, social media took advantage of improving technology, expanding digital networks, and users' insatiable desire to connect with other people. The shift from website-based platforms to phone apps made social media more user friendly. This era of social media is still developing, as individual apps look for ways to distinguish themselves and garner a share of the market. Even as more established brands like Facebook and Twitter integrated improved visual and mobile elements, many new platforms that took advantage of these elements began during the 2010s and have continued to thrive.

One of the earliest pairings of mobile and visual elements was Instagram, which was launched in 2010 as a photo- and video-sharing service. The app began as a way for people to provide their physical locations to other users, similar to other geolocation services like Foursquare. However, it added visual elements to the mix to enhance its users' experiences. The model quickly flipped when the founders realized that the images could drive traffic better than geography. The ability to caption the photos and tweak them through various Photoshop-like options made the app an all-in-one photo studio that anyone could use. Mobile phones with improved cameras gave users an easy way to capture and then share images to the site.

Instagram's founders believed that making the platform mobile would make or break their project.[19] Less than a year after its inception, Instagram had nearly five million users, all of whom were iPhone users. The company didn't release a version of the app for Android users until 2012, when more than one million people downloaded it from the Google Play Store on the first day it was available.[20] That same year, Facebook purchased Instagram for one billion dollars in cash and stock.[21] As of 2022, Instagram had more than two billion active viewers, with six in ten U.S. users visiting the app daily.[22]

A year after Instagram's launch, Snapchat offered a similar successful pairing of visual and mobile elements. Snapchat built on the qualities that made Instagram popular, including its mobile basis that made it ubiquitous and the ability to communicate through visual elements that made it more universal. That said, the creators of Snapchat took the visual aspect in a different direction, relying less on high-quality images and more on quick takes of videos or photos. If Instagram was like a photo gallery exhibition, Snapchat was more like a high school locker door, with simple photos, digital stickers, and cartoonish illustrative options. The default setting on the platform made the visuals disappear ten seconds after the receiver opened the message. The platform also allowed users to save the photos for more permanent use and sharing through a memories function.

Perhaps the most important element that made Snapchat successful was its introduction of incentive **emojis**, small digital icons that expressed emotions or thoughts, based on connections and use.

These icons provided users with the opportunity to label others to indicate different levels of friendship, such as best friends, best friends forever, and super best friends forever. The most valuable icon in terms of inspiring use, however, is the Snapstreak emoji. This fire symbol appears next to a number that indicates how many days in a row two people have sent snaps back and forth. If both users do not snap each other within a twenty-four-hour period, the streak ends and the emoji disappears. This element incentivized use, providing people with a specific reason to log in at least once per day, thus introducing habit-forming behavior. As of 2022, Snapchat has 332 million daily active users, who create an average of 5 billion snaps per day.[23]

Snapchat's use of emojis to reward frequent activity between individuals has helped grow the brand and develop media habits for users.

iStockphoto.com/stockcam

Two apps that emerged around this time paired the Snapchat approach to content with a stronger use of video elements. When Vine launched in 2013, the service offered users the opportunity to share six-second videos with the public or specific segments of their followers. These short clips could be looped for constant play, with the site tracking the number of loops audience members watched. The platform used similar tactics to Snapchat, in that the content wasn't intended to be perfect, while integrating the use of looped motion made popular in animated GIFs. In addition, like other forms of social media, users could connect with friends, celebrities, and anyone else who produced content of interest. Twitter swooped in, buying the app for thirty million dollars before its official release.[24] By 2015, the platform hosted two hundred million active users, but Twitter shut the app down a year later because of financial concerns and increased competition in the video market. Instagram had begun integrating improved video options that allowed longer clips, while Snapchat surged among younger users. In 2016, all video Vines were gone.[25]

A year later, the short-video platform received new life through the popularity of TikTok. After starting in China, merging with the Musical.ly platform, and rebranding itself, TikTok hit the international market in 2017. Within a year, it was available in more than 150 markets and had 133 million users worldwide. By 2022, the app had grown to more than 3 billion total downloads and more than 1 billion active users.[26] The site retained options similar to other social media apps, like filters, messaging, sharing options, and hashtags. The also presented unique features, such as the ability to add musical scores to video clips and socializing challenges, which prompted users to record themselves doing specific activities or lip-synching to certain songs.[27]

FIGURE 10.2 ■ TikTok's Explosive Growth over a Five-Year Span

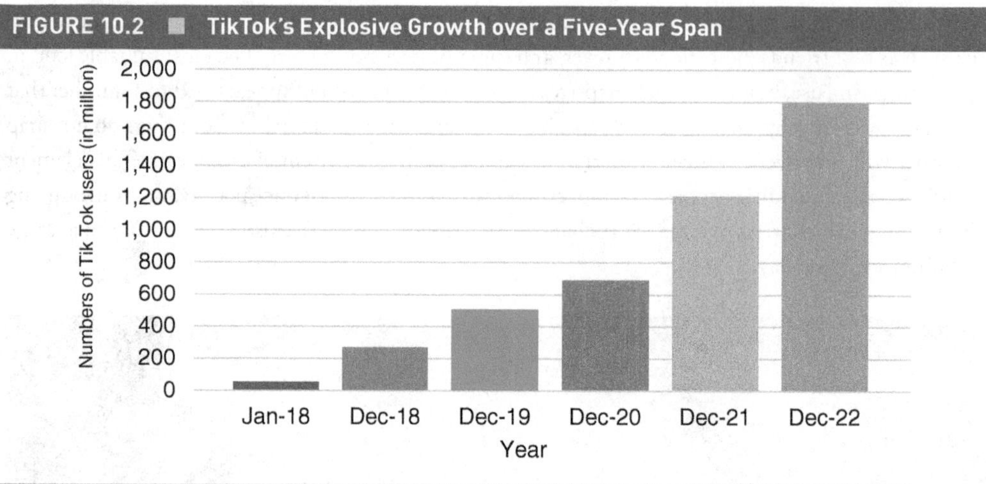

source: Based on data from https://www.omnicoreagency.com/tiktok-statistics/

TikTok also approached content curation in a distinctive way. Rather than relying on a feed of content based on specific people the user follows, TikTok generates a collection of videos for each user based on what they have previously watched. In other words, the computer learns from what you actually do instead of what you say you like, thus providing you with a more accurate and complete collection of content you will likely enjoy.[28]

U.S. officials became concerned, however, about the ability of the app to collect this kind of user data, particularly because the platform's parent company is based in China. As president, Donald Trump demanded that ByteDance sell off the TikTok platform, or the United States would ban the app. Although a deal was in place to make this move, Joe Biden did not enforce Trump's executive order when he took office in 2021, and China remained in control of the app.[29] This became a significant problem in June 2022, when a report based on leaked recordings from TikTok meetings revealed that China has repeatedly accessed U.S. users' private data, despite promises not to do so.[30] In February 2023, the Biden administration required that TikTok be removed from all federal devices, a move mirroring that of multiple other countries.[31]

DEFINING AND DIFFERENTIATING SOCIAL MEDIA

LEARNING OBJECTIVES

LO 2: Discuss the elements that make social media distinctive from other forms of media.

Social media shares many common traits with other forms of communication that we have discussed or will discuss in this book. Here are a few:

- It relies on a sender and a receiver, much like the models outlined in Chapter 1.
- It seeks to engage and inform users on a wide array of topics.
- It allows users to select specific sources, topics, and interests from a wider array of possibilities.

What makes social media special, however, is the ways in which it allows communicators to engage with material in ways not available to them on other platforms. There are hundreds of ways that social media differs from other forms of communication, but for the sake of the big picture, let's focus on just two topics.

- Many-to-many model
- Individualized content selections

Let's take a deeper dive into these two areas.

Many-to-Many Model

We discussed this briefly in Chapter 2, but it bears repeating here, as social media is really one of the key drivers of this approach to content dissemination. The previous forms of media we examined, including books, magazines, newspapers, broadcasting, and films, rely on a one-to-many model of communication. In each case, a single source created a specific message that was delivered to a wide range of readers, listeners, or viewers. The source could be a newspaper or magazine publisher that sent out copies of a specific publication or a broadcasting outlet that sent content along electromagnetic waves to anyone with a radio or television. This approach to disseminating content has been at the core of mass media for generations.

The model for social media differs, because individuals can serve as both senders and receivers of content simultaneously. It also allows individuals to select which sources they receive, creating a large collection of diverse audiences. This approach, known as the many-to-many model, gives people the opportunity to customize the number and type of individuals and organizations they follow. These individuals and organizations, in turn, can decide to reciprocate and "follow back," or choose other people to follow (see Figure 10.3).

FIGURE 10.3 ■ Social Media Model

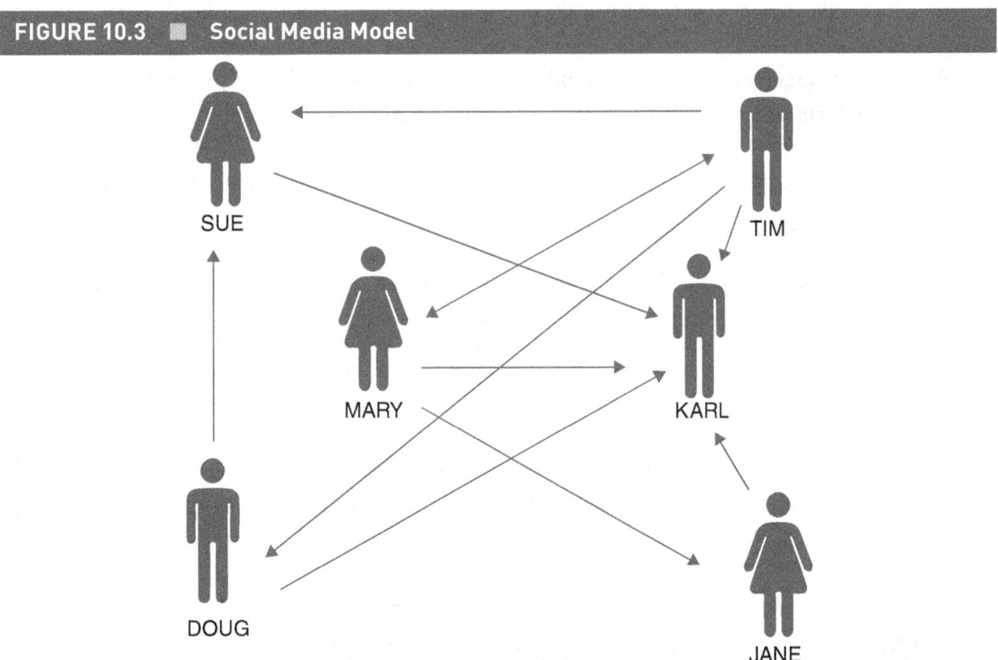

In Figure 10.3, Mary follows Tim, Jane, and Karl on Instagram. Tim follows Mary back, but he also follows Sue and Doug. Doug follows Mary, but not Sue or Tim. Karl doesn't follow anyone, but everyone follows him. At any point, any of these people can choose to follow or unfollow anyone in this matrix or millions of other people who are also on this social media platform.

What also makes this model distinctive is that individuals can decide at which level they wish to participate as senders and receivers. Some people have massive followings, thanks in large part to their national or international fame, but choose not to consume content from a wide array of people. For example, as of April 2023, musician Nicki Minaj has more than 216 million followers on Instagram but has chosen to follow only 651 people on the platform. In other cases, people choose to send and follow equally, or to simply follow accounts without actively creating content of their own, something commonly called **lurking**.

Individualized Content Selection

In a standard one-to-many model, the media outlet itself becomes the source of information as well as the beacon of trust. People choose to believe what they read in the *New York Times*, see on CNN, or hear on National Public Radio. Over the years, these outlets have developed a reputation of putting forth reliable and valuable content, even as the individual reporters, editors, producers, and other staff members change over time. As noted in Chapter 1, some individual journalists on traditional platforms, such as Walter Cronkite, became trusted sources of information in their own right, but the media outlet itself still had significant importance to readers and viewers.

Social media shifts the model significantly in favor of **individualization**. This means that social media users can select specific people to follow, like, and support instead of relying on the monolithic presence of a specific media outlet. A Twitter user can decide the only reporter at the *Jackson County Journal* worth reading is Kareem Howe and follow his Twitter account, while a different user might follow three or four reporters' accounts as well as the newspaper's general account. People interested in political news might follow the local political reporter at the nearby radio station, but not the sports and finance reporters. Each choice is individualized.

The individualized approach also gives people outside of mainstream media outlets a voice. The social media arena gives people the ability to grow their own audiences and wield influence over them based on the expertise they have and the trust they inspire in users. In other words, a teenager who posts fashion ideas to a well-liked and heavily followed Instagram account can sway public opinion about what's hot and what's not more than a veteran reporter at a mainstream fashion magazine. People who have established themselves as valuable sources of information in a given area of social media are called **influencers**.

Influencers do exactly what the term implies: they influence their followers to value certain things, buy certain products, or live in specific ways. Influencers often fall into one of several categories:

- Celebrities (people who are world famous, like athletes, politicians, actors, musicians)
- Niche experts (people with smaller, but engaged followings on specific topics)
- Insta-famous (people who have earned large followings based primarily on their social media presence or lifestyle brand)
- Content creators (people who develop material across various platforms for the benefit of expression and knowledge dissemination)

Given the heavy use of social media and the level of engagement users have with these individuals, marketing agencies and advertising firms have shifted from focusing on mainstream media and global stars to influencers on social media.

A DEEPER LOOK: INFLUENCERS CASH IN

The concept of influencers is not a new one, in that certain people have always had the ability to shape the ways in which people think. Celebrity endorsers in the predigital era included movie stars, musicians, and professional athletes. If actor Humphrey Bogart told people to buy a Whitman's Sampler of chocolates, opera singer Patrice Munsel endorsed Camel cigarettes for throat health, or baseball star Yogi Berra said that Yoo-hoo was worth drinking, people tended to believe it.

In today's social media realm, those same kinds of people hold similar sway over large populations of people, with actor Zendaya, entertainer Jennifer Lopez, and soccer star Cristiano Ronaldo all dominating Instagram. These and other stars have used their social media influence to earn big money through sponsored posts. Ronaldo earns approximately $1.6 million per sponsored post, while movie star Dwayne "The Rock" Johnson and singer/actor Ariana Grande each earn about $1.5 million for each social media promotion.[32]

However, the influencer market goes far beyond famous people who engaged with social media, as social media itself has made people famous. Charli D'Amelio became a multimillionaire at the age of eighteen. The competitive dancer has more than 141 million followers on TikTok, making her the most followed user of the platform as of 2022. Her lip-synch and dance videos have garnered sponsorship gigs with Dunkin' and Hollister as well as her own show on Hulu.[33]

Her story isn't unique, as individuals with significant followings on social media platforms have profited greatly from their efforts. Influencers in many cases are specifically tied to niche aspects of life in which they have cultivated a form of expertise that users admire.

For example, Huda Kattan is a makeup artist who started a blog in 2010 to share her tips and techniques. She currently promotes her work and her own cosmetics line through social media platforms like Instagram, where she has more than fifty million followers as of 2022. Chiara Ferragni started her fashion blog, The Blonde Salad, at age twelve in 2009. In 2012, the model and influencer made her first post on Instagram, and a decade later she has more than twenty-seven million followers and earns about $12,000 per sponsored post.[34]

In some cases, social media influencers have seen their work undercut their marketability. For example, on YouTube, both Shane Dawson and Felix Arvid Ulf "PewDiePie" Kjellberg have millions of subscribers to their channels, but both saw advertisers pull away from them when they used racially insensitive material in their videos. Both men have also been accused of presenting other offensive content, such as anti-Semitic and sexually distasteful statements. However, both influencers remain immensely popular and continue to profit from their work on social media. (We will touch more on this approach to advertising and marketing in Chapter 13.)

Social media has both a larger overall reach and a different target audience than traditional media. Table 10.2 offers a brief look at which U.S.-based outlets and individuals top the list in their respective categories

TABLE 10.2 ■ Traditional versus Influencer Connections

Primary Communication Method	Traditional Leader (U.S.)	Social Media Leader (U.S.)
Text	Newspaper: *USA Today*, circulation 2.3 million	Twitter: former president Barack Obama, 131 million followers
Photos	Magazine: *AARP Magazine*, circulation 35 million	Instagram: reality TV star Kylie Jenner, 347 million followers
Audio	Broadcast radio program: *Marketplace*, 14.8 million weekly listeners	Spotify: *The Joe Rogan Experience*, 11 million listeners per episode
Video	Broadcast TV program: *NCIS* (CBS), 10.9 million viewers per episode	YouTube: Cocomelon - Nursery Rhymes, 135 million subscribers TikTok: Charli D'Amelio, 141.5 million followers

EXAMINING SOCIAL MEDIA APPROACHES

LEARNING OBJECTIVES

LO 3: Compare and contrast the various types of popular social media platforms.

Even using a relatively restrictive definition of social media, the number of different platforms, each with its own approach, can seem overwhelming. To help organize the field, digital marketing expert Garima Kakkar created specific areas into which most social media platforms fall.[35] In applying the social media definition we are using in this chapter to her categorical approach, we can better understand the types of social media that exist and what benefits they each distinctively provide to users (see Table 10.3).

Network-based sites are intended for the user to get acquainted with other people who have similar interests and needs, or to just share valuable information in a discussion-style format. Many of the social networking sites, like Facebook and LinkedIn, allow the users to pick people with whom they wish to connect, based on a broad array of personal and social interests. Others, like TripAdvisor and Reddit, allow people to talk about shared interests, like if a football team overpaid for a free agent or

TABLE 10.3 ■ Kakkar's Categories of Social Media Sites

Category	Example	Purpose
Social networking	Facebook, LinkedIn	• Keep in touch with friends and family members • Develop relationships among people of similar interests • Socialize and share opinions with others
Media sharing	Instagram, YouTube	• Create and share content that is of interest to users • Connect with content creators • Provide entertainment
Discussion forums	Reddit, Quora	• Seek knowledge from experts on various topics • Express opinions on important issues • Keep up to date on news and trends
Content curation	Pinterest, Pocket	• Find inspiration in hobbies and activities from other like-minded people • Share ideas and content to provide value to other users • Store important content for later use online
Consumer reviews	Yelp, TripAdvisor	• Seek information on products and services to make informed decisions • Contribute personal experiences regarding products and services to benefit other consumers • Gain honest information from fellow users as opposed to self-promoting organizations
Self-publishing networks	WordPress, Medium	• Develop an online presence on a topic in which one has interest and expertise • Cultivate an audience of users with an interest in a topic • Sharpen writing skills and build a portfolio of material

what was the worst movie ever made. In addition, some sites give people the opportunity to share expertise, such as providing someone information about the quality of a certain city's restaurants, or engage in collective problem-solving efforts, such as how to fix a garbage disposal or what strategy was most successful in getting past a certain level of a video game.

Content-sharing sites provide users with the opportunity to collect information for themselves and provide it to other users who might find that information useful. Curation sites, like Pinterest, tend to be more about sharing found material, much in the way you might tape a funny cartoon to your computer monitor or copy a favorite recipe out of your grandmother's personal cookbook. On the other hand, Instagram and YouTube offer these options as well as the chance for people to develop their own content for dissemination on the platform.

Some individuals have a desire to find their own place to create, develop, and share informational content on topics with which they can demonstrate particular expertise through diary-style text posts on a **blog**. Blogging began as a phenomenon around 1999 when LiveJournal gave users the opportunity to post their thoughts and daily activities to the web, much in the same way people used to write in personal diaries. While some of these personal journals gained traction, it was the next phase of blogging that occurred over the next decade that made this a legitimate form of social media and information sharing.

In this next phase, individuals and blogging collectives hosted specific sites at which they would write about given topics for an interested audience. Blogs about cooking, politics, parenting, journalism, and more emerged, with the more popular ones gaining social media followings in the hundreds and thousands. For example, Ree Drummond began writing in 2006 at the blogging site TypePad about her life as a mother and a down-home cook from Oklahoma. As the blog's popularity grew, she registered her own domain name, thepioneerwoman.com, and continued to post information about ranch life. Her empire exponentially expanded over the next fifteen years, and she won blogging awards, wrote books, and became a television star. As of 2023, her net worth is estimated at fifty million dollars.[36]

THE VALUE OF SOCIAL MEDIA

LEARNING OBJECTIVES

LO 4: Evaluate the role social media plays in the media ecosystem.

As is the case with most emerging forms of media, it can take a while for a larger section of society to get a handle on what they do and why they matter. (As we noted in Chapter 9, the mainstream media dismissed the value of the internet pretty quickly, only to look quite foolish in retrospect.) Social media has many of the same valuable traits as other forms of media, such as the ability to keep users informed, to meet the needs of specific audiences, and to create a collective base of information from which users can draw. It also has some specific elements that make it distinctive within the larger media ecosystem:

- Constant media access
- Exponential audience expansion
- Transitive trust

Let's unpack each of those aspects one at a time.

Constant Media Access

The movement from traditional computers to mobile devices marked a giant shift in how people obtain information. If we start with the earliest forms of mass media, like newspapers and books, it could take days, weeks, or even months before whatever writers had to say made it to readers. When radio and television broadcast emerged, the speed at which we could gain access to information improved drastically. Instead of getting news once a day in a paper, we could see full news broadcasts at 5, 6, and 10 p.m. and hear news updates once per hour. However, the devices on which we could get that information were usually limited, based on the need for power, the size of the device, and the broadcaster's geographic reach. Furthermore, we got information only when the people in charge of publishing papers or broadcasting reports decided to create and disseminate the content.

The shift to the internet model opened up more doors, because content providers could publish as often as they saw fit, and users could access that material whenever it was convenient. The only true limitation was access to an online portal and a power connection for the computer. In moving media to an app-based, portable-device system, the last barrier to constant media access essentially fell.

Anywhere someone has a phone and a signal, they can be as plugged in to social media as they want. Acting as both senders and receivers, social media users can constantly feed an interested and engaged audience while simultaneously collecting feedback to adjust their approach to subsequent messages and posts they disseminate. This allows users to spend much more time engaging with social media than they otherwise would if it had limitations similar to more traditional forms of media. The average user spent 2 hours and 27 minutes per day on social media in 2023. The Philippines had the highest use, at more than 4 hours, while U.S. users spent 2 hours and 14 minutes each day on various social media platforms.[37]

Exponential Audience Expansion

The size of an audience matters a great deal when it comes to how much influence a media outlet can have. Building a traditional media audience can take months, years, or even decades, which is what makes social media's reach so impressive. For example, the highest circulation ever recorded for a traditional newspaper was when *Komsomolskaya Pravda* in the former Soviet Union peaked at 21.9 million in 1990, 65 years after its founding.[38] In comparison, K-pop star Kim Tae-Hyung, better known as V in the group BTS, set several world records for the fastest to reach 1 million and 10 million followers on Instagram.[39] As of April 2023, he had more than 58 million followers.

Influencers often tally audiences in the millions, as users flock to them to stay aware of whatever they post. In addition, content from one individual can be shared repeatedly throughout a platform, expanding the reach of that message far beyond the person's initial group of followers. Social media users refer to this kind of rapid, exponential spread of content as a post's going **viral**. One good example involved Procter & Gamble's #DistanceDance campaign, begun after the company heard about problems certain states had in getting younger people to practice social distancing during the pandemic. The firm hired Charli D'Amelio in April 2020 to post a TikTok dance challenge, with a message for people to stay home. The video received 8 billion views in a week, and about 1.7 million social media users posted their own versions of the dance.[40]

Social media users have demonstrated the passion they have for the individuals, groups, and brands they follow. When influential members of their online community put forth an idea or challenge, these users respond individually and share the information throughout their own networks, making it much easier for more people to connect with that message quickly.

Transitive Trust

Credibility rests at the core of all good media messages. News reporters, public relations practitioners, and advertising agencies work tirelessly to find ways to show an audience that their work should be trusted. A particularly valuable feature of social media is that it allows the credibility of one source to be shared throughout a network. Traditional media operates like a centralized network when it comes to trust. The source itself is either trusted or not trusted by each individual user. Social media is based on individuals' placing trust in other individuals, meaning that trust is spread through a distributed network (see Chapter 9). Therefore, it is much easier to gain credibility within that type of media ecosystem.

Think about it this way: let's say Claire trusts Bob and Bob trusts Jackson. If Jackson gets a message from Company X on Twitter and decides to share that message, Jackson is essentially saying, "I trust this message and I think you should, too." When Bob sees Jackson's message, he might forward it to his followers, including Claire, who knows nothing about Jackson or Company X. However, because Bob sent it and Claire believes Bob, she believes Company X's message. As long as each individual user trusts the person before them, the message retains its credibility as it moves through the network.

This approach can be fantastic when people or organizations want to spread a message across a wide swath of people in a short time. Conversely, it can be terrible if that message has a mistake in it, makes the sender look stupid, or in some other way runs counter to the ideology of a big portion of the social media community. The name for this kind of viral misstep comes with its own hashtag: **#fail**.

MEDIA LITERACY MOMENT: HOW TO AVOID #FAIL ON SOCIAL MEDIA

Social media can provide people with a broad array of opportunities to do amazing things. This form of communication can also lead to epic disasters, known throughout the internet as #fail. Not every online mistake is avoidable, but many mistakes come from a few basic places. Here are some key things that often create problems on social media and the best ways to avoid them.

Spelling and Grammar

When it comes to ways in which people undercut their own arguments, nothing beets spelling and grammar. (See what I did there?) Editing a social media post before making it public can feel almost quaint, but catching small errors can be the easiest way to limit disasters. Simple mistakes like using the wrong "your" or an incorrect homonym ("berry the hatchet") can have other people questioning how much they should trust you. Even worse, some misspellings can cause your mistakes to go viral. For example, in 2019, CBBC's Dave Benson Phillips used Twitter to remind people about daylight savings time when he wrote, "Have a good night whatever you're doing...and don't forget to put your cocks back." As thousands of Twitter users shared and commented on his error, Phillips issued several other tweets to make it clear he meant "clocks."[41]

Get Dirty

The ability to quickly write a text to send out on social media can lead to errors, especially when your audience has a dirty mind. One key way to avoid these kinds of mistakes is to read everything from the perspective of a twelve-year-old boy, because kids of that age have a way of making everything sound obscene. This can help you avoid making double entendres like "Grandpas say they still enjoy their nuts at Christmas." This basic rule also applies to making sure hashtags don't have similar problems, like the time in 2012 when the Chester Literary Festival in the United Kingdom marketed itself on Twitter with the hashtag #CLitFest.[42]

Research Hashtags

Aside from avoiding awkward hashtags, it will benefit you to avoid hopping on a trending tag before figuring out why it's trending. For example, during the Egyptian Revolution, #cairo became a way for people to keep track of a dangerous, developing situation. The marketing team at Kenneth Cole hopped on Twitter, using the hashtag to promote the fashion brand's upcoming spring lineup.[43] Entenmann's made a similarly tone-deaf mistake in 2011, when a jury announced that Casey Anthony did not kill her daughter, Caylee. As the #notguilty hashtag went viral in that moment, the baked-goods company joined the discussion with a tweet asking "Who's #notguilty about eating all the tasty treats they want?!"[44] Both companies apologized for their mistakes, but the damage was done.

Prepare for Disaster

One of the biggest ways to avoid becoming a cautionary tale on social media is to consider the worst-case scenario for everything you publish. This is particularly important if you are operating social media accounts on behalf of an organization. For example, many social media efforts ask users to participate, not thinking for a minute that users might engage with them in a less-than-positive way. Two campaigns involving police in 2014 fell into this situation, leading to a great deal of backlash on Twitter. CNN used the hashtag #askacop to solicit audience engagement for the network's *Cops Under Fire* segment. Many users took to the hashtag to question issue of police brutality and racism.[45] A similar response occurred when the New York Police Department asked people to share pictures of themselves with officers under the #myNYPD hashtag. The tag was flooded with hundreds of images that showed police officers striking or tackling people during arrests.[46]

Not every social media disaster can be avoided, but these ideas can help prevent some simple mistakes. Prior to publishing, edit the content carefully, consider any way in which the material can be misinterpreted, and take care to avoid connecting your content with anything that could be problematic. Then, be ready to respond to whatever the social media universe throws back at you. As always, being polite, clear, and respectful can make life a lot easier.

THE NEXT STEP: Search the internet for examples of social media failures that have gone viral or have at least attracted some media coverage. Which of the problems that we identified apply to these disasters? Then, go through your social media feeds and apply the above methods to find potential #fail moments. Where do you see the biggest room for improvement? Write a short essay on your findings.

USES AND GRATIFICATIONS OF SOCIAL MEDIA

LEARNING OBJECTIVES

LO 5: Assess the ways in which social media use meets people's needs.

Research on social media use has often focused on the way people rely on these platforms for entertainment and to avoid boredom. These habit-based engagements provide a relatively basic set of reasons for people to scroll through an Instagram feed or snap back at a friend via Snapchat. However, several other uses and gratifications have also emerged in a variety of research studies. Taking the findings on the whole, these needs fit into one of three basic areas:

- Interpersonal connectivity
- Informational awareness
- Social comparison

Let's take a look at the specifics of each area of need.

Whitney Wolfe Herd, founder and CEO of Bumble.

Vivien Killilea/Stringer/via Getty Images

Interpersonal Connectivity

Humans are social creatures, and as such, they have a need to associate with others. The goal is to find like-minded people who share their interests and beliefs as they build a community of friends and colleagues. Social media is a key way for people to achieve this socialization, because it provides easy access to other people with similar interests and overcomes geographic limitations that limited the ability of like-minded people to interact.[47] In this way, social media has become the new town hall, local diner, and singles bar for people today.

For example, apps like Tinder have taken the face-to-face socialization effort of finding love and moved it to handheld devices. As of 2022, the app has more than seventy-five million users and makes more than thirty million matches every day.[48] Since its launch in 2013, it has become the most popular dating app in the world, introducing terms like "swipe right" into the social media lexicon. One of the site's founders, Whitney Wolfe Herd, left Tinder in 2014 amid claims of a toxic workplace environment. She went on to found Bumble, the second most popular dating app in North America. Bumble puts women in charge of the process, giving them the ability to make the first online move. The app's success helped make Herd the youngest self-made female billionaire in the world.[49] Other apps cater to niche audiences, such as the LGBTQ+ community, participants in specific religions, and even pet owners.

Connectivity on social media has also benefited underrepresented groups and social justice causes. Social media user Ashley Weatherspoon is credited with creating Black Twitter when she posted an amusing anecdote in September 2009 with the hashtag #uknowurblackwhen. The message spread quickly and others began adding their own experiences and thoughts about their community. The underlying concept of a set of shared cultural experiences within a larger society isn't new, but social media provided these users with what one writer called "voice and community, power and empowerment" over a group with an expansive reach and an all-seeing lens.[50] The Pew Research Center found in 2020 that Black and Hispanic social media users reported that the sites are extremely valuable to them when it comes to issues of social justice and community affairs. The data revealed that 72 percent of Black users were likely to rely on social media for some form of political activism. In addition, both Black and Hispanic users were more likely than white users to rely on social media to get involved with political or social movements.[51]

Social media satisfies our crucial need for socialization. An analysis of why people use social media placed the need to "stay in touch" with friends and family as the primary reason people gave for using these platforms. This ability to network and to reach other people with similar interests also placed in the top five explanations people gave for taking part in social media.[52] Research done during the COVID-19 outbreak demonstrated that as isolation protocols became more prominent, more people said social media was a great help to them because they were able to remain connected with important others.[53]

Informational Awareness

As noted in Chapter 2, people have an instinctive need to be aware of their surroundings. In prehistoric times, that awareness could mean the difference between life and death, with violent weather and dangerous animals threatening people's lives at a moment's notice. The importance of staying aware of one's surroundings on social media isn't quite so dire, but the concept of FOMO (fear of missing out) can drive individuals to frequently check the status of their accounts on various platforms to keep as current as possible. Researchers found that the more individuals feared being left out or falling behind on important topics, the more heavily they used social media to remain current.[54]

Social media can also provide individuals with important alerts or information that they can use. Influencers provide social media users with information on everything from how to pick the best makeup palettes to how best to prepare porcini mushrooms. Entertainers can also use these channels to alert fans to upcoming events and promote partnerships with brands. Subscribers to specific social media feeds place value in the information provided on topics that matter greatly to them. As users engage with the influencers' content, they feel more knowledgeable about each subject.

Social Comparison

Social media's social aspect can be uplifting or deflating, depending on the users and the channels to which they subscribe. Humans have always defined themselves through comparative measures, seeking out other people like them or near them to determine where they stood overall in society. Think of it this way: are you tall? Although you can measure yourself in feet or inches, no true standard exists in which everyone agrees what "tall" means. Therefore, you determine the state of your "tallness" by looking at other people around you. If you put yourself in a class filled with kindergarteners, you're a giant; however, compared with members of the New York Knicks basketball team, you're tiny.

As we discussed in Chapter 8, social comparison research looks at the ways in which individuals determine their own worth in relation to the status of others. This can lead to significant benefits and harms, particularly when social media is involved, because the group of people to whom users compare themselves is exceptionally large and diverse. Researchers have found the most popular lifestyle influencers exude social prestige, meaning that they make their followers see their lifestyle as something desirable. Followers will often look at these people for guidance on how to live, where to eat, or what to wear. In one study examining this level of need, scholars found that young adults who identified with the values of a social media influencer were more likely to click an advertisement attached to that individual's feed and express an intent to purchase that product.[55]

Conversely, media scholars have found that social comparisons on social media can undermine users' sense of personal value, leading to depression and hopelessness. One study found that social media is a relevant contributor to negative mental health symptoms.[56] Another researcher found that users reported higher levels of anxiety and increased depression when they compared themselves with influencers who displayed aspirational lives.[57]

In other cases, social media enhanced self-esteem through downward social comparison, as we discussed in Chapter 8. In this way, users seek out people who have less status than they do and find social enhancement through negative comparisons. A 2021 study found that while users who saw people living their best lives online reported feeling worse about themselves, users who could compare themselves favorably with online profiles reported increased self-esteem.[58] In other words, if you feel lousy about who you are or what you have, you can look at someone on social media who has it worse than you do and think, "At least I'm not that poor slob."

JOBS RELATED TO SOCIAL MEDIA

Now that you better understand the field of social media, here's a handy overview of a few job opportunities within it.

Career Opportunity	Common Tasks
Social media manager	• Grow online presence for a brand or a client through day-to-day social media interactions • Connect with social media users through comments, direct messages, and other forms of contact • Post and share content relevant to the organization and interesting to your audience
Social media strategist	• Develop and implement overall social media strategy for an organization • Create campaigns across various platforms and through paid and unpaid communication • Establish a brand and voice for an organization on social media
Social media analyst	• Examine data related to key performance indicators to determine the impact of an organization's social media • Report on social media engagement to key players in an organization to assist them in improving its online presence • Develop and assess search engine optimization efforts to enhance user engagement
Social media coordinator	• Collaborate with sales and marketing professionals, editorial staff members, and social media team members to create successful campaigns • Serve as point person for social media campaigns and development opportunities • Coordinate with analysts, strategists, and managers to create a cohesive approach to an organization's social media efforts

CHAPTER REVIEW

LO1 Identify key moments in the history of social media.

- Social media's first steps took place in 1996, when Andrew Weinreich launched Six Degrees, a platform that connected friends in an online environment.
  - Subsequent sites like Friendster and MySpace made similar efforts in the early 2000s but failed to retain their market share.
  - Of the earliest social media sites, LinkedIn was the most successful, opening its doors in 2003 and growing to more than 830 million users as of 2022.
- In the mid-2000s, several sites came to dominate the social media landscape.
  - Facebook, Twitter, and YouTube all went live in the middle of the decade and grew exponentially in the subsequent years. As of 2022, Facebook has more than 2.9 billion active users, while YouTube and Twitter have 2.6 billion and 330 million active users, respectively.
- The technological improvements to mobile digital devices helped social media become exceptionally popular.

- ○ With the launch of the iPhone and Android marketplaces, app developers were able to give social media users access to their favorite platforms without needing to rely on wired internet connections.
- ○ The rise of visual storytelling on these platforms helped Snapchat, Instagram, and TikTok become among the most used social media services.

LO2 **Discuss the elements that make social media distinctive from other forms of media.**

- Many-to-many model: Unlike traditional media in which a newspaper or television station serves as a single point of content dissemination, social media puts into the hands of all users the ability to send and receive content. Users can choose to serve primarily as a sender or a receiver in this model, or balance both roles as they see fit.
- Individualized content selections: Social media users can choose individual sources to follow, instead of relying on a specific media outlet for all their information. Users can choose to follow organizations, teams, and companies or specific individuals within those groups. This gives individuals not associated with mainstream media outlets the ability to produce content of interest to users and grow an audience based on the value of that content.

LO3 **Compare and contrast the various types of popular social media platforms.**

- Social networking sites like Facebook and LinkedIn allow individuals to keep in touch with family and friends, connect with people who share their interests, and socialize.
- Media sharing sites like YouTube and Instagram give users the chance to create content for others to view and connect with content creators.
- Discussion forums like Reddit and Quora allow users to seek knowledge from experts on a broad array of topics, keep up to date on what is happening around them, and express opinions on important issues.
- Content curation sites like Pinterest and Pocket provide users with inspiration for their hobbies and activities as well as allow them to share ideas that could be of value to other people and collect information in one online space for later use.
- Consumer review sites like Yelp and TripAdvisor allow users to contribute their own opinions to the pool of collective knowledge regarding products and services. They also allow users to seek information and make informed choices about what products and services to buy.
- Self-publishing networks like WordPress and Medium give users a chance to develop an online presence, practice content creation, and develop a portfolio.

LO4 **Evaluate the role social media plays in the media ecosystem.**

- The ability to access social media platforms anywhere and everywhere through mobile devices allows users to stay constantly connected.
- Unlike traditional media, social media platforms can reach quickly extremely large audiences. The distributed nature of social media's networks allows a message to be passed along from source to source and amplified through each individual's followers. The ability to spread a message in this fashion is called going viral.
- Trust is crucial for all media practitioners, and social media makes it easier for trust to follow a message. Because each individual user puts a certain amount of faith in the credibility of each source they follow, a message that originated from some far distant and unknown source can still be trustworthy, if it comes from a valued source within one's own network. This form of transitive trust helps messages spread easily and be more believable.

LO5 **Assess the ways in which social media use meets people's needs.**

- Interpersonal connectivity: Social media provides online spaces for users to reach out to other like-minded people for a variety of reasons, including promoting social causes, finding romantic partnerships, and shared interests.

- Informational awareness: Users of social media can keep abreast of important events and activities happening in their world and build knowledge on topics that have personal or professional value.
- Social comparison: Some individuals follow people they aspire to be, such as celebrities or lifestyle influencers, while others choose to follow people to whom they can feel socially superior in some way.

KEY TERMS

Blog
Emojis
#fail
Individualization
Influencers
Lurking
Microblogging
Social media
Viral

DISCUSSION QUESTIONS

1. How has the ability to access social media on your phone changed the way in which you consume media during the day? What habits have you built into your life that revolve around these apps and platforms?
2. In looking through your social media feeds, who do you follow? Do you rely more on individuals or organizations? Famous people or personal contacts? What benefits do you think you get as a result of following these sources?
3. In reviewing the six types of social media formats discussed in the chapter, what category does most of your social media use fall into? Has this changed since you started using social media? Do you foresee it changing in the future?
4. How important is social media in connecting you to broader social issues? Do you see social media as an opportunity to change and grow as a society or more as something to pass time with and entertain people?
5. When you review profiles constructed by influencers, how representative of reality do you think those profiles are? How do you feel after you review these profiles? Better? Worse?
6. Does social media improve your life in a meaningful way? If so, how? If not, why not?

A woman plays a video game online, competing against other people who are playing at various places throughout the world.

iStockPhoto.com/gorodenkoff

VIDEO GAMES AND GAMING AS MEDIA

INTRODUCTION

1. *How are video games similar to the other forms of media you use on a daily basis? How are they different?*
2. *What benefits do you think video games provide to individual users as well as the overall media ecosystem?*
3. *Do you have any concerns about the impact playing video games could have on players? If so, what are they and why do they concern you?*

Video games are a growing part of the overall field of media, whether through the expansion of gaming opportunities or the way they cross over into the world of books, films, magazines, and more. This chapter examines the history, development, and growth of video games as they moved from science labs and computer stations to arcades, home machines, and even arenas, filled with screaming fans. It also outlines the various forms of gaming and what they do for and to us. Additionally, we will examine the psychological aspects of gaming, such as the concept of "flow," that state of perfect harmony between player and game.

LEARNING OBJECTIVES

After completing this chapter, you should be able to:

1. Explain the importance of key moments in the history of video games.
2. Describe game typologies, listing an example of each type.
3. Evaluate video games' role within the media ecosystem.
4. Analyze how video games fulfill gamers' needs.
5. Describe the concept of flow and how it applies to video gaming.

A BRIEF HISTORY OF VIDEO GAMES: FROM CATHODE RAYS TO *FORTNITE*

LEARNING OBJECTIVE

LO 1: Explain the importance of key moments in the history of video games.

Video games have existed for less than eighty years but have developed an exceptional place in global culture. Experts estimate that the gaming industry involves nearly 2.5 billion people worldwide and is set to reach almost $257 billion in revenue by 2025.[1] To better understand how video games became part of our daily lives, we need to look at the evolution of the games and their uses over time.

Here are some key points in the history of video games:

- The early years
- Video games move into the mainstream
- The golden age of gaming
- Mobile and internet gaming takes off

Let's dig into each of these eras.

The Early Years

In the late 1940s, scientists and technicians saw an opportunity to study human-computer interaction by having subjects participate in enjoyable activities in laboratory settings. In 1947, physicists Thomas Goldsmith Jr. and Estle Ray Mann patented the "cathode ray tube amusement device." The game's concept had the user firing a light gun at a target that was displayed on an oscilloscope, an electrical device similar to the radar screens the military used during World War II. Although the unit was never mass-produced or marketed, it represented the first step toward computer-based gaming, and both the oscilloscope and its cathode ray screen became crucial elements of future video game efforts.

In that early postwar period, researchers often used games in their work in the emerging computer science field. For example, in 1952, British professor A.S. Douglas developed *OXO* as part of his doctoral dissertation. The computer program allowed humans to play tic-tac-toe against a machine, with the program responding to each human move. Other researchers developed programs that allowed people to compete against nonhuman foes in simple games like blackjack and checkers, with less emphasis on human enjoyment and more concern with how the computer performed its tasks.

A turning point in video game development came in 1958, when Brookhaven National Laboratory introduced *Tennis for Two*, a game run through an analog computer. Physicist William Higinbotham's invention drew hundreds of visitors to his lab for a chance to knock a digital ball back and forth on an oscilloscope screen. *Creative Computing* magazine noted this was likely the first true video game, and it showed researchers that people enjoyed interacting with computers in gaming environments.

In 1962, Massachusetts Institute of Technology student Steve Russell invented *Spacewar!*, which took the gaming world beyond the simplicity of a bouncing ball. Russell and his colleagues at MIT built the game as a way to get people to engage with computers. The game involves two ships orbiting a central star and fighting each other. What made this product revolutionary was that Russell's group

TABLE 11.1 ■ A Few Key Names in Video Games

William Higinbotham	Mabel Addis	Tomohiro Nishikado	Gerald "Jerry" Lawson	Taneli Armanto	Zoë Quinn
• A physicist who created *Tennis for Two* in 1958, the first interactive analog computer game. • Responsible for the expansion of graphic displays as part of gaming.	• A schoolteacher who worked with IBM and Boards of Cooperative Education to combine educational opportunities and video games. • Developed the *Sumerian Game* between 1964 and 1966, which gave players the opportunity to rule over a city. • Credited as the first woman to design a video game.	• An engineer who helped usher in the "golden age of arcade gaming" when he developed games for Taito in Japan during the 1970s. • Created *Space Invaders*, the first "shooting" arcade video game. • Continued developing games for arcades, home consoles, and handheld devices into the 2000s.	• An electronic engineer who was one of the earliest developers to use microprocessors in his arcade and home console games. • Created Fairchild's Channel F in 1976, the first home gaming system that used cartridges, allowing users to swap among multiple games on a single console. • Honored for his pioneering work in the video game field by the International Game Developers Association in 2011.	• A computer programmer who spent more than fifteen years working for Nokia as part of its mobile phone division. • Credited with programming *Snake* for the Nokia 6110 in the mid-1990s, the first widely distributed video game for mobile phones.	• A video game developer and writer known for developing the interactive game *Depression Quest*. • Became one of several women in the field who received online threats for their feminist views related to gaming, a controversy later known as #gamergate. • Helped found Crash Override in 2015, which helps victims of online harassment and abuse.

made the computer coding open source, thus allowing other computer enthusiasts to use and modify it as they saw fit. This allowed the game to spread and grow beyond its original format.

Zoë Quinn was one of several prominent women involved in the #gamergate online controversy, suffering targeted harassment for speaking about feminism in video games.

John Lamparski / Contributor/via Getty Images

Video Games Move into the Mainstream

Once video games moved outside of lab and university settings, they developed along two distinctive tracks from the early 1960s through the late 1970s: home-based versus arcade-based video gaming. Early gaming pioneers like Ralph Baer sketched out his first idea for a home gaming system in 1966, which he named "game box," to allow people to play sports and adventure games on their own TVs. Often called "the father of home video games," Baer was responsible for the launch of Magnavox's Odyssey home video game system as well as the popular toy Simon, which is still sold today.

Early versions of video game systems featured only a single game, which limited their appeal because people would master the games and become bored with them. In 1975, Gerald "Jerry" Lawson, a pioneer in the video game field, solved the problem by introducing the first cartridge-based video game system for Fairchild Camera and Instrument. This system, called the Channel F, allowed users to purchase specific game titles for a standard machine that could play them all. Although not as popular as the Atari 2600—which came out a few years later and used the same cartridge-based approach—Lawson's innovation dramatically improved the home gaming market and gave gamers a wider array of titles from which to choose.

In contrast to engineers who were developing home-based games, arcade-style developers saw video games as the next step forward in socialized game play in public areas. In 1972, Atari released the arcade version of *Pong*, setting off the arcade revolution. Players would gather at local hangouts and pump quarter after quarter into these machines to play a game similar to *Tennis for Two. Pong* first proved the financial viability of arcade games, as the company sold more than eight thousand units by 1974.

The Golden Age of Gaming

Arcades and home-based games continued to evolve during the late 1970s and early 1980s, with well-known names like Atari, Sega, and Nintendo actively participating in both markets. Both arcades and home-based games would see significant growth in revenue through the decade.

Games like *Space Invaders* and *Pac-Man* appeared in the arcades, where players of all ages came in droves to test their skills against one another in a public venue. By 1980, researchers estimated that owners of coin-operated arcades spent about nine hundred million dollars to stock them with the latest and most popular games on the market. In 1978, that number was only fifty million dollars. Anecdotally, owners told stories of having to empty the bins that collected the money every hour to prevent them from overflowing. Statistically, the industry as a whole made more than five billion dollars a year at its peak.[2]

Although both markets began to sag in the mid-1980s, technological improvements resurrected the home-based game systems near the end of the decade, beginning with the classic Nintendo Entertainment System. Nintendo offered improved graphics and multiple button controllers that gave gamers a more complex experience. Companies like Sega, Sony, and Microsoft soon followed with their own increasingly engaging consoles, reinvigorating sales, and introducing a whole new generation of players to the field.

Mobile and Internet Gaming Takes Off

The largest shift in video gaming occurred at the end of the 1990s and the turn of the new millennium, when gamers were able to participate in games outside of a fixed physical or digital environment. In other words, games were no longer tied to one device in one house or one arcade in one building. This not only made video gaming more a part of people's lives, but it also created higher levels of social interactivity around the games. This happened in two key ways.

First, in 1997, Nokia included designer Taneli Armanto's game *Snake* on its phones. The game involved moving an ever growing "snake" around the screen while capturing a dot, which reappears after each successful effort. If you crashed into a wall or any part of your snake, you lost. Although it pales in comparison with today's games, this game launched a revolution in mobile digital gaming. As of 2023, mobile gaming represents 52 percent of all video gaming activities.[3]

Second, video games found ways to connect users via the internet for interactive play. Online gaming dates back to the late 1970s, when Roy Trubshaw, a student at the University of Essex, developed the first MUD (multiuser dungeon). However, these games lacked graphic interfaces and widespread use. It wasn't until 1987, when computer programming student Stuart Cheshire developed *Bolo*, that a graphically driven game allowed individuals from multiple internet domains to connect effectively for game play. This tank game was among the first to allow up to sixteen players to collaborate and compete using different computers. The game pitted teams of individuals to fight for control of bases with mines, "pillboxes," and tank fire. In addition, the game led to the development of social subcultures online through game-based chat, newsgroups for enthusiasts, and webpages promoting the game.

By the 1990s, not only had the quality of these internet-connected games drastically improved, but so had the enthusiasm of gamers who wanted to test their skills against competitors from around the world. In 1997, the online tournament for the game *Quake*, dubbed the Red Annihilation, was the world's first major event for these games. Approximately two thousand people took part in the event, with the grand prize winner receiving a Ferrari.

As video games continued to evolve, individuals' ability to connect not just with the consoles and games but with others from distant lands became possible. In 2004, the company Blizzard Entertainment released *World of Warcraft*, an online game that allowed people from all over the world to enter a fantasy realm and connect with one another. At its peak in 2009, the game had nearly ten million players worldwide. Although data more than a decade later are somewhat spotty, video game experts note that the game still has almost five million paid subscribers as of 2023, with the most recent estimates placing the game's total revenue at about fourteen billion dollars.[4]

The most recent megahit in online gaming is Fortnite, which launched in 2017 and has more than 350 million players worldwide as of 2020.[5] The game began as a four-player **cooperative game** that allowed each team to "save the world" from increasingly difficult levels of attackers. However, *Fortnite* became exponentially more popular when Epic Games introduced the *Battle Royale* version of the game. In this version, one hundred players compete to be the last person standing, relying on a wide array of weapons and building tactics to survive to the end of the game. Although the game is free to download and play, the company has earned about $1.8 billion annually through the use of in-game purchases, such as specialized character costumes and mapmaking abilities unavailable to free players.[6]

Fortnite is a very popular video game, with over 350 million players worldwide.

Lenscap / Alamy Stock Photo

GAME TYPOLOGY AND GENRES

LEARNING OBJECTIVE

LO 2: Describe game typologies, listing an example of each type.

Video games have come a long way since the 1940s, when they could be played only in laboratory settings. Their themes, actions, and approaches have expanded exponentially over the past few decades, thanks in large part to rapid growth in technology and internet speed and communication capabilities.

Here is a list of gaming types, along with a few genres and games that will help illustrate them. This is not an exhaustive list, but it is meant to show you how the games developed different strategies to connect with users.

- Arcade-style gaming
- Edu-gaming
- Asynchronous gaming
- Massively multiplayer online gaming

Here's a deeper look at each of these gaming formats.

Arcade-Style Gaming

Arcade-style gaming actively engages the player with the machine, as opposed to games that require less frequent and less direct interaction. In an arcade setting, a player had to insert a coin to initiate the game; for this reason, games were designed to be of increasing difficulty so that one player would not monopolize a machine for a long period of time. More turnover of players led to increased revenue for the operators of the arcades.

Arcade-style games included maze and platform games like *Pac-Man* and *Donkey Kong*, in which a player attempted to complete a task in the face of increasingly difficult opposition. For example, in *Pac-Man*, the goal is to collect all of the dots on the board without being touched by one of four ghosts (named Inky, Pinky, Blinky, and Clyde). Four "power pellets" allowed the player to eat the ghosts for a brief time period and send them to their home base to regenerate so they could continue their pursuit of the player. Upon the completion of the board, the player would advance to the next level, where the ghosts were slightly faster and their pursuit was slightly more aggressive. This level-up approach continued until the player lost all of his or her lives.

Arcade games like *X-Men* and *Mortal Kombat* offered players the ability to compete against or cooperate with fellow players. A player could select a competitor with a given skill set and engage in a series of one-on-one battles with that player. After one of the players defeated the other in a best-two-out-of-three format, the losing player had a chance for a rematch. *Teenage Mutant Ninja Turtles* offered a cooperative gaming setup; the game had four joystick and button sets, one for each potential participant. Throughout the game, players could "jump in" at any time and join other players engaged in a battle. The game relied on a storyline, which continued as long as at least one player was actively participating.

These game formats are played in real time, with the participants constantly taking action and making choices based on what the computer does. The players have to be actively engaged with the content, lest they lose a life, sustain damage, or fail at the task. In addition, most of these games presented the players with discernable patterns, which allowed the players to get better each time by mastering each level through practice. For example, in *Pac-Man* the ghosts always go in the same directions when pursuing the player on level 1. Thus, the more you play, the better you get at figuring out this pattern to win at that level. Then, the second level has a different pattern, speed, or approach, and you have to start all over again.

An outgrowth of these competitions were esports, online competitions that mirrored the "real world" of championships that offered cash prizes for winners and excitement for spectators. These competitions have grown into a business generating more than a billion dollars in revenue, with millions of online viewers.

A DEEPER LOOK: ESPORTS

Although worldwide competitive gaming has existed since 1980, when Atari hosted the National *Space Invaders* Championship, the concept of video gaming as a full-fledged sport really started taking hold in the late 1990s.

In 1997, the Red Annihilation tournament for the game *Quake* offered competitors the opportunity to test their skills against thousands of other gamers, with the winner receiving a 1987 Ferrari 328 GTS. A decade later, the Championship Gaming Series began, with the promise of more than one million dollars in prize money for players of games including *Counter-Strike*, *FIFA 07*, and *Motorsport 2*. The series folded after two years, leading one journalist in 2008 to note sarcastically that "watching a TV broadcast of other people playing video games only *just* beats chewing tinfoil." He continued, "Is this the end of the 'e-sports' craze? Perhaps the dingy LAN party and living room full of drunken friends is all the glitz and glamor video game tournaments need after all."[7]

His gloomy forecast for the future of esports proved to be way off base. In 2014, esports drew more than thirty-two million viewers, more than those who watched the NBA Finals or the World Series.[8] According to Nielsen data, esports fans follow about 5.7 games across multiple genres. Approximately two out of every three U.S. gamers surveyed said they livestream esports, with more than one-third of the survey participants saying they have attended a live esports event.[9] The fans support specific players and teams in the same way traditional sports fans do.

For games like *League of Legends* and *Dota 2*, championship events have sold out major sporting venues, including the Staples Center in Los Angeles and Madison Square Garden in New York. Like their counterparts in traditional sports, esports stars have gained international fame and earn high salaries. Tyler Blevins, better known as Ninja to *Fortnite* fans, grew a following of more than eighteen

The League of Legends World Championship is hosted annually by Riot Games and draws tens of millions of fans. In 2022, the event's grand final set a record with 5.1 million concurrent viewers, as DRX rallied for a 3–2 win over T1 to claim the seventy-pound Summoner's Cup and a portion of the $2.23 million prize pool.

Riot Games/Contributor/via Getty Images

million on Twitch, making him the most followed account on the platform.[10] His gaming-related revenue earned him a net worth of more than forty million dollars as of 2023.[11]

The total annual revenue associated with esports is estimated at approximately $1.4 billion and growing as of 2022, with experts predicting that it will eclipse more than $5.4 billion by 2029.[12] The 2022 *Dota 2* international championships offered competitors a prize pool of $19 million. Gaming companies are selling franchises for more than $20 million each, and bankers are valuing some of them at more than $50 million, thanks to the continued double-digit increases in growth each year.[13] Experts expect esports to continue on an upward trajectory in financial growth and fan base over at least the next five years.

Edu-Gaming

Edu-gaming applies familiar video game designs for students to achieve learning goals. Like a traditional video game, educational software relies on known characters, increasingly difficult tasks, and rewards based on accomplishment to engage students and reinforce knowledge gain. For example, students can solve math problems to blast asteroids or fix spelling errors to gain in-game currency.

Educational opportunities have existed in gaming for generations, with programmers seeking to provide both game-based learning titles and edutainment games that leaned heavily on the gaming aspects to improve student engagement. One of the first edu-games was designed by New York schoolteacher Mabel Addis. In 1964, Addis realized that early computer programs could help students learn in an entertaining environment. During her summers, she worked with IBM to develop the *Sumerian Game*, a program that allowed the user to rule the city-state of Lagash, making choices about resource management and societal health. Her program made her the first female video game writer and designer, with the endeavor forecasting other educational games like *Oregon Trail*.

The *Reader Rabbit* franchise was born in 1984 and targets multiple skill groups, ranging from toddlers to grade school students. It has sold more than fourteen million copies across thirty spinoff products.[14] Educational gaming companies have also developed software for math, science, and geography with the launch of products such as *Logical Journey of the Zoombinis* and *Where in the World is Carmen Sandiego?*

When constructed well, educational games can provide students with opportunities for cognitive development and build problem-solving and critical-thinking skills. A University of Michigan study showed that more than half of the K–12 teachers the researchers surveyed used games on a weekly basis as part of their educational efforts. These games were used most often to improve student engagement with material and to prepare students for state or district testing. Survey participants overwhelmingly felt that the games were effective for motivating them and reinforcing previously taught content.[15]

Psychologists, however, warn that educational games aren't a substitute for in-class activities or traditional learning methods. A review of the available scholarship in the area revealed that in most cases, the "either/or" studies ignored the fact that nobody learns solely from a human teacher or a computer game. The quality of the content available, the logical nature of the interface, and the overall design of the products were the most important factors in determining their effectiveness in teaching students important concepts.[16]

Asynchronous Gaming

The goal of early video game play was to create constant engagement and activity, drawing the user into the action and keeping the player paying attention to the game. In the early to mid-2000s, **asynchronous gaming** shifted game designers' focus to habit building and use over time. The classic game *FarmVille*, for example, drew more than thirty-two million people on a daily basis at the height of its popularity.[17] Unlike a traditional game in which you can play as long as you have quarters or feel like staying awake in front of a screen, asynchronous games placed time restrictions on users before they could make the next move. For example, in a game like *FarmVille*, users could plant crops at one point but could not immediately harvest them and move on. The "plants" needed time to "grow," thus forcing the user to wait for a certain amount of time to pass before moving forward.

The asynchronous gaming movement redefined video game design in two significant ways. First, it allowed action to take place whenever and wherever a participant felt like playing. By integrating the games into Facebook and offering free versions in app stores, the companies made the games seem familiar while also allowing the players to put the games on their mobile devices. The games could be played whenever the user had time, without having to be on the game constantly or at the same time as other players.

Second, the user also could take a "shortcut" to advance more quickly. One of the common shortcuts was to pay a nominal fee to get help from the game, such as buying extra rolls in *Yahtzee with Buddies* or a superfertilizer in *FarmVille*. Instead of paying for the game, the user was paying for advantages within it.

Researchers found that these games encouraged users to find ways to make peer connections.[18] They allowed players to connect with social media friends, thus increasing a population of similarly interested participants, while also rewarding people for bringing in new players. Players in social networking systems can provide friends with help, such as more lives to defeat a challenging antagonist or building materials for a construction project. In addition, the players can work collaboratively on larger jobs, whether it's defeating a common enemy or carrying off a valued bounty.

Massively Multiplayer Online Gaming

In the days of dial-up modems, video game developer Richard Garriott took a gamble by moving his role-playing series *Ultima* online. His goal was to create an interactive environment in which thousands of gamers from all over the world could gather and participate in whatever role and to whatever extent they wanted. This effort served as the starting point for the world of **massively multiplayer online games**, or **MMOs**.[19] (A variation on this theme is the massively multiplayer online role-playing games known as MMORPGs.)

In MMOs, players choose a character based on the game's setting. For example, in *EverQuest*, which was released in 1999, participants could choose from one of fourteen character classes, such as warriors, clerics, and wizards. *Anarchy Online*, released two years later, avoided the magical classes and instead allowed players to choose among a variety of humanoid breeds for their characters. In both cases, the choices provided the characters with specific strengths and weaknesses, thus making each character dependent on the others for its own survival.

MMOs provide a chance for participants to escape everyday life as well as an opportunity for people to redefine themselves on their own terms. Researchers wanted to understand what drove people to take part in these overwhelmingly large world games. One study[20] helped define several classes of participants:

- **Achievers** seek to dominate the game through perseverance and effort. They want to "win" through achieving goals they set for themselves within the game and thus gain both status within the game community and a sense of personal accomplishment.
- **Explorers** want to see as much of the gamescape as they can. Think of them as following *Star Trek*'s mission statement: "To explore strange new worlds; to seek out new life and new civilizations; to boldly go where no one has gone before."
- **Socializers** want to meet other players for the purpose of social interactions. They worry less about taking action within the game and spend more time getting to know other players.
- **Killers** want to make other players' lives a living hell by using the tools of the game to spoil it for as many people as possible. One famous example came from *Ultima*, in which a participant killed Garriott's character while he was making a speech.[21]

Researchers found that the socialization aspect of MMOs is much stronger than initially thought. Early concerns that the games' fantasy aspects would lead to players feeling dissociated from reality turned out to be wrong. Instead, their **escapist fantasy** aspects were mitigated by their building social relationships, leading participants to create a set of norms and values that govern their behavior and communication.[22] While the participants were taking on roles of alien races with powers beyond those of humankind, they were also establishing relationships, participating in commerce, and abiding by in-game law. Furthermore, the heaviest users of these games tended to play them with friends and family members, allowing them to connect with important real-world people.[23]

GAMING CROSSOVERS

LEARNING OBJECTIVE

LO 3: Evaluate video games' role within the media ecosystem.

Between game apps on our phones and the rise of esports as a global phenomenon, video games have positioned themselves as a ubiquitous part of our lives. Much like other forms of media, video games have also found a way to weave into other aspects of our media ecosystem, diversifying their reach across multiple platforms and formats. Here are a few ways in which games intersect with other forms of media that we use.

- Books
- Movies
- Television shows
- Marketing and secondary products
- Advertising
- Video game coverage

Let's take a deeper look into these areas that connect significantly with video games.

Books

In 1982, the editors of *Consumer Guide* produced a 34-page volume titled *How to Win at Pac-Man*. It provided gamers everywhere with a level-by-level explanation of how to eat dots, dodge ghosts, and stretch their quarters to the limit.[24] The market for these types of books grew greatly in the 1980s, because each game required experts to share knowledge to people hoping to hone their skills. Today, similar walkthroughs exist in a digital realm for complex games, such as the *Grand Theft Auto* and *Elder Scrolls* series. Much like the *Consumer Guide*'s collective, today's walkthroughs rely on multiple experts, who post their hints and tips on wikis. Some sites require payment or registration to access this content, while others are open to all enthusiasts. That said, companies still sell print-based walkthrough guides for some of their most popular games. For example, Piggyback published a hardcover, 368-page, collector's edition walkthrough guide for the Rockstar game *Red Dead Redemption 2*.

Beyond these "how-to" guides, books remain an elemental part of the marketing of video games, a broader topic we will discuss later in the chapter. For example, under the pen name Oliver Bowden, author Anton Gill has published a seven-volume book set that novelizes each of the installments of the *Assassin's Creed* video game series, and *Desert Oath*, an official prequel to the series. Publishers have also created comic book series based on video games including *God of War* and *StarCraft*. These types of books and series range from a retelling of the game's narrative to expansive endeavors that tell a character's backstory or further adventures.

Movies

When the movie *Tron* hit the big screen in 1982, the arcade game was right behind it, serving as one of the earliest pairings of film and game. Upon the success of this movie-game connection, movie studios began building total marketing packages that included arcade and home console games related to their films.

However, video games have also inspired movies. The *Tomb Raider* franchise has led to three films based on the game's protagonist, Lara Croft, while *Resident Evil* spawned more than a dozen games that helped launch seven films. These successful adaptations benefited from the presence of well-known characters and gamers who were used to seeing them placed in linear, story-based adventures. (Not all films based on video games have been successful, as pretty much anyone who saw the 1993 live-action *Super Mario Bros.* movie or *Street Fighter* will attest.) In 2022, two of the biggest crossover hits demonstrated that people still have a strong interest in seeing games become movies. *Sonic the Hedgehog 2* and *Uncharted* earned more than $401 million and $404 million worldwide, respectively, making them fourth and fifth highest grossing video game–based films.

Television Shows

Video games have served as the impetus for both cartoon and live-action television programs since the 1980s. *Saturday Supercade*, for example, debuted in 1983, and featured a series of cartoon segments that featured cartoon characters from current hot video games, including *Frogger*, *Q*Bert*, and *Space Ace*.[25] The live-action genre tended to lean toward more violent games, such as *Street Fighter* and *Halo 4*, although educational programming such as *Where in the World is Carmen Sandiego?* also had success. Although many shows lasted only for a few seasons, primarily based on the popularity of the games themselves, shows like *Pokemon*, which debuted in 1997, have continued to churn out season after season of content.

Gaming also inspired the creation of an all-gaming network, aimed at catering to a wide variety of players' interests. In 2002, NBC Universal and Dish Network paired to launch the cable station G4, which featured original programming as well as gaming hints and tips for popular titles.[26] It aired shows like *Arena*, which was a multiplayer gaming competition, and *Pulse*, a news program that focused on important happenings in the gaming industry. Despite gaming's popularity, the channel earned low ratings and closed for good in 2014.[27] In spite of this, the popularity of gaming channels continues on platforms like YouTube and Twitch, where competitions and news reports keep gamers connected to the action.

Marketing and Secondary Products

Video games allow companies to market a wide array of secondary products to interested consumers. Trading cards, plush toys, and board games drew buyers interested in connecting further with the brand, as did T-shirts, hats, and other clothes emblazoned with game-related artwork. Foods based on the games also took their places on shelves, with everything from *Donkey Kong* to *Pokemon* filling the cereal aisles at local grocery stores. Companies also branded drink flavors, fruit snacks, and other kid-friendly products based on games or popular game characters. (Some food products even returned the favor, providing games based on their products, such as Kool-Aid and Domino's Pizza.[28])

Advertising

Television shows and movies have relied on product placement for years to boost the bottom line and create more realistic environments for the actors. Marketers have also plugged their products through placement in video games with equal success. A Nielsen study, conducted a decade ago, already showed signs of the impact of in-game advertising on gamers. The study revealed that the advertising of Gatorade in EA Sports games boosted the household dollars spent on the sports drink by 24 percent.[29]

In the following ten years, developers sought ways to expand their appeal to in-game advertising, and advertisers sought more and innovative ways to reach gamers. Much like advertising in the real world, the messages in the video games range from subtle to unavoidable. Developers of games like the *NASCAR Heat* series integrate advertising on the cars themselves to replicate real NASCAR race cars. Companies like Swiftcover used virtual billboards to advertise an array of products in games like *Guitar Hero* and *Tiger Woods PGA Tour*.[30] Other advertising opportunities allow gamers to earn extra lives by watching a video from a sponsor or to access a special powerup that is given to them from an identified sponsor.[31] During the 2020 presidential race, Democratic candidate Joe Biden advertised in the game *Animal Crossing*, placing "Biden/Harris" and "Team Joe" lawn signs in the field of play.[32] (For more on advertising and its connections to video games, see Chapter 13.)

Video Game Coverage

Magazines provided the most consistent level of news coverage for video games in their early years. The launch of the magazine *Electronic Games* in 1981 provided arcade and home console enthusiasts with information about upcoming titles, trends in the gaming world, and insider news on new developments in hardware and software. Corporations like Atari, which launched *Atari Age* in 1982, developed their own magazines as a form of public relations to promote their own titles and highlight new systems they were readying for launch. Other magazines, such as *Electronic Gaming Monthly* and *Game Informer*, also provided a mix of promotion and insight on key titles and trends within the field.

As print media began to fade, bloggers and social media experts took to the internet to provide game reviews, tip sheets, and walkthroughs. Sites like Kotaku rival traditional media outlets with reviews, profiles, and news features on all things involving gaming. Niche sites like TouchArcade, which focuses primarily on touch-screen mobile gaming, have also found an audience in the digital realm.

Video games received sporadic coverage in mainstream media over time, usually relying on event or trend stories such as the launch (and subsequent failure) of the *E.T.* video game in 1982.[33] Recently, major media outlets have recognized the need for coverage of these activities. ESPN now has a dedicated portion of its website devoted to esports, and the *Washington Post* is hiring video gaming and esports journalists for a variety of positions. In explaining why the *Post* is investing in this area of coverage, assignment editor Mike Hume noted, "It's a multi-billion industry that impacts a market that ranges from kids to adults and has not received much mainstream media attention except when it's been treated as an oddity. It warrants more. We think there are a lot of stories that can and will be told here."[34]

ROLE OF VIDEO GAMES

LEARNING OBJECTIVE

LO 4: Analyze how video games fulfill gamers' needs.

As we discussed in Chapter 2, uses and gratifications theory explains that people actively engage with media for specific purposes with the hopes of satisfying particular needs. Video gaming would seem to be the ultimate representation of active engagement, media selection, and need satisfaction. The theory also notes that not everyone uses the same media for the same reasons, which makes their individual choices of game type, level of participation, and overall sense of interaction with the games important to understand. Here are some of the basic reasons people engage with video games:

- Entertainment
- Escape
- Social connections
- Motivated growth

To get a better grip on why people engage with video games, let's dig a bit deeper into those topics.

Entertainment

As simple as this might seem, a main goal of video games is to provide entertainment to people; based on research in this area, the games successfully fulfill this goal. People tend to find activities that provide fun and enjoyment to be worth pursuing, which is why people will often play video games to avoid boredom or pass the time. In this situation, the gamers aren't necessarily excited about the game, but playing it is more entertaining than whatever else is going on around them. Mobile access to games through portable devices and smartphones gives people the opportunity to play simple games, take turns on asynchronous games, or just try another level on a game while waiting in a long line or sitting through a boring lecture.

A survey revealed that almost three-fourths of gamers would rather give up television, and more than two-thirds would give up movies, than forsake gaming.[35] Survey participants were not motivated solely by pushing buttons or moving digital characters around a screen but found enjoyment in the idea of task completion and story advancement. Whether it was to explore new worlds or match like-colored candies, gamers could derive a simple psychological benefit out of their actions.

Experimental research has shown that gamers who find a game both fun and meaningful are able to derive a higher level of benefits than people who simply play to pass time. Experimental participants not only valued the ability to beat the game or make choices within the game, but they also highly valued the games that had storylines that were relatable and mattered to them. As the authors of one study wrote, "Games provide the opportunity of enhanced identification with characters…and the possibility to experience a broad range of emotions."[36]

Escape

In her 2013 talk at the Game Developers Conference, game designer Jane McGonigal noted that people play video games to escape from the pressures of their everyday lives. This urge to escape from reality is not necessarily a bad thing, she noted. She stated that two forms of escapism among gamers exist: self-suppression and self-expansion.[37] Although the game playing is essentially the same, the intent of the gamer makes the difference. Some people play games because their lives are difficult or painful (self-suppression), while others play as a reward system or to engage in activities that promote mental growth and acuity (self-expansion).

Gaming also allows players to demonstrate competence in a meaningful way, thus expanding their sense of self. For example, you may not have the skills to play basketball at the local playground, but in a video game, you can spin, shake, and shoot with the best of them. Moving the playing field from the physical world to the digital realm can provide you with the advantage you need to showcase superiority in a way previously not available to you. In addition, games provide users with autonomy and self-reliance they don't have in the actual world. These games allow them to move into a realm in which they can make more choices and enjoy additional options for success, put themselves into a better position to demonstrate superiority, and make choices independent of outside forces. Researchers have found that people who feel autonomous and competent while playing these games experience better overall motivation and well-being.[38]

Social Connections

As social animals, human beings seek ways to spend time with others with the goal of sharing information or connecting socially. For generations, places like diners, coffee shops, and saloons served as socialization stations for people within a community. There, they could meet like-minded people and talk about their lives in a way that fostered a sense of belonging. Places like Starbucks coffee shops try to create this type of social environment through placing comfortable chairs and plugs for charging devices to encourage people to hang out.

Sociologist Ray Oldenburg referred to these public areas as "third places," noting that they were environments where people spent time between home (first place) and work (second place).[39] These places provided people with the opportunity to talk about important issues, reconnect with friends, and develop relationships with like-minded individuals. These connections helped establish a sense of community and developed a culture that allowed people to feel as if they were a part of something bigger than themselves.

As much as these places have continued to disappear in the physical world, they are becoming a larger force online, thanks primarily to social media and video games. A 2019 article in *Education Week* noted that *Fortnite* serves as a third place in the classic sense of the term, in that it provides a social environment for children to operate outside of home and school. Authors Kurt Dean Squire and Matthew Gaydos explain that the video game is a place "where kids learn to negotiate conflict, become independent, and explore what kind of person they want to be."[40]

In discussing the way in which these online areas serve purposes beyond the games, journalist Keith Stuart compared them with local skate parks. The parks serve as social spaces and venues for the activity. People who gather can participate, watch others participate, or do both. As Stuart noted, "*Fortnite* isn't a game they play—It's a place they go."[41]

The broader range of characters within video games has provided individuals with more opportunities to find personal representation while playing. Nintendo, for example, introduced the Mii avatars in 2006, which provided individuals with opportunities to personalize avatars for all gaming on the Wii system. These characters allowed individuals to customize not just hair, eyes, and facial features but also gender, race, and other demographic representations. Game designers also helped create areas of inclusion for LGBTQ+ participants by adding distinct sexual orientations for characters in story-based gaming. The website Gayming provides readers with a constantly updated list of games that feature roles or themes related to the LGBTQ+ community.[42]

The large online communities that have been inspired by video games can sometimes lead to unexpected consequences for the games' creators. The #gamergate scandal of 2013 illustrates what can happen when players use these connections to harass or intimidate other gamers. An American video game developer, Zoë Quinn, published *Depression Quest* in 2013, a game based in part on her own experiences with depression and anxiety. After Quinn's ex-boyfriend wrote a negative blog post about Quinn and her game, Quinn not only received multiple death threats, but social media users posted all sorts of personal information about her, sharing these items with the hashtag #gamergate.[43]

Although the #gamergate phenomenon lacked a coherent strategy or purpose, many gamers saw this as an opportunity to attack women and people of color who were members of various video game organizations. For example, Brianna Wu, the head of development for an independent video game studio, received threats of rape and murder in 2014 after she tweeted jokingly about the people involved in #gamergate; she was still receiving threats two years later. Feminist scholar Anita Sarkeesian faced similar threats for presenting her views on the ways in which women are portrayed in video games.

In 2017, Quinn released a memoir titled, *Crash Override: How Gamergate (Nearly) Destroyed My Life, and How We Can Win the Fight against Online Hate*, outlining her experiences with #gamergate and how she continues to work for equality within the field of video gaming.

MEDIA LITERACY MOMENT: VIRTUAL WORLDS, REAL ISSUES

Video games have come a long way in terms of complexity since the days of *Pong*, in which two players could push a white dot across a black screen at each other for hours. The generations of game designers who followed sought to make gaming as realistic as possible, with improved graphics, more complicated controls, and expansive opportunities for players.

These opportunities are not without drawbacks, as virtual worlds have become havens for some of the problems we face in the real world as well. Two of these problems are the prevalence of in-game advertising and the presence of toxic behavior by gamers.

In traditional forms of media, advertising is stringently regulated regarding its target audience, the disclosures it must provide about its products, and the claims it can make. In addition, the advertising is often present in clear-cut formats of which consumers are aware, such as a full-page ad in a magazine or a block ad on the sidebar of a website.

However, the increased opportunities for in-game advertising and product placements have provided corporations with additional access to potential consumers while they are in a state of lowered media literacy and heightened concentration. Research shows that although the relationship between the advertising and the player's intention to purchase the product is indirect, the more prominent the advertising, the more it fits in with the theme of the game, and the more seamlessly it is integrated, the more the players like the advertising and the brand.[44] The overall impact of this advertising remains unknown, but corporations are buying in heavily to reach this audience. Data trends suggest that in-game advertising will account for fifty-six billion dollars in revenue by 2024.[45]

Of greater concern, however, is the degree to which the freedom and anonymity gaming provides players has led them to engage in toxic behavior toward others both in the games and in the real world. The toxicity associated with some online gamers has demonstrated that social ills, such as sexism, racism, and violence, can transcend the real world and become amplified in online gaming. The players' use of pseudonyms and avatars plays a major role in how and why some gamers feel free to act on toxic urges they otherwise would suppress.

In addition, the physical separation from one another and the heavy level of engagement the players feel during online sessions can embolden them to go well beyond what they might say or do in person. For example, a twenty-year-old Maryland man found himself receiving death threats after a session of *Call of Duty*, with gamers posting his home address and calling his phone after he quit rather than respond to the threats.[46] Some players have reported that Black characters in games like *Red Dead Redemption 2* have been "rounded up" for torture or execution by teams of white players, who are reenacting Ku Klux Klan–like behaviors or serving as "slave catchers."[47]

Even for nongamers, these issues can create problems, because the people with whom they interact on a daily basis may be cultivating these toxic attitudes during their gaming sessions and using them as well in the real world. The question of how best to quell this negativity online remains unclear, as law enforcement and technology manufacturers have acknowledged.

THE NEXT STEP: Find a story that deals with toxic behavior in gaming. Read at least two articles on the topic, and see what gaming experts, researchers, law enforcement officials, and others have to say on this topic. Explain what you think should or shouldn't be done in these cases, depending on the level of threat, the type of threat, and the presence of criminal charges. Determine which of your own biases may interfere with your critical thinking process as you work through your answers.

Motivated Growth

While William Higinbotham and others were exploring ways to build early video games, a scholar named Robert White was trying to understand why people generally take part in any form of activity. In 1959, White argued that people have an inherent desire to have an effect on their environment, which means they want to demonstrate that they can change things around them.[48] It's why people hang personal effects in their offices or spray-paint graffiti on overpasses.

Beyond simply creating impact, White noted that people want to demonstrate competence at their activities. It's why children struggle repeatedly to tie their shoes until they become proficient at it. Once they have mastered the skill, the value in that task becomes less important, which is why you didn't wake up this morning, tie your shoes, and immediately Snapchat it to your friends to tell them, "NAILED IT!" Other researchers have also found task mastery to be a motivating factor, adding other rationales for why people take on tasks or persist at certain behaviors.[49]

Early games that allowed participants to play against one another allowed for motivation through interpersonal dominance. The goal of one person was to beat the other person and each subsequent challenger. However, with the launch of games like *Space Invaders* and *Pac-Man* in the late 1970s and early 1980s, motivation to demonstrate competence evolved to include multiple other aspects. First, players could play the games repeatedly to "level up" against increasingly difficult competition from the game itself. In *Ms. Pac-Man*, the first seven levels of the game are represented by a variety of foods, including cherries, pretzels, and pears. A player attempts to reach the next level, and thus the next food item in line, to demonstrate improvement and competence within the parameters of the game. Not only does each level increase the value of the food item available to the player, but it also serves as a demarcation for players' bragging rights. ("I made it to the pear. You're still stuck on the strawberry!")

However, to demonstrate a higher level of competence, game developers began to include a high-score board, where people who scored the most points on an arcade machine were invited to input their initials next to their scores. This not only allowed the gamer to establish a sense of preeminence on the machine, but it also motivated other players to beat that score and thus put their initials up higher on the board than previous participants.

When games moved from arcades to home devices, programmers began looking for ways to create a sense of completion for their participants. They began focusing on quest games, in which players could complete levels and attain additional benefits. For example, *Super Mario Bros.* sends the infamous plumber from the *Donkey Kong* series on a quest to rescue a princess. The player must successfully navigate a total of thirty-two levels spread over eight worlds to accomplish this task. Once it is completed, the game is technically over, although replay and other options exist. The motivation shifted away from continued playing to task completion, with the goal to finish the story.

UNDERSTANDING FLOW AND THE VALUE OF VIDEO GAMES

LEARNING OBJECTIVE

LO 5: Describe the concept of flow and how it applies to video gaming.

When it comes to video games, parents have repeatedly asked kids, "How can you play that thing all day?" The answer could come from a famous Hungarian-American psychologist, Mihaly Csikszentmihalyi, who identified the optimum aspects of motivation and their relation to a highly focused state of attention and production. Csikszentmihalyi studied people who engage in voluntary and pleasurable activities that posed specific challenges. His initial work looked at people like rock climbers and painters as he outlined the concept of **flow**, the state of being in which people become intensively involved in any given activity to the point of locking out all distractions.

Csikszentmihalyi's concept of flow consists of four components: control, attention, curiosity, and intrinsic interest. When all four are operating at peak levels, the person enters the flow state and become totally absorbed in the task at hand. He found that people who enter a flow state report feeling "in the groove" or "on a roll" while accomplishing their work or completing an activity. They feel in control of their environment and often lose track of time and other physiological needs like food, sleep, and even personal hygiene.

In looking back at Csikszentmihalyi's work and that of other flow scholars, researchers outlined nine components as crucial to flow.[50] Table 11.2 illuminates how each of these ideas fits into the realm of gaming.

Few activities check all the boxes in this process, and even fewer can be accomplished without advanced professional training or access to a specific environment. For the rock climbers whom

TABLE 11.2 ■ Nine Crucial Components of Flow

Component	How It Works	How It Relates to Gaming
Challenge-skill balance	• People enjoy repeatedly engaging in tasks that are slightly outside of their initial skill levels. • Tasks that are too easy are boring and tasks that are too hard are abandoned.	• Gamers enjoy playing at levels that challenge them to succeed but aren't impossible. • Initial failure at a level leads to repeated tries with improvement until eventually they succeed at the task.
Merging of action and awareness	• People become aware of only what they are doing, and behavior becomes spontaneous. • Repeated actions turn into reflex-like efforts and require almost no thought.	• The repetitive pressing of specific buttons to create desired actions occurs without thought. • Play within a game becomes driven by the player's instinctive actions.
Clarity of goals	• People need to understand the goals of any activity and how to achieve them. • Lack of understanding of what leads to success creates frustration and task abandonment.	• Games provide players with specific tasks that they need to accomplish to win the game or ascend to its next level.
Unambiguous feedback	• People need to see positive and negative outcomes related to their actions to persist or avoid them.	• Increased scores, extra "lives" for the player, and positive sounds reinforce successful actions, while scoring penalties, "dying," and negative noises punish the player for unsuccessful actions. • The feedback is immediate and is presented in unambiguous ways.
Concentration on the task at hand	• People focus on tasks that draw and retain their attention better than any other task available to them.	• Video games tend to require uninterrupted attention and focus on the actions required to keep playing as long as possible.
Paradox of control	• People in a flow state feel totally in control as they achieve goals and complete tasks beyond what they are normally capable. • Upon realizing this control, they often lose control and fail at the task, thus they need to be in control without acknowledging the situation.	• A player who is pitching a no-hitter in a baseball video game will likely be unaware of this achievement unless someone mentions it. • A player exponentially exceeding the game's high score will be focused entirely on the game play, not the score.

(Continued)

TABLE 11.2 ■ Nine Crucial Components of Flow (*Continued*)

Component	How It Works	How It Relates to Gaming
Loss of self-consciousness	• People are so focused on the task at hand, they become unaware of other needs like hunger or thirst.	• Players who are deeply involved in a game might not notice that they need to take a shower, while others around them recognize how bad they smell. • Players become so involved in the game that they don't realize they haven't used the bathroom in two days.
Transformation of time	• People engaged in an interesting or enjoyable activity will lose track of how long they have been involved in that task. • The phrase "time flies when you're having fun" is a simple way to think about this concept.	• Video games inspire extended play when they are going well for the player, even as minutes turn into hours. • Arcade gamers have played more than three days on a single quarter, not realizing that day became night multiple times while they were playing.
Autotelic experience	• People find satisfaction in the task, regardless of other outside rewards or penalties. • The person and the game become intertwined, and the player continues doing the task out of pure enjoyment.	• Gamers continually return to a game they enjoy and play it repeatedly for no real reason other than they like it.

Csikszentmihalyi studied, they needed to find bigger and more challenging rock formations all over the world to challenge themselves and reach the state of flow. Dancers had to get into better shape, practice more difficult moves, and seek additional ways of gaining feedback to improve their work.

Unlike these other strivers, gamers can just plug in and go. If one game doesn't inspire flow, another is easily obtained. Users can participate in any one of myriad environments, including an arcade, a home, or anywhere they can use a phone. Even more, all of the key elements for flow are clearly attached to game usage and engagement with those games, thus leading to an optimum state of motivation and a state of flow.

JOBS RELATED TO VIDEO GAMES

Now that you better understand the field of video games, here's a handy overview of a few job opportunities within it that relate to media.

Career Opportunity	Common Tasks
Video game critic	• Play and review video games, explaining their good and bad aspects as well as comparing them with other games in the field. • Provide walkthrough guides for users to help them navigate the game or work past difficult stages. • Compare and contrast play across gaming platforms.

Career Opportunity	Common Tasks
Video game tester	● Play games during early development stages to locate bugs and errors. ● Provide feedback to designers regarding quality of play on topics including user control quality, interactivity, and game enjoyment. ● Respond to questions from designers and marketers regarding key aspects of the gaming experience.
Esports promotions	● Create audio, video, and social media content related to esports events, players, and hosts. ● Develop marketing material to help audience members learn about teams, games, and leagues within the discipline. ● Interview players, coaches, fans and hosts to help them connect with fans.
Esports announcer	● Provide play-by-play coverage of events to enhance the experience for fans. ● Use gaming knowledge to analyze the strategy and play of gamers. ● Apply broadcast journalism skills in interviewing players, coaches and team owners before and after competitions.
Video game developer	● Create and pitch gaming concepts to companies within the field. ● Develop and apply the coding necessary to create the games themselves. ● Work with reviewers to finetune and enhance the gaming experience.

CHAPTER REVIEW

LO 1: Explain the importance of key moments in the history of video games.

- Video games were first introduced in the 1940s as part of laboratory experiments to study human-machine interactions.
- The development of video games for personal play and enjoyment led to a burgeoning industry of games in arcades and homes in the 1970s through to today.

LO 2: Describe game typologies, listing an example of each type.

- *Arcade-style gaming* actively engage the player with the machine, requiring the player to complete mazes or platforms with increasing levels of difficulty. The games were initially single-player machines in which the gamers challenged themselves against the machine, or dual-player machines, in which players could compete against each other. An example of a single-player game is *Pac-Man*, while an example of a dual-player game is *Mortal Kombat*.
- *Asynchronous gaming* allow gamers to engage the game whenever and wherever they feel like playing, even allowing days or weeks between gaming sessions. These games inspire peer connections on social media platforms, such as Facebook, where the games are often played. Users receive benefits either through habitual actions over time, such as checking in on the game every few hours, or through purchasing boosts that allow them to take a shortcut past the waiting periods. *FarmVille* is an example of an asynchronous game.
- *Edu-gaming* applies familiar video game designs for students to achieve learning goals, such as completing math problems by blasting aliens. An example of an edu-game is *Reader Rabbit*.
- Massively multiplayer online gaming allows gamers from varied geographic locations to come together and play on a single online platform. Players can create their own characters, develop skills, and interact with other game players' characters. MMOs create a sense of community by drawing people into shared spaces online where they can engage in social interactions. *World of Warcraft* is an example of an MMO.

LO 3: Evaluate video games' role within the media ecosystem.

- Gaming crossovers occur when other media formats, such as books, movies and television shows, center on games' concepts or characters.
- Advertising or other marketing opportunities offer additional crossover potential, including esports television coverage and the creation of items for sale that feature the characters associated with the games.

LO 4: Analyze how video games fulfill gamers' needs.

- Games satisfy obvious needs, such as the desire to be entertained and the need to escape from the rigors of everyday life.
- Games also satisfy deeper needs, such as the ability to connect socially with other people, as well as to build a sense of achievement through motivated growth and task accomplishment.

LO 5: Describe the concept of flow and how it applies to video gaming.

- Flow is the state of being in which people become intensively involved in any given activity to the point of locking out all distractions. Mihaly Csikszentmihalyi studied people who engage in voluntary and pleasurable activities and found that flow occurred when individuals' control, attention, curiosity, and intrinsic interest were at peak levels.
- Video gaming allows players to maintain control of what's occurring on screen, focus their attention on task completion, and seek better ways to complete the tasks before them. Because these are voluntary efforts, the intrinsic interest in the game also serves as an underlying motivational factor.

KEY TERMS

Achievers
Arcade-style game
Asynchronous gaming
Autotelic experience
Challenge-skill balance
Cooperative game
Edu-game
Escapist fantasy
Esports
Explorers
Flow
Killers
MMOs
Paradox of control
Socializers
Video game

DISCUSSION QUESTIONS

1. If someone were to ask you, "Why do people play video games?" how would you answer this question and why?
2. Based on your experiences and what you have read here, do you think video games have value as a media format? Why or why not?
3. Of the various types of video games listed in the chapter (arcade-style, edu-gaming, asynchronous, and massively multiplayer online gaming), which type most appeals to you? Which one is least appealing and why?
4. In your way of thinking, are esports actually sports? In making your case, consider issues like skill, fandom, achievement, and financial support, which are prevalent in all forms of sports.
5. Whether it was in video games or in any other form of activity, have you ever experienced flow as it is described in the chapter? If so, how accurate do you think the description here is based on your own experiences?
6. How prevalent is video game crossover marketing in books, trading cards, clothing, advertising, and other media? In considering your encounters with these crossovers, do you think video games play more or less of a role in your life than you initially thought?

A public relations practitioner speaks to a room filled with journalists as part of a news conference.

iStockPhoto.com/monkeybusinessimages

12 PUBLIC RELATIONS

INTRODUCTION

1. *How aware are you of the role public relations plays in shaping the messages you receive on a daily basis?*
2. *How many people, groups, and businesses attempt to persuade you on a daily basis? What do you think makes their efforts successful? What makes them fail?*
3. *Which type of people do you tend to trust more: people who tell you everything, regardless of how bad it is, or people who tell you only what they think you need to know? Why do you feel this way?*

Public relations (PR) involves conveying important information to multiple audiences and shaping relationships among different constituencies. From a business sending out a message about a new innovation or product to a nonprofit advocating for environmental issues, public relations helps shape public opinion in the best sense of explaining complex issues to the population at large. Despite decades of positive work, some view public relations as little more than propaganda—an attempt to sell ideas that lack merit on their own. However, to more fully understand the modern value of public relations and the people who work in the field, it is crucial to see what it is, what it does, and how best practices within the field can lead to benefits across the board.

This chapter will explain not only how PR came to be and where it is now but also the ways in which it can benefit the general public and use communications to connect clients to valued audiences. In addition, we will discuss the specific approaches to sharing information that make PR successful as well as the tools that **practitioners** have used over time to help them succeed in those efforts.

LEARNING OBJECTIVES

After completing this chapter, you should be able to:

1. Explain the importance of key moments in the history of public relations.
2. Define public relations and explain its role in society.
3. List the six principles of persuasion and explain how each relates to public relations.
4. Explain the three key elements of successful public relations efforts, providing examples of each one.
5. Review the primary tools that public relations practitioners use to do their jobs.

A BRIEF HISTORY OF PUBLIC RELATIONS

LEARNING OBJECTIVE

LO 1: Explain the importance of key moments in the history of public relations.

Despite being little more than a century old, **public relations** has become an important and popular area in the realm of mass media. PR is a booming field, with a recent report indicating that there are now six people working in public relations for every one news reporter.[1] That number is up from approximately a two-to-one ratio just twenty years ago. One reason for this swing is that PR practitioners can now more easily speak on behalf of organizations, communicate directly with their audiences through digital tools, and tell stories in ways that readers understand and value.

Here are some key points in the history of public relations:

- Ivy Lee and early public relations efforts
- Shaping public opinion

- Public relations in the time of war
- Growth, development, and diversification of PR
- The digital revolution

Let's dig a bit deeper into these points.

Ivy Lee and Early Public Relations Efforts

Although public relations has existed in some form or another for centuries, scholars place the start of the field as a paid profession around the turn of the twentieth century (see Table 12.1). One of the most important early PR practitioners was Ivy Lee. Lee founded one of the first public relations firms in the United States, Parker and Lee, and worked on several key incidents that showed corporate America the power of public relations.

TABLE 12.1 ■ A Few Key Names in PR

Ivy Lee	Edward Bernays	Doris Fleischman	Joseph Varney Baker	Betsy Plank	Patricia Tobin
• Early PR practitioner • Wrote the first press release • Pushed clients to tell the truth because it would come out sooner or later	• Called the "father of modern PR" • Dubbed PR "the engineering of consent" • Ran PR campaigns for dozens of major companies, including General Electric and Procter & Gamble	• Began her PR career as a staff writer for the Council on Public Relations • Developed PR campaigns for political candidates and corporate interests in the 1920s and 1930s • Created internal client publications as a key PR tool	• Formed his own PR firm in 1934, the first Black-owned PR firm in the country • Became the first African American president of the Philadelphia Public Relations Society of America in 1958 • Provided PR efforts for dozens of major corporations, including RCA, Chrysler, and U.S. Steel	• Called "the first lady of PR" for her trailblazing efforts in the field • Became the first female president of the Publicity Club of Chicago in 1963 • Established the Public Relations Student Society of America in 1967	• Known as "the queen of PR" for her efforts in networking and event planning • Founded Tobin and Associates in 1983 to improve opportunities for PR professionals of color • Cofounded the National Black Public Relations Society

In 1906, a train derailed near Gap, Pennsylvania, killing fifty people. Lee convinced the railroad officials to work with the press to provide coverage of the event. During this crisis, Lee wrote what is largely believed to be the first press release, providing news reporters with information from the corporation and outlining its stand on the incident.

Eight years later, John D. Rockefeller hired Lee after the Colorado National Guard killed twenty-one people during a coal mining strike. Lee used public relations techniques to cast the Rockefeller family in a more humane light, hoping it would garner public sympathy for them. In addition, Lee gave Rockefeller advice that has become the bedrock of quality PR: tell the truth, because sooner or later the public will find it out anyway.[2]

Shaping Public Opinion

A pioneer in shaping PR theory was Edward Bernays, whose books *Crystallizing Public Opinion* in 1923 and *Propaganda* in 1928 earned him the nickname of the "father of modern PR." He defined public relations as "the engineering of public consent." In other words, people often find it difficult to form opinions on difficult issues. Therefore, they look to experts for help in making choices. "Engineering consent" means using expert opinions to get the public to agree with a client's position. In the earlier

Doris Fleischman and her husband Edward Bernays were key figures in the development of PR. Fleischman was the first American woman to travel with her maiden name on her passport.

Bettmann/Contributor/Getty Images

World War II propaganda posters like this one, featuring Rosie the Riveter, were aimed at drawing women into the workforce to fill holes in various industries left by the men who went off to war.

Office for Emergency Management, War Production Board, 1942.

phases of his career, Bernays often used the terms *public relations* and *propaganda* interchangeably, before the latter term became associated with negative aspects of public manipulation.

The first person Bernays hired for his PR firm, in 1919, was his childhood friend Doris Fleischman, who had extensive experience as a writer at the *New York Tribune*. Fleischman crafted articles and press releases for various clients and causes, ranging from oil companies to politicians. Fleischman and Bernays married in 1922 and shared equal partnership in the firm, which continued to serve clients and grow the field itself.

Bernays and Fleischman were one of a few married teams that shaped the landscape of PR in the mid-twentieth century. Among the most influential were Leone Baxter and Clem Whitaker, who realized that politicians could be much more successful if they understood how to interact better with voters. Their approach to political PR and campaign building remains the standard to this day.

Public Relations in the Time of War

While Andrew Jackson hired newspaper owner Amos Kendall as the country's first press secretary back in 1829, Woodrow Wilson took PR to a new level, understanding the importance of public opinion during the time of war. In 1917, he created the U.S. Committee on Public Information, which served as a publicity and propaganda ministry for the country. Wilson hired veteran journalist George Creel to run the organization, which had a mission of creating public support for U.S. intervention in World War I. Creel and his group used traditional forms of media, such as posters and pamphlets, to inform and persuade the public about the importance of the war.

In the lead-up to World War II, both Allied and Axis forces relied heavily on the power of persuasion and propaganda to win support for their positions. After his rise to power in 1933, Nazi leader Adolf Hitler helped create the Reich Ministry of Public Enlightenment and Propaganda. The ministry crafted a narrative that painted Hitler as a heroic leader who would bring Germany back from the edge of disaster to its proper place as a world leader. At the head of the organization was Joseph Goebbels, who recognized the power in the relatively new media of radio and film to spread Nazi propaganda and anti-Semitism.

Seeing the impact propaganda had in Europe, President Franklin D. Roosevelt created the Office of War Information (OWI) in 1942 to serve as a connection between U.S. citizens and their military forces engaged in World War II. Although it did not embrace the tactics or lack of truthfulness the Reich Ministry employed, the OWI demonstrated the power of propaganda through a wide array of techniques and characters, including using or creating popular characters like Uncle Sam, Rosie the Riveter, and even Bugs Bunny to promote the war effort. By the end of the war, the term *propaganda* had developed strong negative connotations, and most public relations practitioners sought to distance themselves and their work from it.

Growth, Development, and Diversification of PR

In the post–World War II era, public relations continued to grow, but limited opportunities existed for women and people of color in the field. To improve the situation, several trailblazers created their own firms and found success on the state and national level. Joseph Varney Baker, who began the first Black-owned PR firm in 1934, worked with many national clients, including the Pennsylvania Railroad, Scott Paper, RCA, and Procter & Gamble. In 1958, six years before the Civil Rights Act became law, he was unanimously elected president of the Philadelphia chapter of the Public Relations Society of America (PRSA), and in 1960 he served as an assistant to Richard Nixon during his presidential campaign against John F. Kennedy.

A key breakthrough for both women and people of color took place in 1957, when Inez Kaiser decided to quit her job teaching home economics and launch her own public relations firm. Kaiser became the first African American woman to run a PR firm with national clients, most notably 7-Up, Sears, and Sterling Drug. Her work was so respected that both the Nixon and Ford administrations consulted with her on the best ways to connect with minority women and businesses.

Still, a gender barrier remained entrenched within the field. PR trailblazer Barbara Hunter noted that she once attended a meeting of the New York chapter of the Public Relations Society of America that had about two hundred men and only ten women. Hunter and her sister, Jean Schoonover, saw a need for more and better representation, so they pooled their resources and bought the Dudley-Anderson-Yutzy (D-A-Y) firm in 1970. They quickly found that not only were the men at D-A-Y making substantially more money than their women counterparts, but the male employees were uncomfortable working for women at all. Although many men left, taking their industrial accounts with them, Hunter and Schoonover helped the company flourish for more than thirteen years before selling it to legendary firm Ogilvy & Mather in 1983.[3]

In 1984, David Garcia of Fleishman-Hillard recognized that a significant group of Latino practitioners were entering the PR field and felt that the multicultural efforts of various firms didn't meet those workers' needs. As a founding member of the Hispanic Public Relations Association and its first president, Garcia helped develop techniques and opportunities for these individuals. HPRA not only supports and empowers practitioners with a connection to the Hispanic market, but it also reflects a movement toward expanded diversity within the public relations field.

In the current market, diversity and gender equity remain a challenge for the field. A recent study showed that throughout the PR industry in the United States, 8.3 percent of practitioners identify themselves as African American, with 5.7 percent identifying as Hispanic American and 2.6 percent as Asian American.[4] Women have made significant inroads in terms of finding jobs in public relations, but those jobs are often at the lowest possible rungs of the corporate ladder. Today, more than two-thirds of all PR jobs are held by women, although almost 80 percent of the CEOs in the field are men.[5] This continues a pattern first studied in the 1980s, when researchers referred to the process of adding more women to lower level positions within a field while limiting their access to managerial and ownership opportunities as a **velvet ghetto**.

The Digital Revolution

Public relations saw technological advances as opportunities to reach audiences with improved tools. From print media and hand-typed press releases to radio and television presentations, PR remained on the cutting edge of media throughout the twentieth century.

In 1997, Business Wire took the next step in these communication efforts when it introduced the "**Smart News Release**," which pushed PR into the digital age. The company's initial offering included text and images delivered digitally, providing media outlets with much more than the standard text-on-page release could offer. It burnished its reputation as a forward-thinking PR company when it issued a fully multimedia-enhanced press release to promote the film *Pearl Harbor* in 2001. The company continued to improve on this initial effort, with current releases now incorporating downloadable audio, video, and images as well as integrated social media options that allow the sharing of the release across various platforms.

In 2006, PR innovator Todd Defren created the first social media news release through his company, SHIFT Communications. At the time, Twitter was less than a year old when Defren crafted what he called a "**twitrelease**," which connected online media users to social media networks. His work helped practitioners see the potential of using 140 characters (which was then Twitter's limit for the size of its messages) to inform an audience in a simple and direct fashion.

Around that same time, Jason Kintzler developed PitchEngine as an alternative to traditional press release systems by taking advantage of the growth of social media and the algorithms that controlled search engines. By employing tactics that reached more audiences, including bloggers and influencers as well as journalists and consumers, PitchEngine was able to showcase the value of social media releases to organizations and their customers alike.

Today, social media has about 4.59 billion active daily users, of whom 75 percent rely on it to research product purchases they intend to make and 71 percent use it to share information about their experiences with organizations.[6] This makes the continued intersection of public relations and digital marketing crucial for the foreseeable future.

DEFINING AND EXPLAINING PUBLIC RELATIONS

LEARNING OBJECTIVE

LO 2: Define public relations and explain its role in society.

In examining the history of its field, the Public Relations Society of America looked into a variety of ways in which practitioners, scholars, and outside entities attempted to define what PR professionals do and why it has value.[7] Its current official definition of the field, agreed upon by its members around 2012, is "Public relations is a strategic communication process that builds mutually beneficial relationships between organizations and their publics."

Outside of this broad view of PR, professionals often describe their field based on how they interact with the public, create messaging for clients, and build branding opportunities for organizations. Despite the wide array of ways in which you can view public relations, many PR definitions have certain terms in common (see Table 12.2).

TABLE 12.2 ■ Six Common PR Terms

Term	Description
1. Reputation	How an organization or product is perceived by others
2. Deliberate	Employing research, testing, and feedback to conduct a successful campaign
3. Strategic	Carefully planning each step of a campaign for maximum impact
4. Well-performed	Successfully carrying out the strategic plan
5. Mutually beneficial	Equally beneficial to all parties, including the practitioner, client, and audience
6. Responsive	Listening to and incorporating feedback to a campaign

With these definitions in mind, it becomes easier to see what public relations is. These elements account for a broad scope of potential uses and activities in which practitioners can reach out to important publics with specific goals in mind. That said, a large portion of this chapter will use those concepts to help explain what PR is specifically supposed to do and how practitioners do it.

Although the approach practitioners will take can vary somewhat based on the clients involved and the goals of specific campaigns, generally speaking, public relations will significantly involve several key concepts.

1. Inform the public: Tell people important things they need to know.
2. Advocate for a cause or a client: Promote the position, thoughts and ideas of a group, an idea or an organization.

3. Share content among all groups: Make sure everyone involved is kept up to date on what is going on.
4. Create quality outcomes for everyone involved: Try to make everyone involved a winner, or at least avoid making anyone a loser.

Here is a deeper look at each of these concepts.

Inform the Public

Public relations is often thought of as a reactive as opposed to a proactive field, with practitioners seeking to answer allegations, prevent negative stories, and generally play defense for their clients. This is the unfortunate by-product of both the misunderstanding of the broad range of careers within the field as well as the hyperawareness many of us have of the bad actors within it. The truth of the matter is that the goal of PR professionals is the same as any other media writers within the field. PR practitioners work for a company (as newspaper reporters, broadcasters, and other media professionals do) with the goal of disseminating information to an engaged audience on a topic that should be of interest to that audience. The content that these practitioners disseminate should be insightful, intriguing, and helpful to those people. As marketing expert Caroline Forsey writes for HubSpot, "PR isn't just used to influence a story after it happens—it's also used to write that story in the first place."[8]

Advocate for a Client or Cause

Public relations differs from traditional news in that it is based on **advocacy**. While news reporters are expected to maintain objectivity in their work, public relations practitioners seek to provide a point of view to the public. In this way, practitioners are similar to editorial or column writers who use information and opinion to sway readers to think the way they do. For example, a Ferrari has the reputation of being both a high-cost and a high-luxury vehicle, while a Honda is often associated with reliability and fuel efficiency.

PR practitioners working for Ferrari would likely advocate for their client by pointing out all its luxury features and making it clear that people deserve to have the finest things in life. A practitioner communicating on behalf of Honda would stress the affordability, gas mileage, and safety features their vehicle has. In other words, they are emphasizing why a specific car shopper might want to purchase their product.

The goal of advocacy is to show the audience members what matters most to the client and then explain to those readers why that issue should also matter to them. The purpose of advocacy is to increase awareness of a topic with factually based information that is paired with persuasive elements. If this is effective, the audience should feel motivated to act in some way.

Share Content among All Groups

Quality PR requires that practitioners not just speak but that they also listen and respond. Audience centricity is crucial to get individuals to buy into a topic in the short term and to invest in an organization in the long term. Practitioners understand that for a client to succeed in forging a successful, ongoing relationship with its public, the client needs to adjust to the feedback it receives from those in its audience. This is why quality practitioners seek to serve as a conduit of information from the organization to the audience and from the audience back to the organization.

A major example of this occurred with Starbucks in 2018, when an employee at a Philadelphia branch of the coffee chain called the police when he saw two African American men in the store who were waiting for a colleague to arrive. Police arrested Rashon Nelson and Donte Robinson on suspicion of trespassing, setting off a nationwide debate over racism, bias, and justice.[9]

Upon hearing about the incident, Starbucks CEO Kevin Johnson put out a statement, declaring that the incident was reprehensible and that he would work to find a solution. After hearing from various stakeholders and experts, Johnson had Starbucks close all eight thousand of its stores so all of its employees could go through a racial bias education workshop. The store outlined what it would do and how it would do it, to keep all interested parties informed. The move, which cost the chain an estimated twelve million dollars in profits, worked to find a solution that all parties could see and value.[10]

Create Quality Outcomes for Everyone Involved

Practitioners occasionally seek short-term gains or outcomes, such as increasing the number of voters at a particular polling place or getting people to sign a petition on a topic of civic interest. However, practitioners also know that for them and their clients to survive and thrive, they must never sacrifice long-term standing for those short-term outcomes. This is why practitioners focus on activities and results that benefit both the client and the public the client is attempting to reach. Symbiotic relationships between clients and audiences will allow both groups to receive benefits from their interactions, thus building trust between the groups and inspiring future interactive engagements.

Think about it this way: if you were running a yard sale and you wanted to sell one lawnmower one time, just to get rid of it, you might be willing to lie to people because you know you'll never deal with them again. So, if someone asks, "Does it start all the time?" You might say, "Absolutely!" without divulging it usually takes about twenty tries before it starts. Or, if someone asks, "How well does it cut thick grass?" You might say, "See how beautiful our yard is?" and not mention that you cut it with your new mower.

However, if you ran a store that sold lawnmowers, this approach would almost certainly kill your business. Between disgruntled customers who want to return faulty products and bad word of mouth on social media, you would see your client base dry up in a hurry. A current example of this kind of corporate failure is the technology company Theranos and its disgraced CEO, Elizabeth Holmes, who was convicted in 2022 of defrauding investors.

Holmes claimed to have invented a "mini-lab" that would allow medical personnel to run hundreds of tests for a patient with just a few drops of blood, taken from a small finger prick. Holmes used TED Talks, guest lectures and public appearances to pitch the benefits of the machine, including the ability to reduce the amount of blood drawn at one time and the opportunity for patients to monitor changes more judiciously in their bodies. She often stated in her talks that she was driven to do this

Former Theranos CEO Elizabeth Holmes, left, walks with her partner, Billy Evans, after leaving federal court in San Jose, California. The Theranos saga is an example of how an overhyped product and a lack of care for all parties involved in an investment can create a disaster.

AP Photo/Jeff Chiu

work by her fear of needles and the death of her favorite uncle, who didn't find out he had cancer until it was too late. Her promotional efforts helped drive the overall value of the company to more than nine billion dollars in 2013.

In reality, Holmes and her researchers could not get the mini-lab to work as she had promised. She hid the devices away from the public and reporters who wrote glowing profile pieces on her. When she had to do demonstrations for potential investors, she faked the results. By 2015, whistleblowers and inside sources had revealed the fraud to the government and the *Wall Street Journal*. The company had completely collapsed by 2018.[11]

Public relations experts James E. Grunig and Todd Hunt outlined four models of public relations in their book *Managing Public Relations*. Table 12.3 offers a thumbnail sketch of each model.

FIGURE 12.1 ■ A Visual Representation of Grunig and Hunt's Four Models of Public Relations

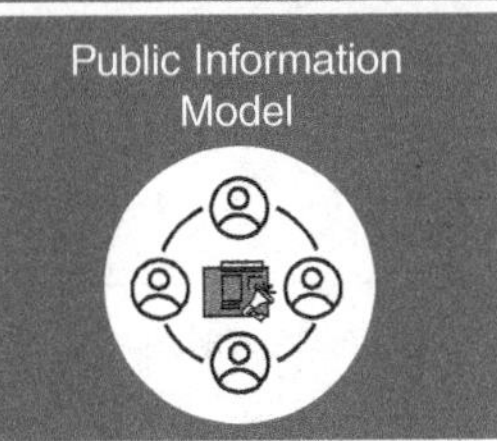

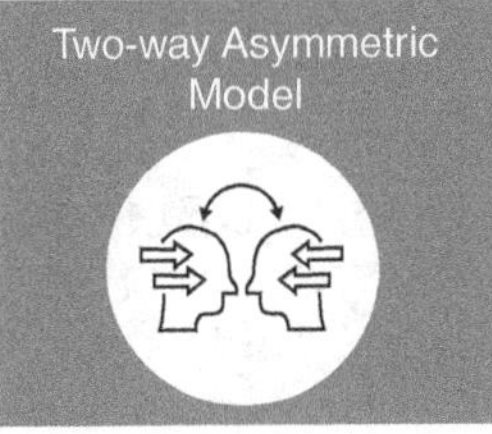

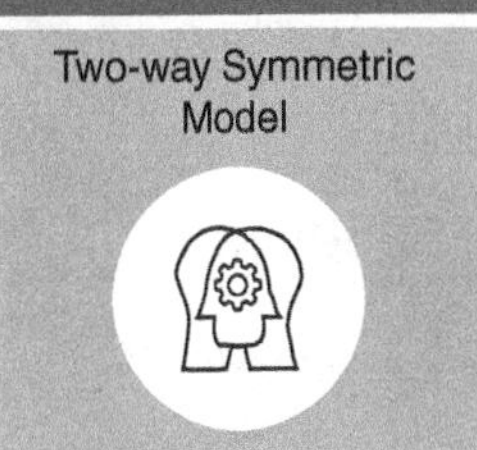

TABLE 12.3 ■ Grunig and Hunt's Four Models of Public Relations

Model	Type	Highlights	Goals	Examples
Press agency/public model	• Most basic model	• All that matters is that the sender gets what the sender wants • Least ethical model, as it places short-term gains ahead of long-term relationships	• To put the sender at the forefront of the audience's mind • To promote content, with little regard as to potential collateral damage	Former Theranos CEO Elizabeth Holmes, who hyped her "blood testing mini-lab" even when she knew it didn't work
Public information model	• A one-way model of communication that sends information from the client to interested publics through various media channels	• This traditional approach uses relationships between PR practitioners and news outlets to alert the public about important issues • Relies on honest and clear communication, making it more ethical than the publicity model	• To develop relationships and make sure that the audience does not think poorly of the client	Ivy Lee's use of press releases and media tours to paint his clients in a favorable light
Two-way asymmetric model	• A two-way model that provides persuasive content based on extensive topic research	• Seeks to not only speak to the audience but hear what audience members think and then respond to those thoughts and concerns • Design allows feedback from the audience to improve the messaging, but the audience remains a secondary concern to the needs of the client	• Allow audience feedback while still promoting a specific message	President Woodrow Wilson's use of the press conference to inform members of the White House press corps on issues concerning the nation

(Continued)

TABLE 12.3 ■ Grunig and Hunt's Four Models of Public Relations (*Continued*)

Model	Type	Highlights	Goals	Examples
Two-way symmetric model	• A two-way model that provides equity among all participants	• Seeks to gather information from all potential stakeholders in the field and continually follow up with them as the practitioner and client make adjustments to a message or campaign • Viewed as the most ethical and most successful model in the field of PR because it allows the broadest level of participation	• Create a symbiotic connection between all parties in PR communication	A university sending out an email survey to gauge its constituents' feelings about its response to the COVID-19 pandemic: after receiving the responses, the school would follow up with each participant

USING PERSUASION IN PUBLIC RELATIONS

LEARNING OBJECTIVE

LO 3: List the six principles of persuasion and explain how each relates to public relations.

The goal of public relations is to present a story in such a way that people will see the world in the same way that you do, that everyone involved will receive a benefit from this information, and that a relationship will form and grow among all the participants. To make all of this happen, public relations practitioners must find ways to persuade their audience members.

Persuasion requires planning and research as well as clear messaging and social connectivity. In some cases, we think of it as an art inherent to the communicator, while in other cases, it comes from the value and logic associated with the message. In an effort to pair the theoretical and the practical, marketing and PR consultant Allen Mireles applied psychologist Robert Cialdini's six key principles of persuasion to public relations (see Table 12.4).[12]

TABLE 12.4 ■ The Six Key Principles of Persuasion

1. The principle of liking	We trust people whom we like
2. The principle of reciprocity	"Do unto others as you would have them do unto you"
3. The principle of social proof	We trust people whom others value
4. The principle of consistency	We like to follow consistent routines
5. The principle of authority	We trust those who show that they have expertise in their fields
6. The principle of scarcity	We like to feel special and have access to things that others can't easily have

The Principle of Liking

In the 1930s, author Dale Carnegie penned a book titled *How to Win Friends and Influence People*, which remains popular to this day. At the heart of the title is the principle of liking: get people to feel friendly toward you, so that you can influence how they act and react in certain situations. Most people want others to like and accept them. In many cases, we tend to trust people we like, thus allowing those people to have a great amount of sway over what we do, where we go, what we eat, and how we live.

The principle of liking is strongly reflected in the social media influencer culture, with people following and liking YouTube and Instagram celebrities. These individuals often promote their lifestyles, their purchases, and even their personal brands through these channels. People who aspire to follow the way that these people will connect with them online and mirror their actions and activities in their own lives.

Mireles notes that finding similar interests between the audience and the client can create or strengthen relationships between them. The key in this case is to be authentic and consistent, because insincerity can really undercut your ability to make any headway toward winning friends and influencing people.

The Principle of Reciprocity

The Golden Rule states, "Do unto others as you would have them do unto you." In short, treat other people how you want to be treated. This truism explains why reciprocity works well in public relations. Mireles says that people are wired to engage in reciprocal behavior, because we don't like to "owe anyone."

An example of reciprocal behavior would be if a classmate asked to copy your notes for this class on a day they missed. If you agree, and the person is grateful, you could easily imagine that person allowing you to copy their notes when you miss a class sometime in the future.

Within public relations, practitioners have ample opportunities to provide stakeholders with access to information and benefits, with the implicit understanding that at some point, those stakeholders will be able to return the favor. In the art of persuasion, it's never a straight-up, contractually outlined trade, but rather a sense of "Happy to help. I'm sure you'll return the favor at some point."

The Principle of Social Proof

To gain a person's trust, you have to demonstrate value to them through various social and personal markers. This means that on social media, people who have more followers are likely to be more influential and seen as more believable than people with just a few likes or shares. People you know are more likely to influence you than people you don't know.

To help improve trust on social media, Twitter introduced its account verification program in 2009, with other social media outlets quickly following suit. Users submit various pieces of information to the social media platform with the goal of being verified as a legitimate source associated with an account. The platform then places the "blue checkmark" on the user's profile, indicating they are a verified source and are accurately representing themselves via that account.[13] This model shifted dramatically in 2022, when billionaire Elon Musk purchased the company and experimented with a "pay-for-play" approach that would allow anyone to purchase this mark for $7.99 per month. Critics argued that this approach to verification could lead to confusion among users and a proliferation of fraudulent accounts that would operate under the mask of authenticity.[14] By 2023, those concerns had become prophesy, as troll accounts that masqueraded as actual celebrities, corporations, and other public figures were adorned with the checkmark. Meanwhile, Musk was essentially gifting the checkmark to famous people and influencers, even as those people took to Twitter to announce that they hadn't paid for the icon and didn't actually want it.[15] Thus, the blue checkmark had become a red flag for users, who saw it more as a farce than proof of legitimacy.

The concept of social connections resonates with individuals throughout public relations, Mireles notes, so it is crucial to demonstrate to your audience members why you should matter to them.

The Principle of Consistency

Human beings are creatures of habit as well as cognitive misers. In other words, when we find something that works and that we don't have to think a lot about, we're totally sold. It's why we tend to follow certain fashion trends, drive certain routes to work, and eat the same thing at our favorite restaurants. When we make an active and conscious choice, we stick with it until either something demonstrably better comes along or that habitual choice betrays us.

We make our media choices in the same way, which is why we visit specific websites and check certain social media feeds repeatedly, even though many other choices exist for us on those platforms. Mireles says PR practitioners should take advantage of habit-building opportunities to create connections between the public and their clients. This will include reminders to readers to sign up for digital newsletters, creating patterns of publishing content for readers, and asking readers to commit to specific causes. The goal is to create habits so that readers consistently consume the content that practitioners place before them.

The Principle of Authority

"Says who?" It's always a fair question when someone proposes an idea that you might not agree with or see as being particularly uninformed. This is why a good answer to this question matters a lot in today's world of public relations.

Authority comes from expertise, experience, and knowledge, all of which is vital in communicating messages to audiences and having those audiences believe what you have to say. Mireles recommends supporting your authority through references to content you have created, sources that cite you, and people who trust you. For example, when reading a press release, a person could think, "Of course they think X is a good idea! They're doing PR for the company!" However, if the *New York Times* or CNN gets that press release and decides to do a story on that topic, citing your work, now you have support from an objective authority figure. When someone says, "I read it in the *Times*" or "I saw it on CNN," that person is likely to be believed, and so is the content they are sharing.

The use of third-party verification is valuable both for practitioners who hope to garner client trust as well as for those who promote their clients' messages in the public sphere with the goal of gaining public trust. The more you can show people why you are knowledgeable, the more likely they are to trust the content you provide to them.[16]

The Principle of Scarcity

The principle of scarcity is based on the idea that the harder a resource is to come by, the more valued it is.

In addition to rarity, exclusivity also plays a role in the idea of scarcity. People enjoy the idea of feeling special, which means getting access to information that other people can't have or being provided with benefits that aren't universally available. This is why promoters make concert tickets available on a presale basis to certain groups, such as frequent customers or people associated with an event's sponsorship. Airlines give people preboarding opportunities if they are part of a "SkyTastic" specialty club. Even stores give people extra discounts for owning a rewards card or using the company's smartphone app.

It would seem that it would be easy to use special and premier offers to connect with the clients' audience members. However, Mireles warns that this method can dramatically backfire if users view the offers as deceptive or the practitioners engage in high-pressure tactics. In relying on this principle, he says, PR professionals should keep an eye on the fine line between offering benefits and being too pushy.

As we've already noted, early public relations practitioners often used the term *propaganda* interchangeably with persuasive PR efforts. Although this is no longer the norm, people who disdain PR often accuse those in the field of engaging in **propaganda**. Table 12.5 outlines the key differences between these two concepts.

TABLE 12.5 ■ Key Differences between Persuasion and Propaganda

Persuasion	Propaganda
Actions are meant to be mutually beneficial, with the goal of a creating a long-term relationship	Actions are meant to benefit only the propagandist and seek short-term gains
Allows people the opportunity to convince one another without threat of recourse	Seeks to change the audience's opinion at all cost, including the use of unethical methods

Persuasion	Propaganda
Attempt to persuade the public through the use of facts, data, and accurate information	Will ignore facts and data or outright lie to convince an audience of a position
Creates a dialogue between the persuader and the audience to create shared understanding; the efforts of the persuader can fail, and that is acceptable in this approach	Lectures the audience continually until the audience gives in and accepts the propagandist's argument; the propagandist will not quit until they win

MEDIA LITERACY MOMENT: INVOLVEMENT, ENGAGEMENT, AND THE ELABORATION LIKELIHOOD MODEL

When a presidential election year comes around, you likely know someone who goes all in on a candidate. They wear T-shirts, buy buttons, and post signs in favor of that person, and they can tell anyone who asks all of the candidate's ideas and why those are the best positions to support. Conversely, you probably also know someone who is vaguely aware of when election day is, skips past every political ad possible, and has no real sense of which candidate is most likely to benefit them.

The difference between these two types of people and the level of persuasion necessary to convince them to change their position comes down to a theory known as the **elaboration likelihood model** or **ELM**. If you understand how this works, you can more easily understand why you can be easily persuaded to do something in some cases while, in others, you'll fight to the death (almost) to bring people around to your way of thinking.

The ELM states that people operate on a spectrum from low involvement to high involvement when faced with making choices. Based on where those people fall on any issue, persuasive efforts are more or less likely to succeed, and certain approaches will work best (see Table 12.6).

TABLE 12.6 ■ The Elaboration Likelihood Model (ELM)

	Low Involvement	High involvement
Personal relevance	People tend to think whatever is happening on a given topic has little impact on their lives	People tend to think whatever is happening on a given topic means a great deal to them
Personal engagement	People will direct very little energy toward doing something about this topic	People will become emotionally invested and invest highly in activities related to this topic
Desire to think	People will avoid putting effort into considering arguments	People will actively engage in active thought processing and scrutiny on the topic
Best path to persuasion	**Peripheral route**: people are more likely to be convinced to act based on peripheral cues, like fun music or beautiful people, or unrelated benefits, like getting a free item to engage in an activity	**Central route**: people will rely on the quality and volume of relevant arguments, often pushing back against weaker positions
Outcome of persuasion	Persuasion of low-involvement people through a peripheral route is weak, short-lasting, and easy to overcome	Persuasion of high involvement people through central route will lead to long-lasting attitudes and stable results

Think of some common methods used to persuade these two groups of people. A commercial for a low-quality light beer aimed at consumers with a low commitment to their current favorite brew is less likely to discuss the inherent intricacies of the malting process or why its nuanced approach provides better flavor to the beer. Instead, it'll show the audience an ad with a lot of beautiful, scantily clad people having fun at a beach volleyball game while they drink their brew. Or they could offer a "Buy a case, get free concert tickets" giveaway to make a consumer pick that beer over a similarly priced discount beer.

However, when it comes to something like selecting a doctor to care for a loved one who is suffering from cancer, people are probably going to be digging deeply into the history of that doctor, the doctor's success rate, and other relevant information. It's highly unlikely that anyone would be persuaded by "Come for cancer surgery, stay for the fun!" ads or a "Get your chemotherapy here and get a free T-shirt!" approach.

If you understand how involved someone is in a topic, you can tailor your approach to best persuade them. You can also be aware of the tactics used to persuade you, thus allowing you to engage in critical thinking before making a decision.

THE NEXT STEP: Think back to the last few purchases you made over the past few days and walk through the steps of the ELM outlined in Table 12.6. To what degree did you feel high or low involvement in terms of personal relevance, personal engagement, and your desire to think in making those purchases? Then, assess which route applied to your purchase decision and the overall outcome of the persuasion. Did some purchases require you to engage in more central or more peripheral routes in terms of your approach? What aspects of the purchase lent themselves to higher or lower involvement in terms of relevance, engagement, and thought? Write a short essay that captures this experience.

KEY ELEMENTS OF SUCCESSFUL PR

LEARNING OBJECTIVE

LO 4: Explain the three key elements of successful public relations efforts, providing examples of each one.

It should be clear that public relations is a complex and wide-reaching field that requires a great amount of communicative skill. How to mount a professional PR campaign—in terms of writing, social interaction, and other similar practices—is beyond the scope of this book. However, here are the three key things that will lead to successful PR efforts:

1. Transparency
2. Clarity
3. Humanity

Let's dig into each of these a bit more deeply.

Transparency

Honesty might always be the best policy, but it doesn't always seem advisable when you are faced with potentially unpleasant consequences. Let's say you were told as a little kid not to drink grape juice while sitting on your parents' new couch, a warning that you ignored. You spill juice on the nice white fabric, and a giant purple stain begins to spread across the middle cushion. What do you do? If you're like a million other kids, you flip that cushion over and hope no one notices. However, the principle of **transparency** requires that you go to your parents and confess to your accident.

Successful PR relies on your willingness to open yourself and your client up to public scrutiny so that the public can examine every aspect of your claims or operations. This can be especially difficult if you are attempting to work through a crisis or scramble to fix a problem. However, experts in PR will tell you that the more you hide something, the worse it is. As Ivy Lee noted years ago, people are going to find out anyway, so don't try to hide it. Transparency enables trust between the organization and the public, leading to a better overall relationship.

Clarity

One of the main reasons you are required to take media writing courses while pursuing a PR degree is the importance of clear and concise messaging. To help you find ways to effectively reach your audience, your writing instructors want you to develop clarity in your writing. When you craft a simple and direct message using a noun-verb-object approach, you can reach your audience with ease. A good clear message is like an expensive steak: it doesn't need a lot of stuff layered onto it to make it palatable. A weak message is like a ten-cent hamburger: you don't get a lot of meat, you have to wonder what that meat is actually made of, and it's going to take a boatload of condiments to choke it down.

FIGURE 12.2 ■ This Sentence Structure Is Clear and Concise and Incorporates the "Holy Trinity" of Good Writing

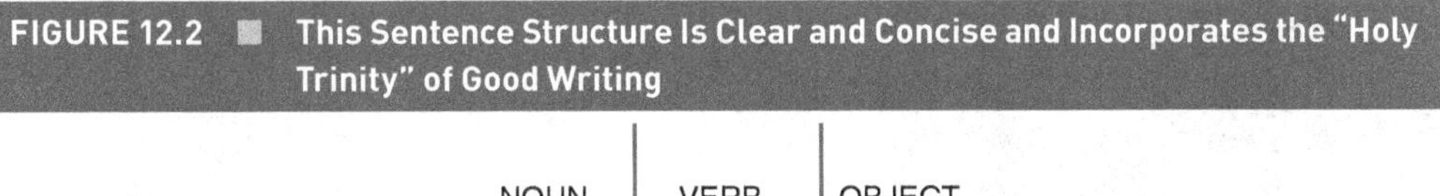

To do this effectively, stick to simple terms in describing your position. Don't try to hide behind a ton of extra verbiage or state something in a way that makes you look untrustworthy. The goal of PR writing is to provide accurate information that enhances trust and improves relationships. Tell people what you know, and be honest about what you don't. If you try to fake your way around something, you will confuse and upset your audience and undermine your ability to persuade them now and in the future.

Humanity

You can be both clear and transparent, but that doesn't always mean you have done your job in this field. Public relations is more than a transactional relationship between two nameless, faceless entities. People exist on both ends of that communicative effort, so you need to embrace the value of humanity, where you show the basic human decency and dignity people respect from one another in society.

An example of how this can go wrong comes from a *Cosmopolitan* social media post made in 2017. The magazine ran a story about a woman who battled a rare form of cancer, and to promote it, the magazine actually sent out this tweet: "How this woman lost 44 pounds without *ANY* exercise." As one person noted on Twitter in response to *Cosmo*'s post: "Cancer is not a diet plan."[17]

It is often much easier to see examples of public relations gone wrong than it is when everything goes well, so PR practitioners often fail to get the proper level of praise for their work. However, the 1982 Tylenol crisis stands not only as a testament to PR done well but also as an instance in which all three elements of successful PR converged to save a brand from certain death.

A DEEPER LOOK: THE TYLENOL CRISIS

In 1982, seven people died in Illinois after ingesting Tylenol that had been laced with potassium cyanide. The product's parent company, Johnson & Johnson, faced a crisis that could have brought down the entire corporation.

Harold Burson, of the legendary PR firm Burson-Marsteller, counseled the company throughout the event, providing advice on how to handle a product recall, how to effectively communicate the company's position on the crisis, and how to rebuild trust in the product itself.

First, the company placed a heavy value on the concept of *humanity*, with company Chairperson James Burke demanding that the question "How do we protect people?" take precedence over any concern over how to preserve the Tylenol brand. In addressing that question, the company immediately put out news releases that told the public not to consume any more Tylenol until the source of the cyanide could be determined. The company also ceased production of Tylenol and issued a nationwide product recall, even though the poisonings were limited to a relatively small area of only one state.

The company also prized *clarity*, as it made simple and direct statements regarding the product. It told people not to take the product during the crisis and informed people what to do if they were concerned that they might have consumed a tainted dose. Once the recall had ended and Johnson & Johnson decided to release a new run of Tylenol, the company communicated its product changes to the public through simple and direct media messaging. Officials explained the purpose of the new plastic safety seal and foil cap on the bottles, as well as what to do if either of them was broken.

Chicago City Health Department employees test Tylenol medicines for cyanide content at a city laboratory. The poisoning scare had citizens avoiding all Tylenol products, for fear of dying. Harold Burson's public relations efforts helped Johnson & Johnson restore confidence in the product and the company.

AP Photo/Charlie Knoblock

Finally, the company demonstrated the importance of *transparency*. The company set up several toll-free telephone lines to allow consumers to call in with concerns and ask any questions they had. To better communicate with the media, the company set up a video center that allowed its press conferences to reach major media outlets. In addition, Burke went on several national television shows, including *60 Minutes* and *Donahue*, to answer questions and provide information to the public.

Despite heavy media coverage that linked Tylenol to the poisonings, the transparency, clarity, and humanity demonstrated throughout the crisis by Johnson & Johnson prevented the brand and the entire company from imploding. Public relations experts have called the handling of this situation a benchmark in crisis communication.

COMMUNICATION TOOLS FOR PUBLIC RELATIONS

LEARNING OBJECTIVE

LO 5: Review the primary tools that public relations practitioners use to do their jobs.

Ivy Lee helped craft and disseminate what was thought to be the first press release within the United States when he worked with the Pennsylvania Railroad after it experienced a disaster. In the more than one hundred years since then, not only has the field grown but so has the array of tools at the disposal of practitioners. Here is a brief list of the most common tools practitioners use on a regular basis:

1. Traditional news and press releases
2. Story pitches
3. Fact sheets

4. Media kits
5. Live events
6. Digital efforts

Let's take a deeper look at these tools and what they do for the practitioners, the organizations, and the audiences who consume them, understanding that these all have both old-school and digital options. Then we can look at two specific areas of digital communication: an organization's website and its social media presence.

Traditional News and Press Releases

The practitioner's most frequently used tool is a traditional news release, a piece of written copy intended to draw the media's attention to something that the practitioner sees as valuable to the public. Practitioners use news releases, or press releases as they are frequently called, to announce an event, react to a situation, localize a broader topic, or simply alert the media to something of value.

The delivery of these news releases can come in multiple formats. Some are written as traditional printed releases like those delivered via mail decades ago, while others are built into the bodies of email messages and delivered to an electronic mailing list. Depending on the media outlet the practitioner is attempting to reach, the content will conform to the writing standards of that platform. For example, a release geared toward newspapers and print-themed online news outlets will use the inverted pyramid, a format outlined in Chapter 5 that puts the most important information at the top of the piece and then includes the remaining information in descending order of importance. On the other hand, releases aimed at radio stations or podcasters will rely on broadcast style and fit within fifteen- or thirty-second formats.

To broaden the appeal of public relations content to television or YouTube viewers, practitioners can use video clips relevant to the topic as well as soundbites from their clients. This approach to creating prepackaged content that mimics the style of television news stories is called a **video news release** (VNR). A VNR can run anywhere from a minute to a minute and a half, and it will usually tell the story of the practitioner's client through standard broadcast techniques. It is prepackaged for insertion into the newscast as a singular element, thus increasing the ease of use and enhancing the likelihood that news stations will use it.

VNRs have come under fire for being so similar to traditional news stories that viewers cannot distinguish them from station-created content. In the early 2000s, the Federal Communications Commission began warning broadcasters to identify VNRs as being the work of outside public relations agencies so people would better understand their source and potential bias.[18]

Story Pitches

To help the media learn about a client, practitioners will often highlight good stories that they see as having value to news outlets in the area. The **story pitch** seeks to interest journalists in a topic that has an opportunity to benefit both the client and the public. A pitch will alert the reporters to the topic, provide rationale as to why it should be of interest to the reporter's audience, and the ways in which the practitioner will help facilitate communication between the client and the journalist. To do this well, you will have to conduct a fair amount of research on the client, the journalist's media outlet, and the audience for that outlet. Then, you need to find ways to use this knowledge to persuade the journalist to consider the idea.

Fact Sheets

Instead of using a narrative approach to tell a story to the media, practitioners will often rely on a **fact sheet**, which contains quick, bullet-point items to get simple bits of information across about a topic, company, or concept. These can include time-date-place information for an upcoming event, fast facts about an organization, or a few bits of trivia about an idea the practitioner wants to promote.

Media Kits

To help a client gain attention and traction within a market, PR firms often will construct a **media kit** that presents crucial information about that organization to the media and the public. Practitioners who used traditional kits might mail them to key audience members or hand out these packets of information at media events. In the digital age, the kits often reside on a company's or an organization's website, thus allowing any interested party the opportunity to download specific elements of interest for consumption or republication.[19]

Live Events

Instead of relying on mediated communication to reach the public, practitioners will often find ways to put the client in front of the audience. The goal of any good live event is to increase interest in the client as well as the topic at hand through the use of personal contact with the media or the audience itself. The most common are **news conferences**, interviews, and media tours (see Table 12.7).

TABLE 12.7 ■ Four Common Live Events

News conferences	A client speaks directly to the public through the media. In some cases, the organization may announce a major, new initiative; in others, it may need to deal with a crisis. Regardless of its purpose, the news conference can relay a singular message in a timely fashion, as well as providing the media the opportunity to ask questions and clarify information.
Interviews	A one-on-one connection between clients and specific reporters that can deepen relationships between organizations and media outlets. In some cases, these are simple phone calls, while other times they may be live interviews for broadcast.
Media tours	Offer the public a glimpse into how an organization works or how a project unfolds. For example, a client in the manufacturing industry might want to show off its new factory or product line to media practitioners who cover that topic.

Digital Efforts

The creation and maintenance of a digital presence for your organization and your clients is crucial in today's media ecosystem. Twenty years ago, simply having a home page that people could find on the web was enough to establish your digital bona fides. Today, you must have a dynamic presence on the web—as well as on other digital platforms—to give potential clients a sense that you can deliver a quality public relations experience for everyone you serve. Let's look at two distinct areas of content: an organization's website and its social media presence.

Website

The website is the digital lobby of the public relations firm, and first impressions matter a great deal. According to Joe Ciarallo of *Adweek*, this digital tool serves as one of the top three drivers for gaining clients and connecting with the public.[20] To that end, what goes on the site and what doesn't can make a huge difference in how the public sees you and your organization.

The website should be clean, simple, and easy to navigate. It must contain content that is relevant, helpful, and engaging for your audience. It must also provide fresh material for readers who visit frequently, while still containing the bedrock elements of a site, including information about your organization and opportunities to connect with you.

Social Media

Platforms like Facebook, Twitter, Instagram, and LinkedIn can give public relations firms and their clients the ability to publish content without relying on traditional media outlets. Writing for the Center for Social Impact Communication at Georgetown University, journalist Paul Bates stated that social media gives you the opportunity to amplify your message, reach larger audiences, and connect on a more personal basis with your public.[21] Your ability to pick the best platforms to reach your audience and your willingness to provide quality content on them will determine your success in this area. If you can make it worth your readers' time, you will continue to have engaged readers on these platforms and be able to rise above the glut of other communicators competing for their attention. If you post infrequently or operate outside some of the "best practices" outlined in Chapter 10, you and your clients will suffer.

JOBS IN PR

Now that you better understand public relations, here's a handy overview of a few common positions in the field of PR today.

Career Opportunity	Common Tasks
Copywriter	• Craft press releases for multiple media platforms • Create social media content for clients • Develop creative ideas for PR campaigns
Spokesperson	• Handle requests for information from various media practitioners • Present information to the public on behalf of a client • Enhance relationships between clients and key publics through direct and indirect communication
Public information officer	• Serve as primary source of information for media outlets seeking information regarding a client • Establish, craft, and maintain key talking points for an organization and its representatives • Plan speeches and press conferences to disseminate information on important events
Event planner	• Plan, host, and troubleshoot conventions, conferences, and other gatherings for a client • Negotiate contracts with facilities and outside vendors for goods and services related to the event • Manage and maintain budgets
Strategic planner	• Conduct research and data analysis to help shape a client's business strategy • Develop plans to assess company performance and overall corporate mission • Assist executives in making educated and effective decisions

CHAPTER REVIEW

LO 1 Explain the importance of key moments in the history of public relations.

- A train wreck in 1906 led PR pioneer Ivy Lee to work with railroad officials to provide information to the press about the crash through what is believed to be the first official press release. Lee also worked with the Rockefellers in 1914 after a coal miners' strike to shape public opinion of the family and create public support for them.
- In his 1923 book *Crystalizing Public Opinion*, Edward Bernays defined public relations as "the engineering of public consent." Bernays and Doris Fleischman ran one of the earliest and most influential PR firms in the United States during the middle of the twentieth century.
- During World War II, both Allied and Axis powers relied on persuasive techniques to gain support for their position among their citizens. Adolf Hitler developed the Reich

Ministry of Public Enlightenment and Propaganda during his rise to power and used it to reinforce his positions and opinions. The United States developed the Office of War Information in 1942 with the goal of garnering support for Allied troops abroad and for austerity measures closer to home.

- In the postwar era, public relations began to diversify by offering increased opportunities for people of color and women. Pioneers like Joseph Varney Baker, Inez Kaiser, Barbara Hunter, Betsy Plank, Jean Schoonover, and David Garcia helped carve out positions within the field for women, African Americans, and Latinos through their efforts.
- Public relations sat at the forefront of the digital revolution through the use of multimedia news releases as far back as 1997. Digital tools, such as websites and social media, have continued to allow practitioners to connect with journalists and audiences.

LO 2 Define public relations and explain its role in society.

- The PRSA defines public relations as "a strategic communication process that builds mutually beneficial relationships between organizations and their publics." The terms *reputation, deliberate, strategic, well-performed, mutually beneficial,* and *responsive* are also used to define PR.
- The role of PR in public includes several key elements:
  - Inform the public: Practitioners reach out to an audience on behalf of a client to explain something of value.
  - Advocate for a cause or a client: Practitioners seek to persuade audience members to see a product, service, or situation the way the practitioner does by communicating factually accurate, persuasive messages.
  - Share content among all groups: PR professionals serve as a hub through which information moves from the organization to the audience and from the audience back to the organization.
  - Create mutually beneficial outcomes: To help forge long-term relationships between clients and the public, practitioners need to ensure that everyone benefits from each interaction among these groups.

LO 3 List the six principles of persuasion and explain how each relates to public relations.

- *The principle of liking*: We tend to trust people we like and allow them to have a great amount of sway over how we live. Public relations practitioners can use this principle to develop relationships with audience members before trying to influence their decisions.
- *The principle of reciprocity*: We interact with other people with the understanding that we will treat them as we would like to be treated ourselves. Practitioners can use this principle as they provide stakeholders with access to information and benefits, with the implicit understanding that, at some point, those stakeholders will return the favor.
- *The principle of social proof*: In a social dynamic, people will extend trust to people who have proven to be trustworthy. In PR, it is vital to demonstrate to your audience members your standing among your peers and the general public on social media.
- *The principle of consistency*: People find comfort in common and repetitive things that can help them develop habits. Practitioners can take advantage of habit-building opportunities to create connections between the public and the clients.
- *The principle of authority*: Audiences will find value in messages delivered by experts and other authority figures. In PR, showing people that they should trust your client because of a high level of expertise is vital in developing a trusting relationship.
- *The principle of scarcity:* The less there is of something, the more valuable it can be in the eyes of the public. People enjoy the idea of feeling special, so practitioners who can give them that feeling will have a leg up on the competition.

LO 4 Explain the three key elements of successful public relations efforts, providing examples of each one.

- *Transparency*: Practitioners and the organizations they represent should not hide things from the public. The more open and honest they are with people, the higher level of trust people will place in them, even in the time of a crisis.
- *Clarity*: PR professionals should be straightforward and simple in how they communicate with the public. Using jargon or complex words can seem dishonest or arrogant to an audience.
- *Humanity*: Accuracy and honesty must be matched with an understanding of feelings and emotions, especially when communicating difficult or painful news. Professionals who embrace the need for a human touch will connect well with the public.

LO 5 Review the primary tools that public relations practitioners use to do their jobs.

- *Traditional news and press releases*: Practitioners use these to draw the media's attention to something that they see as valuable to the public. The releases should tell a simple story and encourage the media to share it with the audiences that they serve.
- *Story pitches*: Pitches tell media outlets of a potential story that could be relevant and useful to that outlet's audience. The practitioner offers to facilitate the telling of that story by connecting the client and the media outlet.
- *Fact sheets*: PR officials use fact sheets to provide simple, factual information about an event or a client to help reporters learn vital background on a relevant topic. This bullet-point approach gives the reporters the who, what, when, where, why, and how of the topic in a direct fashion.
- *Media kits*: These packages contain a great deal of information for reporters to use as they see fit for a single story or their ongoing coverage. A kit can help a client gain attention and traction within a market and serve as a library of content that reporters can access each time they report on this client.
- *Live events*: Press conferences, interviews, and media tours provide media outlets with direct, interpersonal connections with a practitioner's client. The goal of every event is to give the news media information in a format that provides timely content for dissemination and an opportunity to interact with the clients.
- *Digital efforts*: The creation and maintenance of a website and social media presence provide audiences the opportunity to easily access content when it is convenient to them. These are vital elements of establishing connections with the media and the general public.

KEY TERMS

Advocacy
Central route
Clarity
Deliberate
Elaboration likelihood model (ELM)
Fact sheet
Humanity
Media kit
Mutually beneficial
News conference
Peripheral route
Practitioner
Press release
Propaganda
Public relations (PR)
Reputation
Responsive
Smart News Release
Story pitch
Strategic
Transparency
Twitrelease
Velvet ghetto
Video news release
Well-performed

DISCUSSION QUESTIONS

1. Although public relations continues to grow as a field, it has not seen similar levels of growth with regard to the presence of people of color. What are some of the ways in which you would seek to improve this situation within the discipline?
2. Public relations seeks to connect audiences and clients to develop mutually beneficial, long-term relationships. What is the benefit to each group in these types of relationships, and what would be the problem with one group's attempting to maximize its benefits at the cost of the other?
3. Now that you have learned more about public relations, do you feel this information has confirmed what you previously believed about the field or runs counter to what you believed? Has anything in this chapter changed your way of thinking about PR, and if so, how?
4. Which of the three key elements in public relations do you see as most important to being successful in working with the public?
5. Of the six principles listed in the chapter, which ones do you think rate as most vital to successful public relations efforts, and which ones are least vital in that regard?
6. Do you think more traditional media tools or digital efforts are more successful in the field of PR today? Make a case for your position.

People walk past a wall of digital billboard advertising in New York's Times Square.

Mary Altaffer/Associated Press / Alamy Stock Photo

13 ADVERTISING AND MARKETING

INTRODUCTION

1. *How often do you notice advertising in the media you consume each day?*
2. *Do you think that these billboards have an impact on you or people you know regarding what you purchase, use, think, or support?*
3. *What are the benefits and drawbacks of advertising messages like these?*

Advertising is a form of mass communication that has numerous similarities to other forms of media we have discussed throughout the book. In fact, advertising is a key part of newspapers, magazines, television programs, movies, digital media, and more, both in terms of working within the platforms and in the storytelling approaches it takes. It can be as direct as a billboard that says, "Buy This Toy So Your Kid Will Love You." It can also be as nuanced as a character in your favorite show eating a brand-name cereal during a scene or a movie hero wearing a specific type of watch.

Advertising has changed considerably from its earliest form in the United States. In the some of the country's first mass media advertisements, individuals bought space in daily or weekly newssheets to announce the arrival of a ship in port. As companies moved from highlighting only value and functionality to promoting the benefits of status and ego, advertising evolved from a "buy this" to a "live through me" message, in which the products created an entire image based on individual needs, desires, and a sense of self.

At its very core, however, advertising is like the other media we have discussed in this textbook: storytelling content that connects people or groups with shared interests with the goal of inspiring a valuable interaction. In this chapter, we'll discuss the ways in which advertising operates and why this form of media continues to evolve and improve faster than most other forms of mass communication.

The chapter will begin by defining advertising and outlining its key components. We will discuss why advertising exists and what needs it meets for advertisers and consumers, as well as some key criticisms of advertising and how the government and industry have addressed them. Finally, we will look into how advertising companies decide how best to craft messages to reach specified media users.

LEARNING OBJECTIVES

After completing this chapter, you should be able to:

1. Explain the importance of key moments in the history of advertising
2. Define advertising, its key components, and its overall purpose.
3. Outline the types of advertising and the media platforms each uses to reach the public.
4. Understand the role of advertising in society, in terms of both brand identity and consumer value.

A BRIEF HISTORY OF ADVERTISING

LEARNING OBJECTIVE

LO 1: Explain the importance of key moments in the history of advertising.

Advertising has been around since civilizations saw a need to connect consumers and products. Scholars note that ancient Egyptians crafted advertisements to engage citizens in religious or political movements. In one case, a piece of papyrus found in the city of Thebes that dated back to 3000 BC included an ad explaining that the advertiser was missing his slave and was offering to trade a piece of gold in exchange for the safe return of this individual.[1]

In the seventeenth century, advertising took the form of handbills and postings that announced opportunities for the purchase of goods that ships had brought to port, such as coffee, fruits, and sugar from faraway lands. Newspapers also contained notices for travel ventures for individuals seeking their fortunes overseas in the colonies of North America. Ever since, advertising has continued to develop as new technologies and means of communication have evolved.

Here are some key points in the development of advertising:

- Traditional print advertising in the United States
- Broadcast advertising expands message reach
- Advertising agencies assist clients in reaching consumers
- Niche marketing efforts target people of color
- Advertising goes digital

Let's look a bit more deeply at the evolution of this field.

Traditional Print Advertising in the United States

As ships arrived in the New World, advertising for what they were carrying appeared in colonial newspapers. The vessels from overseas offered both exotic products from African and Indian ports as well as products from their homelands that were in short supply in the colonies.

Aside from these kinds of notices, early advertising took the form of what we would come to know as **classified advertising**: ads placed by individuals seeking to buy or sell a specific item or service. One of the earliest examples dates to 1704 when a citizen placed a notice in the *Boston Newsletter* that his Oyster Bay, Long Island, estate was for sale. Given the high cost and limited access associated with print products during the seventeenth and eighteenth centuries, most advertisements were targeted at wealthy individuals and offered expensive products.

When Benjamin Franklin offered multiple pages in his *Pennsylvania Gazette* to "new advertisements," it created an opportunity for readers and sellers alike. The money made from these ads essentially covered the cost of production, so the per-issue cost of a publication could be lowered, allowing more people to purchase the paper. This financial model continued to drive newspapers into the twentieth century, when **display advertisements**, a form of selling that used more space on the page to pair text and visuals, became a prominent form of print ads.

Broadcast Advertising Expands Message Reach

As noted in Chapter 6, the growth of broadcasting opportunities came hand in hand with advertising sponsorships. In 1922, WEAF created the first "pay-for-play" opportunity with its creation of toll broadcasting. This system allowed individuals to purchase ten-minute chunks of air time during which they could present whatever content they liked. The first sponsor was the Hawthorne Court Apartments in New York City.

When television emerged as a viable medium in the early 1940s, advertisers saw another opportunity to reach their audiences. In 1941, Bulova placed the first television ad, a ten-second message that was captioned "America runs on Bulova Time." That $9 ad was the first step toward an advertising explosion that would see companies spend $128 million in 1951 alone. By 1977, television advertising sales would exceed $7.5 billion annually and account for almost 20 percent of all the ad copy placed in all media throughout the United States.

Advertising Agencies Assist Clients in Reaching Consumers

At the forefront of advertising's expansive growth was the creation of the **advertising agency**, a business that worked to connect companies and consumers in a mutually beneficial way. In 1869, F. Wayland Ayer launched Ayer and Son, the first agency that not only purchased space for clients but performed creative and strategic services for them as well. Ayer purchased ad space in bulk, thereby allowing him to

An ad for Schaefer beer.

CBS Photo Archive / Contributor/Getty Images

provide his clients with the best possible rates. In addition, he established an industry-standard rate of a 15 percent **commission**, which is the amount of a total purchase a client owed the agency for its work.

At the start of the twentieth century, most advertising was meant to alert people to the availability of items, such as homes or staple goods for sale. Once a consumer looking for a product knew that it was available, it was hoped that they would purchase it. However, soon advertisers were trying to create demand for their clients' products, not just inform the public of their existence. The staff at the J. Walter Thompson agency sought opportunities to maximize client potential through tools more common to magazine and newspaper stories. Copywriter Helen Lansdowne Resor, for example, used the concept of sex appeal to sell Woodbury Soap in 1911, noting that it provided "a skin you love to touch." Her use of narrative copy and sexualized imagery remained prominent in the company's ads for more than thirty years.

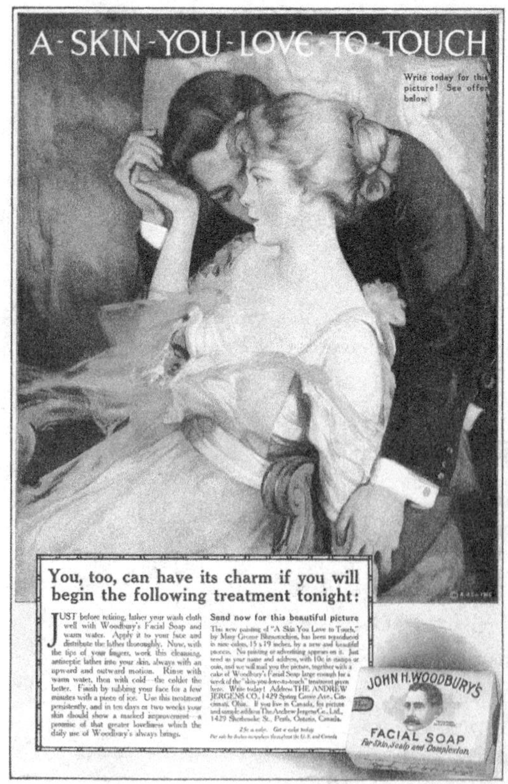

Ads for Woodbury Soap, like this one in the 1916 edition of the Ladies Home Journal, *relied on images promoting sex appeal and text that showcased the benefits of touchable skin.*

Old But Gold / Alamy Stock Photo

Other agencies, like Leo Burnett Company and Ogilvy and Mather, followed in the 1930s and 1940s with this storytelling approach to advertising. Founder Leo Burnett believed in a humanistic approach to advertising copy, with the goal of creating a connection between the audience and the brands he promoted. David Ogilvy, on the other hand, worked from the premise that the sole purpose of advertising was to increase sales. His agency relied on multiple tactics and approaches to expand the bottom line for his clients.

By the 1960s and 1970s, advertising had reached its "golden age," thanks to a creative revolution that relied on psychological approaches to selling consumer goods as well as targeting younger adults with disposable income.[2] The wide array of media outlets, coupled with the competitive nature of corporations, allowed agencies to create content that was not only client specific but also much more niche oriented.[3]

TABLE 13.1 ■ A Few Key Names in Advertising

F. Wayland Ayer	Helen Lansdowne Resor	Leo Burnett	Caroline R. Jones	David Ogilvy	Thomas J. Burrell
• Founded N.W. Ayer and Son in 1869, an early ad firm that provided editing and design services to clients as well as purchasing space for them in publications • Guaranteed that his clients would get the lowest ad rates possible • Established 15 percent as the commission rate for agencies, which remains standard today	• The first female copywriter at J. Walter Thompson in 1908 • Dubbed "the greatest copywriter" in 1964 by the *New York Herald Tribune.* • Known for the first use of "sex appeal" in an advertising campaign	• Founded Leo Burnett Company in 1935, a company that today has a global presence, with more than nine thousand employees in sixty-nine countries • Relied on a "soft sell," humanistic approach to advertising to help build brand equity for his clients • Created memorable characters that linked to his clients' products, like the Keebler Elves, the Pillsbury Doughboy, and Tony the Tiger	• Broke barriers in the advertising industry as the first woman and person of color to serve in executive roles • Formed Zebra Associates in 1968, one of the first full-service advertising agencies with principal officers of color • Her clients included American Express, McDonald's, and the U.S. Postal Service	• Known as the "father of modern advertising" • Cofounded Ogilvy and Mather in 1948, relying on the sole premise that advertising is meant to increase sales • Writer of multiple texts that still guide advertising education	• Became "the first Black person to work in a Chicago advertising agency," moving up from the mailroom to copywriter • Founded Burrell Communications in 1971 with then partner Emmett McBain to develop advertising that spoke directly to the African American community • Famously noted that "black people are not dark-skinned white people," to help clients connect with key elements of Black culture

Niche Marketing Efforts Target People of Color

Advertising has had a long history of targeting a narrow band of consumers, namely middle-class white people who made purchases to maintain a happy lifestyle. However, as the civil rights movement grew and niche marketing opportunities emerged, companies saw a large, untapped area of purchasing power: people of color. Although some media critics argue that early efforts to reach this audience relied on clumsy stereotypes, a few agencies found a way to pair a deeper cultural understanding with targeted outreach that successfully benefitted both clients and consumers.[4]

Thomas J. Burrell founded his advertising agency in 1971 with partner Emmett McBain specifically to create content that reached the African American community.[5] The mantra of Burrell Communications was that "black people are not dark-skinned white people," a simple way of saying that cultural differences existed between these groups and that advertising needed to reflect that. His advertisements for McDonald's and Coca-Cola were based on what he called "positive realism," in which the companies could use people of color in their ads without alienating white consumers. This approach to advertising became as popular among white audiences as it did for the intended Black readers and viewers, leading more companies and agencies to expand their reach into communities of color.[6]

A similar move toward serving one's own community occurred in 1961, when Emilio Azcárraga purchased television stations in Los Angeles and San Antonio to run Spanish-language programming from his Televisa network in Mexico. The creation of SIN/SICC, or the Spanish International Network and Spanish International Communications Corporation, drew large audiences of Latino consumers with content they couldn't find anywhere else, and the advertising dollars soon followed. By 1982, SIN had connected with satellite television operations to reach 90 percent of the nation's

Thomas J. Burrell was the first Black person to work at a Chicago advertising agency.

Ralf-Finn Hestoft / Corbis Historical/ Contributor/Getty Images

Hispanic households and had presented advertisers with a vibrant, diverse, and expansive market.[7] As they became successful here with Spanish-language ads, agencies sought crossover opportunities for more universal products on traditionally white media channels in English. Today, the Hispanic/Latino market represents about one-quarter of the U.S. citizenry, with more than sixty-two million people classifying themselves as Latino in the 2020 census. Advertisers are continuing to cultivate this group through messages that celebrate Latino heritage and present diverse images that represent a wider swath of the community.[8]

Advertising Goes Digital

In 1994 *HotWired* applied the traditional advertising model of using space on a page to promote a product to the World Wide Web, when the publication included **banner ads** for IBM, Volvo, and other companies on its website. These advertisements ran across the top of the page and allowed people to click on them to be transported to the advertiser's website or a larger ad on the publication's website. This is known as **static advertising** because the same ad content was delivered in the same position on the page to all the people who arrived on a given page.

With the development of Google's tracking technology and the launch of Google AdWords in 2000, the model shifted away from static ads to advertising specifically tailored to individual users. **Targeted advertising campaigns** made use of individuals' browsing and search histories to present specific ad messages to people most likely to have an interest in each good or service. This approach helped advertisers avoid blanketing uninterested consumers with messages while also allowing them to fine-tune messages for potential consumers based on the data Google gathered.

As social media became a prominent player in the digital world, advertisers saw the potential of using these platforms to reach interested consumers. Starting in 2007 with the introduction of Facebook advertising, businesses and organizations have used each emerging social media tool to connect with a target audience. YouTube is the most prominent among these platforms, having begun providing advertising opportunities in 2009, as have Instagram, Twitter, and other similar outlets. Research showed that digital advertising in 2022 represented approximately 66 percent of all advertising sales in that year and is expected to increase to nearly 74 percent by 2026.[9]

FIGURE 13.1 ■ Percentage of Advertising Dedicated to Specific Platforms (2019–2022)

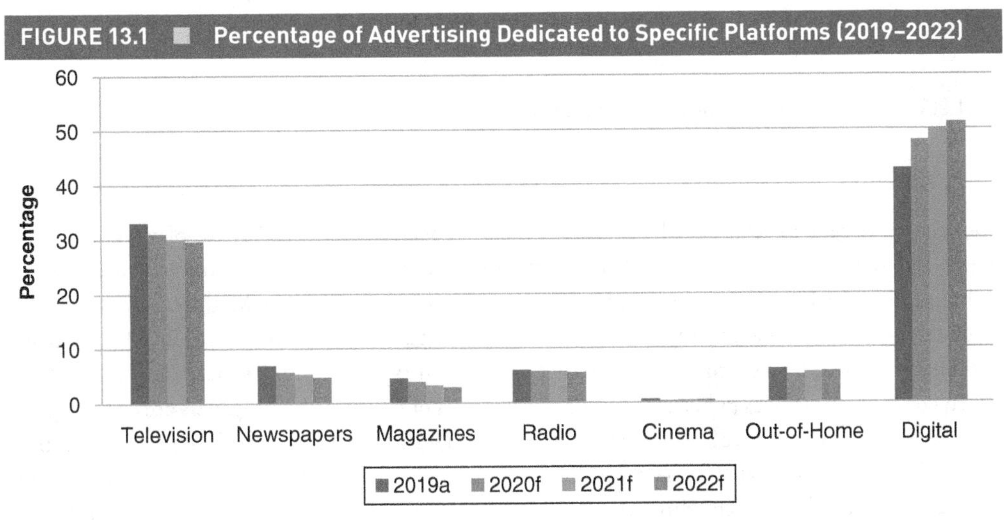

Source: Dentsu.

DEFINING AND EXPLAINING ADVERTISING

LEARNING OBJECTIVE

LO 2: Define advertising, its key components, and its overall purpose.

Advertising is defined as paid, persuasive communication, published with the intent of connecting a client with an audience in hopes of inspiring action. What makes for quality advertising is in the eye of the beholder. One of the most memorable advertisements of all time was the Apple Macintosh advertisement that aired during the 1984 Super Bowl. The spot ran only one time, cost $650,000 to make, and required $250,000 more to purchase the air time. The executives at the company and the agency responsible for running it hated it to the point that they wanted to kill the ad. However, Apple founder Steve Jobs ran the ad, which portrayed other computer companies as "Big Brother" from George Orwell's novel *1984*. All of the people observing a video from "Big Brother" were sitting on sets of bleachers, looking downtrodden. A woman carrying a giant hammer then ran into the room and destroyed the video of the leader. A voice-over then announced how "1984 will not be like *1984*," thanks to the wonderful things the Macintosh will provide. The ad generated more than $155 million in Mac sales in the three months after it aired, becoming both the most well-recognized and successful Super Bowl ad of all time.[10]

Regardless whether an advertisement is a once-in-a-lifetime visual masterpiece or a simple request to "Eat at Joe's," all ads require certain key elements (see Table 13.2).

TABLE 13.2 ■ Key Aspects of an Advertising Message

1. Paid speech	The client provides money to acquire space or time from a media outlet to provide a message of the client's choosing.
2. Known sponsor	The person or group disseminating the advertisement must be listed in some way in the advertising itself.
3. Information plus persuasion	The content of the ad combines factual content with convincing opinions to encourage audience members to do something the client wants them to do.
4. Delivered to an audience	The message must reach content consumers via some media platform.
5. Promotes products, services, or ideas	The advertisement must connect to a tangible item ("Buy a Toyota"), an engagement opportunity ("Hire HandiMaid to clean your house"), or a specific concept ("Be kind").

Let's take a deeper look at how each of these elements works.

Paid Speech

The crucial element associated with advertising is that it operates under a "pay-for-play" model. **Paid speech** requires an organization to contract with a media outlet for a certain amount of money in exchange for a specified amount of space, time, impressions, or distribution. Within these contracted set of parameters, the organization places content that it sees as beneficial to its mission, whether that's to get people to vote for a specific client or to buy a particular type of running shoe.

In comparison, articles published in the news portions of websites or newspapers are chosen based on independent assessments of the media outlet's editorial staff. The writers decide what will be important to the audience and pitch stories to editors, who approve or reject them. This is done without any outside or undue influence regarding what to cover.

In the case of public relations (PR), practitioners attempt to engage media outlets on behalf of their clients through the concept of earned media. In other words, the PR professionals present the writers with enough good information and valuable insight about a product, service, or idea that it compels the journalists to write about them. Although organizations do pay for public relations and expect to receive some form of media attention, they don't make direct cash payments to get the content into the media.

Known Sponsor

One key aspect of all advertising that is often overlooked is that its sponsor must be made known to the consumers. What must be said and how it must be said varies based on the purpose of advertising. In the case of political advertisements, the sponsor must state its name and association in an obvious fashion at the front or end of the advertisement. That's why you often hear, "Paid for by Nate Nelson for Comptroller" or something like that near the end of a commercial on TV or radio. In some instances, candidates legally are required to state who they are and that they approve the message.

In the wake of court rulings that allow special interest groups to place advertisements regarding candidates or political races, the **known sponsor** can be more than a little vague. Political action committees often have nebulous-sounding names like "Concerned Citizens Expressing Concerns about Our Concerns," which is about as helpful as a glass door on a public restroom stall. However, if you are interested in finding out more about that group, you can do some more digging into the history of the group and perhaps find the source of its money.

In the case of more traditional corporate advertising, the identification requirement is often a bit more relaxed when the ads are relatively pedestrian and the source is fairly obvious. For example, a TV advertisement for Diet Coke that features people drinking it from cans and bottles while the logo dances in the background essentially identifies the sponsor. During the final frames of message, some text outlining that the content is copyrighted to the Coca-Cola company based in Atlanta, Georgia, can help codify that message even more. Still, there is little room for confusion as to who is running this ad.

However, if an ad shows people drinking Diet Coke, and they all suddenly grab their throats, start coughing, and drop dead, it's also pretty clear that this ad *isn't* the work of Coca-Cola. What must be made clear is who purchased and placed the ad in this spot. Is it the work of nefarious Pepsi marketers who are tired of hearing that their product is second-rate stuff? Is it a health group trying to make the point that Diet Coke isn't good for you? Is it a rogue stock trader who is trying to "go short" on Coca-Cola and make money by tanking the company? People have the right to know who is behind the ad, which is why the sponsor must be identified in some meaningful way.

Information Plus Persuasion

All good forms of mass communication have information at their core. Whether it's a detailed news story that disentangles an international peace plan or a tweet from your cousin telling you what she's eating for lunch, the point is to tell you something you didn't know already. If the communication is done well, it will make clear to you why you should care about it and maybe even inspire you to ponder it a bit more deeply.

In the case of advertising, the content requires information to be paired with persuasive elements with the overall goal of inspiring action from the audience members. The best advertising provides specific facts that will have value to the audience, such as explaining how safety features on a car will improve the driver's likelihood of surviving a crash. It then uses persuasive messaging to help consumers to see why they need these features and thus should purchase this automobile.

Universities have dedicated an inordinate amount of attention and resources toward this aspect of advertising in recent years. Although providing clear information about the benefits of a specific university or major has always been a part of the admissions process, a significant shrinkage of enrollment in the United States has had institutions of higher education developing persuasive messages that target potential students. Researchers in this area found that in the wake of the shutdowns caused in 2020 by the pandemic, colleges had to reboot their approach to connecting with students who now felt less sure of what to do with their lives. These efforts included aligning the institutions' values with those of generation Z, providing more digital connections for these digital natives, and demonstrating the inherent value of the schools to specific potential students.[11]

How far an advertisers can go in making claims to inform and persuade is often a matter of law. The Federal Trade Commission (FTC) and the Federal Communications Commission prohibit companies from making unsupportable claims in their ads, such as that a pill can give a bald man a full head of hair in a day. However, these commissions provide advertisers some latitude regarding exaggeration and hyperbole, a concept known as **puffery**.

MEDIA LITERACY MOMENT: FACTS VERSUS PUFFERY

Advertising is bound by law to provide truthful representations of a product's qualities, uses, craftsmanship, and more. Thus, if an advertisement for an adhesive product claims that a single drop of glue could suspend a car from the underside of the Golden Gate Bridge, it had better be able to do so. However, as we will discuss in Chapter 14, not every claim made in media is intended to be a statement of fact. In advertising, organizations are allowed to engage in a concept called "puffery."

The Federal Trade Commission, which protects consumers and companies against unfair or deceptive business practices, defines puffery as "the exaggerations reasonably to be expected of a seller as to the degree of quality of his product, the truth or falsity of which cannot be precisely determined."[12] In making this statement, the FTC essentially allowed marketers to fudge the truth here and there for the sake of hyperbole to sell their products, noting it won't pursue cases against "advertising claims that the ordinary consumers do not take seriously." Thus, companies that make claims about having the "best ever homemade spaghetti sauce" or that they run "the tightest ship in the shipping business" aren't likely to run afoul of the law with such claims.

However, there can be a fine line between what makes for over-the-top boasts and false advertising. For example, the FTC reached a $9.3 million settlement in 2020 with clothing retailer

Fashion Nova over claims related to the speed of its shipping. The company made claims of "Fast Shipping" with promises to consumers to "Expect Your Items Quick!" However, the company's shipping delays and its unwillingness to offer consumers full refund options led to complaints of false advertising.[13]

In another case, the FTC filed suit against cosmetics maker L'Oréal for deceptive marketing practices regarding its Lancôme Génifique and L'Oréal Paris Youth Code skin care products. The FTC noted that many claims put forth by makeup manufacturers, such as L'Oréal's "because you're worth it" tagline, fit firmly within the realm of puffery. However, when advertisements stated that these two skin care lines provided antiaging benefits that targeted users' genes, these claims were subject to being objectively proven or disproven. Because L'Oréal could not demonstrate scientific evidence to support these statements, it agreed to a settlement with the FTC that barred the company from making these claims in future marketing material.[14]

The FTC and other consumer watchdog groups continue to examine the ways in which advertising presents information to audience members, with the goal of being fair to both sides. Thus, you can always expect a little exaggeration when it comes to claims of something being "the best" or "the most amazing" product you've ever seen. However, when fact-check-worthy claims appear in advertising, they had better be true.

THE NEXT STEP: Take a look at two or three advertisements for a product that you use and compare the claims associated with the product to how you think the product actually works. Is the messaging in the ad close to what you have experienced? If so, does that make you feel better about your choice to use that product? If not, do the claims upset you or make you feel like you have been cheated?

Delivered to an Audience

As you recall from the media models outlined in Chapter 1, you can see the importance of the medium in conveying a message from the sender to the receiver. Although those models apply to all forms of communication, the definition of advertising mandates that the message reach an audience. If the message fails to reach the target, it fails entirely.

These are two key elements in ensuring that an advertising message reaches its intended audience. First, advertising and marketing professionals clearly define their potential target audience, relying on surveys, focus group data, and market research to ascertain who is likely to use a given product, purchase a specific service, or be attracted to a certain idea. They use demographic, psychographic, and geographic data (see Chapter 2) to define that audience, and they dig deeply into this information to determine not only who they need to reach but also which messages are most likely to appeal to them. For example, experts in university marketing have promoted a shift from stiff, authoritative-sounding slogans and vague institutional promises to highlighting specific strengths and concrete value for students.[15] Marketers in this area also suggest that universities tell better stories about themselves and look for ways to "find their voice" in reaching out to today's students, who have learned to tune out generic messaging and one-size-fits-all marketing.

Second, advertisers must be attuned to changing trends in the market for their products. For example, in the 1990s, cognac producers such as Hennessy and Courvoisier found themselves in a down market as their primary target (older, rich men) continued to dwindle. However, the hip-hop community had long connected with these products, even though it wasn't viewed as a target market. When certain rap stars began mentioning specific brands in their song lyrics, some companies shifted their approach to target marketing to reflect the burgeoning interest among the music's audience.[16] Today, rappers like Nas are spokespeople for brands like Hennessy, playing prominent roles in commercials and serving as "brand ambassadors" for the product.[17]

Promotes Products, Services, or Ideas

The goal of marketing rests on connecting companies to potential buyers, so most advertising relates strongly to the products themselves, such as a computer or a refrigerator. This form of product advertising tends to dominate the media landscape, including everything from billboards to sponsored tweets. However, it is important to understand that advertising does more than get people to buy a generic item: in many cases, it's about buying a specific brand of computer or a particular model of refrigerator.

This is also true about services and ideas. A good ad for a service will get its audience to consider the need for automotive repair or gutter cleaning. An even better one will help them think about contracting with a specific repair place or cleaning service. An idea ad can similarly sponsor a neutral concept ("Go Vote") or a specific directive ("Vote Nelson for Comptroller").

EXPLORING ADVERTISING OPTIONS

LEARNING OBJECTIVE

LO 3: Outline the types of advertising and the media platforms each uses to reach the public.

As we've said, advertising is a paid form of media communication that can range in price based on numerous factors. The nuts and bolts of how to create the largest return on your investment for any particular product or advertising approach is best left to textbooks that specifically deal with advertising. However, you can simplify the entirety of advertising by boiling it down to what you're actually buying: eyeballs.

In trying to explain how to navigate the massive changes to the media advertising landscape, media expert Todd Butler outlined what he called the "four horsemen of conversion" for measuring an ad's effectiveness, regardless of the platform it was on or what approach the client took in sharing the message. Of these four potential measurements, he saw the number of eyeballs an ad reached as the most important factor and "the only currency that can truly bridge all media platforms today."[18]

Where you want to place your ads or what form you want those ads to take relates specifically to connecting with those eyeballs (the people who you want to view your ad). As we discussed in Chapter 2, understanding the demographic, psychographic, and geographic elements of your audience members can improve your ability to connect with them.

Here are some ways in which we can reach eyeballs through various media platforms:

- Buying space
- Buying time
- Buying clicks
- Beyond the basics: advertising in other ways

Let's take a look at some of the specifics associated with this aspect of advertising.

Buying Space

Advertisers who seek to reach consumers have long relied on purchasing space to get their messages across.

Outdoor advertising, also known as out-of-home sales, relies on placing messages in public places where people frequently congregate. The use of **billboards** along highways, kiosk signage in big cities, and even fliers stapled to electrical poles on college campuses can effectively draw people's attention to ads for food, jewelry, or events.

Out-of-home advertising continues to incorporate these static forms of outreach, while taking advantage of technology and innovation to keep their messages in front of their audiences. The integration of digital billboards allows multiple organizations to use a single chunk of space to advertise as part of a slideshow of messages. Agencies have applied similar technology to taxis and even delivery services to present a set of rotating ads on LED screens mounted within or outside the vehicles.[19]

As we've noted, newspapers, magazines, and other print products have long allowed businesses to purchase chunks of space within their publications to promote their goods and services. This form of display advertising remains prevalent in these products, but other forms of marketing and outreach have cut substantially into its dominance in the field.

The print-based model of advertising bases costs on several factors common to all advertising, such as the number of times the advertisement will run and the overall number of copies in one edition of the publication (better known as its **circulation**). With these factors in mind, the media outlet can set its rates for advertising based on how much space an advertiser wishes to purchase.

Publications determine costs based on how large an advertisement is, either by measuring the ad in column inches or determining what portion of a page an advertisement covers. For example, a newspaper might operate on a grid that determines that each page is five columns wide, while the length of the page is twenty inches. If an advertisement covers the lower quarter of the page, it will run five columns across and five inches deep, for a total of twenty-five column inches. The newspaper could then charge the advertiser the rate per column inch times twenty-five to determine the final cost. Discounts are often available for buying larger ads or running them more frequently over the course of a week or a month.

Advertisers, like BMW, can purchase chunks of space from newspapers or magazines and place their messages next to editorial content.

picturelibrary / Alamy Stock Photo

In a magazine, a publication might set rates for a quarter page, a half page, and a full page, thus charging advertisers based on how much of that page they wish to cover. This eliminates the need to calculate the number of inches and the going rate, but it also forces advertisers to limit their ad sizes and shapes to predetermined specifications. Again, discounts are available for repeat sales, and premium costs can be charged for prime placements, like having your ad on the back cover or just inside the first page of a publication. Advertisers are often charged more for these placements because they command more attention.

Buying Time

Radio, television, and other video and audio services provide opportunities to purchase slivers of time within a broadcast day to advertise products, services, and ideas to an interested public. The length of the advertisements has shrunk over the years, moving from full-minute ad spots to those as short as fifteen seconds, because of the costs associated with ad placement and the shrinking attention spans of viewers. One particularly ingenious campaign involved Geico's "Unskippable" ads that ran ahead of videos online in 2015. Each ad lasted only five seconds and included the tagline "You can't skip this ad, because it's already over."[20]

The length of advertisements determines their cost, as does the platform, with television ads being more expensive than radio spots. Each station or media conglomerate sets its own prices, based on several factors, including the number of listeners or viewers it gets. Nielsen serves as the preeminent ratings organization, measuring the number of people who consume specific forms of media at various points in time. The more people watching or listening, the higher the cost.

In addition, the time of day when the advertisements run can lead to variations in costs. Broadcast stations divide twenty-four-hour periods into multiple segments called dayparts, with the idea that some of these will be more valuable to specific advertisers based on who is consuming content. In radio, the five key dayparts are drive time, midday, afternoon drive, evenings, and overnight. These segments not only outline the general portions of the day but also when people are most likely to be near a radio, such as during their daily commute. In television, the day includes the early morning, daytime, afternoon, prime time, and late news or late night, with several "fringe" areas included between those parts to account for local programming or audience choices.

Buying Clicks

The question associated with all forms of advertising is "Does it work?" In other words, if Company X places an advertisement with Media Company Y and runs it Z number of times, will that company see a benefit of some sort? Advertisers in traditional media platforms were able to demonstrate how many copies of a newspaper included an ad or how many people the ratings agency said were watching TV while an advertisement ran. Companies could also measure outcomes after ads ran and make some logical inferences regarding the impact those ads had.

For example, if Forever Clothing Company ran one full-page ad each day for five days in a local newspaper with a circulation of one hundred thousand, it would know how many people had access to the ad. If the ad was for a "buy a sweater, get a sweater for free" campaign, it could measure how many sweaters were sold under that promotion. It could then compare these sales data with the sales data from a previous promotion (or even last year's sweater promotion) to see if more people took part during the new advertising campaign.

This is a rather rudimentary way to determine if something works, because the data are correlative, not causal. It might be that it was colder earlier this year, so more people bought sweaters. It could be that a group of local singers needed sweaters for their annual caroling, so they came en masse to buy sweaters, thus jacking up the sales. Several things could have happened that had nothing to do with the ads that led to the sales.

Digital media advertising literally and figuratively bridges that gap because it can not only track how many eyeballs saw the ad, but what people did after they saw it. The sale of digital advertising is measured in **impressions**, or the number of times users will potentially see the ad itself.

In digital media, many advertisers are buying space and attention much in the same way that they do using traditional media outlets. The advertisements appear as banner ads, block ads, integrated promotional posts, and other forms of messaging. However, digital media marketers can provide much more important data to potential clients, such as how many of the people who saw the ad clicked on it. They can compare these data to other information available from a website: Did the user click on other things on the website that the ad directed them to? Did the users "convert" from viewers to buyers? How much time did people spend while on the site the ad took them to?[21]

Digital advertisements, like the Visa debit banner ad on CNN's home page, connect web readers with brands based on users' characteristics and browsing histories. Interested readers can click the ad and be taken to Visa's website, where further interaction between consumers and Visa is possible.

NetPhotos / Alamy Stock Photo

Measuring the "cost per click" or "cost per action" allows advertisers to see how much money or engagement each advertisement brings on a given platform. This approach also allows media platforms to precisely explain the benefit the advertisers are getting. In short, it's a much better way to prove if the ad "works" or not.

TABLE 13.3 ■ Types of Ads

Form	Placement Media	How It Works	Example
Outdoor/ out-of-home	Billboard, kiosk	Advertisers place content on large spaces in public areas to draw attention to their messages.	A large sign along a freeway, alerting drivers that a fast food restaurant is open at the next offramp; a flier taped to a lamppost stating that a promising local band is playing at the student union on Saturday at 7 p.m.
Print	Newspaper, magazine	Advertisers contract with publishers to purchase a specified amounts of space (display advertising) within publications.	A full-page image of a red sports car with information on how and where to purchase it; a small block of space on a page, explaining that the local cheerleading team is having its annual popcorn sale to raise money for new uniforms.
Traditional audio and video	Radio, television	Advertisers purchase specified amounts of time from broadcasters during specific times of day to put out messages.	A thirty-second spot during the Super Bowl that showcases a new James Bond film headed for theaters later this year; a disc jockey at the local radio station promotes a local window company, offering a personal testimonial about how good his house looks with new windows.

Form	Placement Media	How It Works	Example
Traditional digital	Websites, apps, social media	Advertisers work with digital media platforms to purchase opportunities to place static ads or linked material in or around content on screens.	A theater chain purchases a banner at the top of a movie review website that users can click to buy tickets to upcoming films; creators of a puzzle app buy a fifteen-second spot in between stages of a popular arcade app to entice people to download the puzzle game.
Native advertising	Newspapers, magazines, radio, television, internet, social media	Advertisers work with information providers to create material that mimics nonadvertising content so as to blend in with this material.	A skin care company creates "sponsored content" for a beauty magazine's website that looks like the other articles around it; a television station runs a late-night infomercial that looks like a cooking show, which promotes a meal delivery service.
Product placement	Television, movies	Advertisers work with companies to integrate specific products into the action of films or shows.	The hero of an action movie drives a Ford Mustang, which Ford has paid to include in the film; a sitcom character drinks a Diet Coke while snacking on a box of Wheat Thins, instead of a glass of water and a bowl of popcorn.

Beyond the Basics: Advertising in Other Ways

Aside from the simple billboards, print ads, TV commercials, and promoted content you see every day, marketers have found various other ways to use storytelling techniques and advertising approaches to convince people to buy what they're selling. Here are a few of the better-known other ways in which they reach readers and viewers.

The judges on American Idol aren't drinking Coke products by chance. This use of drinkware with Coca-Cola labels on it is part of a product placement arrangement between the company and the soft drink company.

Cinematic Collection / Alamy Stock Photo

Product Placement

Television shows and movies often show characters interacting with various items that most people use every day. A parent on a sitcom answers a phone to speak with a child who is in the middle of a wacky mishap. A bar patron in a cop drama orders a beer. An international spy in a thriller movie gets into her car before heading off to a tension-filled rendezvous. What brand of phone that parent answers, what type of beer that barfly orders, or what model of car that spy drives will depend a great deal on a negotiation between producers and marketing professionals.[22]

Product placement allows advertisers to insert their brands into the landscape of a show or movie in a way that they receive attention, thanks in part to characters' using the items or interacting with the brands. When Daniel Craig's final turn as legendary spy James Bond hit the theaters in 2021, the movie was saturated with a wide array of product placements. *No Time to Die* was the second most brand-filled Bond movie of Craig's tenure, particularly in its use of automobiles and new technology. Cars made by Aston Martin, Toyota, and Land Rover were given ample screen time in the film, and characters relied on LG, Microsoft, and Dell electronics to complete important tasks.[23]

Native Advertising

As consumers find ways to skip past TV ads, switch radio stations when the ad breaks hit, or skim past print ads, advertisers have responded by embedding advertising into their lives. **Native advertising** takes advantage of storytelling techniques and visual cues to camouflage advertising so it looks like the rest of the content in a print product or on a website.

These ads carry with them certain markers, such as a tag that notes "sponsored content" or "suggested for you." They can appear as promoted links or listings that come up during an internet search or through a series of content recommendations. Marketers note that these surreptitious advertisements draw 53 percent more attention than traditional advertisements on the same platforms. In addition, people who click on these ads are 18 percent more likely to buy something than those who click on a banner or block ad on a website.[24] Media professionals continue to debate the ethics of these advertisements, because they often cause confusion among unsuspecting users, and they can present a conflict of interest for news outlets that use them.[25]

Television channels have long relied on a form of native advertising called the **infomercial**. This blending of the words *information* and *commercial* describes long-form television programs that mimic the style of other product demonstrations or standard programs. They last about twenty-eight to thirty minutes and tend to have three key components: tell the story of the product, explain the features and benefits of the product, and present testimonials for the product to inspire sales at the end of the program.

ADVERTISING AND SOCIETY

LEARNING OBJECTIVE

LO 4: Understand the role of advertising in society, in terms of both brand identity and consumer value.

As we have noted for other forms of media, advertising exists because it performs certain functions within our society. The media platforms, the methods of delivery, and the approach to content have grown and changed over the centuries, but the goal remains unchanged. Like most approaches to communication, when an advertising format or approach proves effective, organizations will flock to it, applying tweaks to the format to make it their own and enhance its benefits.

At the core of all advertising, however, are several key elements that dictate what it does for us and why we continue to use it, even as we complain about the quality of TV commercials, the ubiquitous presence of internet popups, and the overwhelming nature of the billboards that dot our landscape.

Let's look at a few of the reasons that advertising exists:

- Satisfying wants and needs
- Developing connections beyond purchase
- Shaping brand association
- Showcase benefits and characteristics
- Alert consumers to important information

Let's take a deeper look at how advertising performs these tasks.

Satisfying Wants and Needs

Advertising first and foremost is about connecting consumers with products. If you have a headache, you need something that is going to treat it so you can go about the rest of your day without pain. If you are hungry, you need to find a place that serves food you can afford near you. The goal of an advertisement is to show you what will help with your headache and where you can buy some food. This concept isn't rocket science, but it is at the core of what we see in traditional advertising.

However, advertising reaches beyond this simple need satisfaction. Researchers have found that advertising has helped develop a **consumer culture**, in which wants and desires are transformed into base-level needs. Ads showcase goods and services that will satisfy those "needs" in a way that only that specific product can. In other words, it's not just important to buy a coat because winter is coming and you don't want to be cold. You need to look amazing while wearing that coat, lest you be thought of as a dweeb by your peers. Fortunately for you, the advertisement explains, our coat can not only keep you warm but make you look absolutely amazing.

The goal of advertising in a consumer culture is to continually showcase newer, better, and cooler things that will establish you as a cut above other people. Advertising helps direct you to the things that represent and can supposedly deliver an aspirational lifestyle in ways that nothing else can.[26]

Developing Connections beyond Purchase

In consumer culture, people approach purchasing things in several ways that relate to their connection to the products. The two primary types of approach consumers take are **transactional purchases** and **relational purchases**.[27] Let's look at each one individually.

Transactional Purchases

Let's say that you flew across the country to attend your cousin's wedding, and the airline lost your suit bag with the outfit you planned to wear to an event that night. You still have shoes and underwear, but you need to buy some outerwear in a hurry, so you head to a nearby mall. If you're a man, you might be thinking "dress shirt, tie, and decent slacks." If you're a woman, you might be thinking "tasteful black cocktail dress." You browse at a few stores until you see an advertisement in one place that says, "All clothing 50 percent off today ONLY!" You go there, try on a few things, make a purchase, and head off to the wedding. The wedding happens, you dance at the reception, and catch your flight home, grateful that you were able to avoid a disaster.

This is the core of a transactional relationship. You made a purchase based on a specific need, without thinking about much other than getting the purchase completed. You shopped a bit, but you didn't focus on the name associated with the clothes or the celebrities who were endorsing that particular clothing line. You also didn't really care what store you patronized, as you've never been to that mall before and you're not planning to be back there any time soon. In a transactional purchase, the customer is simply buying an item based on a logical need, with no intention of thinking beyond that single interaction.

Relational Purchases

The goal of advertising is to develop deeper bonds between the products a company makes and the customers who intend to purchase them. In other words, advertisers want to develop relational purchases that will allow companies to predict sales beyond single interactions.

Companies invest billions of dollars annually into creating and maintaining public images that reflect their values and that resonate with an audience, a concept better known as a **brand**.[28] Brands provide people with connections on both cognitive and emotional levels that guide their purchasing decisions. From a cognitive sense, brands allow people to understand what it is that they are getting, regardless of where or when they buy it. In providing people something that is familiar and safe, brands help customers develop purchasing habits. From an emotional standpoint, brands allow people to think beyond a single transaction, choosing a single product on a single day. They form emotionally driven ties that will inspire them turn out in droves to see a movie's sequel or buy a band's new album.

Let's return to your trip to attend your cousin's wedding. The service ends at noon and the reception doesn't start until five, so you'll need to find something to eat in the meantime. You don't want to eat anything that might upset your stomach, which could make for a long night. You also don't have a ton of money to spend, because purchasing new clothes drained your finances.

As you drive along, you see multiple potential restaurants, including some local mom-and-pop places. You could stop and try something new, but you don't know if the food will be any good. Even more, you don't know how much the stuff will cost. Instead, you notice a Burger-O-Rama restaurant about a block away. The logo is the same as the one back home, and it has the same layout as the ones you've seen at every other Burger-O-Rama you ever visited. Even more, the menu is the same, so much so that you can order your Big Bucking Burger, Rama Fries, and Diet Coke by simply telling the counter worker, "I'd like a number three, please."

This is an example of a relational transaction. The local restaurants might serve better food than what you would get at Burger-O-Rama. They might also offer cheaper prices and better service. However, they are an unknown, so they present concerns that you won't have to think about if you stick with what is familiar. Burger-O-Rama has put a great amount of branding money into its logo, its approach to franchising, and its advertising to reinforce your connection with the company. In conditioning you to think of the brand beyond any one purchase, the company's advertising can help secure you as a customer for life.

Shaping Brand Association

The concept of branding is one that helps audience members conceive of a company or an organization and its wares in a specific way. Continually exposing the audience to advertising that has a specific tone and feel to it can reinforce the intended sense of what that brand has come to represent. This is why the concept of "shoes" can mean something different to so many people. Nike has grown a sporting brand that ties its shoes to high-performance athletes who can achieve amazing feats on the court and the field, which is why LeBron James is wearing a specially designed pair of them in 2021's basketball/cartoon film *Space Jam 2*. Christian Louboutin has developed a brand that speaks of elegance and elite quality, which is why when Gal Gadot puts her feet up on a desk in the 2021 sexy spy thriller *Red Notice*, she's sporting a pair of their boots.

In continuing to provide the tone, feel, and overall "vibe" associated with the brand to potential customers, advertising can help shape how individuals view themselves in relation to the products. For example, Nike was first known as a maker of specialized running shoes for people who had high athletic standards. As the brand continued to evolve, it created other items that fell into that same realm, such as workout clothing and exercise gear. It signed marketing deals with individual athletes to help tie the brand to those high-performing professional athletes, who would wear the clothes and shoes and endorse the products in a variety of ways. Eventually, Nike began working with professional leagues, like the National Football League, which recently extended its contract with the brand for another eight years at a rumored price tag of one billion dollars.[29]

Audience members who watch the ads that feature athletes in Nike gear or catch games in which the Nike "swoosh" is prominently displayed on uniforms and shoes build mental connections between Nike and high-end athletics. Thus, people who think of themselves as being athletes might be more likely to gravitate to that brand when they make their shoe or clothing purchases. Even more, people who aren't great athletes but aspire to be more talented will likely buy Nike products because they believe they will make them run faster or jump farther. In short, you might not be able to jump like Giannis Antetokounmpo or dribble a soccer ball like Cristiano Ronaldo, but if you put on those Zoom Freak 3s or a pair of Mercurial Superfly cleats, you can get in on a piece of their skills.

A DEEPER LOOK: WHAT DOES ALL THIS AD EXPOSURE DO TO YOU?

In the 1970s, experts estimated that an average person would see between 500 and 1,600 advertising messages per day. By 2007, that number grew to nearly 5,000 per day, and a 2022 report stated that it has likely doubled to 10,000.[30] The largest driver of this is the explosion of online and mobile advertising, which has become a multibillion-dollar business. Recent figures suggest that Google and Facebook together have make more than two hundred billion dollars annually in advertising revenues, which translates to a lot of people on a lot of screens seeing a lot of ads.

As we mentioned in Chapter 1, research shows that media messages don't have a direct and immediate impact on audience members. An advertisement for McDonald's might remind you that you are hungry, but it doesn't compel you to drive to a local McDonald's and order everything to the left of the McRib on the menu. That said, this lack of a direct effect doesn't mean that advertisements don't have an influence over your actions or even your subconscious. Advertising does shape how we think and feel about ourselves and our actions in ways we don't necessarily perceive. Research has shown that heavy and persistent exposure to ads can manipulate the emotional side of our brain, thus giving us a negative sense of who we are and what can be done to improve ourselves.[31]

Ads tap into our insecurities using messages that show us how certain aspects of our lives are bad. An ad from a cosmetic company might show a beautiful model who asks if viewers have tiny lines or wrinkles that make them look older. These viewers might not usually give much thought about wrinkles or getting older, but now the ad has made that a key concern.

The ad then presents a solution to that concern: a new form of makeup that covers wrinkles or a new cream that rejuvenates skin. The model then continues to explain how this works, what makes it superior to other products, and why it has value to consumers. The implication is that purchasing this product will fix a flaw and make viewers happier with their overall sense of self.

Advertising critics have long noted that sales messages pick at our insecurities and then tell us everything we need to fix them is available for purchase. The approach corporations take in connecting with audience members ties products to happiness, thus providing a continual loop of consumerism that we often don't notice. (This is not to be confused with the concept of **subliminal advertising**, in which undetectable messages are slipped into media with the goal of mentally "tricking" people into action.)

This isn't to say that all advertising is bad or that it lacks value, because advertising can provide a series of benefits to you as a consumer. However, like most other things, we should engage in critical thinking when it comes to what we are consuming and what we think about that content. The awareness we have regarding the presence of messages and the things they are trying to tell us can allow us to better determine which things we actually need and which ones we can avoid.

Showcase Benefits and Characteristics

Much of what goes into well-developed advertisements that provide a direct path to immediate action fits into one of two key areas: **benefits** and **characteristics**. If the advertising is done well, both will serve as crucial components of the pitch to consumers. If the advertising is done extremely well, these elements will be clearly interwoven to show how they act in concert to meet the needs and wants of the consumers. In the simplest of terms, characteristics are features associated with the product, service, or idea that can be demonstrated clearly or quantified easily. Benefits are the ways in which the product can make your life better when you use it.

A DEEPER LOOK: HOW BENEFITS AND CHARACTERISTICS WORK TOGETHER

If an advertisement works properly, it will take concrete characteristics of the product and pair them with specific benefits each one provides. In doing this, the advertisement connects with both the logical interests and emotional passions of the consumer.

For example, the 2022 Ford Mustang Shelby GT500 edition generates 760 horsepower and 625 pound-feet of torque.[32] It also has a carbon fiber handling package that includes twenty-inch carbon fiber wheels, adjustable strut top mounts, a Gurney flap, and splitter wickers. These are features that can be measured and examined as part of the car. For example, engineers can assess the level of horsepower the V-8 engine produces and measure the size and composition of the wheels on the car. These elements represent product characteristics associated with the car.

To sell a car like this 2022 Ford Mustang, advertisers must pair the characteristics of the car's many elements with specific benefits that those characteristics provide. Simply saying, "It's really cool looking" is probably true, but it isn't going to sell a lot of cars.

AP Photo/David Santiago

However, the question remains for many readers: "What the heck is all this stuff and why do I care?" That's where the benefits come in.

The higher the horsepower, the better the overall acceleration, which means you can go faster with less stress on the engine. Torque measures how fast the car can accelerate from a dead stop, which is important if you're trying to get out into traffic quickly or blow someone off the line in a race.[33] Carbon fiber wheels will reduce the weight of the vehicle, which means the engine has less mass to pull, thus improving speed. In addition, the wheels will assist the suspension of the car so that it rides better, even over rougher roads and at high rates of speed.[34] We could spend paragraph after paragraph explaining everything from the Gurney flap[35] to the splitter wickers, but the point is, each of these items provides a distinct benefit to the performance of the vehicle.

Good advertising relies on both elements in tandem to make the case that this is the vehicle you want to buy if you plan to go really fast. It's not enough to rely on the tech specs to make the case, as you could see from the earlier description. However, audience members are unlikely to just trust an ad that says, "We go really fast and steer well"; they want some information to support that statement. Through showcasing benefits and characteristics, advertising can satisfy both the emotional and analytical sides of people's minds and make them more willing to purchase an item.

Alert Consumers to Important Information

As we noted in Chapter 1, humans have a need for information about the events happening around them. In many cases, people rely on trusted sources, like friends or family, to inform them directly about something that matters. In other cases, they rely on trusted media sources like news anchors, social media influencers, and newspapers to convey important content to them.

Advertising also takes care of this important need for surveillance, connecting with audience members to make sure they are aware of events that will likely matter to them. A familiar example of this approach could be alerting people to a "going out of business" sale that could help the company sell off its remaining assets, while providing consumers with quality products at discounted products. Similarly, if a company's products were found to be defective, a recall notice could alert people to avoid eating certain foods or driving a vehicle until something could be repaired on it.

JOBS IN ADVERTISING

Now that you better understand advertising, here's a handy overview of a few common positions in the field today.

Career Opportunity	Common Tasks
Sales representative	• Solicit new clients for the advertising firm • Develop advertising strategies based on clients' goods and services and the audiences they hope to reach • Conduct advertising buys in media outlets to reach clients' target audiences
Copywriter	• Develop the text-based content for advertisements across multiple media platforms • Edit and proofread advertising copy for errors or problematic word choices • Coordinate with visual and creative specialists in the creation of advertisements
Market analyst	• Analyze consumer data to assist clients in developing a marketing strategy • Conduct market research to assess sales and marketing trends in their clients' fields • Interact with multiple stakeholders, including clients, colleagues, and vendors, to develop a marketing strategy
Creative/production specialist	• Craft and develop the visual elements for clients' advertisements • Coordinate with copywriters to create complementary messaging and tone between text and artwork • Compose advertisements for production using graphics, text, photographs, videos, and other media tools
Media planner/buyer	• Evaluate content and platforms to determine the best outlets and times in which clients can place their ads • Analyze audience interests and needs to determine the amount, type, and tone of advertising individual clients should use • Assess past plans to assist in the development of future ad buys for their clients

CHAPTER REVIEW

LO 1: Explain the importance of key moments in the history of advertising.

- Advertisements existed as far back as 3000 BC, with people posting notices for goods and services they wanted to provide or receive.
- In colonial America, newspapers began the practice of running what would now be considered classified advertisements, public notices from individuals looking to buy or sell items. The papers also provided display advertising to alert readers about the products available from overseas ships and local merchants.
- The development of broadcasting devices, like televisions and radios, led advertisers to offer "pay-for-play" opportunities.
- Advertisers who sought strategies to get the most out of their messaging turned to advertising agencies in the late nineteenth and early twentieth centuries. These agencies still serve clients in terms of negotiating rates with media outlets, writing copy, developing marketing strategies, and building advertisements.
- As advertisers realized the need to reach untapped markets, they began to seek ways to effectively produce content that connected with people of color. Advertising agencies like Burrell Communications crafted messages that spoke directly to the Black community, while television pioneers like Emilio Azcárraga provided advertisers with opportunities to tap into Latino markets.
- With the advent of the internet, advertisers developed strategies to deliver tailored messages to specific audience members in personalized ways. From the advent of banner ads in 1994 to the development and expansion of Google's AdWords program, targeted marketing strategies seek to individualize a reader's advertising experience.

LO 2: Define advertising, its key components, and its overall purpose.

- Advertising is defined as paid, persuasive communication, published with the intent of connecting a client with an audience in hopes of inspiring action
- The key elements associated with advertising include the following:
  - Paid speech: A client purchases space or time from a media outlet to put forth a message of its choosing.
  - Known sponsor: The source of the advertisement needs to be identified in the ad.
  - Information plus persuasion: The advertising must include both facts and opinions to get a message across to potential consumers.
  - Delivered to an audience: The material must use a media platform of some kind to reach readers, viewers, or listeners.
  - Refers to products, services, or ideas: The advertisement must promote an item, an amenity, or a concept the client wishes to showcase in hopes of creating influence over an audience.

LO 3: Outline the types of advertising and the media platforms each uses to reach the public.

- *Outdoor/out-of-home:* Advertising placed in public areas where people tend to congregate. An example of this would be a billboard along the highway that promotes a nearby restaurant.
- *Print:* Advertising of varying sizes placed on the pages of newspapers and magazines. An example of this would be a quarter-page newspaper display ad that promotes a "buy one, get one" turkey sale at the local grocery store.
- *Traditional audio and video:* Advertisements of various lengths that run during radio programming or television shows. An example of this would be an ad for a new pickup truck that runs during an episode of *Monday Night Football.*
- *Traditional digital:* Advertisements placed on websites that promote a client's interest and allow the user to click on them to learn more. An example of this would be a block ad placed near the top of the NBC's website that promotes its streaming service.

- *Native advertising:* Content produced and placed by advertisers that is created to look like the surrounding editorial content on a website or social media platform. An example of this would be a listicle from Lysol, titled "8 Things You Should Disinfect Daily," that runs alongside other listicles on BuzzFeed.
- *Product placement:* An agreement between an advertiser and a media organization to display or use the company's product in a television show or movie in exchange for financial compensation or brand exposure. An example would be the use of Sony TVs and radios in the 2021 film *Venom: Let There Be Carnage.*

LO 4: Understand the role of advertising in society, in terms of both brand identity and consumer value.

- *Satisfying wants and needs:* Advertisements provide consumers with information about products that can improve their lives, solve their problems, or just make them feel happier.
- *Developing connections beyond purchase:* Advertisers want to create long-term relationships between consumers and their products. The goal is to build buying habits that will lead to purchasing intentions for current and future goods and services.
- *Shaping brand association:* Advertising connects the consumer to products through transactional purchases and relational purchases.
- *Transactional purchases* are simple exchanges of money for goods, regardless of the underlying image of the company. These purchases are individual events based on basic needs.
- *Relational purchases* are based on connections between the consumer and the company brand. These purchases are often made because of familiarity with the product, a shared sense of values with the company and general comfort with the product.
- *Showcase benefits and characteristics:* Advertising presents information about the products by presenting benefits and characteristics associated with the items.
- *Characteristics* are specific, quantifiable elements of a product, such as the size of a car's engine or the amount of caffeine in an energy drink.
- *Benefits* are useful outcomes associated with the product's characteristics, such as how fast a car can go, thanks to its more powerful engine, or how long you can stay awake after consuming an energy drink, thanks to the caffeine in it.
- *Alert consumers to important information:* Advertising satisfies the surveillance need people have by keeping them up to date on product launches, sales, and updates.

KEY TERMS

Advertising
Advertising agency
Banner ad
Benefits
Billboard
Brand
Characteristics
Circulation
Classified advertising
Commission
Consumer culture
Display advertisement
Impression
Infomercial
Known sponsor
Native advertising
Outdoor advertising
Paid speech
Product placement
Puffery
Relational purchase
Static advertising
Subliminal advertising
Targeted advertising campaign
Transactional purchase

DISCUSSION QUESTIONS

1. To best reach people in a short advertising message, companies need to rely on easily understood examples and situations, such as pairing a "traditional mom" with a minivan or showing a child arguing with a parent about getting a new phone. Based on this understanding, how can advertisers reach demographically, psychographically, and geographically diverse audiences successfully without relying on harmful, negative stereotypes?
2. Of the types of advertisements listed in the chapter, which approach do you think most speaks directly to you and people in your social group? Which approach do you think is least effective in reaching you and your peers? Why do you think so?
3. Based on the concerns some critics have regarding the amount of advertising that people are exposed to, how concerned are you about the impact advertising has on you, your friends and your family? Why?

The cover of a supermarket tabloid featuring salacious, attention-grabbing headlines.

Stephanie Keith / Stringer/ Getty Images

14 MEDIA AND THE LAW

INTRODUCTION

1. *When you are on the supermarket checkout line, are you tempted by these types of headlines to purchase the tabloid? Why or why not?*
2. *Do you think there should be a limit to what kinds of stories journalists are allowed to publish? If so, what are those limits and who should set them?*
3. *How often do you think about the owners of images, stories, and other content you take off the internet to use as you see fit? Do you worry about their rights as creators? Why or why not?*

Among the five freedoms delineated in the **First Amendment** to the U.S. Constitution are two that remain crucial to media practitioners to this day: freedom of speech and freedom of the press. In theory, the First Amendment provides citizens the rights to operate newspapers, express unpopular opinions, and communicate with each other without fear. In reality, the courts have spent more than two hundred years trying to determine what people can and cannot do under this blanket order of protection.

This chapter will outline what the First Amendment is and does, as well as how people tend to misinterpret it and run afoul of the law. In addition, it will examine two additional areas of legal concern: invasion of privacy and copyright infringement. We will examine the concept of "fair use" and how it applies to you when using content creating by others.

LEARNING OBJECTIVES

After completing this chapter, you should be able to:

1. Understand the First Amendment and relate how it establishes a free press.
2. Describe how government regulations apply to specific media platforms.
3. Define libel and identify the key elements that can successfully support this charge and the most prominent defenses against them.
4. Describe the ways in which media practitioners can engage in invasion of privacy.
5. Define copyright and explain the ways in which copyrighted content can be legally used.

FREE SPEECH, FREE PRESS, AND THE FIRST AMENDMENT

LEARNING OBJECTIVES

LO 1: Compare and contrast the basic global media systems.

When Brandi Levy didn't make the varsity cheerleading team at Mahanoy Area High School in 2017, she took to Snapchat to voice her complaints about school, dropping several F-bombs along the way. The post lasted only a day and didn't disrupt anything at the school, but her coach decided to ban Levy from all cheer activities for one year.

Levy and her parents sued, winning the case and several appeals, as the courts repeatedly found that the school was not within its rights to ban Levy from the squad. In June 2021, the Supreme Court affirmed Levy's rights to free expression, ruling eight to one in her favor. The court in this case stated that public schools generally lack power to punish students for things they say online while they aren't at school.[1]

When the United States ratified the Bill of Rights in 1791, the **First Amendment** to the Constitution established that this country's citizens have several basic rights, including freedom of speech and freedom of the press. Ever since that time, the First Amendment has been the subject of legal cases that have led to new interpretations and applications of the law. Despite the general simplicity of its text, people have dramatically misunderstood the First Amendment and what it allows them to do or what it protects them from. Despite what you might think, the First Amendment does not give you total freedom.

Here are some of the most common limitations:

- You can't publish anything you want.
- Not all expression is protected and protected equally.
- Journalists don't operate under a higher level of protection than regular citizens.
- The First Amendment doesn't shield you from any harm associated with the things you publish.

Let's take a deeper dive into these issues and separate myth from reality regarding your rights and responsibilities under the First Amendment.

You Can't Publish Anything You Want

The first words of the First Amendment state, "Congress shall make no law...," which might seem to leave the door open for the president or a governor to make a law that impinges upon these rights. Fortunately, the courts eventually interpreted this to mean that no governmental agency can prohibit you from enjoying the freedoms outlined in the amendment.

However, this doesn't mean other organizations or authorities can't prevent you from producing or publishing content. Newspapers and magazines often are privately owned, which entitles the owner or the owner's designees to determine if a story should be published. If you work at the local newspaper and you want to publish a story about how a local landlord is ripping off tenants, your editor, the paper's managing editor, the editor-in-chief, or the publisher could decide to kill the story before it saw the light of day. It could be because they don't think the story is accurate or it might be because the landlord is the publisher's brother-in-law.

When you sign up with various services to host or run a website or a blog, you agree to terms of service (that giant document that you just keep clicking "I agree" on until it eventually goes away), which outlines what you can and can't do. At any point, the company can decide to cut your content, remove your site, or block your access because you violated those terms. For example, Twitter permanently blocked Infowars founder Alex Jones in 2018 for violating the platform's rules against "abusive behavior."[2] Twitter also banned then president Donald Trump from its platform in 2021, saying that he incited rioters in the January 6 attack on the U.S. Capitol.[3] When Elon Musk bought Twitter in 2022, he restored the former president's privileges on the social media site. As a private company, Twitter has the right to do these things, without having to concern itself with the First Amendment.

Even though the First Amendment states that the government can't intrude upon your rights to expression, Congress has actually passed laws that limited citizens' rights to do so. Laws like the Espionage Act (1798) and the Sedition Act (1918) have limited people's rights to criticize the government during times of war, while the Smith Act (1941) made it illegal to advocate the overthrow of the government. See Table 14.1 for some examples of limitations on free expression placed on Americans by our government.

Not All Expression Is Protected and Protected Equally

The actual protection of speech varies depending on its time, manner, place, and medium. States and municipalities have enacted many laws meant to provide quiet hours for citizens to sleep at night, limiting others' rights to play loud music deep in the night. The Supreme Court has applied the First Amendment in a wide variety of cases, including whether forcing a rock band to use a different sound board violated its rights[4] and the constitutionality of a law prohibiting the location of adult theaters within residential zones.[5] Courts have ruled that material like child pornography has no redeeming value and thus is not protected under the First Amendment.

TABLE 14.1 ■ Examples of Governmental Limitations of Expression

Law	Year	Meaning	Outcome
Sedition Act	1798	Congress made it illegal to "write, print, utter, or publish...any false, scandalous and malicious writing" against the government. Those who violated the act could be imprisoned, fined, or deported.	It was massively unpopular among citizens and was allowed to expire in 1801.
Comstock Act	1873	The act, named for moral rights crusader Anthony Comstock, prohibited the "circulation of obscene literature and articles of immoral use." It prohibited the advertising of abortion services, the shipping of contraceptive devices, and other things deemed indecent.	Various court cases over the years have overturned or redefined portions of the act, especially in relation to adult reading materials, contraception, and abortion.
Espionage Act	1917	This law made it illegal for anyone "to cause insubordination, disloyalty, mutiny, or refusal of duty, in the [U.S.] military or naval forces" or to "willfully obstruct the recruiting or enlistment" for these services.	The act remains law. One of the more recent and more famous cases involves Wikileaks founder Julian Assange, who was charged in 2019.
Sedition Act	1918	This law prohibited anyone from criticizing the government, the Constitution, or the flag.	The act was repealed in 1921.
Smith Act	1941	Also known as the Alien Registration Act, this law made it a crime to advocate the violent overthrow of the government.	A series of Supreme Court decisions struck down the key elements of it by the end of the 1950s.
Communication Decency Act	1996	This was the first major attempt to regulate the content on the internet. The act criminalized the distribution of "obscene" and "indecent" material, particularly pornography, online.	In 1997 the Supreme Court ruled in *Reno v. American Civil Liberties Union* that the suppression efforts in the act were unconstitutional, but other portions of the act remain in play.

Additionally, what "counts" as free speech seems to be variable at best. The Supreme Court has held that burning a U.S. flag is a legal form of protest, despite multiple state and federal efforts to prohibit it.[6] Meanwhile, the act of burning a draft card, which multiple young men did to protest the war in Vietnam, was a crime and not protected speech.[7] The court held that high school students were within their legal rights when they wore black armbands to school to protest the Vietnam War, with Justice Abe Fortas noting that students do not "shed their constitutional rights to freedom of speech or expression at the schoolhouse gate."[8] However, four decades later, the Supreme Court ruled that a school was legally within its right to ban a sign at a school-sponsored event that announced "Bong Hits 4 Jesus" and to suspend the student who made it.[9]

The medium of expression has also been considered in determining the limits of the First Amendment. The government has placed heavier restrictions on over-the-air broadcasting operations, stating that the electromagnetic spectrum is a limited resource and is therefore in need of careful regulation. For example, the Radio Act of 1927 created the Federal Radio Commission to oversee and license these broadcasting efforts, with lawmakers requiring the use of the new medium to be in the public interest (see Chapter 6).

In addition, in a 1942 case the Supreme Court found that commercial speech did not enjoy the same rights as other segments of "the press."[10] It wasn't until 1976 that the law provided free-speech protections for advertising, when the Supreme Court struck down a statutory ban in Virginia that prohibited pharmacists from listing drug prices.[11] Other forms of commercial speech have been given various levels of protection over the years as well.

Journalists Don't Operate under a Higher Level of Protection Than Regular Citizens

The United States does not license journalists, something some other countries do, so journalists are not defined as a special class of individuals. In fact, what makes a person a "journalist" is often up to debate, given that anyone with internet access and a few simple tools can publish content that everyone in the world can see.

However, even prior to the digital era, courts held that journalists don't have some sort of special waiver when it comes to the law. A 1972 case, *Branzburg v. Hayes*, determined that courts could compel journalists to disclose confidential sources or demand confidential information that they received from sources. The Supreme Court held that average citizens are often forced to provide information against their wishes during legal proceedings, and the same should be applied to journalists.[12] (Some states did pass press shield laws in the wake of this decision to limit courts' abilities to force reporters to divulge such information.)

Reporters have no more rights than average citizens to enter private spaces, compel individuals to provide them with information, publish content, or exercise any other First Amendment rights. If a reporter at the *New York Times* is legally allowed to do something, so is the average citizen in most cases. Courts have provided less protection for student journalists operating in private institutions and high school media outlets, unfortunately. For example, the administration of Westside High School in Omaha, Nebraska, initially censored a student editorial that called for the end of the censorship of student journalism! Although the administrators allowed the editorial to run a week later, the paper's adviser had already resigned, citing a "year-long assault on student speech and press rights."[13] The high school had the legal right to censor the publication, thanks to the Supreme Court's decision in *Hazelwood v. Kuhlmeier* (1988) allowing schools to censor material journalism students write as part of a class and that might lead to disruption of the school's normal routines.

The First Amendment Doesn't Shield You from Any Harm Associated with the Things You Publish

The First Amendment is not a sword that allows you to attack people with impunity. It's more of a shield against oppression, and even then, it won't keep you safe in every situation. The amendment essentially protects you from prior restraint by governmental bodies. The government can't stop you from publishing content (although, as we noted above, others can). The amendment also gives you some protection against retaliation from the government if officials don't like what you have to say or write. In many cases, however, once you publish something, you are responsible for it, and you might end up in legal trouble.

Content that defames other people can get you sued, as we will discuss later in the chapter under the concept of libel. You can invade someone's privacy by publishing anything from information about their health to photos of them that could be embarrassing or shocking. Beyond these concerns, you can get sued for copyright infringement if you publish content that you don't own, you could get fired from a private company if they don't like something you write, and you can get arrested if you incite violence. (We'll dig into each of these specific situations later in the chapter.)

In short, you do have a lot of leeway when it comes to deciding what you will publish, but once you put it out there, you must answer for it.

BEYOND THE FIRST AMENDMENT: REGULATORS AND REGULATIONS

LEARNING OBJECTIVES

LO 2: Describe how government regulations apply to specific media platforms.

Although the freedom of the press appears to be wide reaching, you can already see there are some limits on when and where people can express themselves and what they can say or do. The government exercises oversight over specific forms of media, creating limitations on what can and can't be communicated. To do so, it has established three agencies that oversee the legality of certain forms of communication (see Table 14.2).

TABLE 14.2 ■ Government Agencies That Oversee the Media

Government Agency	Date Founded	Responsibilities Involving Media
Federal Trade Commission (FTC)	1914	Protects consumers by preventing advertisers from making false or misleading claims
Federal Communications Commission (FCC)	1934	Oversees and regulates broadcasting, including the licensing of broadcast outlets and responding to public complaints about content
Food and Drug Administration (FDA)	1906	Establishes rules for the content of pharmaceutical advertising and oversees advertising pertaining to things people eat and drink

Let's take a deeper look at what these organizations do for the public to regulate communication.

Federal Trade Commission

To protect consumers from false or misleading advertising, the government has empowered the Federal Trade Commission (FTC) to place restrictions on commercial speech.[14] The commission's rules and regulations prohibit the use of deceptive advertising on any medium to entice buyers with false promises. Deceptive advertising is defined as content that misleads consumers through unsubstantiated claims or omitting crucial elements of a sales process. For example, the cannabidiol (CBD) company Kushly Industries LLC made multiple false or unproven claims that its products could treat illnesses including cancer, multiple sclerosis, Parkinson's disease, and Alzheimer's disease. In addition, Kushly's marketing material falsely stated that scientific research supported these claims. In May 2021, the FTC reached an agreement with the company in which it agreed to pay a thirty thousand dollar fine and stop making these and other unsupported medical claims.[15] The FTC also took on for-profit colleges in 2021, sending 70 of these institutions warning letters regarding their claims of graduation rates, job placements, and other potentially deceptive marketing practices. Two years prior to that, the University of Phoenix paid $191 million to settle FTC claims that the educational institution deceived students through its false claims of connections with companies like Microsoft and Twitter.[16]

FTC officials also evaluate the degree to which an advertiser's claims are unfair, which means balancing whether the item or process is likely to lead to substantial and unavoidable injury with whether that injury is outweighed by the product's benefits. A home workout routine might leave you sore after you do it, but you are losing weight and gaining muscle as a result, so that would be fine. However, an advertisement for "Jimmy's Weight Loss Machete" that requires you to lop off a leg to lose twenty pounds would clearly not be a good trade in the injury/benefit department.

Federal Communications Commission

In 1927, the federal government decided that the airwaves were a limited public resource and, as such, needed oversight for the benefit of all people (see Chapter 6). This led to the creation of the Federal Radio Commission, which became the Federal Communications Commission in 1934. The FCC oversees and regulates broadcasting, which includes the use of radio, television, satellite, cable, and wire transmissions within the United States.[17] It also regulates the ownership and licensing of radio and television stations, determining how many outlets any particular ownership group can have in a specific area or on a specific platform.[18]

The commission uses its oversight power to examine content and respond to consumer complaints regarding it. Although the FCC clearly states that both the First Amendment and Section 326 of the Communications Act prohibit it from censoring content, it notes that "if you are offended by a station's programming, we urge you to make your concerns known in writing to the station licensee."[19] In addition, it has noted that material deemed "indecent" or "profane" can lead to action from the FCC if it is broadcast when children are likely to see it: between the hours of 6 a.m. and 10 p.m. Finally, the FCC is integral in the ratings associated with television programming and parents' ability to block it with the use of a V-chip, a digital element embedded in television sets that uses these ratings to help parents weed out potentially objectionable content.[20]

Billy McFarland, the director of Fyre Festival, was charged with wire fraud and pleaded guilty to the charges in 2018.

Mark Lennihan/ Associated Press / Alamy Stock Photo

In more recent years, the FCC is taking a stronger stance on how social media influencers present content, particularly if they are paid for their actions. For example, in 2017, entrepreneur Billy McFarland and musician Ja Rule launched the disastrous Fyre Festival in the Bahamas, which purported to be a luxury concert event, featuring supermodels and the ultrafamous. The organization then launched a full social media campaign by having more than four hundred influencers post a plain orange tile on their social media feeds, which some referred to as an "orange out" campaign.

The influencers, however, were not doing this out of the goodness of their hearts or because they knew the festival was going to be amazing. The organizers had promised many of the influencers free food and lodging at the festival in exchange for that one post. In one case, Kendall Jenner was paid $250,000 for a single Instagram post, in which she promoted the event and intimated that Kanye West and others would be performing at it.[21] However, none of the celebrities who were promoting the event made it clear that they were part of a paid promotional campaign.

The festival never got off the ground, with all the musical acts getting canceled, and hundreds of participants were stranded without food, water, or even a way to get home. Less than a day after the first arrivals, the organizers officially pulled the plug. In the wake of heavy social media criticism, several of the influencers apologized for their role in what became an epic failure, and Jenner settled a lawsuit regarding her post for ninety thousand dollars.[22]

The infamous "wardrobe malfunction" resulted in the FCC's levying a fine against CBS for "indecent exposure" and created a media storm about the incident.

James D. Smith/Icon SMI 901/James D. Smith/Icon SMI/Newscom

(A similar incident occurred with Jenner's half-sister, Kim Kardashian, who was paid $250,000 to promote the cryptocurrency Ethereum on her Instagram account. Even though she included "#ad" hashtag at the bottom of the post, the

Securities and Exchange Commission stated that this wasn't enough to satisfy its disclosure rules. Kardashian and the commission agreed on a $1.26 million settlement in 2022.[23])

In response to this growing trend in which influencers are paid to endorse products,[24] the FTC has issued guidelines for social media users that explain what they need to disclose to remain transparent.[25] Not only are influencers expected do more than include the tag "#ad" at the bottom of a post, but the companies that pay the influencers are expected to make clear these relationships.[26] Table 14.3 outlines some key actions the FCC has taken to enforce these rules.

TABLE 14.3 ■ Key FCC Actions against Broadcast Media

Date	Action
1975	In response to criticism that TV programming was becoming too violent and sexually charged, the FCC established a policy that all three television networks must run "family-friendly" programming from 8 to 9 p.m. Eastern time. Amid protests from producers, directors, and actors, a district court ruled that the FCC's mandate was unconstitutional, and the "family viewing hour" was ended by 1977.
1978	After a radio station aired comedian George Carlin's "filthy words" monologue during an afternoon broadcast, the FCC received a complaint and acted against the station. The Supreme Court ruled in *FCC v. Pacifica* that the FCC can regulate this kind of speech, even if it doesn't reach the standard of obscenity, because radio and television are pervasive and accessible to children. The courts did note, however, that the government lacks the power to ban all such speech.
2001	The FCC issued the first television indecency fine in U.S. history, penalizing WKAQ-TV $21,000 for airing a series of bawdy comedy skits. The variety show *No Te Duermas* featured a scene showing a man and a woman in a bubble-filled bathtub engaging in physical contact and excessive sexual innuendo.
2004	The FCC levied the largest single fine for indecency in history to Clear Channel Communications. The radio chain was fined $755,000 for sexually explicit content that aired between 6:30 a.m. and 9 a.m. on the *Bubba the Love Sponge Show*, in which the host described sex acts between humans and cartoons as well as describing male and female genitalia.
2004	During the Super Bowl halftime show in 2004, singer Janet Jackson's bare breast was briefly exposed on stage during her act with Justin Timberlake. The "wardrobe malfunction," as it became known, led the FCC to impose a $550,000 fine on CBS for indecency. CBS challenged the fine, with the Supreme Court eventually ruling in favor of the broadcast company.
2022	The FCC implemented a rule that required broadcasters to investigate and disclose if a foreign governmental body paid them to air content. The FCC stated that this was meant to prevent the infiltration of Russian and Chinese propaganda into U.S. broadcasts. A federal court blocked the FCC's effort, saying that the investigation portion placed an undue burden on broadcasters.

Food and Drug Administration

Although it maintains a narrow area of interest, the Food and Drug Administration (FDA) does play a key role in regulating advertising. It works with the FTC and the Department of Agriculture to oversee claims made in food advertising regarding its nutritional content or health properties.[27] It also serves as the primary agency for examining claims made regarding prescription drugs.

The FDA does not work with the companies to make the ads, nor does the agency get to see them prior to their publication. However, it has established rules for these types of ads, including listing at least one approved use for the drug and all the risks associated with using it. Consumers who believe that an advertiser has violated these rules can submit a complaint to the FDA and request an investigation.

DEFAMATION, LIBEL, AND SLANDER

LEARNING OBJECTIVES

LO 3: Define libel and identify the key elements that can successfully support this charge and the most prominent defenses against them.

In March 2021, Dominion Voting Systems filed a $1.6 billion lawsuit against Fox News, claiming that the media outlet had made patently false statements regarding the software company's role in the 2020 election.[28] The suit stated that Fox hosts and guests lied to the public by stating that Dominion had rigged the outcome of the presidential race to favor Democratic candidate Joe Biden. In April 2023, Fox settled with Dominion for $787.5 million, acknowledging that the during the lead-up to the settlement, the court found "certain claims about Dominion to be false." In addition, information from the case had leaked to the public, showing that some Fox personalities knew the network was helping spread disinformation about the voting company and the election.[29]

As we've already noted, the First Amendment isn't an impenetrable shield that protects you from harm when you publish content. One of the most common claims people make when they see something written about themselves that they don't like is that the media has defamed them. Although unpleasant statements are made every day, and many media outlets publish things people wished they hadn't, it doesn't necessarily follow that a form of defamation has occurred.

People often misunderstand the concept of defamation or who can be charged with it. The two words most directly attached to claims of defamation are **libel** and **slander**. In the simplest terms, libel is written defamation, while slander is spoken defamation. Courts generally view libel as more damaging, because slander tends to involve spoken words of limited reach. For example, if someone at your school stood up on a table in student union and used a bullhorn to tell everyone that Professor Jane Smith was taking money from students who wanted better grades, this could be a case of slander. If that person, instead of standing on the table and yelling about it, published a column in the student newspaper making similar claims, this could be a case of libel.

The Student Press Law Center (SPLC) in Arlington, Virginia, defines libel as "the publication—in words, photos, pictures or symbols—of false statements that harm another's reputation."[30] Given that this covers most of what you'll be doing in a career as a media professional, let's look at what libel involves and how you can defend yourself against it.

Before we do, however, it's important to understand that you run the risk of libel every time you engage in public discourse. This is not meant to scare you, but it's important to understand that, although professional news publications are usually the defendants in libel cases, it doesn't mean that only newspapers and magazines can libel someone. Public relations practitioners, advertisers, and social media users who put content into the public sphere run the risk of creating libelous content and can be held accountable for their actions.

The SPLC outlines four key things necessary for a person to bring a legitimate libel suit against an individual or media outlet (see Table 14.4).

TABLE 14.4 ■ Four Key Elements of a Libel Suit

Action	Key Question	Examples
Publication	Did you share the content with anyone other than the person claiming to be libeled?	• Writing an article in the school newspaper • Posting something on social media • Running an advertisement on a website
Identification	Can the public determine who is the subject of your content?	• Stating the person's name within the text • Running a photo of the person • Describing the person in a specific way ("The principal of Omniconne High School")
Harm	Has the person's reputation suffered because of shame, ridicule, disgrace, or injury?	• Accusing a professor of taking money for grades • Stating that your roommate has a "raging sexually transmitted infection"
Fault	Negligence standard: Did you fail to act in a reasonable manner? Actual malice standard: Did you act recklessly and publish knowingly false content?	• Failing to adequately fact-check a story before publishing it • Posting lies about a professor who gave you a bad grade, accusing them of using racial slurs in class

Defenses against Defamation

In looking through these four points, it's pretty clear that people who work in the media run the risk of defaming someone every day. A reporter can publish a story about a person who is accused of robbing a store. A public relations practitioner can put out a press release stating that a company violated safety standards. An advertiser can run a commercial that attacks a politician's record on international affairs.

Although you do run some risks every time you publish, it's not always as risky as it seems, if you understand the rules associated with libel. What we just outlined are the four key elements that someone has to prove just to get into the game, so to speak. Table 14.5. outlines the defenses you can use to keep them from winning.

TABLE 14.5 ■ Defenses against Libel

Defense	Explanation	Example
Truth	The information shared, regardless of how damaging it is to a person's reputation, is factually accurate.	A newspaper story accusing a U.S. senator of child trafficking is supported by a video confession the senator made to the police
Privilege	The information comes from an official source, acting in an official capacity.	A website that quotes a judge delivering a guilty verdict, where he calls the defendant a "vile murderer," even though the man insists he didn't commit the crime
Opinion/commentary	The information is meant to demonstrate the thoughts of the writer, not a statement of fact.	A movie reviewer who explains why *Fast and Furious 22: Wheelchairs of Speed* is terrible
Hyperbole/satire	The information is so outlandish that no one could believe it to be factually accurate.	A comment on a sports site that says, "This coach was so stupid, he would probably fail a blood test"
Actual malice	The information was published without a reckless disregard for the truth.	A broadcast story accusing a man of murdering his wife that turns out to be false, despite the reporter's making every effort to gather and report the facts accurately

Here's a deeper look at each of these defenses.

Truth

Recall that libelous content must be "false" by definition. That means that if you can prove that what you published is true, you will likely walk out of court a winner. **Truth** is the best possible defense against libel, and it's the one we strive for every time we publish an item. People won't like hearing negative things about themselves, but if you can prove that what you have published is true, they have very little basis for a libel suit. The courts have long held that a story about a person arrested on suspicion of robbing a store, a press release about a company's violating safety standards, and a political attack ad all have a place in public discourse if they are accurate.

Truth wasn't always a defense against libel. Before the courts ruled in favor of John Peter Zenger in 1735, telling the truth could get you in trouble.

Zenger published opinions in the *New York Weekly Journal* that criticized William Cosby, a recently appointed public official. Cosby, the colonial governor of New York, proclaimed that Zenger had engaged in scandalous and seditious activities.

John Peter Zenger's court case set a precedent for how we handle libel claims, namely, that it can't be libel if it's true.

GRANGER

In 1735, Zenger was tried for libel because of his publications, but his attorneys argued that statements like Zenger's couldn't be libelous, because they were true. A jury agreed, returning a not-guilty verdict in about ten minutes. The Zenger case laid the groundwork for truth as a defense against libel claims.

Privilege

This defense against libel falls into two areas: **absolute privilege** and **qualified privilege**. Absolute privilege is granted to people like judges and governmental officials, which allows them to say things, regardless of their factual basis, while acting in their official roles. Other statements that fall under absolute privilege are those made in public meetings or during court testimony. So, during a meeting, a city council representative could argue that a plan to build a megastore in town "will kill every local merchant, and anyone who supports this plan knows that" without fear of being sued for libel. A witness to a crime can testify that a defendant "kept stabbing that woman like he was possessed by pure evil" and is safe from a defamation claim.

Journalists operate under the area of qualified privilege, which means they can quote these official sources of information without fear of being charged with libel. A broadcaster can run footage of the city council representative on the nightly news, or a newspaper journalist can post a story online quoting the witness in the murder trial without fear. This defense covers media outlets of all kinds, including social media and press releases.

Opinion and Commentary

Courts have ruled that people are entitled to their own opinions and that only factually based statements can be the sources of libel suits. Therefore, the plaintiff in a case must prove that the libelous material includes statements of facts. If you can show that the material in question is an **opinion**, you have a decent chance of defending yourself against libel.

Some statements are easy to differentiate along the fact-opinion spectrum. "Mint chocolate chip ice cream tastes delicious," is clearly one person's opinion. "Wisconsin is a state" is clearly a fact. Unfortunately, many media outlets these days have gotten quite adept at blending fact and opinion while passing it off as pure truth. To that end, it's important to understand the way in which the courts view facts and opinions.

In the case of *Ollman v. Evans*,[31] the courts developed a test to decide if a statement is a fact or an opinion, which included the ability to prove the statement true or false, the social context of the remark, and what the words commonly mean. For example, let's say you're writing a column about your college football coach after he decided to punt instead of going for a first down. In your article, you wrote, "When the team needed his leadership most, Coach John Smith was gutless and spineless." It's clear that you meant that he was cowardly or afraid of making a mistake, not that he lacked a complete set of intestines and a central nervous system.

Commentary is judged by the same rules. If you are reviewing a band, a movie, or a restaurant you are allowed to offer your opinion on the music, the film, or the food without fear, so long as you keep the facts around that opinion straight. You can write on a site like Yelp that "The food at La Pizzeria is bland, cold, and overpriced," because that is clearly your commentary on your meal. However, if you wrote, "La Pizzeria's food is horrible, but it doesn't matter to the owner, because the restaurant is just a front for the Mafia," you are putting yourself at risk by introducing information that could be proven true or false.

Hyperbole and Satire

Courts have ruled that **hyperbole**, things that are so outlandish that no reasonable person would believe them to be true, is protected speech and therefore cannot be libelous. In 2019, comedian John Oliver, on his show *Last Week Tonight*, explained how he eventually prevailed in a libel suit that coal magnate Bob Murray filed against him. Oliver used hyperbole to poke fun at Murray during a 2017 piece on the coal industry, comparing him to "a geriatric Dr. Evil," and having a staff member in a squirrel costume tell him to "Eat shit, Bob." Murray lost the suit, but an appeal reached the West Virginia Supreme Court before Murray eventually withdrew his claim. The lower court's ruling said that the statements Oliver made about Murray's looks and demeanor in his piece were so ridiculous that no reasonable person could consider them to be facts.[32]

Satire of a political nature, such as impressions of political figures on *Saturday Night Live*, falls under similar protections, the courts have held. The use of humor to draw attention to hypocritical actions or bad ideas in the form of political cartoons also receives this protection.

Actual Malice

In determining fault, the courts tend to look at two standards: **negligence** and **actual malice**. Negligence is easier to prove than malice, because it simply requires that the plaintiff show that the defendant failed to act in a reasonable manner to avoid publishing the defamatory content. Actual malice requires that the plaintiff show that the defendant acted recklessly and knew that the published content was false. In this case, the defendant did something on purpose to defame someone, knowing all along that it was untrue. In determining the validity of a libel charge in the United States, private citizens must show negligence, which is much easier to prove, while public figures must prove actual malice, which means the plaintiff has to prove the journalist intended to harm him or her.

Therefore, in some cases, if all else fails, a defendant can win a case if they can demonstrate that they did not act with reckless disregard for the truth. For example, in 2011, the Georgia Supreme Court made its final determination that the *Atlanta Journal-Constitution* did not libel security guard Richard Jewell when it published stories declaring him a suspect in the 1996 Olympic Park bombing. Jewell sued multiple media outlets, claiming that they portrayed him as an overzealous wannabe cop who likely planted the bomb that killed two people and injured more than one hundred others in order to portray himself as a hero. The court ruled that Jewell should be viewed as a limited-purpose public figure, which means he was viewed as a public figure when it came to news about the bombing because he put himself in the public eye for this specific instance, and thus he had to prove actual malice before the courts could side with him. Table 14.6 presents some famous cases of defamation, and why they matter.

TABLE 14.6 ■ Key Defamation Cases

Case	Year	Ruling	Importance
Patterson v. Colorado	1907	The Supreme Court upholds Colorado newspaper owner Thomas Patterson's conviction after he was found guilty of publishing content critical of the state's courts.	The first press freedom case of its kind that stated that freedom of the press allowed people to publish what they want, but it did leave them open to "subsequent punishment."
Chaplinsky v. New Hampshire	1942	The court found that Walter Chaplinsky was correctly arrested for his disparagement of a town marshal as a "damned Fascist."	The court ruled that words intended to "inflict injury or tend to incite an immediate breach of peace" are not protected under the First Amendment. This case established the "fighting words" standard for judging speech that can lead to harm.
New York Times *v. Sullivan*	1964	Alabama's public safety commissioner, L. B. Sullivan, thought a *New York Times* advertisement regarding Martin Luther King, Jr.'s perjury charges had libeled him, and a state court agreed, awarding him $500,000. However, the Supreme Court reversed that decision, siding with the newspaper.	The Supreme Court required public officials to show that any defamatory falsehood against them was made with a reckless disregard for the truth. This decision improved the protections for media when it came to covering public figures and established the "actual malice" standard for libel claims involving them.
Flynt v. Falwell	1988	The founder of the Moral Majority, the Reverend Jerry Falwell, won a $150,000 judgment in state court after Larry Flynt published a spoof advertisement in *Hustler* magazine suggesting that Falwell had sex with his mother and a goat. The Supreme Court reversed that decision, siding with the magazine.	The court ruled that the First Amendment protects parodies of public figures from such liabilities, if the patently offensive speech could not reasonably be believed.
Grace v. eBay, Inc.	2004	After Roger Grace posted negative comments about an eBay seller, the seller responded by saying that Grace should be banned from eBay and was "DISHONEST ALL THE WAY!!!!" When the company refused to remove the comments about him, Grace sued for libel.	A California appellate court found that publishers can be held liable for defamatory material, but not if a user agreement specifically absolves them of responsibility for the postings of others.
The Alex Jones/Sandy Hook lawsuits	2022	Parents of children killed during the Sandy Hook school shooting in Connecticut sued Infowars founder Alex Jones multiple jurisdictions after he repeatedly stated on his news program that the shooting was fake and that the children who were killed were actually "crisis actors" who never died.	Courts in Texas and Connecticut found Jones and Infowars guilty of defamation and collectively awarded the plaintiffs approximately $1.5 billion.

A DEEPER LOOK: LIBEL IS AT THE TIPS OF YOUR FINGERS (OR MAYBE THUMBS)

Social media has made it easier for us to share our thoughts, opinions, and ideas with hundreds, or even thousands, of people in an instant from anywhere we are. We can tweet about the "brain-damaged future pedophile working the register" at our local fast food restaurant. We can post a Photoshopped picture on Instagram that shows a teacher punching a student. After a really bad breakup, we can head to TikTok and tell all our viewers *exactly* why our "ex" was the worst person on Earth.

We might think that postings like these are funny or normal social media behavior, but these kinds of actions can put us at risk of libel suits. The courts have found that social media posts count as publication and that libel suits involving them can proceed to trial. Musician Courtney Love faced multiple libel suits regarding her Twitter and Instagram posts. In a 2014 case, Love claimed on Twitter that her former attorney was "bought off" while working on a fraud case for her. The court found that Love did not libel Rhonda Holmes, and Holmes also lost a 2016 appeal. However, Love had to pay fashion designer Dawn Simorangkir more than $750,000 after Simorangkir sued Love for defamation twice. In the first case, Love settled for $430,000 in 2011 after a tweet storm in which she called Simorangkir numerous insulting things, including an "asswipe nasty lying hosebag thief."[33] In 2015, Love agreed to pay Simorangkir another $350,000 after another Twitter outburst in which she said that the designer was abusive, a drug dealer, and a prostitute.[34]

In 2019, Tesla CEO Elon Musk successfully defended himself against a suit from a British cave explorer, who was upset that Musk called him a "pedo guy" on Twitter. Legal experts noted that this might be a case of a celebrity getting a break, or the courts could be raising the bar regarding what constitutes libel on social media. In either case, the courts reaffirmed that actions taken on social media can be actionable.[35]

Every time you pop open a social media app and share content, you are a publisher, held to the same standards of newspapers, magazines, and other publications. That means that you need to take these actions seriously, particularly when the language could be taken seriously, or the information passed on could lead to harm. It might seem funny or harmless to tweet out that a teacher was leering at an underage student or that someone in your school is the kind of kid who would bring an assault rifle to class. However, those quick, thought-free missives can cause long-term harm and lead you into a courtroom. Moral reasoning aside, the law tends to side with private citizens who are harmed through the publication efforts of others, so follow the advice your mother likely gave you as a kid: "If you can't find anything nice to say about somebody, don't say anything at all."

INVASION OF PRIVACY

LEARNING OBJECTIVES

LO 4: Describe the ways in which media practitioners can engage in invasion of privacy.

Individuals in the United States have an inherent right to be left alone if they so choose. The degree to which the public has a right to know certain things about anyone relates directly to the individual's actions. Therefore, a person who decides to run for Congress has chosen to enter the public eye and thus will sustain more scrutiny than a person who works at a restaurant and generally leads an unremarkable life. However, if that restaurant worker kills three people with a carving knife, that person has now entered the public eye as well and will likely be of interest to people in the community. Table 14.7 presents four key elements that define **invasion of privacy**.

Let's dig into each of these a bit and see how each one works.

Intrusion

Individuals have a right to prevent people from trespassing on their property or surveilling them using technology. For example, in 2022, a student at Northwest Missouri State University pleaded guilty to

TABLE 14.7 ■ Four Key Elements of Invasion of Privacy

Action	Explanation	Example
Intrusion	Violation of a person's right to be left alone in private places.	You use a drone to take video of your neighbor's kids playing in the backyard for your website.
False light	Incorrectly implying something about someone that could be illegal or humiliating.	A newspaper runs a photo of a farmer and his pigs right next to an unrelated story about a man's arrest for bestiality.
Disclosure	Publishing embarrassing facts about a private person that, while true, the public has no right to know.	A blogger publishes documents from a cosmetic surgeon's office, detailing his clients' names and the procedures that they've had.
Misappropriation	Using someone's image or likeness without that person's permission.	You include a photo of your professor on your campaign posters for student government president without the professor's approval.

invasion of privacy after admitting that he used his mobile phone to film women while they took showers in one of the school's residence halls.[36] Protection from this kind of **intrusion** is meant to allow you to behave as you see fit in the privacy of your own home and to allow you to feel secure in your environment.

Journalists have no more rights than average citizens in this regard, so a reporter can't hop a fence to enter a private farm and take pictures of animals he believes are being abused. A videographer can't climb up the outside of your house and gather footage of you while you're sleeping, or fly a drone over your backyard to grab photos of you sunbathing. Journalists can enter private places that are open to regular citizens, like restaurants or shopping malls, but they must leave when the owner or an owner's representative asks them to do so.

Intrusion also applies to hidden devices in public areas where people would reasonably expect privacy. The city government building in your town is a public building, but most people would expect to be free from surveillance in the bathroom there. Therefore, while you can record the mayor engaging in a loud argument with someone in the hallway, you can't stick a mini-recorder behind the toilet in the restroom. In 2013, gossip-news site TMZ was sued for the use of hidden microphones in a California court. Alpha Walker, who was in court on charges that he attempted to extort singer Stevie Wonder, sued after officials found that microphones had been placed on the judge's bench and on both lawyers' tables. Although the judge had allowed recording to occur in the courtroom, the secret placement of the microphones meant that TMZ could record private conversations between the attorneys and their clients as well as between the judge and the attorneys during sidebars that were intended to be private.[37] The case was later dismissed.

False Light

The core of a **false light** claim is that published material incorrectly implies something untrue and damaging about a person. Some states, like Colorado, don't recognize the concept of false light, because their courts view it as too close to defamation to distinguish between the two.[38] However, the distinction is important for media participants to understand, because it often involves inadvertent actions as opposed to errors in active reporting.

False light claims tend to put two true things close enough together that people will see them as related, even if they're not. In cases like these, the court is looking at the "gist" of the material to see if a falsehood is implied. In *Solano v. Playgirl, Inc.*, actor José Solano won a false light suit after the magazine published his photo along with headlines implying that he had posed nude in the magazine, which he had not.[39]

However, a court ruled against a New Hampshire couple in 2021 regarding their false light claim against the *North Woods Law* reality television show. The couple appeared in an episode titled "Weed Whackers" that depicted authorities questioning them about a patch of marijuana growing near their home. The couple's faces were blurred, and the law enforcement officers noted that they weren't suspects after being questioned; however, the couple said that people recognized them anyway and thought they still had something to do with the pot plants.[40]

Disclosure

One of the key tenets of libel law is that the truth is a silver-bullet defense. If a reporter can prove something to be true, that person will likely avoid being convicted of libel. However, the courts have ruled that not everything that is true should be made available to the public, which is where **disclosure** comes in.

The public disclosure of private information that can embarrass someone can land journalists in hot water with the courts, even if that information is true. The primary elements in weighing a disclosure charge is the importance to the public to know this information versus the individual's right to keep things private. Disclosure cases often are based on revealing medical situations, educational records, or sexual conduct. As we explained when discussing libel, private individuals have higher levels of protection than do public figures. That's why a private person only must prove negligence in a defamation case, while public figures have to prove actual malice.

A similar level of protection applies to private versus public figures regarding disclosure. This is why you can read all about how likely it is that actress Gwyneth Paltrow had breast augmentation surgery[41] or that supermodel Gisele Bündchen and NFL legend Tom Brady got a divorce.[42] As people in the public eye, journalists are allowed to claim the information involved in these, and many other, incidents is newsworthy. It is also why you read about the sordid details of politicians' lives, such as those involving former president Donald Trump and his interactions with adult film actress Stormy Daniels.

The courts are less forgiving when reporters provide similar details about regular people. Is it in the public interest to know if your mail carrier is having an affair? Why is it important for everyone on your campus to know if your roommate had cosmetic surgery? Does it really need to be front-page news if a professor and her husband are getting a divorce? Unless you can show a clear and valid reason for this information to be made public, you could lose a lawsuit.

Misappropriation

People have a right to decide how their own images and likenesses are used in the public sphere. Nobody has the right to use a person's photographic image, personal likeness, voice, name, or other identifiable feature without that person's permission.[43] While copyright provides protection against the use of content that you create, **misappropriation** protects you as an individual against being used in other people's content.

Rapper Cardi B found herself in the middle of such a lawsuit in 2021, when Kevin Michael Brophy, Jr., sued her over the "misleading, offensive, humiliating and provocatively sexual" use of his image on an album cover. Brophy's distinctive full-back tattoo of a tiger battling a snake was photoshopped onto the back of another person, who is depicted performing oral sex on Cardi B while she drinks a beer. A court ruled in favor of the singer in October 2022, and an appeals court affirmed the decision later that year, although Brophy attempted to restart the litigation in January 2023.[44]

MEDIA LITERACY MOMENT: BALANCING ACCESS AND PRIVACY

Journalism has always been a balancing act between the public's right to know and the individual's right to be left alone. Who gets to draw that line and where it should be drawn often leads to legal wrangling and a debate over the tastefulness of individual actions. For example, in 2021, Vanessa Bryant sued Los Angeles County for the actions of rescue personnel who took personal pictures of the helicopter crash that killed her husband, basketball icon Kobe Bryant, along with their daughter and seven other people. The invasion-of-privacy suit states that several employees of the sheriff's office and fire department took photos of the grisly scene and shared them with others "without any legitimate governmental purpose." The county's legal team replied that although officials didn't condone the employees' actions, they did not do anything illegal.[45]

The battle over how best to deal with private and painful moments can be difficult from a legal standpoint. (We will discuss the ethical concerns in Chapter 15.) When race car driver Dale Earnhardt died in 2001 after crashing into a wall during the Daytona 500, the *Orlando Sentinel* made an open-records request to have the autopsy photos made available to them. While NASCAR fans, legislators, and even other journalists decried this seemingly invasive and ghoulish action, the *Sentinel* pointed to its investigative series on NASCAR safety and argued that a professional review of the images might help save future lives. When the photos were released, the *Sentinel*'s assumptions about safety protocols were found to be accurate and gave experts opportunities to prevent similar future deaths.

Contrast this with a request from *Hustler* magazine in 2010, when the publication requested crime scene photos taken during the investigation of the death of Meredith Emerson. The twenty-four-year-old Georgia woman was found nude and decapitated in a wooded area in 2008. A homeless drifter, sixty-one-year-old Gary Michael Hilton, had kidnapped her and held her hostage in his van for three days before killing her and dumping her body.[46] Fred Rosen, a veteran true crime author, made the request for the images after receiving an assignment to write a piece for *Hustler*, a pornographic publication. Georgia law enforcement officials refused to comply with the open-records request, and the state rushed through legislation titled "The Meredith Emerson Memorial Privacy Act" to prevent the release of all photos of this type.[47] In an opinion column written two years after the request, Rosen noted that the photos would be the only way he could verify or dispute Hilton's statements to police, something that could have value in examining unsolved murders with a similar M.O.[48]

Open-records law is intended to afford all people equal access to material gathered by governmental agencies for the purpose of creating a more informed citizenry. Based on that standard, is it fair in your mind that one publication got access to a death-scene photo while another did not? Privacy law, and other rules regarding media content, tends to offer a greater level of protection to private citizens than it does to public figures. With that in mind, does it matter that one person was a famous race car driver who died during a major public event while the other was a little-known person who was killed in a van?

These are some of the issues courts consider in determining who gets more or less protection from the prying eyes of the media.

THE NEXT STEP: Take this concept a step further and find a story that deals with an invasion-of-privacy claim. Read at least two articles on the topic, and if a lawsuit has been filed, see if you can get access to the court documents. Determine what biases are most likely to interfere with your critical-thinking process and then work through the three As again, making sure to push back against your preconceived notions of what should or shouldn't be held private.

THAT'S MINE! COPYRIGHT LAW AND PROTECTIONS

LEARNING OBJECTIVES

LO 5: Define copyright and explain the ways in which copyrighted content can be legally used.

Copyright is an intellectual property law, which has its roots in the U.S. Constitution, and provides individuals with the right to content they have authored.[49] This form of law covers anything from screenplays and news articles to photographs and songs. The goal of copyright law is to provide individual writers, artists, composers, and other authors of content with the ability to safeguard their creations from theft or misuse. Courts will often look at issues of ownership, use, and the weight of the public good against the right of the owners when it considers how best to decide these kinds of cases. Here are a few key concerns the courts will examine when determining if copyright infringement occurred.

Fair Use

To balance the needs of the public with the rights of a copyright owner, the law has carved out several opportunities for people to use copyrighted material without permission. **Fair use** is one of the most frequently used of these provisions, because it allows certain uses of a limited amount of content without the permission of the owner.

For example, the U.S. Supreme Court ended an eleven-year battle between Google and Oracle in 2021 regarding Google's use of about 11,500 lines of Oracle's computer code as part of its smartphone development. The court ruled six to two that Google's copying of the code constituted a legal use of the material and fell under the fair-use exception to the copyright law.[50]

According to the U.S. Copyright Office,[51] several factors are key in determining fair use (see Table 14.8.).

TABLE 14.8 ■ Key Factors for Determining Fair Use

Factor	Question at Hand	Answers
Nature of the use	What are you doing with the material?	People who use the content for private purposes, educational work, and news dissemination get more protection under fair use than do those who use it for commercial purposes or financial gain.
Nature of the material	What kind of content are you using?	People who use factual or historical material would have a better fair-use claim than people who use fictional or creative work.
Amount of the material used	How much of the original material did you take for your purposes?	The more you take, the bigger the risk. That said, courts have ruled that certain core elements of content (deemed "the heart of the source") deserve protection, regardless of its overall size in relation to the whole of the original.
Impact on the market	How will this harm the owner of the original material?	If your use makes it difficult or impossible for the copyright owner to benefit from the original work, you are at a greater risk of violating fair use than if your use doesn't harm the owner in any meaningful way.

Nature of the Use

News organizations often are given more leeway by the courts than commercial enterprises when it comes to fair-use provisions. Therefore, a news organization might be able to copy a photo of a person from a social media site without permission and use it in a story about that person winning a major award or being arrested for a crime. On the other hand, an advertising firm that takes a copy of a picture of a sunset over a famous landmark from that same site without permission and uses it to promote local tourism would receive less protection. Educational and other nonprofit enterprises also are more likely to receive fair-use exemptions compared with money-making efforts.

Nature of the Material

Courts look at to what degree material is creatively or factually based, as the goal of fair use is to encourage creative expression. The material from the U.S. Copyright Office website that is the source for this portion of the text, for example, would receive more rights to a fair-use claim than would creative works, like a song, novel, or movie.

The Amount of the Material Used

If you visited your school's library or photocopy center lately, you might have noticed a sign near the copier explaining that they will only let you copy one article out of a journal or 10 percent of any book. Although the courts have not truly established a bright line on exactly how much "borrowing" is too much to support a fair-use claim, the courts do lean toward the argument that the less you take, the safer you are. However, the courts have ruled that you can take a small but vital part of a copyrighted work—in other words, the "heart" of it—and not be covered by fair use.

A dispute of this nature occurred between the Rolling Stones and fellow musicians The Verve regarding the song "Bitter Sweet Symphony." The Verve received permission to use a portion of an orchestral version of the Stones' "The Last Time" as a sample within the band's song. After the song became a hit in 1997, the Stones' management sued, stating that The Verve used much more of the original tune than the two sides initially agreed to. This led The Verve to lose control of the song and the copyright until 2019, when the Stones' Keith Richards and Mick Jagger agreed to hand back the rights to The Verve.[52]

The Impact on the Market

If someone takes an article that you wrote for a class and sells it to the local newspaper, you won't be able to sell that same article to that same newspaper or any other area publications. In short, that person's actions have killed the market for your work and limited your ability to profit from it. The more detrimental someone's actions are to the market or your ability to operate within it, the more likely it is that they violated copyright.

Other Ways to Avoid Copyright Infringement

If you are unsure whether your use of someone else's material falls under fair use, you can take some other simple steps to remain on the right side of the law.

Get Permission

In many cases, people who own the copyright on certain materials are happy to work with you if you want to use their work. You just have to ask before you do it. In some cases, a simple exchange of emails will provide permission to post something on your website or use some material for a broadcast. In other cases, you might need to work out a formal contract that would explain what you planned to use, how you planned to use it, and what cost, if any, is involved.

Use Creative Commons Work

Copyright and trademark law provide owners with "all rights" to the content that they create and requires you to get permission prior to using that material (with the exceptions outlined in the discussion of fair use). However, some content creators want you to use their work without having requiring lengthy legal negotiations. To meet this need, Creative Commons licenses were developed to indicate what you are allowed to use, what you can do to the material itself, and how you are allowed to use it.

For as long as copyright has been enforced, the phrase "all rights reserved" has accompanied it. This phrase gave the owner of the copyright complete control over how the work would be used, as opposed to content that was in the **public domain** (see the next section), which everyone can use for free. However, with the advent of digital media, shared content, and "remixing" opportunities, content creators found the on/off switch approach to copyright overly restricting, which is where Creative Commons stepped in.

Founded in 2001, the nonprofit network provides people with the opportunity to allow others to share and use their content legally without first gaining permission. The model they use is known as a "some rights reserved" approach, which gives the artists and authors of creative works the opportunity to specifically state how the work can or can't be used. The current structure of Creative Commons provides six potential licenses for users, each of which requires the user of the content to provide credit to the original owner. Other than that, the uses range from any purpose to only noncommercial purposes and from any level of remixing to complete retention of all elements from the original work.

For example, an artist might provide a license that gives anyone the right to use a drawing for any noncommercial use without having to ask for permission. Another artist might say anyone can use a drawing for any use, but the art can't be altered in any way, including changing its coloring or cropping out any part of it.

Critics fear that this system may undercut the ability for copyright owners to truly control their own work if they so choose in the future. However, this approach to content sharing has a global network of satisfied users who have produced and shared more than two billion works as of 2023.[53] For more information on how this works, you can go to creativecommons.org.

Use Work without Copyright

Some works exist in the public sphere without the presence of copyright. These works are said to be in the "public domain" because no one can claim ownership to them. Copyright law has changed over the years. The duration of the copyright protection for works created prior to 1978 varies greatly, depending on what actions the creators took in protecting their content. Works created after 1978, however, have copyright protection that lasts for the life of the author plus seventy years.[54] Check to see which works don't have those protections and use them.

Create Your Own Content

One of the easiest ways to avoid copyright infringement is to be the owner of the copyright. This happens when you create your own content and use it as you see fit. When it comes to guarding the copyright of your work, you do not have to register it to have copyright law apply to it. However, if you plan to take legal actions against people who are infringing upon your rights, you will need to register the material with the copyright office prior to engaging in a lawsuit.

JOBS IN MEDIA LAW

Now that you better understand the field of media law, here's a handy overview of a few common positions in the field today.

Career Opportunity	Common Tasks
Entertainment lawyer	• Negotiate contracts between talent and production companies • Approve promotional and distribution agreements for a client • Advise clients on contracts and other legal affairs
Media lawyer	• Advocate for clients in a court of law • Handle contract negotiations for content acquisitions • Review content for potentially libelous content
Telecommunications lawyer	• Review FCC regulations for changes or updates that could affect a client • Provide advice related to issues associated with broadcast television, cable content and digital communication • Represent broadcasting clients during legal matters
First Amendment lawyer	• Work with legislators to craft laws that abide by the dictates in the First Amendment • File "friend of the court" briefs to support the First Amendment in cases that affect free speech or free press • Help media outlets that are under threat of having their First Amendment rights abridged
Copyright lawyer	• Prevent the unauthorized use of a client's intellectual property • Offer advice regarding potential copyright infringement to clients seeking to use content they do not own • License copyright use of client's material

CHAPTER REVIEW

LO 1 Understand the First Amendment and relate how it establishes a free press.

- The First Amendment addresses freedom of the press, of speech, of religion, of the right to petition the government for redress of grievances, and of the right to peaceably assemble.
- Common misinterpretations of the First Amendment include the following:
  - Nobody can stop you from publishing content.
  - All expression is protected and protected equally.
  - Journalists operate under a higher level of protection than regular citizens.
  - The First Amendment shields you from any harm associated with things you publish.

LO 2 Describe how government regulations apply to specific media platforms.

- Federal Trade Commission (FTC): Reviews claims of false advertising, works with companies to abide by the law, and fines organizations that continue to deceive the public.
- Federal Communication Commission (FCC): Oversees and regulates broadcasting, which includes the use of radio, television, satellite, cable, and wire transmissions within the United States. It also oversees the licensing process for all broadcast stations and reviews claims of indecency from the public.
- Food and Drug Administration (FDA): Examines advertising claims related to the potency of medicine and food. It requires that all ads for medicines include at least one approved use and all possible risks of using it.

LO 3 Define libel and identify the key elements that can successfully support this charge and the most prominent defenses against them.

- Libel is defined as the publication—in words, photos, pictures or symbols—of false statements that harm another's reputation.
- To demonstrate libel occurred, a person must prove publication, identification, harm, and fault.
- To successfully defend oneself against a libel suit, a person must prove at least one of the following:
  - The statement was true.
  - The statement came from a privileged source.
  - The statement was opinion or commentary
  - The statement was so hyperbolic or outlandish that no reasonable person would believe it.
- In some cases, a defendant can prove they did not act with "actual malice," which is when they knew something was wrong but published it anyway. Public figures must prove this to successfully win a libel suit.

LO 4 Describe the ways in which media practitioners can engage in invasion of privacy.

- Intrusion: Entering a private place without permission to gather material for publication.
- False light: Presenting information in such a way that it leads to a harmful and erroneous conclusion about a person.
- Disclosure: Publishing true but harmful information about a private citizen that the public has no right to know.
- Misappropriation: Using a person's likeness or image without that person's permission.

LO 5 Define copyright and explain the ways in which copyrighted content can be legally used.

- Copyright is an intellectual property law that gives individuals the right to control the use of content they have created.
- Copyrighted material can be used with permission of the creator, under the exceptions carved out for fair use and public domain or through a Creative Commons license.
- Material you create yourself can also be used as you see fit, as the author of that material

KEY TERMS

Absolute privilege
Actual malice
Commentary
Copyright
Disclosure
Fair use
False light
Fault
First Amendment
Harm
Hyperbole
Identification
Intrusion
Invasion of privacy
Libel
Misappropriation
Negligence
Opinion
Press shield laws
Public domain
Publication
Qualified privilege
Satire
Slander
Truth

DISCUSSION QUESTIONS

1. Which of the misperceptions related to the First Amendment that are listed in the chapter surprised you the most and why?
2. The FCC is cracking down on social media influencers who fail to identify their posts as paid advertising. Do you think it makes a difference to most social media followers if the tag "#advertising" is included in these posts? Should the FCC do more or less regarding these kinds of regulations on social media? Explain your position.
3. How much thought have you given to the concept of libel when you post content to social media platforms or share information digitally? Do the legal ramifications discussed in this chapter concern you? Why or why not?
4. Of the four ways in which an individual can claim an invasion of privacy, which one would be most troubling to you if you were to be the victim of it? What makes that invasion more concerning to you than the others listed?
5. Have you ever downloaded and used digital media content that was copyrighted without obtaining permission for doing so? Has anyone ever used content you have created without your permission? Based on these experiences, what is your overall feeling regarding the protections and punitive measures associated with copyright law?

New York governor Andrew Cuomo and his brother, CNN anchor Chris Cuomo, faced a conflict-of-interest situation when Andrew was accused of sexual misconduct and Chris used his position in the media to help his brother. Political advisers and media professionals publicly rebuked both men for this ethical breach.

Dia Dipasupil / Staff/Getty Images Entertainment/Getty Image

15 ETHICS: WHAT WE VALUE

INTRODUCTION

1. *When you think about ethics, do you prefer a "black or white" sense of ethics or more of a "shades of gray" version of what is or isn't ethical? Why?*
2. *How often do you think ethics play a role in what you see in the media you consume? Do you think the people producing the content have your best interests in mind? Why?*
3. *What ethical standards matter most to you when you decide what kinds of information you share with other people through social media?*

Veteran journalist Katie Couric revealed in her 2021 book *Going There* that during her interview with Supreme Court justice Ruth Bader Ginsburg five years earlier, Ginsburg made several negative comments about Black athletes and their "take a knee" protests during sporting events. Couric said she purposefully withheld those quotes and others to "protect" Ginsburg, because she really liked the Supreme Court justice.[1]

Around this same time, emails between sports journalist Adam Schefter and Washington Commanders president Bruce Allen were leaked to the press, in which Schefter appeared to give Allen final say over a story about a leaguewide labor dispute. Schefter went so far as to call Allen "Mr. Editor," implying that if Allen didn't want something published, it would remain unseen.[2]

In both of these cases, the journalists faced public backlash and scrutiny. Fellow journalists and media organizations stated that these decisions were unethical, because they provided powerful people with benefits that would not be afforded to average citizens. They also argued that Couric and Schefter allowed their personal relationships to shape public perception of important people and issues.

In this chapter, we will examine why ethics matter, explaining the importance of ethical behavior within a society. This examination will help us understand our own ethics as well as how ethics relate to our roles as mass media practitioners. We will also touch on a few well-known ethical models so you can assess your own sense of ethical values. Finally, we will examine the best ways to work through ethical dilemmas and the best things you can learn from doing so.

LEARNING OBJECTIVES

After completing this chapter, you should be able to:

1. Understand the concept of ethics and why they matter in society, particularly for mass media professionals.
2. Identify and explain the four basic ethical philosophies outlined in the chapter.
3. Define the key ethical tenets associated with mass media practitioners and how they apply to their work.
4. Outline the steps in working through an ethical dilemma and explain the value of each one as a part of the process.
5. Examine several principles that guide ethical development to help you shape your own approach to ethics.

WHAT ARE ETHICS AND WHY DO THEY MATTER?

LEARNING OBJECTIVES

LO 1: Understand the concept of ethics and why they matter in society, particularly for mass media professionals.

The term ethics is derived from the Greek word *ethos*, meaning "character," and the Latin word *mores*, meaning "customs."[3] The term serves to represent the ways in which we should act to demonstrate our personal character for the betterment of society. How we perceive our own sense of ethics and how we relate to others in society can vary widely from person to person. Furthermore, the importance of ethical behavior itself is often up for debate, with some arguing that ethics no longer matter to people as much as they once did. Let's look into how ethics work and to what degree they matter in the realm of mass media.

Conceptualizing Ethics

Socrates, one of the greatest thinkers of the modern world, explained that we each need to understand who we are and why we matter, both as individual people and as part of society. Through this knowledge, he argued, we could become virtuous and ethical people who could improve life for everyone. Based on this code of conduct and his philosophy of humanity, it would be interesting to see what Socrates would think about today's internet trolls, who seem hell-bent on sowing hatred and misinformation for their own amusement.

In Chapter 14, we discussed the legal considerations that relate to mass media and its practitioners. Although we demonstrated that the law itself isn't absolute, it was clear that media laws dictate strict "rules of the road" that, if broken, can result in serious penalties. In short, if you break the law, something bad will happen to you in a predefined fashion.

Comparatively speaking, ethics can feel a little squishier and more ill defined. Unlike the law, no one establishes a set of ethical norms that all people in a society are required to follow. Your code of ethics might differ drastically from that of your roommate, for example. Therefore, while you might rigorously fact-check every social media post you receive before sharing it with others, your roommate might put out every conspiracy theory on full blast, simply to enjoy the ensuing chaos.

Additionally, the penalties for violating one's own or society's ethical code can vary widely, with some bad actors allowed to act with impunity while others are shunned for minor offenses. It's like when one of your siblings gets away with everything, but Mom cracks down on you for one faux pas because "You're the good one and you should know better!" Perhaps the best way we can look at ethics, especially in comparison with the law, is that the legal system outlines *what you can and can't do*, while ethics help you figure out *what you should or shouldn't do.*

Why Ethics Matter

If we have a legal system that sets standards, establishes order, and punishes the guilty, ethics would seem to be superfluous at best and annoyingly limiting at worst. Organizations often establish ethical codes that outline lofty goals stated in self-righteous terms, sometimes projecting an arrogance as to how they see themselves and what social mores they will support. Ethics often serve as a scapegoat when people fail, as occurs when some argue that they refused to lower themselves to the standards of their "unethical competitors" in order to get ahead. However, the problem with saying that ethics are not needed in light of the existence of laws is that the law steps in only *after* someone has behaved in a way that violates societal rules. The goal of ethics is to establish a set of agreements we can each value and abide by for the betterment of society.

Think about it this way: if you are late for your final exam and the only parking spot available is designated for drivers with disabilities, would you park there? A lot of people wouldn't do it, because in most places the fine can run into the hundreds of dollars, and you'll spend half the day trying to get your car back from the impound yard. However, if you knew that the person who checked the parking lot for vehicle violations was on vacation that week and that no one would catch you, would you do it then? That's where ethics and moral reasoning start to come into play.

Ethics allow us to self-regulate our behavior to be the best versions of ourselves and help us interact with others in a better way. Here are the things that ethics do for us every day, whether we know it or not:

Establishment of Trust

Each day we engage in behaviors that we have no real right to expect will turn out well for us. Here are three simple scenarios you might face at any point in your college career:

1. You need to wake up early for a test, so you ask one of your roommates to make sure you're conscious and moving by 7 a.m.

2. A friend asks to borrow your car for the night, and you agree, as long as she returns the car with a full tank of gas before you have to go to class in the morning.

3. Your tuition bill is due tomorrow by noon, so you call home to remind your parents that they promised to cover the bill this semester. Mom says she will deposit some money in your bank account so you can pay it before the deadline.

What gives you any right to expect that any of these people will do what they promised? Or worse, why didn't your roommate get you good and drunk in a game of beer pong so you'd not only oversleep but wake up with a splitting headache? Why didn't your friend not only fail to fill the tank, but let the car run in the driveway until the tank was empty? Why didn't Mom head to a local casino, saddle up at the roulette table, and put your tuition money on 23 red?

Did you ever consider any of those things as a real possibility, even though none of them were illegal?

Of course you didn't. You like your roommate enough to live with them every day, you have a long-term relationship with your friend who always lives up to her word, and Mom always came through for you in the past, so there's no reason to think she wouldn't now. In each case, you have essentially extended a form of societal credit to these people in the form of trust. What ethics do is allow us to extend similar credit to more people, more often, and on much more important topics.

Ethics allow us to develop trust in other people, with the idea that their words and actions have value both in a given exchange and during a protracted relationship. The more often people behave in an ethical format, based on how we define ethics, the more likely we are to trust them and value our interactions with them. Without ethics, we would have no real reason to trust anything that anyone does.

Shared Understanding of Values

Ethical codes embody a society's common understanding of how each individual should behave. Societies, organizations, and even loosely connected groups of people who choose to spend time together need to have a set of norms and values that outline what everyone believes in so that they can coexist. The collective then comes to follow these rules of conduct, with corrective action applied to people who violate the ethical standards. People who continue to act in a way that doesn't live up to these shared values will likely be removed from the group so that it can continue to function as a whole.

These ethical **paradigms**, or patterns of basic assumptions and shared understandings, do not cover every possible ethical approach people will take to social interaction. In some cases, people find themselves vacillating between two or more ethical codes, while in other cases, people have forged their own approaches to ethics that make sense to them. Think about it this way: if two people witnessed an armed robbery and they both knew the robber, the ethical standards each holds might make a difference in their actions. One of the people might feel compelled to seek out the police, identify the robber, and even help the authorities bring this person to justice. The other person might abide by a code that states, "Don't be a snitch." Therefore, that person chooses not to say anything to the police about the crime and might even deny knowing the robber if asked about it. This difference between what each person values would likely lead to a conflict between them in relation to a shared sense of values.

An ethical code that provides equality among participants places a high value on fairness. A code that values outcomes will place a limited value on the importance of procedure or process. The degree to which we individually see merit in these and other values will allow us to gravitate toward other people who are willing to act in ways we accept and appreciate.

Respect for All Participants

Ethics outlines the way in which all participants within a group, organization, or society are expected to respect others and how they can expect to be treated by other members. This level of shared respect allows the continuation of societal activities because people understand their roles as well as the roles of others. Therefore, they spend less time concerning themselves with each action they take but rather are guided by an overall sense of what is right and wrong, based on that respect they have for each other. In short, it is not about you and me, it is about us.

SOME BASIC ETHICAL MODELS

LEARNING OBJECTIVES

LO 2: Identify and explain the four basic ethical philosophies outlined in the chapter.

Ethics tend to operate on a sliding scale in which the needs of individuals, the values of society, and the sense of "doing good" vary based on personal interpretation and cultural understanding. Along that scale are various forms of ethical understanding that tend to fall into one of two typologies: **absolute ethics** and **situational ethics**.

People who follow absolute ethics, or absolutists, rely on a concept of clear demarcations between right and wrong, with ethical behaviors fitting into one or the other of these categories. If an action is found to be "right," the ethical standard dictates that the individual will react in a specific way; if the action is found to be "wrong," the ethics demand that the individuals pursue a separate set of actions.

People who follow situational ethics, or situationalists, view ethical cases on an individual basis, relying heavily on moralistic reasoning and rational choices. People who operate under situational ethical codes tend to look for ways to explore nuances associated with their decisions, relying on relativism to help them determine the best possible outcomes.

In other words, if absolutism is about black-and-white choices, situationalism spends more time in the gray areas. Instead of the "yes/no" dichotomous answer an absolutist would present, a situationalist would usually answer, "It depends."

Numerous ethical experts and authors have outlined several of the better known ethical standards, which are listed here so you can see which ones typify which typologies.[4] Read on and see if you can find where your own sense of ethical behavior lies (see Table 15.1).

Immanuel Kant came up with the categorical imperative, an absolutist approach to ethics.

iStockPhoto.com/PanosKarapanagiotis

Aristotle's golden mean is an example of an ethical philosophy that falls under situational ethics.

iStockPhoto.com/Grafissimo

TABLE 15.1 ■ Ethical Philosophers and Philosophies

Paradigm	Philosopher	Basic Concept	Example
Golden mean	Aristotle	● Ethics are best served when equality among participants is promoted, thus leading to the highest level of collective good. ● The golden mean seeks to find the "sweet spot" in which all participants receive as much benefit as possible without costing any other participant too much. ● The goal is to make everyone relatively happy or to keep everyone relatively unharmed.	● A public relations practitioner needs to create a press release for a client regarding a recall of broccoli salad because of the presence of a deadly bacteria. ● The practitioner would want to alert the public in a way that allows shoppers to avoid the food, without unnecessarily damaging the client's reputation, thus providing all participants with a benefit.
Categorical imperative	Immanuel Kant	● This absolutist approach believes that all cultures provide a set of moral principles that dictate what is right and what is wrong. ● Within each of these cultures, there exists an ethical code that dictates how someone should or should not act. ● People within a culture will come to an agreement as to how to act and expect that everyone will follow it.	● Reporters at a news organization believe that lying in furtherance of a story is unethical. ● Not only do the reporters prize the value of honesty within their organization, but they also believe that their sources should also prize honesty as an ethical standard.
Principle of utility	John Stuart Mill	● The goal is to maximize the overall net benefit or minimize the net harm for the group as a collective, even if it disadvantages individuals within that group. It places the needs of the many above the needs of the few.	● A reporter might find out that a local company is dumping toxic sludge into an area river, contaminating the drinking water of the 50,000 nearby residents. ● After the reporter breaks the story, the company is sued and goes out of business, costing one hundred local people their jobs. However, the fifty thousand residents can drink the water safely.

Paradigm	Philosopher	Basic Concept	Example
Veil of ignorance	John Rawls	• This form of absolutism states that equality is the key to ethical behavior, thus offering no favor or privilege to anyone based on status, social condition, or other differences among people. • This is best reflected in the statement that "justice is blind," allowing all people equal access to benefits or requiring that all people share in negative outcomes.	• A football coach institutes a curfew and states that anyone who breaks it will be benched for the championship game. • The star quarterback and the backup punter break curfew and get caught. • Clearly, the quarterback is more valuable to the team than the backup punter. It might also be true that the quarterback broke curfew by only five minutes, while the punter was out until breakfast the next day. • However, under this philosophy, both players will be treated equally and neither will play in the game.

These and other ethical models invite individuals to determine what they value and how that relates to their actions. Although individuals or even groups can disagree with certain ethical rules, the presence of ethical standards means that individuals will be held to account for their actions as they support or undermine the social contract that governs a society.

A DEEPER LOOK: ETHICS REQUIRE ACCOUNTABILITY

Regardless of how well any of us tries, we are going to screw up in life. Our mistakes can be held to account in numerous ways, depending on what we do and how we do it. For example, if you're supposed to wear gloves while working with a tool and you fail to do so, the tool could cut you, leading to a nasty wound and a subsequent scar. If you fail to turn in your homework on time or blow off your final exam, you might fail a class and be forced to pay to take it again next semester, setting your graduation date back a year. If you steal a car or rob a bank, you will likely be arrested, tried, convicted, and sent to prison for an appreciable part of your life.

Like these other personal failures, ethical breaches carry consequences as well and we must be held to account for our actions. Unlike these other mistakes, the cause and effect of the actions and our punishments aren't guaranteed or instantaneous. In our previous examples, the tool doesn't know it's hurting you, and it's not looking for you to make amends of some kind. The professor and you will both move forward, as you can both blame the other for this negative outcome, but it won't really matter, so long as you pass the class next time. Even in the case of a crime, you never have to actually admit that you committed the offense or show any sense of remorse for your actions. The court can convict you without forcing you to admit anything or apologize for it.

When we fail ethically, we create a rift of credibility between us and the society in which we live. When it comes to mass media outlets, ethical mishaps can lead people to think less of the media organizations and disbelieve individual practitioners' work. This limits media professionals' ability to be effective as they try to provide their consumers with information, help them make decisions, or purchase products. To that end, ethical failures require members of the media to fess up when something goes wrong and explain how they're going to work to make things right in the future.

No one likes admitting to being wrong but, interestingly enough, when you do so, people tend to be more willing to forgive your transgressions and more willing to believe you the next time. That said, you can only apologize so many times for making errors before people will give up all hope that you know anything at all, so the overall goal is to make sure you keep your ethical lapses to a minimum.

Beyond simply admitting fault, it can be important to explain the how and the why associated with mistakes. Some mistakes are errors based on simple things like mishearing a quote or transposing a couple of letters in someone's name while typing. Those aren't as egregious as ethical lapses, such as publishing completely fabricated stories while maintain that there are true.

That said, repeated small errors can lead to an erosion of trust, so fixing them and apologizing can make a difference. So can explaining what happened and how you plan to prevent it from happening again. When people see you as honest, contrite, and forward thinking, they are more willing to believe you are being accountable. This can help restore lost credibility and keep your relationship strong moving forward.

THE BASIC ELEMENTS OF MEDIA ETHICS

LEARNING OBJECTIVES

LO 3: Define the key ethical tenets associated with mass media practitioners and how they apply to their work.

Within the field of mass media, practitioners rely on various codes and standards that outline how they should behave while they conduct their work, including the ways in which they interact with the public and the content they publish for their audiences. Organizations like the Society of Professional Journalists, the National Press Photographers Association, the Public Relations Society of America, the American Advertising Federation, and others have established ethical codes for practitioners within their disciplines to help guide their choices.

Although each discipline varies on how it approaches formulating its ethical standards, several elements remain at the core of what professional media operatives should and should not do.

Here is a brief overview of those elements and how they can play out in the field:

- Honesty versus deceit
- Accuracy versus misrepresentations
- Diversity versus stereotyping
- Independence versus conflicts of interest

Let's look more closely at how these issues play into ethics.

Honesty versus Deceit

Credibility is the currency of all forms of mass media, and without it, practitioners aren't going to be worth very much. One of the easiest ways to destroy credibility is to engage in deceptive practices, which is why most media ethical codes emphasize honesty above all else. For example, in June 2022, *USA Today* retracted 23 articles that staff member Gabriela Miranda wrote over the previous year after an internal audit revealed that she likely fabricated sources. Miranda resigned during the audit. Her college paper, *The Red & Black* at the University of Georgia, underwent a similar audit after the *USA Today* situation came to light. The staff there found an additional fourteen articles that could not be substantiated, leading them to make corrections or clarifications to their archives.[5]

Media practitioners need to tell the truth to the people with whom they interact. News reporters are expected to identify themselves as such before approaching potential sources. Writers of books and movies are expected to avoid taking the works and ideas of others to claim as their own. Advertising professionals are expected to communicate honestly with clients regarding what is and is not acceptable when it comes to ad campaigns. Public relations practitioners are expected to maintain honest relationships with news reporters, outside organizations, and others who rely on their honesty to make decisions. Honesty and openness is often referred to as transparency, the idea that media workers are not attempting to hide something from public view.

All media professionals are to hold themselves to the highest standards in working with others, especially those who are less familiar with what they do. Therefore, they shouldn't make promises they can't keep, trick a source into telling them something they wouldn't otherwise disclose, or plagiarize the work of others. Professionals need to treat others with dignity and respect while they conduct their business.

Accuracy versus Misrepresentations

Both honesty and accuracy relate to the concept of fairness. Both require media professionals to be on their best behavior while gathering information and producing content. A distinction you can make is that honesty and fairness tend to relate to *how* we work with other people, while accuracy and fairness tend to reside *in* the work product itself.

Mass media workers have the unenviable and almost impossible task of needing to be right all the time. You can publish five hundred pieces of content that are perfect, building your credibility one grain of sand at a time, only to have one error arise and wash it all away like a tidal wave. It can feel frustrating and completely unfair that this is how things work, but the public has imbued in us a sacred trust that requires us to do everything we can to tell them only what we can prove, so we need to take that to heart.

To be accurate above all else, which multiple ethical codes state as a core principle, media practitioners are expected to verify all the information they put forth as fact. As we noted in earlier chapters, fields like advertising are allowed to engage in certain levels of puffery, and some websites can rely on occasional hyperbole to communicate their intentions without breaking the public trust.

It isn't enough to publish factual information in today's digital age; we must also diligently avoid misrepresenting reality. Individual events should not be reported without the context in which they occurred. For example, in 2021, social media users and some television commenters paired two of President Joe Biden's tweets from different times to make a point that Biden was being hypocritical. In one tweet, he had condemned then president Donald Trump's efforts to limit travel to the United States from certain African countries. In the second one, he stated his decision to restrict travel from other countries on that continent. On its face, this would seem to be a legitimate concern, but the context of the tweets is crucial. The earlier tweet was in reference to Trump's attempted expansion of a ban on people from largely Muslim countries. The later tweet was in reference to health concerns regarding a spike in COVID-19 cases in the countries targeted for restricted travel.[6] To what degree people agree or disagree with either policy is a matter of opinion, but it is important to understand the context of each policy statement before making a decision.

Diversity versus Stereotyping

The media serve as the window through which many people see things they will never personally experience. What we show them through that window and how well it represents the totality of a human experience requires us to go outside of our comfort zones and push back against our own biases. Beyond showcasing people of all backgrounds, areas, and experiences, we need to make sure we are representing them in a way that avoids characterizing them through simplified and generalized traits.

This concept is called often called stereotyping, but that's not entirely accurate. **Stereotypes**, in and of themselves, are useful shortcuts your brain builds over time to help eliminate your need to relearn everything every time you encounter a situation. Think about the last time you went through a drive-through at a coffee chain: you probably didn't even look at the menu, because you knew what you wanted. The shiny silver box talking to you didn't confuse you, because you've heard people take your order through it before. You just made your order, drove around, and paid for your coffee. What makes this possible is the stereotyping your brain does to get you from point A to point B to point C without having to think a lot.

When this becomes problematic is when this mental process applies to negative constructs about individual people based on preconceived notions regarding a specific aspect of that person's being. This is better known as **negative social stereotyping**, and it's where media professionals need to be careful about how they portray individuals. When this occurs, it evokes prejudices and discrimination based on race, gender, sexual orientation, creed, social status, and more. It can occur in how news agencies report events, how movie writers craft roles, or how advertisements promote products.

Ethical codes in mass media require practitioners to reject stereotypes and challenge assumptions that are likely to promote ignorance and reinforce biases. For example, in 2018, Heineken ran an advertisement for its new light beer that drew sharp criticism for being racist. The ad shows a bartender sliding a bottle of Heineken Light down the bar to a patron past several people of color. When the bottle arrives at a woman with the lightest skin of all the patrons, the narrator says, "Sometimes lighter is better."[7] The company apologized for its approach and pulled the ad from circulation.[8]

In 2020, the *Kansas City Star* newspaper used the occasion of its 140th anniversary to apologize retroactively for its long history of disenfranchising people of color in its coverage. The paper dug deep into its archives to reveal the ways in which Black citizens were stereotyped while white citizens were often treated preferentially. In addition to running a six-part series on the paper's shameful past, the editor wrote an open letter to the public, outlining specific stereotyping transgressions and discussing ways in which the paper would work to regain the trust of all community members moving forward.[9]

Diversity is also a crucial element within media institutions themselves. In 2021, the World Economic Forum's Global Future Council on Media, Entertainment and Sport released a report titled "Tackling Diversity and Inclusion in the Newsroom." This study noted that a lack of diversity within media institutions will lead to a fundamental lack of trust and legitimacy in the eyes of the public. The report noted that both the #MeToo and Black Lives Matter movements revealed how a lack of gender and racial diversity within newsrooms led to journalistic failures in how these efforts were covered.[10]

The report also noted that diverse media companies outperform those that lack in diversity, as the collective base of social knowledge is often broader and deeper in the organization. These institutions also have a more complex understanding as to how best to cover issues related to gender, race, and sexual orientation.

Media practitioners should work not only to defeat negative social stereotypes but also to amplify voices that often go unheard. This country has long protected speech, the press, and free expression with the idea that if everyone has a voice is given an opportunity to be heard, the best possible ideas will emerge, and we will all be better for having listened. A key way in which this can occur is through the diversifying of media operations and the expansion of perspectives associated with this improved diversity.

Independence versus Conflicts of Interest

As we discussed, the purpose of ethics is to provide a shared understanding of societal values. When bias or pure self-interest enters the equation, that shared understanding can be undermined quickly and lead to negative outcomes for everyone involved. This is why most ethical codes prize independence and integrity as essential to operating in the best possible way.

In news media, independence relates to the way in which we do not allow our work to be swayed by outside influence. These influences could come in the form of a source asking us to avoid covering their arrest for drinking and driving, or a business owner offering us some free gift cards if we write a glowing review of their store. In advertising or public relations, we can see influence in terms of threats, in which clients will ask us to go against our own sense of right or wrong, lest they take their business (and money) to a competitor.

Radio suffered through a difficult scandal during the late 1950s, in which disc jockeys were provided with money and gifts from record promoters to play certain songs and bands in heavy rotation. This "payola" controversy cost numerous people their jobs, including famous radio personality Alan Freed, and undermined the music business for years to come.[11] These individuals were manipulated into furthering the careers of some individuals while undercutting the careers of others through their actions. Abiding by an ethical code that prized independence would have had these disc jockeys turning down bribes and playing music based on their own independent choices, allowing listeners to determine what was or wasn't worthy of praise.

A conflict of interest, such as the one in the payola scandal, is a situation in which the independence of an individual is called into question because of potential biases. In many cases, media practitioners find themselves internally conflicted because of competing loyalties. As we discussed at the beginning of the chapter, New York governor Andrew Cuomo was battling to save his political career in 2021 after multiple allegations of sexual harassment emerged in the media. His brother, Chris Cuomo, found himself in the middle of a potential conflict of interest because of his role as a news anchor for CNN.[12] Journalism ethics codes suggest that journalists recuse themselves when situations like this arise to avoid the appearance that the journalists might be biased. Instead, Chris not only consulted with his brother's office to keep him up to date about what was being reported, but he also dictated statements for his brother to use in the media. Chris also actively reached out to news sources and other journalists for information about the situation. Andrew resigned in August 2021 amid the scandal, and CNN fired Chris in December 2021 upon learning of these actions (see Table 15.2).[13]

TABLE 15.2 ■ Case Studies in Ethics

Situation	Question to Consider	Real-World Outcomes
When a person is arrested, law enforcement officials take a "mug shot" photo of them as a part of the person's criminal record. Media outlets often run these photos along with stories about the arrests, arguing that they can enhance media coverage. Some civil rights organizations say that these images of unconvicted citizens can remain online for years, damaging their reputations and furthering stereotypes.	Should media outlets run mug shot photos online in association with reports on arrests?	In 2021, media outlets, including chains like Gannett, implemented policies against running these photos. In addition, they have removed previous mug shot galleries from their websites, stating that these images feed into negative racial and social stereotypes.
To obtain information otherwise unavailable, reporters will occasionally "go undercover" to get a story. This often entails pretending to be someone they aren't, lying to a source, or relying on other forms of deception.	Should journalists deceive people to get a story if they can't get it any other way and that story is in the public's interest to know?	• In 2007, journalist Ken Silverstein went undercover as a member of an investment group with ties to a Stalinist dictatorship to expose how willing Washington, D.C., lobbyists were to work with them. He was criticized for his efforts but was otherwise unscathed. • In 2015, a student journalist from the University of Missouri went undercover at rural gas stations to find out if they were selling a synthetic form of marijuana called Spice. She then interviewed experts about how stores were getting around laws meant to regulate this kind of product. Her efforts won her a Kansas City Press Club award.
Online comments and reviews can provide people with information about everything from a restaurant's food quality to a hotel's cleanliness. Some organizations hire companies to monitor sites that host reviews and request that negative reviews be removed. On some company websites, social media managers are able to delete negative comments.	Is it right to eliminate legitimate questions or criticisms from online outlets just because a company doesn't like them?	In 2012, Paspaley jewelry received scores of negative Facebook comments after a news report looked into the death of one of the company's pearl divers. The comments that questioned the company's safety record were deleted, with a spokesperson saying it did so because the posts were "offensive." The company later apologized for the deletions.

(Continued)

TABLE 15.2 ■ Case Studies in Ethics (Continued)

Situation	Question to Consider	Real-World Outcomes
In the music industry, more popular artists receive larger portions of certain types of revenue, including money paid to streaming services. Some industry professionals and third-party organizations have found ways to rely on "streaming farms" of bots to artificially inflate the number of times a song or artist is played, often for a fee.	Is this approach to increasing streams fair to musical artists and streaming services?	In 2019, major music labels and streaming services signed a code of conduct that declared streaming manipulation unethical, with each signatory vowing not to engage in the practice. However, in 2021, multiple third-party organizations were still engaging in streaming manipulations on behalf of artists who sought "astronomical" numbers.
Online influencers often discuss certain products or brands as part of their social media posts or web-based content. Some influencers do this because they are provided with free samples of products or they are paid a certain amount of money to promote a brand.	How transparent should influencers be about their financial relationships with the companies they promote online?	In 2019, the Federal Trade Commission published a series of guidelines and suggestions for online influencers to help them disclose sponsorships and promotions to the public.

WORKING THROUGH ETHICAL DILEMMAS

LEARNING OBJECTIVES

LO 4: Outline the steps in working through an ethical dilemma and explain the value of each one as a part of the process.)

Whether you are an advertising executive assessing a creative brief, a movie producer casting a role, or a news reporter working through an important story, you will face ethical dilemmas that require you to make choices and deal with consequences. One of the most important things to understand about ethical dilemmas is that they rarely have a simple solution, and you won't always feel you did the right thing at the end of the day.

The ethical paradigms and the professional organizations' ethical codes that we have studied will give you extra guidance. In addition, most companies or organizations that might employ you will have an in-house ethical code, which can outline the expectations of how you should act as a member of their group.

These useful tools can help you understand the ethical foundations by which you should abide, but they don't cover every possible situation. Even more, they rarely outline a process you can use to work through a dilemma once one presents itself. To help you with this, consider these steps that can help you determine how to make the best possible decision when faced with a specific situation:

- Assess the situation
- Identify the values
- Discuss the issue with others

Let's analyze how each step plays into this ethical process.

Assess the Situation

Before you decide how to proceed, you want to have as complete of a picture of the dilemma as possible. This means understanding the issue at hand, the decisions you are being asked to make, the pro and con arguments related to it, and the possible ramifications of any action you take. The more fully you understand each of these aspects of the problem, the better the chances are that you will make a better choice in what to do.

Mistakes occur when people attempt to act before they consider every aspect of the problem, hoping to cut off any further problems by acting quickly. Mistakes can also happen when people try to avoid making a decision as the situation continues to get worse while they try to wait it out. The goal of a media practitioner is to do research, ask relevant questions of the key players in the situation, make a choice of action, and stick with it. This first step also will help you better explain to others why you made the choice you did. This can help tamp down discord among people who might not understand your approach or choices.

Identify the Values

Many decisions we make are about the "what" (as in "What should we do?") and the "how" (as in "How are we going to get this done?). However, ethics requires you to answer the "why" of your choice: "Why am I doing what I'm doing?" For individuals, this can be difficult, because it requires self-reflective activities that can yield some uncomfortable answers. For media practitioners, it becomes even more difficult because you aren't in this alone.

In identifying the values you are promoting when making any choice of action, you are determining what needs you are satisfying for yourself, your organization, your audience, and your society. For example, a local radio personality might have access to a famous pop star's newest song before anyone else, but they have been asked not to play the song before a certain date. Should the DJ play it or respect the request? That depends on the values involved. The DJ will likely become known as the person who played the song, perhaps bringing them personal fame. The band's management and ownership group will likely be displeased, leading to some potential conflicts later between the station and the band. The station might become famous or it might get sanctioned. The fans, however, might love it and be grateful to hear it early, thus supporting both the station and the DJ.

The choices you make in a situation like this reflect the values you hold dear. If you put yourself above others, it can isolate you in a way that limits your ability to function in the field later in life. If you put loyalty to an audience above loyalty to a corporate entity, it might benefit the people you serve, while simultaneously undermine your ability to serve them effectively in the future. Again, the choices you make will have consequences, and knowing what you value will help you live with those consequences.

Discuss the Issue with Others

One of the many benefits of working in a media organization is the collective knowledge of your coworkers. If you join a newsroom, television or radio station, public relations firm, or advertising agency, you will become part of a group of people who have done the job for quite some time. This institutional memory and experience will allow you to learn things without having to act totally on your own. These people can be your guides and your safety nets as you navigate the tasks associated with the job.

An ethical decision may be the responsibility of a single person who makes the final choice, but that choice can be better informed if it comes from a discussion with colleagues. These people not only bring prior experiences to the table, but they bring varied viewpoints based on their life experience as well. This is where diversity can play a huge role in making the best possible decisions. The voices of people who are not like you can give you various angles to consider that go beyond your own experiences. In addition, they can help you assess the way in which certain segments of your audience will react to the choice you make, and help you understand what the ramifications of that choice will be.

MEDIA LITERACY MOMENT: GAINING ACCESS WHILE RETAINING ETHICS

Recall the Adam Schefter and Katie Couric situations that we related at the beginning of the chapter. These renewed the debate in media about the ways in which journalists gain access to important information.

Katie Couric declined to publish disparaging comments Supreme Court justice Ruth Bader Ginsberg made about the "take a knee" movement because she was fond of Ginsberg and didn't want to make her look bad.

Keith Beaty/ZUMA Press/Newscom

To become a successful media professional, you need to have information that matters to people and the ability to get it out to your audience first. This means you need access to sources who know things and are willing to share those things with you.

Journalists work hard to gain the trust of sources by presenting information they receive accurately and fairly. They seek to balance the public's right to know with individual's rights to be left alone. They also develop relationships with individual sources or specific organizations to demonstrate their honesty and integrity. That said, journalists are also human, so they know that sources who provide them with something will inevitably expect some sort of favor in return.

Journalists don't provide sources with money or gifts in exchange for access (at least the good ones don't), but that doesn't mean their close relationships with sources are harmless. A journalist with a strong connection to a good source is unlikely to dig into a rumor about that source that could lead to the source's suffering some negative consequences. In common parlance, people tend not to bite the hand that feeds them.

For example, in 2021, a story emerged that officials in the Biden administration required journalists to submit quotes they wanted to use from White House personnel for approval if they wanted to attach that person's name to the quote. This practice gave the administration editorial discretion to approve or veto each quote, regardless of the degree of accuracy that quote contained. Although the practice became public during President Joe Biden's first term, reporters said that both the Trump and Obama administrations had done this as well. The reporters frequently acquiesced because they were afraid that refusing to do so would cut off their access.[14]

Conversely, in 2019, the staff at *The Panther* at Chapman University turned down an incredible opportunity to be the only press allowed to cover former President George W. Bush's speech during a private event on campus. The students declined the invitation because it came with the caveat that Bush's people would have to approve everything *The Panther* had planned to run before it published anything. Louisa Marshall, the editor of the paper, said that her staff refused to bend its ethics with regard to prior review, even if it meant an exclusive story.[15]

In these and other cases, the choices these journalists make both benefit and harm their audiences. Without the sources providing information, the public would be uninformed about subjects that are of interest to them or that could influence their lives. Conversely, the sources who require journalists to restrict content or journalists who decide to shield their sources from public criticism often paint an incomplete or inaccurate picture for their readers.

Apply some critical thinking skills to examine the Schefter and Couric cases, as well as the quote-approval policy, to determine what you think about these requests and their subsequent outcomes after the fact. It might also be helpful to discuss this with your classmates.

THE NEXT STEP: Based on what you have learned to this point about ethics, determine how you would have chosen to act if you were put in a position to disclose or withhold information you received from a valuable source. Apply whichever ethical paradigm that you feel best fits your approach to ethics. Discuss your decision with your classmates and see how other would have proceeded.

DETERMINING YOUR OWN APPROACH TO ETHICS

LEARNING OBJECTIVES

LO 5: Examine several principles that guide ethical development to help you shape your own approach to ethics.

You might wonder how your own values and beliefs can lead you to adopt the best possible ethical code as a media practitioner or at least a decent member of society. Unfortunately, personal ethics aren't like a vision board, where you paste up a bunch of creeds and mottos and think your job is done. You can't sit down with a pen and paper and make an "ethics list" that you will abide by forever. Even the concept of what is and isn't acceptable behavior can shift over time.

Ethics require you to understand what type of person you hope to be as you relate to other people. In addition, it requires you to assess the type of people you want to relate to from the position of who you are and what you do. If you see practitioners in your area of the discipline acting in a certain way, it doesn't necessarily follow that you need to act that way to succeed. If you object to certain actions or behaviors because they don't "feel right," that can go a long way to helping you craft your own sense of ethics as well.

Although there isn't a kit or a formula to developing ethics, consider the following thoughts as you work on yours:

- Seek humanity
- Predict the impact of your actions
- Learn from experience
- Review and respect the codes of others
- Learn to live with your choices

Let's walk through these steps.

Seek Humanity

Ethics start with personal choices and then move to broader outcomes from those choices. Inherent within each ethical code is a simple goal: do the right thing. What "right" is often lies in the eye of the beholder, but certain shared values can help you determine how best to establish an ethical paradigm that you believe to be "right" for yourself, the people you care about, and the broader society at large.

Craig Silverman of the Poynter Institute noted that media ethics are "most effective when they flow from human values, emotions and, of course, action." He noted that, as much as technology has forced us to reexamine how we practice media ethics, ethical principles must come from our humanity.[16]

If there is one thing that ethics attempt to provide people, it is the ability to coexist in a harmonious way. At the core of this is a need to seek humanity in all of our ethical actions. Shared goals, social justice, collective beliefs, and societal growth all emerge when we aspire to improving the human condition for as many people as possible in every ethical choice we make.

Predict the Impact of Your Actions

Reflection is a crucial part of establishing and shaping personal ethical standards. This process allows us to see what we did and what the results were. As media professionals, our actions have impacts that reach far beyond ourselves and even those people we assume will be affected. Like tossing a pebble in a puddle, we create ripples that continue on long after our initial action.

In 2021, rumors began circulating on TikTok that students across the United States were preparing for a national day of school violence on December 17. The threats were vague and didn't have a specific source, but a number of them recommended that fellow students stay home to avoid mass shootings, bomb attacks, and other similar terrorist actions. The more people saw these messages, the more they passed them along, warning others of these potential dangers and helping the message go viral.

In the end, no school reported a violent attack, but that didn't mean that these posts didn't lead to harm. School districts added security or closed school on that day, for fear of what could happen. The U.S. Department of Homeland Security stated that it could not locate evidence this was a credible threat, but it remained on alert for potential outbreaks of violence, as did the Federal Bureau of Investigation.[17]

Our ability to foresee those impacts and the people affected by them can make the difference in how we choose to act. In many cases, the impacts are easy to see, based primarily on the simplicity of your choice and the number of people involved. In other cases, the most devastating impacts injure people or groups you hadn't even considered. The degree to which you are willing and able to examine your potential actions in relation to potential outcomes will establish the degree to which you are successful at building an ethical code with which you can live.

Learn from Experience

Many of the colloquialisms we use demonstrate the value of experience: "Practice makes perfect" and "Experience is the best teacher" are just a few ways in which we say that we learn a lot from doing things over and over again. Working through ethical dilemmas and using them to shore up your own sense of ethics is no different.

In June 2020, UK broadcast editor-at-large Dorothy Byrne spoke at a Reuters Institute for the Study of Journalism seminar, where she explained the ways in which journalists had erred in their coverage of the COVID-19 pandemic. She explained that many of the problems in the earliest coverage of the outbreak were based on weak data literacy among reporters, a failure to seek informed scientists as sources, and the lack of diversity among sources. Byrne said that her own newsroom was just as guilty of this as any other media outlet, but that she and her colleagues worked to learn from these shortcomings.[18] To improve future coverage, Byrne suggested seeing where the media fell short in its reporting and then looking for ways to correct it through improved research, closing knowledge gaps, and looking beyond familiar sources for a better and broader set of views. Continued use of critical thinking will improve future outcomes, she added.

Each time you make a choice, you see a result. That result will provide you with feedback on how you feel about the choice you made. In a personal sense, you have to live with those choices. As a mass media practitioner, a lot of other people will have to live with the results of those choices as well. In reflecting on each choice and outcome, you will see your ethics continue to develop. If your choices yield outcomes you find acceptable, you will codify your ethical approach. If you decide the outcomes are unacceptable, you will likely modify your ethical approach when making future choices. Each choice will help fine-tune your sense of ethical behavior, a process that will continue for as long as you value ethics.

Review and Respect the Codes of Others

It's not enough to establish a series of ethical principles for yourself and live with them. You must understand that you will not conduct your actions in a vacuum, where only your thoughts and choices matter. Many times, you will find yourself at odds with people who do not play the ethics game the same way you do and don't understand your approach to ethical dilemmas at all. This diversity of opinion can lead to a broadening of your own ethical ideas or a case of butting heads over the choices that need to be made.

Jeanne Bourgault, the president and CEO of Internews, noted in 2021 that gender, racial, and social diversity in a media operation can expand the diversity of thought within the organization, giving it an opportunity to better succeed in the long term. As the world becomes more diverse, media operations must act to match that diversity if they wish to see improvements in public trust and credibility. As individuals from varied backgrounds interact, they can see the social, political, racial and economic forces that helped shape each other's ethical perspectives. Remaining open to those differences and respecting the experiences of others can improve both internal operations and external perceptions of media organizations.[19]

You need to understand that ethics are both a personal and a professional component of life, particularly in relation to mass media fields. What is acceptable in PR might be abhorrent to a news journalist, or vice versa. What you personally believe may come into direct conflict with the perspective your boss has about a situation. To find both the best ethical path forward as well as a peaceful solution to a specific problem, you need to review the ethical codes of other people and find ways to respect their positions. You may not necessarily agree with them, but respecting them means allowing others to provide you with information and opinions that they value. From there, you can look for ways to further the discussion in a productive way. After that, you can even reassess your own approaches based on what you have learned from these interactions.

Learn to Live with Your Choices

As we have discussed, no ethical decision is ever perfect. Regardless of your strong adherence to ethical codes, your discussions with others you respect, and your best of intentions in making a choice, someone (or many people) will not be happy with the choice you made. The louder those voices of displeasure get, the more compelled you may feel to change your mind or try to make everyone happy with another decision that can undercut your original decision.

The goal of working through an ethical dilemma step by step is to make the best possible choice. Even situations that have nothing but bad outcomes have one option that's somehow better than all the others. Once you go through this process before you make the choice, you have to learn to live with it, even as negative outcomes and personal criticism occur.

A concept familiar to race car drivers and off-roading enthusiasts might help you here: you need to pick a line and drive. In the case of a crash on the track, drivers are told to pick a spot on the track and drive directly to it. The more the driver tries to weave in and out of the wrecks and the flying metal, the more dangerous it will be. In terms of driving off road, a driver is taught to pick a destination and then assess which way is least likely to damage their vehicle or get it stuck.

The same kind of thinking needs to apply to your ethical choices. The more you start to flip-flop after making a decision, the greater the chances that more people will become exceedingly displeased with you. The more you try to avoid danger by dodging and ducking after the fact, the higher the risk that you'll do more harm than good.

This doesn't mean that you should never change your mind after making a choice. If it turns out you incorrectly understood something or circumstances change in a way that makes your choices foolish, you should reassess what is happening and work through the process again. At that point, if you want to change your mind, it might make sense to do so.

However, if every change you make is based on "Well, this person is now mad and I don't like that," you are destined to fail in this situation and erode the credibility you have built in the eyes of other people who are watching you.

Think about everything as best you can. Make a choice. Live with it.

JOBS IN MEDIA ETHICS

All media outlets require some level of ethical behavior for their employees, so ethics should be considered a crucial element in any form of media employment. Here are a few jobs in media that rely predominantly on ethics in their everyday operations.

Career Opportunity	Common Tasks
Ombudsman	• Address complaints levied against media outlets that require an outside examination • Mediate discussions between the public and media outlets • Work with media outlets to help them remain accountable to the audiences they serve
Independent fact checker	• Examine information spreading virally on the internet for accuracy • Research statements to determine their sources and the degree to which they might be rumors or misinformation • Present accurate content that sets the record straight for consumers concerned about the validity of the information they read elsewhere
Media ethics educator	• Develop educational content for businesses and organizations in media to help guide their employees • Outline specific rules and guidelines for "best practices" a business or organization should follow • Discuss specific ethical dilemmas as they relate to the organization and the particular area of the media field in which it operates

CHAPTER REVIEW

LO 1 **Understand the concept of ethics and why they matter in society, particularly for mass media professionals.**

- The term *ethics* is derived from the Greek word *ethos*, meaning "character," and the Latin word *mores*, meaning "customs." It is meant to explain the ways in which we should act for the overall betterment of society.
- Ethics help us determine how to behave as we look to be the best versions of ourselves. This improves our ability to interact with other people in society.
- Ethics also allow us to establish trust and share values with other people while we provide dignity and respect for all people

LO 2 **Identify and explain the four basic ethical philosophies outlined in the chapter.**

- The golden mean, which is usually associated with Aristotle, is a situational approach to ethics that states society is best served when equality among participants exists, thus leading to the highest level of collective good. This approach tries to balance positive or negative outcomes among all people in a group.
- The principle of utility, which is usually associated with John Stuart Mill, is a situational approach to ethics that seeks to maximize the overall net benefit or minimize the net harm for a group, even if it disadvantages individuals within that group. It places the needs of the many above the needs of the few.
- The categorical imperative, which is usually associated with Immanuel Kant, is an absolutist approach to ethics that indicates that all cultures provide for their people a set of moral principles that dictate what is right and what is wrong. Within each of these cultures, then, exists an ethical code or a set of ethical edicts that dictate how someone should or should not act.
- The veil of ignorance, which is usually associated with John Rawls, is an absolutist approach to ethics that offers no favor or privilege to anyone based on status, social condition, or other differences among people. This approach is best reflected in the statement that "justice is blind."

LO 3 Define the key ethical tenets associated with mass media practitioners and how they apply to their work.

- **Honesty:** Promotes truthfulness in all the ways that media professionals work with members of the public or gather and disseminate information. Practitioners attempt to avoid deceit whenever possible, because it can erode their credibility.
- **Accuracy:** Reinforces the importance of truth and improves the relationships between audience members and journalists. Practitioners attempt to avoid misrepresentations of information, regardless of how it could benefit them or a source, to demonstrate their commitment to serving their audience.
- **Diversity:** Promotes a wider array of perspectives and experiences to be showcased and shared among audience members by acknowledging differences among various races, genders, sexual orientations, or ethnic backgrounds. Practitioners attempt to avoid negative social stereotyping, because it reduces our understanding of others, and undercuts our shared human experience.
- **Independence:** Allows media professionals to perform their work without bias or compromise to serve only the public interest. Practitioners attempt to avoid conflicts of interest, because they create real or perceived biases that can diminish public opinion of the practitioners, their work, and their media outlets.

LO 4 Outline the steps in working through an ethical dilemma and explain the value of each one as a part of the process.

- **Assess the situation:** Before you decide how to proceed, you want to have as complete of a picture of the problem as possible. The more fully you understand it, the better the chances are that you will make a good decision regarding what to do.
- **Identify the values:** Good practitioners will understand what values exist in each aspect of the dilemma and what values any particular choice will represent. In other words, you are determining what needs you are satisfying for yourself, your organization, your audience, and your society in any ethical choice you make.
- **Discuss the issue with others:** To make the best possible decision, good practitioners tap into their coworkers' collective knowledge. This institutional memory and experience can expand their overall understanding of a situation and help them avoid mistakes.

LO 5 Examine several principles that guide ethical development to help you shape your own approach to ethics.

- **Seek humanity:** The goal of ethics is to assure people within a society that they are operating in a fair and decent environment. Shared goals, social justice, collective beliefs, and societal growth all emerge when we aspire to improving the human condition.
- **Predict the impact of your actions:** The concept of "look before you leap" can allow you to see the importance of exploring how your actions will affect others. Just like a stone creates ripples in a puddle beyond the initial impact, your actions have consequences you need to consider before you act.
- **Learn from experience:** Your previous successes and failures in making choices of an ethical nature can help you learn what to do and not to do in a given situation. If you can learn from each experience you have, you will build a storehouse of knowledge from which to draw each subsequent time you need to make an ethical decision.
- **Review and respect the codes of others:** Even when people disagree about ethical codes or choices, a shared sense of the value of ethics can help them come together. To understand that what you perceive to be "right" or "wrong" could differ from the perception of others is to help people coexist within a diverse society.

KEY TERMS

Absolute ethics
Categorical imperative
Ethics
Golden mean
Negative social stereotyping
Norm
Paradigms
Principle of utility
Situational ethics
Stereotypes
Veil of ignorance

DISCUSSION QUESTIONS

1. Based on what you read in this chapter, do you think ethics matter more or less in media compared with other occupations or organizations? What about compared with the interactions you have in your daily life? Why?
2. Of the four ethical paradigms discussed in the chapter, which one do you feel is closest to your own set of ethical values? If you have difficulty determining this, can you explain if you feel more like an absolutist or a situationalist? What about this ethical paradigm or position feels right to you?
3. In reviewing the four key values associated with media practitioners (honesty, accuracy, diversity, and independence), which is most important to you when you consider your media choices? Which one matters the least? Why?
4. Think back to a previous ethical dilemma you have faced. Did it turn out the way you thought it would? If you had a chance would you go back and do it differently? Do you think the three-step approach described in the text would have been helpful to you? Why or why not?

GLOSSARY

#fail: A hashtag that refers to an online mistake by a content creator that leads to a viral spread of the individual's embarrassing moment.

Absolute ethics: An approach to ethical behavior in which people rely on concepts of right and wrong to dictate how best to proceed in a given situation.

Absolute privilege: A right in the United States granted to judges and political officials to say things in their official roles without fear of being convicted of libel, regardless of the factual accuracy of their statements.

Achievers: Video game players who attempt to dominate the game through perseverance and effort.

Actualities: See **sound bites**.

Actual malice: A standard of fault in libel cases that requires the plaintiff to show that the defendant had a reckless disregard for the truth in publishing potentially libelous content. This is the standard public figures must prove to be successful in a libel suit.

Advertising: A form of mass communication that uses paid speech to persuade consumers to engage with a product, service, or idea.

Advertising agency: A business that connects companies and consumers in a mutually beneficial way for the purpose of engaging in paid, persuasive speech.

Advocacy: A public relations technique in which practitioners speak out in favor of their clients.

Affiliate: A broadcast station that is part of a larger network.

Agenda setting: Through emphasizing a topic in its coverage, media makes people think about a certain topic but does not influence *how* they think about it.

Amplitude modulation (AM): A form of radio broadcast that uses variations in signal strength to send messages via radio waves.

Arcade-style game: A type of video game in which a single player actively competes against the machine in a series of increasingly difficult tasks.

ARPANET: Created in 1966 as the first functional version of the internet.

Aspirational viewing: A reason people view television programs that focus on society's high achievers that inspire envy among their viewers.

Asynchronous gaming: A type of gaming in which players can choose to participate in various tasks whenever and wherever they see fit.

Audience: Individuals or a group of individuals who receive messages from senders.

Audion: Invented in 1906, this radio tube was the first practical amplifier used to boost the signal and improve audio quality.

Authoritarian system: A media structure in which content is controlled by the financial and governmental elites and authorities for the supposed good of society to reinforce the norms and values of the ruling class.

Autotelic experience: A component of flow that forges a connection between game and gamer in which people find satisfaction in the task regardless of outside rewards or penalties.

Banner ad: A form of online advertising in which a hyperlinked message is placed at the top of a webpage.

Bechdel test: A way to examine a movie for the prevalence of sexism. To pass the test, a movie must include two named female characters who speak to each other about something other than a man.

Benefits: The portion of an advertising message that explains the inherent value of product or service characteristics to potential buyers.

Bias: A form of prejudice for or against a specific topic, individual, or concept.

Billboard: A form of outdoor advertising that places large messages in public areas.

Binge watching: An approach to television viewing in which multiple episodes are consumed in a single sitting.

Blog: A shortened form of the term "web log," it serves as an online place for users to create, develop, and share informational content through diary-style posts.

Book banning: A censorship process in which governments or other organizations prevent individuals from purchasing or reading books through various official means.

Book challenge: An effort to prevent a book from being used in school curricula or being accessible in school environments.

Book pitch: A document presented from an author to a potential publisher that identifies the purpose and market for a book, as well as the credentials of the author.

Brand: A public image that reflects the values of an institution that resonates with an audience.

Broadcast radio: A form of audio communication that relies on over-the-air transmissions from senders to receivers, as opposed to digital or computerized transmission.

Browser: A software program or application that allows users to access information on the World Wide Web.

Campfire TV model: The earliest form of television viewing, in which people would gather around a single television at a given time and watch whatever was on at that point.

Categorical imperative: An absolutist approach to ethics in which all cultures rely on a set of moral principles that dictate what is right and wrong for all members of the collective, with the expectation that all members will abide by those principles.

Censorship: The elimination of content from the public environment.

Central route: Describes a path to persuasion that requires individuals to rely on the quality and volume of relevant information to be adequately convinced of a position. See **elaboration likelihood model (ELM)**.

Chain: A group of newspapers that serve different local markets but are owned by one individual or organization.

Challenge-skill balance: A component of flow that requires tasks to be slightly outside the individual's initial skill level.

Characteristics: The portion of an advertising message that outlines specific features associated with the product, service, or idea that can be clearly demonstrated or easily quantifiable.

Cinématographe: A film device pioneered by the Lumière brothers that was able to record film and project movies onto a screen.

Circulation: A measurement of reach for print publications that explains how many copies of a given issue are printed and distributed.

Citizen journalist: Anyone who serves as a source of information through an internet connection and a digital media device.

Clarity: A crucial aspect of public relations that requires practitioners to provide direct and effective messaging to the audience.

Classified advertising: One of the earliest forms of this type of communication, these messages are placed in text-based media by individuals who wish to buy or sell a good or service in hopes of connecting with someone capable of meeting their needs.

Commentary: A right to present one's own opinion without fear of engaging in libel, as part of a review or other non-news form of content.

Commission: The portion of an advertising sale that is given to the representative who sold the ad.

Common carriers: Businesses that provide services so vital to citizens that they are required to provide equitable services to the public.

Community antenna television: Also known as CATV, this approach to broadcasting used a single antenna to capture broadcast waves, with cables used to connect the users to that signal. This was a popular approach in communities where mountains or distance blocked direct individual access to broadcast waves.

Conflict: One of five interest elements that explain why a piece of media content has value to a reader. This element explains how mutually exclusive goals can create friction between people or organizations.

Conflict of interest: A potential entanglement that can call into question the independence and fair-mindedness of an individual because of potential biases.

Conglomerates: Extremely large multinational media companies that control multiple outlets across multiple platforms.

Consumer culture: A criticism of advertising stating that companies have used their messages to change desires into needs with the intent of increasing sales and profitability.

Consumer magazine: A form of publication that reaches out to people with an interest in a specific hobby, activity, or culture.

Content editor: An individual who works with the author to develop the structure of a book and assists in the drafting and rewriting stages of it.

Convergence: An approach to media that came to prominence in the late 1990s and early 2000s whereby news organizations operated as collective entities instead of separate media outlets, in an attempt to reach readers and viewers through print, broadcast, and online resources.

Cooperative game: A type of video game in which a collection of players operate collaboratively, with the goal of completing a difficult task or defeating the game itself.

Copy editor: An individual who reviews content for factual, grammatical, and style errors during the writing of a book.

Copyright: An intellectual property law that provides individuals with ownership writes over content they have created.

Credibility: The nature of being trustworthy, believable, and dependable that reflects an honesty of character and reliability.

Critical thinking: The ability to take charge of one's own mind for the purpose of making better overall decisions through intensive analysis.

Cross-ownership rule: A 1975 FCC rule that forbid newspaper ownership groups from purchasing and operating a television station within the same market. The rule was eliminated in 2001.

Cultivation theory: A mass media research area that examines the ways in which heavy television viewing influences people's worldviews compared with light viewing.

Cuneiform: The first known form of writing, in which individuals used river reeds to press wedge-shaped symbols into clay tablets.

Cyberbullying: A form of online harassment in which children and young adults are targeted by their peers with persistent threats and intimidation.

Cylinder press: An advancement in publication that emerged in the 1810s, which significantly increased the speed and efficiency of the printing press.

Decentralized network: A structural approach to connecting computers that relies on multiple hubs of communication through which individual computers access a specific hub and those hubs are connected to one another.

Decode: An attempt by a message recipient to understand the content and meaning of a message.

Deepfake: Audio and video content that appears to be real but is created for the purpose of deceiving the public.

Deliberate: A crucial aspect of public relations that requires practitioners to take a calculated and measured approach to communicating on behalf of their clients.

Demassification: The expansion of media sources and channels to provide more choices to potential consumers.

Demographics: A key element in defining an audience that refers to a collection of relatively stable personal elements that allow researchers to create basic categories of individuals withing a larger population. Examples of these are race, age, and gender.

Development editor: See **content editor**.

Digital media: Content that users access through computer-based platforms as opposed to through traditional means, such as printed publications or over-the-air broadcasting.

Digital video recorder (DVR): A device that allowed users to capture televised content onto a computer hard drive within the machine, allowing easy organization and replay options.

Dime novels: Books that gained popularity in the 1860s, as their reduced price made them accessible to the general public.

Disc jockeys (DJs): Radio personalities who played music and entertained the listeners.

Disclosure: A form of invasion of privacy in which a media outlet reveals something about a private citizen that is true but offends public sensibilities.

Display advertisement: A traditional form of print or digital advertising in which text and visuals are paired, with the intent of creating a persuasive message for the audience.

Distributed network: A structural approach to connecting computers in which all terminals are equal and thus can talk to any other computer to which they are connected. This is the form of the current internet.

Distribution: The process of providing a completed movie to theaters and/or streaming services for the purpose of public viewing.

Downward social comparison: A need outlined in uses and gratification theory in which media users take joy in the misfortunes of others to boost their own self-esteem.

Doxing: A cybercrime in which individuals are attacked for the purpose of public embarrassment or harassment.

Dub: A process in which actors rerecord the dialog of a film in a studio environment to make it clearer for the audience.

DVD: Also known as a "digital video disc" or a "digital versatile disc," this was the first significant challenger to the VCR, as it allowed content to be captured and retained on a laser-readable medium for improved quality and wear resistance.

Edu-game: A type of video game in which individuals complete tasks that reinforce knowledge and information gain.

Elaboration likelihood model (ELM): A persuasion-based communication theory stating that people operate on a spectrum from low to high involvement on any issue. Depending on their level of involvement, specific persuasion tactics will be more or less successful.

Elevator pitch: A brief overview of a film's content.

Emojis: Small digital icons that express emotions or thoughts.

Encode: An attempt by a message sender to construct the content and meaning of a message.

Entertainment: An aspect of uses and gratifications theory that explains people's desires for content that amuses them and makes them feel good.

Escape: An aspect of uses and gratifications theory that explains people's desire to mentally free themselves from the problems they experience in their daily lives.

Escapist fantasy: An approach to video game playing in which users become dissociated from reality.

Esports: Online competitive competitions that mirror real-world championships that offer cash prizes for winners.

Ethics: Derived from the Greek word for character and the Latin word for customs, it refers to the way in which people are expected to demonstrate personal character for the betterment of society.

Ethnic press: Also known as immigrant press, this form of specialty press is written for people from other countries who have just arrived and are seeking insight from others who came from their homeland to a new country.

Explorers: Video game players who try to discover as much of the gamescape as possible, without concerning themselves with other aspects of the game.

Fact sheet: A public relations tool that provides media members with short, bullet-point items about a topic that matters to the practitioner's client.

Fairness Doctrine: A 1949 rule established by the Federal Communications Commission that required broadcasters to use some of their time to discuss controversial issues of public interest. The rule also required that the stations allow contrasting views on these topics. It was eliminated in 1987.

Fair use: The right to use small pieces of copyrighted content for the purpose of informing the public about an important issue.

Fake news: A term that rose to prominence in the mid-2010s that refers to either false and misleading content purposely provided to an audience or content any individual does not like and seeks to dismiss as irrelevant.

False light: A form of invasion of privacy that presents information in such a way that it leads to harmful and erroneous conclusions about a person.

Fame: One of five interest elements that explain why a piece of media content has value to a reader. This element explains how well-known people draw the interest of media consumers.

Fault: An aspect of libel law that determines whether the defendant failed to act in a reasonable manner in creating and publishing the content.

Feedback: Information provided from a message's initial receiver to its initial sender regarding the message itself.

First Amendment: A forty-five-word statement in the Bill of Rights that provides multiple freedoms, including freedom of the press and freedom of speech.

Flow: A psychological concept first introduced by Mihaly Csikszentmihalyi that describes the state of being in which people become intensively involved in an activity to the point of locking out all distractions.

Framing: A media theory that explains that media practitioners place emphases on specific aspects of a topic, thus shaping the way in which consumers view it.

Frequency modulation (FM): A form of radio broadcast that relies on a consistent signal but alters the number of times the audio wave moves to encode messages on radio waves.

Gatekeeping: A media theory that explains how a message passes through multiple decision points before it reaches its audience. The decision points dictate whether that message moves forward to the audience or not.

Gay press: A form of specialty press meant to serve the needs of the LGBTQ+ community.

General-interest magazines: Weekly and monthly publications that thrived in the first half of the twentieth century by providing short bits of information to readers on a broad array of topics alongside vibrant photographs.

Geographics: A key element in defining an audience that refers to the physical location of an audience.

Golden mean: A situational ethics approach in which the goal is to find a way in which all participants can benefit in some way without unduly harming any individual participant.

Great Migration: A large population shift of Black U.S. citizens from southern to northern states at the turn of the twentieth century.

Hack: An illegal entry into a computer network.

Harm: An aspect of libel law that attempts to determine if a person's reputation has suffered as a result of shame, ridicule, disgrace, or injury.

Hedge funds: Private equity ownership groups that pool their money to purchase investments with the goal of earning significant returns in the shortest amount of time possible. More than half of all daily newspapers in the United States are now owned by these organizations.

Hieroglyphics: An image-based form of writing developed by the Egyptians in ancient times.

Humanity: A crucial aspect of public relations that requires practitioners to pair accuracy and honesty with understanding and empathy when communicating difficult or painful information.

Hyperbole: A form of speech that is so outlandish that no reasonable person could reasonably believe it to be true.

Hypertext: An approach to digital communication in which files are stored in a specific repository, but they can be accessed through linked text on the World Wide Web.

Hypodermic-needle model: See **magic-bullet theory**.

Identification: An aspect of libel law that attempts to determine if the public can determine the identity of the person who is claiming to have been libeled.

Identity theft: A scam in which a criminal steals personally identifiable information from an individual and then uses it to commit financial fraud.

Illusion of choice: A psychological phenomenon whereby individuals mistakenly believe they have more control over the media content they consume than they actually do.

Image dissector: An electronic method of scanning images for broadcast that was introduced in the late 1920s.

Immediacy: One of five interest elements that explain why a piece of media content has value to a reader. This element explains how information that is more current has greater value than older information.

Impact: One of five interest elements that explain why a piece of media content has value to a reader. This element explains the need for content to have a direct relationship to the lives of the consumers for it to significantly matter to them.

Imposter scams: A form of theft in which criminals trick people into sending money to them under false pretenses.

Impression: A digital advertising measurement that counts how many times users could see an advertisement during a campaign.

Individualization: An approach to social media that allows users to select specific individuals to follow as opposed to being required to connect with an overarching organization.

Influencers: Social media participants who have established themselves as experts in a way in which their actions and suggestions can sway how their followers react.

Infomercial: An early form of native advertising that combines the informational approach of a television show or news program with the sales aspects of a commercial.

Infotainment: A form of content that blends information dissemination with entertainment elements to better convey content to an audience.

Interactive model: An approach to communication that focuses on how participants share roles as senders and receivers. An example of this would be a question-and-answer session between a professor and a student.

Internet protocol: See **TCP/IP**.

Intrusion: A form of invasion of privacy in which an individual violates a person's right to privacy in a nonpublic space.

Invasion of privacy: The violation of an individual's right to be left alone.

Killers: Video game players who attempt to make life miserable for all other players.

Kinetograph: Thomas Edison's motion picture camera.

Kinetoscope: Thomas Edison's motion picture viewer.

Known sponsor: A crucial element of advertising that requires advertisers to tell consumers who is responsible for the content of the advertising.

Legacy platform: Newspapers, television, and other mass media that predate the digital age.

Libel: The publication in words, photos, pictures, or symbols of false statements that harm another person's reputation.

Libertarian system: A media structure in which content creators in the general public have expansive freedom publish without governmental interference. This approach also allows media outlets to examine, question, and even mock the ruling class.

Limited-effects model: An approach to media theories that presupposes that media does not have strong, direct effects on how people behave after consuming media.

Linear model: A communication approach that explains how a message flows from a sender, through a media channel, to a receiver. The path is viewed as a straight line from transmission to reception.

Line of sight: An explanation as to how radio waves must be unimpeded between sender and receiver for them to function properly.

Location scout: A member of the film crew who assesses the viability of a filming site, based on internal and external shooting needs of the script.

Lurking: A process by which individuals follow others on social media but remain unengaged when it comes to creating their own content.

Magic-bullet theory: A now-disproven theory of communication stating that messages are simple and direct, penetrating the minds of consumers and creating specific direct actions.

Many-to-many model: An approach to communication in which multiple senders and receivers exist.

Mass communication: A technique of disseminating information from one source to many receivers.

Mean world syndrome: A finding of cultivation theory that explains how heavy television viewers perceive society in an exceedingly negative way.

Media: A form of communication that includes discussions of content, platform, and information that is disseminated and received.

Media bubble: An isolation chamber of an individual's own creation in which the continual filtering of content can limit the perspective of that person.

Media kit: A public relations tool that puts all relevant information regarding a client's efforts into a single packet for the benefit of the news media.

Media literacy: The ability to decode messages within the media for the purpose of determining how those messages can create personal influence, so an individual can act effectively on them.

Medium: A portion of a communication model that explains the platform on which a message travels, such as a broadcast wave or a newspaper.

Microblogging: A form of social media in which individuals use short bursts of text to provide diary-like posts on issues of interest to their audience.

Microtargeting: A form of messaging in which individuals are specifically targeted based on niche interests.

Misappropriation: Using a person's likeness or image without that person's permission.

MMOs: Stands for "massive multiplayer online games," in which individuals from all over the world come together to participate and take part in an entire world of activity.

Mood management: The use of mass media, particularly television, to enhance or change an individual's emotional state.

Movable type: A process popularized in the mid-1400s that allowed metal letters to be reused throughout printing. This made it much easier and cheaper to create consistent copies of a pressed page.

Mutually beneficial: A crucial aspect of public relations that requires all communication between the client and the public to benefit both of them in some meaningful way.

Native advertising: A form of content that is produced by advertisers to mimic the surrounding content and blend into the remainder of the editorial content in a publication or on a digital platform.

Negative social stereotyping: A mental process in which a person applies negative constructs about individual people based on preconceived notions about that individual's racial, gender, social, or other group-based affiliation.

Negligence: A standard of fault in a libel case that requires a plaintiff to prove that a defendant did not take reasonable care in their work to avoid libel. This is the standard private individuals must prove to be successful in a lawsuit.

Net neutrality: An approach to internet services dictating that all content is treated equally in terms of the speed in which it is moved to users.

Network: A collection of broadcast stations that would share programming across portions of the country.

News conference: Also called a press conference, these events are used for practitioners or their clients to speak directly to the media in a specific setting.

News desert: A community without a viable, reliable media outlet, due in large part to media consolidation efforts and corporate ownership.

Niche content: Programming meant to appeal to smaller segments of an audience, through the use of specific types of material.

Noise: A portion of a communication model that explains potential forms of interference that can undermine or inhibit the success of a message reaching a receiver.

Nonpartisan press: A form of journalism in which a media outlet operates with the goals of fairness and neutrality in its news coverage.

Norm: A form of acceptable behavior agreed upon by a social group.

Oddity: One of five interest elements that explain why a piece of media content has value to a reader. This element emphasizes rare feats, strange occurrences, and "news of the weird."

One-to-many model: An approach to communication that involves a single sender and multiple receivers.

One-to-one model: An approach to communication that involves a single sender and a single receiver.

Opinion: A defense against libel stating that the material in question was only the writer's own thoughts and feelings, not facts.

Option: The process of securing the rights to a script from its author.

Oral communication: The use of auditory sounds to convey information.

Originator: Another term for the sender in a communication model.

Osgood-Schramm Model: See **interactive model**.

Outdoor advertising: See **billboard**.

Packet switching: An approach to computer communication in which large pieces of information are broken down into smaller chunks and sent along the fastest routes possible to their destination, where the information is reassembled.

Paid speech: A crucial element of advertising the distinguishes it from other forms of mass media in that money is provided in exchange for space in a publication or time during a broadcast.

Pamphleteer: A person who published political arguments in short publications and distributed them to readers in the hope of persuading them. These individuals were prominent in the United States in the pre-Revolutionary period.

Papyrus: An early form of paper that made it much easier for scribes to produce and transport content.

Paradigms: Patterns of basic assumptions and shared understandings.

Paradox of control: A component of flow that describe the way in which individuals feel totally in control of their goals beyond the regular capabilities, until they realize they have this control, at which point they quickly fail at the task.

Parallel construction: A film technique in which two scenes are intercut to build drama and tell stories.

Parasocial relationship: An aspect of uses and gratifications theory that explains the connection media users make between themselves and individuals in the media they consume, in effect forming one-way friendships.

Parchment: A form of paper composed of animal skins that was much less fragile than its predecessors.

Penny dreadful: A cheap, weekly text produced in London during the 1830s that told wild tales and appealed to the masses.

Penny press: A form of mass publication in which publishers sold newspapers for a penny per copy, well below the standard market rate, to reach common citizens and make up for losses through increased volume.

Peripheral route: Describes a path to persuasion that requires individuals to rely on less informative, more engaging cues, like entertaining music or beautiful people. See **elaboration likelihood model (ELM)**.

Personal identity: An aspect of uses and gratifications theory that explains how people enjoy seeing content that involves people to whom they can relate on some level.

Phishing: An email-based attack in which a criminal sends a mass email to a potential target organization, in the hope that one or two people will reveal important information.

Phonograph machine: A device that can record and replay sounds on a physical medium, such as a wax cylinder or disc.

Platform: The delivery format in which information is disseminated, such as a printed newspaper or a social media app.

Platform neutrality: An approach to media that focuses more on the content individuals send and receive than the format or device on which it is delivered.

Podcast: A form of digital communication in which individuals can create downloadable MP3 files that users can listen to at their leisure.

Practitioner: A common term to describe an individual who works in public relations.

Press release: A public relations tool that practitioners use to inform the media about an event involving a client.

Press shield laws: Rules that limit a court's ability to force reporters to divulge information they garnered during the course of their journalistic efforts.

Principal photography: The part of filmmaking in which the majority of the shooting takes place.

Principle of utility: A situational ethics approach in which an action should maximize overall benefits or minimize group harm, regardless of its impact on any individuals within the group.

Product placement: A form of native advertising in which real products are used during movies or television programs in exchange for financial compensation or brand exposure.

Propaganda: A term used to describe fact-free forms of social manipulation for the goal of forcefully persuading an audience to think as the propagandist thinks.

Proposal: See Book Pitch

Psychographics: A key element in defining an audience that refers to the degree of importance individuals place on certain personal traits.

Publication: An aspect of libel law that requires the plaintiff to prove the potentially libelous content was disseminated to people other than the plaintiff.

Public Broadcasting Act: A 1967 governmental ruling that established the Corporation for Public Broadcasting, with the goal of creating and disseminating noncommercial content that was in the public interest.

Public domain: Content that exists free from copyright and that can be used by any individual for any reason.

Public relations (PR): A form of strategic communication through which practitioners serve the needs of clients and audiences to create a mutually beneficial relationship between them.

Puffery: A form of hyperbolic speech used in advertising to enhance the image of a product in a way that is not meant to be seen as demonstrably true or false.

Pulp fiction: No-frills magazines produced on cheap paper in the late 1890s and into the early twentieth century, which gave the public access to less expensive reading options.

Punditry: The use of hyperbolic language and heavy speculation to provide opinions to an audience as part of a news broadcast, rather than relying on facts and balanced coverage.

Qualified privilege: A right in the United States granted to journalists to quote judges and political officials who say things in their official roles, regardless of the factual accuracy of their statements, without fear of libel.

Radio Act of 1912: A governmental ruling that required all broadcasters to be licensed by the government and established a portion of the electromagnetic spectrum for emergency services.

Radio receiver: The piece of equipment that picks up a signal to play it back for the listener.

Ransomware: An attack in which cybercriminals take control over an organization's computer system and threaten to destroy it unless they are paid not to.

Reality TV: A form of programming that assembles a group of nonactors to participate in a contrived scenario as a form of entertainment.

Recce: Short for "reconnaissance." See **site survey**.

Receiver: (1) The audience for which a message was constructed and sent. (2) In radio, the piece of equipment that picks up a signal to play it back for the listener.

Recipient: See **receiver**.

Relational purchase: A form or commerce based on the connection between the individual consumer and the brand itself, with brand loyalty and familiarity leading consumers to favor a company for future purchases.

Reputation: The way in which an organization or a product is perceived by others.

Responsive: A crucial aspect of public relations that requires an organization to listen to and connect with audience members seeking to provide feedback.

Roper question: A survey question meant to determine which media platform was most believable.

Satellite television: A form of broadcasting in which content is beamed from a sending unit to an orbiting broadcast machine in space and then disseminated to individual users.

Satire: A form of humor and discourse that courts have deemed to be protected from claims of libel.

Second unit: A collection of crew members who capture sequences outside the main action of a film for later inclusion in the movie.

Self-awareness: A psychological state in which one is reflective of specific aspects of one's life and being.

Sender-Message-Channel-Receiver model: David Berlo's proposed approach to communication that followed content through each stage of its development and delivery, taking into account various contributing factors that would enhance or diminish the likelihood of successful communication.

Server: Computer hardware that stores, processes, and delivers content to users on the World Wide Web.

Site survey: The process a location scout uses to determine the viability of a shooting location.

Situational ethics: An approach to ethics in which people review cases on a case-by-case basis and rely heavily on moralistic reasoning and rational choices to make nuanced individualized decision.

Slander: False spoken statements that harm a person's reputation.

Smart News Release: One of the earliest forms of digital public relations.

Social comparison: The reliance on the status of others to determine an individual's own personal value.

Socializers: Video game players who take part in the game for the purpose of meeting other people and connecting with them on an interpersonal level.

Social media: A form of online communication that offers opportunities for users to participate as both senders and receivers on a given platform.

Social-responsibility theory: An approach to media that balances freedom of expression with the responsibilities of the media to key publics within society. Media outlets remain privately owned, and media practitioners abide by a set of ethical codes to inspire public trust.

Social utility: An aspect of uses and gratifications theory that explains how people feel the need to connect with other people in society.

Sound bites: Audio or video clips from an interview that are used as part of a broadcast news story.

Source: The creator and disseminator of a message.

Soviet-communist system: A nationalistic media model in which the government controls all media outlets for the purpose of enhancing and promoting the actions of the ruling class.

Spear phishing: A nuanced form of email attack in which individuals within an organization are targeted by criminals posing as known senders who are seeking private information.

Special effects: Technological additions to a film that use computerization, stunts, and other similar techniques to improve the storytelling of a movie.

Specialty publication: A form of media that serves specific social interests, often created by individuals in a "by us, for us" approach. This term refers to media like the ethnic press, the gay press, and the prison press.

Spiral of silence: A media theory stating that the more a person's opinion is in the majority, the more likely that person is to speak out on an issue. Conversely, the less a person's opinion is in the majority, the quieter that person will remain on an issue.

Split screen: A film technique introduced in the early 1900s that placed two characters in different shots performing separate actions on the screen at the same time.

Static advertising: Content that does not change dependent upon the needs or interests of the audience.

Stereotypes: Shortcuts created by your brain that help you engage in simple actions without having to relearn a process each time you encounter a certain situation. These can become dangerous when applied to social groups. See **negative social stereotyping**.

Storyboarding: A process that uses illustrations and limited text to indicate the way in which the filmmaker plans to set scenes and portray characters throughout the movie.

Story pitch: A public relations tool in which a practitioner presents an editor or producer with a ready-made piece of content for inclusion in the publication or newscast.

Strategic: A key term associated with public relations that explains the importance of carefully planning each step of a campaign for maximum impact.

Streaming: The use of the online access to watch video content on internet-enabled devices.

Studio system: A form of oligopoly that dominated U.S. cinema in the 1930s and 1940s, in which five major studios controlled every aspect of filmmaking and the exhibiting process.

Subliminal advertising: A form of advertising in which hidden messages are inserted into the content with the goal of subconsciously persuading audience members.

Subscription-based TV: Television that is not free over the airwaves but requires the purchase of a cable or satellite service.

Surveillance: An aspect of uses and gratifications theory that explains how people feel a need to be aware of what is happening around them.

Take: The recording of actors performing a scene.

Talkies: A term used to describe early films that included audible dialogue.

Targeted advertising campaign: A form of digital advertising in which an advertisers makes use of an individual's browsing and search histories to prevent specific purchase options to that consumer.

TCP/IP: The universally adopted languages of computers that outlined the speed, structure, and format in which data would be sent (transmission control protocol) and the system in which computers would identify themselves online (internet protocol).

Technicolor: A filming process that used a three-color system to create a full-color film.

Terrestrial radio: See broadcast radio.

Third-person effect: A media theory stating that people drastically overestimate the influence messages have on other people while drastically underestimating the impact the messages have on themselves.

Time sharing: The earliest form of computer use, in which a mainframe computer would receive multiple users' commands from multiple input stations and then process them in a prescribed order.

Time-shifting: The ability to take broadcast content presented at one point in time and consume it at another point in time.

Trade publications: Also known as business journalism, these publications are created to provide relevant news to people who work in certain industries.

Transactional model: A dynamic approach to communication that proposes ways in which individuals share space within a communication zone, thus allowing them to operate as senders and receivers at various points in the process.

Transactional purchase: A form of commerce based on a specific, logical need without an underlying connection to the company that created the product, the store that sold the product, or any other brand-related issues.

Transistors: Solid-state radio components that delivered better broadcast quality and reach than tube-based technology. These devices made radios portable, thus expanding the reach of radio.

Transmission control protocol: See **TCP/IP**.

Transmission model: See **linear model**.

Transparency: A crucial aspect of public relations that requires practitioners to be honest and open, even during bad situations, in hope of increasing credibility.

Treatment: The second key stage of a script, in which the initial pitch is fleshed out with title information, key characters, and a summary of the story.

Truth: A defense against libel stating that content, no matter how damaging to a person's reputation, is protected from libel claims if it is factually accurate.

Twitrelease: A press release disseminated through Twitter.

Uses and gratifications: A media theory stating that users make choices on the content they consume based on specific needs they have and the ability of certain content to satisfy those needs.

Vanity press: A self-publishing operation in which authors pay to print and advertise their own books as opposed to working with an established publishing house.

Veil of ignorance: An absolutist ethical position that offers no favor or privilege to anyone based on status or social condition, espousing the philosophy that "justice is blind."

Velvet ghetto: A term used to describe the way in which public relations is heavily skewed toward female participants, but the majority of the executive positions remain in the hands of male participants.

Vertical integration: An approach to cinema in the 1930s and 1940s where five major movie studios controlled production, distribution, and exhibition outlets, giving them total control of films from start to finish.

Video cassette recorder (VCR): A device popular from the 1970s through the 1990s that allowed individuals to record and play movies at home.

Video game: A form of entertainment in which players control actions displayed on an electronic screen.

Video news release: A premade press release that mirrors the form of a broadcast story.

Viral: A rapid, exponential spread of a piece of content throughout the online universe.

Visual communication: A form of expression that relies on images to disseminate content.

Vitaphone: A system developed by Warner Brothers Studio in the 1920s that linked a film's audio and visual elements electronically, thus providing improved synchronicity between the two parts of the movie.

Vulture capital strategy: A financial acquisition strategy in which investors find distressed or nearly bankrupt businesses and purchase them at reduced prices before stripping them of whatever value they had left and discarding them.

Web 2.0: A system of internet behavior that emerged in the mid-1990s, in which users were more active participants in creating and sharing content.

Well-performed: A key term associated with public relations that requires practitioners to enact their work in a way that leads to successful outcomes.

Wireless telegraphy: An early term for broadcast radio.

Written communication: A form of expression that relies on text-based languages to disseminate content.

ENDNOTES

CHAPTER 1

1. Claude Shannon and W. Weaver, *The Mathematical Theory of Communication* (Urbana: University of Illinois Press, 1949).
2. David Berlo, *The Process of Communication* (New York: Holt, Rinehart, & Winston, 1960).
3. Wilbur Schramm, *The Process and Effects of Mass Communication* (Urbana: University of Illinois Press, 1954).
4. Dean C. Barnlund, "A Transactional Model of Communication," in *Communication Theory*, ed. C. D. Mortensen (New Brunswick, NJ: Transaction, 2008).
5. Harold Lasswell, *Propaganda Technique in the World War* (Cambridge, MA: MIT Press, 1927).
6. Paul F. Lazarsfeld, Bernard Berelson, and Hazel Gaudet, *The People's Choice: How the Voter Makes Up His Mind in a Presidential Campaign* (New York: Columbia University Press, 1948).
7. Chinenye Nwabueze and Ebere Okonkwo, "Rethinking the Bullet Theory in the Digital Age," *International Journal of Media, Journalism and Mass Communications* 4, no. 2 (2018): 1–10.
8. David Manning White, "The 'Gate Keeper': A Case Study in the Selection of News," *Journalism Quarterly* 27 (1950): 383–91.
9. Kurt Lewin, "Forces Behind Food Habits and Methods of Change," *Bulletin of the National Research Council* 108 (1943): 35–65.
10. Natalia Aruguete, Ernesto Calvo, and Tiago Ventura, "News Sharing, Gatekeeping, and Polarization: A Study of the #Bolsonaro Election," *Digital Journalism* 9, no. 1 (2021): 1–23.
11. Maxwell E. McCombs and Donald L. Shaw, "The Agenda-Setting Function of Mass Media," *Public Opinion Quarterly* 36, no. 2 (1972): 176–87.
12. Bernard Cecil Cohen, *The Press and Foreign Policy* (New York: Harcourt, 1963).
13. Molly Ball, "How COVID-19 Changed Everything about the 2020 Election," *Time*, August 6, 2020, https://time.com/5876599/election-2020-coronavirus/.
14. Tim Wallace, Karen Yourish, and Troy Griggs, "Trump's Inauguration vs. Obama's: Comparing the Crowds," *The New York Times*, January 20, 2017, https://www.nytimes.com/interactive/2017/01/20/us/politics/trump-inauguration-crowd.html.
15. Eliza Collins, "Report: Photos of Trump's Inauguration Were Edited to Seem Like Crowd Was Large," *USA Today*, September 8, 2018, https://www.usatoday.com/story/news/politics/onpolitics/2018/09/08/trump-inauguration-photos-edited-make-crowd-appear-bigger-report/1238838002/.
16. Dietram A. Scheufele, "Framing as a Theory of Media Effects," *Journal of Communication* 49, no. 4 (1999): 103–22.
17. Brooke Singman, "Trump Threatens to Close Border 'Next Week' if Mexico Doesn't 'Immediately Stop' Flood of Illegal Immigrants," Fox News, March 19, 2019, https://www.foxnews.com/politics/trump-threatens-to-close-southern-border-next-week-if-mexico-doesnt-immediately-stop-illegal-immigrants-from-trying-to-cross-into-us.
18. Ted Laguatan, "Immigrants Are Human Beings Who Just Want a Better Life," Inquirer.net, February 16, 2017, https://usa.inquirer.net/1644/immigrants-human-beings-just-want-better-life.
19. Elisabeth Noelle-Neumann, "The Spiral of Silence: A Theory of Public Opinion," *Journal of Communication* 24, no. 2 (1974): 43–51.
20. Patricia Moy, David Domke, and Keith Stamm, "The Spiral of Silence and Public Opinion on Affirmative Action," *Journalism and Mass Communication Quarterly* 78, no. 1 (2001): 7–25.
21. Xudong Liu and Shahira Fahmy, "Exploring the Spiral of Silence in the Virtual World," *Journal of Media and Communication Studies* 3 (2011): 45–57.
22. W. Phillips Davison, "The Third-Person Effect in Communication," *Public Opinion Quarterly* 47, no. 1 (1983): 1–15.
23. Mina Tsay-Vogel, "Me Versus Them: Third-Person Effects among Facebook Users," *New Media & Society* 18, no. 9 (2016): 1956–72.
24. Laramie D. Taylor, Robert A. Bell, and Richard L. Kravitz, "Third-Person Effects and Direct-to-Consumer Advertisements for Antidepressants," *Depression & Anxiety* 28, no. 2 (2011): 160–65.
25. Hyungjin Gill, Moonhoon Choi, and Swee Kiat Tay, "Fake News and Partisan Blame Attribution: Exploring Mediating Role of Self-Enhancing Perceptual Bias among Young Adults," *Atlantic Journal of Communication*, March 17, 2023, https://www.tandfonline.com/doi/full/10.1080/15456870.2023.2191202.
26. Michael Barthel, Amy Mitchell, and Jesse Holcomb, "Many Americans Believe Fake News Is Sowing Confusion," Pew Research Center, December 15, 2016, https://www.journalism.org/2016/12/15/many-americans-believe-fake-news-is-sowing-confusion/.
27. Clay Calvert, "Fake News, Free Speech, and the Third-Person Effect: I'm No Fool, but Others Are," *Wake Forest Law Review*, 2017, http://wakeforestlawreview.com/2017/02/fake-news-free-speech-the-third-person-effect-im-no-fool-but-others-are/.
28. Hernando Rojas, Dhavan V. Shah, and Ronald J. Faber, "For the Good of Others: Censorship and the Third-Person Effect," *International Journal of Public Opinion Research* 8, no. 2 (1996): 163–86.
29. S. Dixon, "Number of Social Network Users in the United States from 2018 to 2027," Statista, February 23, 2023, https://www.statista.com/statistics/278409/number-of-social-network-users-in-the-united-states/.
30. National Association of Colleges and Employers, "The Key Attributes Employers Seek on Students' Resumes," November 30, 2017, https://www.naceweb.org/about-us/press

/2017/the-key-attributes-employers-seek-on-students-resumes/.

CHAPTER 2

1. Jennifer Kyrnin, "About.com Guide to Web Design: Build and Maintain a Dynamic, User-Friendly Web Site Using HTML, CSS and Javascript," Adams Media, 2007.
2. Affinio, "Demographics vs. Psychographics and Why Culture Matters Most," December 19, 2016, https://social.affinio.com/blog/demographics-vs-psychographics-and-why-culture-matters-most/.
3. U.S. Department of Transportation, National Highway Traffic Safety Administration, "Overview of Motor Vehicle Crashes in 2019," December 2020, https://crashstats.nhtsa.dot.gov/Api/Public/ViewPublication/813060.
4. Media Literacy Now, "What Is Media Literacy?" https://medialiteracynow.org/what-is-media-literacy/.
5. David Folkenflick, "Walter Cronkite, 'America's Most Trusted Man,' Dead," National Public Radio, July 18, 2009, https://www.npr.org/templates/story/story.php?storyId=106770499.
6. Paige Steinman, "Are You Tuning In? These Are the Most and Least Trusted News Anchors on Television," IcePop, August 10, 2020, https://www.icepop.com/most-least-trusted-news-anchors-television?amp.
7. Benjamin Mullin and Katie Robertson, "*USA Today* to Remove 23 Articles after Investigation Into Fabricated Sources," *The New York Times*, June 16, 2022, https://www.nytimes.com/2022/06/16/business/media/usa-today-fabricated-sources.html.
8. Elahe Izadi, "Darnella Frazier, the Teen Who Filmed George Floyd's Murder, Awarded a Pulitzer Citation," *The Washington Post*, June 11, 2021, https://www.washingtonpost.com/media/2021/06/11/darnella-frazier-pulitzer-george-floyd-witness/.
9. Gwen Aviles, "Kendall Jenner to Pay $90,000 Settlement for Promoting Fyre Festival," NBC News, May 21, 2020, https://www.nbcnews.com/pop-culture/pop-culture-news/kendall-jenner-pay-90-000-settlement-promoting-fyre-festival-n1212011.
10. Society of Professional Journalists. "SPJ Code of Ethics," https://www.spj.org/ethicscode.asp.
11. Jessica Bennett, "One Family's Fight against Grisly Web Photos," *Newsweek*, April 24, 2009, https://www.newsweek.com/one-familys-fight-against-grisly-web-photos-77275.
12. Jill Cowan and Vik Jolly, "Jury Awards Vanessa Bryant $16 Million in Suit over Kobe Bryant Crash Photos," *The New York Times*, August 24, 2022, https://www.nytimes.com/2022/08/24/us/vanessa-bryant-verdict-crash-photos.html.
13. Janna Anderson and Lee Rainie, "The Negatives of Digital Life," Pew Research Center, July 3, 2018, https://www.pewinternet.org/2018/07/03/the-negatives-of-digital-life/.
14. Ibid.
15. Monica Anderson, Emily A. Vogels, Andrew Perrin, and Lee Rainie, "Connection, Creativity and Drama: Teen Life on Social Media in 2022," Pew Research Center, November 16, 2022, https://www.pewresearch.org/internet/2022/11/16/connection-creativity-and-drama-teen-life-on-social-media-in-2022/.
16. Emily A. Vogels, "Teens and Cyberbullying 2022," Pew Research Center, December 15, 2022, https://www.pewresearch.org/internet/2022/12/15/teens-and-cyberbullying-2022/.
17. Brian A. Primack et al., "Social Media Use and Perceived Social Isolation among Young Adults in the U.S.," *American Journal of Preventative Medicine* 53, no. 1 (2017): 1–8.
18. Foundation for Critical Thinking, "Our Concept and Definition of Critical Thinking," https://www.criticalthinking.org/pages/our-conception-of-critical-thinking/411.
19. "Hoax Email Saying Classes Canceled Sent to Needham Middle School Parents," CBS Boston, February 15, 2022, https://www.cbsnews.com/boston/news/needham-pollard-middle-school-fake-email-classes-canceled/.
20. Thomas E. Ruggiero, "Uses and Gratifications Theory in the 21st Century," *Mass Communication and Society* 3 (2000): 3–37.
21. Brad J. Bushman and L. Rowell Huesmann, "Short-Term and Long-Term Effects of Violent Media on Aggression in Children and Adults," *Archive of Pediatric Adolescent Medicine* 160 (2006): 348–52.
22. Albert Bandura, Dorothea Ross, and Sheila A. Ross, "Imitation of Film-Mediated Aggressive Models," *Journal of Abnormal and Social Psychology* 66, no. 1 (1963): 3–11.
23. Albert Bandura, "Influence of Models' Reinforcement Contingencies on the Acquisition of Imitative Responses," *Journal of Personality and Social Psychology* 1, no. 6 (1965): 589.
24. L. Rowell Huesmann and Lucyna Kirwil, "Why Observing Violence Increases the Risk of Violent Behavior by the Observer," in *The Cambridge Handbook of Violent Behavior and Aggression*, eds. D. J. Flannery, A. T. Vazsonyi, and I. D. Waldman (Cambridge, UK: Cambridge University Press, 2007), 545–70.
25. Craig A. Anderson et al., "Violent Video Game Effects on Aggression, Empathy, and Prosocial Behavior in Eastern and Western Countries: A Meta-Analytic Review," *Psychological Bulletin* 136 (2010): 151–73.
26. Anna T. Prescott, James D. Sargent, and Jay G. Hull, "Metaanalysis of the Relationship between Violent Video Game Play and Physical Aggression over Time," *Proceedings of the National Academy of Sciences* 115, no. 40 (2018): 9882–88.
27. Nicholas Negroponte, *Being Digital* (New York: Knopf, 1995).
28. Mark Jurkowitz and Amy Mitchell, "About One-Fifth of Democrats and Republicans Get Political News in a Kind of Media Bubble," Pew Research Center, March 4, 2020, https://www.journalism.org/2020/03/04/about-one-fifth-of-democrats-and-republicans-get-political-news-in-a-kind-of-media-bubble/.
29. Mostafa M. EL-Bermawy, "Your Filter Bubble Is Destroying Democracy," *Wired*, November 18, 2016, https://www.wired.com/2016/11/filter-bubble-destroying-democracy/.
30. Andrew Perrin and Monica Anderson, "Share of U.S. Adults Using Social Media, Including Facebook, is Mostly Unchanged Since 2018," Pew Research Center, April 10, 2019, https://www.pewresearch.org/fact-tank/2019/04/10/share-of-u-s-adults-using-social-media-including-facebook-is-mostly-unchanged-since-2018/.

31. Ethan Cramer-Flood, "US Time Spent with Media 2022," *Insider Intelligence*, June 15, 2022, https://www.insiderintelligence.com/content/us-time-spent-with-media-2022.

32. Jeffrey M. Jones, "In U.S., 40% Get Less Than Recommended Amount of Sleep," Gallup, December 19, 2013, https://news.gallup.com/poll/166553/less-recommended-amount-sleep.aspx.

33. Joseph Firth et al., "The 'Online Brain': How the Internet May Be Changing Our Cognition," *World Psychiatry* 18, no. 2 (2019): 119–29.

34. Mary E. McNaughton-Cassill, "We're Consuming Too Much Media. It's Time to Detox Our Brains," *Vox*, February 23, 2017, https://www.vox.com/2017/2/23/14669710/reprogram-brain-media-overload-political-fake-news.

35. S. Nayyar, "Digital Media and Society Report," World Economic Forum, 2016, http://reports.weforum.org/human-implications-of-digital-media-2016/downsides-and-risks/.

36. Eliane Bucher, Christian Fieseler, and Anne Suphan, "The Stress Potential of Social Media in the Workplace," *Information, Communication & Society* 16, no. 10 (2013): 1–29.

37. Elizabeth Hoge, David Bickham, and Joanne Cantor, "Digital Media, Anxiety, and Depression in Children," *Pediatrics* 140 (2017): S76–80.

38. "Raye Boyce (ItsMyRayeRaye)," https://celebslifereel.com/raye-boyce-itsmyrayeraye/.

CHAPTER 3

1. Asad Ismi, "Whoever Controls the Media, Controls the Mind," *The Monitor*, July 1, 2021, https://monitormag.ca/articles/whoever-controls-the-media-controls-the-mind.

2. Fred Siebert, Theodore Peterson, and Wilbur Schramm, *Four Theories of the Press* (Champaign: University of Illinois Press, 1984).

3. Shraddha Bajracharya, "Authoritarian Theory of Mass Communication," Businesstopia, January 6, 2018, https://www.businesstopia.net/mass-communication/authoritarian-theory-mass-communication.

4. Gregory T. Wuliger, "The Moral Universes of Libertarian Press," *Critical Studies in Mass Communication* 8, no. 2 (1991): 152–67.

5. Denis McQuail, *McQuail's Reader in Mass Communication Theory* (Thousand Oaks, CA: Sage, 2002).

6. David Shedden, "Today in Media History: First Colonial Newspaper Published in 1690," *Poynter*, September 25, 2014, https://www.poynter.org/reporting-editing/2014/today-in-media-history-first-colonial-newspaper-published-in-1690/.

7. University of Illinois Library, "American Newspapers, 1800–1860: City Newspapers," https://www.library.illinois.edu/hpnl/tutorials/antebellum-newspapers-city/.

8. American Antiquarian Society, "The Early Nineteenth-Century Newspaper Boom," https://americanantiquarian.org/earlyamericannewsmedia/exhibits/show/news-in-antebellum-america/the-newspaper-boom.

9. Steven R. Swartz, "Hearst President & CEO Reflects on the Record Year," Hearst Media, January 22, 2019, https://www.hearst.com/-/hearst-president-ceo-reflects-on-the-record-year.

10. Rafael Abreu, "What Is the Studio System—Hollywood's Studio Era Explained," Studiobinder, July 11, 2021, https://www.studiobinder.com/blog/what-is-the-studio-system-in-hollywood/.

11. Justia, "*United States v. Paramount Pictures, Inc.*, 334 U.S. 131 (1948)," https://supreme.justia.com/cases/federal/us/334/131/.

12. Douglas Gomery, *The FCC's Newspaper-Broadcast Cross-Ownership Rule* (Washington, DC: Economic Policy Institute, 2002).

13. Vincent F. Filak, "Cultural Convergence: Intergroup Bias among Journalists and Its Impact on Convergence," *Atlantic Journal of Communication* 12, no. 4 (2004): 216–32.

14. Adam Levy, "The Big 6 Media Companies," The Motley Fool, April 29, 2022, https://www.fool.com/investing/stock-market/market-sectors/communication/media-stocks/big-6/.

15. Ben Bagdikian, *The New Media Monopoly* (Boston: Beacon, 2004), 9

16. Edward Helmore, "Fears for Future of American Journalism as Hedge Funds Flex Power," *The Guardian*, June 21, 2021, https://www.theguardian.com/media/2021/jun/21/us-newspapers-journalism-industry-hedge-funds.

17. Joshua Benton, "The Vulture Is Hungry Again: Alden Global Capital Wants to Buy a Few Hundred More Newspapers," November 22, 2021, https://www.niemanlab.org/2021/11/the-vulture-is-hungry-again-alden-global-capital-wants-to-buy-a-few-hundred-more-newspapers/.

18. McKay Coppins, "A Secretive Hedge Fund Is Gutting Newsrooms," *The Atlantic*, October 14, 2021, https://www.theatlantic.com/magazine/archive/2021/11/alden-global-capital-killing-americas-newspapers/620171/.

19. Rick Edmonds, "What You Need to Know about Hedge Funds—and Their Affinity for Newspaper Organizations," *Poynter*, August 3, 2020, https://www.poynter.org/locally/2020/what-you-need-to-know-about-hedge-funds-and-their-affinity-for-newspaper-organizations/.

20. Amelia Tait, "25 Years on, Here Are the Worst Ever Predictions about the Internet," *The New Statesman*, August 23, 2016, https://www.newstatesman.com/science-tech/2016/08/25-years-here-are-worst-ever-predictions-about-internet.

21. David McClintick, "Town Crier for the New Age," *Brills Content*, November 1998, https://web.archive.org/web/20000819015036/http://www.brillscontent.com/features/cryer_1198.html.

22. Andrey Mir, "The Press Now Depends on Readers for Revenue and That's a Big Problem for Journalism," *Discourse*, July 28, 2021, https://www.discoursemagazine.com/culture-and-society/2021/07/28/the-press-now-depends-on-readers-for-revenue-and-thats-a-big-problem-for-journalism/.

23. Scott S. Bateman, "Classified Advertising Still Producing Big Money Online," Promise Media, https://www.promisemedia.com/online-advertising/classified-advertising-still-producing-big-money-online.

24. Sara Fischer, "U.S. Digital Newspaper Ad Revenue Expected to Surpass Print by 2026," *Axios*, June 21, 2022, https://www.axios.com/2022/06/21/digital-newspaper-ad-revenue-print.

25. Patrik Wikström, "The Music Industry in an Age of Digital Distribution," 2014, https://www.bbvaopenmind.com/en/articles/the-music-industry-in-an-age-of-digital-distribution/.

26. Ryan Waniata, "The Life and Times of the Late, Great CD," Digital Trends, February 7, 2018, https://www.digitaltrends.com/music/the-history-of-the-cds-rise-and-fall/.

27. Mark Harris, "A Short History of Napster," *Lifeiwire*, March 2, 2022, https://www.lifewire.com/history-of-napster-2438592.

28. Elliott Obermaier, "Napster: The Black Market That Publicly Dominated the Music Industry," in *Perspectives on Black Markets*, Vol. 3, ed. P. Andrews et al. (Indianapolis: Indiana University Press, 2014).

29. John Martellaro, "The Day Steve Jobs Launched the iPod and Changed Apple Forever," *Mac Observer*, July 27, 2017, https://www.macobserver.com/columns-opinions/editorial/the-day-steve-jobs-launched-the-ipod-and-changed-apple-forever/.

30. Zoe Bernard, "The Compact Disc Industry Is Officially Dead," *Business Insider*, February 16, 2018, https://www.businessinsider.com/the-compact-disc-industry-is-officially-dead-charts-2018-2.

31. Donna L. Halper, "Where Does Radio Go from Here?" *RadioWorld*, February 19, 2021, https://www.radioworld.com/news-and-business/programming-and-sales/so-where-does-radio-go-from-here.

32. Evan Tarver, "Social Media Networks before Facebook," *Investopedia*, November 9, 2021, https://www.investopedia.com/articles/markets/081315/3-social-media-networks-facebook.asp.

33. Josh Getlin, "Time Spent Watching Television Increases," *The Los Angeles Times*, September 22, 2006, https://www.latimes.com/archives/la-xpm-2006-sep-22-fi-tv22-story.html.

34. Stuart Dredge, "YouTube Was Meant to Be a Video-Dating Site," *The Guardian*, March 16, 2016, https://www.theguardian.com/technology/2016/mar/16/youtube-past-video-dating-website.

35. Jeff Ward-Bailey, "YouTube Killed the TV Star: How Online Video Is Replacing TV," *Christian Science Monitor*, January 8, 2016, https://www.csmonitor.com/technology/2016/0108/youtube-killed-the-tv-star-how-online-video-is-replacing-tv.

36. "The State of Online Video 2020," Insight for Professionals, 2020, https://www.insightsforprofessionals.com/it/software/the-state-of-online-video-2020.

37. Dan Avery, "Americans Spend a Third of Waking Hours on Mobile Devices in 2021, Report Finds," CNET, 2022, https://www.cnet.com/tech/services-and-software/americans-spent-a-third-of-waking-hours-on-mobile-devices-in-2021-report-finds/.

38. Paul Lewis, "'Utterly Horrifying': Ex-Facebook Insider Says Covert Data Harvesting was Routine," *The Guardian*, March 20, 2018, https://www.theguardian.com/news/2018/mar/20/facebook-data-cambridge-analytica-sandy-parakilas.

39. Juliana Gruenwald Henderson, "FTC Imposes $5 Billion Penalty and Sweeping Restrictions on Facebook," Federal Trade Commission, July 24, 2019, https://www.ftc.gov/news-events/news/press-releases/2019/07/ftc-imposes-5-billion-penalty-sweeping-new-privacy-restrictions-facebook.

40. Will Oremus, "Are You Really the Product?" *Slate*, April 27, 2018, https://slate.com/technology/2018/04/are-you-really-facebooks-product-the-history-of-a-dangerous-idea.html.

41. University of North Carolina Hussman School of Journalism and Media, "Do you Live in a News Desert?" 2020, https://www.usnewsdeserts.com/reports/expanding-news-desert/loss-of-local-news/local-news-void/#easy-footnote-bottom-7-3754.

42. Penelope Muse Abernathy, *The Rise of a New Media Baron and the Merging Threat of News Deserts* (Chapel Hill: University of North Carolina Press, 2016).

43. Penelope Muse Abernathy, "The Loss of Local News: What It Means for Communities," University of North Carolina Hussman School of Journalism and Media, https://www.usnewsdeserts.com/reports/expanding-news-desert/loss-of-local-news/.

44. J. Clara Chan, "U.S. Newsrooms Lost a Record 16,160 Jobs in 2020, Study Finds," *The Wrap*, January 7, 2021, https://www.thewrap.com/2020-newsroom-layoffs-data/.

45. Nick Bilton, "Why Hollywood as We Know It Is Already Over," *Vanity Fair*, January 29, 2017, https://www.vanityfair.com/news/2017/01/why-hollywood-as-we-know-it-is-already-over.

46. Patricia Lancia, "The Ethical Implications of Monopoly Media Ownership," The Institute for Applied & Professional Ethics Archives, July 27, 2009, https://www.ohio.edu/ethics/2001-conferences/the-ethical-implications-of-monopoly-media-ownership/index.html.

47. Arlin Cuncic, "What Is the Illusion of Choice?" *Verywell Mind*, April 28, 2022, https://www.verywellmind.com/what-is-the-illusion-of-choice-5224973.

CHAPTER 4

1. Rachel Wegner, "Tennessee School Board's Removal of Holocaust Book, 'Maus' Draws International Attention," *The Tennessean*, January 27, 2022, https://www.tennessean.com/story/news/education/2022/01/27/tennessee-school-board-removes-holocaust-mausart-spiegelman/9237260002/.

2. Jonathan Zimmerman, "Book Banning Is a Bipartisan Game," *Dallas Morning News*, May 8, 2020, https://www.dallasnews.com/opinion/commentary/2020/05/08/book-banning-is-a-bipartisan-game/.

3. Aymann Ismail, "There's a Simple Reason That Demands to 'Ban' Books Like Maus Are Soaring," *Slate*, January 31, 2022, https://slate.com/human-interest/2022/01/maus-banned-tennessee-holocaust-graphic-novel.html.

4. The Morgan Library and Museum, "Written in Stone: Historic Inscriptions from the Ancient Near East, ca. 2500 B.C.–550 B.C.," https://www.themorgan.org/collection/Written-in-Stone.

5. Laura Schumm, "Who Created the First Alphabet?" History.com, August 22, 2018, https://www.history.com/news/who-created-the-first-alphabet.

6. Ismail Serageldin, "The Ancient Library," http://www.serageldin.com/ancient_Library.htm.

7. History.com Editors, "The Printing Press," History.com, September 24, 2021, https://www.history.com/topics/inventions/printing-press.

8. Rachel Rosenberg, "Dime Novels and the Cheap Book Boom," *Book Riot*, March 11, 2021, https://bookriot.com/dime-novels/.

9. Pamela Bedore, *Dime Novels and the Roots of American Detective Fiction* (London: Palgrave Macmillan, 2013).

10. Mike Ashley, "The Golden Age of Pulp Fiction," The Pulp Magazines Project, May 2005, https://www.pulpmags.org/contexts/essays/golden-age-of-pulps.html.

11. Thomas W. Ennis, "Robert F. de Graff Dies at 86; Was Pocket Books Founder," *The New York Times*, November 3, 1981, https://www.nytimes.com/1981/11/03/obituaries/robert-f-de-graff-dies-at-86-was-pocket-books-founder.html.

12. Louis Menand, "Pulp's Big Moment," *The New Yorker*, December 29, 2014, https://www.newyorker.com/magazine/2015/01/05/pulps-big-moment.

13. Taylor Locke, "Jeff Bezos Thought There Was a '30% Chance' Amazon Would Succeed," CNBC, September 3, 2020, https://www.cnbc.com/2020/09/03/jeff-bezos-thought-there-was-a-30percent-chance-amazon-would-succeed.html.

14. Kenrick Cai, "Jeff Bezos Is Once Again the Richest Person in the World, Even as Amazon's Stock Skids," *Forbes*, August 18, 2021, https://www.forbes.com/sites/kenrickcai/2021/08/18/jeff-bezos-again-richest-person-in-world/?sh=1be0b4c257cb.

15. Edzer Huitema and Ian French, "How E Ink Developed Full-Color E-paper," *IEEE Spectrum*, January 22, 2022, https://spectrum.ieee.org/how-e-ink-developed-full-color-epaper.

16. Rob Errera, "Paper Books vs. Ebooks Statistics, Trends and Facts," Toner Buzz, February 18, 2022, https://www.tonerbuzz.com/blog/paper-books-vs-ebooks-statistics/.

17. Jesse Maida, "E-book Market: 6.04% Y-O-Y Growth Rate in 2021," *Technavio*, January 20, 2022, https://www.prnewswire.com/news-releases/e-book-market-6-04-y-o-y-growth-rate-in-2021--market-size-share-facts--factors-301463965.html.

18. Hattie Troutman, "Liberty University Student Set to Self-Publish Her Own Book 'Listening to the List,'" *Liberty Champion*, October 13, 2019, https://www.liberty.edu/champion/2019/10/liberty-university-student-set-to-self-publish-her-own-book-listening-to-the-list/.

19. Sarah Millar, "How a Failed Author Made $2 Million from E-Books," *Toronto Star*, March 3, 2011, https://www.thestar.com/entertainment/books/2011/03/03/how_a_failed_author_made_2_million_from_ebooks.html.

20. Claire Wingfield, "The Surprising History of Indie Publishing," March 26, 2017, https://www.clairewingfield.co.uk/blogfeed/2017/3/26/the-surprising-history-of-indie-publishing.

21. Smithsonian American Art Museum, "Literacy as Freedom," https://americanexperience.si.edu/wp-content/uploads/2014/09/Literacy-as-Freedom.pdf.

22. James Clear, *Atomic Habits* (New York: Avery Publishing Group, 2018).

23. Steven Piersanti, "The 10 Awful Truths about Book Publishing," Berrett-Koehler Publishers, June 24, 2020, https://ideas.bkconnection.com/10-awful-truths-about-publishing.

24. Jim Milliot, "Book Publishing's Rousing First Half of 2021," *Publishers Weekly*, September 10, 2021, https://www.publishersweekly.com/pw/by-topic/industry-news/publisher-news/article/87347-book-publishing-s-rousing-first-half-of-2021.html.

25. "Academy of Achievement," John Grisham, https://achievement.org/achiever/john-grisham/.

26. History.com Editors, "Socrates," History.com, October 29, 2021, https://www.history.com/topics/ancient-history/socrates.

27. Michael Taylor, "What Not to Read: Book Censorship in Early Modern Europe," University of New Mexico Libraries, September 26, 2017, https://libguides.unm.edu/blog/what-not-to-read-book-censorship-in-early-modern-europe.

28. Paul Halsall, "Modern History Sourcebook: Council of Trent: Rules on Prohibited Books," 1999, https://sourcebooks.fordham.edu/mod/trent-booksrules.asp.

29. Amy Brady, "The History (and Present) of Banning Books in America," *Literary Hub*, September 22, 2016, https://lithub.com/the-history-and-present-of-banning-books-in-america/.

30. "*The Hunger Games* Reaches Another Milestone: Top 10 Censored Books," *Time*, September 26, 2008, https://entertainment.time.com/2011/01/06/removing-the-n-word-from-huck-finn-top-10-censored-books/slide/the-adventures-of-huckleberry-finn/.

31. "Book Burnings in Germany," PBS, https://www.pbs.org/wgbh/americanexperience/features/goebbels-burnings/.

32. Kathleen McLaughlin, "Allies to Wipe Out Pro-Nazi Books," *The New York Times*, May 14, 1946, https://timesmachine.nytimes.com/timesmachine/1946/05/14/93103717.html?pageNumber=1.

33. Illinois State Library Heritage Project, "The Book-Banning Controversy," https://www.ilsos.gov/departments/library/heritage_project/home/chapters/years-of-transition-the-1950s/the-book-banning-controversy/.

34. American Library Association, "Banned and Challenged Classics," https://www.ala.org/advocacy/bbooks/frequentlychallengedbooks/classics.

35. *Board of Education, Island Trees Union Free School District No. 26 v. Pico by Pico*, Oyez, https://www.oyez.org/cases/1981/80-2043.

36. American Library Association, "Banned Books Week 2022," https://www.ala.org/news/mediapresscenter/presskits/bbw.

37. Scott Simon, "Brooklyn Public Library Makes Banned Books Available to Teens for Free," NPR, August 27, 2022, https://www.npr.org/2022/08/27/1119795623/brooklyn-public-library-makes-banned-books-available-to-teens-for-free.

38. Elizabeth A. Harris and Alexandra Alter, "Book Ban Efforts Spread across the U.S," *The New York Times*, February 8, 2022, https://www.nytimes.com/2022/01/30/books/book-ban-us-schools.html.

39. Michael Agresta, "The Year We Banned Books," *Texas Monthly*, November 23, 2022, https://www.texasmonthly.com/arts-entertainment/the-year-we-banned-books/.

40. Niki Griswold, "Texas Association of School Boards Expresses Confusion over Abbott Letter on Removing 'Pornographic' Books," Spectrum News 1, November 2, 2021, https://spectrumlocalnews.com/tx/south-texas-el-paso/news/2021/11/03/educators-react-to-abbott-letter-on--pornographic--books.

41. Mike Hixenbaugh, "Banned: Books on Race and Sexuality Are Disappearing from Texas Schools in Record

Numbers," NBC News, February 1, 2022, https://www.nbcnews.com/news/us-news/texas-books-race-sexuality-schools-rcna13886?utm_source=pocket-newtab.

42. Jay Parini, "Banning Books Is a Nasty Habit, Whether It Comes from the Right or Left," CNN, September 17, 2021, https://www.cnn.com/2021/09/17/opinions/york-pennsylvania-school-district-book-ban-parini/index.html.

43. American Library Association, Office for Intellectual Freedom, "Banned Books Weeks: About," https://bannedbooksweek.org/about/.

44. Alison Flood, "Alex Gino's Children's Novel *George* Retitled *Melissa* 'to Respect Trans Heroine,'" *The Guardian*, November 2, 2021, https://www.theguardian.com/books/2021/nov/02/alex-gino-childrens-novel-george-retitled-melissa-to-respect-trans-heroine.

45. Jeremy C. Young and Jonathan Friedman, "In Higher Education, New Educational Gag Orders Would Exert Unprecedented Control over College Teaching," Pen America, February 1, 2022, https://pen.org/in-higher-education-new-educational-gag-orders/.

46. Eliza Relman, "Florida Gov. Ron DeSantis Signs Law Punishing Student 'Indoctrination' at Public Universities and Threatens Budget Cuts," *Business Insider*, June 23, 2021, https://www.businessinsider.com/desantis-signs-law-to-punish-student-indoctrination-at-florida-universities-2021-6.

47. Nicole Chavez, "There Are 'Educational Gag Orders' for How History and Race Are Taught in 24 States, Report Says," CNN, November 8, 2021, https://www.cnn.com/2021/11/08/us/critical-race-theory-ban-pen-america-report/index.html.

CHAPTER 5

1. Larry Muhammad, "The Black Press: Past and Present," *Nieman Reports*, September 15, 2003, https://niemanreports.org/articles/the-black-press-past-and-present/.

2. Stanley Nelson, "The Black Press: Soldiers without Swords," PBS, 1999, https://www.pbs.org/blackpress/news_bios/newbios/nwsppr/freedom/freedom.html.

3. Kevin McGruder, "The Black Press during the Civil War," *The New York Times*, March 13, 2014, https://opinionator.blogs.nytimes.com/2014/03/13/the-black-press-during-the-civil-war/.

4. Nelson, "The Black Press."

5. Monica Davey and John Eligon, "The Chicago Defender, Legendary Black Newspaper, Prints Last Copy," *The New York Times*, July 9, 2019, https://www.nytimes.com/2019/07/09/us/chicago-defender-newspaper.html.

6. "History of the Chicago Defender," *The Chicago Defender*, https://chicagodefender.com/history-of-the-chicago-defender/.

7. "To Write in the Light of Freedom," Zinn Education Project, 2015, https://www.zinnedproject.org/materials/to-write-in-the-light-of-freedom/.

8. The Editors of *Encyclopaedia Britannica*, "Ebony," *Encyclopaedia Britannica*, 2017, https://www.britannica.com/topic/Ebony-American-magazine.

9. Robert Channick, "*Jet* Magazine Ending Print Publication," *The Chicago Tribune*, May 7, 2014, https://www.chicagotribune.com/business/ct-xpm-2014-05-07-chi-jet-magazine-ending-print-publication-20140507-story.html.

10. Gloria Steinem, "Gloria Steinem in Her Own Words," 2013, http://transcripts.cnn.com/TRANSCRIPTS/1302/03/se.01.html.

11. "Ethnic American Newspapers from the Balch Collection, 1799–1971," Readex, https://www.readex.com/content/ethnic-american-newspapers-balch-collection-1799-1971.

12. Daffodil Altan, "Ethnic Media in the U.S.: A Growing Force," PBS, 2007, https://www.pbs.org/wgbh/pages/frontline/newswar/part3/ethnic.html.

13. Tracy Baim, *Gay Press, Gay Power: The Growth of LGBT Community Newspapers in America* (CreateSpace Independent Publishing Platform, Prairie Avenue Productions, 2012).

14. Jeff Taylor, "The Fascinating Story of the First Lesbian Magazine in North America, Plus Where to Read It," *Qnotes*, 2018, https://goqnotes.com/54559/the-fascinating-story-of-the-first-lesbian-magazine-in-north-america-plus-where-to-read-it/.

15. "ONE National Gay and Lesbian Archives at the USC Libraries," https://one.usc.edu/about/history.

16. *One, Incorporated v. Olesen*, 355 U.S. 371, 1958, https://supreme.justia.com/cases/federal/us/355/371/.

17. Dick Leitsch, "Police Raid on N.Y. Club Sets Off First Gay Riot," *The Advocate*, September 1969, https://www.advocate.com/society/activism/2012/06/29/our-archives-1969-advocate-article-stonewall-riots.

18. Baim, *Gay Press*.

19. Ibid.

20. Michael Specter, "Public Nuisance," *The New Yorker*, May 6, 2002, https://www.newyorker.com/magazine/2002/05/13/public-nuisance.

21. Baim, *Gay Press*.

22. "Vibrant Prison Press in 20th-Century U.S.," https://www.acrosswalls.org/prison-press-us/.

23. Wilbert Rideau and Linda LaBranche, "Can a Free Press Flourish behind Bars?" June 15, 2014, https://www.thenation.com/article/archive/can-free-press-flourish-behind-bars/.

24. *Candle* front page.

25. Rideau and LaBranche, "Can a Free Press Flourish."

26. "Prisoner Publications Have Largely Vanished," https://www.acrosswalls.org/prisoner-publications-vanished/.

27. Vincent O'Bannon, "Pelican Bay's New Podcast, 'Unlocked.'" *The San Quentin News*, March 16, 2020, https://sanquentinnews.com/pelican-bays-new-podcast-unlocked/.

28. Bill Crider, "Prison Success Story," *The Evening Independent*, March 7, 1980, https://news.google.com/newspapers?id=sAAMAAAAIBAJ&sjid=sVgDAAAAIBAJ&pg=3020,1652647&dq=george-polk-award+sinclair&hl=en.

29. "Eleventh Annual Thurgood Marshall Awards Announced," Death Penalty Information Center, 2007, https://archive.deathpenaltyinfo.org/node/2161.

30. "Top Twenty Daily Newspaper Chains 1995 Circulation," http://www.cptech.org/telecom/newspapers2.html.

31. Tali Arbel, "The Country's Two Largest Newspaper Chains Announce Merger as Industry Struggles," *HuffPost*, 2019, https://www.huffpost.co

m/entry/newspaper-chain-gatehouse-buying-gannett-usa-today_n_5d488415e4b0ca604e36ab17.

32. Milos Djordjevic, "22 US Newspaper Circulation Facts You Should Be Aware Of," *Letter.ly*, April 6, 2021, https://letter.ly/us-newspaper-circulation/.
33. Sui-Lee Wee, "Japan and Thailand Confirm New Cases of Chinese Coronavirus," *The New York Times*, January 15, 2020, https://www.nytimes.com/2020/01/15/world/asia/coronavirus-japan-china.html.
34. "Editorial: Governor Evers Is Right. With Coronavirus Raging in Wisconsin, It Is No Time to Have an in-Person Election," *Milwaukee Journal Sentinel*, April 6, 2020, https://www.jsonline.com/story/news/solutions/2020/04/03/editorial-wisconsin-election-should-not-happen-person/2945865001/.
35. Shorenstein Center, "Announcing the Winner of the 2021 Goldsmith Prize for Investigative Reporting," April 13, 2021, https://shorensteincenter.org/announcing-the-winner-of-the-2021-goldsmith-prize-for-investigative-reporting/.
36. Sherry Liang, "How UGA IFC and Panhellenic Recruitment Hinders Diversity," *Red & Black*, September 8, 2020, https://www.redandblack.com/uganews/how-uga-ifc-and-panhellenic-recruitment-hinders-diversity/article_dea51fe6-f16a-11ea-857e-37254cb0ce6b.html.
37. Kalen Luciano and Heena Srivastava, "In Focus: Loopholes in Federal Lead Law Left 5th Ward in the Dark about What Is in Its Water," *Daily Northwestern*, December 20, 2020, https://dailynorthwestern.com/2020/12/22/featured-stories/in-focus/lead-on-loopholes-in-federal-lead-law-left-5th-ward-in-the-dark-about-what-is-in-its-water/.
38. Thomas Carlyle, *On Heroes, Hero-Worship, & the Heroic in History* (London: James Fraser, 1841).
39. Meagan Flynn, "A Small-Town Iowa Newspaper Brought Down a Cop. His Failed Lawsuit Has Now Put the Paper in Financial Peril," *The Washington Post*, October 10, 2019, https://www.washingtonpost.com/nation/2019/10/10/iowa-newspaper-cop-investigation-leads-libel-lawsuit-financial-peril/.
40. Douglas McLennan and Jack Miles, "A Once Unimaginable Scenario: No More Newspapers," *The Washington Post*, March 21, 2018, https://www.washingtonpost.com/news/theworldpost/wp/2018/03/21/newspapers/.
41. Tara Law, "COVID-19 Is Ravaging Local Newspapers, Making It Easier for Misinformation to Spread," *Time*, January 22, 2021, https://time.com/5932520/covid-19-local-news/.
42. Meg James, "Coronavirus Crisis Hastens the Collapse of Local Newspapers. Here's Why It Matters," *The Los Angeles Times*, April 17, 2020, https://www.latimes.com/entertainment-arts/business/story/2020-04-17/coronavirus-local-newspapers-struggle.
43. Kali Hays, "Magazine Ad Revenue Continues Decline Despite Some Audience Growth," *WWD*, 2019, July 22, https://wwd.com/business-news/media/magazines-ad-revenue-continues-decline-despite-some-audience-growth-1203224173/.
44. McLennan and Miles, "A Once Unimaginable Scenario."
45. Derek Thompson, "This Is the Scariest Statistic about the Newspaper Business Today," *The Atlantic*, March 18, 2013, https://www.theatlantic.com/business/archive/2013/03/this-is-the-scariest-statistic-about-the-newspaper-business-today/274125/.
46. Michael Barthel, "5 Key Takeaways about the State of the News Media in 2018," Pew Research Center, July 23, 2019, https://www.pewresearch.org/fact-tank/2019/07/23/key-takeaways-state-of-the-news-media-2018/.
47. Sophie Gilbert, "Breslin and Hamill: Deadline Artists," *The Atlantic*, January 30, 2019, https://www.theatlantic.com/entertainment/archive/2019/01/breslin-and-hamill-deadline-artists-review/581527/.

CHAPTER 6

1. "About College Radio," Radio Survivor, March 14, 2023, https://www.radiosurvivor.com/learn-more/about-college-radio/.
2. Joe Wood, "History of the Radio: From Inception to Modern Day," 2014, https://www.techwholesale.com/history-of-the-radio.html.
3. U.S. Census Bureau, "Radio Ownership during the Great Depression," March 2015, https://www.census.gov/history/www/homepage_archive/2015/march_2015.html.
4. Elizabeth Howell, "Was the 'War of the Worlds' Radio Broadcast an Early Deepfake?" Space.com, October 29, 2021, https://www.space.com/war-of-the-worlds-radio-broadcast-deepfake-podcast.
5. A. Brad Schwartz, "The Infamous 'War of the Worlds' Radio Broadcast Was a Magnificent Fluke," *Smithsonian*, May 15, 2015, https://www.smithsonianmag.com/history/infamous-war-worlds-radio-broadcast-was-magnificent-fluke-180955180/.
6. Christopher Klein, "Inside 'The War of the Worlds' Radio Broadcast," History.com, October 28, 2019, https://www.history.com/news/inside-the-war-of-the-worlds-broadcast.
7. Mark Memmott, "75 Years Ago, 'War of the Worlds' Started a Panic. Or Did It?" NPR, October 30, 2013, https://www.npr.org/sections/thetwo-way/2013/10/30/241797346/75-years-ago-war-of-the-worlds-started-a-panic-or-did-it.
8. Jefferson Pooley and Michael J. Socolow, "The Myth of the War of the Worlds Panic," *Slate*, October 28, 2013, https://slate.com/culture/2013/10/orson-welles-war-of-the-worlds-panic-myth-the-infamous-radio-broadcast-did-not-cause-a-nationwide-hysteria.html.
9. "Jack L. Cooper Biography," Radio Hall of Fame, https://www.radiohalloffame.com/jack-l-cooper.
10. Bill Brewster and Frank Broughton, *Last Night a DJ Saved My Life: The History of the Disc Jockey* (New York: Grove, 2014).
11. "Power, Politics and Pride: Durham's Destination Freedom," WTTW, https://interactive.wttw.com/dusable-to-obama/durhams-destination-freedom.
12. Emma Raddatz, "Golden Age of Black Radio," Choice360, September 7, 2018, https://www.choice360.org/feature/golden-age-of-black-radio/.
13. "Steinberg, Martha Jean 'The Queen,'" *Encyclopedia of Detroit*, Detroit Historical Society, https://detroithistorical.org/learn/encyclopedia-of-detroit/steinberg-martha-jean-queen.
14. Ted Nelson, "The Effects of Music on Teens of the 1950s," Our Pastimes, September 15, 2017, https://ourpasti

mes.com/the-effects-of-music-on-teens-of-the-1950s-12570973.html.

15. "Radio Transmission: You Try It," PBS, 1998, https://www.pbs.org/wgbh/aso/tryit/radio/radiorelayer.html.
16. Mary Lu Carnevale and John J. Keller, "Cable Company Is Set to Plug into Internet," *The Wall Street Journal*, August 24, 1993, https://www.proquest.com/docview/398478408?parentSessionId=qKl1udb5KQ3utqiisTYAG%2FNX0D2cd4bPLNwGYA9BrFE%3D&accountid=9355.
17. Edmund L. Andrews, "F.C.C. Plan for Radio by Satellite," *The New York Times*, October 8, 1992, https://www.nytimes.com/1992/10/08/business/fcc-plan-for-radio-by-satellite.html.
18. Marie Charlotte Götting, "Number of Sirius XM Subscribers in the United States from 1st Quarter 2011 to 4th Quarter of 2022," *Statista*, March 4, 2023, https://www.statista.com/statistics/252812/number-of-sirius-xms-subscribers/.
19. J. Bishop, "A Brief History of Podcasting," One Fine Play, March 10, 2021, https://www.onefineplay.com/blog/a-brief-history-of-podcasting.
20. Ross Winn, "2021 Podcast Stats & Facts," Podcast Insights, August 25, 2021, https://www.podcastinsights.com/podcast-statistics/.
21. Daniel Ruby, "39+ Podcast Statistics 2022," Demand Sage, August 20, 2022, https://www.demandsage.com/podcast-statistics/.
22. Nik Popli, "Spotify's Joe Rogan Controversy Isn't Over Yet," *Time*, February 11, 2022, https://time.com/6147548/spotify-joe-rogan-controversy-isnt-over/.
23. Fred Jacobs, "The Biggest Challenge Facing Radio?" Jacobs Media Strategies, June 12, 2019, https://jacobsmedia.com/the-biggest-challenge-facing-radio/.
24. Bill Rosenblatt, "New Survey Bears Good News for Spotify and Podcasts, Bad News for Radio," *Forbes*, March 12, 2021, https://www.forbes.com/sites/billrosenblatt/2021/03/12/new-survey-bears-good-news-for-spotify-and-podcasts-bad-news-for-radio/.
25. Jacobs, "The Biggest Challenge."
26. Elias Leight, "'The Culling Has Begun': Inside the iHeartMedia Layoffs," *Rolling Stone*, January 15, 2020, https://www.rollingstone.com/pro/features/iheartmedia-mass-layoffs-937513/.
27. Dan Kennedy, "Local Radio Follows Local Newspapers down the Drain of Corporate Chain Ownership," WGBH, January 21, 2020, https://www.wgbh.org/news/commentary/2020/01/22/local-radio-follows-local-newspapers-down-the-drain-of-corporate-chain-ownership?utm_source=TWITTER&utm_medium=social&utm_term=20200124&utm_content=3067694501&utm_campaign=WGBH+News.
28. Lance Venta, "More Names from Last Week's iHeartMedia Layoffs," *Radio Insight*, April 3, 2023, https://radioinsight.com/headlines/250563/iheartmedia-layoffs-ongoing-this-week/.
29. Robert D. Putnam, *Bowling Alone: The Collapse and Revival of American Community* (New York: Simon & Schuster, 2001).
30. "Record Industry Pushes Back against Radio's Fresh Efforts to Keep Royalties at Bay," *Inside Radio*, May 5, 2021, http://www.insideradio.com/free/record-industry-pushes-back-against-radio-s-fresh-efforts-to-keep-royalties-at-bay/article_dc7f5a5a-ade0-11eb-b656-6b2d510aaf6f.html.
31. BetterHelp Editorial Team, "Why You Should Listen to LGBTQ+ Podcasts," BetterHelp, February 6, 2023, https://www.betterhelp.com/advice/general/why-you-should-listen-to-an-lgbtq-podcast/.
32. Jason Villemez, "Go beyond Netflix with These LGBTQ Streaming Services," *Philadelphia Gay News*, April 28, 2020, https://epgn.com/2020/04/28/go-beyond-netflix-with-these-lgbtq-streaming-services/.
33. "We've Uncovered Top Insights on Our Black Podcast Listeners," SXM Media, November 4, 2021, https://www.sxmmedia.com/insights/weve-uncovered-top-insights-on-our-black-podcast-listeners.
34. Nidia Serrano, "Five Ways Podcasts Are Redefining Black Representation," *AdWeek*, https://www.adweek.com/partner-articles/5-ways-podcasts-are-redefining-black-representation/.
35. Brian Ward, *Radio and the Struggle for Civil Rights in the South* (Gainesville: University of Florida Press, 2006).
36. Adam Gabbatt, "*Serial*: How a Podcast Helped Adnan Syed Become a Free Man," *The Guardian*, September 21, 2022, https://www.theguardian.com/tv-and-radio/2022/sep/21/adnan-syed-serial-podcast-case.
37. Michael Levenson and Abbie VanSickle, "Court Reinstates Adnan Syed's Murder Conviction in 'Serial' Case and Orders New Hearing," *The New York Times*, March 28, 2023, https://www.nytimes.com/2023/03/28/us/adnan-syed-serial-conviction-reinstated.html.
38. Alissa Zhu, "How an Investigative Podcast Helped Free Curtis Flowers," *Mississippi Clarion Ledger*, September 10, 2020, https://www.clarionledger.com/story/news/2020/09/10/how-investigative-podcast-in-dark-helped-free-curtis-flowers/5747054002/.
39. W. Kohler, "Gay History—July 15, 1962: New York's WBAI Radio Broadcasts Talk Show Featuring Eight Gay Men," Back2Stonewall, July 15, 2021, http://www.back2stonewall.com/2021/07/gay-history-july-15-1962-wbai.html.
40. R. Richard Wagner, *Coming Out, Moving Forward: Wisconsin's Recent Gay History* (Madison: Wisconsin Historical Society Press, 2020).
41. Susan Dunne, "Gay Spirit Radio Was Connecticut's 'Original Queer Social Media,' *Hartford Courant*, October 30, 2020, https://www.courant.com/news/connecticut/hc-news-gay-spirit-radio-hartford-20201030-z3xces2vijgfvgrwkeuymslw5y-story.html.

CHAPTER 7

1. "History of Edison Motion Pictures," Library of Congress, https://www.loc.gov/collections/edison-company-motion-pictures-and-sound-recordings/articles-and-essays/history-of-edison-motion-pictures/.
2. Kyerstin Hill, "Auguste Lumière & Louis Lumière," International Photography Hall of Fame and Museum, https://iphf.org/inductees/auguste-louis-lumiere/.
3. Christopher McFadden, "How Edison and the Lumière Brothers Gave the World Cinema," Interesting Engineering, September 21, 2021, https://interestingengineering.com/how-edison-and-the-lumiere-brothers-gave-the-world-cinema.
4. Richard Green, "The Great Train Robbery," National Archives: Unwritten

Record, December 3, 2013, https://unwritten-record.blogs.archives.gov/2013/12/03/the-great-train-robbery/.

5. Caryn James, "Lois Weber: The Trailblazing Director Who Shocked the World," BBC, March 20, 2019, https://www.bbc.com/culture/article/20190318-lois-weber-the-trailblazing-director-who-shocked-the-world.

6. "Changes in Film Style in the 1910s," Wisconsin Center for Film and Theater Research, https://wcftr.commarts.wisc.edu/index.php/exhibits/the-harry-roy-aitken-papers/changes-in-film-style-in-the-1910s/.

7. Michael Freedland, "You Ain't Heard Nothin' Yet," *The Guardian*, October 7, 2017, https://www.theguardian.com/film/2017/oct/07/how-al-jolson-jazz-singer-1927-changed-film-industry-foreever.

8. "'Talkies' Are 88 Years Old," *Playout*, April 14, 2014, https://playout.tvnewscheck.com/2014/04/21/talkies-are-88-years-old/.

9. David Rylance, "Breech Birth: The Receptions to D.W. Griffith's *The Birth of a Nation*," *Australasian Journal of American Studies* 24, no. 2 (2005): 1–20.

10. Todd Boyd, "*Gone with the Wind* and the Damaging Effect of Hollywood Racism," *The Guardian*, June 13, 2020, https://www.theguardian.com/film/2020/jun/13/gone-with-the-wind-hollywood-racism.

11. Loree Seitz, "*The Jazz Singer* and Blackface: How Hollywood's Origins Will Always be Entwined with Racism," *MovieMaker*, August 6, 2020, https://www.moviemaker.com/jazz-singer-blackface-birth-of-a-nation/.

12. J. A. Ball, "The Technicolor Process of Three-Color Cinematography," *Journal of Motion Picture Engineers* 2 (August 1935): 127–38.

13. Madeleine Muzdakis, "Technicolor: The Vibrant History of Hollywood's Early Introduction to Color Films," My Modern Met, September 4, 2020, https://mymodernmet.com/technicolor-films/.

14. Johnnie L. Roberts, "The VCR Boom," *The Chicago Tribune*, September 22, 1985, https://www.chicagotribune.com/news/ct-xpm-1985-09-22-8503040687-story.html.

15. Jack Valenti, "Hearing before the Committee on the Judiciary," 1982, https://cryptome.org/hrcw-hear.htm.

16. "First DVD Recorder Debuts," *Wired*, August 9, 2000, https://www.wired.com/2000/08/first-dvd-recorder-debuts/.

17. "It's Unreel: DVD Rentals Overtake Videocassettes," *The Washington Times*, June 20, 2003, https://www.washingtontimes.com/news/2003/jun/20/20030620-113258-1104r/.

18. Christopher McFadden, "The Fascinating History of NetFlix," *Interesting Engineering*, July 04, 2020, https://interestingengineering.com/the-fascinating-history-of-netflix.

19. Fi O'Reilly Sánchez, "'CODA' Brings Home Oscar for Best Picture, a Historic Win for Deaf Community," NPR, March 27, 2022, https://www.npr.org/2022/03/27/1088526640/oscar-best-picture-coda-wins.

20. Paul Whitington, "How the Great Depression Inspired Hollywood's Golden Age," *Independent.ie*, October 4, 2008, https://www.independent.ie/entertainment/movies/how-the-great-depression-inspired-hollywoods-golden-age-26481978.html.

21. Stephanie Zacharek, "Now Is the Perfect Time to Revisit Movies That Brought America Comfort in the Past," *Time*, March 18, 2020, https://time.com/5805777/coronavirus-comforting-movies-great-depression/.

22. Peter Stack, "Hollywood in Wartime," *San Francisco Chronicle*, September 23, 2001, https://www.sfgate.com/entertainment/article/Hollywood-in-wartime-Films-of-the-World-War-II-2876083.php.

23. Phil Archbold, "What It Was Really Like to See Star Wars in 1977," *Looper*, September 18, 2020, https://www.looper.com/249198/what-it-was-really-like-to-see-star-wars-in-1977/.

24. Sean Hutchinson, "Modern Blockbuster Escapism Resonates Now More Than Ever," *Inverse*, November 23, 2016, https://www.inverse.com/article/24000-star-wars-rogue-one-trump-escapism.

25. Rebecca Rubin, "'The Batman' Flies Even Higher with $134 Million Debut at Domestic Box Office," *Variety*, March 7, 2022, https://variety.com/2022/film/box-office/box-office-the-batman-opening-weekend-bigger-than-expected-1235197903/.

26. The Editors, "Dorothy Davenport's Message Movies," Silentfilm.org, 2016, https://silentfilm.org/dorothy-davenports-message-movies/.

27. Emily Kubincanek, "'Where Are My Children?' and Lois Weber's Trailblazing Films about Women," Film School Rejects, March 24, 2021, https://filmschoolrejects.com/lois-weber-where-are-my-children/.

28. "Oscar Micheaux," Sioux City History, http://www.siouxcityhistory.org/notable-people/122-micheaux-oscar.

29. Tambay Obenson, "How John Singleton Made History as the Oscars' First Black Best Director Nominee," *IndieWire*, April 29, 2019, https://www.indiewire.com/2019/04/john-singleton-oscars-first-black-best-director-nominee-boyz-n-the-hood-1202129312/.

30. Christopher Hooton, "Please Stop Calling It the Bechdel Test, Says Alison Bechdel," *The Independent*, August 27, 2015, https://www.independent.co.uk/arts-entertainment/films/news/please-stop-calling-it-the-bechdel-test-says-alison-bechdel-10474730.html.

31. Walt Hickey, "The Dollar-and-Cents Case against Hollywood's Exclusion of Women," FiveThirtyEight, April 1, 2014, https://fivethirtyeight.com/features/the-dollar-and-cents-case-against-hollywoods-exclusion-of-women/.

32. "Bechdel Test Movie List," https://bechdeltest.com/index.pl/statistics/.

33. Kyle Deguzman, "What Is a Film Treatment? Examples from *E.T.* to *The Shining*," Studio Binder, December 6, 2020, https://www.studiobinder.com/blog/what-is-a-film-treatment-definition/.

34. Alyssa Maio, "What Is a Storyboard? The Fundamentals to Get You Started," Studio Binder, March 5, 2020, https://www.studiobinder.com/blog/what-is-a-storyboard/.

35. Philip Walker, "The Most Important Things to Know about Film Budgeting," The Film Fund, November 19, 2020, https://www.thefilmfund.co/the-most-important-things-to-know-about-film-budgeting/.

36. "F9: The Fast Saga (2021)," The Numbers, https://www.the-numbers.com/movie/F9-The-Fast-Saga-(2021)#tab=summary.

37. Eva Contis, "What Happens during Principal Photography?" Careers in Film, July 20, 2019, https://www.care

ersinfilm.com/principal-photography/.

38. Jay Holben, "The Ins and Outs of 2nd Unit," *American Cinematographer*, March 18, 2019, https://ascmag.com/blog/shot-craft/the-ins-and-outs-of-2nd-unit.

39. Anna Keizer, "The Post-Production Process in Film: What Comes After a Movie is Filmed?" *Careers in Film*, November 29, 2021, https://www.careersinfilm.com/post-production/.

40. Stephen Lambrechts, "*Army of the Dead*: See How Tig Notaro Was Digitally Inserted into the Movie," *Tech Radar*, June 7, 2021, https://www.techradar.com/news/army-of-the-dead-see-how-tig-notaro-was-digitally-inserted-into-the-movie.

41. Jon Burlingame, "'All Quiet on the Western Front' Composer Volker Bertelmann Wins Original Score Oscar," *Variety*, March 12, 2023, https://variety.com/2023/artisans/awards/original-score-oscar-all-quiet-western-front-volker-bertelmann-1235549505/.

42. Erin Pearson, "The Complete Guide to Film Distribution," *Topsheet*, August 10, 2020, https://topsheet.io/blog/complete-guide-to-film-distribution.

43. Jasmine Garsd, "Universal, Banking on Home Audiences, to Stream Movie Releases," *Marketplace*, March 17, 2020, https://www.marketplace.org/2020/03/17/movie-studios-release-movies-straight-streaming-covid19/.

44. "The Production Code of 1934," https://censorshipinfilm.wordpress.com/resources/production-code-1934/.

45. David Espar, "Hollywood Censored: The Production Code," PBS, February 2, 2000, https://www.pbs.org/wgbh/cultureshock/beyond/hollywood.html.

46. William Crawford Green, "*Burstyn v. Wilson* (1952)," 2009, https://www.mtsu.edu/first-amendment/article/92/burstyn-v-wilson.

CHAPTER 8

1. Iain Logie Baird, "Television in the World of Tomorrow," *Echoes*, Winter 1997, https://www.bairdtelevision.com/television-at-the-1939-new-york-worlds-fair.html.

2. Gregory Clary, "50th Anniversary of Satellite Telstar Celebrated," CNN Lightyears Blog, July 13, 2012, https://lightyears.blogs.cnn.com/2012/07/13/50th-anniversary-of-satellite-celebrated/.

3. Phillip Swann, "2022 Prediction: Will DirecTV and Dish Merge?" The Answer Man, December 21, 2021, https://tvanswerman.com/2021/12/10/2022-prediction-will-directv-dish-merge/.

4. CalBroadband, "History of Cable Broadband," https://www.calbroadband.org/broadband-facts/history-of-cable-broadband/.

5. Ibid.

6. Cristel Antonia Russell and Sidney J. Levy, "The Temporal and Focal Dynamics of Volitional Reconsumption: A Phenomenological Investigation of Repeated Hedonic Experiences," *Journal of Consumer Research* 39, no. 2 (2012): 341–59.

7. Dolf Zillmann and Jennings Bryant, *Selective Exposure to Communication* (New York: Routledge, 1985).

8. Dani Anguiano, "Sex and the City Fans Shocked over Character's Death by Peloton," *The Guardian*, December 10, 2021, https://www.theguardian.com/tv-and-radio/2021/dec/10/sex-and-the-city-fans-shocked-over-characters-death-by-peloton.

9. Sarah Berger, "Here's How Many Americans Watched Prince Harry and Meghan Markle's Royal Wedding," CNBC.com, May 21, 2018, https://www.cnbc.com/2018/05/21/ratings-for-prince-harry-and-meghan-markle-royal-wedding.html.

10. "On This Day: 1981: Charles and Diana Marry," BBC, July 29, 2005, http://news.bbc.co.uk/onthisday/hi/dates/stories/july/29/newsid_2494000/2494949.stm.

11. Paul Farhi, "Dear Readers: Please Stop Calling Us 'the Media.' There Is No Such Thing," *The Washington Post*, September 23, 2016, https://www.washingtonpost.com/lifestyle/style/dear-readers-please-stop-calling-us-the-media-there-is-no-such-thing/2016/09/23/37972a32-7932-11e6-ac8e-cf8e0dd91dc7_story.html.

12. Donald Liebenson, "How *The Fugitive*'s Heart-Pumping Finale Changed TV Forever," *Vanity Fair*, August 29, 2017, https://www.vanityfair.com/hollywood/2017/08/the-fugitive-tv-show-series-finale-judgment-anniversary-kimble-one-armed-man.

13. Marc Bernardin, "How Binge-Watching Has Changed TV Writing," *The Hollywood Reporter*, June 15, 2018, https://www.hollywoodreporter.com/tv/tv-news/has-binge-watching-changed-tv-writing-1118988/.

14. Stuart Heritage, "The Proof Is In: TV Really Does Rot Your Brain," *The Guardian*, September 13, 2021, https://www.theguardian.com/tv-and-radio/2021/sep/13/the-proof-is-in-tv-really-does-rot-your-brain.

15. Rachael Rettner, "Too Much TV May Be Bad for Your Long-Term Brain Health," Live Science, May 20, 2021, https://www.livescience.com/tv-watching-midlife-brain-health.html.

16. Jennifer Maas, "'Euphoria' Season 2 Viewership Is Up Nearly 100% from Season 1," *Variety*, February 1, 2022, https://variety.com/2022/tv/news/euphoria-season-2-ratings-viewership-up-1235167603/.

17. Sara M. Moniuszko, "'Euphoria' Nudity, Controversies Make Viewers Uncomfortable, but Not Enough to Turn It Off," *USA Today*, February 4, 2022, https://www.usatoday.com/story/entertainment/tv/2022/02/04/euphoria-makes-us-uncomfortable-so-why-cant-we-look-away/9286707002/.

18. Trina Young, "Why Elvis Presley Was Censored on 'The Ed Sullivan Show'," Elvis Biography, September 9, 2020, https://elvisbiography.net/2020/09/09/why-elvis-presley-was-censored-on-the-ed-sullivan-show/.

19. American Psychological Association, *Violence & Youth: Psychology's Response. Vol. I: Summary Report of the American Psychological Association Commission on Violence and Youth*, 1993, https://www.apa.org/pi/prevent-violence/resources/violence-youth.pdf.

20. L. Rowell Huesmann et al., "Longitudinal Relations between Children's Exposure to TV Violence and Their Aggressive and Violent Behavior in Young Adulthood: 1977–1992," *Developmental Psychology* 39 (2003): 201–21.

21. Caroline Fitzpatrick, Tracie Barnett, and Linda Pagani, "Early Exposure to Media Violence and Later Child Adjustment," *Journal of Developmental Behavior in Pediatrics* 33, no. 4 (2012): 291–97.

22. Rebecca Collins et al., "Does Watching Sex on TV Influence Teens' Sexual Activity?" Rand, 2004, https://www.rand.org/pubs/research_briefs/RB9068.html.

23. Christopher Ferguson, "Sex on TV: Less Impact on Teens Than You Might Think," The Associated Press, August 1, 2016, https://apnews.com/article/b2b2fd04178049809cded04556b6ca0c.

24. Robin L. Nabi and Karyn Riddle, "Personality Traits, Television Viewing, and the Cultivation Effect," *Journal of Broadcasting and Electronic Media* 52, no. 3 (2008): 327–48.

25. Daniel Romer, Kathleen Hall Jamieson, and Sean Aday, "Television News and the Cultivation of Fear of Crime," *Journal of Communication* 53, no. 1 (2003): 88–104.

26. Kaiser Family Foundation, "Generation M2: Media in the Lives of 8- to 18-Year-Olds," January 1, 20120, https://www.kff.org/other/poll-finding/report-generation-m2-media-in-the-lives/.

27. Rebecca Moody, "Screen Time Statistics," Comparitech, March 21, 2022, https://www.comparitech.com/tv-streaming/screen-time-statistics/.

28. Thomas C. O'Guinn and L. Schrum, "The Role of Television in the Construction of Consumer Reality," *Journal of Consumer Research* 23, no. 4 (1997): 278–94.

29. Alanna Bennett, "The 'Friends' Apartment Would Cost Way More IRL," *Bustle*, January 27, 2015, https://www.bustle.com/articles/60983-how-much-would-the-friends-apartments-cost-in-real-life-lets-just-say-theyve-always-been.

30. L. Schrum, James E. Burroughs, and Aric Rindfleisch, "Lifestyles of the Rich and Famous: Does Television Make Us More Materialistic?" Association for Consumer Research, https://www.acrwebsite.org/web/acr-content/803/lifestyles-of-the-rich-and-famous-does-television-make-us-more-.

31. Georg Szalai, "79 Percent Say More On-Screen Diversity Is Needed in Film/TV, ViacomCBS Study Finds," *The Hollywood Reporter*, October 28, 2021, https://www.hollywoodreporter.com/business/business-news/diversity-representation-study-viacomcbs-film-tv-1235037655/.

32. Louis Staples, "The 'Gay Best Friend': Has TV's Laziest Cliché Finally Fallen Out of Fashion?" *The Guardian*, August 7, 2021, https://www.theguardian.com/culture/2021/aug/07/the-gay-best-friend-has-tvs-laziest-cliche-finally-fallen-out-of-fashion.

33. Jessica Wolf, "TV Shows with Diverse Writers Rooms, Casts Resonated with Pandemic Audiences," UCLA Newsroom, October 26, 2021, https://newsroom.ucla.edu/releases/hollywood-diversity-report-tv-diverse-casts-pandemic-audiences.

34. "Record Number of LGBT Characters on US TV, Study Says," BBC News, February 1, 2022, https://www.bbc.com/news/newsbeat-60429942.

35. Beth Montemurro, "Toward a Sociology of Reality Television," *Sociology Compass*, 2007, https://compass.onlinelibrary.wiley.com/doi/full/10.1111/j.1751-9020.2007.00064.x.

36. Sarah Shevenock, "Reality TV Is Having a Second Renaissance on Streaming," *Morning Consult*, October 5, 2021, https://morningconsult.com/2021/10/05/reality-tv-the-circle-netflix/.

37. Shondell Varcianna, "12 Reasons Why Reality TV Is Ruining Society," The Richest, September 24, 2015, https://www.therichest.com/entertainment/12-reasons-why-reality-tv-is-ruining-society/.

38. "Viewer Beware: Watching Reality TV Can Impact Real-Life Behavior," NPR, August 24, 2014, https://www.npr.org/2014/08/24/342429563/viewer-beware-watching-reality-tv-can-impact-real-life-behavior.

39. Emine Saner, "'They Sell You a Dream': Are Reality Shows Such as Love Island Failing Contestants?" *The Guardian*, June 3, 2019, https://www.theguardian.com/tv-and-radio/2019/jun/03/they-sell-you-a-dream-are-reality-shows-such-as-love-island-failing-contestants.

40. Michiko Kakutani, "Is Jon Stewart the Most Trusted Man in America?" *The New York Times*, August 17, 2008, https://www.nytimes.com/2008/08/17/arts/television/17kaku.html.

41. Jason Linkins, "Online Poll: Jon Stewart Is America's Most Trusted Newsman," *Huffington Post*, August 22, 2009, https://www.huffpost.com/entry/time-magazine-poll-jon-st_n_242933.

42. Ashton Yount, "Delivering the News with Humor Makes Young Adults More Likely to Remember and Share," Annenberg School for Communication, January 6, 2021, https://www.asc.upenn.edu/news-events/news/delivering-news-humor-makes-young-adults-more-likely-remember-and-share.

43. Matthew E. Popkin, "The Role and Impact of *The Daily Show with Jon Stewart*: Taking Satire Seriously on a 'Daily Show' Basis," *Inquires Journal*, 2012, http://www.inquiriesjournal.com/articles/693/the-role-and-impact-of-the-daily-show-with-jon-stewart-taking-satire-seriously-on-a-daily-show-basis.

44. Debbie Elliott, "The 'Daily Effect': Cynical, Yet Informed," NPR, July 9, 2006, https://www.npr.org/templates/story/story.php?storyId=5544604.

45. Jeremy Littau and Daxton R. Stewart, "'Truthiness' and Second-Level Agenda Setting: Satire News and Its Influence on Perceptions of Television News Credibility," *Electronic News*, 2015, https://journals.sagepub.com/doi/full/10.1177/1931243115581416.

46. Paul Farhi, "We Have Reached Peak Punditry," *The Washington Post*, June 2, 2016, https://www.washingtonpost.com/sf/style/2016/06/02/pundits.

47. Amy Mitchell et al., "Distinguishing between Factual and Opinion Statements in the News," Pew Research Center, June 18, 2018, https://www.journalism.org/2018/06/18/distinguishing-between-factual-and-opinion-statements-in-the-news/.

48. Michael Dimock, "How Americans View Trust, Facts, and Democracy Today," *Pew Research Center Trust Magazine*, February 19, 2020, https://www.pewtrusts.org/en/trust/archive/winter-2020/how-americans-view-trust-facts-and-democracy-today.

CHAPTER 9

1. James Pelkey, "Chapter 4—Networking: Vision and Packet Switching 1959–1968," *The History of Computer Communications*, https://historyofcomputercommunications.info/section/4.1/the-intergalactic-network-1962-1964/.

2. Ibid.

3. David Shedden, "Today in Media History: The Internet Began with a Crash on October 29, 1969," *Poynter*, October 29, 2014, https://www.poynter.org/reporting-editing/2014/today-in-media-history-the-internet-began-with-a-crash-on-october-29-1969/.

4. L. Sawyer, "Elizabeth Feinler and the History of the Internet," New York Historical Society, November 13, 2020, https://www.nyhistory.org/blogs/elizabeth-feinler-and-the-history-of-the-internet.

5. Gavin Wright, "What Is ARPANET?" Tech Target, November, 2021, https://www.techtarget.com/searchnetworking/definition/ARPANET.

6. "Internet History of the 1970s," Computer History Museum, https://www.computerhistory.org/internethistory/1970s/.

7. Benj Edwards, "The Foundation of the Internet: TCP/IP Turns 40," How-to Geek, September 1, 2021, https://www.howtogeek.com/751880/the-foundation-of-the-internet-tcpip-turns-40/.

8. Laura Mears and Scott Dutfield, "World Wide Web: Definition, History and Facts," Live Science, March 31, 2022, https://www.livescience.com/world-wide-web.

9. Will Kenton, "Web 2.0," Investopedia, February 3, 2022, https://www.investopedia.com/terms/w/web-20.asp.

10. "Global Ecommerce Sales (2020–2025)," Shopify, April 26, 2022, https://www.shopify.com/blog/global-ecommerce-sales.

11. Sabrina-Lee, "AOL Stops Charging for Time Spent on the Web—and Instead Switches to Flat Rate Monthly Rate—Changing the Web Forever," Famous Daily, http://www.famousdaily.com/history/aol-switches-to-flat-monthly-rate.html.

12. Luke Dormehl, "Today in Apple History: iBook Ushers in a Wi-Fi Revolution," Cult of Mac, July 21, 2016, https://www.cultofmac.com/439013/today-in-apple-history-ibook-ushers-in-a-wi-fi-revolution/.

13. Tony Smith, "Wi-Fi Trade Body Approves First WLAN Mobile Phones," *The Register*, October 22, 2004, https://www.theregister.com/2004/10/22/wifi_phones_certified/.

14. Simon Kemp, "Digital 2022: Global Overview Report," Data Reportal, January 22, 2022, https://datareportal.com/reports/digital-2022-global-overview-report.

15. Paul Bischoff, "Internet Censorship 2022: A Global Map of Internet Restrictions," Comparitech, January 25, 2022, https://www.comparitech.com/blog/vpn-privacy/internet-censorship-map/.

16. Lauren Mak, "Censorship in North Korea: How to Stay Safe Online," VPN Overview, June 7, 2022, https://vpnoverview.com/unblocking/censorship/internet-censorship-north-korea/.

17. David Auerbach, "When AOL was GayOL," *Slate*, August 21, 2014, https://slate.com/technology/2014/08/lgbtq-nerds-and-the-evolution-of-life-online.html.

18. Neil Patel, "How Niche Communities Are Changing Online Conversations," https://neilpatel.com/blog/niche-communities/.

19. "About the Internet Archive," https://archive.org/about/.

20. Louise Matsakis, "The Gawker Archives Aren't Going Anywhere," *Wired*, January 31, 2018, https://www.wired.com/story/gawker-archives-freedom-of-press-foundation-toast-la-weekly/.

21. Kayla Harris, Christina Beis, and Stephanie Shreffler, "Parts of the Web Are Disappearing Every Day. Here's How to Save Internet History," Fast Company, August 17, 2021, https://www.fastcompany.com/90666430/parts-of-the-web-are-disappearing-every-day-heres-how-to-save-internet-history.

22. Lauren Feiner, "House Democrats Say Facebook, Amazon, Alphabet, Apple Enjoy 'Monopoly Power' and Recommend Big Changes," CNBC, October 6, 2020, https://www.cnbc.com/2020/10/06/house-democrats-say-facebook-amazon-alphabet-apple-enjoy-monopoly-power.html.

23. Alyson Shontell, "The Greatest Comeback Story of All Time: How Apple Went from Near Bankruptcy to Billions in 13 Years," *Business Insider*, October 26, 2010, https://www.businessinsider.com/apple-comeback-story-2010-10#2007-the-iphone-revolutionizes-the-mobile-industry-apple-tv-is-announced-11.

24. Nancy Western, "Apple Net Worth 2022," CA Knowledge, June 17, 2022, https://caknowledge.com/apple-net-worth/.

25. Kif Leswing, "Apple's 'Monopoly Power' over iPhone App Distribution Gives It Outsized Profits, Antitrust Committee Says," CNBC, October 6, 2022, https://www.cnbc.com/2020/10/06/house-antitrust-subcommittee-apple-has-monopoly-power.html.

26. Mark MacCarthy, "The Epic-Apple App Case Reveals Monopoly Power and the Need for New Regulatory Oversight," Brookings Institution, June 2, 2021, https://www.brookings.edu/blog/techtank/2021/06/02/the-epic-apple-app-case-reveals-monopoly-power-and-the-need-for-new-regulatory-oversight/.

27. Sara Morrison, "How Much Control Should Apple Have over Your iPhone?" *Vox*, December 8, 2021, https://www.vox.com/recode/22821277/apple-iphone-antitrust-app-store-privacy.

28. Juan Carlos Perez, "Amazon Records First Profitable Year in Its History," *Computerworld*, January 28, 2004, https://www.computerworld.com/article/2575106/amazon-records-first-profitable-year-in-its-history.html.

29. Todd Bishop, "Amazon Tops 1M U.S. Employees," Geek Wire, February 9, 2022, https://www.geekwire.com/2022/amazon-tops-1m-u-s-employees/.

30. Nancy Western, "Amazon Net Worth," CA Knowledge, June 6, 2022, https://caknowledge.com/amazon-net-worth/.

31. James Anthony, "74 Amazon Statistics You Must Know," Finances Online, 2021, https://financesonline.com/amazon-statistics/.

32. Adrianne Jeffries and Leon Yin, "Amazon Puts Its Own 'Brands' First above Better-Rated Products," The Markup, October 14, 2021, https://themarkup.org/amazons-advantage/2021/10/14/amazon-puts-its-own-brands-first-above-better-rated-products.

33. Dana Mattioli, "Amazon Scooped up Data from Its Own Sellers to Launch Competing Products," *The Wall Street Journal*, April 23, 2020, https://www.wsj.com/articles/amazon-scooped-up-data-from-its-own-sellers-to-launch-competing-products-11587650015.

34. Aditya Kalra and Steve Stecklow, "Amazon Copied Products and Rigged Search Results to Promote Its Own Brands, Documents Show,"

Reuters, October 13, 2021, https://www.reuters.com/investigates/special-report/amazon-india-rigging/.

35. Isabel Reynolds, "Facebook Net Worth 2023: (Meta Platforms) Revenue Assets," CA Knowledge, January 4, 2023, https://caknowledge.com/facebook-net-worth/.

36. Simon Kemp, "Facebook Statistics and Trends," Data Reportal, January 22, 2022, https://datareportal.com/essential-facebook-stats.

37. M. Martin, "39 Facebook Stats That Matter to Marketers in 2022," Hootsuite, March 2, 2022, https://blog.hootsuite.com/facebook-statistics/.

38. "FTC Alleges Facebook Resorted to Illegal Buy-or-Bury Scheme to Crush Competition after String of Failed Attempts to Innovate," Federal Trade Commission, August 19, 2021, https://www.ftc.gov/news-events/news/press-releases/2021/08/ftc-alleges-facebook-resorted-illegal-buy-or-bury-scheme-crush-competition-after-string-failed.

39. Keach Hagey and Jeff Horwitz, "Facebook Tried to Make Its Platform a Healthier Place. It Got Angrier Instead," *The Wall Street Journal*, September 15, 2021, https://www.wsj.com/articles/facebook-algorithm-change-zuckerberg-11631654215?mod=article_inline.

40. Keach Hagey and Jeff Horwitz, "Facebook's Internal Chat Boards Show Politics Often at Center of Decision Making," *The Wall Street Journal*, October 24, 2021, https://www.wsj.com/articles/facebook-politics-decision-making-documents-11635100195?mod=article_inline.

41. Georgia Wells, Deepa Seetharaman, and Jeff Horwitz, "Is Facebook Bad for You? It Is for About 360 Million Users, Company Surveys Suggest," *The Wall Street Journal*, November 5, 2021, https://www.wsj.com/articles/facebook-bad-for-you-360-million-users-say-yes-company-documents-facebook-files-11636124681?mod=article_inline.

42. "Facebook to Pay $100 Million for Misleading Investors about the Risks It Faced from Misuse of User Data," U.S. Securities and Exchange Commission, July 24, 2019, https://www.sec.gov/news/press-release/2019-140.

43. Cecilia Kang, "Facebook Faces a Public Relations Crisis. What about a Legal One?" *The New York Times*, October 26, 2021, https://www.nytimes.com/2021/10/26/technology/facebook-sec-complaints.html.

44. R. Choudhary, "Google Net Worth 2022," CA Knowledge, June 5, 2022, https://caknowledge.com/google-net-worth/.

45. Jeff Desjardins, "This Chart Reveals Google's True Dominance over the Web," *Visual Capitalist*, April 20, 2018, https://www.visualcapitalist.com/this-chart-reveals-googles-true-dominance-over-the-web/.

46. Matt Rosoff, "This Is Not the Google We Knew and Loved—It's Turning into a Portal," *Business Insider*, January 17, 2012, https://www.businessinsider.com/google-is-looking-more-and-more-like-a-portal-2012-1.

47. Adrianne Jeffries and Leon Yin, "Google's Top Search Result? Surprise! It's Google," The Markup, July 28, 2020, https://themarkup.org/google-the-giant/2020/07/28/google-search-results-prioritize-google-products-over-competitors.

48. W. DiAntonio, "Do People Click on the Second Page of Google?" Reputation 911, November 18, 2015, https://reputation911.com/do-people-click-past-the-first-page-of-google/.

49. Cecilia Kang, David McCabe, and Daisuke Wakabayashi, "U.S. Accuses Google of Illegally Protecting Monopoly," New York Times, October 20, 2020, https://www.nytimes.com/2020/10/20/technology/google-antitrust.html.

50. David McCabe and Daisuke Wakabayashi, "10 States Accuse Google of Abusing Monopoly in Online Ads," *New York Times*, December 16, 2020, https://www.nytimes.com/2020/12/16/technology/google-monopoly-antitrust.html.

51. Leah Nylen, "36 States, D.C. Sue Google for Alleged Antitrust Violations in Its Android App Store," *Politico*, July 7, 2021, https://www.politico.com/news/2021/07/07/36-states-dc-sue-google-for-alleged-antitrust-violations-in-its-android-app-store-498622.

52. Klint Finley, "The Wired Guide to Net Neutrality," *Wired*, May 5, 2020, https://www.wired.com/story/guide-net-neutrality/.

53. Tim Wu, "Network Neutrality, Broadband Discrimination," *Journal on Telecommunication and High Tech Law*, 2, no. 2 (2003): 141–76.

54. Barack Obama, "Net Neutrality: President Obama's Plan for a Free and Open Internet," https://obamawhitehouse.archives.gov/net-neutrality.

55. T. J. York, "FCC's Simington Welcomes Congressional Action on Net Neutrality," Broadband Breakfast, June 1, 2022, https://broadbandbreakfast.com/2022/06/fccs-simington-welcomes-congressional-action-on-net-neutrality/.

56. David Schultz and David L. Hudson, "Marketplace of Ideas," *The First Amendment Encyclopedia*, June 2017, https://www.mtsu.edu/first-amendment/article/999/marketplace-of-ideas.

57. "Imposter Scams: Year: 2022, Quarter: 4," https://public.tableau.com/app/profile/federal.trade.commission/viz/FraudReports/FraudFacts.

58. Maddie Rosenthal, "Must-Know Phishing Statistics: Updated 2022," Tessian, January 12, 2022, https://www.tessian.com/blog/phishing-statistics-2020/.

59. Sean Michael Kerner, "Colonial Pipeline Hack Explained: Everything you Need to Know," *Tech Target*, April 26, 2022, https://www.techtarget.com/whatis/feature/Colonial-Pipeline-hack-explained-Everything-you-need-to-know.

60. Christina Wilkie, "Colonial Pipeline Paid $5 Million Ransom One Day after Cyber Attack, CEO Tells Senate," CNBC, June 8, 2021, https://www.cnbc.com/2021/06/08/colonial-pipeline-ceo-testifies-on-first-hours-of-ransomware-attack.html.

61. Dino Grandoni, "Ashley Madison, a Dating Website, Says Hackers May Have Data on Millions," *The New York Times*, July 20, 2015, https://www.nytimes.com/2015/07/21/technology/hacker-attack-reported-on-ashley-madison-a-dating-service.html.

62. Tom Lamont, "Life after the Ashley Madison Affair," *The Guardian*, February 27, 2016, https://www.theguardian.com/technology/2016/feb/28/what-happened-after-ashley-madison-was-hacked.

63. Editorial Board, "The Cost of Free Speech: On Wellesley, Palestine, and Student Journalist Solidarity," *Harvard Crimson*, November 2, 2022, http

s://www.thecrimson.com/article/2022/11/2/editorial-wellesley-bds/.

64. Ari Lazarus, "Hey College Students: Have You Seen This Scam?" Federal Trade Commission, December 2, 2020, https://consumer.ftc.gov/consumer-alerts/2020/12/hey-college-students-have-you-seen-scam.

65. James Caunt, "Professor Reads out His Own Terrible 'Rate My Professor' Reviews in Front of the Class, and They're Absolutely Brutal," Bored Panda, 2017, https://www.boredpanda.com/funny-professor-review-stories/?utm_source=google&utm_medium=organic&utm_campaign=organic.

66. "19 Brutally Honest 'Rate My Professors' Reviews That Are Worse Than Attending a Lecture Hungover," https://cheezburger.com/2199813/19-brutally-honest-rate-my-professors-reviews-that-are-worse-than-attending-a-lecture-hungover.

67. Emily A. Vogels, "The State of Online Harassment," Pew Research Center, January 13, 2021, https://www.pewresearch.org/internet/2021/01/13/the-state-of-online-harassment/.

68. Ivana Vojinovic, "Heart-Breaking Cyberbullying Statistics for 2022," DataProt, March 15, 2022, https://dataprot.net/statistics/cyberbullying-statistics/.

69. Sameer Hinduja and Justin W. Patchin, "Bullying, Cyberbullying and Suicides," *Archives of Suicide Research* 14, no. 3 (2010): 206–21.

CHAPTER 10

1. Matthew Jones, "The Complete History of Social Media: A Timeline of the Invention of Online Networking," History Cooperative, June 16, 2015, https://historycooperative.org/the-history-of-social-media/.

2. Chenda Ngak, "Then and Now: A History of Social Networking Sites," CBS News, July 6, 2011, https://www.cbsnews.com/pictures/then-and-now-a-history-of-social-networking-sites/.

3. Evan Tarver, "3 Social Media Networks before Facebook," *Investopedia*, November 9, 2021, https://www.investopedia.com/articles/markets/081315/3-social-media-networks-facebook.asp.

4. Angie Renfro, "The Rise and Fall of Friendster," *Medium*, March 19, 2018, https://medium.com/@the.angie.renfro/the-failure-of-friendster-71efaab34774.

5. Lori Kozlowski, "New Life: How MySpace Spawned a Start-Up Ecosystem," *Forbes*, May 15, 2012, https://www.forbes.com/sites/lorikozlowski/2012/05/15/how-myspace-spawned-a-startup-ecosystem/?sh=7b292a9940ba.

6. Josh Halliday, "Justin Timberlake Buys Own Social Network with MySpace Investment," *The Guardian*, June 30, 2011, https://www.theguardian.com/technology/2011/jun/30/myspace-internet.

7. Debra Zahay et al., *Social Media Marketing: A Strategic Approach*, 3rd ed. (Boston: Cengage, 2022).

8. Marissa Storrs, "Looking Back at the History of LinkedIn," Pennington Creative, https://penningtoncreative.com/history-of-linkedin/.

9. Lewis Howes, "LinkedIn Goes Public: What Does This Mean for IPOs?" CBS News, May 20, 2011, https://www.cbsnews.com/news/linkedin-goes-public-what-does-this-mean-for-ipos/.

10. Maddy Osman, "Mind-Blowing LinkedIn Statistics and Facts (2022)," Kinsta, June 15, 2022, https://kinsta.com/blog/linkedin-statistics/.

11. "Me at the Zoo," https://en.wikipedia.org/wiki/Me_at_the_zoo.

12. Danny Donchev, "40 Mind Blowing YouTube Facts, Figures and Statistics – 2022," FortuneLords, June 22, 2022, https://fortunelords.com/youtube-statistics/.

13. "YouTube User Statistics 2022," Global Media Insight, April 18, 2022, https://www.globalmediainsight.com/blog/youtube-users-statistics/.

14. Biz Stone, "What's Happening?" Twitter, November 19, 2009, https://blog.twitter.com/en_us/a/2009/whats-happening.

15. Danny Maiorca, "10 Twitter Hashtags That Shaped History," Make Use Of, May 1, 2021, https://www.makeuseof.com/twitter-hashtags-that-shaped-history/.

16. Victor Luckerson, "Twitter Goes Public," *Time*, November 7, 2013, https://business.time.com/2013/11/07/live-updates-twitter-goes-public/.

17. Kate Conger and Lauren Hirsch, "Elon Musk Completes $44 Billion Deal to Buy Twitter," *The New York Times*, October 22, 2022, https://www.nytimes.com/2022/10/27/technology/elon-musk-twitter-deal-complete.html.

18. Natalie Neysa Alund, "Twitter Lost More Than 1.3 Million Users in the Week after Elon Musk Bought It," *USA Today*, November 8, 2022, https://www.usatoday.com/story/tech/2022/11/08/mit-report-twitter-elon-musk-users-lost/8300611001/.

19. Somini Sengupta, Nicole Perlroth, and Jenna Wortham, "Behind Instagram's Success, Networking the Old Way," *The New York Times*, April 13, 2012, https://www.nytimes.com/2012/04/14/technology/instagram-founders-were-helped-by-bay-area-connections.html.

20. Jeff Blagdon, "Instagram for Android Breaks 1 Million Downloads in Less Than a Day," *The Verge*, April 4, 2012, https://www.theverge.com/2012/4/4/2924600/instagram-android-1-million-downloads.

21. Jenna Wortham, "Facebook to Buy Photo-Sharing Service Instagram for $1 Billion," *The New York Times*, April 9, 2012, https://bits.blogs.nytimes.com/2012/04/09/facebook-acquires-photo-sharing-service-instagram/.

22. J. Chen, "Instagram Statistics You Need to Know for 2022," Sprout Social, March 15, 2022, https://sproutsocial.com/insights/instagram-stats/.

23. Jack Shepherd, "21 Essential Snapchat Statistics You Need to Know in 2022," Social Shepherd, June 16, 2022, https://thesocialshepherd.com/blog/snapchat-statistics.

24. John Herrman, "Vine Changed the Internet Forever. How Much Does the Internet Miss It?" *The New York Times*, February 22, 2020, https://www.nytimes.com/2020/02/22/style/byte-vine-short-video-apps.html.

25. Josh Constine, "Vine Reboot Byte Officially Launches," TechCrunch, January 24, 2020, https://techcrunch.com/2020/01/24/vine-byte/.

26. Mansoor Iqbal, "TikTok Revenue and Usage Statistics (2022)," Business of Apps, June 14, 2022, https://www.businessofapps.com/data/tik-tok-statistics/.

27. John Herrman, "How TikTok Is Rewriting the World," *The New York Times*, March 10, 2019, https://www.nytimes.com/2019/03/10/style/what-is-tik-tok.html.

28. Ali Arslan, "10 Reasons Why TikTok Is Actually Good," Make Use Of, January 13, 2022, https://www.makeuseof.com/reasons-why-tiktok-is-actually-good/.

29. Andrew Ross Sorkin et al., "Biden's TikTok Problem," *The New York Times*, June 21, 2022, https://www.nytimes.com/2022/06/21/business/dealbook/biden-tiktok-china.html.

30. Emily Baker-White, "Leaked Audio from 80 Internal TikTok Meetings Shows That US User Data Has Been Repeatedly Accessed from China," *Buzzfeed News*, June 17, 2022, https://www.buzzfeednews.com/article/emilybakerwhite/tiktok-tapes-us-user-data-china-bytedance-access.

31. AP, "TikTok Banned on U.S. Government Devices, and the U.S. Is Not Alone. Here Is Where the App Is Restricted," CBS News, March 1, 2023, https://www.cbsnews.com/news/tiktok-banned-us-government-where-else-around-the-world/

32. Cynthia Bowman, "How Much Do Instagram Influencers Make? 2022 Top Earners," GO Banking Rates, June 6, 2022, https://www.gobankingrates.com/money/entrepreneur/how-much-do-instagram-influencers-make/.

33. Yasmine Leung, "The 6 Highest-Earning TikTok Stars Scored up to $17 Million in 2021," HITC, June 21, 2022, https://www.hitc.com/en-gb/2022/06/21/the-6-highest-earning-tiktok-stars-scored-up-to-17-million-in-2021/.

34. E. Enjte, "How Much Does Chiara Ferragni Pay for a Post on Instagram," Class Lifestyle, January 24, 2019, https://www.classlifestyle.com/news/33767/how-much-does-chiara-ferragni-pay-for-a-post-on-instagram/eng/.

35. Garima Kakkar, "Types of Social Media," Digital Vidya, January 14, 2022, https://www.digitalvidya.com/blog/types-of-social-media/.

36. "Ree Drummond Net Worth," Celebrity Net Worth, 2022, https://www.celebritynetworth.com/richest-celebrities/richest-celebrity-chefs/ree-drummond-net-worth/.

37. J. Howarth, "Worldwide Social Media Use," Exploding Topics, April 10, 2023, https://explodingtopics.com/blog/social-media-usage.

38. Guinness World Records, "Highest Ever Daily Newspaper Circulation," https://www.guinnessworldrecords.com/world-records/67027-highest-ever-daily-newspaper-circulation.

39. Vibha Hegde, "BTS V Breaks Two Guinness World Records for Fastest Instagram Account to Hit 1 Million and 10 Million Followers," Sportskeeda SK Pop, December 14, 2021, https://www.sportskeeda.com/pop-culture/bts-v-breaks-two-guinness-world-records-fastest-instagram-account-hit-1-million-10-million-followers.

40. Lindsay Stein, "P&G, TikTok and Grey Make a Difference with #DistanceDance Campaign," *PR Week*, April 6, 2020, https://www.prweek.com/article/1679533/p-g-tiktok-grey-difference-distancedance-campaign.

41. Alicia Adejobi, "CBBC's Dave Benson Phillips Accidentally Reminds Us to 'Turn Our C***s Back' and Twitter Is Finished," *Metro*, October 27, 2019, https://metro.co.uk/2019/10/27/cbbcs-dave-benson-phillips-accidentally-reminds-us-turn-cs-back-twitter-finished-10991006/.

42. Steve Hand, "The 10 Worst Twitter Hashtag Fails of All Time," Miappi, https://blog.miappi.com/10-worst-twitter-hashtag-fails-time.

43. M. Kennedy, "5 Biggest Hashtag Fails of All Time," Set Fire Creative, March 19, 2021, https://setfirecreative.com/5-biggest-hashtag-fails-of-all-time/.

44. Hand, "The 10 Worst."

45. Danielle Young, "CNN Uses #AskACop on Twitter & You Know What Happened...," Hello Beautiful, December 17, 2014, https://hellobeautiful.com/2760163/cnn-ask-a-cop-hashtag/.

46. "NYPD Social Media Outreach Backfires When Twitter Answers #myNYPD Campaign," NBC New York, April 22, 2014, https://www.nbcnewyork.com/news/local/nypd-twitter-backlash-mynypd-fail-negative-photos-flood-social-media/2001371/.

47. K. Mueller, "11 Reasons Why People Love and Use Social Media," *Business 2 Community*, March 17, 2014, https://www.business2community.com/social-media-articles/11-reasons-people-love-use-social-media-0812775.

48. Liam Barnett, "Tinder Statistics 2022 & Fun Facts That You Didn't Know Before," Dating Zest, March 8, 2022, https://datingzest.com/tinder-statistics/.

49. Angel Au-Yeung, "Bumble Founder Whitney Wolfe Herd Fortune Rockets Past $1 Billion as Dating App Goes Public," *Forbes*, February 11, 2021, https://www.forbes.com/sites/angelauyeung/2021/02/11/bumble-founder-whitney-wolfe-herds-fortune-rockets-past-1-billion-as-dating-app-goes-public/?sh=ca1887578d99.

50. Jason Parham, "A People's History of Black Twitter," *Wired*, July 15, 2021, https://www.wired.com/story/black-twitter-oral-history-part-i-coming-together/.

51. Brooke Auxier, "Social Media Continue to Be Important Political Outlets for Black Americans," Pew Research Center, December 11, 2020, https://www.pewresearch.org/fact-tank/2020/12/11/social-media-continue-to-be-important-political-outlets-for-black-americans/.

52. Olivia Valentine, "Top 10 Reasons for Using Social Media," GWI, January 11, 2018, https://blog.gwi.com/chart-of-the-day/social-media/.

53. Colleen McClain et al., "The Internet and the Pandemic," Pew Research Center, September 1, 2021, https://www.pewresearch.org/internet/2021/09/01/the-internet-and-the-pandemic/.

54. Sebastian Ocklenburg, "FOMO and Social Media," *Psychology Today*, June 13, 2021, https://www.psychologytoday.com/us/blog/the-asymmetric-brain/202106/fomo-and-social-media.

55. Emmelyn Croes and Jos Bartels, "Young Adults' Motivations for Following Social Influencers and Their Relationship to Identification and Buying Behavior," *Computers in Human Behavior* 124 (2021): 1–10.

56. Dan Warrender and Rosa Milne, "How Use of Social Media and Social Comparison Affect Mental Health," *Nursing Times* 116, no. 3 (2020): 56–59.

57. Carly A. Parsons, Lynn E. Alden and Jeremy C. Biesanz, "Influencing Emotion: Social Anxiety and Comparisons on Instagram," *Emotion* 21, no. 7 (2021): 1427–37.

58. Benjamin K. Johnson, "Look Up, Look Down: Articulating Inputs and Outputs of Social Media Social

Comparison," *Journal of Communication Technology* 4, no. 1 (2021): 28–53.

CHAPTER 11

1. Teodora Dobrilova, "How Much Is the Gaming Industry Worth in 2021?" Tech Jury, August 5, 2021, https://techjury.net/blog/gaming-industry-worth/.
2. Mark J. P. Wolf, *The Video Game Explosion: A History from Pong to PlayStation and Beyond* (Westport, CT: Greenwood, 2007).
3. Jason Wise, "Mobile Gaming Statistics 2023: Industry Size, Revenue & Demographics, April 9, 2023, https://earthweb.com/mobile-gaming-statistics/.
4. Matija Ferjan, "Latest *World of Warcraft* Player Count & Subscription Numbers (2023)," Headphones Addict, February 21, 2023, https://headphonesaddict.com/world-of-warcraft-player-count/#WoW-subscription-numbers.
5. C. Gough, "Registered Users of Fortnite Worldwide from August 2017 to May 2020," Statista, November 6, 2020, https://www.statista.com/statistics/746230/fortnite-players/.
6. Akhilesh Ganti, "How Does Fortnite Make Money?" *Investopedia*, September 10, 2020, https://www.investopedia.com/tech/how-does-fortnite-make-money/.
7. Austin Modine, "Championship Gaming Series Runs Out of Quarters," *The Register*, November 19, 2008, https://www.theregister.co.uk/2008/11/19/championship_gaming_series_closes/.
8. Nick Schwartz, "More People Watch eSports Than Watch the World Series or NBA Finals," *USA Today*, May 19, 2014, https://ftw.usatoday.com/2014/05/league-of-legends-popularity-world-series-nba.
9. Dean Takahashi, "Nielsen: Esports Fans Follow an Average of 5-7 Games," *Venture Beat*, October 2, 2017, https://venturebeat.com/2017/10/02/nielsen-esports-fans-follow-an-average-of-5-7-games/.
10. Streams Charts, "Most Watched Twitch Streamers, Last 30 Days," https://streamscharts.com/channels?platform=twitch&time=30-days&sortBy=followers.
11. Emmy Wallin, "Tyler Ninja Blevins Net Worth," Wealthy Gorilla, April 9, 2023, https://wealthygorilla.com/tyler-ninja-blevins-net-worth/.
12. "Esports Market Size Share & COVID-19 Impact," *Fortune Business Insights*, September 2022, https://www.fortunebusinessinsights.com/esports-market-106820.
13. Andrew Webster, "*Dota 2*'s The International Returns in August with $40 Million Prize Pool," *Forbes*, May 21, 2021, https://www.theverge.com/2021/5/12/22432042/dota-2-international-esports-tournament-stockholm-date.
14. Abigail Cain, "The Rise and Fall of the Company behind 'Reader Rabbit' and All Your Favorite Educational Games," *The Outline*, September 26, 2018, https://theoutline.com/post/6293/reader-rabbit-history-the-learning-company-zoombinis-carmen-sandiego?zd=1&zi=y45gdjet.
15. B. Fishman, M. Riconscente, R. Snider, T. Tsai, and J. Plass, "Empowering Educators: Supporting Student Progress in the Classroom with Digital Games" (Ann Arbor: University of Michigan, 2014), http://gamesandlearning.umich.edu/wp-content/uploads/2014/11/A-GAMES-Part-I_A-National-Survey.pdf.
16. Amy Novotney, "Gaming to Learn: Do Educational Computer Video Games Lead to Real Learning Gains? Psychologists Say More Research Is Necessary," *American Psychological Association Monitor on Psychology*, April, 2015, https://www.apa.org/monitor/2015/04/gaming.
17. Tracey Lien, "'FarmVille 2' Represents the Next Generation of Social Gaming, Zynga Says," *Polygon*, September 5, 2012, https://www.polygon.com/gaming/2012/9/5/3290747/farmville-2.
18. Dong-Hee Shin and Youn-Joo Shin, "Why Do People Play Social Network Games?" *Computers in Human Behavior* 27, no. 2 (2011): 852–61.
19. Steven Messner, "A Brief History of MMO Games," *PC Gamer*, July 28, 2017, https://www.pcgamer.com/a-brief-history-of-mmo-games/.
20. Richard Bartle, "Hearts, Clubs, Diamonds, Spades: Players Who Suit MUDS," 1996, http://www.mud.co.uk/richard/hcds.htm.
21. Justin Olivetti, "The Game Archaeologist: The Assassination of Lord British," Massively Overpowered, October 3, 2015, https://massivelyop.com/2015/10/03/the-game-archaeologist-the-assassination-of-lord-british/.
22. Elizabeth Kolbert, "Pimps and Dragons: How an Online World Survived a Social Breakdown," *The New Yorker* 77, no. 13 (May 28, 2001): 88.
23. Nick Yee, "The Daedalus Project," 2006, http://www.nickyee.com/daedalus/archives/001468.php.
24. Consumers Guide Editors, *How to Win at Pac-Man* (Pocket Publication, 1982).
25. IMDb, "Saturday Supercade," https://www.imdb.com/title/tt0085008/?ref_=nv_sr_1?ref_=nv_sr_1.
26. Daniel Sieberg, "24-Hour Videogame Channel Set to Launch," CNN, April 12, 2002, http://www.cnn.com/2002/TECH/ptech/04/12/video.game.channel/index.html.
27. Merrill Barr, "NBC Shutting Down G4 Network on November 30th," Screenrant, November 17, 2014, https://screenrant.com/g4-tv-network-canceled-2014/.
28. Heidi Kemps, "12 Games That Existed Just to Sell You Junk Food," *Wired*, August 2, 2013, https://www.wired.com/2013/08/games-and-junk-food/.
29. Gerardo Guzman, "Videogame Advertising Playing to Win...and Sell," September 14, 2010, https://www.nielsen.com/us/en/insights/article/2010/video-game-advertising-playing-to-win-and-sell/.
30. Michael Barnett, "In-Game Advertising: Mind Games," *Marketing Week*, February 26, 2014, https://www.marketingweek.com/in-game-advertising-mind-games/.
31. I. Ciobotaru, "4 In-Game Native Advertising Examples (and What All Mobile Publishers Can Learn from Them)," October 21, 2015, https://pubnative.net/blog/in-game-mobile-native-advertising-examples-and-learnings/.
32. Kevin Roose, "How Joe Biden's Digital Team Tamed the MAGA Internet," *The New York Times*, December 6, 2020, https://www.nytimes.com/2020/12/06/technology/joe-biden-internet-election.html.

33. Aljean Harmetz, "New Faces, More Profits for Video Games," *Times Union*, January 15, 1983.

34. M. Koretzky, "*Post* Game Report," July 28, 2019, https://journoterrorist.com/2019/07/28/post-games/.

35. Peter Vorderer et al., "Playing Video Games as Entertainment," in *Playing Video Games: Motives, Responses, and Consequences*, eds. Peter Vorderer and Jennings Bryant (Mahwah, NJ: Lawrence Erlbaum Associates Publishers, 2006), 1–7.

36. Mary Beth Oliver, et al., Video Games as Meaningful Entertainment Experiences, Scholarship and Professional Work—Communication (Indianapolis: Butler University, 2015), 145–59.

37. Philip Kollar, "Jane McGonigal on the Good and Bad of Videogame Escapism," *Polygon*, March 28, 2013, https://www.polygon.com/2013/3/28/4159254/jane-mcgonigal-video-game-escapism.

38. Richard M. Ryan, C. Scott Rigby, and Andrew Przybylski, "The Motivational Pull of Video Games: A Self-Determination Theory Approach," *Motivation and Emotion* 30, no. 4 (2006): 347–63.

39. Ray Oldenburg, "Our Vanishing 'Third Places.'" *Planning Commissioners Journal* 25 (1996–97): 5–10.

40. Kurt Dean Squire and Matthew Gaydos, "No, Fortnite Isn't Rotting Kids' Brains. It May Even Be Good for Them," *Education Week*, August 8, 2018, https://www.edweek.org/ew/articles/2018/08/08/no-fortnite-isnt-rotting-kids-brains-it.html.

41. Keith Stuart, "Fortnite Is So Much More Than a Game," *Medium*, August 17, 2018, https://medium.com/s/greatescape/fortnite-is-so-much-more-than-a-game-3ca829f389f4.

42. Aimee Hart, "LGBTQ Video Games Coming Out in 2022," *Gayming Magazine*, September 29, 2022, https://gaymingmag.com/2022/09/lgbtq-video-games-coming-out-in-2022/.

43. Simon Parkin, "Zoe Quinn's Depression Quest," *The New Yorker*, September 9, 2014, https://www.newyorker.com/tech/annals-of-technology/zoe-quinns-depression-quest.

44. Soebandhi Santirianingrum and Yuan Andriansyah, "In-Game Advertising: Analyzing the Effects of Brand Congruity, Integration, and Prominence towards IGA Attitude and Purchase Intention," *Jurnal Manajemen Teknologi* 16, no. 3 (December, 2017): 258–70.

45. "In-Game ad Revenue Will Reach $56B in 2024, but Getting Your Share Depends on Your Genre," *Venture Beat*, November 9, 2020, https://venturebeat.com/2020/11/09/in-game-ad-revenue-will-reach-56b-in-2024-but-getting-your-share-depends-on-genre-vb-live/.

46. Noah Smith, "Racism, Misogyny, Death Threats: Why Can't the Booming Video-Game Industry Curb Toxicity?" *The Washington Post*, February 26, 2019, https://www.washingtonpost.com/technology/2019/02/26/racism-misogyny-death-threats-why-cant-booming-video-game-industry-curb-toxicity/.

47. Patricia Hernandez, "Playing *Red Dead Online* as a Black Character Means Enduring Racist Garbage," *The Verge*, January 15, 2019, https://www.theverge.com/2019/1/15/18183843/red-dead-online-black-character-racism.

48. Robert W. White, "Motivation Reconsidered: The Concept of Competence," *Psychological Review* 66, no. 5 (1959): 297–333.

49. Edward L. Deci and Richard M. Ryan, "The 'What' and 'Why' of Goal Pursuits: Human Needs and the Self-Determination of Behavior," *Psychological Inquiry* 11, no. 4 (2000): 227–68.

50. Clive J. Fullagar and E. Kevin Kelloway, "'Flow' at Work: An Experience Sampling Approach," *Journal of Occupational and Organizational Psychology* 82 (2009): 595–615.

CHAPTER 12

1. Alexandre Tanzi and Shelly Hagan, "Public Relations Jobs Boom as Buffett Sees Newspapers Dying," Bloomberg, April 27, 2019, https://www.bloomberg.com/news/articles/2019-04-27/public-relations-jobs-boom-as-buffett-sees-newspapers-dying.

2. Tim Morris, "Ivy Lee and the Origins of the Press Release," PR Academy, August 25, 2014, https://pracademy.co.uk/insights/ivy-lee-and-the-origins-of-the-press-release/.

3. Barbara Hunter, "Oral Histories: Barbara Hunter," May 18, 2016, https://www.bellisario.psu.edu/page-center/oral-histories/barbara-hunter/.

4. Srikant Ramaswami, "Diversity and Inclusion in the PR Profession: The Case for Change," *PR Week*, September 27, 2018, https://www.prweek.com/article/1494228/diversity-inclusion-pr-profession-case-change.

5. Tina McCorkindale, "Achieving Gender Parity in Public Relations," Center for Public Relations, December 12, 2019, https://annenberg.usc.edu/research/center-public-relations/achieving-gender-parity-public-relations.

6. Maryam Mohsin, "10 Social Media Statistics You Need to Know in 2022," Oberlo, September 12, 2022, https://www.oberlo.com/blog/social-media-marketing-statistics.

7. Public Relations Society of America, "About Public Relations," https://www.prsa.org/all-about-pr/.

8. Caroline Forsey, "What is Public Relations? The Definition of PR in 100 Words or Less," HubSpot, April 20, 2018, https://blog.hubspot.com/marketing/public-relations-definition.

9. Morgan Winsor and Kelly McCarthy, "Men Arrested at Starbucks Were There for Business Meeting Hoping to Change 'Our Lives,'" ABC News, April 19, 2018, https://abcnews.go.com/GMA/News/men-arrested-starbucks-business-meeting-hoping-change-lives/story?id=54578217.

10. "What You Can Learn from the All-Time Best Managed PR Crises," Prezly, https://www.prezly.com/academy/the-best-managed-pr-crises-of-2018.

11. Sara Ashley O'Brien, "Elizabeth Holmes' Trial Is Set to Begin: Here Is What You Need to Know," CNN, August 30, 2021, https://www.cnn.com/2021/08/30/tech/elizabeth-holmes-theranos-trial/index.html.

12. Allen Mireles, "Persuasion: 6 Principles That Power PR Success," LinkedIn, September 28, 2017, https://www.linkedin.com/pulse/persuasion-6-principles-power-pr-success-allen-mireles/.

13. Craig Kanalley, "Why Twitter Verifies Users: The History of the Blue Checkmark," *Huffington Post*, March 12, 2013, https://www.huffpost.com/entry/twitter-verified-accounts_b_2863282.

14. Emma Bowman and Raquel Maria Dillon, "Twitter Begins Advertising a Paid Verification Plan for $8 Per Month," NPR, November 6, 2022, https://www.npr.org/2022/11/05/1134561542/twitter-blue-check-paid-verification-elon-musk.

15. Shirin Ghaffary, "Elon's Blue Check Disaster Is Getting Worse," *Vox*, April 25, 2023, https://www.vox.com/technology/2023/4/25/23697830/elon-musk-twitter-checkmark-removal-blue-kara-swisher-lebron-james-doja-cat.

16. Brittany Mclaughlin, "Why Brand Authority Matters and How to Achieve It," Idea Grove, August 20, 2020, https://www.ideagrove.com/blog/why-brand-authority-matters-and-how-to-achieve-it.

17. Travis M. Andrews, "Dear *Cosmopolitan* Magazine: 'Cancer Is Not a Diet Plan,'" *The Washington Post*, April 12, 2017, https://www.washingtonpost.com/news/morning-mix/wp/2017/04/12/dear-cosmopolitan-magazine-cancer-is-not-a-diet-plan/?utm_term=.a37d67041c28.

18. NNA, "FCC Warns Broadcasters to Identify Source of Video News Releases," *PBS News Hour*, April 14, 2005, https://www.pbs.org/newshour/nation/media-jan-june05-vnr_04-14.

19. Jennifer Shore, "9 Things That Must Be in Your Electronic Press Kit," SmartBug, March 20, 2018, https://www.smartbugmedia.com/blog/9-things-that-must-be-in-your-electronic-press-kit.

20. Joe Ciarallo, "Five Things Every PR Agency Website Should Include," *Adweek*, October 25, 2011, https://www.adweek.com/digital/five-things-every-pr-agency-website-should-include/.

21. Paul Bates, "Why Public Relations Should Play a Role in Your Social Media Marketing," Georgetown University Center for Social Impact Communication, http://csic.georgetown.edu/magazine/public-relations-play-role-social-media-marketing/.

CHAPTER 13

1. "The Origins of Marketing and Advertising," *Anchor Digital*, July 19, 2019, https://anchordigital.com.au/the-origins-of-marketing-and-advertising/.

2. "What Marketing Looked Like in the 50s & 60s," *Color Fire*, March 16, 2019, https://www.colorfire.com/marketing-50s-60s/.

3. Alexander Vijay Smith, "The Art of Advertising—The Golden Age of Advertising," North Central Louisiana Arts Council, September 4, 2012, https://www.nclac.org/news-blog/the-art-of-advertising-the-golden-age-of-advertising.

4. Lenika Cruz, "'Dinnertimin' and 'No Tipping': How Advertisers Targeted Black Consumers in the 1970s," *The Atlantic*, June 2015, https://www.theatlantic.com/entertainment/archive/2015/06/casual-racism-and-greater-diversity-in-70s-advertising/394958/.

5. "Thomas J. Burrell," The HistoryMakers, June 5, 2001, https://www.thehistorymakers.org/biography/thomas-j-burrell-40.

6. "Thomas J. Burrell," Advertising Hall of Fame (Washington, DC: American Advertising Federation, 2004), http://advertisinghall.org/members/member_bio.php?memid=832.

7. J. Rodriguez, "Latinos and Advertising," Race & Ethnicity in Advertising: America in the 20th Century, https://raceandethnicity.org/exhibits/show/latinos-and-advertising/latinos-and-advertising.

8. Nidia Serrano, "Understanding Hispanic and Latino Diversity Is the First Step to Celebrating This Audience," *Adweek*, https://www.adweek.com/partner-articles/understanding-hispanic-and-latino-diversity-is-the-first-step-to-celebrating-this-audience/.

9. Ethan Cramer-Flood, "Worldwide Ad Spending 2022," *Insider Intelligence/eMarketer*, May 18, 2022, https://www.insiderintelligence.com/content/worldwide-ad-spending-2022/.

10. Aaron Taube, "How the Greatest Super Bowl Ad Ever—Apple's '1984'—almost Didn't Make It to Air," *Business Insider*, January 22, 2014, https://www.businessinsider.com/apple-super-bowl-retrospective-2014-1.

11. Jamie McCrary, "College Branding: 5 Steps to Making Your Brand Stand Out," *Lead Squared*, October 1, 2021, https://www.leadsquared.com/college-branding/.

12. Scott Berinato, "The Power and Perils of Puffery," *Harvard Business Review*, May 11, 2010, https://hbr.org/2010/05/the-power-and-perils-of-puffer.

13. Lesley Fair, "$9.3 Million FTC Settlement Suggests Mail Order Rule Compliance Is Always in Style," Federal Trade Commission, April 21, 2020, https://www.ftc.gov/news-events/blogs/business-blog/2020/04/93-million-ftc-settlement-suggests-mail-order-rule.

14. Diane Bartz, "L'Oreal Settles over Skin Care Ads That U.S. Termed Deceptive," Reuters, June 30, 2014, https://www.reuters.com/article/us-l-oreal-advertisement-ftc/loreal-settles-over-skin-care-ads-that-u-s-termed-deceptive-idUSKBN0F52KU20140630.

15. Steve Harvey, "University Branding: Your Clever Guide to Higher Education Branding," Fabrik, https://fabrikbrands.com/university-branding-and-higher-education-branding/.

16. Charles Passy, "How Liquor Companies Are Breaking into Minority Markets," MarketWatch, August 13, 2015, https://www.marketwatch.com/story/booze-business-vies-for-lucrative-minority-market-2015-08-13.

17. E. Bell, "10 Things You Should Know about Hennessy Cognac," Vine Pair, March 2, 2018, https://vinepair.com/articles/best-hennessy-cognac/.

18. Todd Butler, "The Only Four Metrics a Converged Campaign Needs," Media Ocean, December 17, 2018, https://www.mediaocean.com/blog/only-four-metrics-converged-campaign-needs.

19. Yee Yin, "The 5 Hottest Outdoor Advertising Trends in 2021," The Perfect Media Group, December 29, 2020, https://theperfectmediagroup.com/the-5-hottest-outdoor-advertising-trends-in-2021/.

20. Tim Nudd, "How the Best Ad Campaign of 2015 Hilariously Hacked the Lowly Preroll Ad," *Adweek*, December 13, 2015, https://www.adweek.com/brand-marketing/how-best-ad-campaign-2015-hilariously-hacked-lowly-preroll-ad-168614/.

21. L. Kim, "Cost Per Action (CPA): How to Lower Your CPA in AdWords," WordStream, https://www.wordstream.com/cost-per-action.

22. Hitesh Bhasin, "What Is Product Placement? Examples and Importance in Marketing," Marketing91,

July 21, 2020, https://www.marketing91.com/product-placement/.

23. "'No Time to Die' Top 10 Product Placement Brands," Concave Brand Tracking, October 1, 2021, https://concavebt.com/no-time-to-die-top-10-product-placement-brands/.

24. "What Is Native Advertising?" Outbrain, https://www.outbrain.com/native-advertising/.

25. Demian Farnworth, "Is Native Advertising Ethical? Depends on Who You Ask," Copyblogger, May 5, 2014, https://copyblogger.com/is-native-advertising-ethical/.

26. Mike Featherstone, "Consumer Culture and Its Futures: Dreams and Consequences," Pp. 1–46 in *Approaching Consumer Culture: Global Flows and Local Contexts*, edited by Evgenia Krasteva-Blagoeva (New York: Springer, 2018).

27. "Transactional vs. Relational Purchasing for Your Apparel Brand," The Apparel Logistics Group, January 4, 2017, http://www.apparellogisticsgroup.com/Blog/January-2017/Transactional-vs--Relational-Purchasing.aspx.

28. Neil Patel, "Which U.S. Brands Are Spending the Most on Advertising?" https://neilpatel.com/blog/top-ad-spenders/.

29. Ahiza Garcia, "NFL and Nike Sign 8-Year Contract for Uniforms," CNN Business, March 27, 2018, https://money.cnn.com/2018/03/27/news/companies/nike-nfl-gear-contract/index.html.

30. Jordan T. Prodanoff, "How Many Ads Do We See in a Day?" Web Tribunal, October 6, 2022, https://webtribunal.net/blog/how-many-ads-do-we-see-a-day/.

31. Deo Mishra, Gyan, "What Advertising Does to Your Brain, Effects of Unconscious Exposure," *Medium*, April 26, 2019, https://medium.com/@gyandeo/what-advertising-does-to-your-brain-effects-of-unconscious-exposure-d6bea9d39760.

32. Eric Stafford, "2022 Ford Mustang Shelby GT500," *Car and Driver*, 2021, https://www.caranddriver.com/ford/mustang-shelby-gt500.

33. Cherise Threewitt, "Why Does Horsepower Matter?" *US News & World Report*, May 11, 2017, https://cars.usnews.com/cars-trucks/why-does-horsepower-matter.

34. "Ford GT Will Utilize New Carbon Fiber Wheels," Brandon Ford Blog, May 19, 2016, http://www.brandonford.com/blog/benefits-of-carbon-fiber-wheels/.

35. Evan Williams, "What's a Gurney Flap and Why Is the GT350 Getting One?" All Ford Mustangs, October 3, 2017, https://www.allfordmustangs.com/threads/whats-a-gurney-flap-and-why-is-the-gt350-getting-one.1090414/.

CHAPTER 14

1. Pete Williams, "Supreme Court Gives Cheerleader Victory in School Free Speech Case," NBC News, June 23, 2021, https://www.nbcnews.com/politics/supreme-court/supreme-court-says-schools-don-t-have-free-hand-punish-n1272107?icid=related.

2. Avie Schneider, "Twitter Bans Alex Jones and Infowars; Cites Abusive Behavior," NPR, September 6, 2018, https://www.npr.org/2018/09/06/645352618/twitter-bans-alex-jones-and-infowars-cites-abusive-behavior.

3. Brian Fung, "Twitter Bans President Trump Permanently," CNN, January 9, 2021, https://www.cnn.com/2021/01/08/tech/trump-twitter-ban/index.html.

4. "*Ward v. Rock Against Racism*," Oyez, https://www.oyez.org/cases/1988/88-226.

5. *City of Renton v. "Playtime Theaters, Inc.*," Oyez, https://www.oyez.org/cases/1985/84-1360.

6. "*Texas v. Johnson*," Oyez, https://www.oyez.org/cases/1988/88-155; "*United States v. Eichman*," Oyez, https://www.oyez.org/cases/1989/89-1433.

7. "*United States v. O'Brien*," Oyez, https://www.oyez.org/cases/1967/232.

8. "*Tinker v. Des Moines*—Landmark Supreme Court Ruling on Behalf of Student Expression," ACLU, https://www.aclu.org/other/tinker-v-des-moines-landmark-supreme-court-ruling-behalf-student-expression.

9. "*Morse v. Frederick*," Oyez, https://www.oyez.org/cases/2006/06-278.

10. "*Valentine v. Chrestensen*," Justia, https://supreme.justia.com/cases/federal/us/316/52/.

11. "*Virginia State Board of Pharmacy v. Virginia Citizens Consumer Council, Inc.*," Oyez, https://www.oyez.org/cases/1975/74-895.

12. "*Branzburg v. Hayes*," Oyez, https://www.oyez.org/cases/1971/70-85.

13. Sian Shin, "Nebraska High School Censors Student Editorial about Censorship and Journalism Adviser Resigns," Student Press Law Center, February 25, 2021, https://splc.org/2021/02/nebraska-high-school-journalists-face-delays-self-censorship-after-newly-enforced-prior-review/.

14. Federal Trade Commission, "Advertising and Marketing on the Internet: Rules of the Road," https://www.ftc.gov/tips-advice/business-center/guidance/advertising-marketing-internet-rules-road.

15. Federal Trade Commission, "FTC Announces Latest Enforcement Action Halting Deceptive CBD Product Marketing," https://www.ftc.gov/news-events/press-releases/2021/05/ftc-announces-latest-enforcement-action-halting-deceptive-cbd.

16. Carol Kando-Pineda, "For-Profit Colleges on Notice," Federal Trade Commission, October 6, 2021, https://consumer.ftc.gov/consumer-alerts/2021/10/profit-colleges-notice.

17. Federal Communications Commission, "What We Do," https://www.fcc.gov/about-fcc/what-we-do.

18. Federal Communications Commission, "FCC Broadcast Ownership Rules," https://www.fcc.gov/consumers/guides/fccs-review-broadcast-ownership-rules.

19. Federal Communications Commission, "The Public and Broadcasting," https://www.fcc.gov/media/radio/public-and-broadcasting#SPEECH.

20. Federal Communications Commission, "The V-Chip: Options to Restrict What Your Children Watch on TV," https://www.fcc.gov/consumers/guides/v-chip-putting-restrictions-what-your-children-watch.

21. Mary Hanbury, "Kendall Jenner, Bella Hadid, and Other Models Who Appeared in the Viral Fyre Festival Ad Could Be Forced to Reveal How Much They Got Paid to Promote It," *Business Insider*, January 28, 2019, https://www.businessinsider.com/kendall-jenner-top-models-could-face-fyre-festival-subpoena-2019-1.

22. Gwen Aviles, "Kendall Jenner to Pay $90,000 Settlement for Promoting

Fyre Festival," NBC News, May 21, 2020, https://www.nbcnews.com/pop-culture/pop-culture-news/kendall-jenner-pay-90-000-settlement-promoting-fyre-festival-n1212011.

23. Gonzalo E. Mon, "SEC Is Latest Agency to Keep Up with the Kardashians," *Ad Law Access*, October 3, 2022, https://www.adlawaccess.com/2022/10/articles/sec-is-the-latest-agency-to-keep-up-with-the-kardashians/.

24. Mitchell Katz, "CSGO Lotto Owners Settle FTC's First-Ever Complaint against Individual Social Media Influencers," Federal Trade Commission, September 7, 2017, https://www.ftc.gov/news-events/press-releases/2017/09/csgo-lotto-owners-settle-ftcs-first-ever-complaint-against.

25. Federal Trade Commission, "Disclosures 101 for Social Media Influencers," November, 2019, https://www.ftc.gov/system/files/documents/plain-language/1001a-influencer-guide-508_1.pdf.

26. Paolo Zialcita, "FTC Issues Rules for Disclosure of Ads by Social Media Influencers," NPR, November 5, 2019, https://www.npr.org/2019/11/05/776488326/ftc-issues-rules-for-disclosure-of-ads-by-social-media-influencers.

27. Federal Trade Commission, "Enforcement Policy Statement on Food Advertising," https://www.ftc.gov/public-statements/1994/05/enforcement-policy-statement-food-advertising#Introduction.

28. Michael M. Grynbaum and Jonah E. Bromwich, "Fox News Faces Second Defamation Suit over Election Coverage," September 23, 2021, https://www.nytimes.com/2021/03/26/business/media/fox-news-defamation-suit-dominion.html.

29. David Bauder, Randall Chase, and Geoff Mulvihill, "Fox, Dominion Reach $787 M Settlement over Election Claims," Associated Press, April 18, 2023, https://apnews.com/article/fox-news-dominion-lawsuit-trial-trump-2020-0ac71f75acfacc52ea80b3e747fb0afe.

30. Student Press Law Center, "Four Elements of Libel Law," June 1, 2001, https://splc.org/2001/06/libel-law/.

31. "*Ollman v. Evans*," Casetext, https://casetext.com/case/ollman-v-evans.

32. Melissa Locker, "John Oliver Picks a New Fight with Coal Boss He Called 'a Geriatric Dr. Evil' on 'Last Week Tonight,'" *Time*, November 11, 2019, https://time.com/5722305/john-oliver-coal-fight-last-week-tonight/.

33. Matthew Belloni, "Courtney Love to Pay $430,000 in Twitter Case," Reuters, March 3, 2011, https://www.reuters.com/article/us-courtneylove/courtney-love-to-pay-430000-in-twitter-case-idUSTRE7230F820110304.

34. James Grebey, "Courtney Love Pays $350,000 to Settle Twitter-Based Defamation Lawsuit," *Spin*, August 31, 2015, https://www.spin.com/2015/08/courtney-love-350000-dollars-defamation-lawsuit-twitter-dawn-simorangkir/.

35. Tom Hals, "Musk's Defamation Win May Reset Legal Landscape for Social Media," Reuters, December 6, 2019, https://www.reuters.com/article/us-musk-lawsuit-landscape/musks-defamation-win-may-reset-legal-landscape-for-social-media-idUSKBN1YB023.

36. Sidney Lowry, "Fainter Enters Guilty Plea in Invasion of Privacy Case," *Northwest Missourian*, October 12, 2022, https://www.nwmissourinews.com/news/article_a59fcd1a-4a71-11ed-99a4-efc0b7c59d67.html.

37. Eriq Gardner, "TMZ Sued for Placing Hidden Microphones in Courtroom," *Hollywood Reporter*, April 2, 2013, https://www.hollywoodreporter.com/business/business-news/tmz-sued-placing-hidden-microphones-432279/.

38. Wendy Tannenbaum, "A Recent Decision Calls False Light Outdated," Reporters Committee for Freedom of the Press, 2002, https://www.rcfp.org/journals/the-news-media-and-the-law-fall-2002/recent-decision-calls-false-l/.

39. "*Solano v. Playgirl, Inc.*," Casebriefs, 2002, https://www.casebriefs.com/blog/law/torts/torts-keyed-to-dobbs/communication-of-personally-harmful-impressions-to-others/solano-v-playgirl-inc/.

40. Mark Hayward, "Supreme Court Ruling Favors 'North Woods Law' in Privacy-Invasion Case," New Hampshire Union Leader, 2021, January 8, https://www.unionleader.com/news/courts/supreme-court-ruling-favors-north-woods-law-in-privacy-invasion-case/article_ead8d027-314a-5bae-9b4e-ea83198f5c5a.html.

41. Staff, "Gwyneth Boosts Her Boobs! Experts Spot Sure Signs of Surgery," *National Enquirer*, February 17, 2020, https://www.nationalenquirer.com/celebrity/gwyneth-paltrow-plastic-surgery-breasts/.

42. Jesus Jimenez and Kevin Draper, "Tom Brady and Gisele Bundchen Divorce after 13 Years," *The New York Times*, October 28, 2022, https://www.nytimes.com/2022/10/28/sports/football/tom-brady-gisele-bundchen-divorce.html.

43. "Misappropriation of Personal Image and Possible Remedies," HG.org, https://www.hg.org/legal-articles/misappropriation-of-personal-image-and-possible-remedies-46776.

44. Dylan Smith, "Cardi B Faces Yet Another Round in 'Back Tattoo' Lawsuit," *Digital Music News*, January 26, 2023, https://www.digitalmusicnews.com/2023/01/26/cardi-b-back-tattoo-lawsuit-new-trial/.

45. Brent Schrotenboer, "County of Los Angeles Responds to Vanessa Bryant's Lawsuit over Photos of Helicopter Crash," *USA Today*, May 3, 2021, https://www.usatoday.com/story/sports/nba/2021/05/03/lawsuit-kobe-bryant-widow-vanessa-triggers-response-la-county/4933158001/.

46. Christian Boone, "Ten Years Later, Hiker's Murder Still Haunts Those Closest to Case," *Atlanta Journal-Constitution*, January 4, 2018, https://www.ajc.com/news/crime--law/ten-years-later-hiker-murder-still-haunts-those-closest-case/CSgydKXZNfG738F34UdWYN/.

47. Walter C. Jones, "'Hustler' Wants Crime Scene Photos of Slain Hiker," *The Augusta Chronicle*, March 8, 2010, https://www.augustachronicle.com/article/20100308/NEWS/303089950.

48. Fred Rosen, "Why I Requested Slain Hiker's Crime Scene Photos," *Atlanta Journal-Constitution*, August 11, 2012, https://www.ajc.com/news/opinion/why-requested-slain-hiker-crime-scene-photos/2PmN2O3oTCOJKq7mBuvgfL/.

49. "Copyright in General," U.S. Copyright Office, https://www.copyright.gov/help/faq/faq-general.html.

50. J. Alexander Hershey & Bryon M. Chowka, "*Google v. Oracle* Provides Freedom for Developers, Caution to

Copyright Holders," April 22, 2021, https://www.law.com/thelegalintelligencer/2021/04/22/google-v-oracle-provides-freedom-to-developers-caution-to-copyright-owners/?slreturn=20210419102248.

51. "More Information on Fair Use," U.S. Copyright Office, April 2020, https://www.copyright.gov/fair-use/more-info.html.

52. Anastasia Tsioulcas, "Not Bitter, Just Sweet: The Rolling Stones Give Royalties to the Verve," NPR, May 23, 2019, https://www.npr.org/2019/05/23/726227555/not-bitter-just-sweet-the-rolling-stones-give-royalties-to-the-verve.

53. https://creativecommons.org.

54. "Duration of Copyright," U.S. Copyright Office, April 2020, https://www.copyright.gov/title17/92chap3.html.

CHAPTER 15

1. Daniel Bates, "EXCLUSIVE: Katie Couric Covered up RBG's Dislike for Taking the Knee," *The Daily Mail*, October 13, 2021, https://www.dailymail.co.uk/news/article-10088027/Katie-Couric-admits-editing-Ruth-Bader-Ginsburg-interview-protect-late-justice.html.

2. Joe Rivera, "What Did Adam Schefter's Email Say? Why NFL Insider's Reported Email Situation Is a Big Deal," *The Sporting News*, October 14, 2021, https://www.sportingnews.com/us/nfl/news/what-did-adam-schefter-nfl-insider-email-say/vuva5491y7x6188sbbmwmifyt.

3. Cornell Law School, Legal Information Institute, "Ethics," https://www.law.cornell.edu/wex/ethics.

4. Philip Patterson and Lee Wilkins, *Media Ethics: Issues and Cases*, 8th ed. (Boston: McGraw-Hill, 2013); Joseph Dominick, *The Dynamics of Mass Communication*, 10th ed. (Boston: McGraw-Hill, 2009); Patrick Plaisance, *Media Ethics*, 2nd ed. (Thousand Oaks, CA: Sage, 2013).

5. Jeremy Barr and Paul Farhi, "*USA Today* Removes 23 Articles, Says Reporter Fabricated Sources," *The Washington Post*, June 16, 2022, https://www.washingtonpost.com/media/2022/06/16/usa-today-gabriela-miranda-retractions/.

6. Saranac Hale Spencer, "Social Media Post Misrepresents Old Biden Tweet on Travel Ban," December 3, 2021, https://www.factcheck.org/2021/12/social-media-posts-misrepresent-old-biden-tweet-on-travel-ban/.

7. Oli Lynch, "Do Controversial Ads Work? And How Can You Make Them?" https://www.clickcease.com/blog/examples-of-controversial-ads/.

8. Mike Snider, "Heineken Pulls 'Lighter Is Better' Commercial after Some Call It Racist," *USA Today*, March 27, 2018, https://www.usatoday.com/story/money/business/2018/03/27/heineken-pulls-lighter-better-commercial-after-some-call-racist/461395002/.

9. Mike Fannin, "The Truth in Black and White: An Apology from the *Kansas City Star*," *Kansas City Star*, December 22, 2020, https://www.kansascity.com/news/local/article247928045.html.

10. "Tackling Diversity and Inclusion in the Newsroom," World Economic Forum Global Future Council on Media Entertainment and Sport, July 2021.

11. Lynda Hutchinson, "Alan Freed and the Radio Payola Scandal," *Performing Songwriter*, August 20, 2015, https://performingsongwriter.com/alan-freed-payola-scandal/.

12. Michael M. Grynbaum, John Koblin, and Jodi Kantor, "CNN Fires Chris Cuomo amid Inquiry into His Efforts to Aid His Brother," *The New York Times*, December 4, 2021, https://www.nytimes.com/2021/12/04/business/media/chris-cuomo-fired-cnn.html.

13. Brian Schwartz, "CNN Host Chris Cuomo Used His Media Sources to Find Out Info on Brother Andrew's Accusers, Records Show," CNBC, November 29, 2021, https://www.cnbc.com/2021/11/29/cnn-host-chris-cuomo-used-sources-to-find-info-on-andrew-cuomo-accusers-records.html.

14. Alex Thompson and Theodoric Meyer, "Reporters Fume at White House 'Quote Approval' Rules," *Politico*, May 10, 2021, https://www.politico.com/newsletters/west-wing-playbook/2021/05/10/this-email-is-on-background-with-quote-approval-492792.

15. Vincent Filak, "Ethics versus Access: An Interview with the Chapman *Panther* Editor Who Said, 'No Thanks' to Covering George W. Bush's Private Event on the Campus," Dynamics of Writing, October 21, 2019, https://dynamicsofwriting.com/2019/10/21/ethics-versus-access-an-interview-with-the-chapman-panther-editor-who-said-no-thanks-to-covering-george-w-bushs-private-event-on-the-campus/.

16. Craig Silverman, "Journalism Ethics Are Rooted in Humanity, Not Technology," Poynter Institute, October 26, 2012, https://www.poynter.org/reporting-editing/2012/journalism-ethics-are-rooted-in-humanity-not-technology/.

17. Brian Fung and Geneva Sands, "Vague and Viral TikTok Warning of School Violence Is Not Credible but Has Schools and Law Enforcement on High Alert," CNN Business, December 17, 2021, https://www.cnn.com/2021/12/17/tech/tiktok-school-threat-december-17/index.html.

18. Hannah Storm, "What Journalists Can Learn from Their Mistakes during the Pandemic," Ethical Journalism Network, June 22, 2020, https://ethicaljournalismnetwork.org/what-journalists-can-learn-from-their-mistakes-during-the-pandemic.

19. Jeanne Bourgault, "Diversity in the Newsroom can Build Better Media. Here's Why," World Economic Forum, December 1, 2021, https://www.weforum.org/agenda/2021/12/diversity-in-news-media/.

INDEX